The Envy of Angels

University of Pennsylvania Press
MIDDLE AGES SERIES
Edited by
Edward Peters
Henry Charles Lea Professor
of Medieval History
University of Pennsylvania

A listing of the available books
in the series appears at the
back of this volume

The Envy of Angels

Cathedral Schools and Social Ideals in Medieval Europe, 950–1200

C. Stephen Jaeger

University of Pennsylvania Press

Philadelphia

Permission is gratefully acknowledged to reprint illustrations in Appendix A (a noted) from:

Hans Reinhardt, *La cathédrale de Strasbourg*. (Strassburg: Arthaud, 1972).

Otto Schmitt, *Gotische Skulpturen des Strassburger Münsters* (Frankfurt am Main, 1924), volume 2.

The "Orpheus" sections of Chapter 5 appeared originally in *Mittellateinisches Jahrbuch* 27 (1992): 141–68. They appear here revised by permission of the editor.

Chapter 9, "Humanism and Ethics at the School of St. Victor," appeared originally in *Mediaeval Studies* 55 (1993): 51–79. A revised version appears here by permission of the publisher. Copyright © 1993 by the Pontifical Institute of Mediaeval Studies, Toronto.

Library of Congress Cataloging-in-Publication Data
Jaeger, C. Stephen.
    The envy of angels : cathedral schools and social ideas in medieval Europe, 950–1200 / C. Stephen Jaeger.
        p.   cm. — (Middle Ages series)
    Includes bibliographical references (p.   ) and index.
    ISBN 0-8122-3246-1
    1. Education, Medieval — Europe — Philosophy. 2. Church schools — Europe — History. 3. Education, Medieval — Social aspects — Europe — History. I. Title. II. Series.
LA95.J34   1994
370'.94'0902 — dc20
                                                                    94-16677
                                                                    CIP

This book is dedicated to
KATIE JAEGER

O, how composed does discipline render every posture of your girlish body, and even more so, of your mind! It sets the angle of the neck, arranges the eyebrows, composes the expression of the face, directs the eyes, restrains laughter, moderates speech, suppresses appetite, controls anger, arranges the gait . . . What glory can compare to virginity thus adorned? The glory of angels? An angel has virginity, but no body; he is happier for it certainly, but not stronger. The best and most desirable is that ornament which even angels might envy.

— Bernard of Clairvaux, Letter to the virgin Sophia

. . . those meant to be formed by artist's hand from wet and malleable clay into vessels of glory on the wheel of discipline . . .

— Goswin of Mainz, Letter to Walcher, ch. 27

Why do you suppose, brothers, we are commanded to imitate the life and habits of good men, unless it be that we are reformed through imitating them to the image of a new life? For in them the form of the image of God is engraved, and when through the process of imitation we are pressed against that carved surface, we too are moulded in the likeness of that same image . . . We long to be perfectly carved and sculpted in the image of good men, and when excellent and sublime qualities . . . stand out in them, which arouse astonishment and admiration in mens' minds, then they shine forth in them like the beauty in exquisite statues, and we strive to recreate these qualities in ourselves.

— Hugh of St. Victor, *De institutione novitiorum* ch. 8

Contents

Acknowledgments

My work on this book began in a sabbatical year made possible by a fellowship from the John Simon Guggenheim Foundation. I am grateful to the foundation for its support on both the research and the printing of this book. An invitation from Professor Marianne Wynn of Westfield College, University of London, gave me the opportunity to work out the general shape of the study. My particular thanks are due also to the Fulbright Commission, which supported my work with a fellowship in 1991–92. I had help with difficulties in the Latin school poetry from Peter von Moos, Peter Godman, and Anders Winroth. Sieglinde Pontow rendered invaluable aid by checking and correcting my translation of the letter of Goswin of Mainz with the kind of acumen and patience without which no one could read that author's prose. It is especially gratifying to be able to thank Dianne Zimmer and Dale Johnson of the Graduate School Fund of University of Washington for support that invariably came with charm, good humor, and a sense of faith in my work and in research in the humanities generally. The chapter on Gothic style in sculpture would not have been possible without the materials of the Princeton Index of Christian Art which Adelaide Bennett of Princeton University sent me in quantities that left the embarrassed beneficiary awe-struck. My thanks also to Shirley Wargon for materials from the Index of Christian Art at UCLA. A lecture on Boethius by my colleague JoAnn Taricani at University of Washington inspired the section on music and morality. Robert Benson and John Baldwin read the finished manuscript and made many valuable suggestions. Sheila Prieur, Peter Dy-Liacco, and Lisa Eschenbach helped with the preparation of the manuscript.

For their encouragement and kindness over the past years I am grateful to Gerhild Scholz Williams, Joe Voyles, Charles Barrack, Hans Bänziger, Wolfgang Harms, Horst Wenzel, Ursula Peters, Joachim Bumke, Klaus Speckenbach, and Michael Curschmann. My deepest gratitude is due to my wife Alison for her faith and support, and to my daughters Rosalind, and Katie, to whom this book is dedicated.

Abbreviations

AHDLMA	*Archives d'histoire doctrinale et littéraire du moyen âge.*
AKG	*Archiv für Kulturgeschichte*
AHR	*American Historical Review*
BAR	*British Archeological Reports*
BGPTMA	*Beiträge zur Geschichte der Philosophie und Theologie des Mittelalters*
CCCM	*Corpus Christianorum, Continuatio Mediaevalis*
CHFMA	*Classiques de l'histoire de France au moyen âge*
CSEL	*Corpus Scriptorum Ecclesiasticorum Latinorum*
CTSEEH	*Collection de textes pour servir à l'étude et à l'enseignement de l'histoire*
DA	*Deutsches Archiv für Erforschung des Mittelalters*
DGQ	*Deutschlands Geschichtsquellen im Mittelalter*
DVJS	*Deutsche Vierteljahrsschrift für Literaturwissenschaft und Geistesgeschichte*
HJb	*Historisches Jahrbuch*
HZ	*Historische Zeitschrift*
JEGP	*Journal of English and Germanic Philology*
LB	*Lebensbeschreibungen einiger Bischöfe des 10.–12. Jahrhunderts.* Trans. Hatto Kallfelz. Ausgewählte Quellen zur deutschen Geschichte des Mittelalters: Freiherr vom Stein Gedächtnisausgabe.
MGH	*Monumenta Germaniae Historica*
MGH SS	*MGH Scriptores*
MGH SS rer. Germ. in us. schol.	*MGH Scriptores rerum Germanicarum in usum scholarum*
MIÖG	*Mitteilungen des Instituts für Österreichische Geschichtsforschung*
NLH	*New Literary History*
PBB	*Beiträge zur Geschichte der deutschen Sprache und Literatur*

PL	*Patrologia Latina, ed. J. P. Migne*
RHE	*Revue d'histoire ecclésiastique*
RS	*Rerum Britannicarum medii aevi scriptores: Rolls Series*
RTAM	*Recherches de théologie ancienne et médiévale*
ZfdPh	*Zeitschrift für deutsche Philologie*
ZRPH	*Zeitschrift für romanische Philologie*

Introduction

The humanist strain in twelfth-century culture represented by figures like Bernard Silvester, John of Salisbury, and Alan of Lille has its roots in the late tenth and eleventh centuries. C. H. Haskins knew very well that the movement he called the "Renaissance of the twelfth century" grew out of developments in the preceding age, and he called the eleventh century "that obscure period of origins which holds the secret of the new movement."[1]

What especially favors that obscurity and guards that secret is the apparent poverty of intellectual and artistic achievement in the centers of worldly learning, the cathedral schools. Those schools produced no great works of philosophy or imaginative fiction, very little poetry worth reading, no autobiography or personal reminiscences, and no compendia of learning like those of Hugh of St. Victor and Thierry of Chartres from the twelfth century.

The scholarship on education in the earlier Middle Ages has drawn a picture of the arts curriculum based largely on the seven liberal arts[2] and scriptural studies in monastic learning.[3] The logic of looking for something where there is light even when you have lost it in the dark has turned monasteries and continuing Carolingian traditions into the measure for cathedral schools in the era of their rise, 950–1100. The scholarship on education in the period does not distinguish clearly between monastic and secular learning, or between the learning of the eleventh century and its Carolingian predecessors, or for that matter between the eleventh and the twelfth centuries.

In terms of availability of sources, the eleventh-century cathedral schools are hemmed in on all sides by comparatively well documented institutions, and in the middle is a blank. There are critics of whatever was in that blank: Peter Damian and Otloh of St. Emmeram in the eleventh century, and Peter Abelard in the twelfth. A number of young men at monastic schools in the late tenth century left them to go off to study in that blank space, and they emerged again as prominent bishops, as advisors to kings, as saints.

The obscurity of the cathedral schools is hard to dispel given the dearth of sources. Writings from the monasteries are abundant, and writings from the cathedrals are scarce. From the late tenth to the late eleventh century, some very vital schools produced remarkably few written documents. We have letters and letter collections, some lists of *auctores*, some library catalogues,[4] schematizations of studies, and discussions of them. There are some descriptions of education in history and biography, and a handful of mediocre commentaries and tracts. There is also a body of learned poetry, generally in a Latin so obscure as to thwart interest rather than reward it.

That is the best we can do for primary documentation of the cathedral schools in the period roughly from 950 to 1070. Given the privilege that modern historians of culture grant to the "monuments" an age creates for itself, the period appears extremely threadbare. But that privilege directs us where there is no path and blocks the one that is open.

In odd contrast to the dearth of monuments is the enthusiastic praise by contemporary observers of whatever was happening in the blank. The centers of learning are regularly referred to as "a second Athens," "a second Rome"; the masters are called "our Plato," "our Socrates," "a second Cicero." There are many expressions of fervent love of student for master and master for student. We hear about great crowds of students and a flourishing school life, and we can observe keen competition between schools (see below, Chapter 3). Something was going on at the early cathedral schools that is not transmitted clearly by the sources or set in intelligible structures by current frames of explanation. The result of this unfavorable array of sources is that the school life of the period often seems like an enclosed garden protected from exploration, and the would-be-explorer stands before it like an Alice in Wonderland, who fits through none of the available doors and can only get oblique looks through undersized and inconveniently placed windows into a vivid and alluring world. And there are no documents labeled "eat me," or "digest me," or "include me in the discussion."

"Eat Me": Letters and Manners

For this study the entry into the world of the schools is the phrase "letters and manners." What essentially happened at cathedral schools has its formula in that phrase. Students acquired *mores* along with letters. I translate *litterae* throughout as "letters," though "literature" would be an appropriate rendering, a field of meaning still held firm in our phrases "letters and sciences" or "humane letters." The meaning of the word *mores*, and the way they were taught and studied, are the subject of most of what follows. The quotations at the beginning of the introduction are good idealizing statements of the conception and goal of this learning. Goswin of Mainz (Gozechinus) used the image of the teacher as potter, forming students "by artist's hand from wet and malleable clay into vessels of glory on the wheel of discipline."[5] The discipline of *mores* turned them into living works of art by teaching them conduct. The mode of behavior cultivated was based largely on classical models: on Cicero and Seneca, on the Roman orator and statesman. This educational model privileged eloquence and "wisdom," the former the concern of letters, the latter of *mores*. But as we will see, the two assimilated so closely to each other that sharp distinctions are not possible. Essentially a student's and teacher's time was spent in the discipline of conduct and the study of prose and verse composition based on classical models. The liberal arts likewise assimilated to *mores*, which was also called *ethica, moralis disciplina, moralis philosophia* or *moralitas*.[6]

Given this orientation of studies an inventory of the books read and the intellectual goals pursued has only a secondary value. We have to put aside the conception of school learning as primarily the transmission of knowledge: lecturing, note-taking, book-learning, the generating of understanding, the cultivation of critical thought. Studying the "scholarly," "intellectual" side of cathedral school learning is like writing history of the theater from lists of plays performed and from theoretical treatises by actors. If in a particular period the repertoire does not change much and there are no theoretical treatises (and there never are—actors do not ordinarily theorize), then we might conclude that that period was not original or productive. And if from the same period that we have just judged unoriginal and unproductive we have many rave reviews from critics, then we might say that given the lack of originality and productivity in the theater, such reviews must be taken as an indication of the low expectations and bad taste of the period.

Of course, that interpretation is based on a fundamental misunderstanding of what a theater is and what it does. This is the predicament of historians of education for the eleventh century. There is a great deal of talk about flourishing schools and great teachers. But there are no intellectual achievements, and therefore the schools are judged to "show little vitality from within."[7]

The apparent poverty of the age is misleading. The vitality and continuity in secular learning in the period 950–1100 are not to be found in texts and artifacts, but in personalities and in the cultivation of personal qualities. Its real accomplishment was what came off the "wheel of discipline." Its works of art are men whose "manners" are "composed." This composition, the well-tempered man, was a major contribution of the eleventh century to "philosophy" (as defined in Chapter 5) and to culture. It is the best answer to the question how the age could have been glorious while inhabiting a blank spot in intellectual history.

Our education and intellectual life are based on texts. We do not have a model of learning and philosophy that is not oriented to the written word. The result is that written monuments exercise a jealous tyranny in the writing of intellectual and cultural history, telling us that they are the thing itself and we shall have no other criteria before them. But the culture of the cathedral schools was what I will call a charismatic culture. It cannot be assessed by weighing and measuring its documentation, which by its very nature it tends not to produce; such texts as are produced are only recorded by chance, not because documentation and representation are the media of cultural productivity.

I want to sketch in the following comments an explanatory framework that will accommodate the available sources on eleventh-century school culture better than the current model of schools as educators of intellect in a textualized culture. This model will also help us to see the eleventh century in its relation to the twelfth.[8]

The culture of the early cathedral schools was complex and sophisticated. It cultivated the Latin language to the highest degree of complexity it attained in the Middle Ages. A particular kind of intentionally obscure Latin poetry was its dominant literary form. It was a poetry that produced its effect in performance with music, and the written form is a petrified artifact that can give virtually no clues of its vital social function. The culture was highly literate but at the same time more or less indifferent to textuality. To call the cathedral schools "oral" would be misleading, especially in analogy to oral-formulaic literature. The "sacred simplicity of the illiterate" has nothing to do with this culture, and to associate it with the "rusticity" of orality as opposed to the "urbanity" of written Latin is not possible.

Charismatic Culture Versus Intellectual Culture

The transition from the eleventh to the twelfth century plays out a contest between two stages of culture which is not restricted to one historical setting but recurs at various points in western history: in fifth- and fourth-century Athens, in Rome from the republic to the empire, in the European Middle Ages from the eleventh to the twelfth centuries, and again from the late Middle Ages to the Renaissance. We can call the two stages charismatic and intellectual. The shifts from the one to the other are not linear; it is possible for charismatic culture to supersede intellectual. The new stage always appears wrapped in the aura of "rebirth," "renaissance," and renewal, and the older stage always laments the advent of the new with complaints of the collapse of culture and civilization.

This model regards the two stages as engaged in a productive, dynamic contest. It allows us to avoid the blinders of a progressive model of historical development. It takes seriously the sense of superiority of the old and its feeling that culture suffers diminution and trivializing from the new, and it is as much concerned with what is lost as with what is gained in historical and cultural change. It makes it possible to deal with the "return" of charismatic culture, an event that took place, for instance, when Renaissance humanism confronted scholasticism in the fourteenth and fifteenth centuries. Finally, the model is useful, I believe, in part as an answer to a basic fallacy that hovers around the discussion of the shift from an oral to a literate culture: that idea that growing literacy represents improvement, increasing sophistication, a move from an archaic and primitive to an advanced culture.

"Charismatic versus intellectual culture" is the embracing category that contains the problem, oral versus written. We can define and authenticate this antinomy by starting with Cicero's scheme of the development of Roman philosophy. He had a clear conception of the poles of culture I have called charismatic and intellectual, and presented them as distinct but related contexts of philosophy. He formulated this opposition and gave it a historical framework in the *Tusculan Disputations*. He observed that philosophy was a fairly new discipline in the Rome of his time, although the Greeks had long since developed it to a high level of sophistication. He explains this "deficiency" to the advantage of his countrymen: it may be, he says, that the philosophy of the early Romans was Pythagorean, and the Pythagoreans were careful to transmit their wisdom secretly, hermetically, in the form of poems and songs.[9] The early Romans also used to sing songs at banquets in praise of the merits of illustrious men. Therefore it is clear that they had a culture of poetry, and this may have accommodated some aspects of philosophy. He can point to some written monuments: laws, orations, family traditions. But for the most part the early Romans, either because of the grand undertakings of state they were caught up in, or because they sought to guard their knowledge from the ignorant, practiced "the most bountiful of all arts, the discipline of living well."[10] They preferred to do this — and here is the main point — in the conduct of life and public affairs rather than in written words (*vita magis quam litteris*).

After this period in which philosophy and life were identical came a period of writings. The first Roman to publish his writings, Cicero says, found many students, in part because the crowd found him "easy to understand" (*cognitu perfacilis*). And soon after, many teachers followed his example and "took Italy by storm," a development of which Cicero disapproves (cf. *Tusc. Disp.* 4.3.6–7).

Cicero's view of Roman intellectual history is based on a scheme in which a poetic, hermetic, elitist culture, whose "philosophy" is based on "virtue," personal merit, and physical presence, gives way to one which communicates and teaches numbers of people through writings aimed at generating understanding (*cognitu perfacilis*). This model applies well to the eleventh century and the transition to the twelfth.

The example of fifth- and fourth-century Athens is also useful to fill out this model. Socrates is a good representative of a charismatic culture. He wrote nothing. He taught by dialogue and question. He mistrusted the written word, and regarded writing as lethal to the mind's highest faculty, memory. Texts represented the rigidifying of thought, which develops in the living dialogue through assertion, challenge, and response. Writing everything down mummifies thought and threatens the death of the mind.[11] The fragmentary nature of pre-Socratic philosophy shows a similar disregard of the written word as the medium of philosophy. The charismatic teaching central to Greek Stoicism is embedded in the same matrix.

Two opposing lines of influence follow from Socrates[12]: on the one hand there are Aristotle and the peripatetics; on the other Plato, Xenophon, Antisthenes, and Aeschines of Sphettus. The first is a rationalist reaction against the master's doctrine. It speaks a simple language aimed at communicating, not evoking and creating; employs myth and poetry only as objects of study, not as bearers of doctrine, and relocates reality in things and in created nature, not in transcendent ideas. The second commemorates the master and continues his traditions in biography, memoirs, dialogues, histories. A variety of new forms develop around the attempt to reproduce the incomparable presence of Socrates (see n. 11 above). The first abolishes charisma by demystifying the process of cognition and depersonalizing the art of teaching (put everything in writing); the second attempts to restore charisma and physical presence by textualizing it. The first tends towards the condition of empirical natural science; the second tends toward the condition of imaginative literature.

The humanism and pre-scholasticism of the twelfth century reproduce these two trends in their reaction to eleventh-century cathedral school learning.

Charismatic Culture

The major areas in which transition registers from the eleventh to the twelfth centuries are well known and much discussed[13]: in theology the move from authority to reason; in the understanding of the eucharist, from real to symbolic presence; in philosophy, from realism to nominalism; in literature, from oral to written. An essential shift in the exercise of political power is the move from itinerant to "administrative" kingship,[14] and in church administration from what Gerd Tellenbach and Hayden White have called "charismatic leadership" to canonical procedure in the election of bishops and abbots.[15] The shared characteristic is the shift from real presence to symbolic, from performance to representation.[16] "Real presence" is the essential feature of a charismatic culture. I will use the term in the generalized sense of a defining and legitimizing factor in charisma, not just in the conventional sense of Christ's presence in the eucharist.

The charismatic presence — whatever the historical setting — tries to root itself in the supernatural, to indicate that a god is present in the living flesh. This is evident in the case of political charisma. The king is charged with a force instilled directly by God: his authority is God's, his will is the will of God. In the context of cathedral school learning, the teacher is the bearer and conveyor of real presence. His person is the lesson; it communicates "knowledge," wisdom, and eloquence.

Charismatic teaching also appeals to a higher realm of which the master is the emissary or at least the interpreter. The ideas mediated are not his own: they exist independently in a higher realm of immutable Truth and are given to the master as an exclusive gift, the way *heil* is given to the ruler. Both charismatic rulers and teachers bind their disciples by strong emotional ties that grant them god-like authority over the individual.

A charismatic culture makes the body and physical presence into the mediator of cultural values. The controlled body with all its attributes — grace, posture, charm, sensuality, beauty, authority — is the work of art of the eleventh century. The human presence was the raw material ready to be shaped and formed like the clay on the potter's wheel or the sculptor's marble block; the end product a disciplined human being.

It is useful to think of the eleventh century as a "heroic" age of culture. To do so is not to glorify the period or turn its representatives into titans, but rather to clarify its relationship to the twelfth century. "Heroic" suggests action and not reflection; presence and not representation; the glorifying of the lived moment, the *kairos*, and of the elegant human response to it, not art and the symbolic representation of the human being. The glorifying of representation is a phenomenon of the next age, a restorative phase when real and present charisma is passing out of existence and artists and poets are struggling to rescue and preserve it in texts, pictures and statues, as the disciples of Socrates and Christ strove to hold firm the physical and spiritual presence of the dead master.

The irreplaceable center of the cult of charisma is the body. The mind and soul of Socrates and Christ are certainly the more precious parts, but the impact on students, disciples, and lovers is inseparable from the unique physical presence. The effect of the master is deepest and most abiding when the charismatic body is tortured, mutilated, destroyed. The love of the living master may be a strong inducement to live according to his model; his martyrdom is stronger yet. The elegance of Socrates's death and the agony of Christ's had equally wrenching impacts on their followers. These masters' deaths by violence established their cult as much as did their teaching. The tragic demise in each case laid foundations deep in the souls of the disciples, cemented them in place with an emotional force beyond tragedy, a force far more lasting than anything as comparatively trivial as knowledge and understanding.

Physical presence is accordingly the anchor of charismatic culture. The body of the virgin Sophia, not her virginity, is what the angels envy in the passage from Bernard of Clairvaux that begins this book and furnishes its title. Angels, frozen in their state of everlasting spirituality, have all the virtues, as well as the condition from which they all derive. Those are things that any angel can have. What they can never have is a body shaped into the work of art and staging ground of those qualities. Sophia is heroic ("strong"), while the condition of the angels is merely "happy." Their "envy" suggests a sense of living in trivial felicity, a wan eternal goodness, barred from ever attaining the condition Sophia has attained in heroic struggle against temptation and vice. They can never become physical presence, and they long for the state that is denied to them.

In this study I develop the angels' "envy" into a historical principle: it refers to a certain posture of the twelfth century toward the eleventh. The greatness of its art, its sculpture and architecture, its literature, its learned humanist allegories, is in part a response to nostalgic desire, the testimony to a vast project aimed at capturing in symbolic representation the fading charisma that the previous age enjoyed — real, full, vital, embodied, and functioning as bearer of cultural ideals. The humanist educational ideals of the eleventh century did not register in sculpture, art or fiction because that age had or sought the thing itself. The twelfth century sensed its passing and strove to restore it. The results of that striving in the intellectual and artistic realm are what we call the "twelfth-century renaissance."

"Envy" as a historical principle is a response to the shift from charismatic to intellectual culture. The humanists of the twelfth century wrote out of nostalgia, not out of the vaulting self-confidence of an age of Renaissance. Their works are shoring to stave off the inevitable collapse of a culture passing out of existence.

Inner and Outer

The identification of physical appearance and bearing with the character and the state of the inner life is a defining feature of cathedral school culture, one which registers clearly in language. One of the problems in writing this book has been translating into modern English a number of Latin terms from moral philosophy that do not distinguish the inner from the outer world. Here are some of them:

Mores: the range of the word is indicated in the English words "morals" and "mores." It includes an internal disposition to the good and the outward behavior that brings it to expression. Any English translation of this term (and of those that follow) represents a narrowing of its meaning: "character" and "morals" are common translations; likewise "manners," "conduct," and "behavior." There is no term that accomplishes the bridging, or rather fusing, of inner and outer world that occurs in the Latin *mores*. I translate it ordinarily with "manners." "Proper conduct" and "good" or "elegant conduct" are paraphrasing translations that approximate the sense of it.

Habitus: The word can mean "attitude," "inner posture," "frame of mind," or "[physical] posture," "stance," "position." At its most external, it means "clothing," as in the "habit" of a monk or nun. It has the range of meaning of the English word "posture" understood as both the position taken on an issue and the position in which the body is held.

Motus: The range of the word is indicated in the two English cognates, "motion" and "emotion." The Latin of the schools tends to distinguish between *motus corporis* (= gesture, carriage) and *motus mentis* or *animi* (= emotions, impulses). But often it stands by itself and only the context indicates a more specific reference. The blurring of boundaries that (for the modern reader) occurs here is especially significant for the discipline of *mores*. The motion of the body is perhaps the most visible means of registering the inner state: the way of gesturing and walking (external *motus*) indicates the way of feeling or the inner state (*motus animi, status animi*). Identifying motion with impulse sets a pedagogic imperative. The education in manners aims precisely at the governance of impulse, and if this is identical with the way of carrying the body, then control of the body means control of mind, and the body in motion is the locus for the contest of reason and nature.

One of the results of this identification of inner with outer world was a highly sophisticated external culture. This took two directions. The first was pedantic caution in the regulating of behavior. The customary of the community of St. Victor at Paris spins every moment of the day into a web of regulations, seemingly trivial ones: how to hold the soup bowl, what direction to swing the legs when climbing into bed — along with minute prescriptions for greater issues like receiving and training novices, welcoming guests, and arranging the liturgy. The second was overrefinement, luxury, cultivated fashion in dress, gait, posture, speech.

Both tendencies are implicit in the assumptions of moral discipline, the identification of inner and outer behavior. The first is the extreme to which it tended in a non-monastic religious community; the second in worldly and ecclesiastical courts. In both of these contexts, the cultivators of external refinement would appeal to their clothes, gestures, their whole modus of carriage, as outward signs of an inner virtue.

The Body and the Text

The body consequently is meant to be "read." The well-composed body is itself a text-book of virtue; it is the curriculum for beginners in the study of *mores*. Hugh of St. Victor described this relationship with the image of the seal impressing its carved surface into wax. The teacher is the seal and the student the wax. In another work he talks about the two books written for man in Christ: the one is within him, the book of contemplation; the other is his outward form, "to be read for the purpose of imitation."[17] Education becomes a process of transmitting personal qualities through the charismatic effect of a well disciplined, well "composed" teacher, and this can be described in the metaphor of "reading" the text of the outer man. Herbert of Bosham played on this idea to make a witty transition in his biography of Thomas Becket:

> Let us turn back the pages of our new exemplar [= Thomas himself] and continue to read in it. For acts of virtue are certainly read more fruitfully in men themselves than books, just as deeds speak more effectively than words.[18]

Masters and students of *mores* oriented teaching and learning to an "aesthetic of the body" and a "hermeneutic of the body."[19] In the man composed according to this aesthetic the outer presence relates to the inner world as literal level to meaning in a poem. A person's carriage is the symbol, the narrative and the lyric poem conveying his character.

The sense of the physical presence as a text is preserved in the language of the period.[20] Some of the basic concepts of older poetics are borrowed terms for the human body and its postures. Quintilian pointed to this in defining the rhetorical "figures of speech" against the model of the grace and vitality of the human body:

> A body held stiffly upright possesses virtually no grace; the eyes stare straight ahead, the arms hang down straight, the feet are as though tied together, and the entire form makes an impression of rigidity. But a certain curve and, if I may put it that way, motion, confer vitality and force. Nor are the hands held to a single posture, while the face has a thousand moods . . . This same gracefulness and charm are conferred on speech by the rhetorical figures.[21]

The fluid borders between body and text are evident in the middle Latin term, *documentum*. In modern usage a "document" is a piece of paper with a text on it. For the earlier Middle Ages it was also the human presence charged with pedagogical force. Here are a few examples, some of which defy translation into a language that no longer can convey the sense of living presence as text book and curriculum:

. . . inter alia vivendi documenta saluberrimum abstinentiae vel continentiae clericis exemplum reliquit.	along with other "documents" of the good life, he left the clerics a most salubrious example of abstinence and self-control.[22]

veluti maternis ab eius colloquio documentis venustatis habitum et honestatis gravitatem moribus . . . exornabat.	By her manners in conversation, as though by a mother's teachings [*documentis*], she shed lustre on her beauty of posture and the dignity of her conduct.[23]
. . . exemplum et documentum factus est omnibus	he became an example and a "document" for all . . .[24]
His vivendi documentis non tantum initiatus, sed ad plenitudinem institutus.	We are not so much stirred to emulation as trained and disciplined fully by these documents of the good life [= the lives of the abbots][25]

The word can also mean "example" or "teachings."[26] The blurring of the borders between physical presence of a teacher and the contents of a lesson is the important point. By the later Middle Ages, the word's predominant meaning is the one known to us.[27]

The same movement from physical to textual is also evident in the rhetorical terms "scheme," "trope," and of course "figure."

From Disciplined Body to Virtue

In the disciplined person the body is the perfect mirror of the soul. That means that learning to walk and gesture elegantly, to speak persuasively, to hold the head and the body in dignified, grave, modest postures, and to compose facial expressions appropriate to any given emotion, are the first steps in the cultivation of virtue. Hugh of St. Victor spoke for school practice of the previous century when he claimed:

> The members of the body are to be restrained . . . through discipline, so that the condition of the mind may be firmed up within and strengthened to the point where exterior vigilance is set against interior flightiness. . . . Little by little, as it becomes habitual, that same image of virtue is impressed on the mind which is maintained through outward discipline in the disposition of the body. . . . The perfection of virtue is attained when the members of the body are governed and ordered through the inner custody of the mind.[28]

Defined in this way, virtue is accessible through training. Hugh's definition presupposes two stages in the process: one where discipline is imposed from without, by a teacher; the other where it is imposed from within, by the individual. The lessons of *mores* become internalized and form part of the character of the mature student. In this way the process of discipline continues throughout life within the self-contained classroom of the individual.

The discipline of the body is preparation for the true job of teaching, the "composing" of the inner man. Like a musical instrument, the inner world can be "tuned" through adjusting the outer. In the apparently mechanical procedure of tuning a stringed instrument, highly sophisticated laws of harmonics and musical proportion are at work, even when the instrument tuner does not know and master them, and when the instrument sounds in tune its physical presence becomes a medium of those laws. The "tuning" of the body works similarly. If the student walks and gestures gracefully, speaks confidently and persuasively, and holds his head and eyes in a moderated and controlled way, then the inner world will be held to the laws of grace, restraint, moderation that are in force in the outer. This musical metaphor was well known in the eleventh and twelfth centuries, and it seems probable that in Rheims, Chartres, and Bamberg, as in fifth-century Athens, music as an ethical discipline played an important part in the formation of character (see below, Chapter 5).

From Virtue to Social Ideal

The virgin Sophia described by Bernard has many of the qualities that "cultivation of virtue" promises. She walks beautifully, and the tilt of her head and the position of her eyes, her voice, her expression all beam virginity, or rather domination of desire and impulse. Here the classroom is self-enclosed, but the first stage is bypassed. She has no teachers of self-control. She just is an ideal. She comes that way. This attitude of Bernard's would appear to any remaining representatives of the old discipline (the letter was written some time prior to 1145) as wishful thinking. Bernard in turn would appear as a kind of moral Cornifician, who represents virtue as a thing that comes by nature and grace and is obtainable without discipline. By 1145 no cathedral school masters — or very few, perhaps in Germany and far in the provinces of France — were whipping virtue into their students and turning vessels of perfection off the wheel of discipline. But virtually all of aristocratic society recognized, credited, and — to an extent that it is now hard for us to assess — actually strove for the qualities that had constituted the curriculum of *mores* from the previous century. What had been an educational goal had transformed itself into a social value, and this transformation took place just at the time when the institutions of that learning were being radically transformed and *mores* and *ethica* were being thrown overboard. When the virtues cultivated in moral training no longer had formal educational institutions to convey them, they survived as widely admired social values.

Charismatic Texts

A prominent development in the transition from the eleventh to the thirteenth century was the gradual fictionalizing and aestheticizing of *ethica*. This is the fate of charisma in the transition to an intellectual culture: it becomes enfabulated, an object for study and reading. The real presence is no longer the bearer of culture, but rather the symbolic presence. Moral discipline registers in artifacts, not in human beings. This development follows the course of the memorializing of Socrates: the master was bottled and packaged in various kinds of texts. The "heroic age" when philosophy was inseparable from presence passed away, and was supplanted by an age of texts, often highly impressive, refined, and sophisticated, but created out of "envy," lacking the force and vitality of what had preceded. It is that nostalgic urge to recapture the incomparable personality and moral heroism of the eleventh century out of which many of the great artifacts of the twelfth were born. Viewed in this way, the twelfth century relates to the eleventh as Plato to Socrates.

The evidence for the survival of the old learning is accordingly very different from that provided by the age in which it was alive. The documents are not letters and portraits of real people, but rather fiction, sculpture, and didactic and imaginative literature. *Ethica* is much more prominent, but somehow also much less real. As a practiced discipline it is mainly present in complaints about its absence. The discipline has moved out of real life and has become thoroughly "textualized."

The "perfect man" occurs as a grand philosophical abstraction in Bernard Silvester's and Alan of Lille's allegorical poems, and both of them draw on ideas from "moral" instruction of the previous century.

We also have a variety of manuals of instruction for princes whose content owes much to the moral discipline of the eleventh-century cathedral schools: John of Salisbury's *Policraticus*, Gerald of Wales's *De principis instructione*, and a work that is an amalgam of *ethica* and what comes to be known as courtly ideals, Thomasin von Zirclaere's *Der welsche Gast*.

A new genre of fictional narrative becomes a prominent bearer of "ethical" ideals: the courtly romance. It shows idealized knights and ladies behaving with sublime courtesy, charm, humanity, restraint, polish — even when shaken with passion. The Arthurian romance was a charismatic text in the highest degree. It provoked imitation.

*   *   *

This introduction gave a sketchy frame of the education which this book studies. It is a wholly unintellectual, even anti-intellectual discipline, transmitted above all by a kind of body-magic that I have called charisma; it makes the teacher's presence into a seal and the student into wax receiving his imprint.

Germany — France — Italy

In defining the sources appropriate to this study, again, "letters and manners" were my guide. I have followed this formula as extensively as I could. The result is a large body of evidence that suggests common foundations of the cathedral schools of Germany and France. There are no doubt local differences, but those do not become evident until an overview of the spread of this learning is available and it is possible to compare one center with another. In any case, my purpose is to define common features, not local ones.

I was guided by the scholarship on particular centers, and could have gotten nowhere without it. But research has concentrated on local influences and has tidily separated Germany from France. The intellectual history of twelfth-century France and the early history of schools and universities have been written largely without any reference to German sources.[29] And that seemed to an earlier generation both good methodology and common sense.

The value of local historical studies is obvious. But an overview of the larger relationships has oddly not seemed necessary. Some of the most important figures and works of the period are totally unlocatable, and that could not be the case if local or national differences were at all sharply definable. Here are some questions for the advocates of carefully — especially nationally — narrowed bases of sources.

(1) Who is the author of the long, learned didactic poem "Quid suum

virtutis"? It is central to the study that follows and comes up in a number of chapters. The attempts at attribution show an erratic spread. The abbot Thierry of St. Trond was one of the candidates for authorship, Hildebert of Lavardin another. The poem was accordingly dated ca. 1100. The most recent editor dates it reliably to ca. 1043–46.[30] She also suggests the author was possibly a member of the chapel of emperor Henry III writing for the instruction of the prince.

These conjectures pretty much sweep the social and geographic spectrum of the learned world north of the Alps: the author was from the lowlands, France, or Germany; he was a monk, a bishop or a court cleric. Paravicini's dating also broadens the spectrum of time: from mid-century to the end of the century. Barthélemy Hauréau found this poem "the most interesting and admirable work of Hildebert," and E. R. Curtius saw in it "the true, genuine and consistent statement of Hildebert on the nature of poetry."[31] I know of no better confirmation of the unity of learning in the eleventh century than the identification by these eminent scholars of a poem — written probably before Hildebert's birth and possibly by a German — with the core of Hildebert of Lavardin's poetics.

(2) Who was Master Manegold, teacher of William of Champeaux and Anselm of Laon and "master of the modern masters"? A Frenchman or a German? Or a conservative anti-imperial reformer from Alsace?

(3) Who was Honorius Augustodunensis? A German from Augsburg? Or from Regensburg? Or was he a Frenchman from Autun? Or perhaps an Englishman or Irishman? What place does *Augustodunensis* refer to? Did he study at Chartres, Laon, St. Victor, or Canterbury? Or at all these schools?

(4) Who was Hugh of St. Victor? Was he from Saxony, the low countries, or Lorraine?

These personalities are not obscure and mute figures concealing their identities by their silence. They are prolific and central players in the school life, and the fact that their large body of writings does not supply the clues to their backgrounds underscores my point: local background and national origins played no significant role in their writings. The perspectives of local history have severe limits for our period. The cathedral schools formed a cultural unity and need to be studied from that perspective as well as from that of local and national history.

An important factor in the formation of the northern schools were those south of the Alps. The Italians Stefan and Gunzo of Novara were important influences in the early formation of cathedral schools. Adelman of Liège indicates that students of Fulbert of Chartres regularly traveled to Italy in search of instruction. Anselm of Besate and Benzo of Alba are also witnesses to a rich culture in Italy in the tenth and eleventh centuries, one which has left few traces, and those mainly when Italians moved to the north. I have not found access to those schools, and they remain an obscure factor in the education described here.[32]

Most of the following chapters are structured as commentaries on particular texts. The literature of the cathedral schools is little known, and it has seemed to me important to include many excerpts in English translation. I hope this will serve to some extent to encourage a rescue operation for that rich but neglected culture.

Part One

The Old Learning

1. Two Models of Carolingian Education

Carolingian education is oriented to the practical and spiritual needs of two institutions: the royal/imperial court and the church. The first looks toward civil administration, the second toward the religious life. Court education is a minor subject in Carolingian times. It affects few people at the highest level of lay society and is badly documented. The church and religious education virtually monopolize the records. The phrase "Carolingian educational revival" refers to a broad program of learning whose content is Christian but whose beneficiaries are both lay and clergy.[1] We begin with a look at this dominant and better understood model.

Ecclesiasticae disciplinae

An education in a cathedral or a monastery served a limited range of purposes: the rudiments of letters and the liberal arts, the reading and understanding of the Bible within the traditions of patristic scholarship[2]; preaching and converting; a Christian life according to the Benedictine rule; other more specific purposes within the sphere of church functions, among which music and the performance of the liturgy were especially prominent. The liberal arts occupied an important position, but were ancillary to the study of scripture. The description of the education of Sturmi, founder and first abbot of Fulda and a student of Boniface, in his biography by Eigil (written in the 790s) illustrates some of these concerns:

> . . . this holy priest strove to instruct the lad Sturmi for the service of God Almighty. . . . Having committed the Psalms to memory, and having learned a great many readings in incessant study, the boy began to understand sacred scripture in its spiritual sense; he also took pains to learn with the utmost diligence the mysteries of the four gospels of Christ. He strove to the limits of his capacity to store in the treasure chamber of his heart both the new and the old Testament through assiduous reading. Night and day his thoughts were, as it is written, on the law of the Lord.[3]

The list of texts holds no surprises. The biographical literature corroborates what is common knowledge about Carolingian education, that "sacred letters" are its main object.[4] The summary is useful for showing something of the spirit of scriptural studies at Fulda. Everything is memorized, not only the Psalms (*memoriae traditis*), but also the spiritual meaning of scripture, absorbed through the incessant memorization of interpretations; the mysteries of the gospels are "added on through learning" (*addiscere*). Eigil's idea of learning is memorizing a fixed body of knowledge. "Mysteries" are learnable texts, as are Psalms and gospels. The working of some creative faculty of understanding or intuition is not even postulated. The basic requirement of learning is effort, for which Sturmi certainly received an A plus. His memory is "tenacious"; the interpretations memorized are "as many as possible", his study "incessant"; his learning of the mysteries *studiosissime*; his "assiduous" reading of both testaments at the limits of his capacity, his meditations on the law continue "day and night." Brute memorization fueled by a zeal for the service of God is the essential orientation of Sturmi's education.[5] The passage shows us the great strength of Carolingian learning: energy and robustness; and its great weakness: uncritical acquiring of a fixed body of knowledge.[6] We may imagine Sturmi and the Carolingian student in general accumulating knowledge through the exertion of strong intellectual muscles. If there is deftness and versatility of genius in writings from the period, it is borrowed, with few exceptions, from an earlier age when penetration and dialectical sharpness were weapons of the Christian thinker against a pagan intellectual tradition daunting in its sophistication. The church in Carolingian times needed new books, reliable texts, a clergy who commanded the rudiments of learning, not intellectuals on the cutting edge of European thought. Mental muscle served these needs, and genius might have seemed an irrelevant luxury. There are times when a blunt instrument is just right to provide the cutting edge.[7]

If eloquence is praised in Carolingian vitae, it is ordinarily in the context of preaching and converting. Liudger's Life of Abbot Gregory of Utrecht (ca. 800) gives a good example. Gregory, like Sturmi a student of Boniface, is reading one day under the master's supervision. The master asks his pupil for an explanation of the text, but stops him when he starts in Latin, and asks him to use his native language. Gregory protests he cannot; Boniface then does it for him, and his eloquence flows miraculously (through his stomach) over into Gregory, who preaches to his teacher and his whole family. Knowing that the Holy Spirit had come over Boniface, Gregory becomes a disciple and follows him "to study the sacred books."[8]

This is a text book example of the Carolingian concern for letters and preaching in the vernacular and its religious purpose of conversion.[9] These concerns helped form the Carolingian educational ideal of the Christian orator, formulated for instance in Hrabanus Maurus's *De institutione clericorum*. When in addition to the liberal arts and knowledge of scripture the student has acquired the four cardinal virtues, then he is prepared to fulfill the duty of orator worthily in the church:

> The ancient definition affirms this: [the orator] ought to be a good man, skilled in speaking. If then this definition was observed in the orators of the pagans, then it is appropriate that it be observed so much the more in orators of Christ, who must make not only their speech, but the conduct of their entire life into a course of instruction in the virtues.[10]

For Hrabanus the wisdom of the orator stands in direct relation to his knowledge of the Bible:

> A man speaks more or less wisely to the degree that he is proficient in sacred scripture.[11]

The liberal arts were part and parcel of this ecclesiastical education.[12] This role is so well known, it would hardly deserve more than a mention here, except that the relation of secular to divine studies changed in certain areas in post-Carolingian education, and it is important to point here to their good relations in all areas so as to emphasize the later contrast. In Carolingian sources hints of a conflict between secular and divine studies are uncommon. They emerge in the course of the tenth century. The norm is a conciliatory climate, evident in the Life of Aldric of Sens (d. 836):

> When after some time he was sent by his parents to be educated in the liberal arts . . . he began . . . to receive in addition instruction in religion according to the course of doctrinal studies, so that he was learned not only in liberal disciplines, but also in spiritual ones.[13]

Aldric was a pupil of Alcuin, and this course of studies can be taken as consistent with the ideals of Carolingian educational policy, conceived and formulated in large part by his teacher. It aimed at literacy, and grammar, rhetoric and dialectic were the necessary foundation.

CONVERSATIO — CONVICTUS

The "moral" side of this education interests us by contrast to the Ottonian model, the main object of our inquiry. The young student learned *conver-*

satio according to the *norma vivendi*. The biography of Aldric of Sens continues from the passage quoted above,

> Recalling, as the word of Wisdom has stated, that character is formed by the shared life of teacher and pupils [*mores ex convictu formari*], he took pleasure in continued discussions with his fellow monks and delighted in the colloquies of religious men. (PL 105, 800C)

The formation of character through a life shared by students and master is part and parcel of education in antiquity and the earlier Middle Ages.[14] This principle applies whatever the locus of education: royal courts, monastery, cathedral. *Convictus* is the arrangement within which moral/ethical formation takes place. The church in the Carolingian period had its own vocabulary of *sancta conversatio* and its own concepts of the virtues appropriate to a monk and cleric. A few examples will serve to contrast with the notions which later supplanted them.

Bishop Rimburg of Hamburg (d. 888) as a young man at school had advanced through his studies to maturity "in both knowledge and in virtue" (PL 126, 993B). Pope Leo IV. was sent to school "for the study of letters . . . where he not only learned letters, but persisted in the study [or zeal for] a holy way of life, not in the manner of a boy . . . but like a perfect monk."[15] Walafrid Strabo praises the learning of St. Otmar in similar terms: "raised aloft in the knowledge of letters, this pursuer of virtue and possessor of praiseworthy manners advanced to the level of the priesthood."[16] Alcuin wrote to the monks of Murbach in 804 urging them to educate the young boys of the community "in chastity and sanctity and ecclesiastical discipline, so that they may be worthy to assume your position after you."[17] Late Carolingian descriptions of education tend to fall into a slightly mechanical rehearsal of the areas: letters, sacred scripture, ecclesiastical disciplines.

Bishop Stephen of Laon gives the education of St. Lambert in some detail (the *Vita* from 920). As a boy he was sent to "highly skilled men for an education." He distinguishes himself in "ecclesiastical religion," and "down to his very heart he is inflamed with the burning love of divine mysteries," and he drank from the streams of the liberal arts all the more swiftly for being filled with the love of God. At length he is thoroughly trained in "divine teachings" and is strengthened by mastery of "monastic rules." Striving with all his might to become a "perfect man," Lambert is finally sent by Theodard of Utrecht to the royal court for further education, since the bishop observes Lambert's "high nobility and the most elegant form of his body."[18]

The Carolingian edicts on education give some clear insights into the relationship of these two branches of learning, letters and *conversatio*. The *Epistola de litteris colendis* takes for granted the learning of *honestas morum* and introduces the study of letters as the cure for what ails the church and kingdom:

> . . . we consider it useful that it be incumbent on the cathedrals and monasteries given into our rule by the favor of Christ to strive to teach, along with the order of the regular life and the mode of conduct appropriate to holy religion, also the discipline of letters, to those who are able to learn, each according to his own capacity. Just as the rule of living ordains and embellishes upright behavior, so also let the activity of teaching and learning order and embellish the flow of our speech, so that those who seek to please God by right living may not neglect to please Him by right speaking.[19]

This two-fold thrust of learning dominates in the letter. The recipients are praised as "men inwardly dedicated and outwardly learned, chaste through living well and scholarly through speaking well."[20] But the wording makes clear that subject is not *De religiosa conversatione colenda*. The reform of morals among the clergy had been the project of an earlier generation.[21] Now it is the study of letters that is lacking and is commended to the church as an addition to the discipline of good behavior.[22] Moral instruction here may be little more than the teaching and enforcement of the monastic or canonical rule of life. But it is presented as a part of an old and established curriculum that now has to expand to include a new element, letters.[23] Letters are patched on to the established curriculum in *conversatio*.

THE PERFECT MAN

The ideal that emerges from Carolingian vitae is that of the *vir perfectus*. It has a long history in Christianity,[24] but a few portraits from Carolingian vitae will allow us to distinguish the notion of the perfect man of the ninth century from that of the twelfth. Recall that Bishop Rimbert of Hamburg matured in *gravitas* at the same time as he advanced in *liberales disciplinae*. In a few years time he distinguished himself for perfection of learning and of virtues.[25] The portrait of the young Sturmi gives some of the desirable virtues:

> . . . his understanding was profound, his thoughts wise, his speech prudent, his appearance handsome, his gait composed, his manners upright, his life unspotted. Through his charity, his humility, his gentleness and versatility, he won the love of all men.[26]

Liudger was popular and beloved while in school at Utrecht as a "man of marvelous gentleness, of cheerful countenance though restrained in his laughter, combining in all of his acts prudence and temperance." But the explanation of his amiability is not charm or any qualities of character, but only his diligent culling of God's praise from scripture: " . . . he was an assiduous student of Holy Scripture and especially of whatever pertained to the praise of God and to catholic doctrine."[27] He was "in his accustomed way dear to all, because he was adorned with good manners and saintly striving."[28] Good manners, affability, gentleness, saintly striving and popularity have a context in social life in general; but the critical problem for the Carolingian church was to maintain the balance between the worldliness and the saintliness of these qualities in favor of the saintly. Agobard of Lyon cautioned monks and clerics not to cultivate them for the sake of advancement:

> Anyone placed in charge of others, be he cleric or monk, if he strives to appear benevolent, gentle and affable in order to win the hearts of his subjects to exalt himself and his own praise, is a deceiver, and ought never to undertake the care of souls.[29]

It was important that popularity should result from holiness, not ambition, all the more so since "perfection" was indeed a means of advancement in a career. The much quoted anecdote of Charlemagne reproving the lazy aristocrats and praising the diligent poor boys of his palace school shows at least Notker's acceptance of this qualification. According to his life of Charlemagne, the emperor promised the diligent students "magnificent bishoprics and abbacies" if they would "attain to perfection."[30]

MONASTERY AND CATHEDRAL

If there are differences between education at cathedral and monastic schools during this period, they are negligible. One of the striking features of the program of education conceived by Charlemagne and Alcuin is its universality. The whole range of social contexts in which learning could have a place is included in their pronouncements on education. The kinds of men who attend school in a monastery certainly varied from those who received their learning at a cathedral or at the royal court, but at all three the dominant goal of education was *ecclesiasticae disciplinae* as described earlier.[31] Monks educated in the cloister might be called to court service and eventually made bishop; courtiers educated clerically at court might become abbots or bishops. A virtually complete interchange among these three dominant centers of intellectual and civil/administrative life seems to be one result of the universality of education. It is not likely in this earlier period that a diocese would complain at receiving a monk as its bishop (as the diocese of Mainz did in 1031 when Bardo, formerly abbot of Hersfeld, became its bishop), or that the imperial courtiers would object to the installation of a monkish bishop who had not learned the art of governing at the royal court (as they did when the ascetic Wazo was elected Bishop of Liège in 1042[32]). The Carolingian capitularies on education do not make distinctions between cathedral and monastery schools; they enjoin the same education on both. The *Epistola de litteris colendis* is directed to Abbot Baugulf of Fulda, who is to send copies to all bishops and monasteries.[33] The differences in rules of life of monks and clerics will have guaranteed some differences in the discipline of *mores* and *conversatio*. But any differences that may distinguish the two in the teaching of letters do not register in the main sources on education. The unity and uniformity of the Carolingian reform were one of its great strengths, a trend toward cultural unification of the empire one of its great accomplishments.

Court Education: *Civiles Mores/Aulicae Disciplinae*

An education in *ecclesiasticae disciplinae* was available at the royal court under Charlemagne.[34] This sharply distinguished the Carolingian "palace school" from the court schools of the Merovingians, whose sole purpose was training in military and civil disciplines.[35]

Ecclesiastical education was available at the court, and it probably differed little from that offered in Alcuin's school at St. Martin's of Tours, at Fulda, or at St. Gall. But we also find reference to something called *aulicae disciplinae*. It is not easy to form a picture of what the phrase indicates. It is a minor subject in the history of education in the period, but its small rivulet swells into the mainstream of the eleventh century.

SCHOOLS AT COURT/THE COURT AS A SCHOOL
Hincmar of Rheims wrote a letter of instruction for Louis the German, in which he described the "palace school" under Charlemagne:

> The king's court is properly called a school, that is a course of discipline [*schola, id est disciplina*], not because it consists solely of schoolmen, men bred on learning and well trained in the conventional way, but rather a school in its own right, which we can take to mean a place of discipline, that is correction,

since it corrects men's way of dressing [or behaving: *habitus*] and walking, their speech and actions, and in general holds them to the norms of restraint appropriate to a good life.[36]

Hincmar was far from regarding the main object of education at court as sacred or divine letters. On the contrary, he sets the discipline of behavior against the usual school disciplines (*non tantum scolastici, id est disciplinati . . . sicut alii*), and the passage implies that it is this other kind of discipline that makes the court a school.

The idea of a "court school" is open to misunderstanding. The source of this misunderstanding is our conception of a school as an institution devoted exclusively to a kind of instruction where some people teach and lecture and others learn and read.[37] To recover the earlier notion it is useful to remove from the word "school" the suggestion of learned instruction. What remains is the sense of membership in a group with common characteristics, habits, and interests. In Merovingian times *schola* commonly refers to the court entourage.[38] It is useful to take this definition of the word as our point of departure: a group with common characteristics, customs, and interests.

Monastery, cathedral, and court all have their individual institutional identities, even if the special concerns of education do not register them. But the court is distinguished from the other two in that it combines the center of political power with the center of social life. Under Charlemagne it also became the center of intellectual activity and continued as such in varying degrees with successive emperors. That peculiar constellation accounts for tensions in the life of the court that tend toward the creation of an etiquette of behavior. Indeed, our vocabulary of politeness is still strongly marked by reminders of its origins at worldly courts: "courtesy," "curtsey," to "pay court." A code of refined manners seems to be a constant of life at a prince's court. The courts of Europe, the orient, Arabia, and India all produced ideals of courtly behavior.

The curriculum of institutional identity and the pedagogy of individual charisma were as strongly in force at worldly courts as in monasteries or cathedrals. The possibilities for diversity were far greater at court, however. There is no ideal of uniform dress and behavior (*aequalitas morum*). On the contrary, there is a tendency toward personalized and individualized forms of behavior that grew stronger in the course of the high and late Middle Ages, and became a striking feature of Renaissance courts. Fashion and a tendency toward the aestheticizing of behavior, hence toward artificiality, are features of European court life that distinguish it from customs of religious communities.

Hincmar stated that the king's court is itself a school, which "corrects men's way of dressing and walking, their speech and actions, and in general holds them to the norms of restraint appropriate to a good life." In part the language is that of ecclesiastical disciplines: *disciplina, correctio, bonitatis continentia.*[39] It departs from that language by omitting any reference to sacred learning, scripture, or divine law. *Habitus, incessus, verbum*, and *actus* are not common among the topics of praise of Carolingian clergy,[40] but they will loom large in the eleventh century.

The education of the royal family under Charlemagne included behavior, *mores*. We learn this from Einhard who tells that the emperor arranged for the education of his children

> first in liberal studies, to which he himself was devoted. Then, as soon as their age permitted, he had his sons instructed in horseback riding, weapons, and hunting, as is the custom of the Franks, while his daughters learned spinning and weaving . . . and he ordered them instructed in every element of good behavior.[41]

A witness to the training at the court school is Ermenrich of Ellwangen, who wrote a letter to his teacher, Grimald, former member of the palace academy, associate of Alcuin and Paulus Diaconus, and Abbot of St. Gall from 841 to 872. It praises him as

> dressed in the seven-fold garment Sophia wove, adorned with the gems of all virtues [humility, justice, fortitude, prudence, temperance, zeal for God, patience and lenience, good cheer in adversity, humility in prosperity]. And you well deserve to fly above others on the wings of these virtues, since from the first flower of youth you were nurtured in excellent manners among the courtiers of the blessed emperors [Charlemagne and Louis the Pious]. From them you learned not only the whole range of school subjects, but also the norm of right living . . .[42]

From this description we learn at least that the education of an imperial courtier excited extravagant praise in ornate language, which pares down in the above passage to *liberales disciplinae* and *decentissimi mores*. The list of virtues is consistent with other descriptions of Carolingian clergy (Hrabanus Maurus' treatment of the virtues in *De institutione clericorum* comes close) and with writings on the virtues by Grimald's teacher, Alcuin. This catalogue of virtues has a more worldly cast than some: it dwells on the four cardinal virtues, and Grimald's patience and twice-mentioned humility are Stoic as well as Christian virtues, not specific to a social context. Descriptions cited earlier combining liberal arts, sacred scriptures, and ecclesiastical discipline highlight this worldliness somewhat by contrast, but they do not show one set of virtues specific to the court and another specific to the monastery/cathedral. While the worldly setting of the court and the emperor's presence impress this writer particularly, little in the passage suggests a distinction between the pattern of Grimald's education and that common to Carolingian programs generally, except that Ermenrich did not mention ecclesiastical disciplines.

Paschius Radbertus's Vita of Adalhard, Abbot of Corvey (d. 826) shows a similar admiration for courtly upbringing. The nephew of King Pipin, cousin of Charlemagne, Adalhard was educated at court along with "the neophytes of the palace," assigned to the same masters as the young prince. The biographer gives nothing more than a hint at the nature of that education: he was "instructed in every form of worldly wisdom" (*omni mundi prudentia eruditus*).[43] The only conclusions we can draw from this phrase are that *prudentia mundi* formed part of the instruction at the palace, and that Paschasius Radbertus's description of Adalhard's education is fragmentary. "Worldly prudence" does not emerge as a course of studies separable from "ecclesiastical disciplines." The fact that Adalhard eventually became Abbot of St. Gall attests to his mastery of, or at the very least his extensive exposure to, the latter.

This is the context in which we turn to Alcuin's writings for the court. We know that students of the palace school received the whole range of education available in the period: instruction in liberal disciplines, sacred letters, and some form of moral/ethical formation. A formulation like "worldly wisdom" or *morum honestas* gives us no entry into the contents of ethical instruction.

Alcuin's work *De rhetorica et virtutibus* is singular among his writings in that its ethical vocabulary and concepts are clearly distinguishable from that of *conversatio* and *mores* in the majority of Carolingian texts. The work is one in a series of dialogues between Alcuin and his pupils: *De grammatica, De rhetorica et virtutibus*, and *De dialectica*.[44] They form a sequence that aims at a comprehensive course on the trivium. There are references in one dialogue to questions disputed in the previous one (cf. PL 101, 951D). The work *De orthographia* forms a part of this sequence, but its form is purely expository, not dialogic, and it lacks the general philosophical framework in which each of the others is situated.

The *De rhetorica* operates squarely in the context of civil administration, and this is its most distinctive feature. The introductory verses explain that it was written by Charlemagne and Alcuin together while they carried on the business of the court.[45] Charlemagne begins the dialogue by asking Alcuin for instruction:

> I recall your once mentioning that the entire thrust of this art is directed at civil questions. But, as you know better than anyone, the affairs of the kingdom and the concerns of the palace place us in constant contact with this sort of question, and it seems ridiculous to have remained ignorant of the precepts of an art so necessary to my daily occupations.[46]

This stress on the practical application of the art of rhetoric in secular government continues throughout.[47] The work is about *civiles mores*, and the introductory verses invite all interested in this art to learn its precepts:

> Whoever wishes to learn civil manners, I say,
>   Let him read the precepts in this book.[48]

The dialogue begins with a definition of rhetoric and its application: "[rhetoric] is concerned with civil questions" (p. 68, l. 57). The particular form in which Alcuin conceives the art excludes administrative tasks in the church, as Charlemagne states outright late in the dialogue: "Those who are deemed destined for civil matters and *secular affairs* must cultivate the art of oratory with great diligence from youth on."[49] This shows the social-political context for Alcuin's dialogue on rhetoric: its lessons apply to men at the royal court who will use the art of oratory in their public life, and who ideally will receive training in the discipline from their youth.

We should be careful not to confuse this with "lay education." Alcuin's view of the education of a layman is clearly expressed in his "breviary" for Count Wido, the letter-tract, *De virtutibus et vitiis*, basically a guide to piety.[50] By contrast, the *De rhetorica et virtutibus* provides us with a glimpse of a rarity in Carolingian education: a purely secular discipline.

Alcuin's work is central to a sociology of rhetoric in the Carolingian period.[51] It borrows so heavily from Cicero's *De inventione* as to appear in places a cento of quotations. Its other sources are ancient — Quintilian and the fourth-century writer Julius Victor, through whom Cicero's *De oratore* reached Alcuin. Earlier suggestions of strong influence from Cassiodorus and Isidore have proven unfounded.[52] Its rhetorical doctrine is so close to that of Cicero that the search for peculiarly Alcuinian elements is not rewarding. Its general conceptual framework is an abbreviated version of Cicero's philosophy of the orator. Alcuin lifts Cicero's myth assigning the origins of civilization to eloquence, from the beginning of *De inventione*, and places it without change at the opening of *De rhetorica*. The ethical thrust of Cicero's work, inseparable from that myth, is also part and parcel of Alcuin's work. It is about rhetoric *and the virtues*. Appending "the virtues" to his title served the author's purposes, even though they are the subject of only the final section.

Cicero's point of departure was that eloquence has two faces: good and evil. When the orator is a good man, whose eloquence is allied with wisdom, then oratory is a civilizing force, uniting men in harmony and guiding the state rationally.[53] Speech and conduct are linked in Cicero's scheme of the discipline of oratory, and the training of a statesman requires long exercise in both.[54]

Alcuin leads into the ethical aspect of the orator's education with his discussion of the fifth and last division of rhetoric, delivery (*pronuntiatio*, p. 138. ll. 1088ff). It is defined as "dignity of phrasing, the congruence of meaning and expression, and the control of the body." Proper delivery requires long and arduous training of voice and body. This training must begin in youth; it cultivates a confident voice, an even flow of speech, and decorous movement of the body. The court is the appropriate place for this exercise and training; it is to the orator what the military camp is to the soldier.[55] The law of speech and of conduct is moderation and temperance; it governs speech and conduct alike:

> ... let your words be well chosen, proper, lucid, simple, let your speech be full, your demeanor serene, your face well composed. Do not laugh immoderately, and speak without raucousness. For there is a law of the golden mean [*bonus modus*] in speech as in carriage, in walking calmly, without springing, without hesitating, allowing every move to show forth temperance and moderation, which is one of the four cardinal virtues, from which the others procede as from their roots. In these are located nobility of mind, dignity of conduct, probity of manners and praiseworthy discipline.[56]

This discourse brings home to Charlemagne the meaning of the philosopher's saying, "nothing in excess": it applies no less to conduct than to speech (*non solum moribus, sed etiam verbis*, l. 1177). Then follows a brief treatment of the four cardinal virtues, ending with the reminder that God and salvation are the goals of all human striving.

These quotations give some of the major themes of the orator's education inherited from Cicero, Quintilian, and the entire Roman tradition which flowed into Alcuin's work. They also state the major themes of training in *mores* in the cathedral schools of the eleventh century. The ideals of "nobility of mind," "dignified conduct," and moderation in speech and bearing, move from these traditions into a scene dominated by "ecclesiastical" education.

In Alcuin's work we find discipline of manners linked to eloquent speech. The two are inseparable, since an eloquent speech loses its effectiveness when delivered with inappropriate and undisciplined gestures (cf. pg. 139. ll. 1093ff.). Disciplined conduct and bearing are then an indispensable part of an orator's education. In ecclesiastical education the linking of letters and conduct was much looser. The two elements were separable, and Charlemagne's efforts first to add letters to conduct, then to reinforce conduct when it was neglected in favor of letters, show the tendency of the two to separate. No pressing social need held them together; no philosophical coherence was threatened with rupture by their separation. The same was not true of civil rhetoric. Well composed manners were as much a part of it as well composed speeches.

The type of the virtuous orator, then, comes across in Alcuin as part of the discipline of delivery and oratorical training in general: one requires the virtues for effective delivery. Virtue had been part of the overarching philosophical framework of oratory and public service: in Cicero virtue makes the orator good; in Alcuin it makes him effective. But the requirement of training in *mores* for the statesman remains the same in both.

Classical, not ecclesiastical, models provided the guidelines for Alcuin's orator. He is at pains to argue the legitimacy of the ancient philosophers as authorities on conduct.[57] One particular phrase in Alcuin's dialogue will prove useful later in locating and defining classical ideals of behavior. At the end of the work a few lines of verse are appended corresponding to the verses with which the work opened.[58] They urge young men to put the days of their youth to good use, learning good speech and cultivating the virtues, learning to treat their "cases" (*causas*) with eloquence, so that they can provide their people defense, protection, and well-being. The poem ends with the lines,

Disce, precor, juvenis, motus moresque venustos,
    Laudetur toto ut nomen in orbe tuum.

"Learn, I beg you, young man, beauty of gestures and of manners, so that your name will be praised throughout the land." "Beautiful gestures and manners" is a classical ideal. I have not found an occurrence of it in personal descriptions from the period. The phrase is uncommon in Alcuin, though not completely isolated.[59]

Alcuin's dialogue on rhetoric in general is a work so isolated in the Carolingian period that it appears anomalous. Its focus on secular administration isolates it within Alcuin's own works on the trivium. It lacks the distinctive feature of Carolingian learning, the submersion of classical models in Christian ones. This absence is evident if we compare the dialogue with a Carolingian presentation of rhetoric that does show that feature, that of Hrabanus Maurus—Alcuin's pupil—on rhetoric in the *De institutione clericorum*. The chapter begins,

> Rhetoric, as the masters agree, is the science of speaking well in secular letters and in civil questions.

This could have been a lesson learned from Alcuin's rhetoric.[60] But immediately there follows the element lacking there:

> But this definition, though it seems to pertain to worldly knowledge, still it is not wholly foreign to ecclesiastical discipline. For whatever an orator and preacher of divine law profers eloquently and decorously, or whatever he puts forward aptly and elegantly in speech, is in accord with the dictates of this art; nor should it be considered sinful for a student to practice this art at an appropriate age.[61]

The taint of sin clung to rhetoric in the first generation of students following Alcuin, and Hrabanus had to free the art of this taint and pronounce it legitimate as an early stage in the education of a preacher. We noticed earlier that Hrabanus adapted the figure of the orator and its classical definition to the purposes of the Christian preacher.[62] He clearly understood the position of rhetoric in the arts and appropriated a classical model for ecclesiastical purposes; he indicates that this art, ancient and pagan though it may be, has a modern application in "secular letters and civil questions."

The civil education of a prince is an obvious necessity of rule, and the silence of sources should not be taken as proof of its absence, particularly in a period as conscious of both lay and clerical education as the Carolingian. Eloquence was of practical value to the ruler. Sedulius Scottus makes it into one of the "eight pillars which . . . uphold the kingdom of a just king . . . ": "the fourth [pillar] is persuasiveness or affability in speech," and a line of verse restates the thought, "the fourth, eloquence, utters pleasing words."[63] The description of Charlemagne's education in Einhard's biography points to his study of rhetoric with Alcuin,[64] and that gives some minor corroboration to the program of the *De rhetorica et virtutibus* as a practiced curriculum of rhetoric. But again, we are limited to the figure of Charlemagne himself and his teacher Alcuin. If Alcuin's introductory verses to those who "desire to learn civil manners" applied to many courtiers, the traces of this wider instruction are lost. The picture of lay literacy in Thompson's study shows no signs of rhetorical/oratorical training among the Carolingian laity generally[65]; their education is not essentially different from that of the clergy — at least it is described in formulae that are not essentially different. Alcuin's tract represents training in rhetoric and civil manners as actually available at the Carolingian court, but it was probably restricted to Charlemagne and the narrow circle around him. On the other hand, the manuscript tradition shows that the work was popular and fairly widely distributed in the ninth century.[66] What we can conclude from it is that there was an awareness of the classical model of the orator's education at the center of power and educational reform in the late eighth/early ninth century. Since no Carolingian statesman was actually described in the terms that traditionally convey this form of education, however, we must at least consider whether it existed mainly on paper. We can say with some certainty that when educational programs were translated into practice, the ideal of the statesman/ orator was subordinated to that of the Christian prince or the preacher and converter.

If the program suggested in the *De rhetorica* was a reality in the palace school of Charlemagne, it must have been a kind of "underground" project. Long and arduous training in "beautiful manners and gestures" may have existed, but it would have been pulled constantly into the orbit of Christian recastings of *bona conversatio* and *honestas morum*. The training of a secular statesman/orator in *civiles mores* would have been in a constant state of assimilation to the far more powerful force in educational reform, *ecclesiasticae disciplinae*.

This picture was to change radically in the middle of the tenth century.

2. Court and School in Ottonian Times

A New Model: *Disciplina Brunonis*

Brun of Cologne, brother of Otto the Great, archchaplain and imperial chancellor (ca. 939–953) and Archbishop of Cologne (953–965), was an educator and statesman. That the two roles are hard to separate from each other is a symptom of a new model of education that emerges in the mid-tenth century and comes to dominate in the eleventh.

We approach it via two texts that describe Brun's activity as teacher. The first is from his biography, written around 968–969 by Ruotger, a cleric of Cologne and his former student. He tells of Brun's life at the imperial court, to which his brother summoned him from his studies at Utrecht. The court in Ruotger's idealized picture is a kind of philosopher's academy that reached its highpoint through Brun's influence. He describes it as a place where "through studies, whatever was obscure in the world could be illuminated." The court attracted anyone with a sense of his own worth; men oppressed by calumny received asylum. In Brun they found an exemplar of wisdom, piety, and justice beyond anything in human memory. Those who came with notions of their own learning went forth again chastened and convinced of their ignorance. God made Brun his vessel, and filled him with the spirit of wisdom and understanding. Brun stimulated thought on philosophical questions, common and abstruse, and he restored the seven liberal arts, which had long since fallen into neglect, to a place of prominence. Whatever new and grand things the historians, orators, poets, or philosophers bruited about, he diligently scrutinized with learned men of whatever language, and if one of them distinguished himself for his understanding, Brun humbly made himself that man's pupil. Debates took place between the most learned of the Latin and Greek doctors on the most subtle and highest questions of philosophy, and Brun served as mediator. He raised the level of Latin eloquence at court, not only his own, but that of many others, and he did this with no arrogance, but with courtly grace and urbane gravity. He was a diligent reader, even carrying a portable library with him when the court traveled.[1]

Ruotger considered the subject of Brun as a learned courtier important enough to devote three chapters of his biography to it. His description stresses intellectual activities. Philosophical debate focuses on obscure and difficult questions; the seven liberal arts loom large, and Ruotger sees this as a renewal of a neglected subject; reading and eloquence appear as autonomous subjects, not as applied and practical aspects of a statesman's activities. "Letters" in the general sense predominate. The idea of an ethical formation is not absent, merely inconspicuous. Ruotger says that Brun himself provides an exemplar of wisdom, piety and justice. On questions of behavior, Brun was the text that others studied. This two-fold orientation of teaching activity at court is indicated in the two-fold gift that Brun received from God: *sapientia* and *intellectus*. A court "education" means absorbing the double light of these two beams that illumine the "student"'s mind and manners.

The second text presents more fully the ethical thrust of Brun's pedagogy, only hinted at in his biography. It also shows us that something essential has changed from Carolingian to Ottonian times. This text describes the education of one of Brun's pupils at the cathedral school of Cologne, Dietrich, first bishop of Metz by that name (965–984). The informant is Sigebert of Gembloux, who wrote a biography of Dietrich around 1050–60. Dietrich, born of high Saxon nobility, had his first education at the cathedral school of Halberstadt. From his efforts there he began to show the rich fruits of "inborn nature and manners" resulting from his "sublime education."[2] After his early studies, he follows his cousin Brun to Cologne, and becomes the pupil and inseparable companion of the archbishop. Now begins his "education" by Brun; it is worth quoting the passage in full:

> And because he was destined one day to do civil battle in the militia of the church, he was exercised now over long periods beneath [Brun's] tutelage in an apprenticeship of liberal studies at the school of the holy church of Cologne, and laudably stood the test in lengthy exercises. He who would one day have many men subject to him to their own utility, learned now humbly to subject himself; he learned to benefit his subjects, governing most usefully with humility and discretion. There were in each of these men talents that each embraced in the other, and, as steel sharpens steel, the one was edified in emulation of the other's good qualities.[3]

In the following lines Sigebert stresses the friendship that bound the two men to each other and strengthened the ties of blood that joined them. This relationship had its higher significance:

... a man destined to so great and important a role in Christ and in the church, whom mother church had educated as an ornament and a firmament [foundation] to itself, whom nature — or rather the creator of nature himself — had provided with the native gift of genius: such a man well deserved to be instructed and polished in the study and the tutelage of such a master. As a certain poet puts it,

Learning promotes inborn talent,
And the right exercises strengthen the muscles,
But when manners falter,
Failings mar native virtue. [Horace, Ode 4,4]

The two texts give us a picture of Brun active as a teacher at both court and cathedral school. The first feature of this picture we should notice is the absence of Carolingian educational goals. The understanding of Holy Scripture is never mentioned; preparation for pastoral care and the edification of religion is nowhere in evidence. Dietrich's "role in Christ and the church" will be "civil battle." The motives and goals of education in the two texts are secular. Ruotger's description places the stress on reading and intellectual activity in itself, not on any religious motive, and if he praises Brun as an exemplar of justice, wisdom, and piety, the lack of any dramatization of this last quality shows the small corner into which it shrinks in this biography[4] as opposed to virtually any Carolingian vita. Likewise Brun's instruction as school master and bishop of Cologne prepares Dietrich of Metz above all for the worldly affairs of the empire and the church of Metz.

Here we do learn the goals and motives of education. The long and demanding discipline imposed on Dietrich by Brun aims at the preparation of one who is to do "civil battle" on behalf of the church: *civiliter militaturus* is a key phrase. We have seen the role of education in civil matters in Carolingian times. It was present, but minimal, restricted to an education in rhetoric at court for the emperor and those (apparently few) who wished to learn *civiles mores* — an education that had little profile in itself, but lived a life borrowed from its source, Cicero. In Brun's pedagogy preparation for "civil" activity is located in the cathedral. Dietrich is to administer the church and govern many subjects, and again the civil life is more in the biographer's eye than the religious. Sigebert stresses the "utility" of Dietrich's destined rule: "he was to govern many for their own utility and to benefit his subjects most usefully." The civil causes of the church are also the end of liberal learning: "because he was to exert himself in civil causes, he was exercised in an apprenticeship of liberal studies" (" . . . quia erat . . . civiliter militaturus . . . liberali tyrocinio est exercitatus" — *Vita Deod.*,

p. 464, l. 48). In the next chapter he describes Dietrich as "a man born for the utility of many" ("vir ad utilitatem multorum nat[us]" — p. 465, l. 17); his stewardship of the church of Metz was given him "for the profit of many" ("profectui plurimorum" — p. 465, l. 19). This education subtly shifts the relationship of *praeesse* and *prodesse* — ruling and doing good — as received from the Benedictine Rule. The rule enjoins the abbot to attempt "to do good rather than govern."[5] The relation between "governing" and "benefiting" is particularly important here. Christian tradition prior to the Ottonian period continues the priority given to benefiting as against commanding.[6] From Ottonian times on, "governing" or ruling rises in importance: *praeesse* in equal measure with *prodesse* becomes the formula for a bishop's authority; not so much *praeesse* as *prodesse* the abbot's.

The essential point in the passage from Sigebert's Life of Dietrich is that governing becomes part of an education preparing more for statesmanship than for pastoral duties. Insufficient training in "governing" was to be invoked against the nomination of Wazo to the bishopric of Liège: he had neither learned to govern, nor had he served the emperor in his chapel. This training in *praeesse* was clearly in the context of imperial service, and Wazo's election shows us the imperial tradition asserting itself against a monastic one intruding into episcopal elections (see below, Chapter 7).

The learning of human qualities predominates in the description of Dietrich's education. This element was present in Carolingian education, of course, but there it was more appropriate to speak of "spiritual formation" than of ethics. Two features of Brun's influence are especially striking. First is the role of his personal presence. This is not *disciplina regularis*. He is not instructing his cousin in some textbook curriculum of manners. He is shining on him the beam of his personality. His personal charisma is a course of studies, and his mere presence is the textbook. This is the thrust of Sigebert's metaphor, "as steel sharpens steel, the one was edified in emulation of the other's gifts." Brun's person was exemplary: this is an observation Sigebert shared with Ruotger. The latter showed Brun as a mirror of justice, piety and wisdom at the emperor's court "beyond anything human memory can recall," and throughout he stresses this quality in Brun.[7] The motive of writing his biography is to retain the force of his personal presence in the written word: "We believe that many others can be taught by the example of his way of living if we recount it summarily from his youth" (ch. 2, p. 3). Ruotger was trying to capture and preserve in the form of the written word the transforming effect of Brun's personality.

It is worth noting that Sigebert describes this relationship not only with the metaphor of steel sharpening steel but also with vocabulary borrowed from Neoplatonic conceptions of the creation. Not nature but its *auctor* gives Dietrich his inborn genius; God makes him in his own image, transforming him in turn into an *opifex* who is to shape good works in the workshop (*officina*) of the bishopric (line 18). Brun has the power to imprint himself on others like a Platonic archetype on raw matter.

The second striking feature is Sigebert's stress on the role of natural talent. Dietrich is a product of nature, or of the creator of nature, from whom he has received the native gift of genius: " . . . quem natura, immo ipsius auctor naturae, nativo ingenii bono ditabat. . . ." God of course has more gifts at his disposal to give future bishops, and we might intuitively expect some of these as well as *ingenium* to fall to Dietrich's lot: powers of prophecy, sanctity, contempt for worldly vanity and so forth. Instead, he receives not any particular characteristic but rather intellectual potentiality, a tabula rasa of high quality material.

But here we have touched on what was no doubt a major influence of the figure of Brun. Suddenly the stress on the supernatural in the making of men gives way to the natural. The talents inborn in men had provided Ruotger with the opening of his biography. He tries to deal with the mysterious process by which divine grace parcels out its gifts. On the one hand, man has nothing he has not received (1. Cor. 4: 7); on the other, man in some way deserves what he receives. It is a theocratic view of man juxtaposed with an aristocratic one. For the apostle, all gifts are given, and the man without them is dust. For the aristocracy such a democratizing of privilege is absurd; merits must be inborn and course in the blood, and the elect of noble birth develops them by discipline. The compromise position for the Christian is that inborn merits lure divine grace more strongly than inborn faults. And this is Ruotger's explanation for Brun's talents:

> The ineffable providence of God's goodness confers on the elect the abundant and free gifts of grace. And yet in some sense they merit what they receive, the one more, the other less. The one and unique spirit follows its own will in parcelling out to individual men whatever it wishes, according to the force at work in each.[8]

Well might Ruotger call the diversity of human talents "an amazing problem" (*admirabilis questio*). His own formulations can do nothing to resolve the paradox with which it confronts him; they only heighten it. They show divine grace both operating by its own free will and compelled by the forces at work in its beneficiaries.

The recurrence of this stress on natural talent in Sigebert's Vita of Dietrich is no coincidence but an important part of the new model. Sigebert is well informed about Brun. In a sense, Brun is the leading character of Dietrich's biography, and Dietrich stands somewhat in his shadow. Brun made Dietrich what he is through education, made him in the image and likeness of himself. Sigebert praises one quality especially in Brun: his eye for men of talent and his success in employing them in the administration of the empire:

> To the other skills in which he abounded there is this to add: that he bestowed his favor and friendship on princes of whatever rank, in whom he perceived the innocence of the dove, the cunning of the serpent, and especially the simplicity of sound faith. For men like this he . . . sought and won the favor of the king two- and three-fold. If perchance a private life had kept any such man out of the limelight, he perceived the apt moment for raising him into positions vacated through the death of illustrious men, and urged them on to good action. He truly became all things to all men . . . [9]

The description fluctuates between Brun as proselytizer and Brun as talent scout, though the man with the eye for religious charisma is clearly overlay and decoration, and the man with the eye for administrative talent and usefulness in the affairs of the empire clearly the essential point. He commended his "finds" not to God's but to the king's favor.

Dietrich's promotion to Bishop of Metz is reported as one such find, and the lengthy praise of Brun's talents preceding it places the student in the shadow of his teacher.

The idea of natural talent became part of the tradition of memorializing Dietrich I of Metz. It was not Sigebert's invention. Alpertus, a monk of St. Symphorian, writing a history of the bishops of Metz ca. 1006, half a century before Sigebert, testifies to Dietrich's inborn talents in turns of thought not far from Ruotger's. After reciting the swashbuckling story of Dietrich's rescue of Otto II near Rossano in 982,[10] he defends Dietrich against the reproach of disloyalty to Otto III, arguing his superiority to any of his contemporaries:

> When I ponder the affairs of all the eminent men of our church, I find nothing in them that is not surpassed by the elegance of his life. And anyone who presumes to compare his own conduct favorably to Dietrich's brings down on himself the charge of arrogance; for many are rendered rich or illustrious by what others give or steal for them, not by their own merits. But Dietrich had far more to commend him than high birth and illustrious ancestors: his fame rested also on the great wealth of endowments he was born with.[11]

There is one further point to make before we try to locate these texts in a social and historical setting. The education of Dietrich of Metz shows us clearly a new goal of learning, but not its content. The textbook is Brun himself; "learning" it makes a good governor of the church. But what is written in it? The only answer Sigebert provides is "humility": "There he learned to subject himself humbly and to benefit his subjects through a humble and judicious administration" ("Discebat ibi humiliter subesse . . . et subiectis humili et discreta praelatione utillime prodesse"). Both parts of the sentence place this virtue in the context of administration, and both make it clear that it is a virtue of a ruler and governor, not that of a saint; it is a lesson that applies particularly to a man "destined to be placed above many" ("qui debebat multis aliquando utiliter praeesse"). It is a virtue closer to aristocratic deference than to Christian self-denial.[12] It is in a sense less valuable in itself than as a counterbalance to the pride inevitably generated by the "great man's" sense of self-worth (Ruotger's epithet for Brun, *Vita Brun.*, chapter 3, LB, p. 184: *magnus vir*).

Sparse as this indication of Brun's discipline is, it remains consistent with our reading of Dietrich's education as a preparation for statesmanship.

*   *   *

These passages show us some important features of a new model of education. It is by and large secular though given and received by clerics; it is for the civil administration of the church; it integrates the liberal arts into the formation of *mores*; its ethical side relies on the charisma of the "great man"; it focuses more on the development of human talent than the acquisitions of normative, rule-imposed qualities; notions of supernatural intrusion into the process of education function more as metaphor than as literal exposition of that process; it aims at the preparation of administrators and statesmen; it makes great men greater for civil purposes; its context is the imperial church, the secular and episcopal court.

The texts discussed do not give us a paradigm of that education. They are too selective. Their information is suggestive of grand lines. They give us the general contours of this new education, which we can draw in sharper detail by reference to other texts.

Some readers will have wondered about the value of Sigebert of Gembloux's testimony to Brun's teaching. He lived and wrote nearly a century after Brun, but it is easy to validate his testimony. The biography was written during his tenure as school master at St. Vincent of Metz

(1050–ca. 1070/75). While he had grown up in the reformed community of Gembloux, his years at Metz clearly brought him into close contact with an imperial see. We have already seen that he shares a number of concerns central to Ruotger's biography: the role of natural talent, the humility appropriate to the great man, the importance of statesmanship and exemplary teaching. Virtually every feature of his description of Brun's teaching finds corroboration in Ruotger's biography. But after all Brun "as he actually was," or as his contemporaries actually observed him, is not at issue. At issue is the model of education we can infer from these texts.

Another work by Sigebert is helpful on this score. In the section he wrote of the history of the abbots of Gembloux (*Gesta abbatum Gemblacensium*),[13] he describes the education of his own teacher, Abbot Olbert. It is very different from the education of Dietrich of Metz. Olbert was educated from his early youth "in the discipline of monks according to the rule" ("in disciplina monachica regulariter" — chapter 26, p. 536). Also he was "excellently educated in the disciplines of letters" ("in studiis litterarum adprime eruditus" — loc. cit.). He studied the seven liberal arts for the sake of later scriptural studies. His own teaching was directed at the liberal arts, sacred scripture, and moral improvement. The latter is described at length.[14] It is a glimpse at "spiritual formation" in an eleventh-century monastery. There is not a single echo of Brun's teaching as presented in Sigebert's *Vita Deoderici*.

Sigebert distinguished clearly between an education appropriate to the monastery and one appropriate to the cathedral, a distinction it was not possible to make sharply in Carolingian times. The two passages from Sigebert show us two directions in education: one older, monastic, a survival from Carolingian reforms; the other a new direction, recently emerged. The latter was placed by Sigebert squarely in a historical/political context he revered and idealized: the Ottonian empire.

The Imperial Church

The term, "imperial church system," describes the integration of the church into the administrative apparatus of the empire that occurred as part of a program implemented by Otto I and his successors.[15] The Saxon emperors benefited in the establishment of an imperial church from two bequests of Carolingian rule: a quasi-divine aura surrounding the king, and the conception of the king/emperor as the heir and continuator of the Roman empire and of Roman traditions of rule. This latter pillar of imperial ideology was developed and articulated in Ottonian times beyond what was possible in the Carolingian period. The Ottos also transformed the administrative apparatus in ways that led them well beyond their Carolingian predecessors. They took a more aggressive role in the selection and seating of bishops, and they did not shrink from placing their own relatives and friends in vacant sees, men strictly loyal to the emperors and to imperial interests. In this way the Ottos built up a network of political alliances in the kingdom that served as a buffer against the traditional political opposition of the nobility. And they created an ecclesiastical institution with an entirely new and much more worldly cast: the *ecclesia regni* or *ecclesia imperii*.

Court and Cathedral

The royal/imperial court played a significant role in this transformation of the power structures in the empire. A close personal relationship to the emperor became one of the decisive elements in determining a man's suitability (*idoneitas*) for the office of bishop. Young men were groomed at court, under the eye of the emperor, for service later in the kingdom. In this way the court chapel became a training ground and a "school for imperial bishops."[16] The emperors sought men of talent in monastic and cathedral schools, invited them to court, and eventually promoted them to the bishopric. This was a common sequence in the career of an Ottonian bishop: from cathedral school to court chapel to bishopric.

Courtier Bishops

This development brought a new figure onto the political and cultural scene, the "courtier bishop," or, in the pithy German phrase, "geistlicher Fürst," "spiritual prince."[17] Brun of Cologne is the prototype of this figure.[18] His brother Otto singles him out (in Ruotger's version of events) for an important diplomatic mission in time of political crisis, and explains his choice to Brun:

> What consoles me most in my present straits is that I see a royal priesthood sent by the grace of God Allmighty to the aid of our empire. For you combine in your person the religion of a priest and the strength of a king. . . . And I have long noted that the mother of all noble arts and the virtue of true philosophy is yours, and it is she who has educated you to modesty and greatness of soul.[19]

An extraordinarily illuminating speech — whether Otto actually spoke it or Ruotger invented or embroidered it. It gives us one of the dominant political conceptions of Ottonian rule: the "royal priesthood," borne by the clerical prince who combines his ecclesiastical duties with obligations to the state (*res publica*), and who requires a wisdom and virtuosity gained in the study of "philosophy." It was a combination of activities that was not unproblematic for his contemporaries. Ruotger is at pains to legitimize this mingling of pastoral duties with secular ones and to protect Brun's name against reproaches leveled at him of excessive worldly preoccupations. He refers to Old Testament figures who were both priest and judge and shows all the good that Brun accomplished in the service of the state: "All that he did was for the good and the benefit of our republic" ("Honestum namque et utile nostre rei publice fuit omne, quod fecit" — chapter 23, p. 214). This formulation states one of the major goals of clerical political activity (we have already seen it in passing in Dietrich of Metz's biography: *utilitas ecclesiae, utilitas rei publicae*), and it draws on categories borrowed from Cicero's work on statesmanship, *De officiis*. The two ethical spheres, *honestum et utile*, structure Cicero's work; the task of the statesman is to reconcile them.

The discussion of Otto's letter ordinarily focuses on the phrase *regale sacerdotium*. But what interests us here is the role of "philosophy." It is evident from the above that education plays a major role in the office Otto has mapped out for his brother. He admires both his priestly princehood and his education through philosophy; again, as earlier in Ruotger and later in Sigebert of Gembloux, the result of this education is an array of virtues that combines deference with greatness, *modestia* and *magnitudo animi*. Ruotger said earlier that Brun "remained meek and gentle, though placed at the very pinnacle of nobility" ("in maximo nobilitatis fastu humilis et mansuetus erat" — ch. 11, p. 11); and Dietrich learned from Brun how to remain humble while ruling over many subjects. Probably there is a reflection of the same ideal in Sigebert's observation that Brun had an eye for men who combined "the meekness of the dove with the cunning of the serpent" (cf. Matt. 10: 16). At least it shows a similar tension between skill and a virtue restraining and tempering it. Is this combination then an individual characteristic of Brun? Since it is repeated by various sources in formulations that owe nothing to each other, the historian is tempted to believe it. But it is one of those perplexing situations where the rules for critical reading of texts are not adequate to the task at hand. Otto the Great (or Ruotger putting words in his mouth), in praising the influence of philosophy on Brun, has borrowed another formulation from Cicero, who wrote of philosophy's influence in the *Tusculan Disputations*, " . . . philosophy, the mother of all arts . . . instructed us first in their worship [i.e., the gods] . . . then in modesty and greatness of soul . . . "[20] Whether or not this is a personal characteristic of Brun described by Ruotger in a classical formulation does not matter. It is one of the central educational ideals of the Ottonian courtier bishop: greatness tempered by humility. It becomes a common formula in praise of courtier bishops.[21] Ruotger's testimony allows us to trace it to the figure of Brun, who was instrumental in creating, embodying, and transmitting the ideals of this office, and to observe its literary source in Ciceronian ideals of the statesman. Other sources show its diffusion to men in the same milieu. It is one of many ideals of the office of imperial bishop. It is instructive in this context because it shows us the importance of humanist educational tradition (Cicero) and of educational practice (Dietrich of Metz's education) in the making of a courtier bishop. There is a form of education peculiarly tailored for the political/cultural circumstances of the Ottonian empire. Sigebert names precisely Brun's pedagogy as the factor that made the next generations of bishops distinguished: they were "rendered illustrious *through Brun's teaching*" (*ex disciplina Brunonis*).[22] This new education was to exercise a powerful transforming influence on European society and culture long after the political circumstances that produced and nurtured it had passed from the scene. Brun was in a position to assure its spread, since his influence in placing bishops was immense.[23]

Cathedral Schools

The bearers of this new education were the cathedral schools in alliance with the royal/imperial court.[24] The transformation of the institutions of education registers in the composition of the court chapel under Otto the Great. The chapel tripled in size during his thirty-seven-year reign. A specific constituency accounted for the increase: clerics of high nobility attached to a cathedral. The number of monks in the chapel decreased. It is possible to observe clear stages of this shift.[25] Before 953, the year in which Brun assumed the archbishopric of Cologne, Otto's policy with regard to the seating of bishops did not differ markedly from that of his predecessor, Henry I. After 953 appointments, particularly in Lorraine but also elsewhere in the kingdom, suddenly began to fall predominantly to former pupils of Brun from the cathedral school of Cologne. In 967, two years after Brun's death just as suddenly and dramatically, the chapel took over the task of supplying candidates. It appears that Brun transformed the cathedral school of Cologne into the testing and training ground for future bishops. Upon his death, this function, which during his lifetime had proven its value, was taken over by the court chapel. But from the middle of the tenth century on, there is a steep rise both in the prominence of cathedral schools and in their role in providing royal chaplains and bishops. A cathedral school education becomes virtually a requirement for higher office in the imperial church.[26] Monastic education plays a minor role; in fact it can be a negative factor (the case of Wazo of Liège).

Otto the Great and Brun of Cologne evidently found a consistent and sustaining purpose for the institution of cathedral schools, and this gave those schools a profile they had not had in Carolingian times. They take on the task of training talented young men in statesmanship and administrative duties. Cathedral school education becomes identical with preparation for service at court, be it secular or episcopal. This development is of funda-mental importance for our understanding of the social and political context of the new model.

This view of the new purpose of cathedral schools is also borne out by the observable growth of the schools in both Germany and France in the period. In the mid-tenth century they begin to flourish dramatically. We hear praise of the Magdeburg school in mid-century, of the great crowds of students there, of the intense interest in secular studies aroused by the "second Cicero," Master Ohtricus, a teacher of such distinction and learn-ing that he was later to debate with Gerbert of Aurillac in Ravenna before Otto II and his court.[27] By 952 Würzburg is flourishing under an Italian master, Stefan of Novara, called to the north by Otto the Great and Bishop Poppo of Würzburg. By 953 the Cologne school comes into prominence under the episcopacy of Brun. This school will produce some of the most illustrious intellectuals, statesmen, educators, and bishops of the next gen-eration. By 954 we hear Hildesheim praised as a center of learning; by 956 Trier. In the last quarter of the century, under the guidance of the next generation of scholars — many of them students of Brun — Worms, Liège, Mainz, Speyer, Bamberg, and Regensburg come to life. In France Rheims experiences a renewal under Gerbert, and some decades later Chartres comes to prominence under Gerbert's pupil, Bishop Fulbert (1006–1028). These schools are regularly referred to as "a second Athens," the better loved teachers as "noster Plato," "noster Socrates," "alter Cicero." In a commemorative poem from around 1012, Bamberg is praised as the "city of letters [or learning], [its citizens] no wit inferior to the Stoics, greater than the Athenians."[28]

In short, some twelve major cathedral schools arose — with the direct impetus of imperial patronage — in the comparatively brief space of sixty years, and others that had existed in varying degrees of obscurity emerged into the light. This is just the first generation of foundations. The students of Gerbert and Fulbert of Chartres founded or revived the major cathedral schools of France in the middle and later eleventh century.[29] This sudden and dramatic renewal is consistent with the other developments in the kingdom mentioned earlier. It represents the institutionalizing of the education developed to serve a church integrated into the system of imperial administration.

Humanist Learning at the Schools

Ottonian politics required the transmission of ideals of an office that proved so useful to the emperor's interests. The institutionalizing of this task has to be reckoned one of the great accomplishments of Ottonian times. The new or renewed cathedral schools now taught a new curriculum. Certainly learning in itself remained an object of interest and admiration, but the fundamental purpose was the formation of men who would work well at court and in the episcopate and serve the *utilitas ecclesiae et rei publicae*, the kind of men Brun was praised for seeking: "energetic and industrious men, who with loyalty and all their might will look after the republic, each in his own place" (*Vita Brun.*, chapter 37, LB, p. 234).

This goal of caring for the state and defending its interests commended the model of classical education to these new institutions. Indeed, there was no other model for the education of statesmen than a classical one, formulated most prominently by Cicero, Seneca, and Quintilian. Christianity, understandably, had responded only very sluggishly to this need. Statesmanship required an affirmation of worldly values such as the active life, secular affairs, and service of the state. It also required education of a kind that Christian orthodoxy never could fully and unreservedly affirm. Virtually the only canonical work of a Christian author that attempted such a resolution of classical education with the Christian life was Ambrose's *De officiis ministrorum ecclesiae*, which itself appropriated large parts of its model, Cicero's handbook of statesmanship, *De officiis*. Bernard of Clairvaux's *De consideratione* is the closest the High Middle Ages came to combining orthodoxy with statesmanship. The role of Christian orthodoxy was to limit, never to extend, the bounds of what could legitimately be rendered unto Caesar; it tended to subordinate the art of governing (*praeesse*) to the pastoral duty of helping (*prodesse*). But when policy imposed such an extension the stocks of Cicero, Seneca and the Roman classical tradition invariably rose.

Letters and Manners

Our entry into the new education is the formula mentioned in the Introduction, letters and manners. Carolingian education had also been two-fold. If the formula occurred, it was not programmatic, just descriptive. But the intention and nature of this combination of intellectual and ethical learning changed in Ottonian times. The two became closely and logically knit. The nature of "manners" changed radically compared with the "ecclesiastical disciplines" of the earlier period, and the influence of "manners" on letters in the new model is another strong distinguishing factor. After the mid-tenth century the phrase "letters and manners" became the bearer of a program.

It occurs in a variety of forms in descriptions of cathedral school education: *litterae et mores, sapientia et mores, ingenium et mores*. As school master at Trier (ca. 957) Wolfgang, later Bishop of Regensburg, taught not only "liberal learning" but also "moral doctrines."[30] Wazo as school master at Liège (1008–1042) is said to have given instruction in the disciplines "of manners as well as letters."[31]

The education of Bernward of Hildesheim (d. 1022) gives us an interesting insight into the social context of the formula. In his youth he was sent to school "to be imbued with letters and trained in manners" (*litteris imbuendus, moribus etiam instituendus*). Later he entered the imperial court during the regency of Theophanu, and became the favorite of the empress. She entrusted her son, the future emperor Otto III, to Bernward, "to be imbued with letters and trained in manners."[32] For this biographer it was possible without any qualifications to describe a future bishop's and a future emperor's education with the same terms. This indicates the process of assimilation that took place between education at court and at cathedral school in the period.

These phrases are certainly not topoi without much content cribbed from ancient notions on the education of an orator. Examples that occur outside the standard topical section of a vita on the subject's education show clearly the vitality of the formula. A student, or several students, at Würzburg wrote a poem in 1031 in answer to an attack on their school by the scholars of Worms. The poem praises the virtues of their school at length and calls it a flowing spring out of which one drinks the "doctrine of eloquence and of proper conduct of life" ("recte vivendi et dogma loquendi").[33] That is, their school teaches rhetoric, oratory and poetry (proper speaking), and ethics (proper living), clearly a variant of "letters and manners." In the context of an answer to an attack the phrase had to convey something of substance. Whether or not the school of Würzburg poured forth this two-fold doctrine as abundantly as its students claimed, such a doctrine had to exist. The students of Worms could not have been answered with an empty phrase.

A more telling example is from a letter written around 1060 by the Bamberg school master Meinhard, later bishop of Würzburg (1085–1088). The letter must be considered an important text in the history of education in the eleventh century. Meinhard answers a request from his bishop, Gunther of Bamberg, for a book on the Christian faith. He begins,

> First you entangle me in all the busy cares of a headmaster, and now you are after me . . . for another work, a task not just arduous but downright impossible.

He goes on with this interesting complaint:

> If the only task placed in my care were the instruction of young minds in the liberal arts — and many earlier writers argue for this single curriculum — then the rigors of the task and the reputation gained by it would be sufficient pay for me. Now however, those placed at the head of schools are taxed in a dual function for the profit of the church: for they spend the first part of their fortunes in forming manners and squander the second part in teaching letters.[34]

Here "letters and manners" cannot be an empty topos. School masters do not groan under the burden of meaningless formulae, certainly not when they explain to their bishops why they lack the time to write books. And bishops cannot be persuaded how hard their staff is working by the appeal to non-existent schemes of studies, any more than deans and provosts now can. Meinhard actually taught something called "manners," and it took much of his time, time he would rather have devoted to liberal studies. He teaches this "subject" as part of a required curriculum, one not of his own design but imposed on him by considerations of the "church's profit" (*usus ecclesiae*). Meinhard's sense of the history of this double instruction within other schemes of studies is also interesting. It is comparatively recent. He can refer to a time when masters got along without it. And while it is, unfortunately, not clear who or what is meant by the *studia veterum*, Meinhard knew Cicero and Quintilian well enough not to include them among the earlier writers who argued for a curriculum in the liberal arts alone. In any case it is the school masters of the present ("Verum *nunc* qui prefecti scolarum habentur") who are taxed doubly, not just in Bamberg but at schools generally. The passage shows us "letters and manners" as a program and imposed curriculum of studies, the two inseparable from one another. It shows us a school master complaining about the problems of maintaining the union of the two. It also tells us a goal of this "double instruction": it is given *pro ecclesiastico usu*, for the profit of the church.

All this is good testimony to the institutionalizing of a program of studies and to its applied goal. Ethical instruction is not given *pro scholarium usu* alone, but for the service of the church. But apparently this instruction has next to nothing to do with Christian doctrine and scriptural studies. These are not, as in Carolingian times, the content of an education useful to the church; at least they are not specifically mentioned as such. After all, Meinhard is protesting that this instruction is preventing him from writing his work, "On the Faith" (*De fide*, which eventually got written). In this letter he is far from seeing common ground between his teaching duties and his interest in the faith. Also we have it from a contemporary of Meinhard, Goswin (Gozechin), school master first at Liège, later at Mainz, that Meinhard — along with Hermann of Rheims and others — eventually gave up his worldly studies to devote himself to theology.[35] The passage does not tell us the content of those "ambitions abandoned, labors and studies abdicated," but it does show us a constellation common in the eleventh century: "studies" at the schools are something different from what Goswin calls *theologia*. *Usus ecclesiae* and *utilitas ecclesiae* are served by studies, and the pursuit of theology means a kind of retirement from the life of the schools.

Meinhard gives us a second piece of testimony to the reality of this formula. In another letter he commiserates with an unknown recipient on the death of the master of his school: now studies have died, the "light of letters" (*lumen litterarum*) is snuffed out, and "the moral discipline most excellently established and of long standing" is dead and buried. But Meinhard acknowledges with gratitude the arrival at Bamberg of a youth from this bereaved diocese, who has been sent to the Bamberg "workshop" for an education, so that those two marks of the school's former excellence, "letters and manners", may be revived upon his return.[36] Again, this is an extraordinarily clear example of the real existence of "letters and manners" as a scheme of studies. The diocese seeking a new master clearly feels an obligation to retrain its candidate according to this program. The scholar does not shape the curriculum; the curriculum shapes the scholar.

The choice of the Bamberg school as a "workshop" to prepare a master of "letters and manners" made good sense. Bamberg gained a reputation for precisely this orientation of studies. In 1115 the canons of Bamberg received a letter from their colleagues at Worms commending their bishop elect, Burchard II, and requesting Bamberg's support for his appointment. Burchard is a former student of Bamberg, they say (*vestris institutis fundatus a puericia*), a "son of Bamberg . . . in the science of letters, in skill for practical affairs, in good manners, in the gift of good judgment."[37] Whether this is flattery, panegyric, or a deserved reputation, it shows a desirable curriculum for a school of future bishops: letters and manners, skill in governing or administering (*rerum agendarum pericia*), and good judgment, presumably the kind a bishop/administrator, not an intellectual, requires.

3. The New Education Institutionalized: Schools of Manners

The cathedral schools of Germany and France became the institutional locus of this program in our period. This Chapter surveys the major schools and the sources that indicate instruction in *mores*. The arrangement is roughly chronological, starting from the earliest documents that mention ethical training. This will allow us to scan the descriptions of studies and form an idea of common educational programs, of their development, and of the conceptual vocabulary of *mores*.

Cologne

Brun and his school at Cologne were the center from which civil education radiated. The main documents from the second half of the tenth century were discussed in the previous Chapter. For the eleventh the sources are not rich. They suggest that the reputation of Cologne as a center of learning was maintained, but that the actual accomplishment was small and little noted. The school did not produce a single bishop in the period 1002–1125.[1] It nonetheless offered the full range of studies, as we see in the description of Wolfhelm of Brauweiler's education during the episcopacy of Heribert (999–1021):

> . . . in addition to the pages of sacred scripture, he penetrated all that the poet sang, all that the eloquent orator declaimed, all that the philosopher thought out, borne on the wings of higher understanding. . . . There was such gravity and maturity of manners [*gravitas, maturitas morum*] in him that all who saw him recognized in him a chosen man. . . . He ignored the foolish stories and wanton pastimes of other youths, he abhorred the venomed tongues of flatterers. His gravity was like an anchor, holding him safe from foolish speech and a wanton gaze, and controlling all the gestures and stirrings of his body [*totius motus corporis anchora cohibebat gravitatis*]. The master of the schools, seeing his progress in the disciplines of all the virtues [*in omnium virtutum disciplinis*],

rejoiced to have imposed studies on him, since he saw him attaining the pinnacle of perfection.[2]

As a result of these qualities, the school master made Wolfhelm his assistant, and the school attracted many students.

While he studied scripture, literature, and "philosophy," his progress in virtue is what predominates in the passage; his personal qualities account for his advancement. The passage contains a phrase of considerable importance for our purposes: "His gravity was like an anchor holding him safe from foolish speech and a wanton gaze, and controlling all the gestures and stirrings of his body." Virtue is a force that controls the motions and gestures of the body. In other words, he walked, spoke, and gestured well, and these are the visible signs of his inner "gravity and maturity of manners." It is a short step from this to the pedagogic conclusion that the disciplining of the body to ideals of grace, moderation, and self-control is a means of cultivating virtue.

Wolfhelm's biography was written between 1110 and 1123. The author was a monk of Brauweiler, Konrad, whose personal acquaintance with Wolfhelm dates from 1070 (see *DGQ* 2.645–46). It seems fairly likely therefore that his conception of Wolfhelm's education derives from the eleventh century, even if it cannot be taken as an infallible witness to the actual education of Wolfhelm in the first half of that century. The least we can conclude is that Konrad of Brauweiler was familiar with this pedagogy at the latest by 1123, and that probably it was functioning at the school of Cologne considerably earlier.

Liège

Liège, not Cologne, is the crucial center for the diffusion of the new model of education developed under Brun. Bishop Eraclius (959–971) was the first to restore learning to Liège after the decline in late Carolingian days.[3] He was a Saxon, a student of Brun and Rather of Verona. Eraclius was appointed bishop through the direct intercession of Brun of Cologne.[4] Anselm of Liège's comments about his influence on the schools are often referred to but seldom read in context. The passage in Anselm's *Gesta* reads as follows:

> Because Eraclius was firmly grounded in elegant probity of manners and the liberal learning of virtue [or good behavior: *honestas*], and because he had long

since completed from beginning to end the course in liberal studies and memory with our countrymen from that time, he took pains to establish schools throughout the churches.[5]

It not only credits him with founding schools, but gives his credentials, which are two-fold: "elegant probity of manners and knowledge of virtue" on the one hand, and liberal studies on the other.[6] The passage is instructive. We learn from it that Eraclius brought "elegant manners and virtue" to Liège from the royal chapel and court. "Liberal studies" were what he received "long since" from masters in or near Liège (*aput nostrates*). On the origin of the Liège school the passage is unambiguous: it was established on the basis of a two-fold learning: elegant manners or probity (*honestas*) and liberal studies.

The successor of Eraclius was Notker of Liège (972–1008), a Swabian, who is generally credited with establishing Liège as a great city and center of education.[7] Notker's biographer, writing at the end of the eleventh century, gives the lines of his early career:

> And so from his studies of letters he also received ornaments of his manners and, having progressed laudably in both disciplines, he deservedly was called from the schools to the palace. There among wise and good men — only wise and good men attended the king at that time — he shone so brightly for the strength of his counsel and his action, that because of his gift of *honestas* he passed from the palace to the leadership of the church of Liège, having been chosen by the vows and demands of clergy and populace and by the favor of the prince. There at long last this most illustrious man found the place in which his virtue would become effective. . . .[8]

Anselm praises Notker as "highly distinguished for the elegance of his manners, though a German."[9] Again, virtue and learning are the moving forces in his advancement to the court chapel and the bishopric of Liège. Unfortunately we do not know where Notker took his early studies.[10]

Wazo was school master under Notker (ca. 1005–ca. 1030) before becoming bishop (1042–48). Anselm describes him as "imbued with the example [of Notker] and instructed in his learning, but also adding his own virtues, received as a divine gift."[11] Anselm was in awe of Wazo and described how the bishop's presence could bring him out of countenance:

> Woe to me, miserable as I am — I hardly dare admit it — so unworthy and filled with confusion, when he would deign to speak to me with his sweet speech, excellent knowledge and elegant genius.[12]

As school master Wazo taught both letters and manners, and he favored those who excelled in manners over those who were merely skilled in letters. Students left his school instructed in letters, manners and religion.[13]

Anselm wrote around 1056 and complained about the collapse of discipline in the schools. He praised the "golden age" of Bishop Notker, "when in the chapels of the emperor no less than in those of bishops nothing more was pursued than the discipline of manners along with the study of letters!"[14] We learn from this that "letters and manners" had been the curriculum alike of emperor's chapel and bishops' schools, and that by the mid-eleventh century a member of the Liège community could lament its passing from the schools.

Anselm's contemporary Gozechin or Goswin taught at Liège between 1044 and 1057.[15] In his letter to his former student at Liège, Walcher, he contrasts the schools of the present (i.e., ca. 1065) with Liège in its heyday: "[Liège] guides, educates and instructs [its students] in all things civil, and in manners."[16] That was in the past. Nowadays, he continues, the schools suffer from rejecting *mores* and *disciplina*; young students flee instruction in "the gravity of moral discipline" (XXVII, p. 31). He looks back on the golden age of the schools, when the gravity of discipline ruled and all studies were for the utility of the republic and of *honestas*, when the beauty of virtues and the liberal arts flourished. He laments the passing of this age (chapter XXXIV, pp. 36–37). Goswin located all that was good in the schools in Liège, and clearly "moral discipline," civil matters, and the study of virtue loomed large.

Rheims

The learning of Rheims in our period has its beginnings in the efforts of Archbishop Adalbero to revive the school, beginning in 969. But the flowering of these efforts occurs under Gerbert of Aurillac.[17] The sources that describe his teaching say nothing about instruction in *mores*.[18] The priorities of the sources may have filtered out the subject of *mores*. But there can be no doubt that Gerbert exerted influence in this area, even if we have no reports of it in the narrower context of his teaching at Rheims. Otto III's letter inviting Gerbert to his court in order to banish their "Saxon rusticity"[19] may indicate the emperor's perception of his usefulness in regard to manners and conduct, though the only areas of instruction expressly mentioned are composition and mathematics. But the emperor also says he is to exercise the *studium correctionis* and advise him in state affairs, and this indicates areas closer to *mores* (though "correction" applies as well to composition as to behavior).

In Gerbert's answer the teacher's concern with the discipline of conduct is evident when he praises the dual studies of his future pupil, mathematics and moral philosophy: ". . . unless you embraced the gravity of moral philosophy, humility, guardian of all virtues, would not thus be impressed upon your words."[20] It is worth noting in this connection that Gerbert described himself as a "a faithful executor of the precepts of Cicero in both state affairs and in leisure,"[21] and claimed that he always strictly identified the "study of living well" with the "study of speaking well," in accordance with the precepts of philosophy and of Cicero.[22] This dual study became programmatic for the schools, and the Ciceronian formulation, *studium bene vivendi*, was taken over directly. Gerbert's mention of moral philosophy and *studium bene vivendi* in relation to his state affairs and tutoring of the emperor reminds us again that the new education had a dual context: court and cathedral school.[23]

These are the few clues to a teaching of *mores* through Gerbert, and it is curious that the testimony is sparse and indirect. But we can complement them with accounts from the Rheims community more or less contemporary with Gerbert.

A poem by a monk of St. Remi of Rheims written in the mid-980s gives us a good introduction to the ethical vocabulary and concepts at the disposal of a learned member of the Rheims community contemporary with Gerbert. It also shows us the intellectual atmosphere of that community very clearly. It is a fulsome panegyric on Constantine, school master of Fleury and later Abbot of Micy, a close friend and correspondent of Gerbert. Its diction and grammar are abstruse; its dense and hermetic learned allusions and its many Greek words make it hard to read. But its description of Constantine speaks the language of *cultus virtutum*.[24]

Constantine is a man of great merit, not only for his high birth (he descends from the long-haired Frankish kings — 2–3), but also because of nature's gifts. His character is of high distinction: he is made "all things to all men" (26); Wisdom herself was his educator from youth on; she has built herself a temple in this "man magnificent above others and always loveable" and has ornamented it with "the excellent light of virtues" (33–40); he combines the chastity of the dove with the cunning of the serpent (44–47); he beams "nobility of merits" like a light, and is famed for his "probity of manners" (*morum probitate celebris* — 70–71); he is a "mirror of justice, hosanna of kings,"[25] illumination of the learned, an ornament and model for monks" (90–91). He is also impressive physically, and his beauty is the visible symbol of his inner excellence (*Vultu conspicuus, mentis pietate decorus* — 87). The point is stressed, and it is an important element of portraits of men in this milieu:

> Since, finally, it is regarded as true that the body's acts are the sign of the mind, and the intellect displays itself in action, you are, in our judgement, worthy of that great praise of your body that fame bruits about the whole world.[26]

Constantine is also distinguished for his learning and mental acumen.[27] He searches the peaks of high heaven (25); he is the "light of the study of rhetorical speech" (*fandi / Rethorici cultus lumen* — 53); the poet claims that his own wit and skill come entirely from Constantine (54); he is the "light of the learned" (91). The skill given the highest profile is the composition of poetry: the phrase *psalmatio regum* (90), which I translate as "hosanna of kings," probably makes him into a harpist on the model of David before Saul; he has written "many an ode" for the poet, who promises to cherish them perpetually since they allude to their happy love: "These pages will bring happiness when your presence cannot" (106–8). The poet imagines himself climbing up Parnassus and conjuring from there the words and matter of praise for his song: "Ah, dear lyre, sing songs, flowing forth in apt tones, for the man who deserves worship for the probity of his manners, but only such [songs] as are worthy of the Sophoclean stage" (62–64).[28]

Nothing indicates that his learning is in the area of sacred scripture. There are scriptural reminiscences in the poet's diction, but the classical tradition predominates in his conceptualizing of poetry and composition.

The poem shows a cult of friendship in full blossom. Constantine is a "beloved companion" and "sweetest doctor" (52). Anyone who had loved him happily for ages must wish to have him as "patron, constant companion, lord" (84–85). These lines indicate a courtship in progress. Perhaps Constantine is a candidate as bishop or abbot. The writer stresses that the "brothers of the Remigian cottage" are his faithful friends (75), who miss him, and jokingly complains that he has not fulfilled his promise to visit them (99–105); if he were to become their "greatest part" he would receive love and devotion equal to his honor (95–98).

But the language of friendship is not explainable just in terms of

Constantine's candidacy for the abbacy. This language is establishing itself at the imperial court and the cathedral community — or the community of the educated clergy at Rheims more generally — at just this time. This cult of love and friendship is an important characteristic of the cathedral schools of the period.[29] Gerbert himself may be its prime mover, or one of them. At least the tone of love that characterizes the poem to Constantine is present in Gerbert's letters and tracts and at the court of Otto III.[30]

One final observation: The poem came from the monastic community of St. Remi in Rheims, not the cathedral. It was written by a monk for the school master of Fleury (also a monastic community) and future abbot of Micy. But the worldliness of its tone is evident. None of the themes of reformed monasticism are in evidence. On the contrary, it is clearly a community of men who define themselves as scholars, poets and statesmen/administrators (Constantine is among those who "wish to function well and laudably in the world through their actions"; "Qui . . . vigere cupit seclo laudabilis actu" — 18).

Though the testimony to Gerbert's influence on the teaching of manners is scant, it is certain that the subject was prominent at the cathedral school of Rheims in the late tenth and early eleventh century.

Bishop Gerhard I of Cambrai (1012–1051) had his early education there and probably was a student of Gerbert.[31] The author of the *Gesta episcoporum Cameracensium* describes his education there as follows:

> Beneath the liberal teaching [of his relative Archbishop Adalbero of Rheims (969–989)] he would experience both the norm of religion appropriate to the church and the discipline of worldly ethics.[32]

The passage is valuable for showing the "norm of religion" as distinguishable from "worldly ethics" (*mundana honestas*), and for showing both as subjects of "liberal" education.

Hugh of Flavigny, writing at the turn of the eleventh to the twelfth century, gives a broader picture of the subjects taught at Rheims in the early eleventh century. Virtue, manners, behavior loom large:

> At that time this church flourished so brilliantly in religion, and it did itself such honor in the virtuous multitude and seemly virtuousness of the men of nobility and of religion whom it educated, that in respect to religion it outshone all other churches of Belgium, and it was for all a model of the virtuous life and of proper behavior [*forma honeste vivendi recteque conversandi*], in chastity, in learning, in discipline, in the correction of behavior, in its display of good works.[33]

The education of Richard of St. Vannes, described by his biographer at the beginning of the twelfth century, is consistent with this picture. Richard was sent to Notre-Dame of Rheims as a young boy, "to be taught letters and to be instructed in the canonical rule." The result of his learning was that he advanced so far, "both in the gift of learning and in the elegance of his life and manners" that he was appointed precentor and deacon in the church of Rheims.[34] Elegance and learning appear here as qualifications for office acquired in a cathedral school education. It may be that Richard also was a student of Gerbert (Lèsne, *Les écoles*, 1: 280). But a few formulations in the above passages caution us against reading them straight. At the Rheims cathedral school he is said to have received "instruction in the canonical rule." This is a technical term in the training of novices (see below, Chapter 9), something different from *mores* or *honestas*, which are distinguishable from anything called *regula*. Probably both Hugh of Flavigny and the biographer of Richard looked back from the perspective of a religious reform whose more ascetic ideals had become entrenched and had in part dislodged the more worldly ethical training, at least in the imaginations of biographers writing the lives of the movement's leaders. The atmosphere of St. Remi of Rheims, as represented in the poem to Constantine — its focus on poetry, friendship, and personal virtue — is not in evidence in the descriptions of Richard's education at Rheims. But that is a bias of the texts, not a reliable insight into moral training under Gerbert and his successors.

The texts described below were written several decades earlier (though they describe a period a few decades later) and they are not subject to that bias.

In 1023 Archbishop Ebalus of Rheims (1021–33) received a letter from Fulbert of Chartres commending his former student Hubertus, presently studying at the school of Rheims. He transferred to Rheims, Fulbert says, "for the sake of learning proper behavior" (*causa discendae honestatis*),[35] and he adds that this was the same subject that had brought him to Chartres. Apparently the form of *honestas* taught at Rheims was different enough from that of Chartres that the transfer seemed sensible to Fulbert.[36]

Rheims clearly excelled in the subject. Meinhard of Bamberg wrote a letter (ca. 1057–67), reminiscing nostalgically about his own studies. It probably refers to his two years at Rheims under master Hermann:

> That way of living [*convictus*] into which you received me in so profoundly humane a manner was more free and noble, more effective and practical [*ad utilitatem efficacius*], more scrupulous in the cultivation of elegance [*ad elegan-*

tiam accuratius], more conducive to the highest a man can attain [*ad sub-limitatem exquisitius*] than any other whatsoever, even if my thickness of mind deprived me of its richer fruits.[37]

Meinhard is not recollecting challenges of the mind or intellectual activity of any kind. This learning cultivates a personal quality, called here "elegance," through a shared life of master and pupil. Its practical benefits are indicated directly in *utilitas*, and less directly, though still distinctly, in *sublimitas*, which may mean both the perfect life and the highest rank or office a man can attain. It does not indicate piety and the religious life, though that undoubtedly formed part of the teaching at Rheims, as other sources have indicated. The secular nature of the shared interests that still bound the Bamberg master to his former teacher is underscored by his request in the same letter for a copy of Cicero's Verrine orations and a commentary on Terence.

Bruno, founder of the Carthusian order, probably succeeded Hermann as *magister scholarum*.[38] One of his epitaphs says of him, "Bruno both possessed and transmitted the true knowledge and prudence of the liberal arts and the other cardinal virtues."[39]

Godfrey of Rheims succeeded Bruno as chancellor and school master in 1076 or 1077.[40] He represents the highpoint of humanist poetry at Rheims and is mentioned alongside Hildebert, Baudri and Marbod as one of the highpoints of Latin poetry of the Middle Ages.

Baudri of Bourgueil wrote a poem in praise of Godfrey, in which he includes a brief survey of the schools.[41] He praises the Rheims school as the most flourishing of all the flourishing schools of France, a second Rome. He describes Bruno as "a mirror of the study of the Latins" (l. 100). Herimannus was a "bright beacon of study" (l. 102). Godfrey himself is praised as a resident in the home of the muses; the spirit of the ancient poets lives in him; he possesses the gravity of Virgil and the lightness and wit of Ovid (cf. ll. 5–8, and Williams, p. 31). He praises mainly Godfrey's poetic gift: he has the power to immortalize those he sings of. Baudri hopes to receive some of the immortality he has to bestow. The poem aims at knitting the friendship between the two men, and only touches in general reflections on the moral power of poetry (cf. ll. 159–62, 181–82, 197–98).

Godfrey's own poems give us a much richer picture of the cultivation of *mores*, but they appear to convey the ideals of *mores* as general social values, useful in poetic portraits, and not specifically learned habits taught in school (see below, Chapters 4 and 5). The problematic figure of Manasses I of Rheims, whose person and manners contradicted much that *moralitas* aimed at, may have something to do with the sparsity of references to the school training in the subject in the late eleventh century at Rheims (see below, Chapter 5).

Chartres

Fulbert studied at Rheims with Gerbert. The student he recommended to Ebalus of Rheims had originally come to Chartres to study *honestas* (p. 60 above). The biographer of Angelran of St. Riquier calls Fulbert Angelran's "guardian and instructor in both manners and letters."[42] Adelman of Liège praised his former teacher Fulbert, in his poem *De viris illustribus sui temporis* in telling phrases:

> Ah, with what dignity and diligence in questions of *mores*,
> With what gravity in subject matter,
> What sweetness in words
> He explained the mysteries of higher knowledge.[43]

The praise is directed to the teacher's manner: dignity, gravity and eloquence are qualities of Fulbert, not of the text he discusses. Here again the person of the teacher, his virtues and his carriage rouse students' enthusiasm. Eloquence and noble bearing were what students wanted from Fulbert, probably as much as illumination of the "mysteries of higher knowledge." Fulbert's student Hildegar is praised in the same poem for having taken over and made his own the master's facial expression, tone of voice, and manners.[44] This same Hildegar who made himself into a copy of Fulbert wrote a letter to the master with two requests: to correct a little work of his (*opusculum*) and to correct his vice of anger.[45] Hildegar clearly regarded both his literary and his moral improvement, his letters and his manners, the province of his teacher. I find no references to the teaching of *mores* from the time of Fulbert until Bernard of Chartres.[46]

Speyer

Walther of Speyer, writing in 984, describes liberal studies at Speyer in detail, but makes no mention of instruction in *mores*.[47] We can learn from his *Libellus scolasticus* that that same artificial and overladen classicizing style of poetry we observed in the poem to Constantine from Rheims was thoroughly entrenched at Speyer in the same period. It may be that the strict adherence to the seven liberal arts with no mention of *mores* is the continuing tradition of St. Gall, which Walther's teacher, Bishop Balderich (970–986) introduced into Speyer.[48]

Speyer's role in imperial politics came not with the Ottonian, but with the Salian dynasty, and its school grew in size and stature in the eleventh century. In the major school text from Speyer in mid-century, behavior and manners suddenly loom large. Onulf of Speyer in his *Colores rhetorici* subordinates the entire discipline of rhetoric to "elegance of manners, composition of bearing and dignity of behavior."[49]

Adelman of Liège was school master in Speyer between 1044 and 1050. Though no sources testify to his activity there, we can assume that the influence of both Liège and Chartres will have come with him.

Benno of Osnabrück studied at Speyer in this same period. His biographer makes a remark that is worth pointing to in this context, if only to call for an explanation. He says that at that time the "brilliant imperial study, including the study of letters," burned bright everywhere, but nowhere so brightly as at Speyer, and this attracted throngs of students.[50] Speyer had close contacts with the imperial court, and the term "school for diplomats" may not be altogether appropriate, but the Speyer school educated prominent members of the court and prominent imperial bishops.[51]

Bamberg

The school at Bamberg appears to have played an important part in the staffing of imperial offices virtually since its founding in 1007.[52] We have cited a number of significant references to the teaching of *mores* by Meinhard, school master from about 1060 until his appointment as Bishop of Würzburg in 1085 (pp. 50–52 above). The fundamental unity of educational purpose tying Bamberg to Liège is evident in a letter from Bishop Hermann of Bamberg (written ca. 1065–1075 by Meinhard in the bishop's name) to the bishop of Liège, in which Hermann commends a student of Bamberg to the school of Liège, "so that, once tempered in the workshop of your school in regard to both manners and discipline . . . , he may be resplendent as an ornament of our church," and he closes by reminding his fellow bishop that the educational traditions of Bamberg had their origins in Liège.[53]

Bishop Otto of Bamberg is the embodiment of what an education in manners aimed at.[54] We touch on him again in a later Chapter, since his biographies are all from the mid-twelfth century. However we have a letter from Bishop Otto, at least written in his name, offering a scholar (addressed only as F.) the vacant position of school master. The letter, dated ca. 1103, begins,

> Because the quality of your manners, the conduct of your life, and the maturity of your liberal studies is known to us from the time of your stay with us, we have decided unanimously on you and invite you to join our community.[55]

This is not panegyric, but a list of qualifications for the office of school master. It sets behavior before liberal studies. In this case no mention is made of religion.

The canons of Bamberg received a letter around 1115 from the canons of Worms requesting help in securing the confirmation of their bishop elect. They list among his qualifications his studies at Bamberg, which have left their mark:

> I see clearly [the letter is written in the first person singular] that he is a son of the church of Bamberg in his knowledge of letters, in his skill in administrative affairs, in the uprightness of his manners [*in honestate morum*], and in his gift of good judgment.[56]

This passage is useful not only for showing the qualities cultivated in education at Bamberg, but also for putting these qualities forward as qualifications for the bishopric. They are personal integrity, wisdom and practical skill, and they do not include piety or knowledge of scripture.

Würzburg

We end this survey with a more detailed look at the school of Würzburg, one made possible by some remarkable documents from the 1030s.

Würzburg's school was rescued from the obscurity of its Carolingian beginnings when Otto the Great and Bishop Poppo summoned the learned Italian master Stefan of Novara in the early 950s.[57] The school flourished under his direction. It attracted many students, among whom two were particularly distinguished, Wolfgang of Regensburg (972–994) and Heinrich of Trier (956–964). Their move to Würzburg is vividly recorded in Otloh of St. Emmeram's Life of Wolfgang, and it is worth recounting.[58]

Wolfgang excelled in the learning of letters as a young boy, mastering in a few years not only the superficial historical meaning of texts but also their hidden inner meanings. Not content with private studies, he sought learning in the place where "in German lands at that time studies most flourished," and moved with his father's blessing to Reichenau. Here he befriended Heinrich, later Archbishop of Trier, who persuaded him to go with him to Würzburg, where Heinrich's brother, Poppo, was bishop, and "a certain master Stefan from Italy . . . , who was able to satisfy all who desired learning," directed the schools. Otloh's enthusiasm for the monastic school and his faint praise of Stefan may have to do with his own monastic background and mistrust of worldly learning, or with his good relations with the monks of Reichenau and his not particularly happy period as a canon in a rustic parish of Würzburg.[59]

Wolfgang's own intellectual talent was a danger to his character. His teachers at Reichenau kept a sharp eye out for signs of pride in one so gifted, but found none. But at Würzburg it broke out. Master Stefan did not explain certain problems in Martianus Capella to the satisfaction of his students, Otloh tells us, and they turned to Wolfgang. His superior command of the text roused the envy of Stefan, and Wolfgang eventually left to become school master at Trier. Here he instructed his students "not only in liberal teachings, but also in moral disciplines" (chapter 7, p. 529, ll. 3–4). This is the first mention of *morales disciplinae* in a description that looks otherwise exclusively at the study of letters. It is not unreasonable to assume that Wolfgang is teaching a discipline he learned at Würzburg. Nothing encourages us to think he learned it at Reichenau.

Apart from this testimony, we have a vague reference in a poem Stefan wrote when he left Würzburg in 970 to return to his homeland. He says that he had given himself, in his years at Würzburg, to the "teaching and study of wisdom."[60] But the conventional phrase hardly even implies anything about the teaching of *mores*.

Wolfgang's move from famous and flourishing Reichenau to Würzburg was probably not motivated just by the arm-twisting persuasion of his friend Heinrich, brother of the bishop of Würzburg. It is a move of some historical significance. Promising young men heading for bishoprics were apparently better served in Würzburg than in Reichenau. At least the role of education for bishops passes in just this period from the monastic to the cathedral schools. Since there is no reason to doubt that instruction in liberal arts was excellent at Reichenau, it may well have been the *morales disciplinae* of the cathedral school that now constituted the essential preparation.

The roughly eighty years separating the departure of Wolfgang of Regensburg from the next recorded events at the Würzburg school represented the school's heyday.[61] But they are lost in the same silence that enfolds most of the life of the cathedral schools prior to the twelfth century. Bishop Heribert of Eichstätt (1022–1042) received his education there. Under Bishop Meginhard (1019–1034) a school master named Pernolf emerges to figure in an episode that becomes one of the few points of illumination from the schools of the period. The chronicler of the Eichstätt bishops known as Anonymus Haserensis tells that the newly elected Bishop Heribert found a master named Gunderam in charge of the schools. He would have fired him, since he accounted anyone ill-educated who, like Gunderam, had studied "at home, not along the Rhine or in Gaul."[62] A visit from Pernolf, "that famous master of Würzburg," is the occasion to test Gunderam. Pernolf stands high in the esteem of the former student of Würzburg, Heribert. Possibly the bishop had even studied in Pernolf's school. Gunderam's lecture impresses the Würzburg master, who persuades Heribert to drop his resolve to "throw him out and replace him with another."[63]

Nothing else is known about this "famous master of Würzburg,"[64] and he would remain a player in a minor anecdote from an all but unrecoverable epoch of school history, were it not that one or perhaps several of his students wrote a polemical poem glorifying the Würzburg school and its master. This poem was at the center of a quarrel between the schools of Würzburg and Worms, which is also addressed in several letters from the Worms letter collection. Suddenly, in the darkness of documentation, these texts casts a brilliant light on the school, its goals, its program, its self-conception, and its teacher.

The poem is available in several editions with good philological commentaries, and it is surprising that it has not loomed larger in the history of cathedral schools.[65] In reading this poem and the scholarship on the schools of Worms and Würzburg, the limits of the writing of local history become evident. Viewed as local history, the dispute between the two schools appears as a historical curiosity, isolated and anomalous. Viewed from the perspective of cathedral schools in eleventh-century France and Germany, it illustrates some of the characteristic features of those schools.

The poem is a response to some students of Worms, one of them evidently a Würzburg alumnus, who wrote, in the autumn of 1030, a poem criticizing the school at Würzburg and its master and extolling their own. The Worms poem, now lost, may well have begun as an exercise in composition,[66] as its originators claim, but it involved a taunt and quickly turned serious. In the first months of 1031, the perpetrators from Worms write nervously to some of their fellow students, possibly at the royal court and in a position to pick up gossip, asking what they know about the progress of their altercation. They strike a nonchalant posture: "If anyone is curious in what state of mind they have done this [i.e., failed to answer until now], let anyone inquire who is losing sleep over it. We care little about it" (*Wormser Briefsammlung*, epist. 15, p. 32). But they care enough to pursue the rumor that the royal chancellor Bruno (from Worms, later Bishop of Würzburg) has received an answer from the Würzburg students, of which they have until now seen neither hide nor hair. They ask their colleagues to send it along post haste, if they get a copy.

They received their answer soon enough and surely did not sleep more soundly for it. It is a poem in Leonine hexameters. Addressed to no one in particular, it is a laudation of the Würzburg school, its master, its atmosphere of studies, and its disdain for contention. It is crushingly lofty and towers from the moral high road down upon the pranksters who were to rue provoking it. Here is a summary and partial translation[67]:

Just as this city bears the name of health-giving herbs that restore the body, so also it is the progenitor of perfect students. It administers teaching as the medicine of the unlearned. It drives away the illness of vice. Let all lepers, unclean, vice-ridden, and ignorant come to us: our learned discourse will restore their minds better than herbs can restore their bodies. Our rector is a man of no mean honor and a pillar of the church. This prince of those primates who explain the secrets of the poets/prophets [*vatum*] surpasses the pinnacle of all honors of this world. He shines with the radiance of many a poet. His one care is the study of composition.[68] He is a cultivator of virtue and of eternal salvation, who received from the allmighty the gift of so great a mind. The model (or example or teaching) of this man (*huius documentum*) is an ornament to us; his honors increase constantly, like the springtime foliage. Bringing the light and acumen of his mind to the unlearned, he instructs them in the elements of grammar and in all the arts. Nor does he cease at night time to give forth the sayings of the poets and grammarians (36). Demanding and just, laden with the gems of virtue, this generous Argus provides throughout the night a feast of his example [or his teaching (*fercula documenti*)]. With painstaking care, he watches over his own flock. He never favors the more advanced and skilled students over the beginners. He firms up the wisdom of the one and corrects the ignorance of the other. By a common vow we are all joined together into a single community. Our gathering is happy about its prince; even the shrewdest, hardest working, brightest of us reveres him. The word of such a teacher brings the joys of life. For his sake people gather here from diverse regions, not only from the vicinity. Many who have wandered from afar seek him out (54). When the sons of the nobles win his love, then submission to his tutelage does them no dishonor. Whoever works at his side is shaped according to his paternal example, to his own benefit. No mortal masters the arts as he does (*pollet artificalis*). While this sage lacks not one of all eight virtues, yet he retains humility as the glory of a mind so laden with ornaments. Replete with virtues, he is serene in his prosperity. Harm stays away, and with sadness banished, he rejoices in the security which surrounds him; the joys of true peace [enjoyed at Würzburg] are widely celebrated (67).

He merits heaven by his marvelous virtue, and when God calls men to account before His heavenly throne, he [the master] will shine like the sun for the merits of a life so adorned with teachings, and he will lead in joy all those students who have demonstrated the moderation learned from him (78). This group will include among its number the highest pontiffs, his followers, alumni of the school.

Before moving on to the rest of the poem, very different in tone, it is time to analyse the concerns of its first third. The unnamed teacher is on center stage. His stature, his rank and standing are foremost among the subjects of praise: he is "of no mean honor" (18), he has set new standards of worldly honor (*Mundi cunctorum transcendit culmen honorum*, 22). He is the "highest pillar of the church" (19). The most persistent term of praise is "virtue": he is a "cultivator [or worshiper] of virtue" (*cultor virtutis* — 27), "laden with the gems of virtue" (40), he "lacks none of the eight virtues" (61), he is "replete with virtue" (64), his "marvelous virtue" will merit salvation (70).

The praise of his teaching stresses two areas: poetry (including grammar and the arts), and virtue.

Poetry. The epithet "prince of primates who reveal the mysteries of the poets" (*Princeps primatum, qui pandunt abdita vatum*, 21) suggests a teaching hierarchy, mixed of equal elements of worldly ranks (*princeps*) and ecclesiastical (*primates*). The explainers of the poets'/prophets' secrets are ranked along this hierarchy, with the Würzburg master placed at the top. These *vates* are almost certainly the Latin classical poets, as line 24, "the refulgence of many poets," implies. Christian poetry/prophecy and holy scripture are not mentioned in the entire poem. We must read line 26 carefully: "His only concern is the study of *scriptura*" ("Preter scripture studium nihil est sibi cure . . ."). The usage of this poem and of the locale makes it evident that this means "the study of composition."[69] It is certainly not correct to read the line, "the study of scripture is his sole concern."

Classical learning plays a large part in the poem. The polemic which follows the part just summarized is directed in part against the excessive cultivation of pagan learning at Worms.[70] But while he is eager to hurl the reproach of paganism against his adversaries, he does not hesitate to display his own mastery of classical traditions. He invokes in passing Diana, Mars, Hercules and the Hydra, Orpheus and Pluto's kingdom, Argus, the muses, Arethusa, and Plato. In his practice of quoting he favors classical authors, though Biblical reminiscences are not lacking. Horace is far and away his favorite source (cf. Strecker's and Bulst's annotations). Also the display of poetic skill becomes itself part of his advertisement for the school and a weapon against his foes. In one important aspect the dispute is a contest of poetry. The Würzburg master is praised for beaming forth "the light of many poets." It was a poem from Worms, written possibly as an exercise in composition (*exercitii causa*) that started the whole thing (102). Not only its contents, but its form are offensive. The Würzburger calls his opponent the "composer of that repulsive verse, vehicle of lies" (143), which,

> discordant and pedestrian, dictated by some rustic muse, offends the [true] muse by its deceitfulness and sets Arethusa to flight. Its mute syllables show, as soon as they are spoken, that you are ignorant when it comes to setting the correct rhythm in a song. I see you abandoning the laws of grammar when you try your hand as a poet. (143–48)

The lying, ill-modulated verses are the very image of the heart of their maker, he says (159–61). Finally, if they try to prolong the fight and do harm to Würzburg, they will find their opponents "strong athletes and poets" (241). It speaks for the standing of poetry in these schools that it can function alongside muscle as a means of intimidation.

These polemics and the entire poem demonstrate the high cultivation of poetry in the school. The "parts of grammar" and the "other arts" are mentioned in a single line (34).

Virtue. The Würzburg school offers as the second prominent allurement to its students the qualities of its master: his virtue. The opening lines praising the city (and implying the identity of city and school) promise a healing and restoring effect of study, parallel to the restorative effect of herbs, for which the "city of herbs" is named (Herbipolensis = Würzburg). This effect derives from the person of the teacher; hence the stress on his virtue and honor. He is an exemplar; he stamps his own character on that of his students. Those who attend his lessons "take after the father" (*patrissare* — 59). When he enters heaven he will take with him those students "who have shown forth his moderation" (*eius moderamine functos* — 78).

The master's virtues are praised but not enumerated. That is a pity. It would give us some notion of the content of the "dogma of right living." We know only that his "moderation" (*moderamen*), passed on to his students, gains them entry into heaven. One other passage in the poem further illuminates the question. The master, for all his virtues and his stature, has maintained his humility, and that is the true glory of his mind: "His ornamentis humilis stat gloria mentis" (62). The praise here strikes a familiar chord. It reminds us of that quality of Brun of Cologne and other imperial bishops discussed in the previous chapter: the humility appropriate to greatness.

The composing of poetry, then, predominates in the curriculum of Würzburg as we can infer it from this poem. Virtue, honor, and salvation through the master's personal qualities are indicated benefits, but if the poet had wanted to stress that "virtue" is a course of studies, he could have done so. He does give a clear indication toward the end of the poem that he conceives the curriculum of the school within a two-fold scheme: a drink from the fountain of their learning revives the senses and imbues them with "the doctrine of right living and speaking." ("Istinc si discis, statim sensu resipiscis, / Recte vivendi potans et dogma loquendi" — 264–65). These lines are clearly a variant of the formula "letters and manners."

THE SWEET LIFE OF WÜRZBURG

Now we turn to the rest of the poem. At line 83 the tone changes from commendatory to polemical:

> The "distinguished child" [author of the offending poem] with his slanderous muttering about the superiority of the Worms master is playing with fire and now has kindled them. The slanderer himself is riddled with vices and filthy habits, unworthy of his clerical standing. Those who have seen his writings claim this at least. He wrote an abusive poem, they say, because of his own crime, and he is now in trouble for it (102). He is a sower of wrath and destroyer of friendships, sending messages of contention. Does he not know of the sweet life at Würzburg? ["An nos mellitam nescis hic ducere vitam" — 108]. It is peaceful and uncontentious. Harsh words do not assail them, and if their opponent had ceased his snarling, they would never have come looking for a fight. Even now the words of this poem are spoken in hope of reconciliation. If he wants war, he'll get war; if he wants peace, he'll get that: "You have felt, along with me, the noble doctrine of our master, who educates and adorns us with his elegant wit and his reason. Once you praised him, and that made me deeply happy. Now let the discord and cruel anger between us fade. Let us shun war and become joined as twins in our love. A bond like that of David

and Jonathan will join us. No cruelty will disturb us now or ever more. Those caught up in unending quarrels will marvel to see such a friendship between us" (127–35).[71]

After this extravagant offering of peace and reconciliation, the polemic continues (again I am paraphrasing):

Tell me why you rage so, threatening us with wars, spurning peace, mad with the love of Mars, composing that poem, a foul vehicle of lies? Discordant to common sense and inspired by a rustic muse, you trouble the [true] muse with your deceptions and set Arethusa to flight. Your written verse, when spoken aloud, shows plainly your ignorance of how to arrange the rhythm in a poem. You call yourself a poet but abandon the strictures of grammar (148).[72] Your voice is immense, but your mind is altogether empty of learning. You are an example of the very crime of which you accuse others. What your heart attempts to conceal, your verse reveals: it is false and ill-composed (cf. ll. 141–161).

Now follows a lengthy rehearsal of the "divine wealth" of Würzburg, the saints they venerate and who render them help, patronage, and "the joys of life" (178). They provide supernal defense, and assure peace and security (cf. 167–205).

Turning from this sweeping picture of pious reverence for the saints at Würzburg, he next depicts its negative counterpart at Worms: their paganism. The saints revered there are Mars, Hercules, the gods of the underworld, the "black demons." They all are fomenters of war and strife, and their false religion assures their defeat (206–36). The poem ends with a repeated call for peace after conjuring the certain defeat that awaits all foes of Würzburg. The sick man who has attacked them is invited for a drink from the health-giving spring of their learning with its two-fold fount, the doctrine of right living and speaking.

These passages paint the picture of an ideal landscape of education: peace, love, happiness, affectionate and what our administrators call "supportive" relationships among students and between students and teacher. The language and metaphors depicting this ideal life draw persistently on the language of peace as opposed to warfare. It seems probable that the movements for the peace and truce of God, which were making headway into Germany at just this time, were among the providers of that language (see below, Chapter 5, on "Orphic" poetry). The proponents of that movement could not have wished for a more fully institutionalized model of a life based on peace and friendship than that offered in the Würzburg school, as this poet represents it. The happiness and joy that study brings is a leitmotif of the work. The students are happy about their "prince" (= teacher; *de principe letus* — 49). His word brings the "joys of life" (52; also mentioned later as one of the gifts of St. Stephen — 178). Serene in his prosperity, the master has "shed all sad things and rejoices" (66). Praise of the teacher "gladdens" the writer (129). The poet's offer of reconciliation to the man he is raging against exemplifies the ideal of friendship and forgiveness. He and his school have been wounded deeply, are turned as it were into an armed camp ready to ward off further attacks. But no matter how grievous the provocation, they are ready at any moment to end the contention and hold no grudges. No wrongs will rankle once friendship and love are reestablished. This shows the virtue of "gentleness," *mansuetudo*, an aristocratic turning of the other cheek, a gesture that asserts humility and superiority at the same time.[73]

It is evident that the poem from Worms, which provoked the Würzburg poem, violated some sacred principle of the schools. It did not matter whether or not it was written "for exercise." One element of that principle is the holy and inviolable person of the master: this has been assailed, and that means war. The squabble turns on the person of the teacher as much as it does on the composing of poetry. The second element is the "sweet life" of study, the "celebrated peace" of Würzburg. These things, the master's person and the atmosphere of untroubled happiness, are ideals too central to the mission of the school to tolerate any weakening of it. They are no joking matter, and their proponents lose their sense of humor when these become the subject of exercises. The seriousness is evident in the reaction at Worms. The perpetrator has gotten himself in trouble straightaway,[74] and his fellow students are still trying two years later to turn down the heat and end the conflict, as we will see.

Needless to say, the poem gives a utopian vision. Würzburg is an Elysian realm, an academy of poetry and virtue, its students a harmonious community of loving friends, knit together as "by a single vow" (46). The poem's idealizing is programmatic, not descriptive, and as such it gives us a uniquely clear insight into the values and self-conception of the early cathedral schools. Its documentary value is comparable to the advertising literature of American colleges. They project institutional values. The vision of the Würzburg poet is not an individual's fancy, but a set of widely shared values reflecting the social and intellectual ideals of the schools of France and Germany.

Central to these values is a kind of cult of the teacher's person. He is a charismatic priest / wizard / teacher, a "prince of primates" in his capacity as master. The light of learning flows in a living stream from his breast. His virtue and his standing loom larger than his learning. Worldly honor and rank appear as a major part of his contribution to the school. That is of course because the master's standing is a factor in determining whether the school's students are to join the ranks of *summi pontifices*. Accomplishing that goal requires that the master's honor remain intact. It facilitates promotion in the church and entry into heaven. Awe and reverence towards the teacher shore up his authority, and respond to his honor and his rank. Students do not dispute with a pillar of the church,[75] nor do they tolerate anything that could undermine him. Their own interests are bound up with that inviolable authority.

The arts are important, but virtually the only facets of them mentioned in the poem are reading, interpreting and composing poetry. We see the study of classics in full bloom, though in the same ambiguous light in which it would remain throughout the Middle Ages: one could accuse an opponent of paganism, but one could not omit a demonstration of the mastery of classical traditions from one's own poetic diction.

*   *   *

This squabble has an epilogue. The student or students of Worms got much more than they bargained for. The Würzburgers' threat to flex their muscles as athletes and poets was not an idle one. Two years after it began, the students of Worms are still embattled and are out looking for help. They write to students of the Mainz cathedral school.[76] The dispute between Würzburg and Worms has now turned into "fierce hatred," they write. Both the authorities in Würzburg and now the bishop and princes of Worms have been drawn in as judges, and are evidently dealing with the guilty parties. Some of the Würzburg students have given solemn oaths of their innocence. The writers of the letter are clearly feeling under pressure, and amidst aspersions cast on unnamed culprits, they beg information and advice from their peers at Mainz. The reply from Mainz (epist. 26, pp. 47–48) is a remarkable piece of letter writing; its subtlety is a caution against overestimating the conventional and formulaic nature of medieval letters. Its amicable and diplomatic tone (it greets the recipients with the offer of "seamless friendship and unshaken fidelity") is undercut by an irony that is not always subtle. The letter is marked also by an element of "Schadenfreude," barely concealed satisfaction at the predicament of the Worms students.

The writer opens with a barbed greeting that must have bitten sharply into a group of students still no doubt sensitive to the reproach of excessive devotion to pagan studies: "To the distinguished youth of Worms, who labor in the studies and the arts of the Athenians, R. of Mainz, no Greek, hardly even advanced in Latin . . ." R. of Mainz's wish to win the "love and reverence of all and to participate in the friendship of good men" urges him to write, and he assures them respect and reverence in the same degree as they have "always striven religiously and assiduously for the reverence of friends." The Worms students have gotten themselves off the moral high road, and he sprinkles his letter with snide reminders of the great community of peace-loving friends from which they have cut themselves off, all the time appearing to include them in its ranks: "We are gratified over and over again that you wish to receive us with such heart-felt charity and such loving sincerity into the communion of your friendship." As for their request for advice and counsel, however, he cannot comply with it for fear of forfeiting the friendship of one or the other of the parties to the dispute. He urges them at this late point in the conflict to seek the counsel of those whose counsel led them into it. He assumes such advisors must exist, since wise men like them do nothing without counsel. This response amounts to saying, "You got yourselves into this; now you can get yourselves out." The appeal to his scruples barely conceals his scorn.

Isolated and with the bishop and local princes breathing down their necks, they received in their colleague's letter a reminder of the intact world of friendship and love from which a satiric poem got them banished. Such was the price paid, in the 1030s, for criticism of a master and his school.[77]

*   *   *

Neither the above survey of schools nor the citation of texts was intended to be complete. They simply allow us to locate and identify *mores* joined to letters as an important subject of instruction at the major schools of France and Germany in the eleventh century. This education is regularly tied to advancement either in the church or at the royal court or both. It is peculiar to the cathedral schools. I have not found a single instance where the formula is applied to monastic education.[78]

The education founded on "manners" joined to letters was the distinctive feature of cathedral school education, and the program borne by that formula is an essential unifying element in the life of the schools in France and Germany in the period. Religious studies are regularly mentioned and scriptural learning commonly praised; the seven liberal arts still provide a framework for the intellectual side of learning. But now an intermediate subject swells to create a large territory between theology and the arts. That subject is *mores*, acquired through *disciplina* and *cultus virtutum*.

4. *Cultus Virtutum*

Part 1: Teaching Virtue

Eleventh-century schoolmasters would have lined up solidly on the side of the Sophist Protagoras, who argued against Socrates that virtue can be taught. But how did they teach it?[1] The framework of instruction known to us — reading, commenting, memorizing, lecturing, interpreting — existed and was at work in ethical instruction, but it was a minor element of a more embracing mode: imitation of the teacher. Again it is more useful to set the eleventh century cathedral school against the model of the theater than that of the classroom. If we want to form a conception of what a ballet lesson or a rehearsal consists of, written texts or director's notes will not be of much help. And if that is the only kind of source we have, we will not learn from them what we want to know.

As in the ballet lesson, the physical presence of the teacher demonstrating the subject through his own example is the essence of instruction in *mores*[2]; he is the curriculum; his presence radiates a force to the students, dips them in its magic aura and transforms them in his image and likeness. This quasi-magical creation or transformation of character is reduced by the bald phrase, "teacher imitation," but that was the main element of a pedagogy based on personal charisma.

CHARISMATIC PEDAGOGY

Imitation of the teacher is probably the most ancient form of pedagogy. It works through the diffusion of personal charisma.[3] A strong and impressive personality has the quality of replicating itself, remaking others in its image. An inner force called "virtue" creates this effect. The Renaissance was very aware of this forcefield-like effect of virtue. Shakespeare had Lady Percy describe the dead Hotspur in these terms:

> [his honor] stuck upon him as the sun
> In the grey vault of heaven, and by his light

Did all the chivalry of England move
To do brave acts; he was indeed the glass
Wherein the noble youth did dress themselves.
He had no legs that practiced not his gait;
And speaking thick, which nature made his blemish,
Became the accents of the valiant; . . .
He was the mark and glass, the copy and book
That fashion'd others. . . . . O wondrous him!
O miracle of men![4]

Charisma stimulates imitation. It is to moral development what parental genes are to embryonic development: a powerful principle by which like begets like. It is an irrational principle, which is also the basis of demagogery, hero-worship and cults of personality. But in the ancient world, the earlier Middle Ages, and the Renaissance it provided the foundation of ethical instruction.

The Greek and Roman ideals of paideia were transmitted by a double system of instruction that relied no less on the living model than on the literary.[5] Seneca turned a phrase that had a great future in medieval and Renaissance thinking on education:

The living voice and a life shared by pupil and master [*convictus*] benefit you more than any speech. . . . Long is the path through precepts; brief and effective through examples.[6]

The fuel that propelled the student along the way of examples was fervent attachment to the physical presence of the teacher: "Choose that man as tutor whom you admire more when you see him than when you hear him."[7] The pedagogy of teacher imitation was particularly strong in Stoicism. Zeno the founder of the school urged students to shape every act as if they had to account to their teachers for it.[8] Seneca formulates the precept as follows:

We must attach ourselves through love to some good man and hold him constantly before our mind's eye, and we should live as if he observed us constantly and do what we do as though he were observing.[9]

But the idea of a Stoic tradition founding this kind of pedagogy in the Middle Ages is unnecessary and misleading. The practice of teacher imitation and the pedagogy of personal charisma were far more widespread. We find it in writings on the education of an orator in Roman antiquity.[10] Early Christian tradition presents a particularly nuanced picture.[11] Peter Brown sees this mode of learning as founded on the conviction that the Christian life joins men as links in a chain diffusing the charisma of Christ, first through saints, then through monks and holy men, then bishops and priests, ending in laymen. The internal receptacle of this force is the image of God within, and the presence of the saint or holy man, the "Christ-carrying man," by itself brightens and partially restores this image. This, according to Brown, is "the imitation of Christ" in its early medieval aspect (Brown, "The Saint as Exemplar," pp. 1ff., see n. 11 above).

The classical tradition was another strand in a web of influences the ancient world exercised on the Middle Ages. They are joined in Ambrose, whose *De officiis ministrorum* formulates an ethic based on Cicero for ministers of the church. He recommends that young men should follow wise and famous men, since they form their lives in the likeness of those whom they follow.[12]

The practice was reinforced by Biblical and patristic precept[13]; it became institutionalized in the Merovingian church[14]; and it is everywhere observable in Carolingian education.[15]

In our period it is the foundation of education in *mores*. The biographer of Brun of Cologne, writing just after the mid-tenth century, described Brun as an exemplar of wisdom, piety and justice for the students at the royal court (p. 36 above). And Sigebert of Gembloux said expressly that Dietrich I of Metz learned to govern from Brun in a process of observation and transference of personal qualities: "as steel sharpens steel, the one was edified in emulation of the other's good qualities" (p. 37 above).

Willigis of Mainz rose to the archbishopric of Mainz (975–1011) through service at the royal court in the period immediately following Brun, as chancellor of Otto the Great and Otto II. His biographer, writing between 1019 and 1039, made the educating effect of the archbishop's presence into the dominant motif of his short vita:

> He taught lovers of virtue to live according to moral perfection, in his acts, not in his speech, more with the language of his behavior than that of his words.[16]

The impressive phrase, "language of his manners" (*lingua morum*), makes the person of the teacher into a learnable discourse. The Vita shows Willigis as a living textbook of *mores*: he was "a mirror of the perfectly moral life"; from his way of living "those who strive to live honestly can draw perfect examples of the moral life"; "through his example of faithful reading and honest morality, he incessantly rendered the lives of others honest."[17]

The continuator of *Gesta episcoporum Verdunensium*, writing in the mid-eleventh century, says the same thing more succinctly of Richard of St. Vannes: "The life of this remarkable man rendered the lives of many men remarkable."[18]

From the same period we have a number of witnesses to the effect of Fulbert's presence on his students at Chartres (see Chapter 3, p. 62 above). It is worth repeating two of them here. Adelman's portrait of Fulbert teaching the "mysteries of higher knowledge" is permeated with praise of the master's personal qualities: dignity in questions of *mores*, gravity and eloquence. These constituted the lesson, at least in part. We see this transference of personal qualities as a pedagogic goal clearly in Adelman's praise of his fellow student Hildegar, who succeeded in making himself into a copy of Fulbert "in his facial expressions, tone of voice and manners."[19] This was a major goal of instruction in *mores*: to become like the teacher, better yet, to become the teacher, to transform oneself in his image. Goswin of Mainz praised his student Walcher for his ability to do just this: ". . . while others present at my instruction were hardly able to reproduce their teacher's words in speech or writing, you seemed to transform yourself altogether into your master."[20]

Teaching by example became the dominant pastoral duty in the new houses of canons regular that burgeoned after the second half of the eleventh century.[21] The author of the *Moralium dogma philosophorum*, presumed to be William of Conches, urges imitation of good men in a passage based on the lines from Seneca quoted earlier (p. 77). He defines "reverence" as

> the virtue which accords the honor due to men of some gravity or men elevated in a position of authority. It enjoins us to imitate prominent men. The best course is to follow in the footsteps of men of eminence, if they walked the right path. We must choose a good man and hold his image ever before our mind's eye, and thus we will live as if he were observing our each and every act.[22]

And the Italian-German chivalric didactic poet Thomasin von Zirclaere (writing ca. 1215) draws on both Seneca and William of Conches to say that "a child of the nobility"

> should mind that he observe the behavior of the best men, for eminent men are and should be a mirror to youth. . . . Let him choose in his mind an excellent

man and arrange his behavior according to that pattern. . . . A youth should always behave as if his every act were observed by a man of distinction. . . . Let him willingly follow the man whose actions he can admire more than his words.[23]

Wibald of Stablo had his early education at Liège. The monastic milieu to which he moved as abbot of Stablo was not as limiting in his case as in others. He was "one of the most important statesmen of the twelfth century" (Manitius), counselor to four kings. He wrote a letter to a young school master, Balderich of Trier, which is a major statement of the kind of pedagogy we are dealing with. He urges him,

let your mere presence be a course of studies for your students. . . . Your position requires more than just teaching. You must exercise strict severity, for you are, as you know, also one who supervises the correction of conduct. This teaching and this exercise is more subtle and in its fruits more important than any other.[24]

In another letter, Wibald praised Bernard of Clairvaux for what amounts to a miraculous exercise of teaching through his mere presence: "You need only look on him, and you are instructed; you need only hear the sound of his voice, and you learn; you need only follow him, and you are made perfect."[25]

The physical presence of an educated man possessed a high pedagogic value; his composure and bearing, his conduct of life, themselves constituted a form of discourse, intelligible and learnable.[26] And this form of pedagogy defined one of the central tasks of cathedral schools: the formation of character according to the model of the master or bishop or whoever was charged with the authority to teach by example.[27] A fundamental element of the life of the schools in the period was a kind of cult of personality. The personal authority of the teacher becomes the dominant criterion of pedagogy. This brings us a long way towards understanding the nature and goal of cathedral school education and the role of *magister scholarum*, a position of much greater stature than its modern counterpart, school master. It is a striking fact that the position of master is commonly a stepping stone on the way to the bishopric. A career followed by many of the most distinguished imperial bishops since Ottonian times led from student to school master to court chaplain to bishop, with perhaps stations in between as provost or chancellor.[28] The reason for the close connection of school master and high administrative positions is, above all, that the master had to embody the qualities he "taught," and those qualities were ones that qualified a man for royal service, for administrative and diplomatic duties, for the episcopacy. Therefore a good *magister scholarum* was an obvious candidate for the royal chapel and the bishopric. The personal charisma of the great man, the diplomat, the statesman, the follower of the great Roman statesmen: this was the aura that surrounded the successful teacher at the cathedral schools and it was the main curriculum of *mores*.

This cult of personality functioning pedagogically explains in part the exuberant praise of masters from the period. Students were swept away by the personal magnetism of the man suited for the service of the emperor and probably destined for it. And it mattered less what they knew than what they were. What they wrote did not matter at all, as long as they exuded qualities like *dignitas, gravitas*, and *elegantia*. Peter Abelard, a teacher in a completely different stamp from the masters of the old learning, was astonished that great crowds of students lavished devotion on the venerable Anselm of Laon (whose school offered instruction in *litterae et mores*).[29] Anselm spoke beautifully, but his thought was obscure and he could not deal with the problems of philosophy he raised: "He had a remarkable command of words, but their meaning was worthless and devoid of all sense. The fire he kindled filled his house with smoke but not with light."[30] Here an intellectualized mentality looks back with contempt on a master of the old learning, sees all the faults and weaknesses of a cult of personality, and none of its strengths. Anselm's students understood perfectly what made Anselm great; they felt it in his gestures and his voice. In awe at the dignity of his presence, they could nurse the fiction that his understanding of scripture was profound, confident that none of their circle was vulgar enough to expose it as a fiction.

Another critical observer of cathedral school teaching shows us the same weaknesses from the opposite perspective, that of monks. Guitmund of Aversa, a student of Lanfranc and polemicist against Berengar of Tours in the eucharist controversy, gave us this extraordinary glimpse of the lecturing style of his foe:

> Whatever bespoke grandeur and distinction, he affected. This man, almost wholly ignorant, claimed to be a doctor of the arts, and persuaded people of it by virtue of his pompous posing, by elevating himself above others on a platform, by simulating the dignity of a teacher in his manner rather than by the substance of his teachings, by burying his head deep in his cowl, pretending to be in profound meditation, then finally, when the expectations of the listeners had been whetted by his long hesitation, giving forth in an extremely

soft and plangent tone, which was effective in deceiving those who did not know better.[31]

This text captures, more vividly than any other known to me, the peculiar blend of clericalness and imperial/secular pomp that must have character-ized masters of the old learning. Guitmund illustrates Berengar's "gran-deur" and garish pomposity by an oddly monkish gesture, his theatrical emergence from deep in his cowl with a kind of sung lecture. Guitmund's criticism amounts to a statement that Berengar's grand self-presentation compensates for puny learning. Berengar of Tours is a figure very much on the border between the old learning and the new. His career took him between the cathedral schools and the courts of secular lords,[32] his learning and personal charisma won him many enthusiastic students, but his use of reason and analytic thought set him sharply apart from masters like Fulbert of Chartres (whose student Berengar had been), Hermann of Rheims and Meinhard of Bamberg (both of whom retired out of annoyance with Berengar and his influence, according to Goswin). He had the style of the masters of the old learning, but he combined it with probing and exacting reason. We can put aside Guitmund's criticism of Berengar's learning. It tells us more about the categories of judgment applicable to secular masters in the second half of the eleventh century. Here Abelard and Guitmund would — in the abstract — agree. There is a shared structure of criticism: both Berengar and Anselm of Laon are criticized for knowing little but speaking and acting grandly. Probably many teachers could substitute per-sonal style, intellectually unrigorous moralizing, and grand self-presenta-tion for scholarship: probably many of them "simulated the dignity of a teacher in [their] manner rather than in the substance of [their] teaching," and students were more than willing to accept their education on those terms. Wibald of Stablo complains in the mid-twelfth century that students defend the sayings of their masters, not because they are true, but because they love the men who pronounce them, and he sees one school set against another, not in the pursuit of truth through reason, but "in hate or love of individual teachers."[33]

Personal authority was the basis of teaching manners, and this is starkly at odds with the reasoning intellect. A cult of personality and learning by the magnetism of presence require the numbing of critical judgment, not its sharpening. Charismatic pedagogy has this (and much else) in common with charismatic demagogery.

We may well think that then as now the cult of personal authority was a substitute for genius and a sign of the mediocrity of the age. Certainly to read what masters of the old learning wrote cautions against thinking them a lot of mute, inglorious Miltons. Works of mediocrity and verbosity abound. The *Rhetorimachia* of Anselm of Besate exemplifies grand, loud-mouthed self-inflation. Can the explanation of personal greatness possibly cover all the sins of pedantry and self-congratulation this author commits? Henry III took Anselm into the royal chapel, supposedly as a reward for the *Rhetorimachia* (though we have only Anselm's word on it). Let us hope that the emperor did it because his judgment was numbed by the spell of Anselm's personality.

Part 2: Embodying Virtue

But a fair number of men in Anselm's position and with his ambitions were mute and glorious, whatever the quality of the unwritten works slumbering somewhere in their minds. The problem for us in the twentieth century is to get from the muteness to the glory. Silence means obscurity, and it is a pall over great men and mediocrities alike.

THE CIVIL LIFE AS PRODUCTIVITY: *DISCIPLINA VIVENDI*

The forum in which learning, intellect and brilliance were to be expressed was the active life, public service, not philosophical tracts. A cleric of Worms wrote a letter to his bishop, Azecho, around 1030, in which he set forth an ideal of public administration as the fulfillment of philosophy:

> Divine providence, in foreseeing the necessity of installing you as the governor of our republic, has placed you at the apex of pastoral care in order that you may now translate into acts of public administration those things you have learned in your private studies. The schoolmistress of all virtues [philosophy] has taken up her abode in you, so that in all your undertakings you may follow in her footsteps.[34]

The letter was a job application, and the applicant was not only wheedling, but also putting forward his credentials by showing his mastery of Boethius and of the ideal of the learned administrator whose acts reveal the influence of philosophy. Public administration as a form of philosophy: it is a topic that would lead us back to Roman antiquity and into the heart of medieval humanism. Philosophy in the service of the *res publica* is a much cultivated educational and political ideal, one that required the alliance of schools with the apparatus of government.[35]

It is a major theme of the important letter collection, called by its editors *Die Regensburger Rhetorischen Briefe*. It was written around 1090. The purported narrative has a clerical administrator corresponding with friends and asking them for advice and guidance in the trials and difficulties of public life. The situation is fictionalized, but the sentiments surely are not. The problems treated and the solutions proposed will have been of vital interest to a German clerical administrator in the investiture controversy. The source of advice, consolation, and statesmanly wisdom to which the writers regularly turn is, generally stated, Philosophy. But the philosophy they draw on is almost exclusively Cicero's *Tusculan Disputations*, quoted so often that the letters occasionally appear a cento of passages from that work. It is a work of major importance for the cathedral schools of the eleventh century. Meinhard of Bamberg had termed it the most important work of philosophy from Roman antiquity, and commended it to a young cleric as a guide through the perils of his new career as an administrator at Cologne.[36] The great appeal lay in its combining of asceticism and rejection of the world with a stoically courageous affirmation of state service: persist, suffer through all the tribulations of the active life, and make the cult of virtues — identified with philosophy — into your guide. That is the thrust of *Tusculan Disputations*, and the author of the letters makes it into his theme. The appeal of this attitude to worldly clergy in the German empire in the second half of the eleventh century should be evident: torn between the parties in the investiture controversy, they could find in Cicero's work a rule of life, a philosophy that lent dignity to administrative service while at the same time casting serious doubt on it. It idealized imperial statesmen while placing the emperor himself in the role of Nero, Herod, and Nebuchadnezzar (*Regensburger Rhet. Briefe*, epist. 9, p. 314). It reconciled *contemptus mundi* with service of the state. In one of the most remarkable of these letters the author sets the trials of public life parallel with the sufferings of the martyrs and of Christ, and makes the courageous facing of those trials into an act of Christian fortitude. Here is a passage that shows especially clearly the odd mingling of Christian and Roman heroism:

> He himself [Christ] once fought for us. And should we now refuse to enter the field of battle for his sake? And would we, seeing his wounds, not suffer tribulations for his sake, having won salvation through the hate he faced? Spartan boys face tortures inflicted on them without crying out. Lacedaemonian youths in competitive fighting suffer blows and kicks and even bites, but would sooner suffer death itself than admit defeat. (*Regensburger Rhet. Briefe*, epist. 9, p. 319)

I doubt that the sufferings of Christ have ever before or since been set parallel to the training of Spartan and Lacedaemonian boys. But it shows us a central concern of this author: to legitimize and sweeten a cleric's service to the state by appeal to ancient Greek and Roman ideals, to transform the sufferings of state service into acts of heroism.

But our point of departure was the combining of philosophy and the active life. The *Regensburg Letters* find in the *Tusculan Disputations* a Roman model for this combination, one which must have had a deep resonance in the schools and courts of eleventh century Europe, at least among its statesman/intellectual class. It is the passage from which we developed the opposition of charismatic to intellectual culture in the introduction. The early Romans did not write works of philosophy, Cicero says, because they were so taken up with the great tasks of running the state, and they preferred to practice "that most bountiful of disciplines, the discipline of living well" (*bene vivendi disciplina*). They pursued this more in their lives than in their writings: "Vita magis quam litteris persecuti sunt."[37] It is difficult to do justice in English to the phrase *disciplina vivendi*, and one takes recourse to spelling out its implications. It makes the conduct of public life into a form of philosophical discourse, a program of studies, a textbook. Wibald of Stablo was speaking within this trope when he urged Balderich of Trier to turn his mere presence into a discipline (p. 80 above). And the example of the Roman statesman who turns public life into a philosophical discipline gave allure to this substitute form of productivity: life itself could become a work of philosophy, a composition analogous to an oration or to a musical composition. This work of art, the man of composed *mores*, was a major contribution of the eleventh century to "philosophy"[38] and to culture. It is the best answer to the question how that age could have been mute and glorious at the same time.

THE STATESMAN

By its very nature, then, the end product of *cultus virtutum* is lost to recovery: it is the living administrator functioning at court, expressing philosophy through acts of governing. But we can recover some literary representations of this ideal type in portraits of bishops, in descriptions of an idealized education and of particular virtues within that education. The courtier, administrator and bishop embodied the ideals of a program of education in *mores* and *ethica*. *Cultus virtutum* was a preparation for office. Richard of St. Victor wrote a letter to Robert of Hereford congratulating him on his promotion from schoolmaster to bishop:

> . . . all your students were filled with joyful hope [at the news of the promotion], and the entire school was heartened and roused to the love of letters and the cultivation of virtue through the example of your efforts and your success.[39]

The promotion of a former teacher to the bishopric would not animate students *ad amorem litterarum et cultum virtutum* unless that were seen as the path to office.

The content of that program of studies registers in the idealized portraits of men pursuing that education and those ambitions. I have discussed the figure of the court bishop, his virtues, and their social context elsewhere,[40] and I will not repeat here more than is necessary to lay the foundation for reading a few portraits.

A high clerical administrator, court chaplain, and bishop had to be handsome, preferably tall, at least impressive in appearance. At least these were highly desirable qualities, often mentioned in portraits. There are cases where unworthy bishops or bishops under attack are reproached with their ugliness or puny stature. *Statura procerus, vultu venerandus* are common terms of praise; *splendor* or *nitor personae* sums them up. Lampert of Hersfeld described Bishop Gunther of Bamberg (d. 1065) as "a man replete with all the good qualities of the body, in addition to the glory of his manners and the wealth of his mind." So preeminent was he among other mortals in respect to "elegance of form and overall build of the body," Lampert continues, that on his crusade in Jerusalem crowds of locals gathered in front of a church he was in and prevented him from leaving, so eager were they to get a look at his fabled beauty.[41]

The force of personal presence tends to become a motif of episcopal hagiography, one which humanizes the superpersonal miracles of popular hagiography. William of Malmesbury tells of a bishop, the object of a murder attempt, who turns and faces his assailants, and the splendor of his presence is so dazzling to them that they drop their knives and flee. It is the atmosphere of the saint's life and of miracle, but the event is not strictly speaking miraculous. The bishop is saved by his splendor; there is no supernatural interference.[42]

An important ideal of this milieu is borne by the phrase, "the greater we are," or "the higher we are set above other men, the more we should bear ourselves as their inferiors." The phrase is taken from Cicero, though the same ideal draws on the Biblical "the greater you are, the more you should humble yourself before all men."[43] It is an ideal based more on aristocratic deference than on Christian self-denial. Other qualities often praised are gentleness (*mansuetudo*), affability and popularity. A frequent formula for the latter is the Pauline "he is made all things to all men" (1 Cor. 9: 22), though the context of Paul's letter, proselytizing, plays virtually no role. The phrase designates an adaptable, versatile, amiable personality.

Particularly prominent is a quality called "beauty" or "elegance of manners." It is important for forming a bridge between the teachings of the schools and the entrance into the service of bishop or king.

Part 3: Two Views of Bishop Licinius

Many texts show us the qualities associated with *mores* as a school curriculum. We start with two that describe the education and early career of an obscure Bishop, Licinius of Angers (d. ca. 610). The first is the *Vita Licinii* composed by an anonymous monk some time in the eighth century (the work is not more closely dateable). The second is the adaptation of this *Vita* by Marbod of Rennes, written in the last decade of the eleventh century during Marbod's term as Archdeacon of Angers and after long service as *magister* of the school at Angers. Marbod read and used the older *Vita*. His changes represent a response to his source and show us all the more clearly the conception he imposed on what he received.

Marbod varied freely and modernized unhesitatingly. He changed the archaic vita, written in clumsy and hardly translatable Latin (its style intentionally unimproved in my translation), into an elegant and readable work, and changed the archaic values and educational ideals of the original to reflect the contemporary life of the cathedral schools. For that reason the two texts are a good starting point. The comparison allows us to distinguish ideals of education and courtiership of the eighth century from those of the eleventh.

The following excerpts juxtapose Marbod's version with passages he adapted[44]:

1. *Auctor anonymus*	Marbod
And so most blessed Bishop Licinius, born of the royal line of the kings of France, being highly versatile [*utilis*] and noble and abundantly supplied with the possessions of this world, persisted in the	And so Licinius, sprung from the highest lineage (he numbered kings of France among his ancestors), and supplied by nature with all the gifts of soul and body, increased his felicity through the study of

discipline and faith of Christ and strove for even higher nobility and sublimity. Hence he grew from day to day in faith and maturity, better and more fully, and was replete with the grace of God. (678D)

virtue. Ever since his boyhood, his behavior had been such that in him a pattern of future perfection and a model of extraordinary character shown forth. (1495A–B)

2. *Auct. anon.*

Marbod

In his youth . . . he was handsome and noble, but choice among his family; and within his lineage, he grew amiable. And among servants and friends he stood out for the eminence of his countenance, which flashed forth with every glance he cast. And when his father noted such industry in his son and recognized how blessed he was with every good quality, he rejoiced in his soul, and exulted in his joy, sending infinite thanks to God, who had deigned to send him so decorous a youth for his consolation. (678E)

For apart from his gift of external beauty and modesty of countenance, which won the hearts of all observers, as through the working of some secret talent, other qualities were judged excellent in the boy: that, guided by the grace of God, he spurned those vices, which seem innate in early youth and dominate all as if through some law of nature. For neither was he excessive in playing games, nor crude in his eating habits, nor garrulous in speech. (1495B)

3. *Auct. anon.*

Marbod

And when the time was at hand that he should be sent for an education in letters, he is given soon enough to a preceptor and is instructed by the most learned masters of sacred letters. Among his fellow students, for the sharpness of his mind, for his ample memory, he distinguished himself as amiable. At the urging of the Lord, he was the servant of all, but in respect to obedience, faith and charity, he was exalted above others. Now when his education with these most wise men was over, he returned to the home of his father, and, leaving behind the mind of a boy, passed his adolescence in industrious activity. The spirit of wisdom and the grace of humility shone forth nobly from his deeds, and he grew from virtue to virtue, performing daily good and saintly acts. (678E–F)

And when after learning the first basics, he was sent, as children of the nobility customarily are, to study the discipline of letters, he distinguished himself for the mildness of a noble nature and for an ample genius. What he heard from his masters he easily grasped and retained in his memory. Nor was it fear of the whip that made him attentive, but the love of learning. He knew how to show reverence to his doctors, obedience to his pedagogues, benevolence to his fellow pupils, and humility to all alike. . . . The hostility of his rivals he bore with equanimity and put an end to swiftly. He conquered anger with patience and pride with humility. He lent neither his ear nor his tongue to the back-biting of his fellows. He ignored abuse directed towards him, and reproved that directed towards others. In short, while still a disciple, he developed into a master of manners [*magister morum*]. (1495C–D)

4. Auct. anon.

Marbod

When, thus thoroughly educated, he had come to the age of maturity, straightaway his father commended him to Clotharius, king of the Franks, to whom he was closely related by ties of blood and loyalty. For the father of Licinius was vassal to the aforementioned King Clotharius. For S. Licinius was a wise youth, amiable in appearance, affable in speech, correct in his behavior with the king himself, with holy faith and with every man who entered the court, so that he was agreeable to all good men, but disagreeable to the evil and undisciplined. For he was supreme in appearance, strong and swift, agile, very wise and sweet, but unshakeably chaste, loving and humble.

Having passed the years of his boyhood in this study, and having added no small amount to the knowledge of his masters in divine and secular letters, he was forced to renounce philosophy at the command of his father, who was second only to the king in the palace, and to leave his leisure for affairs of state, his studies for an active life, the benefits of the schools for those of the palace. King Clotharius received him with open arms, as much because of their close relationship, as for the dignity of his excellent appearance and the elegance of manners in which the youth excelled. (1495D–96A)

5. Auct. anon.

Marbod

And when the aforementioned king had found him tried and true in this way, he prepared him for his service, and appointed him Count and custodian of his stable and all its horses. For he possessed in abundance the strength and the power for waging war bestowed on him by God, who watched over all his acts. With his sword he put to flight many troops of the enemy, through God's aid. For he was diligent in prayer and fasting, and tireless in his compassion for the poor. In addition he very often attended to his reading, and, as it is written, he rendered unto Caesar the things which are Caesar's, and unto the Lord the things of the Lord.

. . . honoring him after a brief time with the girding on of the sword, he began to reckon him among his friends, having found him plainly worthy to serve as the man with whom he dealt on affairs of great importance and the administration of the kingdom. For he possessed wisdom in counselling, loyalty in defending, rigor in executing. Nor was he wanting in flowing speech, nor in love of justice. Hence he was regarded as most useful both in pronouncing and executing the law. He bore himself to his colleagues in such a way that he sought to win the favor of each by some act of service. He showed himself affable to all. . . . He helped whomever he could with the king, and he was able to help whomever he wanted. Thus there was no one to whom some benefit did not come through him. . . . He soon came to function as steward of the court. From there it came about that, at the urging of all, the king made him military tribune, which now we customarily call constable. (1496A–B)

The passages in 1. have a common theme. We might call it: nature improved by nurture. But in the archaic Vita nature hardly is recognized as such; its gifts are noble birth and possessions. Social class and wealth constitute identity. In the eleventh-century version, there is a force named Nature who is the giver of the personal gifts, along with those which come by physical inheritance. In other words, Marbod has a conception of individual identity, at least of identity shaped by some gift-bestowing force. Nature shapes his identity and pays no, or little, attention to class and lineage.

In both, education improves this native state, and here the changes by Marbod are striking. The older Life invokes only the "discipline of Christ" which helps him grow in faith and attain the grace of God. Marbod replaces this religious conception of maturing with the "study of virtue," aimed at improving "behavior" (*conversatio*) to the point where it realizes its original potential for exemplarity. The formula for development in Marbod is "natural talent heightened by the study of virtue."

Both excerpts in 2. stress his impressive appearance. Marbod again is at pains to make this outer quality into the result of some inner gift (a "secret talent" — *occulto quodam munere* — working on him). Modesty of countenance is his addition. The older writer wants him not only modest but also daunting. Here we see also the change in, so to speak, the audience of this showpiece. The context in the earlier Life is the family; in Marbod it is broadened to include "all observers." Marbod includes a brief discourse on the vices of youth, specifically of students, which his hero shunned. All of them are overcome by Licinius's restraint and moderation.

The passages in 3. describe Licinius's elementary education. Both mention letters, but the older Life places these in the service of God: he studies with masters of "sacred letters"; his virtues are "obedience, faith and charity"; his acts are "saintly" (*bona et sancta opera*). Marbod has consistently removed any reference to the religious motive of studies. The letters he studies are not qualified; his virtues (not the theological virtues of the older Life) are directed to his teachers and schoolmates. His good deeds are strictly social; they aim at the untroubled conduct of learning. It is the "sweet life" of peace, reverence, and affability we encountered at Würzburg, that Licinius's good qualities look toward. Friendship, affection and smooth social relations are not even hinted at in the older Vita. The archaic Licinius relates to God and his father; Marbod's relates to his teachers and schoolmates. The learning in letters receives short shrift, and Marbod complements it with his mastery of *mores*. His patience, his ability to ignore insults, accept hostility and disregard backbiting, are set in sharp profile. These are not only the oil preventing friction in social life, but also talents of diplomacy and survival in a court.[45] They are evidently the virtues appropriate to the "kindness" or "mildness" (*benignitas*) of a noble nature (*generosae naturae*).

4. describes the departure from school and entry into royal service. In Marbod there is an element of reluctance: he was "forced" to "renounce" studies at his father's "command." The listing of virtues that commend him for the king's service in the older Vita suggest an author cramming alot in out of fear he may leave something out. Affability and amiability are major virtues for this author, along with wisdom and strength. Marbod reduces the list to two: the "dignity" of his appearance and his elegance of manners (*elegantia morum*). He also omits the mention of Licinius's "holy faith."

Finally, their active service of the king is described in excerpts 5. The older Vita makes him into a warrior. His duties as constable are presumably central to warfare, waged with God looking on benevolently. Marbod turns this divine warrior into an administrator, a *vir utilis*. He becomes a knight through the girding on of the sword (a ceremony the older author could not have known), but he never uses his sword. He enjoys the king's familiarity, administers the state at his side, and rises in honors. One of his offices is constable, but rather than describing his activities as "military tribunal," Marbod immediately launches into a description of his ascetic, monkish regimen while at court. The social context in Marbod's version is the life of the court. His ingratiating acts of affability, his granting of *beneficia*, have the odor of strategies of survival and success in a tight knit court where many courtiers vie for favor, and envy and intrigue are constant dangers.

This list of differences has considerable historical value in the greater context of the development of institutions. The older Vita depicted a young hero doing justice to family expectations. The only social category at work is family; even the entrance into the court operates within it: the father passes him to his relative the king. The element of blood relationships plays a part in Marbod's Vita, but the institutional setting is schools and court, and family ties are submerged in a host of qualities and considerations that derive from this broader institutional setting.

The archaic Licinius is a hero; Marbod's is a courtier-philosopher.

The structure of personal development in the older Life has three stations: father-king-God; Marbod's has two — school and court — and presents the dichotomy in sharp focus: "from leisure to state affairs, from studies to the active life, from the schools to the palace" (cf. Marbod, excerpt 4).

The anonymous Life shows an archaic curriculum in letters and religion. In Marbod, the curriculum is letters and manners. The religious life is important and highlighted during Licinius' court service, but oddly enough it plays no role at all in his education. Marbod worked purposefully in this direction, because he had to eliminate so many references to religious training and the guidance of God from his source. The "study of virtues" is central to his hero's education. It culminates in his mastery of manners, such that he himself becomes a *magister* of the subject (the double meaning of *magister* is clearly intentional: he mastered them, he taught them). This mastery gained at school is answered by his entrance into court, where his manners commend him along with his family ties. The same was true of the older Life, where also a list of virtues explains his favor at court. Marbod can eliminate the list, because he has a collective concept for the entire range of virtues that qualify a man for court service: "elegance of manners" ("propter egregiae formae dignitatem ac morum elegantiam . . . suscepit" — 1496A). Those are some general insights we can glean from the comparison. Two specific points deserve a more detailed treatment.

NATURAL TALENT

Marbod's stress on nature-given talent developed through the study of virtue recalls the biographies of Brun of Cologne and Dietrich I of Metz (pp. 36ff. above). This is evident in details of wording:

> Sigebert on Dietrich: ". . . whom nature, or rather the author of nature, enriched with the native gift of genius . . ." (". . . quem natura, immo ipsius auctor naturae, nativo ingenii bono ditabat . . .").

> Marbod: ". . . Licinius, enriched with all the gifts of soul and body . . ." (". . . Licinius . . . bonis omnibus animae et corporis a natura ditatus . . .").

Alpert of St. Symphorian had also praised Dietrich for his inborn talents, and had distinguished sharply between inherited and nature-given gifts:

> Dietrich had far more to commend him than high birth and illustrious ancestors: his fame rested also on the great wealth of endowments he was born with.[46]

Here the distinction implicit in the older and newer Vitae of Licinius, has sharp contours: nobility of birth counts less than nobility of soul. Marbod's

Vita Licinii is symptomatic of the diffusion of that pattern of education we observed in chapter 2: through cultivation of virtue, the talented man develops into a civil administrator. Marbod's work presupposes the Ottonian educational model institutionalized.

The idea that natural talent and not the mere chance of birth determines a man's values has broad social and educational implications. It creates the possibility of "nobility of soul" competing with or even supplanting nobility of birth as a measure of human worth.[47] The cultivation of virtue has a vital role to play when the contents of the soul and their expression in outward behavior become the measure of man. Our period sees a proliferation of epithets referring to human greatness. They work within the logic of this structure: native gifts developed through cultivation of virtue bring forth greatness. A few examples:

Ruotger called Brun a "great man." His ancestors were of the highest nobility, but he surpassed them all in "the grace of his figure, the greatness of his learning and his versatile industry of mind."[48] Notker of Liège is praised for his "the endowments of his mind and his supreme virtue" received as a "singular gift from the spirit of God."[49] Notker's biographer praises his "majesty of person."[50] Meinhard of Bamberg, wishing for the advancement of Benno (later Bishop of Osnabrück), tells him that a demotion in title means nothing as long as there is increase in "splendor of honor and of person."[51] The biographer of Bishop Godehard of Hildesheim praises Godehard's father as a man who "with the elegance of a versatile ingeniousness outdid many puffed up with the arrogant pride of empty nobility. For no one is noble whom virtue does not ennoble."[52]

This formula of praise had its context above all in administrative service. It is perhaps indicative that Richer draws on the same logic in praising Otto II as "an energetic and useful administrator of the republic, a man of great genius and all virtue, distinguished for his knowledge of the liberal arts."[53] Here again a significant and typical constellation: genius, learning, virtue and "useful" administration. In this case it refers to the highest secular "administrator of the republic." Benzo of Alba draws on the logic of these formulae repeatedly in his praise of members of Henry IV's court. He defines virtue as "dignity of mind, nobility of soul, which makes man not just an object of wonder, but divine."[54] He develops an idea of the dignity of man, established by his upright stature, his reason and eloquence, and his lordship over all of created nature.[55] A passage discussing the emperor's obligation of choosing bishops carefully and responsibly is worth quoting in full:

> I wish him [the emperor] to know that some men dare murmur against him, saying that in the creation of bishops he draws too little on his individual judgment (*specialis discretio*), whereas he should note that God himself by His own act conferred on him the right to ordain men to superior positions, just as He himself arranges the ranks of the citizens of heaven. And because he is the vicar of the Creator, he is obligated to attend daily to the duties of his overlordship. Raised to such lofty sublimity by divine favor . . . he ought to exercise in all of his acts a judgment instructed/nourished by the virtues, and thus render honor and glory to Him who made him in His own likeness as a second Creator for human beings.[56]

Here a sentiment against the papal party in the investiture controversy is nourished by the cult of virtues at the schools. The emperor is a second creator, a demiurge of pontiffs, and the criterion of judgment is *virtutes*. This eliminates — at least subordinates — other criteria: canonical procedure, the advice of clergy, populace and pope, and miraculous selection. The emperor is to exercise his own virtues in the recognition of virtue, and arrange the earthly hierarchy accordingly. This is entirely consistent with the picture of Brun selecting men for the high positions in the empire in terms of their talents and virtues. It also shows the principle of charisma at work in the selection of bishops.[57]

ELEGANCE OF MANNERS

This quality or set of qualities apparently became a defining criterion for selecting administrators at worldly and ecclesiastical courts. It has come up often in previous chapters.[58]

Elegance, beauty, suaveness of manners (*elegantia, venustas, suavitas morum*) are formulations inherited from classical Latin. As such they occur from the early Middle Ages on.[59] But the occurrence is sparse and the usage without sharp profile until the end of the tenth century. Then the new educational and social context raises the virtue into prominence. Anselm of Liège praised both Eraclius and Notker of Liège for this quality (Chapter 3, p. 55 above), and he praised Wazo for his elegant genius (p. 55 above). These references are from the mid-eleventh century or later, though they refer to a period a hundred years earlier. From the beginning of the eleventh century we have Alpert of St. Symphorian's praise of Dietrich of Metz for his *eligantia vitae* (Chapter 2, p. 41 above). This quality set him above all his contemporaries, whose distinctions were merely outward and inherited; his "elegance" derived from "great inborn wealth of gifts." It appears as a personal quality here. It is worth noting that all of these men (with the exception of Wazo) were close to Brun of Cologne: Dietrich as his student and relative, Eraclius and Notker as royal chaplains.

From the mid-eleventh century on, numerous references make it clear that "elegance of manners" looms large in the teaching of the cathedral schools and plays a major role in advancement through the ranks of administrative service in secular and ecclesiastical courts. We could infer from Anselm of Liège's praise of Bishop Eraclius that the Liège schools were founded on this quality along with the learning of letters: "Because Eraclius was firmly grounded in elegant probity of manners and the liberal learning of *honestas* . . . he took pains to establish schools throughout the churches." The studies of Richard of St. Vannes at Rheims had the result that he advanced so far "both in the gift of learning and in the elegance of his life and manners" that he became precentor and deacon at Rheims (p. 60 above). Meinhard stated outright that his "studies" (i.e., *convictus*) with his former teacher were valuable for their *utilitas, elegantia,* and *sublimitas.* Here "elegance" was imbedded in two terms that referred to administrative service: the skilled and versatile exercise of it (*utilitas*) and high rank (*sublimitas*).

This quality is learned at the schools and once mastered it leads to advancement. Various references show that it was especially attractive to secular lords.[60] Agnes of Poitou, wife of Henry III, sought out Ulrich of Cluny (Zell) for her service because she admired his "suaveness of charming manners" and sought in him the "pattern of correct conduct."[61] Meinwerk of Paderborn was taken into the royal chapel on the strength of this quality:

> Meinwerk, born of the royal family, is judged suited for the royal service because of the elegance of his manners, and, called to the palace, he is made a royal chaplain.[62]

John of Salisbury makes a comment worth noting in this context. He prefaces his Pseudo-Plutarchan "Education of Trajan" with a letter from Plutarch to the emperor. It begins:

> I had known that modest as you are you did not seek high office, even though you have always striven to merit it by your elegance of manners.[63]

Whether or not John of Salisbury invented the letter with no authentic model,[64] he allowed this striking turn of thought to stand: a ruler merits sovereignty by elegance of manners. Gerald of Wales describes "beauty of manners" (*venustas morum*) as not only "the chief quality useful and appropriate to the individual's governing of his own life," but also claims, "no one requires it more than he who governs the multitude."[65]

Our point of departure was Marbod's comment that King Clothar welcomed Licinius into court service willingly because of his family ties, his impressive appearance, and his elegance of manners. The context of this quality should be clear: it is a summation of what *cultus virtutum* aims at, and it is a preparation and qualification for administrative service at church or court.

Part 4: The Virtues of G's Father

Meinhard of Bamberg wrote a letter to a former student, who was about to take up a high position at the cathedral of Cologne. The master gives the student advice on surviving and prospering in that dangerous city. The letter, in my opinion, is one of the most important documents of eleventh-century humanism. Meinhard refers to the recipient only as G. Erdmann conjectures that he is either archbishop elect or a man being groomed for that position, but he is not able to identify him with a particular archbishop of Cologne.[66]

Meinhard warns him of a war that is to be waged over his soul in Cologne. Two courts will fight to gain his services and to make him a member of their retinue. The one is the noble court of virtues, the other the ignoble court of vices. The court of virtues summons him as its special favorite and places the entire government of the court in his hands because of his perfect, exemplary manners (*specimen morum*) and the sharpness of his mind (again, manners and letters or intellect as the prerequisite to administrative service). The other court calls to him with the allure of its "slippery, silky bodies," and tries to make him into a citizen of the second Babylon, Cologne. The allegory is a sort of psychomachia,[67] but it is fabricated from the real situation of the competition between courts for a gifted courtier.[68] Meinhard reminds him of lessons he tried to impress on him as a student:

> You have often heard me dispute about nobility turning into one of two paths, toward glory or toward ignominy. I stressed what a heavy burden the distinguished service of our ancestors places on the shoulders of descendants, to whom a morally upright life and careful custody of manners is not so much a virtue as a necessity, and who, even if all their acts were performed with the

utmost perspicacity, seek not so much to merit praise as to avoid blame. . . . For if they stray so much as an inch away from the path to the exalted place of virtue, which the glory of their parents paved for them, what a headlong plunge, o my G., their fame, reputation and honor will suffer! This and many things like this . . . you have heard me lecture you on.[69]

This provides a list of subjects on which Meinhard lectured and preached: the necessity of following the examples of illustrious predecessors, the importance of fame, reputation, *honestas*, the obligation to maintain glory in the active life. This no doubt is a clear if limited glimpse into *mores* as a classroom subject. It leads up to the example of G.'s own father, which Meinhard impresses on him particularly. He describes him as

> a man instructed in every kind of virtue, a man who enjoys to an astonishing degree all the charm and grace of humanity, qualities visible far and wide not only in his dazzling blaze of manners [*flagrantia morum*] but also in the bright good humor which shone most graciously from his eyes.[70]

Again, we have an excerpt from Meinhard's "curriculum" in virtues. The passage supplies us with important concepts from that curriculum: grace and charm, humanity, upright character and virtue that radiate like a fiery light from the countenance, gracious good humor which is the sign of those rich inner qualities.

HUMANITAS

The phrase *omni lepore humanitatis mirifice conditus* is striking for the purity of its Ciceronian pedigree, and since the virtues it conveys are received in an education in virtue and are important in administrative service, the student of medieval humanism is tempted to turn bright spotlights on it and reserve it a place on center stage in future studies. Such an impulse should always arouse in the same student the highest critical resistance. This is the place to discuss the problem of medieval *humanitas* by way of establishing the context of Meinhard's resonant comment.[71]

Meinhard had a Ciceronian phrase in his mind when he wrote this passage, not a conventional and widespread usage in the Latin of the eleventh century cathedral schools. Cicero had praised Cinna in the *Tusculan Disputations* (that work which Meinhard commended to G. in the same letter) as an ideal of "humanity, wit, grace (*suavitas*) and charm (*lepor*)."[72] He also lauded Socrates for his "charm, wit and humanity" (*lepore et humanitate*) in *De oratore*.[73] Meinhard not only used Cicero's phrase, combining *lepor* and *humanitas* but he clearly understood the import of both terms. *Humanitas* here is a social quality, an amiable graciousness that shows itself in a higher good humor—not mere jocularity, but an inner warmth that flows outward from virtue; it is gentleness and mildness based on strength, confidence, optimism and a stable and self-assured character. The phrase and the concept are both Ciceronian.[74] Meinhard used the term in this sense in other letters. The letter to his former teacher cited above (pp. 60–61) praised the "most humane manner" in which he had received Meinhard into his school, where his studies set him onto a path of education "more liberal" than any other and highly conducive to "utility, elegance and sublimity."[75] Meinhard's reception, and not the liberal studies themselves, are described as humane. The word *humanus* here is close to "generosity," but in the context of receiving an outsider, there is certainly also a suggestion of a humane spirit of kindness and friendship. The fact that he is being admitted to "liberal" studies may be a chance connection. He is being admitted humanely to liberal studies, not to the *studia humanitatis*.

Meinhard also praised the "humanity" of Cardinal Bishop Leopertus of Palestrina:

> No powers of eloquence suffice to explain how the most sweet savor of your humane nature [*condimenta humanitatis tue*] reigns with its loving, soft and imperious rule in our heart.[76]

Here again is a notion of *humanitas* which asserts a strong sense of the dignity of man: "humanity" represents strong authority reined in and restrained by gentleness, love, kindness.

These usages have their spiritual ancestors in Roman antiquity and Ciceronian humanism. Let us see what if anything they owe to medieval and contemporary usage.

We can quickly rule out the patristic and medieval sense of *humanitas* as human frailty, set against divine permanence, *divinitas*.[77] But *humanitas* also took on a more positive sense of human kindness, mercy, compassion that was Christian and monastic. The Benedictine Rule was the major transmitter of the word in this sense. It calls for a "humane" reception of guests: "[receive a guest by reading the rule to him] and after this let him be shown all humanity."[78] This early usage treads a narrow line between "human feeling of compassion for those in need" and simply "what frail human nature requires to sustain itself." But it came to mean clearly "what one owes out of human compassion to the hungry and needy." Gerbert urged bishops to be hospitable out of a vision guided by *humanitas*.[79] Bishop Radbod of Utrecht was praised for his kindness to paupers, such generosity being among the *studia et officia humanitatis et misericordiae*.[80] There we have the major meaning and context of medieval humanity: compassion for those in need. The specific context is ordinarily hospitality.[81]

But the Ciceronian ideal of affability and charm as defining elements of humanity could find their way into the most ascetic usages. Ulrich of Cluny (Zell) is praised for receiving even his enemy "with a joyous countenance, offering him peace with an embrace and with the kiss of charity, charming him with kind and sweet words, and refreshing him with all the attentive service that humanity demands."[82] *Obsequium humanitatis* does not mean service due to human nature; but rather the service which humane behavior demands. The word conveys here an ideal of benevolent conduct, not a conception of human frailty: the sense of the word has passed from the suffering of the receiver to the kindness of the giver.

The term can be released from its main context, hospitality, to signify compassion and kindness in general. Bernard of Clairvaux was said by one of his biographers to have great compassion with physical suffering, and indeed "his *humanitas* was so great that he commiserated not only with human beings but also with irrational creatures, birds and animals."[83] It occurs commonly in conjunction with *misericordia, mansuetudo*, and *benignitas*.[84] In this connection it becomes a royal virtue,[85] one far removed from the obligatory gesture of reminding the king in his majesty that he is mortal and burdened with frail *humanitas*.[86]

Gerald of Wales tells an anecdote that is a rich picture of this concept in the context of royal liberality. He proposes the Emperor Trajan as the supreme example of *humanitas et benignitas*,[87] and illustrates it with this story:

> Once when he was about to set out on a journey to tend to some urgent business, he had already gotten underway in a great hurry, when a wretchedly poor beggar woman threw herself at his feet and importuned him to restore the pension unjustly taken from her. And when the emperor replied that it must wait for his return, she asked, "And if you never return? What is to become of me?" Without a trace of exasperation, the emperor put off his departure until the woman was provided with letters containing the imperial mandate restoring her right. Because of these and other acts of humanity and because of the infinite virtues conferred on him by nature . . . [Gregory the Great attained redemption for him through prayer][88]

The strands of meaning are particularly rich here. "Humanity and kindness" consist of royal condescension. The least and humblest of his subjects, the story implies, is as important as the pressing affairs of state business. This is medieval *humanitas* in its fullest formulation: the grand world of diplomacy and politics is put on hold for a beggar woman.

But it is not exactly what the historian of humanism and the humanities looks for: the meaningful connection of liberal studies with a conception of *humanitas* taken over from classical Rome. This story and every other example cited, with the possible exception of Meinhard, is quite separate from studies. The Ciceronian notion that liberal studies are humane studies because they render the student human has not yet reappeared.[89]

It seems that the *studia humanitatis* were more vitally at work in the medieval kitchen and refectory than in the classroom and library. The biographer of Bernard of Tiron provides a charming if specious argument for that claim. Writing around 1115, he praises the religious reformer's parents as honest and religious people, who "pursued the studies of hospitality and humanity."[90] The phrase *studia humanitatis* was part of his vocabulary, but the concept has shriveled to hospitality.

Were liberal studies excluded from medieval *humanitas*? Not entirely. Thierry of Chartres uses the term at the beginning of his manual of the liberal arts, the *Heptateuchon*. The seven arts are gathered together in a kind of synod, he says, convoked *ad cultum humanitatis*.[91] The phrase may have been borrowed from his source, but Thierry would hardly have used it in so prominent a place if his conception of *humanitas* were limited to the narrower medieval contexts.[92] The formulation *ad cultum humanitatis* is curious. "For the worship of mankind" is a possible translation. Closer would be "for the enrichment and cultivation of that ideal, *humanitas*." Whatever its specific contours, it must mean an ideal of humanity acquired through study of the liberal arts.

William of Conches provides a gloss on *studia humanitatis* in his commentary on the *Timaeus*. The gloss runs as follows:

> . . . he commends Osium in this way: with his mind flourishing in the studies of humanity. Study is the urgent and energetic application of the mind to action with strong will. But studies are of two kinds, either of humanity, as in practical studies [*practica*, i.e., ethics], or of divinity, as in theoretical. But, while he flourished in both of them, he did best in humanities, because the human being is human[e]. The *studia humanitatis* may also refer to all things that the human being can know, in all of which he flourished.[93]

This groping commentary strengthens the impression that a firm conception of *studia humanitatis* did not exist in eleventh and twelfth century humanism, only an inherited phrase whose meaning in antiquity had been forgotten. What we do learn from this narrowed version of a classical concept is that William of Conches connected *studia humanitatis* with ethical learning: "studia, alia sunt humanitatis ut practice." The alternate meaning, "all that is knowable," leaves the door open for liberal studies, but a meaningful connection of the two is lacking.

One final citation will firm up our understanding of the term without eliminating the impression that the medieval *studia humanitatis* was different from the ancient. Wibald of Stablo wrote a letter to an archdeacon of Liège in 1151 excusing himself from important peace negotiations. His presence is not necessary, he says with a gracious and captious turn of phrase, because his correspondent is far better trained and instructed in *mores* by that regal lady and indoctrinatress of things human and divine, the Magistra and educatrix, Lady Philosophy. She is *umana philosophia*, who does not hesitate to take counsel with sworn enemies when the good of the state is at stake. With her support he can undertake his task "with humanity and placidity of soul" (*cum omni humanitate et placiditate animi*) and strive to guide it to a good conclusion.[94] Earlier in this chapter we quoted a passage from the Worms letter collection written some hundred years earlier describing philosophy as the instructor of men who guide the affairs of the state. This is that same figure, but considerably enriched. She is a teacher of *mores*. The word "human[e]" is a leitmotif in the passage: she teaches things human and divine; she is "human philosophy"; and she looks on his efforts "with humanity." This is close to an allegorical representation of philosophy as characterized by *humanitas*, precisely in her capacity as teacher of the *mores* of statesmen.

This may give us a strong connection between philosophy and *humanitas*, but not a medieval *studia humanitatis* modeled on ancient.

Now it is time to return to the passage from Meinhard's letter to G. His father's *lepor humanitatis* was a learned quality, acquired in instruction in the virtues (*omni genere virtutis instructus*), important in the war against the vices he will wage in administrative service at Cologne. This whole web of ideas and contexts has little echo in the other references cited from the eleventh and twelfth centuries. It appears to be a case of a more or less pure Ciceronian conception of *humanitas* appropriated by Meinhard — one which did not take firm hold. A later humanism will recreate a Ciceronian ideal of humanity broadly adapting something approaching its original conception.[95]

But it should also be clear that Meinhard's *humanitas* is not totally anachronistic and isolated. On the contrary, the atmosphere in which he worked and taught called forth this Ciceronian idea. It happened that the development of medieval *humanitas* did not follow precisely this neo-classical track; it was a blind alley — in terms of word history. That does not alter the fact that the ideal human being who was kind, benign, gracious, charming, compassionate and well-lettered, and who showed these qualities in his outer bearing, his facial expression and motions, was a widely shared ideal of education in *mores*. Whatever name contemporaries chose to apply to this ideal, it was alive and vital in the cathedral schools.

LEPOR AND HILARITAS

Charm, grace and wit (*lepor*) are attributes of *humanitas*. They are expressed not only in the visible radiance of G's father's manners, but also in his serene good humor (*hilaritas*).

Lepor is a courtly virtue. It is both a way of acting (gracious and winning) and a way of speaking (witty and charming.) An eleventh-century glossator gives it as a gloss on *facetiae*: *facetiae: lepos, suavitas verborum, urbanitas*. The twelfth-century *Glossarium Maii* gives the adjectival form as a gloss on *comis* (amiable, friendly): *comis: facetus, urbanus, lepidus, curialis*.[96] Ruotger praised Brun of Cologne for raising the quality of Latin at the court of Otto the Great: "This he did with no arrogance, but with both courtly grace [*domesticus lepor*] and urbane gravity."[97] Meinhard's letter to G. makes it clear that as early as the eleventh century the term spanned both meanings: ironic wit (as in *facetiae*) and amiability (as in *comis, comitas*).

One might well expect to equip a man setting out to do battle against vice with more powerful weapons. But in fact charm and winning grace are qualities vital to survival in the hothouse atmosphere of court life and administrative service. *Lepor* and *hilaritas* have a distinct social context. They fit into a broad field of concepts, virtues, social ideals that includes affability, gentleness, charm and wit. A common formula to describe the successful exercise of these virtues is the Pauline phrase, "all things to all men." It is a formula of success in the favor relationships at court. The utility of this ideal of amiability is evident in Ambrose's praise of the virtue, adapted from Cicero:

> First we should know that there is nothing so useful as to be loved, nothing as inexpedient as the opposite. . . . Goodness is popular and agreeable to all men,

and nothing impresses itself with such ease on humane sensibilities. And if we bring this goodness to fruition through a gentle and polite manner, moderation in commands and affability of speech, respectful choice of words and unassuming form of address and a graceful modesty, it will bring us amazed to the pinnacle of affection.[98]

The same passage is quoted by Gerald of Wales in his tract on the education of the prince, and that indicates the worldly context of this quality in the twelfth-century. Virtually no biography of a clerical administrator that describes his early career and rise to prominence omits mention of the man's winning charm, grace, affability, good humor.[99] The two biographers of Licinius treated in the previous section both placed emphasis on the young man's affability, friendliness to his fellow students and colleagues and to the king. The older vita described him as "amiable" (three times), "affable in speech," "agreeable to all good men," "loving and humble." Marbod said that "he won the hearts of all observers"; his gentleness and patience allowed him to thwart the anger and intriguing of his schoolmates; at the king's court he was "affable to all" and sought to win each man's favor.

These virtues operate in a field of forces where they are set against intrigue, envy, hate, anger, malice, treachery, betrayal of loyalty. Virtues that can overcome these chief vices of court life, far from being light and flimsy weapons, are the guarantors of success. For that reason they are prominent among the manners cultivated in an education in *mores*. A passage that is paradigmatic for the relation of cathedral school education to the virtues of charm and amiability is in the Vita of Norbert of Xanten. His biographer praises his education:

> . . . enjoying the gift of nature in regard to the shape and suppleness of his body, preeminent in eloquence through his knowledge of letters, adorned with the ornament of his manners, he showed himself gracious to all who knew him.[100]

In this passage at least, letters and manners have the result of creating an amiable man, and that will have been an important goal of the *cultus virtutum* in general.

FRIENDSHIP: *AMICITIA*

The grace and good humor of G's father may have been individual virtues, but they were also representative. The atmosphere of *amor* and *amicitia* was an ideal of the schools. We have seen this in the example of the Würzburg-

Worms polemics. The jealousy with which friendship and amicability were guarded and offenses against them punished suggests an ideal with a real power to shape social intercourse in these institutions.

An atmosphere of loving friendship was praised and cultivated, at both schools and court from the early Middle Ages on. Friendship and love were a form of respect, and an atmosphere of loving friendship was the visible or palpable sign of the virtue and high merit of the men who lived in it. This was a central ideal of the most popular of all Cicero's works in the Middle Ages, *De amicitia*: only good, strong and noble men are capable of friendship, because true friendship is the love of virtue in another person.[101] It is not useful to distinguish the philosophical from the social ideal, though *amicitia* is regularly regarded in modern scholarship as some kind of abstract, philosophical notion realized in the cases of some few gifted individuals, as it was in the cult of male friendship in European romanticism in the late eighteenth and early nineteenth-century. In the Middle Ages the social institutions of aristocracy were saturated with this ideal. It governed social intercourse among clergy and at royal courts, and as a result it also bore strongly on the curriculum of behavior at those schools that prepared young men for service to church and state.

The language of favor relationships at court was the language of love.[102] The king "loves" his favored councilors passionately.[103] The more passionate the avowal of love the greater the virtue in both men. The declarations of love common between kings and courtiers have beguiled some readers into thinking that homoerotic relations could color the atmosphere of life at court. That may be true, but it must not be read into the language of love and friendship, which was spoken with no suggestion of physical love. On the contrary, if the love expressed was not Platonic, then the claim of virtue implicit in it was forfeited — and that claim constituted its major social value. The cultivation of friendship at court has been overshadowed by the cult of spiritual friendship in the monasteries since the late eleventh-century. This has to do mainly with the richer documentation of the phenomenon: monks wrote tracts on spiritual love and courtiers did not.[104] A broad-based study of love and friendship in the eleventh and twelfth centuries that regarded the social mores of monasteries, cathedral communities and worldly courts would correct the one-sided notion of a custom centered in and originating from monastic communities. It was a practice and an ideal of aristocratic society generally.[105]

Brun of Cologne introduced an ideal of peace and tranquillity into diplomacy, administration and studies. Ruotger says that Brun was born to be a peacemaker, not only in affairs of state, but in those of the schools. He always cultivated peace, "as if it were the nourishing force and crown of all other virtues." Tranquillity strengthens virtue, while strife weakens it.[106] His quality of *pietas* made warriors timid; the fame of his name put an end to wars, ushered in peace, and *established the study of the arts*. Ruotger places this peace-making activity so clearly in the context of studies, displacing it from the normal context of peace — warfare —, we are justified in wondering whether the ideals of peace, love and friendship were not introduced into the cathedral schools by Brun. We know that he shaped the early curriculum of *mores* and placed the cultivation of virtue in the foreground of studies, and Ruotger states clearly that Brun considered peace the ideal atmosphere for the pursuit of virtue.

However the ideal entered the schools, it was firmly enshrined there. A mutual love joining teacher and student is probably not restricted to any one period. But it gained a sharp profile in the eleventh century and almost certainly was part of a program. There are numerous pronouncements on the obligations of teacher and students to love one another,[107] and there are documents that attest to extraordinarily close, passionate friendships.[108] But it is also possible to form an idea of the atmosphere of mutual reverence and respect, of restrained, modest amiability that predominated in the instruction itself from the letters and poems of the period. The Würzburg school was depicted as a peaceful kingdom, its teacher and students bonded by a "single vow" of love and peace. "Joy" and "happiness" predominated. A similar atmosphere is indicated in the letter of admonition Adelman of Liège wrote to Berengar of Tours, recalling him from his errant ways by invoking the memory of their golden days in the school of Fulbert of Chartres:

> I have called you my fellow suckling and foster brother in memory of that sweetest and most pleasant life of studies [*dulcissimum contubernium . . . iocundissime duxi . . .*] we spent together, you a mere youth, I somewhat older, at the academy of Chartres under our venerable Socrates. We have more cause to glory in the common life of studies [*convictus*] shared with him than had Plato, who gave thanks to nature for bringing him forth as a man rather than as an animal in the days when Socrates was teaching.[109]

The most acerbic exchanges cloak themselves in this idiom of mutual love and admiration of students for each other and for their teacher. Studies in the eleventh-century were by all accounts "sweet and pleasant." The letter of Goswin (Gozechinus) of Mainz to his former student Walcher (see the translation of the letter in Appendix B) wraps the letter's real agenda in a cloud of amiability and mutual love joining teacher and student. Some excerpts:

> I. To his brother and son, united with him in soul, brother Goswin sends his wish that the better part of existence may be a happy coexistence.
> Since you have renewed the many tokens of good will you used to show me so often, I in turn both cherish and pay out a wealth of favor to you, dearest friend, not only for the sweet, pleasant and delectable memory of times past, but also for the joyous receipt of this new gift . . . When I first saw your gift . . . at the same moment my deep affection for you was so fully rekindled as if I had never experienced it before. . . .
> IV. How deeply I rejoiced in your company seeing your maturity of character, your virtuous conduct. What was there in life more gratifying to me, more cherished than you! . . . Our familiarity, in public or in private, only served to enshrine you more deeply in my regard, and each passing day rendered you dearer and fresher . . . V. How could I . . . fail to mention your probity, your diligence, your kindness . . . and moreover, how could I not love you, even if I wished to?[110]

The schools nourished an ideal of amiability, charm, good humor, mutual love and respect in the shared life of student and teacher. Administrative service was the context in which these "virtues" became effective. The love of teacher and students was preparatory to the love of king and court. This constellation was present in Marbod's description of Licinius's school days: his amiability, his talent for ending conflict and living in loving harmony with students and teachers made him preeminently a *magister morum*. It also commended him to the king.

VIRTUE MADE VISIBLE: *DECOR*

The virtues of G's father shone forth from him, broke from him like a bright light, a "dazzling blaze," in his manners and in the good humor which illuminated his face.[111]

Virtue made visible and embodied in a living presence is a major goal of education in manners. This conception impinged on the teaching of virtue in a dramatic way, in fact constituted its foundation. The notion forced an assimilation of the teaching of virtue to external culture. Dress, gesture, speech, tone of voice, table manners, posture and gait are the point of departure for the cultivation of virtue.

A history of external carriage manifesting virtue from Cicero (who insists that outer decorum can never be present without inner *honestas*, nor *honestas* without decorum) to Shakespeare (whose Ophelia asks Hamlet,

"Could beauty, my lord, have better commerce than with honesty?"),
would be a rewarding task. It would begin with Hellenic *paideia* and its
ideal of *kalokagathia*.[112] My intention here is just to observe this virtue in
our period and analyse it in the context of school instruction and administrative service. The texts that follow are meant only to give an idea of the
scope of this structure of thought which makes the outer man an "epiphany
of virtue and spiritual force" (Herwig Wolfram's phrase).

Ambrose echoes Cicero in maintaining that physical beauty is a decoration of inner virtue.[113] The idea occurs in Carolingian panegyric.[114] The
anonymous late tenth-century poem from Rheims honoring Constantine
of Fleury (above, p. 58) praises him as worthy of all the fame and honor
the world heaps on him, since "the action of the body is a sign of the mind,
and the soul expresses itself in deeds."[115] Alpert of St. Symphorian, writing
in the first decades of the eleventh century, praised Count Ansfrid of
Brabant for his eloquence:

> His speech was so tempered with moderation and good judgment that he did
> not disobey the dictum of that satiric writer, "Nothing in excess." But it should
> also be added that those who heard him could infer from his moderation of
> speech the composure and virtuousness hidden in his heart.[116]

Bern of Reichenau has built this quality into the education of Bishop Ulrich
of Augsburg:

> He then began a modest way of behaving to his fellow students . . . and in his
> way of moving, his gesture, his gait, he began to show outwardly, to the degree
> possible at that early age, what kind of mental posture was being formed in
> him inwardly.[117]

At the synod of Mainz in 1049 Pope Leo IX (Bruno of Toul) confirmed the
election of Archbishop Hugo of Besançon in formulas that incorporate the
logic of "virtue made visible" significantly into the investiture of a bishop:

> . . . with this document we concede and confirm also the archiepiscopal
> insignia to this same Archbishop Hugh . . . so that he who displays laudable
> dignity of merits, in the knowledge of virtue as in uprightness of manners
> [*morum honestate*], may display also beauty of ornaments in all plenitude of his
> high office. May he always be mindful to maintain inward beauty along with
> the splendor of his outward trappings.[118]

This turn of thought indicates an ideology of outward splendor in the
exercise of office. The beauty and impressiveness of robes, staff, insignia,
become the guarantors of the inner virtue of the office-holder, and at the

same time they impose on him the obligation to maintain the beauty of virtue along with the beauty of his robes. Those inner counterparts of external magnificence are worth noting: "dignity of merits, knowledge of virtue and *honestas morum*." These phrases and "knowledge of virtue" (*scientia virtutum*) point directly to a kind of behavior acquired in learning.

Lampert of Hersfeld's description of Bishop Gunther of Bamberg (Meinhard's first bishop) is worth referring to in this context, since it is built on the parallel of the inner to the outer endowments of the man:

> This was a man adorned with all the gifts of the body, in addition to the glory of his manners and the wealth of his mind. . . . He was unhesitating in speech and in council, learned in letters both divine and human, in stature and elegance of figure and the overall build of his body, preeminent among all other mortals.[119]

William of Malmesbury has an interesting variant in the description of the beauty of St. Wulfstan:

> The beauty of his body heightened that of his mind, and while I do not include beauty itself among the virtues, I do not altogether exclude it, for just as the art of a craftsman shines forth in a more commodious material, so virtue radiates more brightly in beauty of form.[120]

The notion looms large in the teaching of novices at St. Victor:

> The fullness of virtue is attained when through the internal custody of the mind the members of the body are governed in an orderly way.[121]

John of Salisbury sends a gift of a silver salt cellar decorated with gold to his friend Peter of Celle with this elegant dedication:

> It is an appropriate gift, since you . . . offer salt to God in the refined silver of pure eloquence, and golden images of the virtues shine forth for all beholders in the mirror of your words and deeds, and incite them to desire that they by imitating those virtues may become mirrors for others to gaze upon.[122]

In the thirteenth century Vincent of Beauvais made this relationship between virtue and its outward expression into the basis of the education of nobles, following Hugh of St. Victor's *De institutione novitiorum*. The composing (*composicio*) of *mores* is accomplished by a two-fold discipline, he writes in *De eruditione filiorum nobilium*, inward and outward. The inner "moral composition" consists in the acquisition of virtues like humility, kindness, patience and charity; the outer in the "fitting composition of the members of the body." The rest of the chapter consists largely of long quotations from Hugh's *De institutione*, the basic thought of which is that the disciplining of the body accomplishes the composed ordering of the mind.[123]

The monastic appropriation of this complex is located between the miraculous and the sumptuous. It sat more or less comfortably in the context of the performance of miracles as *manifestatio virtutis*. But in cathedral schools and administrative service, it represents the legitimation of certain kinds of external refinements that can run the gamut from disciplined behavior in walking, speech, table manners to material refinements: splendid clothing. Accordingly the rehearsal of this motif in a saint's life can become the locus for a criticism and rejection of worldliness. It becomes a structuring idea for the early part of Jotsald's Life of Odilo of Cluny (written ca. 1051). Odilo's successor as Abbot of Cluny, Maiolus, noting his "elegance of body and nobility of birth" recognizes "something great and divine" in him with the gaze of his internal eye, and begins to "fall in love with him altogether."[124] Some quality of distinction shone forth in him that made his fellow monks imitate and respect him. This was because the inner state of his mind registered in his outer bearing, Jotsald writes, quoting Ambrose, "Habitus mentis . . . in corporis statu cernitur."[125] This is the occasion of a chapter devoted to his appearance, followed by another devoted to the "composition of his manners" (chapters 5, 6). In physical appearance he was

> of medium height. His face was full of authority and grace. To gentle people he was cheerful and good-natured; but to the proud so terrible they could hardly bear his presence. In his emaciation he was strong, in his pallor ornate, in his greyness, beautiful. His eyes, radiating as it were some sort of splendor were for the beholder both a source of terror and admiration . . . Furthermore there shone forth from his motions, his gestures, his gait, the form of authority, the weight of gravity, and the mark of tranquillity.[126]

After praise of his beautiful, virile voice and his suave, gracious speech, he closes with a reference to Ambrose's comment that physical beauty may not be the locus of virtue, but gracefulness is. The next chapters treat the four cardinal virtues with references to definitions by "the philosophers," but the author fills them with a Christian content: Odilo showed his prudence by constant reading of the bible and singing of hymns, the latter even in his sleep; his sermons and letters bespeak a sweet eloquence and "the beauty of suaveness and grace" (901D). This sampling of his eulogy shows the logic and structure which grounds the first part of the Vita: his activities as a monk and abbot of Cluny represent virtue made visible. A basically Ciceronian scheme is filled with Christian-ascetic content. The vocabulary is by and large Ciceronian-Ambrosian. He knows and draws most directly on Ambrose, *De officiis*. But the received framework now accommodates concepts at odds with the original Ciceronian intent, for instance the phrases "strong in his emaciation, ornate in his pallor." The author stresses his influence, friendship and favor with worldly potentates (chapter 7, 902), and again draws on Ciceronian vocabulary: he was *amicabilis et officiosus*; powerful men magnified him with "friendships, offices and imperial gifts" (*amicitiis, officiis et imperialibus muneribus* — 902B). And this helps us locate the description: it shows us Odilo as the representative of a great, illustrious, as it were imperial asceticism. By the mid-eleventh-century the Cluniacs clearly commanded the idiom of "moral" training at the cathedral schools,[127] but they filled them with a specifically monastic-ascetic content.

However, they had long known the limits of this kind of expression of "virtue" with its ambiguous stress on the exterior. Odo of Cluny takes his Life of Gerald of Aurillac, ca. 935, (whom he praises for making his beauty of body into an expression of beauty of soul) as the occasion for attacking an excessive stress on externals. Some men who profess religion, he says, try to capture the reverence and respect they lack by cultivating luxury of the body. They would spend their time better by cultivating beauty of soul.[128]

At the end of the eleventh century Conrad of Hirsau mounts a polemic against worldly clerics that draws on this idiom in his *Dialogue on the Contempt and Love of the World*. In part it turns on the tensions between external and inner cultivation. He brands the devotion to externals worthless if it is based on false claims of pursuing virtue. External culture must be joined to disciplining of the soul, so that *animus* and *habitus* conform to one another.[129]

Monastic writers became the policemen of virtue. They made themselves wardens of an ideology highly open to abuse: the outward signs of virtue were coveted even by men completely indifferent to inner beauty, composition and discipline. In the early twelfth century Nicholas of Clairvaux mounted an attack on Benedictine luxury in these terms. He accuses them of equating wealth with merit and luxurious vestments with greater virtue.[130]

At the same time as Cistercians policed this scheme, they drew on it to define their own ideals of discipline and behavior. It finds one of its high points in Bernard of Clairvaux. "Beauty of soul" which registers in outer carriage is a prominent motif of his writings.[131] One especially powerful passage will suffice to illustrate it. He is explaining the line from Psalm 92, "The lord desireth your beauty," which he takes to mean beauty of soul (*decor*):

> What then is beauty of the soul? Is it perhaps that quality we call ethical goodness [*honestum*]? Let us accept this for the moment until something better occurs to us. . . . But to understand this quality [*honestum*] we must observe a man's outward bearing, not because morality originates from conduct, but because conduct mediates morality. . . . The beauty of actions is visible testimony to the state of the conscience. . . . But when the luminosity of this beauty fills the inner depths of the heart, it overflows and surges outward. Then the body, the very image of the mind, catches up this light glowing and bursting forth like the rays of the sun. All its senses and all its members are suffused with it, until its glow is seen in every act, in speech, in appearance, in the way of walking and laughing. . . . When the motions, the gestures and the habits of the body and the senses show forth their gravity, purity and modesty . . . then beauty of the soul becomes outwardly visible.[132]

Bernard's *decor animae* has much in common with the virtues of G's father. Both employ a Ciceronian ethical vocabulary; both use the image of a powerful light breaking forth from within as the metaphor for inner virtue in its relation to outward grace and composure. We see the sign of the monastic writer in Bernard's slightly condescending treatment of *honestas* and his preference of good conscience as the inner center which governs outer beauty. In Meinhard's scheme, the outer man had brought *lepor humanitatis* to expression. But in both we are in a conceptual environment where behavior — speech, gesture, dress, gait — is aestheticized and represented as a visible manifestation of inner beauty and harmony.

GESTURES, GAIT, BEARING, AND CARRIAGE

"Virtue made visible" was more than a formula of praise. It registered a pedagogic practice, one in many ways central to the cultivation of virtue. Outer carriage was the staging ground of virtue, and this required a disciplining of gait and gesture. The cultivation of virtue began with the body, with training in gesture, gait, motions (emotions, impulses) of the body, attitude of body and mind, facial expression, voice and speech (*gestus, incessus, motus corporis, habitus corporis et mentis, vultus, vox, sermo*). The other meaning of *habitus* comes to loom large in this discipline as well, namely dress. In the twelfth century we will add table manners. I suspect that the table was as important a schoolroom in the eleventh as well, but the documentation is scanty. The man who walks, talks, stands, and carries himself perfectly is the *magister morum*. He shows in his every gesture what harmony reigns within him; the composition of his body shows the composition of his soul.

The roots of this discipline are classical. Its most influential formulation was in Cicero's *De officiis*. In his discussion of temperance and decorum he says that the pleasing motions of the body are an indication that body and soul are in harmony with nature (1.100). After a long discussion of control of the passions (*motus animi*) he commends *constantia* in all acts, and this brings him to the *motus corporis*:

> . . . the propriety to which I refer shows itself also in every deed, in every word, even in every movement and attitude of the body. And in outward, visible propriety there are three elements — beauty, order and embellishment appropriate to the act it accompanies.[133]

To achieve beauty, order and appropriate embellishment, we need to follow nature in our motions:

> . . . in standing or walking, in sitting or reclining, in our expression, our eyes, or the movements of our hands, let us preserve this decorum. We must avoid especially the two extremes: our conduct and speech should not be effeminate and affected [*effeminatum vel molle*] on the one hand, nor coarse and boorish on the other.[134]

The beauty of conduct is of two kinds, he continues. The one called "loveliness" [*venustas*] is feminine; the other [*dignitas*] is manly. Let a man therefore avoid any *ornatus* of dress that is not dignified, and the same applies to gesture and motion. The golden mean is the ideal to follow [*mediocritas* — cf. 1.130–31]. This means, we should walk and gesture neither too slow nor too fast, since this puts us out of breath, distorts the face, and is a strong indication that inner constancy is lacking.[135] In these passages fitting gait and gesture into a philosophy of "natural" behavior, Cicero represents beauty of gesture as a response to and symptom of an inner harmony. Elsewhere he uses the image of the harmonically composed soul playing inaudible music, a kind of visible melody, on the instrument of the body (*Tusc. Disp.* 1.19–20), and here we see how the disciplines of gesture and music overlap. But also gesture and eloquence. Cicero represents the motions of the body as a kind of language or oratory of the body.[136] When inner constancy and harmony find their expression in natural external gestures the result is grace, beauty and dignity.

Ambrose picked up these ideas in his adaptation of *De officiis* and made proper walking and gesturing into an important duty of the Christian statesman. Composed gesture and movements are signs of *verecundia*, modesty and reluctance to give offense:

> *Verecundia* is to be maintained even in motion, gestures, and gait. The attitude of the mind is perceived in the state of the body . . . And in this way the motion of the body is a kind of voice of the soul.[137]

He demands a kind of gesture and movement which bespeak authority, gravity and tranquillity.[138] Ambrose tells two anecdotes that illustrate the importance of decorous movement: he rejected a friend for membership in the clergy — though his stringent performance of duties commended him — because his gestures were in very poor taste ("gestus eius plurimum dedecerat"). Another, a young cleric, he ordered never to walk in front of him, because his gait offended his eyes, like a slap in the face (49A). Both men met bad ends, which Ambrose believes he could have predicted from their way of walking.

Good carriage occurs as a virtue in Vitae of Carolingian clerics and monks,[139] but it is not common. The Roman ideal appears to have been restricted to the court circle and "civil education."[140] Alcuin gave Charlemagne extensive instruction on gesturing and carriage in his dialogue on rhetoric (PL 101, 941–43), and this subject was placed significantly before the final section on the virtues. Hincmar of Rheims placed instruction in carriage and gait precisely in the context of courtly schooling in his letter of instruction to Louis the German:

> The king's court is indeed called a school . . . since it corrects others in attitude, way of walking, speech and gesture [*habitu, incessu, verbo et actu*], and in general holds them to the norms of a good life.[141]

The rules of the monastic and clerical life regularly point to bearing and gesture as objects of disciplining, but without any reminiscences of the Roman sources or the Carolingian court. They are plain admonitions to inoffensive behavior, not indications of an ideal of elegant bearing.[142]

An ideal of walking and gesturing based on classical models came to prominence from the second half of the tenth century on. We recall the lines of the anonymous Rheims poet praising Constantine, the friend of Gerbert of Aurillac:

> . . . if the common belief is true that the motions of the body are signs of the mind, and the soul expresses itself in the gestures, then in our judgment you

fully merit that praise of body which fame spreads about you through the world.[143]

Bern of Reichenau has a telling description of the education of Bishop Ulrich of Augsburg. The future saint began to show his modesty and respectfulness at an early age, and the gradual forming of virtuous patterns of behavior showed themselves outwardly in "the motion of his body, his gestures, his way of walking."[144] The outward signals of inner virtue here are not just a given of the future bishop's person, but a product of inner formation and development (*qualis habitus formaretur intus in mente*).

Godfrey of Rheims wrote a poem between 1060 and 1095 to Odo of Orleans, in which he represents his friend as he appeared to him in a dream. The description of Odo's appearance makes clear that Godfrey mastered a highly sophisticated and startlingly worldly idiom of external culture:

> There was no mistaking the man:
> Doubt not that his attitude, voice, speech, figure,
> His gait and appearance all gave off signs of an integrating harmony.
> ["habitus, vox, sermo, figura, / Gressus et aspectus consona signa
>   dabant"]
> He was not austere with morose gravity — which I hate —
> But rather serene with bright spirited countenance — which I love.
> His face was not twisted nor intimidating with grim glances,
> Nor were his brows rigid and severe,
> But rather mild, gentle and placid as a dove, [warming] as the
>   summer sun.
> Nor was he so gay and facile to look on
> That he would have neglected a modest appearance.
> Nor would he tempt shame by frivolous speech
> Or turn his appearance into that of a petulant boy.
> For vice is ill-shunned,
> When the shunning yokes you to its opposite vice.
> He has not bathed well who washes away riotousness and gluttony
> Only to immerse himself in as indecent a fault, avarice.
> Odo holds the middle road between both extremes,
> And considers moderation safe from faults.
> He adorns himself so with temperance that his mark is
> Light good humor mixed with gravity.
>   [A line missing in the manuscript]

Temperance drives the swift horses of the sun,
Temperance forms the harvests, mixing heat and cold,
Temperance turns grapes to wine.
This posture, this attitude are decorous; let the wretch stray
Who swells with mendacious religion.
Let him live, mute, bitter and harsh, banished to the wilderness,
The companion of Hyrcanian tigers.
He who condemns joys and approves melancholy
Will be judged like winter and its frosty winds . . .
With such decorousness and such moderation of countenance
The poet's image [i.e., Odo] stood at our bed.
His form was not stumpy and puny,
It was the towering stature of a great man.
A sublime head set on a noble body
Magnified his appearance of height.[145]

The fundamental concepts of this portrait are an "integrating unity" that renders Odo's shape and countenance harmoniously suited to his motion, gestures and speech; the virtues that integrate the parts into a whole are temperance and moderation. This holds the extremes of vice in check, so that virtue becomes the mean between two extremes. The poet creates a rich play on the word *temperies*, which can mean both time, temper, temperament and temperance. He sees that force working to fabricate the products of nature (harvests and wine), and working equally to produce the harmonious balance in Odo's appearance. "Decorousness" is the criterion which is satisfied when the ethical and the aesthetic are in good balance; the body is the location of the visible traces of the "decent": "hic status, hec habitudo decent" (51). The quality of bright, restrained good humor was prized also in the father of G., and is widely held ideal of the cathedral communities.

I included the lines on "mendacious religion" to show the worldly flavor of the portrait. Here and in numerous statements of this ideal of moderated appearance, we will see that the authors have barbs to direct at both extremes of the social scale, against rigorous and extreme asceticism and against unrestrained and affected worldliness.

The point is that the body has become the text in which virtues are read: *moderamen* is a quality visible in facial expression (69). Apparently the art of reading the appearance was of some interest in the French schools. A friend of Marbod of Rennes named Walter (Gualterius) sent him a treatise on physiognomy, an ancient Roman work detailing the science of reading the character from physical signs.[146] It is prefaced by a few lines of verse composed by Walter:

> Well then, it may be small and no bigger than the hand,
> But this is the sort of book that sweet France admires.
> It is marked throughout by rich variety and honey-flowing rivulets.
> To tell the truth, it opens the secrets of nature to view;
> It notes certain things marked with the signatures of secret
>   meanings,
> Like stature, countenance, posture, voice, gestures, grooming.
> It commends men even when you do not know their inner character
>   [and reveals]
> Whether this one is just, beautiful with the flower of virtues,
> Or evil, false, and overly bold at any crime.[147]

These texts show the high level that the culture of the body reached in poetic and personal ideals by the later eleventh-century. This culture is directly connected with the cultivation of virtue, since bearing makes virtue visible. The cathedral schools practiced a pedagogy aimed at creating the balanced, restrained, decorous, "well-tempered" human being, and it is reasonable to assume that this began with the discipline of walking and gesturing.

*   *   *

The texts treated in this chapter familiarize us with some of the ideals of cathedral school education in the eleventh and twelfth centuries. The presentation was not comprehensive; it aimed only at being representative. These texts have brought us into the core of the old learning, not its peripheries. An important concept only touched on is *honestas*. It has come up so often that it should be mentioned at least. To give it the kind of detailed treatment we gave other virtues would not be profitable, since it represents a kind of collective and a summation of all individual virtues. It is the overriding goal of an education in *mores*, as the educational aims of the student named Hubert, who studied this "subject" at both Chartres and Rheims, indicate to us. Humility, modesty, moderation and patience were mentioned frequently, and clearly were important components of *honestas* and *elegantia morum*.

This education was oriented to human qualities, qualities that are effective in regulating social and political life. This distinguishes it sharply from education based on norms derived from dogma. Christian doctrine plays only an oblique role in the descriptions of education from our period. The formula "he is made all things to all men," is representative of this priority. "All things to all men" is synonymous with "affable," "amiable," "beloved of all." What was an ideal of the Christian proselytizer when St. Paul formulated it, becomes a social ideal in eleventh-century cathedral schools.

This is one sense in which that education was humanistic. Another is that the social and ethical ideals were formulated in a discourse inherited most directly from the education of the orator in classical antiquity. Cicero's *Tusculan Disputations* is the work Meinhard commended to G. as he entered administrative service, and that recommendation is paradigmatic for priorities at the cathedral schools. The administrators were Christian pastors in their overarching function, but in the details of their development and self-definition, and in practical matters of administration, they identified with the Roman statesman and senator.[148] Meinhard found Cicero a better guide to the active life than St. Paul.

It has been possible to speak of humanistic education until now without any reference to the other side of its formula: letters. Liberal studies took a major expenditure of efforts from masters and students. Meinhard complained that he squandered the first part of his fortune teaching manners, and the second part on "letters." But letters and liberal studies were inseparable. A detailed look shows them not as instruments to develop the intellect and intellectual skills, but as the handmaidens of ethical training.

5. Ethics Colonizing the Liberal Arts

Learning for its own sake had no legitimate role in this period. Studies had to be subordinated to a higher goal. For secular studies this goal was virtue and "composed manners." These aimed at forming the human being, "attuning" the inner to the outer world through discipline, exercise, rehearsal, and study. Speech and gesture were the activities in which inner man and outer expression met most closely, but all the disciplines and arts could serve that purpose and ideally were pursued "for the sake of learning virtue," *causa discendae honestatis*.

In its relations to the liberal arts and other classroom disciplines, ethics is always at work directing the focus, the methods, the tone and atmosphere of study. A frequently cited scheme of studies subordinates the liberal arts to ethics.[1] In the eleventh century this was not an empty scheme, but pedagogic practice. Ethics colonized the other disciplines. This chapter observes the process in the major disciplines it came to govern.

Philosophy and Ethics

For classical antiquity ethics formed one of the branches of philosophy. Cicero's definition made the formation of life through discipline the highest activity of philosophy, which "promotes a good and happy life" (*bene beateque vivendum*). Its end is virtue:

> If there is really a way to learn virtue, where shall one look for it, when one has turned aside from this field of learning [namely philosophy]?[2]

The *Tusculan Disputations* begins with the observation,

> ... the system and method of instruction in all the arts which have a bearing upon the right conduct of life [*ad rectam vivendi viam pertinerent*] are contained in the study of wisdom which goes by the name of philosophy. (*Tusc. Disp.*, 1.1)

Philosophy is the *magistra vitae*, an epithet widely quoted in our period:

> O philosophy, thou guide of life, o thou explorer of virtue and expeller of vice!
> [*O vitae philosophia dux, o virtutis indagatrix expultrixque vitiorum!*]. . . . Thou
> hast been the teacher of manners and of discipline [*magistra morum et disci-
> plinae*]. (*Tusc. Disp.*, 5.5)[3]

Ciceronian ideas and formulations on philosophy passed to the Middle Ages by the well-known routes.[4] Isidore of Seville defines philosophy as
"the knowledge of things human and divine joined to the study of living
well" (*cum studio bene vivendi*).[5] Alcuin echoes this:

> Philosophy is the investigation of natures, the knowledge of things human and
> divine. . . . Philosophy is also proper conduct of life, the study of living well
> [*honestas vitae, studium bene vivendi*], the meditation of death, contempt of the
> world.[6]

Hrabanus Maurus gives an encyclopedic definition:

> A philosopher is one who has knowledge of things human and divine. He
> holds constantly to the path of the good life [*bene vivendi tramitem tenet*].[7]

He gives the well-worn derivation that makes Pythagoras the first to use the
name philosopher. The three kinds of philosophers are *physici, ethici, logici*.
The ethicists are so called because they deal with manners and morals (*de
moribus tractant*). Ethics is divided into four parts because the cardinal
virtues are four. He sums up, quoting Alcuin with slight variations:

> Philosophy therefore is the investigation of nature, the knowledge of things
> human and divine, to the extent it is possible for human beings to investigate
> them. Philosophy is also the proper conduct of life, the study of living well, the
> contemplation of death and the contempt of the world. (ibid.)

Gerbert of Aurillac articulates this ethical conception of philosophy in
a comment that will come up often in this study. He claims to be a follower
of Cicero in his refusal to separate what is moral from what is useful, and
makes the connection into a law of philosophy:

> Since philosophy does not distinguish between the rules of speaking and the
> rules of conduct, I have always joined the study of eloquence to the study of
> living well. And as good conduct by itself is superior to good speech, it may be
> enough to choose the former over the latter for one freed from the cares of ad-
> ministration. But for us who are caught up in the affairs of state, both are
> necessary.[8]

The practical governance of life in the context of state service figures here as a prominent element of "philosophy." This ideal of conduct joined to the study of eloquence is both a way of life for the public man and a program of studies. In the eleventh century philosophy was the imposition and exercise of discipline to structure behavior and restrain impulse.[9] *Studium bene vivendi* was a form of philosophizing; philosophy shaped *mores*.

We should recall the admonition of a student of Worms to his bishop around 1030, reminding him that public administration is the translation into the active life of the lessons of philosophy: "The schoolmistress of all virtues (*magistra virtutum = Philosophia*) has taken up her abode in you, so that in all your undertakings you may follow in her footsteps."[10] The formulation evokes two models of Lady Philosophy: that of Cicero (*magistra virtutum*) and that of Boethius.

In his complaint to Philosophy, Boethius reviewed their longstanding relationship and showed Philosophy guiding his investigations of the heavens and shaping his *mores* according to the pattern of celestial harmony; she taught him Plato's dictum that the happy state would be governed by students of wisdom, and brought him by that route to devote himself to the service of the state.[11]

Philosophy makes the statesman, and the statesman is a kind of philosopher.[12] This model registers in the usage of the word *philosophus* in the tenth and eleventh centuries. Otto I justified his choice of Brun as chancellor and advisor (in the letter transmitted by Ruotger, see p. 44 above) by pointing to his "education" by philosophy: "The true virtue of philosophy has formed [*erudivit*] you with modesty and greatness of soul."[13] Otto III had likewise invited Gerbert to his court as teacher and advisor, pointing to his philosophical skill as his qualification (Gerbert, epist. 186, ed. Weigle, p. 221). Wipo, in the prologue to the *Gesta Chuonradi*, gives examples of ancient (i.e., Old Testament) "philosophers" advising rulers. They instructed the prince by interpreting dreams and by telling fabulous narratives, "since such figments are by no means adverse to philosophy" (*Die Werke Wipos*, ed. Bresslau, p. 5). The *Ruodlieb* poet placed among the retinue of the *rex minor* a "philosopher, wiser than all the rest, whom neither fear nor favor could divert from the true path in rendering judgment" (*Ruodlieb*, ed. Vollmann, 4.11ff.). It is irony, since this wise man, asked for advice, turns to the king and says, in effect, "whatever you say."

Logic and Ethics in the *Regensburg Letters*

The previous references have the character of *topoi*. They transmit conventional formulations. We can say with certainty that the formation of manners was included in abstract schemes of philosophy and that wise men in various capacities could be called philosophers, but they do not show us philosophy practicing what all these sources preach about it.

The *Regensburg Rhetorical Letters* (ca. 1090) bring us close to philosophy at work shaping conduct. The letters are themselves highly stylized and derivative. Often they appear as a cento of quotations from Cicero's *Tusculan Disputations*. Their conceptions of philosophy and education are saturated with Ciceronian models. But the narrative plot—if I may use that term for these epistolary exchanges—and the content of their debates are immediate and, while it would go too far to call them original, they are unique and vivid sources on the practice of philosophy as it was conceived in the eleventh century. The Ciceronianism is put into practice in these letters in a way that brings us close to the classroom of the cathedral school. Probably they are the product of a single writer. The title (given to them by Fickermann) is slightly misleading. They certainly are exercises, but "rhetorical" does not do justice to their wide spectrum of interests and intentions. They are loosely fictionalized in the sense that individual letters maintain a single author's persona, distinguishable from that of the writer. My references in the analysis to writer 1 and writer 2 should be understood in this sense, as designations of the fictional persona. The basic situation is that a clerical administrator corresponds with friends, debating, exchanging ideas, and giving and receiving advice, guidance and consolation for the rigors of administrative work.

The first letter is written in the person of a man busied in the affairs of administration.[14] He identifies with Cicero. Caught up "in the labors of advocacy and senatorial matters," he has grown unaccustomed to study and discipline. It is the beginning of the *Tusculan Disputations* taken over into the fictive life of the letter writer. Since "study and discipline are the way to living rightly," he turns now to what he has neglected. He breaks out into praises of philosophy, quoting Cicero: "O vite philosophia dux" and so forth. It is philosophy as the "teacher of manners and of discipline" whom he invokes. His intention in taking up philosophy is to pursue virtue, and anything contrary to the faith he would tread underfoot:

> . . . to seek virtue, to cling to the study of virtue, to sweat and strain in the exercise of virtue, these activities serve not only the Good but also the Useful.[15]

Now he proceeds to a logical justification of philosophy:

> All that expels vices ushers in virtues. But philosophy expels vices. It therefore admits virtues. Philosophy, then, admits virtues. But whatever admits virtues

is a thing to be sought after. Therefore philosophy is to be sought. Whatever is to be sought has the approval of the learned. Therefore philosophy has the approval of the learned. (p. 275)

The letter continues at the same level of penetration to prove that all that is good derives from the highest good. This brings him to the source of evil in the world, which he develops from the case of the good and the rebel angels. *Superbia* is the root of all evil, as he proves by citing scripture.

Letter 2 (pp. 276–77) is a reply. The writer notes that his correspondent, taking confidence in his genius, has undertaken things that he himself, mediocrity that he is, has requested. Such things are difficult for great and distinguished men, who are situated in the fortress of argumentative disputation, and whose knowledge is manifold. The writer himself is not educated in that group and has no intention of undertaking or even attempting such tasks. He prefers to amble on the beach of philosophy than to risk drowning in the ocean. A man who speaks like a barbarian should not be a teacher of grammar. It is a modesty formula and at the same time a rebuke to his correspondent, not a very generous position since he himself requested the philosophizing the writer of letter 1 provides. He urges him not to be counted among the philosophers who live badly. And as if to serve notice that he is not incapable of a sharp reply, "Do not judge me toothless until you find I can't bite." Having rebuked writer 1 for philosophizing, writer 2 now criticizes the logic of his letter. The passage is worth quoting at length:

> You have discussed the Good in your letter. Perhaps you are unaware that if you are compelled to train yourself thoroughly in this question, it can happen that your eyelids become glued together with the rheum of doubt, so that you require the help of doctors to cleanse them. But what am I saying? I regret that I have fallen prey to the Charybdis of suspicion. I may appear to envy you, wise man that you are, these profound things. . . . But please do not think I wish to carry on polemics with you and thwart your mind, accepting in myself what I reprove in you. You can turn back on me the words [of Cicero] quoted earlier in defense of Q. Ligurius: "I do not concede that you should attack in another those things that you prize in yourself."

The original writer (1) replies in Epist. 3 (pp. 278–79). A brief paraphrase:

> Everyone but a dunce will know what is right for each person, as long as he knows himself. I did not want to suggest that you are a kind of Proteus, gathering in yourself all the disciplines. It shows little judgment if a man esteems himself wise when the perturbations of the mind trouble him. The mind of the wise man is not inflated or swollen. He shuns vice and he avoids

anger. First you urge me to virtue, then when I labor for virtue, you reject it as though it were empty babbling. Perhaps you object to my mentioning the Good. It was Augustine, not those philosophers you mentioned (the Stoics, Epicureans, Carneades), to whom I was referring. May your teeth remain healthy, but I prefer them blunted or pulled rather than biting me. I may have said many superfluous things, but exercise is delightful even when it does not bear fruit. Do not think I am nagging at you. I delight in your words and embrace the bitter along with the sweet. Where perfect fidelity reigns, danger cannot enter.

The most perplexing feature of this exchange is its evident shallowness, pettiness, and insignificance. We should not exclude the possibility that a contemporary reader would have shared that judgment. The apparatus of thought is extremely skimpy. Its furniture are the syllogism and a handful of authorities. The writer knows Cicero well (17 direct quotations) and clearly has a copy of the *Tusculan Disputations* at his fingertips, possibly in his memory.[16] He knows the *De amicitia* and some of the speeches. He borrows phrasing from the Bible but does not quote it directly. Letter 1 contains a single quotation from Augustine. The reference to Augustine in letter 3 is a reminiscence so general that the editor, Fickermann, otherwise very scrupulous, has not identified the source. Regarded as a "philosophical" disputation on the nature of Good and Evil, there is no way to rescue these three letters from triviality. In content and method they are puerile.[17]

Now we want to look at them on their own terms, not ours. To do so we need to substitute for the conception of philosophy as "knowledge of things" the one at work here, namely philosophy as "teacher of manners." The three letters are thin on ideas and keen reasoning, but rich with postures, *habitus*, and that is what the exchange is about.

Friendship is the overarching virtue of this exchange. It begins with the theme. Writer 1 addresses writer 2 as "his second self" (Cicero, *De amicitia*, 21.80), and ends epist. 3 with reassurances aimed at restoring firm friendship after the debate.

Christian preferred to pagan philosophy is another "virtue" embodied. The writer argues the point shallowly, but strikes the posture forcefully:

Were I to find anything that impugns the sacred faith, I would not only reject it with a shudder, but also, withdrawing my foot, I would turn my back on the defective sentence. (p. 275)

Writer 2 begins his answer (epist. 2, pp. 276–77) with a display of modesty, setting his own *mediocritas* against the *ingenium* of his correspondent. The opening bristles with the kind of barbed reproaches we observed in the Worms — Würzburg polemics. He is checking and correcting the potential vice of intellectual overweening. He holds up the "great and distinguished" philosophers, but undercuts the praise by locating them in the "fortress of argumentative disputation," bad words in the vocabulary of the schools. He points to men who get in over their heads and violate the laws or misuse the instruments of their own discipline, and leaves it to his friend to place himself in their midst. But as if to let him know that the sensed prickliness is intended, he launches the apparent non-sequitur, "Don't judge me toothless." In other words, if you feel rebuked, you have understood my purpose.

The dangers of doubt produced by logical reasoning are touched on. This checks and corrects in advance a sceptical, critical posture.

Writer 2 corrects his own behavior by deploring the envy and fault-finding he might appear guilty of through his criticism.

These three letters contain not a single point of substance. They dissolve into postures: "virtues," corrections, admonitions, some explicit, others insinuated. They are a pattern book of the correct postures in intellectual debate and in life. They are also a set of negotiations on personal relations. The writers come full circle from friendship through disagreement back to friendship. Through exemplary attitudes they encourage virtue and correct vice. This is philosophy as Cicero defined it, a "teacher of manners and remover of vices."

RITUALIZED LEARNING

The biographer of Burchard of Worms, writing shortly after Burchard's death in 1025, has preserved a lucid example of Biblical studies instructing in *mores*. He includes two chapters illustrating Burchard's teaching.[18] Burchard required daily exercises in writing from the students. They prepared *sermones et quaestiunculas* concerning scripture to present to the bishop. He quotes one of these exercises, in which a student requests an explanation of the Bible's claim that Moses and Elijah fasted for forty days. Lest he fall into the "labyrinth of doubt" he turns to Burchard to receive through the master's erudition the "truth of the thing itself." He reminds his teacher of the pitfalls that beset the student of scripture, unless he has cleansed himself through a thorough confession. Out of the deep sorrow at the wounds he has inflicted on his own conscience, and fearing to hide them, he "confesses" to Burchard to make visible what is now hiding within. He offers this inquiry to Burchard, not out of pride, but "so that you may correct me and render me more certain in my investigation" (p. 841, ll. 14–15). He hopes that, having purified himself by his confession and having received illumination from his bishop and teacher, he will participate in his sanctity. Then follows the question: Did Moses and Elijah actually fast for forty days? "Many of us doubt it" (or "are uncertain about it"—l. 25); it seems beyond human power: "I doubt that any man could do this" (l. 27). He pleads with Burchard to relieve him of the burden of doubt on the question, "so that I may avoid the snare of evil and receive the fruit of penitence and true confession" (ll. 35–36).

Burchard's reply is long, eloquent, and packed with scriptural quotations to support his points. The substance of his answer amounts to, "The word of God nourishes spiritual men." But here also the postures struck and the virtues exemplified are the real substance of his answer, and they are represented extensively. He answers the question his student has posed "as if doubting" (*quasi dubitando*—l. 39), because he does not want him to doubt: ". . . te . . . dubitare nolo" (l. 40). He praises him for confessing his doubt as a potentially grave sin. He is glad to answer, because "whoever converts a sinner from his error saves his soul" (ll. 44–45). To wander in error is foolishness. Foolish men do not shun vice and seek virtue. "Therefore every vice is to be shunned. . . . And by the same token every virtue is to be pursued. Wisdom certainly is to be pursued, since it is the virtue of God" (p. 842, ll. 9ff.). He finishes his exposition of the passage and perorates: "Let these few words of correction suffice" (p. 843, l. 33).

The student regards the lengthy answer to his question as a spiritual feast so great that he wishes to share it with others. He divides it among his fellow students, and "'they devoured it, the head with the legs with the purtenance thereof'" (ll. 40–41; cf. Exodus 12:9).

The exchange is about a biblical text and the pious *habitus* appropriate to the study of it. It is from the school of Worms at the beginning of the century. The other documentation on this school from the same period shows a preoccupation with classical learning of which this letter has preserved no trace (see Chapter 3 above). But the illustration of Burchard's teaching shows us something that biblical and secular studies had in common: their highly ritualized character. Learning from Burchard is a sacramental event; student and teacher alike see it as a form of confession, repentance, and absolution. The student's joyous reception of the master's letter becomes a eucharistic event: the students partake of the holy meal of the teacher's words. The other framework is the cultivation of virtue and correction of vice: the student poses a question; questioning means seeking correction; teaching means imparting *verba correctionis*.

The arch-villain of this intellectual world is clearly doubt. It is a sin into which the student falls by wondering about the meaning of the text. It also seems to be a role he plays to provoke correction (*quasi dubitans*), since of course the entire exchange results from the daily assignment imposed by Burchard. The teacher is there to dispel doubt with the benediction of the truth, with absolution and consolation.

STYLE AND SUBSTANCE

The previous two sections reveal a fundamental feature of the intellectual life of the schools in the eleventh century. Understanding is secondary and patterns of conduct are primary. Probing, searching investigation, doubt aiming at truth, have no place in this picture. They are prominent among the vices to be avoided. This principle illuminates the teaching of Fulbert of Chartres. We recall that Adelman's praise of his teaching did not distinguish sharply between the qualities of the teacher and those of the text:

Ah! with what dignity in striving for *mores*,
With what gravity in subject matter,
What sweetness in words,
He explained the mysteries of higher knowledge![19]

Like Burchard, Fulbert exemplifies virtues in explaining scripture: dignity, gravity, and "sweetness of words." Nothing is said about the object of his explications; Adelman had his eye exclusively on personal style. The person of the teacher is the curriculum. This is ritualized philosophy. Ideas and interpretations are accepted as givens, and the process of learning the correct attitudes to those givens is itself the purpose. The student enters into this process the way he sings the liturgy: it is important for him to learn the modalities, but the meaning of texts and the nature of ideas are fixed and unambiguous. At least treating them as such has to be accepted as one of the modalities of learning.

Viewed through the eyes of critics, this is precisely the offending point of the old learning: all style, no substance. That is what Guitmund of Aversa criticized in Berengar of Tours (he "simulates the dignity of a teacher in his manner rather than by the substance of his teaching"), and Abelard in Anselm of Laon (he was able to generate admiration but not understanding). But for Fulbert and Burchard these priorities were perfectly understandable (not for Berengar and Anselm of Laon: the criticism is false or slanted): philosophising was demonstrating *forma vivendi*, and substantial questions of interpretation were a forest of error.

*   *   *

Twelfth-century sources tend to create a hierarchy of studies, subordinating philosophy to ethics rather than identifying the two, as the previous century had.[20] John of Salisbury claims trenchantly, "Any pretext of philosophy that does not bear fruit in the cultivation of virtue [*cultus virtutis*] and the guidance of conduct is futile and false."[21] John still insists on practical ethics as the sole worthy element of philosophy (*virtus unica via est philosophandi*) and the goal toward which all intellectual activity ought to tend. But the tone and intent are polemical. His claims make it evident that he is defending an outmoded program under attack, and not reporting soberly on a practiced course of studies.[22]

Thierry of Chartres calls philosophy "the study of wisdom." It is the "comprehensive knowledge either of speculative and logical reason, or of duty, which pertains to ethics."[23] The language reveals the essentially new conception of ethics: *integra cognitio rationis . . . aut officii*. Ethics moves to the status of a school subject among others. It becomes an object of knowledge and inquiry, and no longer the practical discipline of "living well."[24]

While it no longer structured the life of the schools, the idea of philosophy as a force that primarily molds men's characters and guides them in public life remained an important conception, as we learn from the letter of Wibald of Stablo excusing himself from peace negotiations in Liège:

> That teacher and liege-lady of yours, Philosophy, the *magistra* and instructor of things human and divine, has not shaped and informed our manners [*mores*] as she has yours.[25]

The aura of archaic ethical conceptions wafts from a portrait of Bishop Eraclius of Liège (d. 971) by Reiner of Liège writing around 1180:

> Sent to Cologne for instruction in the rudiments of letters, he later acquired such knowledge in both divine and human studies that he justly was considered the equal of the greatest philosophers, but especially because his splendid manners served as an adornment to the beauty of his body, and, as Solomon says, the face of the wise man shows forth his prudence.[26]

More than his skill in "divine and human studies", the bishop's manners and beauty, his carriage and physical presence, establish him as the equal of great philosophers. By 1180 very few active "philosophers" would have agreed with these priorities.

The Trivium

Eleventh- and early twelfth-century school life was a literary-poetic as opposed to an analytical-philosophical culture of learning. That culture required a literature of examples, not texts that posed problems for solving and for rational penetration. Its dominant arts were grammar and rhetoric, not logic.[27] Of course "literary-poetic" is a subcategory of the culture's overriding character: personal charisma. The two elements — personal presence and literature — met and were resolved in the example.[28] The continuum joining the living example and the literary formulation was an experienced reality of the life of the schools.[29]

Thus the connection of the trivium with ethics was not at all loose or random but central to humanist learning. The combination of speaking well with living well was the overriding justification for the reading and study of the pagan classics.[30]

GRAMMAR
Delhaye has given many examples of the integrating of grammar and ethics. Rather than stir through his material and Rolf Köhn's once more, I will compare in this section two descriptions of the teaching of grammar, one from 1031, the other from 1159.

Here are the lines of the Würzburg poet praising Master Pernolf (see above, Chapter 3):

He himself blazes bright with the beauty of many poets.
He spares the master's rod, as Christ commanded,
He cares for nothing but the study of composition,
He remains a cultivator of virtue and of eternal salvation.
He retains his power of mind by the gift of the Allmighty.
The living stream of learning flows from his breast,
The eternal divinity gives him his flow of speech.
His example [*documentum*] is an ornament to us,
Since his honors grow like springtime flowers.

Bringing the light and acumen of his mind to the unlearned,
He instructs them in the elements of grammar and in all the arts.
Nor does he cease at night time, as during the day,
To give forth the sayings of the poets and grammarians.
To such a pastor no writings are difficult.
Every volume is as luminous to him as sunlight.
Making the earth's orb blossom with his genius,
Demanding and just, laden with the gems of virtue,
This generous Argus provides throughout the night a feast of his
    instruction [*documentum*] . . .
He never favors the more advanced and skilled students over the
    beginners.[31]

John of Salisbury's description of the teaching of Bernard of Chartres
(*Metalogicon*, 1.24) is a major document in the history of medieval education. It has formed our ideas of the teaching of grammar and of the
classroom methods of a famous teacher. Here are excerpts from the chapter:

> Bernard of Chartres, the greatest font of literary learning in Gaul in recent
> times, used to teach grammar in the following way. He would point out, in
> reading the authors, what was simple and according to rule. On the other
> hand, he would explain grammatical figures, rhetorical embellishment, and
> sophistical quibbling, as well as the relation of given passages to other studies.
> He would do so, however, without trying to teach everything at one time. On
> the contrary, he would dispense his instruction to his hearers gradually, in a
> manner commensurate with their powers of assimilation. . . . In view of the
> fact that exercise both strengthens and sharpens our mind, Bernard would
> bend every effort to bring his students to imitate what they were hearing. In
> some cases he would rely on exhortation, in others he would resort to punish-
> ments, such as flogging. . . . The evening exercise, known as the "declination,"
> was so replete with grammatical instruction that if anyone were to take part in
> it for an entire year, provided he were not a dullard, he would become
> thoroughly familiar with the method of speaking and writing. . . . Since
> however it is not right to allow any school or day to be without religion,
> subject matter was presented to foster faith, to build up morals [*edificaret* . . .
> *mores*], and to inspire those present at this quasicollation to perform good
> works. This evening declination or philosophical collation closed with the
> pious commendation of the souls of the departed to their Redeemer, by the
> devout recitation of the Sixth Penitential Psalm and the Lord's Prayer. He
> would also explain the poets and orators who were to serve as models for the
> boys in their introductory exercises in imitating prose and poetry. Pointing out
> how the diction of the authors was so skillfully connected, and what they had
> to say was so elegantly concluded, he would admonish his students to follow

their example. . . . He would also inculcate as fundamental, and impress on the minds of his listeners, what virtue exists in economy; what is praiseworthy in the beauty of things, what is praiseworthy in words; where concise and, so to speak, frugal speech is in order, and where fuller, more copious expression is appropriate; as well as where speech is excessive, and wherein consists just measure [*modus*] . . . he diligently and insistently demanded from each, as a daily debt, something committed to memory. . . . A further feature of Bernard's method was to have his disciples compose prose and poetry every day, and exercise their faculties in mutual conferences, for nothing is more useful in introductory training than actually to accustom one's students to practice the art they are studying. Nothing serves better to foster the acquisition of eloquence and the attainment of knowledge than such conferences, which also have a salutary influence on practical conduct, provided that charity moderates enthusiasm, and that humility is not lost during progress in learning.[32]

The two passages have a number of common features. In both, grammatical study is inextricably linked to reading, composition, and ethics. In both we have the sense of intimate classes and close personal relations between master and students. Both masters hold evening sessions, explaining the poets. Reading and composition are the basis of both methods. Both masters are sensitive to the level of their students. The use of the whip is mentioned in both cases; Pernolf spares it, Bernard uses it when admonition fails.

The two grammar classrooms are not essentially different in their curriculum: students learn to read and compose by studying classical texts. Pernolf "cares for nothing but letters/composition [*scriptura*]"; Bernard is "the greatest font of literary learning [*fons litterarum*] in Gaul." Both live and teach in a literary culture of learning.

But apart from the bare subject matter, the two classrooms are two very different worlds. The earlier work shows the cult of magisterial charisma in full bloom. Pernolf teaches by divine right. He has his genius from the Allmighty and his gift of flowing speech from "the eternal divinity." And it is no doubt this conception of a sacral professorship that generated the extravagant metaphor of learning flowing from the master's breast "in a living stream." Also that puzzling, mystical formulation, "he blazes bright with the beauty of many poets." Learning translates into charismatic light. Pernolf is what he reads. Text and teacher fuse; the teacher is a "document," teaching by luminosity and flood, and suffusing his students with his qualities. The earlier text stresses the transmission of virtue from the person of the teacher much more than the later. He cultivates "virtue and salvation"; he blossoms with honors; he is studded with "the gems of virtues," and these qualities become "ornaments" of his students. While the teacher's virtues loom large in the earlier work, his methods are the focus of the later.

John of Salisbury's account is far more sober, almost scientific in its reportage. There is no teaching by divine right. The master is a trained man mediating skills and a body of material well. The mysticism of the teacher is gone. In Bernard of Chartres's classroom, virtue and charisma have passed over into texts. Poetic language and diction have become the bearer of virtue: the poems themselves show forth "virtue," "elegance," "economy," "moderation." The students are admonished to follow the example of the poets, not that of the teacher. Pernolf was much more than a mediator. *His* eloquence, and not Virgil's or Lucan's, is the model which made the students eloquent. The skill of the ancient poets came to life and luminosity in him and poured forth from him like a stream. The material and the technique of the teacher are far more important in John of Salisbury's account than the person of the teacher.

About 130 years separate these two texts. They show us grammar and literary studies in their ascendancy and in their decline. John was a conservative advocate of a learning that was embattled and passing from the scene, and he is attempting — futilely — to reconcile old and new. His presentation of grammar is overgrown with classifications, systematizing, and technical terminology that put forward his credentials as a man in touch with the current developments in studies. His presentation of Bernard's methods is a nostalgic look back. By 1159 it was no longer possible to commend a master by praise of his personal authority, his virtues, his transforming charisma. On the contrary, John tells us that two continuators of the methods of Bernard of Chartres, William of Conches and Richard the Bishop, were forced into early retirement, and that Richard's personal qualities could not prevent it.

Magisterial authority has shifted away from men and into texts; a document is just a document and not a living being; virtue has relocated into language. Bernard of Chartres is a skillful technician, not a charismatic wizard of diction. His commentary merely illuminates texts; the texts do not illuminate him.

RHETORIC

Eloquence and Wisdom

The second of the seven liberal arts came to the Middle Ages from Roman antiquity with ethics attached to it. The combination was part and parcel of the idealized orator's education,[33] and medieval authors and teachers received it in the major texts from antiquity on rhetoric. Cicero's *De inventione*, widely read and commented on,[34] opens with a discussion of the significance of joining eloquence with wisdom. The separation of the two leads to the harm of the state and the stagnation of intellect. But joined together they are a powerful force in human affairs. The combination accounts for the origins of civil society in a myth which follows: it makes eloquence into the force that effected the primal consent of pre-civilized men to forgo violence in favor of peace, friendship and a sociable life (*De inventione*, 1.1–5). And the work ends with a detailed presentation of the definition and nature of virtue as a topic of deliberative rhetoric (2.157–65).

What was for Cicero one theme among many became for Alcuin the essential division of the art of rhetoric. It had two parts: eloquence and virtue, the structure evident in his title, *De rhetorica et virtutibus*. For Alcuin the study of rhetoric leads to and is inseparably connected with the study of virtue.

Gerbert of Aurillac, explicitly following Cicero, drew an even closer connection between the two by refusing to recognize a distinction between the art of speaking well and the art of living well (epist. 44, ed. Weigle, p. 73). This was a programmatic formulation for cathedral school education, and showed the central role assigned to rhetoric: rhetoric joined to the cultivation of virtue restates the general program, "letters and manners."

At the other end of the period, a poet writing some time in the last two decades of the eleventh century produced a poem that is a summation of the learning of the preceding century. It will occupy us at length in the next section of this chapter, but a few comments on its presentation of rhetoric are in order now. The "De nuptiis Mercurii et Philologie" was written by an anonymous French poet in or near the Rheims circle probably around 1080.[35] An allegorical survey of the seven liberal arts ends in the Orpheus story. Wisdom presides as each of the arts is presented, defined, and praised by one of the muses. The muse Calliope says about rhetoric:

> The art teaches this: it holds kings and laws to the rule of
> moderation,
> It reforms the knighthood, who bear the weapons of Mars,
> Teaching them the doctrine of vigilance and lordly ways.
> It regulates the manners of youths [*iuvenum mores*] and instructs the
> mature,
> Holding them to the civil laws in constant moderation.

It is ornamented and beautified by the four virtues.
It moderates all things with good judgment, and quietly
Tempers everything. It is just in its strength and beautiful in its
    wisdom.
Firmly supported on these four columns [i.e., virtues]
It stands equal-sided as if perfectly squared.[36]

This conception of rhetoric is Ciceronian, but it is anything but schematic. It conceives of rhetoric above all as a civilizing force. Not a single line of the passage has to do with an orator's skills and the narrower "science" of learning eloquent speech. It assigns rhetoric an educating force on society: the harshness of the law is tempered, the knighthood restrained from violence, and the other classes taught manners. Of course the Ciceronian vision of rhetoric establishing the civil order informs the lines, but the poet has his own distinct social program, in which rhetoric plays an important part. The four virtues are the foundation of this rhetoric, but it is worth noting that temperance or moderation predominates. Fortitude and prudence are only briefly mentioned, and justice is present largely to receive the tempering influence of moderation. That influence is rhetoric's main virtue, and it is qualified as "beautiful" (*venuste prudens*).

One of the *Regensburg Letters* (ca. 1090) gives us a portrait of the ideal administrator who joins wisdom to eloquence in the context of his administrative duties. The letter is worth citing for its joining of scriptural ideals and precepts from the Benedictine rule with Ciceronian sentiments. The writer is consoling his friend who is caught up in debilitating administrative affairs, scandals, and intrigues. He is about to retire to a life of meditation, but his friend argues stoutly for the importance of the active life:

> You are in a position to govern [*praeesse*] others. This causes harm if you do not strive also to do good [*prodesse*] for them. But you profit others, and yourself especially if while speaking well you also behave well [*si bene cum loqueris, bene operaris*] . . . if you adapt yourself to all men in such a way that all are in agreement with you . . . if you reward vice with odium and virtue with reverence . . . if you represent for all men an example of chastity, a mirror of restraint, a model of discipline, so that your words may themselves be composed manners [*ut mores compositi verba sint*] and your words conform to your acts, so that all may see in you what it is they should strive after . . . so that you wish more to be loved than feared.[37]

The pairing of *praeesse* and *prodesse* is that important structure for formulating governing inherited from the Benedictine rule and Gregory the Great.

Here, however, the formulation is closer to that given in Sigebert's biography of Dietrich of Metz: the ideal of educating men to govern and do good in the same degree, as against the more ascetic tradition that subordinates governing to doing good. Parallel to this is the duty of speaking well and acting well in the same degree.

We have encountered the passage's subordinate ideals: affability that creates harmony among men, and the exemplary nature of the clerical administrator. This statement is close to a comprehensive portrait summarizing ideals of the cathedral schools. A particularly striking suggestion is that exemplarity of behavior also makes speech into an assertion of "composed manners" (*ut mores compositi verba sint*). Speech and ethical conduct coalesce in this dense formulation. The word becomes a good and elegant deed. The formulation restates the Ciceronian/Gerbertian ideal that makes eloquence a form of ethical behavior and beautiful bearing a form of eloquence.

The short work of Honorius Augustodunensis (d. ca. 1156), *De animae exsilio et patria*, is an allegorical pilgrimage through the arts. It follows the soul's progress from ignorance to wisdom, from exile to homeland. The journey leads through ten cities (the first seven are the liberal arts, the eighth "physics," the ninth economics, and the tenth the mechanical arts). The second city is rhetoric. Its gate is "concern for civil matters" (*civilis cura*). In the city itself the administrators of the church compose decrees, while kings and judges issue edicts. In some places synods are convoked, in others forensic laws are promulgated. Cicero is the teacher:

> In this city Tullius instructs pilgrims in the art of speaking ornately, and he composes their manners through the four virtues. . . . This city is the home of those books known as histories, fables, books of oratory and of ethics, and through these the steps of the mind are to be guided toward the fatherland.[38]

The Cicero this writer evokes is still a teacher of eloquence joined to manners. Honorius has essentially the same vision of the mission of rhetoric as the author of "De nuptiis," though with a strong admixture of book-learning.

Wisdom and Eloquence in the Glosses
Two sets of glosses on *De inventione* a generation apart show us a shift in the understanding of Cicero's myth of social origins. The influential glosses of "Master Menegaldus," the teacher of Anselm of Laon and of William of Champeaux, possibly Manegold of Lautenbach, give us a good example

from the second half of the eleventh century.[39] The glossator refers in key words to the myth, which shows how "the ignorant erred and men were wont to act with arbitrary violence" in the primal state. They operated only on physical strength, not rational counsel. They possessed neither religion nor knowledge and did not know "what brother owed to brother and neighbor to neighbor. And for this reason he says, [they lacked a sense] of human duty, i.e., the knowledge of ethics." The gifted orator ended this:

> A certain man possessing eloquence naturally joined with wisdom reflected how much greater was man's dignity with this intellectual skill than with the others. Having realized the value of this skill, he compelled other men to unanimity. Thence arose cities. Once this was accomplished he taught them to suppress wars, to cultivate friendship and social life. And this he accomplished through wisdom and eloquence.[40]

This vision of progress out of a state of violence is paraphrased from Cicero, but Master Menegaldus no doubt had good reason to highlight just this part of the introduction to rhetoric. The transition from a reign of arbitrary violence to a society based on friendship had deep resonance for the genera-tion engaged in the peace movement. And the vision of an end to violence through eloquence was not just a received idea but an experience with powerful appeal.[41] Eloquence is the force that makes reasonable rule pos-sible:

> Hence it is clear that certain men could enlarge the republic because in them resided the aforesaid *virtus* and authority, i.e., that dignity of person amplified by the highest truth, i.e., eloquence. And this I want to stress because it was an ornament to their authority and through this the "governing of the republic" was possible. (Ward, *Art. Eloquentia*, p. 84)

Indicative of the word-centeredness of this culture is the formulation, *summa veritas, i.e., eloquencia.*

Still in the context of a commentary on wisdom joined to eloquence, he makes an interesting observation on Cicero's cautioning against glib eloquence with the false appearance of wisdom:

> This facile quality I call an imitator of the virtue of perfect men. . . . That is why the authors call whatever they describe strong and beautiful, as if virtue disdained to enter imperfect bodies. (Ward, pp. 77–78)

When we move to the glosses by Thierry of Chartres on *De inventione* and *Ad Herennium*, we find a clearer focus on rhetoric and a weakened, or at least shifted, interest in its connection to virtue. We are in the same conceptual world, but it has become intellectualized. Thierry stresses the beginning of Cicero's work and the joining of eloquence with wisdom, but his definition of wisdom is telling. It is "the thorough knowledge either of 'reason,' which pertains to speculative thinking and logic, or of 'duty,' which pertains to ethics" (*Latin Rhetorical Commentaries*, ed. Fredborg, p. 59). The definition of eloquence, dour in its brevity, is "the study of speech." This statement harmonizes with Thierry's introduction: "The utility of this book [*De inventione*] is the composition of a rhetorical oration" (ed. Fredborg, p. 55). The qualification for civil office is eloquence joined to wisdom, but wisdom is "knowledge of the nature of things": "Nisi enim quis et eloquens fuerit et *naturas rerum bene cognoverit*" (p. 71; my emphasis). Thierry in fact insists on the restricted scope of rhetoric and excludes facets of it that earlier writers would have included:

> if some person skilled in all the arts should assign to the art of rhetoric the duty of encompassing also questions of physics and ethics, this may be possible to him who is perfect in the sciences, but not to the art of rhetoric. (p. 75)

These are the comments of a master for whom studies have become more specialized than they were for Master Manegold. Thierry's Cicero is no longer the teacher in Honorius' second city, who "instructs pilgrims in the art of speaking ornately and composes their manners through the four virtues."

Speech and Manners in Two Rhetorical Treatises

1. *Onulf of Speyer*. An earlier master of letters and manners, Onulf of Speyer (mid-eleventh century), did not agree that questions of ethics fell outside of the realm of rhetoric. This Speyer school master's *Colores rhetorici*,[42] like so many works from the eleventh century, owes its origins and survival to chance, not to any practical need of the schools to record the thought and teaching of their masters. A friend of Onulf, a monk and teacher, requested instruction on the "colors of rhetoric" along with citations from ancient authors, and since he lived at some distance, Onulf could not give it to him in person. The result is a work that is deeply representative for the intellectual-ethical orientation of the schools.

"Letters and manners" provides the background against which its representative character becomes evident.[43] He leads the reader through the ornaments of speech (adapting *Rhetorica ad Herennium*, 4.19ff.) to "ornaments of manners." The work begins with a statement of the subordinate relationship of rhetoric to manners. Unfortunately the first words of the prologue are lost. It opens with the sentence fragment, ". . . arti rethoricae: morum elegantiam, compositionem habitus, vitae dignitatem amplectere" (ed. Wattenbach, p. 369). A conjecture in harmony with the thrust of the work would see this as completing the thought, "The art of rhetoric [is not confined to the framing of speeches, but] embraces the cultivation of elegant manners, composed bearing and dignity of conduct," or, more succinctly, "Manners are the higher form of eloquence." The work is built on the transference of the rules of beautiful speech to rules of elegant conduct. A passage close to the logic and structure of the stunted prologue is the explanation of *traductio*:

> What does such ornamentation [i.e, rhetorical] contribute to your salvation, since the ornamentation of manners and of bearing solely, sole as it is, merits solely the name of ornamentation?[44]

Here and throughout, the rejection of rhetoric in favor of *mores* is the structuring principle. But the same words that reject rhetorical ornament illustrate it. The repetition of *sola* and *exornatio* illustrate the figure at hand.

The work has two parts. Each figure of speech discussed in prose in the first part is repeated in verse in the second. Here is Onulf's definition of *articulus*, in prose:

> Do not exert yourself greatly in attaining knowledge of *articulus*, concerning which orators claim an oration is polished by the staccato setting apart of single words in a sequence. You however should seek to show skill . . . in your manners, your bearing, your knowledge of divine scriptures. (p. 373)

and in verse:

> Manners, bearing and wisdom adorn your mind
> So that you will please young, old, and the throng of youths.
> God, His angel and the learned man himself command, love, and
>   prove this.
> Let man, woman, rich and poor revere, desire and love you.
> Let every age, condition and both sexes revere and honor you.
> Be sweet and amiable in tone of voice, attitude, facial expression.[45]

In rejecting rhetoric, he displays it, and in this way both complies with his friend's request and strikes a virtuous posture. His self-abjuring virtuosity fuses instruction in letters to instruction in manners. He combines the rules of speech and the rules of living, adjuring the reader to "compose" himself according to rhetorical precepts.

It is difficult to draw any clear conclusions about the sociology of this short work. It is written by a teacher at a cathedral school for a teacher in a monastery. The lessons given look toward the contemplative and solitary life, and we cannot be certain that they were at home both in Onulf's school and in that of his addressee. Concerns specific to the school of Speyer with its flourishing "imperial study" emerge in Onulf's treatment of homoeoteleuton (*similiter desinens*):

> *Similiter desinens* occurs when the word endings are similar, although the words are indeclinable. Perhaps you shrink from appearing unlearned, or perhaps you blush to be thought uncultivated; you labor at your exercises of composition in verse and prose, and at those rhetorical ornaments you request of me; you suggest the reading of the authors to your pupils, you strive to answer their each and every question, and unless you can respond to all, you are deeply ashamed. But now listen to what Democritus said, a philosopher and not the least among them. Called upon to play during a banquet, he said he knew no songs on the lyre. To those who then asked what he did know, since he did not know this, he replied, "I have learned something far more excellent: I know how to govern the state wisely, and I know how to make a small state large." And in the same way let the wise knowledge of divine service be the magnifying glory of your learning. (p. 374, parag. 13)

This bit of wisdom from a Greek philosopher seems more apt for students like Benno of Osnabrück (possibly a student of Onulf), a skilled administrator and courtier, than for the monk to whom the work is addressed. The "divine service" must include service of the state. No doubt Onulf's friend was living at an unreformed religious house, the culture of which probably varied little from that of the Speyer clerical community. It is a relationship like that of St. Remi of Rheims to the Rheims cathedral school in the late tenth century (see above, p. 59).

We should not make much of Onulf's "rejection" of literary studies and their classical models. This is the orthodox *habitus* we have observed elsewhere. The masters and students cultivate a language saturated with classical models, and their rejection of antiquity is a thinly disguised admission of a profound debt to it.[46] Onulf himself was probably a student of Walther of Speyer, bishop of Speyer from 1004–1027. Anyone who has struggled even partly through the impenetrable Latin of his *Libellus scholasticus* will realize how large rhetorical ornament and the Baroque diction of Martianus Capella loomed for the previous generation of Speyer masters.

2. *Marbod of Rennes*. Onulf's work has been compared with Marbod of Rennes' *Liber de ornamentis verborum*. This work, written some fifty years later, cites the definitions from the *Rhetorica ad Herennium* and appends a few lines of verse to illustrate the figure. Here is Marbod's treatment of *homoeoteleuton*:

> *Similiter desinens* occurs when the word endings are similar, although the words are indeclinable. In this way:
> You seek increase of wealth, decrease of virtue is the result. But you will never be rich as long as you lack virtue.
> You may speak sweetly, but you will deceive insidiously.
> You may question glibly, but you will act abominably.[47]

The structure is virtually identical with that of Onulf's work: rhetorical precepts are followed by illustrative examples with some moral content. But there is a clear shift in priorities: Onulf's concern is essentially ethical, Marbod's essentially aesthetic. Both contain moral lessons: Marbod's are tags appended to rhetorical lessons; Onulf's are fruit removed from the husk of rhetoric. What Onulf "rejected" has become the main object in Marbod. His work ends with a brief epilogue which shows the development of a sophisticated literary aesthetic:

> If you wish to compose, then hold to
> The natures of things as a mirror and poet's model,
> Keep that as your exemplar, like one who wishes to learn to
>   paint . . .
> Since art emerges from nature when summoned by reason,
> It strives to retain the form of its own origin.   (1692C–D)

The grounding of Onulf's rhetorical teaching is man and the laws of his conduct; that of Marbod's is nature and its representation. This difference is a distinction not just of two thinkers, but of two generations of intellectuals. Art, or "the art," is tending to emancipate itself from its grounding in moral teaching. We will observe this shift from man to art/nature in other contexts.

POETRY

"School poetry" had a role in learning and society in the eleventh century that is easy to underestimate. A much quoted dictum of E. R. Curtius's makes poetry into an assemblage of received learning: "Why did one write poetry? One was taught to in school."[48] The tone in the master's voice here brooked no contradiction and convicted the sensible question, "Why learn poetry?" in advance of impertinence. Curtius notwithstanding, poetry was the art, along with rhetoric, through which training in *mores* most immediately engaged in eleventh-century society.

We can get some impression of the distance that separates the learned eleventh-century poet from the "Vagant" of the twelfth in a satirical portrait of the perfect worldly cleric by Peter Damian:

> Even today there is a brother living in the city of Rome, sprung from the highest French nobility, whose name I shall not mention, for I shudder at the ignominy of a brother. I doubt that he is lacking in anything that qualifies him for office [*aliquid utilitatis*]. He is radiant with the flowers of external goods: noble as the emperor; beautiful to look on; he speaks like Cicero; he writes poetry like Virgil; he is a sounding trumpet in the church; he is learned and sharp in divine law. Disputing like a scholar, his speech flows as though he were reading it from the page; speaking in everyday language, he does not offend the rule of Roman urbanity. What can I say about his mastery of the monastic rule? or of the regulated life of clergy? He knows them equally so that he could teach them as an expert.[49]

This is a man who has covered all his bases. That means, for Peter Damian, a master of speech, the law, and the *mores* of the two main divisions of church communities, monastic and regular clergy. In addition he is of high nobility and handsome appearance. That list touches the major forms of "usefulness." The detail that gives pause is poetry: "ut Virgilius poetatur." Suspending our own picture of alienated poets and deep abysses separating the word from the deed, we could imagine poetry as one of the useful arts in the sense of advanced rhetoric: an aid to speech and eloquent writing, the handmaid of rhetoric.

It was a great deal more than that. The status of poetry in the eleventh century was extraordinary and not to be viewed or appreciated through the optics and aesthetics of other periods. Peter Damian sets poetry parallel to high birth, physical beauty, forensic eloquence, political influence, legal training, and training in *mores*. That is closer to an accurate classification than "handmaid of rhetoric." The learned poet of the eleventh century is more likely to be found in furs and silks in high church positions than wandering homeless and hopeful of patronage for the evening's bread.[50]

Poetry the Fulfillment of Learning

Far from being handmaiden to any art, poetry stood at the top of the hierarchy of studies, it was in fact that skill toward which the other language arts tended. This extraordinary status of poetry is evident in the poem *De mensa philosophie* from the Cambridge Songs. It sets a rich table of philosophical food and drink, but serves only poetry:

Hasten to the table of philosophy, you who thirst,
And drink the seven streams of its threefold feast.
Flowing from a single fountain, they go separate ways.
Here flow the rudiments of grammar, here the stream of poetry,
Here the platter of the satirists, here the applause of the comics,
And the Mantuan flutes [= Virgil's pastoral poetry] bring joy to the
    banquet.[51]

This is not a niggardly "let them eat poetry!"; it is the best dish the host has to offer. The age had a loose hold on the quadrivium, but it had a sense that in poetry Virgil was not always its equal.[52] We have seen much testimony to the fervid devotion to poetry in school.[53] The Würzburg poem from 1031 (above, Chapter 3) shows its stature in that school. The master is praised as "the prince of those primates who expound the poets' secrets" (ed. Bulst, l. 21). He is "refulgent with the light of many poets," he "beams" poetry, as he might exude humanity, grace and charm. Teaching by divine right, he devotes his entire attention to composition ("Preter scripture studium nihil est sibi cure" — 26). He qualifies his students for office, and himself and them for heaven, through learning and virtue (cf. ll. 75ff.).

Not only did poetry enjoy a high status, it was regarded as the end point and fulfillment of studies. There is a grand statement of this conception in the important school poem from around 1080 entitled, like the work of Martianus Capella which it adapts, "De nuptiis Mercurii et Philologie."[54] I would like to call particular attention to this poem. It is a summation of learning at the eleventh-century cathedral schools. Like Alan of Lille's *Anti-claudian*, though on less grand a scale, it is an allegory of the ideal education.

As in the work of Martianus Capella, the poem begins with the marriage of Mercury and Philology. The wedding feast is presided over by *sapientia*. Apollo calls upon the nine muses, who "cling closely to study" (*studio cohibente* — 82). They are to "magnify the arts." Then each of the muses sings the praises of one of the arts. After the celebration of the arts, the "ethereal chorus of philosophy" sings a song praising *sapientia*.

Next Orpheus appears with his wife Eurydice. No reason is given for his entrance. He simply is "there": *Ecce novus vates vatumque ferens novitates* (242). He calls for silence and begins to sing. The song he sings is of no particular importance, though it goes on at some length (242–366). It is a series of "hymns" to gods and heroes, essentially the brief retelling of myths. Eurydice follows and sings of some of the paramours of Jove, and is awarded the laurel wreath, gems and gold for her song.[55] When she ends the feast is over (402).

Now, with no transition, we are into the story of Orpheus and Eurydice. She is bitten by the serpent; he descends to recover her, softens the flinty hearts of the infernal beings, and, following the Ovidian "unhappy ending," loses the redeemed Eurydice by looking back.

What does it mean that a poem celebrating the union of eloquence and wisdom through the muses and the liberal arts ends in the story of Orpheus and Eurydice? Essentially, the message is that education is fulfilled in poetry and music.[56] For this anonymous poet, what Orpheus stands for is what education is about. Martianus Capella's work also ended with music. The ninth and final book of the *De nuptiis* is devoted to Harmony. Banished from earth, she joins the wedding party to celebrate the union in song. Orpheus is also present, along with Amphion and Arion. His song and his failed rescue are mentioned, but with no particular profile. He is one of several emblems of Harmony's working. Martianus Capella's work ends with a long-winded rehearsal of the laws of harmonics and metrics. The two works share the same structure: a survey of studies ends in the art which fulfills them. But the eleventh-century poet thoroughly changed his source to highlight Orpheus and his role.[57]

Toward the end of the period (ca. 1125), when poetry and learning had gone very different ways in France, a learned German, Ulrich of Bamberg, could make the skilled composition of verse and prose into the measure of learning:

> I believe for my own part, my sweetest friend,
> And hope you agree, that no one is thoroughly learned,
> Nor perfect, who is unable to compose something
> Worth hearing. What greater sign is there,
> What stronger argument or more certain testimony
> Of abundant genius, dearest brother, than when
> A poet can soothe ears and minds gracefully?
> Here is what we seek, or nowhere, here, I say,
> Is the fruit of long studies.[58]

Just as the Cambridge poem could make poetry into the only drink at Philosophy's banquet, this poem can make poetry into the measure, and, more strikingly, the final goal, of learning. Ulrich states plainly what the structure of "De nuptiis" implies: poetic skill gives the strongest argument "of abundant genius" and "the fruit of long studies."

Orphic Poetry: A Civilizing Force

There is more here than puerile enthusiasm willing to rank poetasters with Virgil. To get at it we need to study the figure of Orpheus in the period.[59] The age made the Thracian bard into the representative of its lofty conception of poetry. We can approach this conception through close readings of three Orpheus poems, one from the mid-eleventh century, the other two from its last decades. In all three, the underworld scene is the key to the guiding conceptions.

"De nuptiis": The Furies Plead for Clemency. In his visit to hell, as the poem "De nuptiis" depicts it, Orpheus meets the harshest, cruelest, and most inflexible beings God and nature have created, and his song softens their hearts and turns them into advocates of compassion. The fates are present, but are no match for Orphic song. Its force makes them into petitioners, begging the king, Dis, to relent and spare Eurydice: "The fates are softened, and they say: 'O just king, spare her!'" ("Flectuntur Parce, que dicunt: 'Rex pie, parce!'" — 571). The furies, described as "ferocious, cruel, grim" (*ferva, trux, torva*), reproach Dis for his cruelty (574). The tortured in hell forget their sufferings (575).

Orpheus begins his plea to Dis. The dominant tone is sensual nostalgia: "Hymen" has driven him to invade the land of hell (534); Orpheus is "a youth bound by the reins of love" (535); his dead bride had "hardly even in her girlish mind tasted the union with a man, still knew not how to love or be loved" (538–9); Eurydice, roused from the dark regions by her lover's voice, "desires to embrace him" (559).

The romantic pathos seizes the residents of hell and awakens love and compassion in all of them. A chorus of the furies and the damned together plead with Pluto for Orpheus: "Love presses them all with its urgings, from all sides the clamor for forgiveness rings out" (*Omnibus instat amor, venie sonat undique clamor* — 586).

The lord of the underworld was at first irritated and hardened his heart (*Pluto cor indurat neque vati parcere curat* — 588). But this love-inspired plea for mercy from a unanimous chorus softens and renders him "modest and placid" (*Rex prius infestus placida iam mente modestus* — 617), and he "lightens the fatal law" (618). But Orpheus violates his condition. Eurydice is lost forever, and the poet is left with only the consolation of his song, which retains its power to console:

> He mitigates with the art of his lyre the curses of sorrow and anger,
> And whatever mourning beset him, art restores him. (642–43)

The essential moment in the scene is the conversion of the underworld, the remarkable metamorphosis from cold, dead rage and vengeful fury to warmth, compassion and love. This is the power of Orphic music. The love-inspired song soothes and conquers the fury and anger of harsh and cruel beings and softens the hard laws of nature.

A central thought of the poet emerges in the meeting of Orpheus and Dis. It is modeled on a courtroom scene. Orpheus is pleading a case, the chorus of the furies and damned speak in his support, Dis is a king sitting in judgment and enforcing or relaxing laws.[60] This conceit of the poet's makes poetry and judicial rhetoric into allies in legal dealings, and reiterates a remarkable passage earlier in the poem, the praise of rhetoric by the muse Calliope (discussed above, pp. 132–33 and note 36):

> This art [rhetoric] teaches the following: it holds kings to moderation in exercising the law, it reforms [or reeducates] the knighthood, who bear the weapons of Mars, with the doctrine of vigilance and study of lordly ways; it instructs youths in manners and guides the mature; it constantly holds the civil laws close to the rule of moderation. . . . It moderates everything wisely and gently tempers all things. (ed. Boutemy, p. 50, ll. 136–59)

The softening, taming effect of Orpheus's song is answered in this passage by the moderating, tempering effect of rhetoric. In both, a king is "held to moderation in exercising the laws." Judicial pleading and poetry meet in the function of urging clemency by softening the emotions of the judge or king. This correspondence shows us again that the first and second parts of the poem are knit in a unified conception. It also shows us the remarkable symbolic staging that is the high point of the underworld scene: poetry / music joins forces with judicial rhetoric to soothe, and this makes allies of Orpheus and the residents of hell.

Orphic poetry has a civilizing mission like that of rhetoric as the educator of warriors and temperer of royal judgment. It inspires mercy and "brings low impious rage" (*Carminibus vatis occidit furor impietatis* — 600). It replaces cruelty and vengefulness with love.

The conception of poetry as a softening and civilizing force has a long history, and the story of Orpheus and Eurydice was frequently its vehicle.[61] But the eleventh century gave a profile to this role that was not received from classical or earlier medieval sources.[62] Orpheus and Eurydice becomes a defining myth for the mission of the educated man. That explains the logic of concluding a survey of the seven liberal arts with the story of Orpheus in hell: the object and applied goal of education is to exercise the softening, mitigating, peace- and love-bringing effect of "Orphic" song.

"Quid suum virtutis": The Dance of the Monsters. The poem "Quid suum virtutis" ("The Nature of Virtue") is a showpiece of the manneristic style of eleventh-century poetry. It dates probably from ca. 1043–1046, and possibly was written at or for the German royal court.[63] The poem places the story of Orpheus between an opening section castigating contemporary vices and the decline of virtue (ll. 1–498) and a closing section offering lessons in virtue (1025–1190). The placement of the myth again is significant. It is introduced to illustrate the virtues that the present age has lost. Those are study and hard work that develop "art":

> By sweating and toiling in labor joined to native art,
> Orpheus extricated Eurydice.
> He would not have controlled the rivers or moved the stones
> If he had wished to languish in wanton sloth,
> But impelled by fervent study he composed the muses' own odes
> And caressed and soothed all things with their beguiling tones.[64]

Orpheus is the representative of uncorrupted "study" leading to virtue, that is, the embodiment of the instruction the poet offers, essentially, "what is the nature of virtue" ("quid suum virtutis"). If "De nuptiis" shows the arts fulfilled in poetry, "Quid suum" shows poetry fulfilled in virtue, actively rousing compassion and saving lives.

The effects of Orpheus's music before the descent to the underworld are described in terms familiar from the "De nuptiis." It "soothes with its sweetness."[65] His muse is "sweet."[66] It delights and brings happiness.[67] It can create a variety of moods according to the temper of the mode, the "gravity of the spondee" calms anger and brings peace to the soul,[68] though harsher tones stir rage and belligerence (795–96). The learned author integrates these effects into Boethian ideas of cosmic and human music (see the discussion in the section on music, below, pp. 165ff.). The dominant mode of music is conciliating, soothing harmony:

> This man's muse, soothing and delighting the world with such sweetness, shows clearly how the power of harmony tempers the essence of things, reconciling dissonant things in a unanimous bond. . . . And this same law of number in its moderating effect couples the nature of the greater world [= macrocosm] with that of the lesser [= microcosm]. . . . She [Harmony] joins body to soul, the things of the lower world to the supernal. She ornaments manners [*haec mores ornat*] and relieves the body of its pain.[69]

He goes on to derive the inner constitution of man from the effect of music:

> Since the musical temper now soothes, now irritates, and again pacifies the mood of the mind, it is more certain than certain that the totality of man is aptly conjoined by the tempering effect of number.[70]

Man's harmonious constitution renders him susceptible to the tempering and "educating" influence of music, since the "ornament of manners" registers the body's harmonious coherence with the soul, for which song and number are responsible.

The descent and journey through hell are powerfully described, and the representation is based on a conception as distinct and as fundamental to our topic as the corresponding scene of "De nuptiis." Everywhere are scenes of sadness, suffering, cruelty and inhumanity. Orpheus passes through these dead realms singing. His music casts a magic spell, transforming rage and vengefulness into love and gentleness. The "sweetness" of his music softens hell, "destroys the Stygian law," and brings streams of tears to the eyes of the Eumenides:

> Nor is it a wonder to tell, sacred Orpheus,
> That your muse brought such sweet sounds to the gods.
> You softened the realms of hell and destroyed the law of death.
> At your singing the Eumenides wept.[71]

The stones themselves weep (817). The poet's ebullient imagination produced a scene unique in the Orpheus myth: the music of Orpheus sets the monsters of hell dancing:

> All the monsters housed in the Stygian port
>   Step from one leg to the other to the instruments' tune.[72]

They do not dance well (*incompositas . . . choreas*), but then they are not used to music (931–32). The ferryman Charon, who has never experienced a happy day in his life, grows joyful in his bitter old age, and works his pole with renewed pleasure in the task (943–44). The raging waves themselves grow glad (945). Hairy Cerberus now fawns on the poet with wags of his tail and nods of his triple-throated maw; he turns sociable and becomes the companion of the Hydra (951–52). The gloomy aspect of the shades grows cheerful (953), and at the dulcet sounds of the lyre and the "nectar of the voice," pain loses its sting, Rhadamanthus grows cheerful and festive, while cruel (*trux*) Eacus, deeply moved, breaks into smiles (954–56). The "king" of the underworld (*rex Tartareus*) himself sits, as though on a throne (*In cuius medio maiestas fulta tyranni* — 965), in the middle of a black fire that overwhelms the vision[73] and leaps as a sulfurous whirlwind into the heights. Attended by Agony, Lamentation and Horror (the editor stresses the personification by capitalizing the names), he feeds the guilty into his consuming fire.

At the sound of Orpheus's music the tyrant is astonished to see how his teeth-gnashing fury is calmed, and he is transformed from his former self into a gentle creature.[74]

This remarkable scene shows us the cumulative and outbidding impulse of eleventh-century poetic "mannerism," not merely producing poetic flotsam, but engaged in the crucial moment of the poem. The guiding idea is the magical transformation of an entire society from savage inhumanity to courteous sociability. One monster after another turns into a mild-mannered courtier, until the entire underworld is a festive[75] grand ballroom with the guests greeting each other affably, walking arm in arm, dancing, smiling, and making charming and blandishing comments and gestures. The disparity, comical to the modern reader, is high seriousness for the eleventh-century poet. If the model for hell in "De nuptiis" was the king's court dispensing law, in "Quid suum virtutis" it is the king's court as social center.

Finally, in an anticlimactic single line, Orpheus' wish is granted: "Odis empta viro redditur Euridice" (996). Orpheus leads her out, but in this case, as opposed to the "De nuptiis," love works against him. It forces him to look back. And so he whom no effort or exertion could conquer is thwarted by love (1008).[76] Eurydice vanishes. Orpheus is eager to return and work his marvelous effect again, taking courage from the power of his lyre, but is dissuaded by his revulsion at the thought of petitioning evil.[77] But the divine power of song has already enabled him to win a great victory over Styx, and this shows how "art, with the mediation of fervent study, conquers nature, proving that all things yield to Lady Virtue."[78]

Once More: From Cruelty to Kindness. Our next text is a short poem (60 lines) from the so-called "Liège Songs."[79] It dates from the end of the century and was written by a certain "Gautier," who had ties to Marbod and Baudri of Bourgueil and probably was himself active at Rheims.[80] The element of study and education that played such a prominent part in both the other poems is absent. The entire poem is given over to the effects of Orpheus's song on the residents of the underworld. The ideas and the conception — transformation from cruelty to mercy and kindness — differ little from what we have observed so far. But a look at it confirms that these poems speak a widely shared language that we can call from now on "Orphic discourse."

Here also, Orpheus's music is imagined as penetrating all of hell and working its magic on all its denizens: "Orpheus holds the caves of hell spellbound and song-softened. . . . Whatever evil they suffered was mollified by his song."[81] Where there was fury, at the sound of the song there is deep peace and quiet (4). Those bound in chains forget their pain and anger at the love that the lyre spreads (7–8). This Orpheus also changes the laws of hell: "Arte lireque sonis mutavit iura Plutonis" (13). As he proceeds, the "dark faces and loathesome figures" he passes "transform their grim countenances and greet him cordially" (41). Facing the gods of the underworld, Orpheus "takes away their raging fury and alleviates the fierceness of their hearts" ("Sic rabiem demit, sic fera corda premit" — 56). The god of the underworld is overcome, and his "imperial command" returns Eurydice to the poet.

These poems show us that "Orphic" poetry has two major characteristics: it is the fulfillment of learning — liberal and ethical — and it transforms the cruel and vengeful into gentle, loving, compassionate beings. That it "conquers nature" and is an instrument in the pursuit of virtue, as the "Quid suum virtutis" depicts it, is for the eleventh century part and parcel of cathedral school learning based on *cultus virtutum*.

A Civilizing Mission

The eleventh-century poets show an interest in the conversion of the underworld that is unprecedented in any tradition. The poets are far less concerned with the fate of Eurydice than with the civilizing of hell. That mission is the basic manifestation of Orphic poetry.

We know from sources outside the Orpheus poems that these two aspects of poetry (it fulfills education, it soothes hard hearts and creates compassion) were accepted views of its role in studies and life.[82] In this light the lines on poetry by Ulrich of Bamberg quoted earlier (p. 142 and n. 58) have programmatic character:

> no one is thoroughly learned,
> Nor perfect, who is unable to compose something
> Worth hearing. What greater sign is there,
> What stronger argument or more certain testimony
> Of abundant genius, dearest brother, than when
> A poet can soothe ears and minds gracefully?
> Here is what we seek, or nowhere, here, I say,
> Is the fruit of long studies. ("Bamberger ars dictaminis," ll. 32–39)

It is a pithy statement of the conclusion just formulated: poetry that can "soothe," "charm," or "delight" (*mulcere*), attests to thorough learning (*doctus ad unguem*) and virtue (*perfectus*).[83] Ulrich elaborates on the effects of poetry a few lines later. His unnamed friend is known as a man of strong and kind genius:

> . . . who is ignorant of your brilliance?
> Who would deny the kind strain of your mind?
> For in writing sweet verses you soothe breasts,
> And you soothe as well when writing excellent prose.
> With your manners you ornament these [verses],
> Since your will is always bent to Good.[84]

The thought is essentially the same as in the previous passage: genius (*subtilis*) and virtue (*benignus, prona ad bonum*) are shown forth in poems and prose compositions that "charm and delight." Poetry and virtue are again closely joined in the phrase, "moribus haec ornas." The statement is close to the basic idea of both "De nuptiis" and "Quid suum virtutis." Ulrich is defining poetry as "Orphic" without any reference to Orpheus.

Orphic Discourse. Orphic poetry is not an aesthetic idea separable from social circumstances and moral obligations. The concept as the eleventh-century schools developed it analyses situations of conflict. That is, those who observed and described conflict themselves called on the Orpheus myth for their formulations.

The poem glorifying the Würzburg school calls on Orphic discourse to describe the contention between the two parties. The passages that interest us juxtapose the peace of Würzburg with the hell of contentiousness at Worms. The poet depicts Würzburg as an Elysian realm of studies, an academy of poetry and virtue, its students and master a harmonious community, knit together as if "by a single vow" (see above, p. 72). The Worms poet has stormed into this citadel of love as a raging enemy of peace. He is a "sower of wrath and destroyer of friendships" (*sator irarum et destructor amicitiarum* — 105), filled with "frenzied rage, mad with the love of Mars" (*bacharis . . . Martis amore furendo* — 141–42); he has fomented between them the "discord of dire wrath" (*dire discordia ire* — 130); his "message of contention" (*nuncia litis* — 107) disturbs the "sweet life of Würzburg" and the peace that rules on all sides (105–9).

The peace-breaker's penchant to anger, rage and combat is consistent with the studies at his school, the poet claims. At Worms they worship "spiritual monsters" (206); they lack all art and put their faith in the quarrels of Mars (207); they call back to life the gods of the underworld (*Inferni divos . . . redivivos* — 213) and prefer their worship to the society of the living under the "law of instruction" (*ius documenti* — 211); they worship the "black demons," who, while they lived, engaged in "constant contentions" (224–27); they will never prevail in the present combat, "even though the prince of the underworld himself should leave hell to render them aid" (269–70).

We are suddenly in the underworld scene of the Orpheus myth, though there has been no signal of it nor any reference to that story. The "sower of wrath" has chosen to revive the gods of hell, those whom the law of Pluto has condemned to the dragon's jaw, but there is no resonating lyre to soften his (Pluto's) anger. No pleading can rescue those who enter his kingdom.[85] The Worms poet, in other words, is caught in the hell of contention he has created, and has no soothing lyre and no redeeming Orpheus to soften the rage of the beasts he consorts with. Wrathful contentiousness is stylized as a descent to the underworld; hell is the place of anger, fury and war. The poet could evoke the story without telling it; the circumstances themselves called for an Orpheus.[86]

If there is an Orpheus in the poem, it is the Würzburg poet. His foe is in the position of Eurydice, caught in hell and locked into the law of Pluto. It takes an Orpheus with his "conciliating lyre" to redeem him. The poet has cast himself in the role of peacemaker and reconciler. Having railed against the warlike posture of Worms, he makes an extravagant offer of peace: "Now let the discord and cruel anger between us fade. Let us shun war and become joined as twins in our love. A bond like that of David and Jonathan will join us. No cruelty will disturb us now or ever more. Those caught up in unending quarrels will marvel to see such a friendship between us."[87] This posture of unquestioning forgiveness of wrongs, overlooking of insults, and forgoing vengefulness to restore peace and friendship, was an admired one. The poet shows his "gentleness of spirit" (*mansuetudo*)[88] by pouring forth reconciling oil to sooth the dispute. His own poem is the bringer of it. The final lines represent the poet as the redeemer of his wrathful colleague at Worms, sowing seeds of peace in the divine field by his song and praying for aid from God, "by whose gifts I master the melody of reason."[89]

This poem shows us actual social circumstances that commended the figure of Orpheus as a representative of peace and conciliation. Peace, friendship, love in cathedral schools was a sacred law. To violate it was serious.[90] It was important to have people who, Orpheus-like, mastered the "melody of reason," not just in the schools, but in the society generally.

The Würzburg poem is not the only case in which a breach of claustral tranquility conjured Orpheus as the reconciler. Two letters from the Hannover collection show us the same logic at work.

The first is written (between 1054 and 1079) to Bishop Hezilo of Hildesheim by a group of students residing at the Hildesheim cathedral school, evidently as guests (*hospites*), not members of the chapter. They are starving. In their salutation, they sign themselves "famished men whose flesh barely clings to their bones" and wish Bishop Hezilo "the satiety of celestial grace, full of the bread of life."[91] They play changes on their hunger, describing the physical effects in detail. They compare themselves to the tortured in hell, except that their own tortures are worse:

> . . . we feel more wretched than Tantalus who dared not touch those regal feasts set near him, more plagued than Ixion bound to the rolling wheel, more damned than Sisyphus pushing his constantly falling stone back up again and again, worse punished than Tition at whose ever replenished liver an insatiable vulture gnaws, and altogether delivered over in body to infernal suffering. (p. 62)

They beg the bishop to release them from "the jaws of hell" (p. 63). Having set up the bishop for the role of either Pluto or Orpheus, they end discreetly by casting themselves as Orpheus pleading for Bishop Hezilo before God. Just as the lyre of Orpheus liberated Eurydice (whom they call "Erudicen") from hellish creatures who know no forgiveness, they pray that "the cithara of their devotion" will win from God whatever Hezilo wishes.[92]

A letter from Walo, abbot of St. Arnulf in Metz, to Archbishop Manasses of Rheims, written in 1074, is not so discreet. The unhappy abbot heaps vituperation on the Archbishop, who has wronged him. He grieves for the errors of Manasses, as is appropriate to anyone moved by the "affection of true love." He has grieved far more for the "ragings" of his injurer than for the injuries done himself. He shudders to recall the misery he has suffered under the "barbarous rule" (*barbaro dominio*). He declines to enumerate the threats and the curses he has received from Manasses. Had he been anything but a simple fool, he would not have come to so "ungentle, so cruel, so violent, so monstrous a beast" (*ad te tam inmitem tam trucem tam violentam tam inmanem bestiam*).[93] Manasses has had the nerve to suggest that Walo, being a peaceful, humble and quiet man (*pacificum, humilem et quietum*), and constantly given to reading, is not comfortable with the "French manners" of Manasses. Only a monster barren of all virtue, Walo says, could imagine a life tempered by peace, modesty and sobriety to be lower in virtue than one given to harsh and bold combat. The rehearsal of the archbishop's perverse ideas continues: peace weakens the spirits of powerful men, while combat strengthens the weak and idle. But, Walo replies, Cicero has shown the superiority of the toga to weapons. The opposition of peaceful, gentle Walo to fierce and barbarous Manasses gives the structure that invokes Orpheus. Walo says he has tried to mitigate the fury of Manasses by citing scripture and "celestial words":

> Oh how often have I administered to you the medicine of scripture! How often I attempted to mitigate your fury, singing, as it were, the songs of heavenly words! How often I strove—not with the Thracian but with the Davidic lyre—to expel or tame that demon that vexes you! (p. 183)

The rejection of the "Thracian cithara" only confirms the appropriateness of Orpheus in the circumstances. It is a gesture, like the "rejection of the muses" in invocations,[94] that christianizes a domain legitimately occupied by the classical tradition, and in so doing concedes a strong sense of obligation to what it rejects. The reference to the harp of David demonstrates through its isolation how accepted the jurisdiction of Orpheus in the correction of *furor* and *saevitia* was. David curing Saul would have had a higher degree of legitimacy, but the Old Testament singer is seldom invoked as a soother of royal anger, though his poetry is often compared to that of Orpheus.[95]

Sigebert of Gembloux gives us a second example of Christian superseding Orphic opposition to violence and rage in his *Passio Thebeorum* (ca. 1070).[96] He represents Emperor Maximian as the raging king, "barely civil, no friend to his friends, savage in his anger . . . a lion who is never meek at heart or relaxed and gentle, fierce and cruel by nature, barbaric in feelings."[97] He orders the (Christian) Theban legion to slaughter the foe (a rebel Gallic tribe and Christians) mercilessly: "Let no compassion soften you. / Show no restraint, show no mercy."[98] In a speech full of fine ironies (2.2.25–159, pp. 71–75), the emperor's speaker warns the (converted) legion against the dangers of Christianity: their God is taking over, snatching the trident from Neptune, and so on. Soon he will command the underworld — rightly so, since Dis, harder than stone, is deaf to the pleas and blind to the tears of the wretched (says the spokesman of the cruel emperor). Dis could not even be softened by the tearful songs of Orpheus and refused to grant the life of Eurydice:

> Pluto, who is harder than stones of adamant, could not be softened by the tearful songs of Orpheus, who softened the tigers, the mountains, the wild forests and the rivers, to give the singer Eurydice's life as his payment.[99]

But "this new fellow Jesus" (*hic novus Iesus*) hears the pleas of all and has compassion with all, even to the point of returning the dead to life.

This is the only version known to me in which Eurydice is not saved even once and the song of Orpheus fails to soften Dis/Pluto. Sigebert obviously required an inflexible king and a thwarted Orpheus in order to create a space for a Christ whose redeeming mission overcame the ineffectual pagan means of arousing mercy.[100]

The Orpheus story was a structuring myth for conflict in actual social-political circumstances. Sigebert's *Passio Thebeorum* underscores this role, even though it is an imaginative narrative poem. The same narrative metaphor was at the disposal of any learned cleric who described conflict situations. It gave a powerful analogue to the learned man of peace softening the rage of rulers, no matter what the ultimate success.

Orphic Men

The soothing and civilizing role of verse was more than a conceit of school poetry. Orphic discourse formulated important duties of secular clergy: restraining and soothing the anger of princes and rulers, making peace, effecting reconciliations. "Mitigating the fury of kings" is mentioned as a matter of praise in Carolingian sources,[101] though it is not common and Orpheus is not associated with it. Gerbert of Aurillac formulated the task programmatically. He strikes a Ciceronian posture insisting that the art of speaking well must be inseparable from the art of living well. The necessity for combining good speaking and good living is the "mitigating" task of the statesman:

> . . . to us who are taken up with the governing of the republic both are necessary. For there is the highest utility in the ability to speak appropriately to persuade and *to restrain the minds of the raging from violence by gentle oratory*.[102]

The discourse of fury and anger mollified was present in the tenth century, and the man whose charisma had peace-making force was an admired ideal. Ruotger says that Brun of Cologne was born to be a peace-maker, just at the time when his father had "tamed the savageness of the barbarians" (*perdomita barbarorum sevicia*),[103] "turned back the danger of internal strife," and proceeded to rebuild a peaceful kingdom. Brun always cultivated peace, "as if it were the nourishing force and crown of all other virtues." The mere sound of his name put an end to wars, ushered in peace and established the study of the arts. He believed that tranquillity was the atmosphere that strengthens virtue, while strife weakens it.[104]

The first abbot of Gembloux, Erluin (d. 987), was described by his contemporary the monk Richarius, in verses transmitted by Sigebert of Gembloux, as the embodiment of the peacemaking task:

> Who could fully recount
> How patient, how sweet and how kind he always was?
> For with his own gentle ways he softened the hearts of the enraged,
> Recalling them from ferocity to peaceful ways.
> Charming in his speech, modest though marvelously dignified,
> He was not abrasive, not cruel, not violent . . .
> Those he saw mourning or sad or suffering
> He succoured with a father's affection.[105]

It is not likely that this early portrait drew even indirectly on the image of Orpheus doing with his song what the abbot did with his speech and his mere presence. But the language dramatically shows the affinities between a clerical ideal and the Orpheus myth. The "Orphic" personality was an embodied reality first, and moved to take on the status of a poetic emblem. This conception of the peace-bringing personality was probably formed in clerical-monastic circles around the Cluny reform,[106] and then appropriated in the cathedral schools with their stress on poetry and classical learning, to describe the music of Orpheus.

Fulbert of Chartres seems to have radiated the effect of soothing tinged with friendship and love implied in *mulcere*. He received a letter from his disciple Hildegar asking that the master correct his student's vice of anger, since Fulbert "emits the sweetest fragrance of mature holiness" through his virtues.[107] We see Fulbert at work in this capacity in his letter to King Robert the Pious restraining his anger against Bishop Odolricus of Orleans.[108]

In Fulbert this clerical obligation connects with engagement in the peace movement. His poem in praise of peace shows how close the conception of a new civilization based on law, moderation and restraint was to goals of the peace movement.[109] It would be surprising if that movement did not call on the image of the soothing, calm-restoring man of peace mollifying the raging of barbarians, but in fact this language is nowhere in evidence in the legislation of peace and truce, though sermons and orations could draw on it.[110]

Archbishop Manasses I of Rheims with his rough warrior ways seems to have brought out this quality in the gentler clergy around him. One observer described him as the raging barbarian tamed by clerical gentleness:

> ... by nature and by [acquired] manners he was more fierce than appropriate, but he [Abbot Thierry of St. Hubert] behaved to him in so laudable a way that he made him his friend ... And so he put aside his harsh ways to a great extent at his admonitions ... and though to many men he was frequently ungentle and truculent, to this man alone ... he was always gentle and placid.[111]

This complex of concerns comes together in Bern of Reichenau's letters to Henry III praising him as peacemaker.[112] In a letter written in 1044 he explained to the king the significance of his royal title:

> The authority of the ancients attests abundantly that those who are now called kings were once called tyrants because of the ferocity of their manners. But as the pursuit of sacred religion increased they were called "kings" from "right rule" [*reges a recte regendo*], since they restrained their bestial impulses and showed themselves rational through the power of judgment. (epist. 26, ed. Schmale, p. 55)

This is a result of clerical instruction of kings since it occurs "as the zeal of religion grows" (*crescente sacrae religionis studio*).[113] It is a significant connection. It indicates the clergy's sense of being engaged in a mission of civilizing the laity that registers in other sources in the eleventh and twelfth centuries.[114] Bern's letters in praise of Henry III as peace-maker show the language of the peace movement and that of instruction in *mores* intersecting.

The obligation to soothe and calm the ruler registers in *Ruodlieb* and here again is significantly connected with goals of the peace movement, possibly with the amnesties of Henry III.[115] The *rex maior* thanks his "kind and gentle" courtier, Ruodlieb, for dispelling his anger:

> . . . "far be it from me that a guest should be troubled
> From whom I was never in any way stirred to anger,
> But rather when angered, he rendered me gentle as a lamb."[116]

"Soothing the anger" of the king was was no minor bit of personal royal psychological counseling, but rather a fundamental way of doing business, accomplishing personal and political goals. Its role is underscored in Gerbert's comment that the ability to soothe is "necessary and of the highest utility to us who are engaged in governing the republic." There is good testimony to Orphic discourse functioning in royal business.[117] In this context it may be that the king's "anger" at its palest is little more than a circumscription for his refusing requests. The language of royal favor or disfavor is a language of the emotions: the king's favor is "love," his disapproval "hate" or "anger."[118]

The task of soothing, pacifying and instructing princes and moving the lay nobility away from barbarity to *mores compositi* registered in tracts on the obligation to shun anger and cultivate clemency. An early example is Wipo's *Tetralogus*. The last two of the four admonishers of the king in this "tetralogue" are the Law and Grace. *Gratia* urges the softening and moderating of the precepts that *Lex* had urged on him:

> After judgment is rendered, let gentle forgiveness follow . . .
> The Law brings hate on the king who savages the guilty;
> Grace urges the king to remain beloved.[119]

In showing mercy, Henry imitates Jove himself, who punishes crimes by forgiveness (*parcendo crimina punit!* cf. 243–44). Wipo cites a consecration formula for the girding on of the king's sword,[120] built on the antithesis of the killing weapon to the preserving mercy of the king:

> Oh enraged king, turn calm through mercy.
> When the law of moderate reason performs its duties,
> It alternates between softening harsh things
> and hardening the gentle in its flames.
> Hence the hard diamond is softened in the soft blood . . .
> And nature commands that sad things change to glad.[121]

This section of the poem is a verse tract on tempering justice with mercy. The eleventh and twelfth centuries produced a fair number of prescriptive writings on the subject.[122]

The Orpheus figure became an emblem for a certain obligation of clergy in their dealings with lords clerical and secular, and this obligation had wide social and political resonance. But is it anything more than an emblem? Did poetry itself actually function in this capacity? The testimony to learned men singing Orphically in real circumstances is scarce, at least I have not found it in abundance.[123] Wipo's *Tetralogus* and "Quid suum virtutis" might qualify as "orphic" poems in the sense we have given the word, also the Würzburg poem, though its main purpose is polemical, and the "mitigating" intent secondary.

Fulcoius of Beauvais, who lived into the first decade of the twelfth century, wrote poetry advocating the cause of Manasses I of Rheims in his conflict with Rome — ironically, since Manasses does not spring to mind as a deserving beneficiary of Orphic song. Fulcoius has much in common with that ideal cleric whose portrait Peter Damian drew (above, p. 140): both were French nobility, lived in Rome, were skilled in law, rhetoric and poetry.[124] Peter Damian died too early to have had Fulcoius in mind, but he certainly would have recognized in him a representative of the species. Fulcoius wrote several verse epistles to Alexander II and Gregory VII seeking reconciliation. When Manasses was excommunicated by Hugh of Die, Fulcoius wrote a conciliatory letter in verse commending the many good qualities of his patron, arguing against the "hatreds" which beset Manasses, and urging him to exercise mercy before justice and lift the excommunication (epist. 3). Fulcoius is at work with his poetry mollifying the anger of Manasses's foes. It is not improbable on this model to imagine gifted and learned men serving the interests of their lords through poetry. It certainly shows us why Peter Damian and others would have regarded poetry in the eleventh century as *utilis*. It also suggests that a study of the role of poetry at the eleventh-century schools would do well to consider the function of poetry in the practice of law itself. It is certain that students and poets conceived of its importance in advocacy, and the epistles of Fulcoius of Beauvais indicate its actual use in that context.

*   *   *

This discussion sets forth the broader social context which drew the Orpheus figure into its orbit and made of the ancient singer the prototypical softener of royal anger. We know that learned clerics felt an obligation to perform this function, and that poetic composition was part and parcel of their education. A man showed his own *mores compositi* by mitigating the anger of lords, bishops, brothers, and if he ornamented his *mores* with poetry (or vice versa in Ulrich of Bamberg's formulation), then he gave testimony to excellent moral training and powerful genius. Peter Damian's portrait of the perfection of a worldly cleric virtually reiterates (though in a satiric mode) the educational ideals of the poem "De nuptiis." The combination of judicial rhetoric, knowledge of the law and poetic composition, was the best the cathedral schools had to offer. This explains the prominence of the Orpheus figure in some of the major "school" poems of the period.

This conception of the role of poetry virtually died out at the schools after the end of the eleventh century. It hangs on as reminiscences.[125] A passage in the fourth homily on the Virgin Mary of Bishop Amadeus of Lausanne (mid-twelfth century) adapts the earlier view of Orpheus to describe creation, conversion and moral training:

> . . . by the sweetness of his wondrous song, [God] created the sons of Abraham from stones, and the trees of the wild forests, that is the hearts of the gentiles, he moved to faith. He also composed the wild beasts morally, that is [man's] fierce impulses and uncultivated barbarity, and thus he trained men educated out of their [mere] human state, to enter the ranks of the gods.[126]

It is fairly clear that this is an Orphic God, though Orpheus is not mentioned. The twelfth century dissolved the Orpheus of the eleventh into religious or psychological allegories,[127] and Orpheus's civilizing mission was absorbed into the broader role of Orpheus/Christ or Orpheus/Reason.

The fate of Orpheus in the twelfth-century schools does not show that the ancient singer has at last reemerged and come into his own. It shows a concept which had firm contours in the eleventh century losing them in the twelfth. In the eleventh-century the Orpheus figure bore a vital educational ideal with broad social and political significance, and maintained this role in competition with Christ and King David.

Strong Poetry: Res valida ingenium
Poetry's humanizing power was in the foreground of the last section. That function and its mythical emblem, Orpheus, had another aspect that developed significantly toward the end of the century and emancipated itself

from the first: its force. Ulrich of Bamberg took poetic skill as a proof of genius:

> What stronger argument or more certain testimony
> Of abundant genius, dearest brother, than when
> A poet can soothe ears and minds gracefully?
> ("Bamberger ars dictaminis," ll. 34–36)

The poet of "Quid suum virtutis" made the Orpheus story illustrate "the noble acumen of the mind" (1025) and art's ability to overcome nature (1023). His Orpheus found in the strength of the "conciliating lyre" the courage to return a second time to hell and the conviction that his genius would sweep all barriers before it: "His skilled genius promises a positive outcome" ("Sollers effectum nec negat ingenium" — 1018).

The poetic culture of the eleventh century envisioned poetry engaged in grand moral enterprises: "Scale the ladder of art wherever arduous virtue summons you!" exclaimed the poet of "Quid suum virtutis" (line 1033). Art civilizes the individual and the society, and in this way overcomes nature. Nature is brutish and contentious. It is not that morally organized place the twelfth century found in it, a model for man's mind and character, but rather a place much like hell, where the feudal nobles rob, rape and pillage. It is also the condition in which human beings enter the world, a condition that could be greatly improved by study.

But the conquest of nature calls for strong minds and hard study. Sigebert of Gembloux's St. Victor looks back on a long life spent in the pursuit of knowledge, and summarizes the accomplishments of his generation:

> All that happens in the world in so great a variety
> Either study recovers or the gradual passing of time reveals . . .
> Our penetrating mind has increased the totality of nature.
> Just as the frequent exercise of study has extracted many sharpenable
> Mountain stones from the veins of nature,
> So also it has hammered out and fashioned many arts
> As from the mountain marble.[128]

And Sigebert himself sets to work on his poem with the conviction that his obligation is greater than the mass of men who praise God, "since mind and reason render us god-like."[129]

The idea of art overcoming nature and the gods implies an aesthetic. The brilliant blossoming of poetry at Rheims and in the Loire valley at the end of the century realized the aesthetic possibilities of strong poetry, but also tended to move art away from its humanizing mission.

The "Liège Song" on Orpheus in the underworld articulates this strange faith in poetry's power. It significantly removed from the Orpheus story its two functions of fulfilling learning and embodying virtue. The theme of the poem is stated in its proem-like first lines:

> All things that grow will perish and whither after maturity,
> Bronze and gold moulder, only poems remain.[130]

The taming and softening effects of Orphic poetry are still a prominent concern. But on the periphery is the theme of poetry itself and its power. Orpheus's visit to hell was a confrontation, and he was the victor: "Facing the gods, Orpheus conquered them with his song" ("Orpheus ante deos, carmine vicit eos" — 10). This emerging theme alone makes the proem intelligible. It makes the Orpheus story into a symbol of the power and permanence of art, a message it had not conveyed earlier in the century. A new conception is representing itself in the imagery of the old.

Godfrey of Rheims is beyond an obligation to the school tradition. In his dialogue with Calliope he composes an episode of Orpheus from which any trace of compassion and civilizing is absent. It is a display piece pure and simple, its sole purpose to show what power Calliope has.[131] Godfrey's poem to Odo of Orleans evokes Amphion as the proper aid to Odo: "The stones obeyed his lyre when called."[132] The formulation is significant: it is not the *lyra concilians* and *permulcens*, but the commanding lyre. In Godfrey's poem to Enguerrand of Coucy the poet finds the idiom appropriate to his conception of poetry. He sets it against physical force:

> A powerful thing is genius and stronger than the sharp sword.
> The eloquent tongue cuts through the armed duke.[133]

Enguerrand's poetry assured his fame, says the poet. If nature had given him only this one gift, or if it took back all the wealth it had lavished on him, his name would live on in his song, which gives him a kind of magical force over other human beings:

In song if you wish to raise the powerful to the heavens,
In song you can raise whomever you like to the heavens.
In song if you wish to make your friend famous,
In song your friend will become famous.
In song if you wish to do damage to your enemies,
Then your enemy will be damaged in song.[134]

These lines with their tedious anaphoras can characterize Godfrey's magical-utilitarian conception of strong poetry. His verses are glib, overladen, and flat. It is a style consistent with a self-indulgent and self-seeking strain in his thinking. He would seem to be an appropriate courtier for Archbishop Manasses of Rheims, to whom Guibert of Nogent ascribed the quip, "The archbishopric of Rheims would be a pleasant thing if it did not oblige one to be singing masses constantly."[135] The idea that Enguerrand would do quite well if he lost his other qualities and retained his poetry cancels the close bond between poetry and virtue on which Orphic song was based.

A magical, miraculous view of poetry is built into the Orpheus story: he uproots trees and turns rivers back in their courses, he revives — or partially revives — the dead. The style of poetry in the eleventh century developed as if to convey this view. The mannerism of eleventh-century poetry[136] expresses an aesthetic that sets art above nature. The elaborate flourishes, the heavy ornamentation, the slavish regularity of grammar and metrics that overrides any obligation to clarity, and the affected obscurity that seems to offer entry into "the hidden nature of things" (*abdita rerum*): these instruments of virtuosity were the visible, audible testimony to "powerful genius." They show the poet as wizard and word-master exercising magical control over language. The age's love of catalogues; the long lists of trees, birds and animals in "Quid suum virtutis"; the ability to marshal and arrange many things with strange names in metrical orders show the magician's domination of nature. Poets who see their art as superior to nature need the effects that will demonstrate it, and what is above nature is unnatural. "Outdoing the gods and nature" translated stylistically into writing more obscurely than Martianus Capella.

The naively exuberant conviction of genius's power was symptomatic of intellectual energy and optimism, not of decadence, and if it produced much obscure and futile verse-making, it also produced some of the best poetry from the Middle Ages. The work of Hildebert of Lavardin is the high point of eleventh-century poetry. He shares its optimism about poetry and education, but he escapes its excesses. The climactic lines from his Rome poem, "Par tibi, Roma, nihil," are an expression of the received view that art can outbid the gods and overcome nature[137]:

> Human skill could construct a Rome so great
> That the skill of the gods could not destroy it.
> Here the gods themselves look astonished on their carved forms,
> And wish they were the equal of these sculpted faces.
> Nature could not create gods as miraculous
> As the images of the gods that man created.
> Faces improve these gods, and they are better worshipped
> For the sculptor's accomplishment than for their divinity.

The handwork of Nature — gods — is compared with the art of man, to the advantage of man; the gods are not as beautiful or sacred as their statues. In this way human art conquers nature and outbids the gods. The statement is close to the summation of the Orpheus story in "Quid suum virtutis": "Thus art conquered nature with the mediation of diligent study" ("Sic ars naturam vicit, studio mediante." But Hildebert's lines show only the superiority of human art, not that "all things yield to Lady Virtue."[138] The passage just quoted implies an aesthetics released from its subordination to ethics.

The idea of a competition between art and nature, at least between art and the reality it represents, takes an interesting turn in the poetry of Marbod of Rennes. Marbod shares with the eleventh-century schools a high vision of the power of poetry, but its relation to nature shifts notably.[139] His poem "De molesta recreatione," "Troubled Recreation," represents a real event: a young harpist plays to Marbod in the evening to drive away his cares. But his song is of the death of a knight and the lament of his beloved over her lover's dead body. The sweetness of the song and the power of the narration evoke the fictive event with such immediacy and such a strong illusion of reality, that Marbod's mood darkens and his "recreation" is troubled.[140]

Gone are the mythological subject matter, the excesses of style, the obscurity. The word order is nearly that of prose, the hexameter is fitted to the words in rhythms nearly as natural as speech. The internal rhymes of the Leonine form are a feature of external ornamentation that Marbod shares with early poetry, but the clear diction comes like a fresh new wind.

The poem is about Marbod's reception of a song sung to entertain him. The subject is not important. We do not know the identity of the girl or the knight; they are not Priam and Hecuba or Hector and Andromache.[141] He is simply *quidam miles*, some knight. The poem is not about its fable; it is about the song that transmits the fable, about poetry; it reflects on its nature and its effect. It creates a doubled stage: on one the performance and on the other the story performed can be observed.

The harpist's song is of the surpassing and outbidding kind the school poets strove for. In its sweet melody, it surpasses the heavens for subtlety: "Cuius dulce melos transcendit acumine celos" (l. 5). The competition between art and nature likewise is played out, with a slightly different result: art does not overcome nature; it creates a second nature. The harpist's song appears to become reality: "quasi res non cantio fiat" (l. 22). It is a powerful illusion, a cheating of the senses. The artificially produced sounds take the quality of the described experience: "I seem myself to suffer everything I hear from the harpist" ("Meque pati credo, quicquid sonat a citharedo" — l. 27). This effect comes from the artist's skilful imitation of reality: "as he plays, the intertwining of lute and voice imitates remarkably the girl's embraces" ("Dum citharizatur, plus quam satis imitatur / Virginis amplexus fidium vocisque reflexus" — ll. 24–25).

Bond connects this poem with Marbod's programmatic statement in the epilogue of his *De ornamentis verborum*:

> If you wish to compose, hold to the natures of things as the mirror and the poet's model and exemplar, as does the student of painting. . . . Nature is where art begins, Reason summons it [to nature], and it strives to maintain the form of its true origin. (PL 171, 1692C–D)

Marbod's poem still represents a lyric of magical transformation, based on a conception of divinely empowered poetry. But the poetry is not dark magical mumblings, and the magic does not produce supernatural events: the rivers continue to flow downstream, and the laws of Pluto remain in full force, since the dead are not even partially revived. Neither the knight's lady nor the singer who sings her lament is an Orpheus.[142] The strength of poetry is now measured by its ability to be or to seem reality (*imitatio, quasi res non cantio*), to maintain, as Marbod put it, the first and true principle of art. This skill is now credited with a kind of divinity, or something more than divinity.[143] That means that poetry now transcends nature by making words seem to be things.

In this sense (as in others) the eleventh and twelfth centuries meet in Marbod of Rennes. He and Hildebert appear as poets significantly located at the turn of the century. They were "naturalists," but they could still close their eyes to a cold and disenchanting empiricism to the extent of confiding to language the task of conveying reality.[144] They no longer believed that words really restored the dead, but words could seem to make fictions come to life, and so retained the significant illusion of magical revival and transformation. Marbod and Hildebert banish a crude Realism from the practice of poetry, and in this regard have a role in poetics comparable to that of Hildebert's friend and teacher, Berengar of Tours, in theology. Just as Berengar forced symbolic presence to the center of a discussion of the eucharist and dislodged the accepted belief in a real presence, so also the transforming power of poetry shifted under the influence of poets like Marbod and Hildebert from governing to imitating reality. In this sense the Loire poets retain a muted, aestheticized version of the earlier Orphic poetic optimism in their new poetry.

The idea that words are adequate to things always has a nourishing effect on eloquence. Viewed from within a post-structuralist critical atmosphere, the idea seems like a child's dream and a fairy tale world of magic, an abandoned and unrecoverable stage on the ladder of human cognitive development. It seemed every bit as whimsical to the generation following Abelard, whose intellectual mission involved dismantling the eleventh century's world view and in particular the equation of words and things.

Gerald Bond has shown how this turn toward a poetics oriented to nature brings poetry into line with the intellectual trends in the earlier twelfth century. He makes the connection between Marbod's "reading" natural meanings from stones and herbs and his orientation to nature as the criterion of poetry. What we learn from looking back to the eleventh century is what is lost through the advent of the new naturalism. The modern reader can be grateful for the loss of much bombast. But that heavy ballast was the outward expression of a magical Orphic view of the world, in which obscure, pretentious, slightly pagan poetry had a critical role to play. It does not register well now, but neither would the mutterings of a Delphic prophet sung to a reconstructed melody. The effect depends on a world view utterly foreign to us.

The Quadrivium

Music and "physics" were the main loci of ethics in the quadrivium. Astronomy and mathematics as ethical disciplines assimilated to the study of created nature. The moral aspect of mathematics overflowed all boundaries in numerical symbolism. It was a subject to which abundant moral meanings and a lavish hermeneutic practice attached, but no discipline. Music is the art in which mathematical concepts contribute to notions of human perfection. In music proportion and harmony emerge as ethical ideals capable of realization through disipline. For our purposes it is possible to collapse the quadrivium into two subjects, music and physics or cosmology.

MUSIC

Music had a central role in Greek education. Hellenic philosophy situated music within paideia as the means of attuning the body to the soul in accordance with the laws governing the harmonious motion of the cosmos.[145] Mind and body can be "moulded and modulated by music to a pattern of graceful bearing."[146] The relation of body to soul has a significant parallel in the relation of musical instrument to harmony (e.g., Plato, *Phaedo*, 86). Cicero passed this notion to the Middle Ages in the *Tusculan Disputations*:

> Aristoxenus, musician as well as philosopher, held the soul to be a special tuning of the body, like that which in instrumental or vocal music is called harmony. In the same way, the various motions of the body through its nature and its form are said to sing like the sounds produced in vocal music.[147]

The major transmitter of Hellenic musical theory to the Middle Ages was Boethius in his *De institutione musica*. The prologue to this work presented music as a force that ennobles or corrupts human conduct.[148] It is not only a subject for speculation and performance, but also a means of moral instruction (*moralitati coniuncta* — 1.1, ed. Friedlein, p. 179, l. 23). He cites Platonic ideas on music's educating role: music is an important means of maintaining the republic, since the introduction of "lascivious" modes brings about the corruption of morals — p. 180, ll. 22ff.); children are to be instructed in the modes that are "vigorous and simple"; the purity of the mode is to be rigorously maintained, since the slightest changes sink into the soul. "Music of the highest moral character and modestly composed" is a safeguard of the state's welfare as long as it is "temperate, simple and masculine, rather than effeminate, violent or fickle" (ed. Friedlein, p. 181; trans. Bower, p. 4). He gives examples and anecdotes of music inculcating moderation and virtue and calming anger. Its effectiveness in calming and moderating action is rooted in the relation of body to soul; they are joined by musical harmonies.[149]

Boethius divided music into three classifications: *musica mundana*, *musica humana* and *musica instrumentalis* (1.2, 1171Df.). The scheme became standard in the Middle Ages. The music of the world is cosmic music, the music of the spheres. It is inseparable from "human music"; the two are related as macrocosm to microcosm[150]:

> The soul of the universe was joined together according to musical concord . . . when we hear what is properly and harmoniously united in sound in conjunction with that which is harmoniously coupled and joined together within us — and are attracted to it, then we recognize that we ourselves are put together in its likeness. (trans. Bower, p. 2)

Musica humana is the force which unites the parts of the soul to each other and the soul to the body. Harmony effects this joining. This is the "tuning" (*temperatio* — p. 188, l. 30) of body and soul. Boethius promised to elaborate on this subject later in his treatise, but never got back to it.

The musical ideas of Greek paideia survived in a diminished form in the Middle Ages.[151] *Musica humana* was in part assimilated to instrumental music as the particular form produced by the human voice,[152] and that assimilation tended to weaken the notion of music as an ethical force.

Music as an element in the cultivation of virtue emerges clearly in the eleventh century. Bern of Reichenau wrote a letter to Archbishop Pilgrim of Cologne sometime between 1021 and 1036. It was a dedication of his *Tonarius*, which he wrote at the request of the archbishop. In the letter he praises the prelate in terms that indicate a vocabulary of musical ethics and a clearly formed conception of *musica humana*. The *honestas* of moral discipline, so runs the opening of the letter, has composed the "natural motions" of Pilgrim's soul to such an extent that he is progressing rationally to supernal things, which in the present context refers to his request for a work on music. This disciplining is evident in the "splendid forms of the Christian faith" he displays, which show his soul to be a seat of wisdom: "You, whom not only knowledge of the four disciplines of mathematics, renders foursquare, but also the melody of celestial harmony renders vigorously tuned [*caelestis armoniae melos . . . reddit intentum*] with divine praises, you now command me who have only half a voice, who am nearly mute and tongueless in the arts." Bern finds the archbishop's interest in music fully logical and consistent with his character: "your soul delights more sweetly in the sweetness of this art, since the entire connection of our body and soul is joined by a musical coaptation with nature instigating."[153] These lines give a portrait of a "composed" man. Of course the occasion, the sending of a tract on music, encouraged praise of the patron in musical terms, but the sender could not have formulated it as he did without a sophisticated command of conceptions of *musica humana* that go beyond what was available to him in Boethius' tract on music. He understands the principle of grace and outward piety as a musical "tuning" of the soul, and he understands the principle of the music of the spheres providing the model for "human music."

Likewise the author of "Quid suum virtutis," writing, according to the most recent editor, at most one decade later than Bern of Reichenau, is familiar with these concepts. In the passage on Orpheus's music referred to earlier, he represents the power of harmony as a reconciler of differences. It is the force that knits "the same and the different," the basic consituent forces of the soul and the universe in Plato's *Timaeus*. The world soul unites the universe by the law of number, and this same law joins the greater to the lesser world, the macrocosm to the microcosm (cf. ed. Paravicini, ll. 749–64). Within the smaller world, man, music joins the body to the soul, establishes the bond between man and universe, ornaments *mores*, and relieves the pain of the limbs (764). A few lines later, the poet observes the effects of music on the "motions of the soul," and derives from those effects man's basically harmonious, musical nature:

> Since the musical temper now softens, now makes harsh, now pacifies the mind's emotions, it is more certain than certain that it is man's nature to be aptly conjoined by the tempering of number.[154]

These Platonic-Boethian ideas are not new by the time Baudri of Bourgueil takes them up at the end of the century. They have been in the air for some decades. Baudri uses them in his description of the bedchamber of Countess Adela of Blois.[155] The headboard and ivory feet of the bed represent an allegory of Philosophy and the seven liberal arts.[156] Music is located next to Philosophy herself. She "sits at her right hand" (l. 975) or at her feet: "Philosophy had made her second only to herself and commanded her always to be present at her feet. This is because she is the force which holds the other sisters in harmony with each other."[157] The stress in Baudri's allegory is decidedly on the ethical aspects of music, that is, on *musica humana*, though he touches briefly on the other Boethian types. Music has the power to "charm humans with such sweetness that it can recreate the human soul itself. The human condition, the vigor and rhythm [*modulatio*] of life is governed by a certain harmony, I know not which, and it seems to arise from the form of a square." After a few lines on the perfection of the number four he continues, connecting the four elements with the power of music: "And thus the vivifying power corresponds to these four, so that by an equal measure it may give vigor to all things." There is some bonding force in the tetragon, he says, that strengthens it. This force is "the construct of harmony as a visible image" [*harmonie typicalis compotus*]. Together with the celestial rhythms, it governs our bodies.[158]

Baudri's *musica humana* is a force that invigorates and gives order to life. It recreates the soul and governs the body. It is also worth noting that for Baudri music is the liberal art closest to philosophy itself. It performs by itself that integrating function that each of the other disciplines aims at in a limited way. For Baudri music governs the inner and outer conduct of man. In another poem he takes the musical instrument as a metaphor of the harmoniously governed life. The well-modulated life is one lived in a single mode, and this is the way that God "harmonizes our manners and our bodies, so that the mystical symphony of our life will be pleasing."[159] This impressive phrase encapsulates the equation of musical harmony with the governed life.

Bernard of Chartres presents music as part of a discipline of *mores*. In his glosses on *Timaeus* he explains why the creator bestowed hearing on newly created man. Hearing is important, because it serves to correct manners and behavior (*ad correctionem morum*):

> Upon hearing the harmonies of music, we ought to be reformed in our conduct [*mores*] according to the harmony of virtues. For although the soul is constructed according to consonances, yet those consonances turn dissonant when joined to the body, and they must be reformed outwardly through music. And this means: music as a whole is given to man not for his delight but for the composition of his manners.[160]

Rhythm has a similar purpose:

> ... not only musical consonances are valuable for the composition of manners, but also rhythm. Rhythm is an equal number of syllables and, in accord with its equality, a similar equality is to be established in our manners.[161]

Earlier in the work, talking about the two-fold character of the governor of the republic, he makes some striking comments on music's role. Governors of the state need to be both gentle and fierce, and this brings him to the subject of the ruler's education:

The country's wardens are to be educated in such a way that they will be eager for labor and hardships and affable to their obedient subjects. This eagerness is cultivated through exercise, such as running, hunting and gymnastic games. Their gentleness and affability will be cultivated by the solace of music, which through the harmony of its tones teaches harmony of conduct.[162]

In Honorius Augustodunensis's pilgrimage through the liberal arts the fifth city is music. Here the pilgrims learn "to pass by the modulation of manners to the harmony of the heavens."[163]

Hugh of St. Victor articulates Boethius's three kinds of music in his *Didascalicon* and makes some interesting comments on *musica humana*. There are three kinds of "human music": one in the body, one in the soul, and one in the connection of the two. The kind in the body is a regulating force. It governs the balance of the four humors, and it checks the operations of the body, holding them within the bounds of moderation, "which is especially suited to rational creatures." The music of the soul is in the four virtues and the powers of the soul, reason, anger, desire, and so forth. His last category is worth quoting:

The music between the body and the soul is that natural friendship by which the soul is tied to the body, not by physical chains, but by affections of a kind, whose purpose is to give motion and sensation to the body.[164]

We have already noticed the passage in Amadeus of Lausanne where the music of an Orphic God is said to "compose morally the fierce impulses and the rude barbarism" of men and introduce them into the number of the gods.[165]

Adelard of Bath's treatment of "human music" moves the subject toward the discourse of natural science, without weakening the idea of music's educating force. He pushes aside the legend of Amphion and Orpheus building buildings and moving forests with song and argues that such fables are not necessary to confirm the power of music: it calms the soul and disposes it to *pietas*. The ethical force of music asserts itself most strongly in old age, when the hearer is not content with mere concord of voices but calls for a corresponding music of conduct: "[the hearer] rejoices and strives to bring manners [*mores*] and all acts into ethical consonance." Music can move all ages from avarice to generosity and from sickness to health. Therefore it is no minor subject for philosophers. It seems to confirm the conviction of the ancients that the soul descended from higher stars into the body, and that, once placed in a body, it still recognizes the "symphony" which it had heard in its celestial homeland. Adelard also understands the coordination of world soul and individual soul through the medium of music. Harmony and congruence of parts are qualities that the world soul perceives as the highest and most dignified in creatures, and so it strives to infuse this quality into bodies and so harmonize their parts.[166]

The texts cited until now show us something we have not observed in following the alliance between *mores* and the other liberal arts: a strong and consistent tradition of *musica humana* from the eleventh through the twelfth century. Different writers emphasize different aspects of the music of body and soul. But the concept itself as received from Boethius retains firm contours and does not detach from ethics. This continues beyond the twelfth century, and is enriched from the early thirteenth century on by vernacular courtly literature, didactic, and epic.

Gottfried von Strassburg gives an extensive picture of an education in the arts and in manners in the scenes in which Tristan tutors the young princess Isolde.[167] This passage deserves a prominent place in the history of medieval education, and since it posits music as the culmination of learning, it can serve both to summarize and to conclude this chapter. The princess, already having received rudimentary instruction in foreign languages, music and composition, learns various kinds of disciplines from her tutor Tristan, But she devotes most of her attention to the one called *moraliteit*:

> under aller dirre lere
> gab er ir eine unmüezekeit,
> die heizen wir moraliteit.
> diu kunst diu leret schoene site. (8002–5)

Amidst all these forms of learning he included a discipline which we call *moralitas*. This is the art which teaches beauty of manners.

All women, the passage continues, should occupy themselves with this "sweet discipline" from youth on. It teaches them to please God and the world, and without it they will attain neither wealth nor honor. The results of this instruction for Isold:

> hie von so wart si wol gesite,
> schone unde reine gemuot,
> ir gebaerde süeze unde guot. (8024–26)

From this instruction she became well-mannered, of a beautiful and pure temperament, her gestures charming and pleasing.

In the six months of her instruction she improved her "learning and comportment" (*lere unde gebare*) to such an extent that the fame of her talents spread throughout the land. When guests come to court she entertains them with her arts: she sings, writes and reads.

As the culmination of this education, she performs her music before the Irish court at Dublin. Her effect on the audience is stunning, "as often happens when one sees such a miraculous combination of beauty and talent as Isold enjoyed" (ll. 8081–84). The song she sang was two-fold, the poet says, the one song secret, the other public.[168] The open and public song was the audible music produced by instrument and voice. The "secret song" was her marvelous beauty. Her physical presence is an inaudible song, whose instrument is her body. Her aura with all the grace, harmony, and self-control acquired in the discipline of *moraliteit*, comprises a "spiritual song" or "mind song" (*muotgedoene*). Audible and visible songs are parallel compositions, the one is performed music, the other is lived and embodied music.

The passage is one of the most sublime statements of the human presence as a work of art from the Middle Ages and beyond. Gottfried clearly had a conception of the educated, disciplined and restrained physical presence as a kind of music.[169] It is a counterpart to Cicero's idea that music "tunes" the body and makes its motions "sing" a kind of silent music. The virtuosity of conception is in the play on the two types of music, instrumental and human. Isolde is beautiful not only for the music she plays, but for the music she *is*. It is like Baudri's formulation, "the mystical symphony of our conduct." But in the case of *Tristan*, it occurs embodied in a human being, and that rescues the conception from the abstractness of Baudri's and Bernard of Chartres's formulations.

There follows a final summary of the results of her studies with Tristan: it gave her "sweetness of mind" (*suoze gemuot*), lent charm to her manner and her bearing. She mastered all kinds of courtly games and pastimes, she could compose letters[170] and songs (cf. 8132–41).

This description is a vivid picture of a court education close to the old learning. It combines letters with manners and culminates in music charged with an ethical—aesthetic aspect. Furthermore, it is clear that Gottfried masters the language and concepts of *cultus virtutum*. Many of his terms and his turns of thought translate readily into that vocabulary: *moraliteit* corresponds to *moralitas*; it teaches *schoene site*, that is *morum venustas, morum elegantia. Lere unde gebare*, which Gottfried also varies as *rede unde gebare*, comes close to *litterae et mores*. The princess receives from the discipline of *moraliteit* beauty of mind or temperament (*schône gemuot, süeze gemuot*; cf. *decor animi, compositio morum*), and both references to this "well-tempered" quality are followed by the statement that her manners and her comportment, her gestures and bearing were pleasing and charming. The implication is that her pleasant gestures are a result of her spiritual beauty; elegant bearing expresses inner composure. And at its most sophisticated the passage shows the author's mastery of a conception of the ethical force of music. In this case there is no suggestion that the music rendered Isolde beautiful, graceful and so forth (though nothing prevents us from inferring it from the parallel of performed and embodied music). But it is evident that he has a conception of an aesthetic of the human presence describable in terms appropriate to the aesthetic of music and cultivated through training in *moraliteit*.

What we observed first as an ethical ideal taught to aspiring worldly clerics at cathedral schools recurs here as an education in courtliness aimed at princesses and other noble ladies. That education has shed all its religious trappings in this passage and shows the educational goal — refinement of mind and manners — as a means to wealth, honor, and reputation at court, as a prerequisite to administrative skills (writing letters and reading) and court entertainments (games, music, composing).

This idea of the ethics of music does not die out, in contrast to the ethical aspects of the other arts. It would be possible to trace it into the thirteenth century and beyond,[171] but that would take us beyond the scope of this study.

*   *   *

The idea of the human body, its motions and its action, as an expression of inaudible musical proportions, was in the air in the eleventh and twelfth centuries. It provided a scheme of description of the ideally educated, composed and ordered human being. The translation of the Platonic — Boethian idea into practical pedagogy is not as much in evidence as are, say, the ethics of rhetoric and poetry. But all the humanist sources on music cited testify to a widespread conviction of music's ethical force.

COSMOLOGY
The connection of ethics and cosmology is ancient and primitive. In its earliest phase it will have had close ties to astrology. The Middle Ages had it

most directly from Stoic philosophy. The connection is founded on the idea, *natura optima vivendi dux*, Nature is the guide to human actions. A benevolent and providential God has fashioned the world in such a well ordered plan that it provides a pattern of order and harmony for men. Life according to nature leads to the ideal states of *apatheia* or *euthymia*, spiritual peace and well-being. The ultimate goal is *eudaimonia*, the condition of the soul when it resembles God. The means to this end is virtue. The pursuit of virtue proceeds along two main paths: physics and ethics.[172]

For the Stoics the natural law was the primal law inherent in the cosmic order. This was prior to any human legislation. They saw the introduction by men of "positive" or "civil law" as a corruption of the original natural law. These notions made the study of nature and the cosmic order into an ethical obligation. If the chief good of man is life according to nature, then man must have a clear knowledge of nature and of his place in it.

The idea looms large for Cicero, whose philosophical works were the main conduit of Stoicism to the Middle Ages. In *De legibus* he argues that the natural law dominates all moral conduct. The highest goal of man seeking that path is "to follow nature and to live in accord with its law."[173] All particular laws are ultimately rooted in cosmic relationships. Cicero formulated the pithy phrase, "Nature is the best guide to conduct" ("natura optima vivendi dux"—*De amicitia*, 5.19). John of Salisbury is fond of quoting it.[174] The pursuit of nature is for Cicero an important obligation of the statesman. In the *Tusculan Disputations* he traces the route by which public life leads distinguished men to philosophy, then to astronomy, thence to the search for the causes and origins of things, and ultimately to the good life (*Tusc. disp.*, 5.24–25, 68–72).

These ideas are preserved for the Middle Ages in some of the major sources of Neoplatonic thought, which made a comfortable accommodation with Stoic ethics. In the *Consolation of Philosophy* Boethius thanked Lady Philosophy for forming his *mores* in accordance with the celestial order and the movement of the planets: "I searched the secrets of nature with you, when you described to me the course of the stars . . . when you fashioned my *mores* and the manner of my whole life according to the pattern of the celestial order."[175] If the planetary movements are seen as a pattern for man's morals, then the study of astronomy is an object of ethics. Astronomy can form or reform man's character.

For Macrobius the search for the originating causes of virtue and the good life takes the creation of the world as its point of departure. He presents the virtues as rooted ultimately in the mind of God, but having their first embodiment in the planets and their motions. The Good proceeds in progressive emanations from God to cosmic virtue to human virtue, and the study of the former is requisite to the cultivation of the latter. As authority he cites the maxim of Juvenal, also widely quoted in the Middle Ages, "From the sky has come to us the saying, 'Know yourself.'"[176]

It is entirely consistent with this direction of thought that the obligation to self-knowledge come from the heavens. That is the place of origin of the virtues, and their counterparts in the human soul are heaven-seeking qualities, which lift up the souls of the dead into the skies. It was the common coin of Neo-platonist thought that the soul underwent a kind of education during its descent through the heavens toward its destination in an earthly body, taking on the qualities of the heavenly spheres it passed on the way. The idea was passed on to the Middle Ages in Macrobius's commentary on the Dream of Scipio, and in the Hermetic Asclepius. It was to loom large in Bernard Silvester's *Cosmographia*[177] and Alan of Lille's *Anticlaudianus*.

The work which recorded most clearly the pattern of the natural law was Plato's cosmological work, *Timaeus*.[178] The laws of cosmic creation are also the laws of man's harmonious functioning. Therefore the *Timaeus* was regarded as a work of ethics. It was avidly studied in our period. Gunzo of Novara brought a copy of the work with him from Italy to Germany.

The manuscript tradition of the *Timaeus* speaks clearly on its distribution.[179] It virtually begins for the Middle Ages in the eleventh century. From the period 850–900 one manuscript has survived; from 900–950, two; from 950–1000, four. The first half of the eleventh century suddenly produces fifteen manuscripts, most of them from Germany; the second half fourteen, also largely from Germany.

It would be a mistake to form our judgment of the reception of the *Timaeus* in the eleventh century from the "scientific" literature, glosses and commentaries. If we did we would judge the level of understanding puerile, and the comparative wealth of manuscripts would suggest that the Carolingian commentators had used less material to better effect. The commentaries and glosses on both Boethius's *Consolation* and the *Timaeus* are lifeless and derivative. Certainly it is in the nature of glosses that they do not pulse with life and alluring models for *mores*. But one wonders what intellectual stimulation of any kind can be gotten from their sterile logic and the pitter-patter of their syllogisms. Here is an eleventh-century *Timaeus* gloss proving that the world was created:

> Let us pose the question whether the world was made. Everything corporeal is visible. Everything visible is sensible. But everything sensible was made. Ergo the world was made, insofar as it is corporeal.[180]

But again, as in music, so in cosmology, the "scientific" literature shows no particular interest in ethics, and we look to letters and poems for the best evidence for the joining of cosmology and ethics. These sources show the *Timaeus*, the *Tusculan Disputations*, and the *Consolation of Philosophy* providing patterns for the structure and purpose of studies and a poetic-cosmological language for describing the well-educated and well-formed human being.

The poem "Quid suum virtutis" called on Timaean concepts to describe the musical composition of man (749–64, see above, p. 146): the power of music "reconciles dissonant things in a unified node"; it "knits the world soul from same things and different by the fixed law of number"; the same law of number "joins the nature of the greater to that of the lesser world by a moderating act." The poet was a learned Platonist, who could combine Boethian ideas on music with Timaean cosmology to conceptualize the harmonious construction of the human being.

The *Regensburg Letters* show us Ciceronian ethical-cosmological ideas adapted and understood. They place this complex of ideas in the context of court service during the investiture controversy. The narrative voice in the following passage is that of a man caught up in the busy duties of worldly administration. When he considers the state of the world—simony, court intrigues, false friendships, the dangers of imperial service—he decides to turn to the life of philosophy and studies:

> The world being what it is . . . I began to investigate the three-fold power of the wise man's mind. One of these powers seeks to attain knowledge of things and the explanation of nature; the second, to demonstrate which things in life are to be sought and which are to be shunned; the third, to judge what is suitable and what unsuitable for each and every man. . . . What part of worldly studies could be more delightful, more ingenious, more excellent, than to investigate the motions and revolutions of the entire firmament, to observe the innumerable stars studding the heavens, to be in harmony with that heavenly course. . . . My mind, exercising itself in meditations of this kind, overcame the present age and outstripped many times over the nature of those men whose god is the stomach, who in a bestial way rob the mind of its due, which is the exercise of reason, altogether refusing to exert themselves in the pursuit of virtue.[181]

The passage places the study of astronomy in the service of the pursuit of virtues, and represents the courses of the planets as the pattern for human harmony. But it is doubly useful for showing both these forms of "study" in the context of administrative service. The troubled administrator looks to the heavens to find the lost pattern of earthly, human harmony. His "studies" elevate him above the mass of men who live without such a law. This vision of cosmology in politics is directly adapted from Cicero's *Tusculan Disputations* (see Fickermann's detailed identification of quotations), but the adaptation is genuine. The writer would not have looked to the heavens for an end to human disorder unless he understood the ethical basis of the cosmos.

Marbod of Rennes composed a remarkable poem on the beauties of the springtime, in which the vision of a graceful and beautifully ordered nature provides him the model for his own mind:

> Spring's grace forbids me to practice bestial manners.
> I get my mind's model from the elements.[182]

Gerald Bond's studies of Marbod and the Loire circle of poets and scholars show the discovery of a nature that relates to the human being and no longer strictly to some metaphysical reality, as the bestiaries do ("Natural Poetics," pp. 27–28). The lines just quoted show us a poet looking at nature itself, not following some Ciceronian model of investigating the heavens. The feeling toward nature in Marbod's poem is a kind of reverse romanticism. Nature is not a projection of the inner world of the poet, but rather man is the projection of nature. He remakes himself in the image of nature's order and virtue.

The actual nature of *Timaeus* studies in the eleventh century is simply not known. There are many indications of intense interest in the subject but few indications of the results of its study. The discrepancy suggests that at present we do not know what was going on.[183] By the end of the eleventh century the preoccupation with Plato's work was so intense that it provoked a polemic from Manegold of Lautenbach, his treatise against Wolfhelm of Brauweiler.[184] He attacks opinions and interpretations of German *philosophi*, not just of Wolfhelm. Some of these opinions turn up a few decades later in works of Peter Abelard.[185] The thrust of the teaching Manegold opposes is that the *Timaeus* is reconcilable with Christian doctrine. This is of course a favorite idea of the "school of Chartres." It provides the basis of Thierry of Chartres' Hexameron commentary.[186] And the more general problem of reconciling the ancient philosophers with Christian doctrine is the basic focus of Abelard's *Theologia Christiana*. Manegold's concern is that the study of the Platonic work tends to release itself from the realm of morality and reach over into theology, and so to claim a kind of scientific, ontological truth for its view of creation and the universe. Manegold concedes the value of the *Timaeus* in "moral judgments aside from questions of faith." The *Timaeus* is legitimately used in the pursuit of virtues appropriate to the "rectors of the church and governors of the divine republic."[187] Such a comment — the *Timaeus* is to teach morals to church and state administrators — makes no sense unless we assume a thorough integration of cosmology and ethics in the schools of those philosophers studying the work. Given the program of cathedral schools of teaching manners and letters to future "rectors of the church and governors of the republic," it makes sense.

Manegold's polemic is located at the watershed between the old and the new learning, between a moralizing and a scientific orientation to the study of nature. It is just beyond this stage where we encounter the study of the creation of the world in the commentaries of the "school of Chartres." William of Conches begins his glosses on the *Timaeus* by regretting that the many past commentators have paid too much attention to *sententia* and too little to *littera*. He wants to shift the emphasis from the moral sense of the creation myth — its sententiousness — to the literal level, from ethics to physics.[188] Also Thierry of Chartres promises to comment on the literal, historical and "physical" sense of Genesis in his Hexameron commentary and to completely bypass the well-known moral and allegorical readings.[189] Cosmology is shedding its ethical aspects and moving in the direction of natural science.

But some of the major works of twelfth-century cosmological speculation still show distinct signs of the conviction that nature provides the pattern for human *mores*. Hugh of St. Victor gave terse expression to the connection:

> . . . in the meaning of things lies natural justice, out of which the discipline of our own conduct [*mores*] arises. By contemplating what God has made we realize what we ourselves ought to do. Every nature tells of God; every nature teaches man.[190]

"Natural justice" is the core of the *Timaeus*'s teachings for the early twelfth century. William of Conches designates this as the purpose of Plato's work, and comments that natural law is a subject best approached via the creation of the world. Plato's concern about justice in the Republic brought him to cosmology, not vice versa:

> Hence the subject of this book is natural justice, or the creation of the world; for he treats the latter by way of investigating natural justice.[191]

He classifies Plato's work under both practical and theoretical philosophy (*Glosae super Platonem*, p. 60), and in his glosses on Boethius he assigned both the *Timaeus* and the *Consolation of Philosophy* specifically to *ethica*.[192]

William gives an especially good example of the way the creation myth serves ethics in his comments on *Timaeus* 47b, God giving man his eyes. He gave man eyes so that man could pursue philosophy and study the natures of things. Philosophy is given primarily to help man form his *mores* and shape his virtues. The eyes form *mores* by serving "practical philosophy." With his eyes man perceives the dual motions of the firmament and the planets. He connects these to the inner motions of the spirit and the flesh, and arranges his own priorities in accordance with the priorities of celestial motions. As the firmament moves "rationally" and the planets "erratically," so also ideally and properly the spirit moves in its relations to the flesh.[193]

Moralists and "scientific" philosophers alike from the eleventh to the earlier twelfth century regarded the *Timaeus* as a work of ethics. This fact helps explain its manuscript tradition. It became popular in the first half of the eleventh century because it accompanied a new program of ethical education at cathedral schools.

The root impulse for the study of the creation and of nature in the eleventh and twelfth centuries lies in the "moral" perfection of the cosmos. Any "science" based on this conception of the universe was necessarily a "humane" science, directed toward self-knowledge and human perfection, toward good governance of the self and the state. The idea of macrocosm-microcosm, and with it the basic form of some of the most prominent works of twelfth-century humanism, reveal this conception: William of Conches's *Philosophia mundi*, Bernard Silvester's *Cosmographia*, and Alan of Lille's *Anticlaudian*. In each case the point of departure is the cosmos and cosmic perfection, and following upon this, man and human perfection. This form came from the *Timaeus*, but the idea it proclaimed was shared by eleventh- and twelfth-century humanists. Cosmology in the period is in its basic impulse humane and ethical. The progress of the study of nature in the twelfth century toward Aristotelian empiricism, toward new Arabic astronomy, toward "natural science" in a sense approaching our understanding of the term, must be seen as a progress away from the study of nature in a humanistic, Stoic-Ciceronian sense.[194]

Cosmology was an easy subject at eleventh-century cathedral schools. Precise instruments and data were not really necessary.[195] The required materials were the sky and the vision of a cosmos with perfectly ordered "manners." Equipped through the *Timaeus* with the idea of celestial harmony and through self-knowledge and magisterial correction with a sense of microcosmic inadequacy, the student only had to meditate on the implications for the arrangement of his own inner world. That was the reason God had given him eyesight, in the view of Bernard of Chartres and William of Conches. Astronomy as meditation was easy, pleasant, and intellectually warming. It had the feeling of productive thought and "enrichment." Students pursued cosmology the way the governor of the state, in Bernard of Chartres's view, should pursue music, to "tune" him to affability. They did not need to master Pythagoras and Ptolemy to do it. Students studied the heavens the way our undergraduates take courses in art history and music appreciation. The intricacies of a rigorous discipline were less important than the sense of participating in the life of the cosmic works of art and the hope that their harmony and elegance contributed to one's own.

6. Conclusion to Part I: Outbidding the Gods

A Ridiculous Mouse?

Adelman of Liège wrote a poem commemorating Fulbert and his students at Chartres, and had the temerity to send it to one of his former schoolmates, Berengar of Tours. The acerbic intellectual reformer, impatient with the obsequious nostalgia and obscure language of the poem, responded with the line of Horace, "a ridiculous mouse is born."

It would be easy to extend this quip to virtually any poem from the cathedral schools of the day, because it is based on a wholesale rejection of their learning. The eleventh century cannot be rescued as a text-producing age. Its strange, baroque poetry needs apology and explanation. It cannot be enjoyed as poetry and will never loom large in medieval studies. It is best regarded as a hermetic code, hard to crack, rewarding because of what it points to, not because of what it is, like those poems the early Romans wrote more to conceal than to reveal their philosophy. The cathedral schools did not produce a scholar or philosopher whose works are worth serious consideration alongside Anselm of Canterbury, Abelard, John of Salisbury, or Hugh of St. Victor.[1] Seen from the vantage point of these towering peaks, the mountains of the previous age appear foothills whose difficult labor gave birth to nothing but ridiculous mice.

But this criticism should caution us against judging any period through the eyes of the generation that superseded it. The eleventh century requires rescuing from the perspectives of the twelfth (and for that matter, those of the fifteenth to the twentieth). It is in this regard like the Middle Ages as a whole, which is gradually being rescued from the judgment of the Renaissance humanists.

The eleventh-century cathedral schools had one big idea that organized studies. That idea was *mores*: the well-tuned, well composed man. With the partial exception of letters, the other areas of the liberal arts were not studied as rigorous, intellectually demanding disciplines. That would have been contrary to the purpose of study. They were ancillary to self-discipline.

This goal commended the study of grammar, poetry, and eloquence. It accounted for the revival of ancient poetry, philosophy, and mythology. It commended the preoccupation with Neoplatonic ideas, with Stoicism, with Cicero and Quintilian. These subjects, in themselves somewhat dubious, were justifiable as the instruments of *cultus virtutum*.

By 1100 we see an impressive blossoming of neo-classical Latin poetry. The study of the *Timaeus* flourished. The next fifty years produced some brilliant philosophical poetry based on a Neoplatonic vision of man and his place in the cosmos and on a poetic vision of cosmic and human harmony. It produced an interesting body of commentary on classical poetry, dissolving it into allegories of the human psyche and human destiny. It produced some compendia of liberal studies and one defense of the arts of the trivium, John of Salisbury's *Metalogicon*.

The disciplines of *mores* and *ethica* played a major part in the emergence of twelfth-century humanism. They were like a rising tide that raised all the boats. The tide stopped rising toward the end of the century and began to recede in the first decades of the twelfth, leaving the arts it had raised up stranded on shifting soil. They experienced a short but brilliant flourishing. Then the schools abandoned them and went on to other things.

From this perspective, twelfth-century humanism is the last blossoming of a program of studies that had preceded it by some one hundred and fifty years. The most impressive *written* testimony to humanism surfaced well after the establishment of humanist learning in the courts and cathedrals, the administrative centers of Europe. The same is true of humanism in ancient Rome and in fifteenth-century Italy: its ideals were formulated first in the active civil life, then in written testimony. From this perspective also the role of the worldly culture of the eleventh century can be seen more clearly in its relation to the twelfth: it was one of the giants on whose back the "renaissance" of the twelfth century rode.

Sigebert's *Passion of the Theban Legion*

The excursuses in Sigebert of Gembloux's *Passion of the Theban Legion* (*Passio Thebeorum*) capture the spirit of eleventh-century intellectual life in many of its aspects, and they are good texts with which to conclude a treatment of the schools in the period. Sigebert wrote the work around 1075 as a monk of Gembloux, but he had moved there recently from Metz, where he had taught for some twenty years at the school of St. Vincent of Metz. The work has the flavor more of the episcopal town with its imperial traditions than of the reformed community of Gembloux. This narrative poem and other of his writings make it clear that he was steeped in the traditions of the empire.[2] His biography of Dietrich of Metz was one of our best sources on the instruction of Brun of Cologne, Dietrich's teacher. His praise of the golden age of the Ottonians in that work, and his polemical writings in favor of the imperial cause in the investiture controversy, locate his political and to some extent his intellectual obligations. The *Passio Thebeorum* was probably written for his colleagues back at Metz, undoubtedly for clerical advisors to the Emperor Henry IV. He tells us in the prologue that he is "serving the king's servants" in writing it.[3]

The work is a blend of the martyr legend and the heroic epic. It has direct ties to the Latin heroic epic *Waltharius*.[4] It borrows from Frontinus's (second-century) manual of military strategy to describe the training of the Theban troops. It will serve us as a paradigm text to summarize the eleventh century.

VIVACIA TEMPORA NOSTRE VITE

A legion of Roman soldiers from Thebes in Egypt — all of them converted Christians — is sent by Emperor Maximian to attack the Gallic tribe of the Bagaudes. The legion refuse the emperor's command to renounce their faith and worship the pagan gods, and are martyred. The veteran soldier Victor enters the scene at the end of the carnage, is filled with admiration for the martyrs, and sensing the approach of his own death, gives a kind of résumé of his life and of "what things are appropriate to a strong man and a wise man."[5] At the end of his magnificent "oration" or "prayer" he decides to join the Thebans in martyrdom[6]:

> "Perhaps Nature is already counting my [remaining] years on her right hand. The long-lived ravens, the long-lived stags, even the crow who suffers death only after nine ages: these marvel at the vitality of our long life. For me the justification of so long a life was to gather knowledge of many things, all I have seen, its nature, its abundance. . . . As I scaled this ladder of age step by step, Nature has enriched my mind in the same degree as she impoverished my body.[7]
>
> "All that happens in the world in so great a variety either study recovers or the gradual passing of time reveals, [unless][8] unpredictable chance disturbs

our activities. Our penetrating mind has increased the totality of nature. Just as the frequent exercise of study has extracted many sharpenable mountain stones from the veins of nature, so also it has hammered out and fashioned many arts as from the mountain's marble.[9] It polished one stone with another and refined one art with another, and these buffed our rough minds of their dense rust, sharpened and refined them. Thus mighty Nature exercises her power, placing in our breast for her own benefit the law of our kingdom, which she has dominated through all things.

"But cursed be the changeable order of things that has substituted for Nature's rule you, O Fortune, and enshrined you on the throne of domination. This is the unjust and arrogant act of those who refuse to write in their hearts that nothing in the nature of things happens without cause, nothing is fortuitous, nothing random and arbitrary. This is why mutability vexes earthly affairs.

"I have drunk new wine, felt the frosts of winter, seen spring's flowers and autumn's harvests mature; how many times have I seen Phoebus recapture the diadem of Phoebe and watched the aging sun turn youth again. So many hours have flowed through so many years, while I have noted the many weights placed in the swaying balance of human affairs. The mind in its natural state is given to vain cares and, abandoning reason's rudder, bobs uncertainly in the stream and labors to reach either shore, its fate hanging in the balance. When the four humors of the body . . . flowing from one source, overflow the banks in the rising tide or struggle in the ebb, they do not vex the heart so, do not trouble the body so, as the four emotions stir and rouse the restless, fervid breast, scatter its impulses and tear them from the hinges. . . . On this four-branching path [quadrivium], having lost the guide to the true path, the rough roads exhaust you, the swamps plunge you into dangers: here the brambles prick you, the hindering tree-trunks wound you. Thus wretched, vagrant man is driven about on the flux. . . . He who seeks what is worth wanting and he who rejects what is worthless is rare. But the rarest bird of all is virtue. . . . The false course snatches many onto its contrary path. . . . And sure enough the whole world lies wrapped in a dense fog. Thus the darkness encrusts all, so that the way of life is nearly obscured. And what moderation can exist in such foul clouds? The light flowing from light and pouring light back again from light shows us no spark of illumination. . . .

"Realizing these things and pondering them in my mature mind with full emotion and supreme desire—Oh, would that I, sighing and aspiring like an athlete, Oh, would that I could die in a way commensurate with these holy men! . . .

"My heart, my soul, my reason, my mind, my senses, my spirit, or rather the sum total of my soul sing out Christ, desire and love Him. In Christ I live, Christ I worship, and now in Christ I die."

The passage represents a self-assessment of the life of "studies" in the eleventh century. There is nothing of the classroom in it, but then there is little of the life of the warrior either. It is a description of a wise man's career. It begins and ends with enormous vitality, and vitality is the quality that Victor himself sees in looking back over his many years (*nostre vivacia tempora vite*). There is something Faustian about the perpetual drivenness of this "restless, fervid breast," in search first of knowledge and refinement, then of virtue and wisdom, finally of the true path, from which his Faust-like quest diverges. In the end the lost wanderer finds his redemption through Christ. Like Faust, he is a striver after knowledge, who is saved in the last moments of his life. Even the path of error he conjures has a quality of the earthly striving of Goethe's wanderers.

The episode of a final heroic resolve of a wise aged warrior also bears comparison with Tennyson's Ulysses. Both Victor and Ulysses hold their dramatic monologues just before embarking on one last heroic enterprise. Both of them are moved by a restless spirit that seeks experience in every realm, that wants to "drink life to the lees." Answering to Victor's experience in human affairs ("I have noted the many weights placed in the swaying balance of human affairs") is Ulysses's "always roaming with a hungry heart, / Much have I seen and known — cities of men / And manners." Both are moved by the thought of sacrificing themselves at the end of their long lives in a final heroic deed:

Victor:

> "Oh, would that I could die in a way commensurate with these holy men!"

and Ulysses:

> Death closes all; but something ere the end
> Some work of noble note, may yet be done,
> Not unbecoming to men that strove with gods.

And both of them show how contemptible death itself is in the face of such heroic spirits.

MIND OVER NATURE

Victor's life was spent in the pursuit of knowledge of many things. Three forces have dominated it: nature, his own mind and desires, and chance or Fortuna. Nature was his ally, fortune his enemy. Remarkable is the line, "the totality of nature has increased, thanks to our penetrating mind" ("Nature columen per nostrum excrevit acumen" — 2.598). It is not exactly the sense of "virtue conquering nature" expressed in "Quid suum virtutis," nor quite the experience of art outbidding nature and the gods in Hildebert's Rome poem, but a related if more conciliatory position on the connection of nature and human efforts. It posits a nature constituted by the human perception of it.

He sets the formation of the arts parallel to the mining of useful stones for tools and the shaping of stones to tools and statues. Human skills in Sigebert's vision are a contribution to nature, an increase of its potential.

What did "increasing nature," "overcoming nature," and "outbidding the gods" mean for the eleventh century? This is a central question for understanding the age's self-definition. We discussed it in the context of poetry in the last chapter, and will add a few comments here. Overcoming nature is something that happens in the process of education. Sigebert formulated the notion again in the *Passio Thebeorum* in the remarkable section (Sigebert's contribution) describing the military training of the legion. The description uses terms we are familiar with from the schools: "All that the ancient ordering of war dictated, either as received from nature or from you, Mistress Instruction, the Theban youth learned in patient studies."[10] *Natura* and *doctrina* are the two teachers, and the eager student's task is to conquer nature, as the poet indicates when he sums up their learning: "When potent virtue strives to conquer nature, then it is necessary to reach beyond the laws of nature."[11] The lines speak the same language as the conclusion of the Orpheus episode of "Quid suum virtutis": "Thus art conquered nature with the mediation of study, proving that all things cede to Mistress Virtue."[12] "Conquering nature" is the task of virtue, and study equips it for the struggle. Clearly this is a different nature from that norm-giving *Natura* of the twelfth century and of Alanus's *Complaint of Nature.* "Nature" is the condition of uneducated man. It is the world as it is prior to man's intervention, prior to mining, tool-making, prior to the arts, and especially prior to training in *mores*. It is nature unused and unformed, and "conquering" it involves applying art, study and discipline to reach beyond its laws. Marbod of Rennes depicted the early education of Licinius in these terms: he overcame the vices that seem planted "as if through some law of nature" in youth,[13] and we inferred from Marbod's Life of Licinius the formula, "natural talent heightened by the study of virtue." Thierry of Chartres formulated the educational ideal in a pithy gloss: "unde boni naturaliter, sed meliores per doctrinam effecti"; "good by nature, men are rendered better by learning."[14]

Overcoming nature is a pedagogic task, then. But the phrase has the ring of a high ideal. It suggests a superhuman quality in the educated, restrained, disciplined man, a godlikeness. In Hildebert's Rome poem, the skill of the artists of ancient Rome was sufficient to put the gods themselves to shame. Hildebert represented the pagan gods as products of mere nature and constructed a contest of skill between nature's and man's art: "Nature could not create gods as miraculous / As the images of the gods that man created."[15]

Godfrey of Rheims's phrase, "Genius is a powerful thing" (*res valida ingenium*) is a kind of summation of the age's vaulting optimism, indicated also in the formula, "overcoming nature." And Sigebert felt that his own "godlike" gift imposed on him the obligation of using it: "We whom mind and reason have made godlike, let us, having the gift of greater praise, praise more greatly."[16] This tendency to regard the educated human being as something godlike and beyond nature persisted into the twelfth century, and received impressive formulations. Amadeus of Lausanne said that the music of an Orphic God "composed man morally," removing his "fierce impulses and uncultivated barbarism," and "introducing him into the number of the gods."[17] Bernard of Clairvaux was still using the logic and concepts of the old learning when he congratulated the Virgin Sophia on her self-control, which he set above the angels, who have no body as the battle ground on which this string of glorious victories over the self can take place:

> Can the glory of angels compare to this? An angel has no body. He may be happier, but not stronger. Excellent and most desirable is the adornment which even angels might envy![18]

Sophia's discipline "overcomes" or "outbids" the angels, and this thought continues the logic of surpassing the divine well known in the previous century.[19]

CONQUERING FATE

Sigebert's Saint Victor calls out against the perversion of the ideal order of things. Fortune and chance have been enthroned in the place of nature and reason. There is a whole generation of men "who refuse to write in their hearts that nothing in nature happens without cause, nothing is fortuitous, nothing arbitrary." Again, Victor exhibits vaulting optimism. He clearly opposes the rule of fortune, and his martyrdom is in part a refusal to submit to it. The stance is fairly straightforward Boethianism, though at the end, when Victor requires the consolation of Philosophy, he receives the consolation of Christ. The dramatic development of his oration is the move from the pits and swamps of error, through which virtue is his guide, to the certain victory over error through martyrdom. His martyrdom is a willed act of self-sacrifice. He was not a member of the legion. He joins only when he sees what a community of heroes he will be entering and what a glorious death he can choose.

Sigebert places Victor's martyrdom in the context of the strong and disciplined mind overcoming fate and chance. It is clearly related to the motif of the Orpheus poems, "Orpheus's music changes the laws of Pluto and bends the resolve of the fates."

Bernard Silvester was to take up the theme a few decades later in his unfinished poem "Mathematicus."[20] Its Roman hero, Patricida, is destined by a decree of the oracle to be the murderer of his own father. Grown to manhood, distinguished in war and politics, ruler of Rome, Patricida learns of the prophecy and decides to take his own life, sacrificing all the titles and distinctions of his splendid career, rather than commit an atrocity and concede a victory to fate:

> For what purpose is our mind more closely related to the ethereal
>   stars
> If it must bear the dreary necessity of harsh Lachesis?
> Senseless is the divine mind of Patricide
> If our reason is unable to guard its own cause.
> God has created the elements and the fiery constellations
> Not so that man would be the plaything of stars and planets.
> Rather the macrocosmic skill of a pure genius is given man the
>   microcosm,
> So that he may face all barriers successfully.[21]

The context is different from that of the death of Saint Victor. Bernard Silvester's hero dies a noble, Roman, Stoic death (or would have if the poem fragment had been completed), free of any trace of Christian martyrdom. But the principles at stake are the same. Both men die so that fate will be denied its victory over the human mind. What distinguishes both of them from their model — Boethius in prison — is that all their options are open, whereas Boethius was making the best of a hopeless situation. Patricide and Victor choose death over error in heroic acts of the will that represent the ultimate gesture of overcoming fate. It should be evident that Bernard Silvester is still thinking thoughts that have clear precedents in the intellectual world of the eleventh century, and he finds a striking and original medium for them.

Founding the Arts

Sigebert's Victor has the sense that he and his generation created the arts in analogy to a miner mining stones, and refined them like one stone sharpening another: "It [*studium*] polished one stone with another and refined one art with another."[22] The comment makes no sense as the reminiscence of a veteran soldier, but it is intelligible as Sigebert's conception of his own and his generation's intellectual mission. They created the arts. The great age of the cathedral schools started with Brun of Cologne, whom Ruotger praised as the reviver of the arts and whom Sigebert admired as an educator and connoisseur of human talent.

Restless, Fervid Hearts

Victor's and Sigebert's generation is characterized by fervent enthusiasm; the sense of having a mission to fulfill and of having built a civilization with poetry, music, study; the sense that "We taught nature how to improve itself, we changed the laws of Hell, we sent nature herself to school." It also carries a sense of newness and new challenge — the mentality of the innovator, not the reformer.

Again Sigebert gives us a passage that expresses the spirit of the cathedral schools with a freshness and originality not typical in the poetry of the period. It is his morning hymn at the beginning of Book 2. It introduces a more or less conventional invocation, but it begins with an unconventional scene, the poet waking up:

> Now it's time to get up. The way lies before us, and this weighty poem forces me to an early start. Long rest may revive my powers, but it is the tinder of vice and the companion of sloth. The cock, who crows out the hours, see how now he sings out the minutes, prodding me: "Get up now, the day lies in front of you, be on your way!"
>
> What a delight to get off the path of rest! The body is torpid, but the mind alert. All things rejoice in the morning to shake off sleep. That's why the Greek word for morning also means "good." Is there anyone who could ignore the symphony of the birds, which they perform each morning with tune-filled throats? A thousand species of birds give forth a thousand sonorous voices, producing occasional harmony from such variety. That same song-fest relieves you, o wayfarer, of your long tedium. Where that concert plays, the labor of the road is cheated of its due. Here is your singing school; it could teach you the six-voice mode, shrill at the top and grave at the bottom of the register.

Therefore since all creatures praise the true God to the limits of their god-given skills, let us too praise Him, all the more able to praise, since mind and reason render us god-like. I am stirred with all my heart to sanctify the saint of all saints through his saints and to venerate Him. (*Pass. Theb.*, Prol. 2.1–24, p. 69)

WHO NEEDS EXAMPLES? YOU ARE THE EXAMPLE

Sigebert's St. Maurice begins his oration to the Thebans with Christ's urging to passive resistance and martyrdom (2. 441–48), then interrupts his own flow of speech to reject the Biblical example and exclaim: "There is no need for examples [from books]. You yourselves are the example" ("Non opus exemplis: exemplum vos magis estis" — 2.448). Sigebert develops the idea and the opposition of written history to living history in what follows. Maurice cites Biblical examples of heroic martyrdom, then again compares the living men he is addressing with the heroes of the past:

"We have read this, we have heard that. So many triumphs of the saints are reported throughout the world. But here I see with my very eyes those deeds I have read about. Tell me, you wise men . . . is that faith more certain which enters through the ears or through the eyes? . . . . Let others believe in what they hear; I shall believe my eyes.[23] Are not those whom I should imitate and those at whom I should marvel right here in front of me!"[24]

This passage formulates a fundamental principle of eleventh-century culture. Truth is in the immediate presence of a model human being. His personality, his conduct, his bearing is the thing itself, is what study and learning are about. He himself, and not books and texts, is the lesson. The living presence, equipped with the weapons of virtue, outdoes even sacred history.

It is evident from an earlier chapter that the pedagogy of charisma played a greater role than text-bound learning. The age developed extravagant formulae of praise that derive from this faith in the charismatic force of living examples. Constantine of Fleury was "magnificent above other men and always loveable," illumined with "the light of many virtues," and beaming "nobility of merits." Pernolf of Würzburg "shone with the beauty of many poets." G. of Cologne blazed forth all the "charm and grace of humanity," as well as the "bright good humor which shone most graciously from his eyes." These formulae, which draw on religious and imperial forms of representation, are the marks of charisma, of a divine gift made visible in the physical presence of a talented human being. It is the product of nature and education, and it has educating force. But it is located in the human body, lacking which it can have no expression. So marvelous is the force, angels themselves might envy charismatic humans that theater of magnificence, their bodies.

This preoccupation with embodied virtue expressed itself in the admiration of saints' virtue as opposed to their miracles. Sigebert of Gembloux commended St. Wicbert, "Let not his virtues be obscured by his miracles. His miracles merely commended his virtues."[25] The biographer of Bernard of Clairvaux condensed the same thought into an impressive phrase: "He performed innumerable miracles, but the first and greatest miracle was the man himself."[26]

Charismatic Body — Charismatic Text

Miracles were the event that externalized the saint's charisma. For the teacher / philosopher / bishop, his well-composed body, his presence, was the medium that made his charisma communicable. Both media were perfectly adequate for a charismatic culture, but they did not fare well in the advent of twelfth-century rationalism. In a culture that became increasingly oriented to the text, the real presence needed only a kind of fictional representative; in fact, in that form it was far less vulnerable to the unmasking gaze of critical inquiry. This is the general historical dialectic that pushed toward the charismatic text.

A symbiotic relationship exists between persons and texts, and it is worthwhile to reflect briefly on the dynamic that governs this relationship, and to continue at the same time the theoretical reflections begun in the Introduction. It illuminates eleventh-century intellectual life in its relations to the twelfth. These reflections will serve us as a theoretical guide through later sections of this study.

The eleventh century was oriented to personal presence; the twelfth tended more and more toward texts. It is a development closely related to the transition from an oral to a written culture. But the transition of media has received far more attention and intelligent commentary than the more embracing category, the transition from real to symbolic, from physical to textual presence, in the intellectual life of the two periods.[27]

A lucid illustration of this change is pointed out by Guy Beaujouan. He shows that, whereas the eleventh-century schools used the pupil's hand to teach calculation and musical harmony, the twelfth used books.[28] The earlier instruction was oriented to the human body, the later to textbook formulations that made the fingers unnecessary. The shift in the intellectual orientation of the two ages crystallizes in this example.

The relationship between person and text is basically agonal. They vie for each other's prerogatives; each wants what the other has. Texts are lasting and unchangeable; they lend permanence to persons, things, ideas. Real presence has life, vitality, and that force which inspires imitation. Texts constantly want injections of life, vitality, and charisma. Real presence, knowing it is mortal, wants permanence, wants to become a book. Texts, knowing they can only imitate, want the condition of life, being dry and empty without it; the living being hopes to preserve its exemplarity by becoming a text.

The historical dialectic at work in the move from person to text is evident in the life of any charismatic teacher. The effect of real presence in the case of Christ and Socrates (neither of whom wrote texts) is immense, and the pupils want to preserve that effect, to reproduce the man. The medium at their disposal is the text.[29] Ruotger stated this as his basic intention in writing the life of Brun of Cologne.[30] And Wipo developed the thought in his prologue to the life of Conrad II:

> To hold firm the fugitive memory of passing things with the bonds of the written word . . . I've thought it fitting to put forward the *forma bene vivendi*, because a useful example renders the soul of him who imitates it readier and firmer in *rebus agendis*.[31]

The disciple is always disappointed in the biography of the exemplary man, since he finds the force of personality replaced by words and paper, desiccated, robbed of its living energy and *virtú*. But gradually this disappointment is replaced by the realization that words on paper — representation in any form — have their own magic; one must only know how to make it work.[32] This is the basic impulse that creates the charismatic work of art. It originates when the means of representation develop to the point where they can reproduce the qualities of the living human being: immediacy, presence, voice, sensuality, body, force, authority. They have to be able to stir and stimulate that urge to imitate that is the essence of charismatic pedagogy. Don Quixote becoming a romance hero, and Rilke feeling the admonition to change his life which beams from the headless torso of Apollo, are in the forcefield of the charismatic work of art.

The parameters of this competition are the charismatic person, whose real presence texts attempt in vain to capture, and the charismatic fiction, whose hero corresponds to nothing in reality. The historical development of this aesthetic contest has representation first matching and then conquering real presence. The gradual disappearance of personality behind representation is a basic trend of the twelfth century.

The dethronement of real presence and the enthronement of representation has as its inevitable result the advent of charismatic fiction. If the Bruns and Conrads who inspire biography no longer exist in the flesh, — or if the principle of personal authority erodes — then the new master of the charismatic text has to invent his own characters and inject them with artificial charisma. Moral philosophy came to serve as the ethical basis for creating fictional heroes, and in this context *ethica* became gradually textualized and fictionalized in the course of the twelfth century.

From the end of the eleventh century to the thirteenth, moral philosophy passes, as in a massive transfusion, from bodies to texts. By the end of the twelfth century we no longer have the biographies of bishops and kings as a dominant form. But we have the courtly romance, whose hero embodies forms of behavior that were incarnated in the educated man of the previous century. We no longer have charismatic teachers teaching the curriculum of their mere presence and transforming loving students into little copies of themselves. But we have fictional courtly ladies, whose mere presence is elevating and educating, and whose love makes a man courteous, affable, gentle and wise, and we have learned wizards and magicians who become the instruments and administrators of virtue.[33] Virtue gradually becomes enfabulated, projected into the realm of the *merveilleux*, the fictional source of charisma par excellence. It becomes accessible through *aventiure*.

The eleventh century was the period when lessons in *mores* were conveyed through the body and personality of the teacher, just as lessons in mathematics and music were stored on the hand of the pupil. Its literature and works of art were the educated human being, the statesman / administrator. But this figure, like the charismatic personality, is perishable. It requires an act of antiquarian restoration comparable to the discovery and re-editing of old texts. It died with the men who embodied it, and what we gain from the reconstruction are glimpses of its shaping ideals of humanity, deference and elegant comportment.

The following centuries create the "monuments" to those ideals in their lyric, narrative, and sculpture.

*   *   *

Here we part company with Sigebert's *Passio Thebeorum*. It was representative of a number of important trends and positions of the eleventh-century schools. But it does not lead us into two important ones that have to be mentioned in summarizing the intellectual life of the period.

Peace and Friendship

A summary of the schools in the eleventh century would not be complete without some reference to their social atmosphere. Love, friendship and peace were the medium in which instruction took place. The temptation to call the cult of friendship an "ideal" of the schools is best resisted, at least if the word is taken to imply a reality at odds with the ideal. We recall that the students of Worms got themselves into trouble by violating this "ideal." Naturally, wherever love, reverence and friendship are imposed as obligatory forms of behavior, they will also serve as a mask for intrigue and an instrument of hate, envy and anger, which are not abolished by such an imposition. But friendship was an ideal of the schools, just as honesty and respect for the rights of others are important ideals of modern schools, however often they are violated.

Much of the teaching in *mores* in the eleventh century aimed at cultivating personal qualities that inspired love and friendship. Cicero's dictum that friendship is love of virtue in another man fit neatly a school scene which aimed at acquisition of virtue. Adaptability, grace, charm and affability, being all things to all men, were goals of study and training, and the ability to make and keep friends was the visible sign of mastery of these qualities. It attested to the presence of virtue in both parties to the friendship.

This element of *cultus virtutum* was not disengaged self-realization. There was also a social program behind it. This broader goal was to infuse secular society with the ideals of gentleness, friendship and love. This goal is expressed most clearly in the poetry of the age and the definitions of its goal. Orphic poetry was the bearer of that softening, mollifying, civilizing mission that was by no means only a poetic fiction of the age.

In the eleventh century it was perilous to contradict and argue with the teacher, to doubt and to assert the value of one's own opinions over the authority of the text and the teacher. It was a violation of the rule of love and peace. In the twelfth century, it was a serious intellectual posture.

Classicism

The learning of the eleventh century was saturated with classical models. The statesman and orator were central figures. The ideal leans heavily on

Cicero's *De officiis*, and that model is only slightly veiled in its adaptation, the manual of the Christian statesman, Ambrose's *De officiis ministrorum*. The *Tusculan Disputations* likewise had a major role in shaping the statesman's sensibility. Along with Boethius's *Consolation of Philosophy* it played an important part in shaping the sensibilities of a class of clerical administrators caught between conflicting parties in the investiture controversy.

The age's classical Roman cast is for us most evident in its literary style. The elegant Ciceronianism of Meinhard of Bamberg is an exception. Normally it was Martianus Capella who set the tone for composition in prose and, along with Horace, also for verse. That priority ruined the poetry of the age for posterity, even for its immediate heirs. The hermetic mannerism of school poetry must have made an immediate impact in performance by lending the performer aura: he is a man who knows more strange words than even his classical sources and who can scramble syntax into all but insoluble puzzles. One of the results is that a thorough knowledge of Latin poetry was obligatory. Poetry was the best testimony to a thorough education (Ulrich of Bamberg), and no one who lacked a knowledge of Horace, Virgil, Ovid, and Martianus could put forward that testimony.

This kind of accomplishment must have turned up by several degrees the brightness in the beam of poetry that broke from the poet, but it virtually extinguished any illumination the text itself had to offer, or made it so inaccessible that few would go looking for it. The effect of poetry was precisely to make *the poet himself* (or the teacher/reader of poetry), and not the text, into a monument: "he glows with the beauty of many poets." This lack of focus on the text is surely one of the reasons why so little school poetry has survived of the masses that must have been composed.

*   *   *

This summary has been a look at the eleventh-century cathedral schools intact, so to speak, viewed from the point of view of their goals, their values, their ideals, as expressed in an exuberantly idealizing literature, and there is much that encourages us to think that idealizing and norm-giving were identical. These institutions were humanistic in various senses of the word. They aimed at the development of the articulate individual, his integration into society, his active role in politics and administration. They aimed at humanizing the individual and through the humane individual, society. They cultivated poetry, oratory and conduct based on classical models.

The picture we have drawn of the schools intact leaves us with an image of great, modest, and amiable human beings in the masters' chairs, surrounded by talented admirers disciplining their conduct on the model of great men, "as steel sharpens steel" — also with a vision of peace, love, and affability dominating intellectual and social discourse.

But this whole alluring setting had frail foundations. Viewing the old learning intact has allowed us to ignore for a while the forces that pulled it down. These were present from the outset, both inside and outside the institutions, and they gained strength in the course of the eleventh century. When we observe those forces at work, the vivid picture of humanist institutes of learning appears more like a grand house of cards, standing there like the old south at the beginning of *Gone with the Wind*, about to be swept away.

Part Two

The Decline of the
Old Learning

7. Two Crises

The most visible of the forces that undermined and transformed the old learning were the peace movement, the monastic reform, and the investiture controversy. The changes produced by these developments and by whatever underlying forces of change had crystallized them reshaped European society, politics, economy, and intellectual life in the second half of the eleventh century and the first half of the twelfth. They ended the imperial church system and dissolved the particular relationship that had tied cathedral school to imperial court — and that spelled the doom of *cultus virtutum* as a school discipline.

This and the next chapter observe the demise of this discipline — which from now on I will refer to as "the old learning" — at cathedral schools. The present chapter focuses on the social forces, the next on the intellectual forces, which beset it.

Something happens to the *mores* of the aristocracy, lay and clerical, in the course of the eleventh century. There is a restless pressing against and overstepping of boundaries. The work of art that the schools produced — the well-composed man — sought new styles and new modes of self-representation. The trend toward change was answered by a stubborn, conservative retrenching and hardening of boundaries.

The study of this development is at a beginning stage.[1] Some of the basic texts and forms of expression are available for analysis. But its underlying motive forces, its connection with the peace movement and with the monastic reform movement, and its implications for European social forms are far from clear. Also a fundamental problem is the question whether the fashions themselves, or their critics' willingness to voice their disapproval, are new.

There is a dynamic built into the nature of court life itself that drives it toward extravagant forms of representation. These emerge at the imperial courts in Ottonian times, stimulated at least in part by the competition of the western and eastern emperors, both vying for the legitimate title of successor to the Roman emperors.[2]

"Novelties" of conduct break out in full force and blossom in Provence in the early eleventh century.[3] They enter the court of Henry III of Germany reportedly via Henry's marriage with Agnes of Poitou in 1043.[4] The Provençal retainers of Agnes, according to Abbot Siegfried of Gorze, are corrupting the ancient and honorable customs of the kingdom with their obscene modes of dress and behavior. They wear short and tight-fitting clothes, and they cut their beards. Such men win the close favor of the king by their novelties. They escape correction and thereby encourage others to "think up mad novelties on an even greater scale."[5]

The Abbot of Gorze's criticism is based on the opposition of discipline to laxness. The moral strength of previous emperors asserted itself in the strict maintenance of custom, especially military custom. Now obscene novelty goes unchecked, and it spreads like a disease.

This race for novelty among the aristocracy continues throughout the century, and it is regarded and represented by its clerical observers as a corruption of *mores*. Men make women of themselves. Their effeminization saps their moral fibre and extinguishes their will to fight. They wear superfluously rich and soft garments; they eat delicate and overly refined cuisine; they walk in a dainty, effeminate manner, with tiny steps, swinging their hips from side to side.

Many at the cathedral schools observed this transformation of *mores* with concern. Understandably so: the teaching of *mores* and discipline formed a large part of the curriculum, and presumably the obligation to correct manners reached beyond the classrooms to lay and clerical society generally. Innovation in the codes regulating social behavior was bound to have unsettling effects in an educational system based on authority and custom. The two crises of this chapter open those effects to view. They led in various directions. For instance, the resistance to new customs encouraged a severe, rigorous ordering of the religious life in opposition to the new worldly ways, a trend which pulled cathedral and canonical communities into the orbit of the church reformers (Liège). But the worldly ways could also take over a diocese and themselves become an object of instruction in its cathedral school (Hildesheim). Eventually, the reaction also produced an amalgamation of *cultus virtutum* with ideals of the apostolic life.

Henry III

This chapter focuses on the court of Henry III (1039–56) in its relations to the schools. It was one of the most remarkable and culturally rich courts of

the earlier Middle Ages. Henry's reign became representative in later historiography for the high point of the imperial church, an ideal balance of
church and state, and a golden age of peace and culture.[6] The king himself
was well educated,[7] and he cultivated learning both at his court and in the
kingdom. Ekkehard of Aura's praise of Henry III's son shows that the father
regularly gathered learned men around him for readings and discussion:

> Just as his father had, he valued the company of clerics and men of the highest
> learning . . . and he himself occupied himself intensely with the study of the
> liberal arts.[8]

He ushered in an unprecedented cultural flourishing, the result of his zeal
for studies:

> With his active support and efforts a great many men flourished at that time
> both in the arts, in architecture, in [the study of] the authors, in every kind of
> learning. And everywhere studies at their finest arose.[9]

Many of the works that have been major sources for this study were
written either directly for or in the proximity of Henry's court: Anselm of
Besate's *Rhetorimachia,* Wipo's Life of Conrad and *Tetralogus,* the *Sermones*
of Amarcius Sextus, possibly the poem "Quid suum virtutis." Many of the
short pieces that comprise Benzo of Alba's book of instruction, *Ad Heinricum IV imperatorem,* look back to the author's days as chaplain at the court
of Henry III. The Latin romance-epic *Ruodlieb,* probably by a monk of
Tegernsee, has been dated as early as 1042 and as late as 1070.[10] Its stress on
courtesy, court ceremonial, peace and love as the ideal atmosphere of life at
court and in the kingdom, may well be idealized reminiscences of the
emperor's court.

Members of the king's court were placed in more than half of all
German episcopal sees vacated during Henry's reign, a percentage that
surpasses any of his predecessors or successors.[11] That means that court
influence was at an unprecedented highpoint during Henry's reign.

His efforts at creating an institutionalized peace brought him the
reputation of pacifier and civilizer.[12] Bern of Reichenau praises him in terms
that echo distinctly the peacemaking and civilizing role cultivated at cathedral schools prior to the reign of Henry III. In a letter to the king from
around 1044, Bern explains the significance of his royal title:

> . . . those men who are now called kings once were called tyrants because of the
> crude ferocity of their conduct [*ob crudelem morum ferocitatem*], but when the
> zeal for sacred religion grew, they were called kings for ruling rightly [*reges* . . .

a recte regendo], since they suppress bestial urges and prove themselves rational through the force of good judgement.[13]

He has framed his praise so as to make of Henry a kind of royal Orpheus, or at least a Pluto/Dis fully under the influence of pacifying Orphic music.[14] He says that Henry fully merits his title, both for his lineage and for manners and conduct (*moribus et vita*) worthy of his grand ancestry.

This king is the wish-dream of learned clergy, an embodiment of important goals of cathedral schools: a ruler who is equal parts philosopher-king and prince of peace, loving and forgiving, sensitive to the high value of learned clerics.

It is not easy to reconcile this image with the very different one we gather from other sources. Siegfried of Gorze saw a real danger of the corruption of the empire in Henry's marriage with Agnes of Poitou. He saw Henry III as a plaything of flatterers and rewarder of turpitude.[15] The reproach of moral corruption threatened him doubly from his marriage to Agnes, since some critics considered it incestuous.[16] Hermann of Reichenau, a sober observer and near contemporary, described a decline in the later years of Henry's reign:

> At that time not only the great men of the kingdom but also the lesser began to murmur ever more against the emperor. They say he is long since falling away from his original posture of justice, love of peace, piety, fear of God and manifold virtues . . . into avarice and a certain laxness.[17]

This harsh judgment comes from a younger contemporary of Bern of Reichenau, who a decade before had praised him as David and Solomon combined in one.

Whatever else the reign of Henry III was, it was the period in which a crisis of conduct (*mores*) emerged at court and in the schools. The ambivalent judgment of his reign seems consistent with social/political divisions that are forming in the empire.

First Crisis: Wazo of Liège

Anselm of Liège wrote his history of the bishops of Liège in the second half of Henry's reign, approximately 1050–56. Liège still maintained its close relationship to the imperial court (see above, Chapter 3, pp. 54ff.). But the court chapel and the nature of court service had changed — in Anselm's opinion at least. What he observed troubled him, and his comments give us some of the clearest insights available into the close relationship between court chapel and cathedral school in the reign of Henry III, its Ottonian roots and its weakening in the mid-eleventh century. He expresses his concerns in his chapter on Bishop Notker's (972–1008) influence on the school in the previous century, and he compares the schools in their origins with those of the present day:

> His [Notker's] care for the education of the young was very great, and he saw to their instruction in the disciplines of the church. So great was this concern that whenever he traveled, to places near or far, he took with him young students, who would place themselves in the care of one of the chaplains under the strictest discipline, in no way different from that of the schools, and he had them carry along a great supply of books and other weapons of learning. In this way it happened that many of the ignorant and unlettered young men whom he snatched from cloistered walls returned perfectly lettered and a match even for those who earlier had been their teachers.
>
> But I fear that this may provide a bad example for those who seek to break forth from the halls of scholarship[18] into the courts of kings and bishops, and, disdaining the yoke of discipline, strive to surrender their lives to levity. I would judge such men fortunate if they never wandered so much as an inch from the learning of which he [Notker] gave an example. For if in the present age the study of the good arts, as plied amid the hurly-burly of courts, is held equal in value to cloistered leisure, then we do not deny that they ought to flee from the laxer and return to the more rigorous path of learning.[19] But if the opposite is the case, or rather because it is [namely that cloistered learning is more rigorous than that at court], then let this lascivious generation cease its empty pretense of reasons for its unsteady character, since what it neglected in claustral tranquility, it will never attain in the turbulent hustle and bustle of the court. Oh, if only those golden ages could be restored in our times when in the chapels of the emperor no less than in those of bishops nothing more was pursued than the discipline of manners along with the study of letters![20]

The cooperation of court and cathedral school — past and present — is so close that the venues of education are interchangeable. Under Notker, students could get a better education under stricter discipline while wandering with the court than in the cloistral tranquility of the school. Both the court and the school taught, in Notker's day, only "the discipline of manners along with the study of letters." What has changed is not this close relationship, nor the availability of instruction at both places, but rather the discipline at court. It is now laxer than at the schools. It is breeding a "lascivious" generation given to "levity." This laxness of discipline is attractive to students, because it encourages them to "break forth from the halls of scholarship into the courts of kings and bishops and disdain the yoke of discipline." There is now a group of men who chafe under this yoke[21] and hasten to courts, where they may continue their learning relieved of it.

What irritates Anselm is not the double venue of education, but a new spirit of levity and frivolity at the courts. The tensions are between discipline and laxness. In Anselm's report those tensions play themselves out within the structure of claustral quiet opposed to worldly confusion. Anselm gives us a suggestion of something not hinted at in Siegfried of Gorze's letter (notes 5 and 15 above): the court is drawing students away from the schools, since they can escape claustral discipline there. The atmosphere of undisciplined turpitude continues, though Provençal corrupters are no longer cited as the source of it.[22]

Anselm applies to the discipline of school and monastery interchangeably the term we found characteristic of Carolingian education: *ecclesiasticae disciplinae*[23] (see Chapter 2), and while it does not disappear from the description of studies at cathedral schools in the eleventh century, it is comparatively rare. He tends to stress the reforming activities of those who studied at the Liège schools[24] and does not dwell on their court activities or their service to the emperor, except to illustrate opposition to him.

When he does mention the court it is ordinarily in a tone of condemnation. Bishop Wolbodo, while serving at the court of Henry II, angered the king and resolved to pay compensation in order to placate him. But then he considered that it is "pointless to placate the prince of this earth if the ruler of heaven is offended" (208, l. 14), and he gives all the money to the poor. This action increases his fame at court, but makes him offensive to

> other men in charge of administrative duties [*praesules*], who contend to despoil the churches in their care and give their wealth to mimes and other dogs of the court. They themselves do not blush to indulge in scurrilous and obscene adulation toward the king by their inane speech.[25]

Bishop Wazo is mistrusted by the emperor for having favored the church of Liège and is accused of allying himself with Godfrey of Lorraine against "the imperial majesty and the well-being of the kingdom." The emperor is wrong for mistrusting Wazo, Anselm claims, but what can you expect; the life at court deprives a man of good judgment:

> It is difficult for the mind's eye not to be blinded from the light of truth [at court], since here are glory and wealth, here the many concerns of the republic that require administering, here the tongues of a thousand flatterers pulling in different directions.[26]

In short, rigorous religious discipline is a frail and endangered thing for Anselm of Liège, and the force that tends to undermine it are the worldly concerns of the students, especially the ambition to enter that whirlwind of secular cares, the court. "Laxness" and "lasciviousness" are general names for the offending modes of behavior. He is not more specific on the offenses, unfortunately.

*   *   *

Two important events in the life and activity of Wazo of Liège give us a clearer view of what is troubling Anselm. Both turn on administrative styles and the styles of education behind them. Viewing these events from the perspective of *cultus virtutum* and its application in public life allows us to see Wazo's personality and influence as engaged directly in the imperial tradition of the cathedral school of Liège — as a retarding force.

Wazo Versus Provost John

The first event is Wazo's conflict with a canon of Liège named John, who advanced in 1021 to the office of provost and proceeded to destroy what had been a close personal friendship with Wazo.[27] Wazo was not of noble birth, and throughout his life he has trouble with men who are.[28] The critical moment is the debate over his appointment as bishop, but the brawl with Provost John certainly was the most inflamed and dangerous conflict with powerful men of high rank in Wazo's early career.

Anselm tells us outright that the principles at stake in this conflict were the same Wazo defended later, first in his office as provost (Wazo was John's successor), then as bishop.[29] Anselm records Wazo's long letter of protest to Provost John, in order show how consistently Wazo placed himself on the side of justice.

The events occurred between 1021 and 1025. The cause of the quarrel in Wazo's version is that Provost John has regularly overstepped the boundaries of his position. He has arrogated the property and income of the church to himself and given it to whomever he chose. He has made many decisions without consulting the brothers whose consent has made him provost. He has claimed that as provost he also holds the office of prelate. At fault, says Wazo, are John's pride and arrogance, his confidence in his own standing and power,[30] his ambition,[31] and above all his urge to dominate and rule.[32] In setting provost and prelate equal, John is said to set earthly things above spiritual, since the provost administers the house's worldly goods, while the prelate administers the spiritual life:

> Spiritual things are rightly set above secular, in the same way that the rational soul rules over the stolid flesh. The cloisters of the west hold unswervingly to this arrangement, as do all houses of monks wherever they may be.[33]

This ranking of spiritual above worldly becomes a dominant motif of Wazo's thought and administration.[34]

One result of John's disordered administration is that discipline and the study of letters decline.[35] Wazo himself resigns his position as school master:

> I have fled my duty of [maintaining] scholarly obedience — the only sensible step — since neither the zeal to learn nor the ability to compel is present.[36]

John's urge to dominate banishes "subjection, loyalty, humility and obedience" (cf. 212, 35). The "Rule" calls on him to provide an example of canonical behavior for his subordinates (212, ll. 48–49).[37] Instead, John is lazy. He does not visit the chorus, the refectory, the dormitory, in violation of the mandate of the Rule. "Why?" asks Wazo rhetorically, "You are of sound mind, healthy and have plenty of time on your hands" (212, ll. 49ff.). Instead of attending to his mandated duties, John labors from morning to evening over his secular business. While he himself works not at all or only little, he collects all the fruits of others' labors for his own use (213, 1ff.).

That is Wazo's case against Provost John. The issue is clear, and it is formulated by Wazo trenchantly: "administration according to the Rule, not tyranny" ("administrationem secundum regulam, non dominationem" — 213, 38).

The Provost has his own say, and Anselm / Wazo obligingly record his defense. John calls Wazo a troublemaker and hothead[38] who acted out of deep-seated obstinacy. The reproach has weight in itself. A few years later, the Worms students who provoked the students of Würzburg would feel it turned against them, to their consternation.

It also has weight in the particular circumstances. Provost John takes his complaint to Bishop Durandus[39] and persuades both him and the other superiors of the church that Wazo was motivated by a contentious and litigious nature.[40] The result is that Wazo and not John is forced to leave Liège, and apparently not even Anselm's story that the provost had the dormitory set on fire by local wine-suppliers in order to murder Wazo carried more weight with the bishop than John's complaint against Wazo's contumacious nature.

Wazo was indeed an uncomfortable figure, stubborn, contentious, and given to confrontation. For all his humility and self-deprecation, he was a real fighter, "a supremely bold defender of the pure truth," Anselm calls him ("audacissimus purae veritatis assertor"—chapter 65, 228, 44). And he regularly applies the metaphor of war, battle and contention to Wazo's activities.[41] Wazo is not a mediator. Instances in his biography of his seeking compromise and reconciliation are few and far between.[42] He is very different from the smooth men of peace and the middle road the imperial church cultivated, men like Brun, Dietrich I of Metz, Gerbert of Aurillac, and Benno of Osnabrück, who worked hand in glove with the emperor. On the contrary, his differences with the emperor were not merely a difference of opinion that could be settled and reconciled by holding to the golden mean, but rather a "war against the emperor," and Wazo's role the "liberation" of his church.[43] It is consistent with this character that Anselm says Wazo ought to have lived in the times of the Roman persecutions; he would have willingly offered his neck to the executioner, just as he was prepared in the conflicts of Liège to arm himself with the cross and "throw himself into the midst of the armed hosts."[44] Wazo was an aspiring martyr who needed a Nero to oppose him, and if some insufferable tyrant did not exist, Wazo would invent him. He conceived his role as one who "threw himself into the midst of hosts," armed or not. An abrasive defender of spiritual rights can always find weapons turned against him in the hands of worldly men.

There are two sides to the story of the conflict between Wazo and Provost John. The decision of the chapter to banish Wazo and keep John has weight. A provost who was abusing his office in the atmosphere of Liège, as Anselm depicts it, would surely have been out on his ear. The office lent itself to abuse. In the comparatively lax Hildesheim (see next crisis) under Bishop Hezilo, the bishop ejected a provost named Kuno for abusing his office in very much the way Wazo accuses John of doing. In this case, neither Kuno's relatedness to the bishop nor Hezilo's wish to maintain good relations with Bamberg, where Kuno had his training, can rescue the provost.[45]

It is unlikely that the decision to keep John and dismiss Wazo was a frivolous one. Wazo may well have been perceived by Durandus and the seniors of the community as having violated that sacred rule of peace with outbursts of anger and obstinate clamoring against his provost over minor infractions that a man with more imperial values would have found easy to countenance.[46]

Provost John has one other defense. He points to his archdiocese,

Cologne, and says, in effect, that he is not doing anything not done there. We can assume he makes this argument, because Wazo refutes it: "Do not try to strengthen the defense of your presumption by the example of Cologne" (214, ll. 9–10). Liège owed its traditions to Cologne, as did other dioceses of Lorraine, not only as their archdiocese, but above all as the see of Brun. Brun of Cologne had hand-picked both founders of the Liège school traditions, Evraclius and Notker, and they had no doubt continued his tradition. Brun's education of Dietrich of Metz had aimed at creating a prelate who would be adept at both "governing and benefiting" (*praeesse et prodesse*). The man Brun educated was destined for "civil battle." He would require humility because "he would be set above many, to their own benefit" (see above, Chapter 2, pp. 38–39).

The proposed balance between *praeesse* and *prodesse* changes subtly the priorities of church traditions. The Benedictine Rule stipulates that the abbot should seek rather to "benefit" than to "preside."[47] Brun's education of Dietrich sets them equal. Wazo lines up with the Benedictine Rule, and this alignment has an edge against the imperial tradition.

Wazo had a deep mistrust of power. He resisted office every time it was thrust on him; he repeatedly turned down vacant bishoprics. This stance gives weight to Anselm's protestations, for instance, that Wazo served in Conrad II's court "not out of any desire to receive a bishopric, nor any other ambition for domination."[48] This penchant of Wazo was to be confirmed from the side of his opponents in his contested election to bishop of Liège, our second event.

Wazo's Election

When Bishop Neithard died in 1041, "clergy and populace" demanded Wazo as bishop. He is ultimately appointed against the opposition of certain "flatterers" of the king. These men claim that a bishop must be elected from the chaplains of the king, but Wazo had never exerted himself in the royal service, hence had not earned such an honor. It is wrong, they say, to make a man bishop who has not "wandered around"[49] with the king's court. More telling is their argument that it is not appropriate to elect a man who has been trained to the subjection of claustral obedience and who has learned not so much to rule (*praesse*) as to do good (*prodesse*).[50]

The issue turns on questions of education, how the candidate is trained (*informatus*) and what he has learned (*didicerit*).[51] Wazo's opponents state plainly that a bishop should be *educated* to govern (*praeesse*), and that monastic training may well be contrary to this purpose. This is clearly an assertion of the imperial tradition against a monastic one that is injecting itself into episcopal appointments. The king's chaplains want one of their own in the see of Liège, and they are men who have both served at court and learned to wield authority as befits a "spiritual prince."

Here Wazo's own principles are invoked and turned against him in order to disqualify him for office. He devotes his life to the defense of obedience and subjection against the ambition of domination, and on the occasion of his election as bishop, the king's chaplains call for a candidate closer in character to Provost John. Clearly the principle of "administration in accord with the Rule" (*administratio secundum regulam*) could have little weight with the king's advisors.

Wazo is not a spiritual prince; he is not a magnificent wielder of authority in the tradition of Brun and Dietrich of Metz. Otto the Great had wanted men who combined "the religion of a priest with the strength of a king" ("*sacerdotalis religio et regia fortitudo*").[52] Wazo's strength and magnificence were qualities of a martyr, not of a king. He was anything but a successor to the "regal priesthood" (*regale sacerdotium*) of Brun.

Anselm formulated the opposition to Wazo's election in terms consistent with his comments on education under Notker of Liège. He favored training in claustral rigor; these "flatterers" demanded an apprenticeship at the royal court as preparation for a bishopric, and the royal court had been for Anselm a whirlpool of laxness and lasciviousness. The words of Wazo's opponents would seem to encourage precisely those men "who seek to break out of the halls of learning into the courts of kings and bishops." The new breed of students "wander" from discipline, just as the chaplains demand of a legitimate candidate, "to wander with the royal court" ("*in curte regia evagari*"); the students of the present seek to "reject the yoke of discipline," and the king's chaplains reject candidates trained in the "subjection of claustral obedience."

In Wazo's contested election we have a head-on opposition of *disciplina Brunonis*, the education introduced by Brun, to monastic tradition.

*   *   *

The opposition of Wazo and Anselm to the values of the royal court sets Liège at odds with the imperial tradition of education. That tradition was not one-sidedly claustral. It never favored the goal of doing good over that of governing. On the contrary, *praeesse* was set equal to *prodesse*. Far from shunning worldly business, an imperial bishop saw to *secularia negotia* as one of his central activities, "civil battle" for church and state. Brun himself was accused of excessive preoccupation with civil administration.

Liège moves away from that balance, favoring "doing good" and treating "governing" as prideful and ambitious. Some hundred years after Brun's influence asserted itself in cathedral school education, there are clear signs that the close cooperation between court and school is becoming strained. Liège cannot follow the emperor's court in its worldliness and its novelties, and this strengthens a monastic posture toward learning. That is the crisis of Liège.

Goswin of Mainz considered the school of Liège to be on its way downhill by the time he wrote his letter to Walcher (ca. 1065). Whatever it had retained of the glory of its Ottonian traditions, it no longer supplied chaplains and had all but ceased receiving its own bishops from the royal chapel.[53] By the early years of the twelfth century it had lost its position of glory and influence, never to regain it. Charlotte Renardy has studied this decline. She shows its cause to be the church reform and the infiltration of its values into the cathedral school of Liège.[54]

Wazo of Liège is located at the beginning of the decline of the Liège school, and it is probably accurate to say that he is a major cause of it.

Second Crisis: Bishop Azelinus Reforms Hildesheim[55]

At Liège all the problems were at court, and the cure was cloister-like cathedral schools. At Hildesheim in the same period the "problems" infiltrate the cathedral. Bishop Azelinus (1044–54) was a chaplain in the court of Henry III, and when the king appointed him bishop he brought with him the ways of the court.[56] An anonymous chronicler of the Hildesheim church, writing around 1080, makes this bishop responsible for an infusion of "ambitious courtliness." The passage is important, and I quote it here at length. It begins by praising the rigorous discipline under bishops prior to Azelinus:

> . . . the clergy gave itself over to the service of God with zealous piety and pious zeal so great that though professed canons they rejoiced in monastic strictness [*districtio*]. I shall not go into how severe the punishment was for tardiness when entering the choir, the mensa, or the dormitory—not to mention absence! Such presumption could only be excused by grave need or special permission. Once relieved of the yoke of school discipline, they were guided by yet tighter reins in the cloister. . . . So indifferent were they to the

more elegant clothing, which is now all the rage among the clergy, that they knew nothing of gluttony or of fur collars, and they decorated their sleeves with darkened rags and patches, not with robes. . . . In this way they preferred rustic boorishness to courtly sophistication . . . they had no pretenses to things higher than what the cloister provided, so that they who had not yet renounced the world lived in claustral restraint, ignorant of worldliness. This claustral state pleased Emperor Henry [II] . . . so well that he chose for his own church of Bamberg the claustral rigor of Hildesheim combined with the studies of Liège, since he knew that the highly composed posture of the outer man showed forth the religion of the inner man.

This claustral rigor persisted down to the times of our sixteenth bishop, Azelinus. During his administration there crept in an ambitious courtliness, which — being softer and gentler in dress, more elegant and refined in manner of living, more scrupulous in every aspect of culture, seeking to inspire love rather than fear — led to the softening of monastic rigor.[57]

The changes that came with Bishop Azelinus could only have been regarded by this advocate of ascetic discipline as a form of corruption, though he is remarkably reticent in branding them as such. Whatever the new forms of conduct Azelinus imported, their result is to soften monastic rigor, a bad trend in this man's eyes. Liège avoided the fate of Hildesheim, possibly because at the critical moment the severe spokesman of discipline, Bishop Wazo, presided.

It is instructive to compare this report with what we know of the perils of Liège. The Hildesheim writer shows strict discipline maintained especially in entering the choir, refectory and the dormitory. At Liège, Wazo criticized Provost John precisely for relaxing his vigilance over these areas. Driven by ambition and the urge to rule and dominate, he neglected his visitations in choir, refectory and dormitory, while he sweat over his "worldly business." Likewise the "courtliness" of bishop Azelinus is "ambitious," a phrase that can only mean aimed at pleasing the king, finding favor, winning an office through that favor. The cutting issue at Liège also surfaces in the context of changed *mores* at Hildesheim, *praesse* vs. *prodesse*. Immediately after describing the administration of Azelinus, the author of the *Fundatio* praises his successor Hezilo as "a father more than a superior, since he wished to do good rather than to rule."[58] It confirms that bishops who are perceived as close to the emperor are branded as men eager to "rule" rather than to "do good."

So the issues are in some ways the same: claustral rigor opposed to a laxer rule of life that comes from the court. But the results are very different. Azelinus introduces or permits the introduction of "courtliness." Not only does it "creep in," but there are good reasons for thinking that the relaxed and softened style of life won the day. There is no resistance. Criticism is muted, uncertain and indirect. If we removed the praise of claustral rigor from the report in the *Fundatio,* we might well think the writer was praising and not criticising the reforms of Bishop Azelinus. Hildesheim clearly is a very different kind of place than Liège, where the bishop himself lined up squarely against the incursions of manners from the imperial court.

This text is valuable for giving us some details of the phenomenon called here for the first time "courtliness." What we know from this chronicler's report is that fine clothing, delicate and abundant food, a refined form of speech and behavior are the constituents of this new fashion. Like the bishop who brought it, it comes from the court, and is called after its place of origin.

A puzzling feature of "ambitious courtliness" is that "it preferred to be loved rather than feared": "amari quam timeri maluit." The phrase may refer to the atmosphere of friendship, harmony, and love that other sources lead us to believe predominated at the imperial court (see above, pp. 104ff.). It is clear that the writer countenances a stern and rigorous asceticism. He regrets the passing of the days when canons were whipped for appearing late at choir, and we can infer that this did not happen under Azelinus. This writer may well regard the affectionate affability of courtly manners as a form of laxness. But he seems oblivious to the stipulation of the Benedictine Rule that the abbot should strive to be loved rather than feared.[59] His extreme sternness does not countenance even sanctioned forms of humane and pleasant social intercourse. We observed this opposition from the other side — advocacy of humane affability against monastic rigor — in the poem of Godfrey of Rheims quoted earlier. He praises his friend Odo of Orleans:

He was not austere with morose gravity — which I hate —
But rather serene with bright spirited countenance — which I love.
His face was not twisted nor intimidating with grim glances,
Nor were his brows rigid and severe,
But rather mild, gentle and placid as a dove, . . .

Godfrey opposes stern religious rigor, and banishes it to the wilderness to live with the merciless tigers:

. . . let the wretch stray
Who swells with mendacious religion.

Let him live, mute, bitter and harsh, banished to the wilderness,
The companion of Hyrcanian tigers.
He who condemns joys and approves melancholy
Will be judged like winter and its frosty winds.[60]

The Hildesheim chronicler, writing a few years before Godfrey, idealizes precisely rigor and rusticity, and it seems probable that the comparison taps into a real social tension: the opposition of courtly affability to monastic severity. The conditions the author of the *Fundatio* countenances would seem to be those Godfrey banished to the "wilderness" and the company of fierce, untamed animals. There is no disagreement on the forms of behavior, only on the judgment of them.

If we had only the report of the *Fundatio* and other critics of court style to rely on, we would judge Bishop Azelinus a corrupter of his diocese. Fortunately there are other sources. It is curious that no historian of this church criticizes Azelinus for his reforms (not even the author of the *Fundatio,* though his judgment is implicit). In other reports, Azelinus comes across as a successful, well-connected bishop,[61] whose contribution to the diocese was limited only by the unfortunate chance that the church burned down early in his administration and he did not live long enough to complete the job of rebuilding.

The changes to a softer and gentler style of life were a reality at Hildesheim, not the invention of a disgruntled advocate of severe order. Otloh of St. Emmeram is probably the earliest writer to observe the change. He tells in one of his *Visiones* (written ca. 1062–66) of an odd incident at Hildesheim. An angel appeared repeatedly to one of the priests and warned him against the "extremely precious vestments" worn by the clergy. The cleric places the blame on the bishop. He tries to pluck up his courage and "correct" the bishop's ways, but hesitates. Finally, overcoming his timidity, he warns the bishop and clergy, telling them of the apparition. Still they refuse to give up their "noxious frivolity of voluptuous ornament." The angel finally runs out of patience and sends lightning to destroy the church. Thereupon they finally abandon "not only the superfluous ornaments of clothing, but also the useless refinements of manners" (*inutilia morum fastigia*).[62]

This story supposedly was told to Otloh while at Hersfeld, where he lived in the 1020s. But it could hardly refer either to the revered Bernward of Hildesheim (993–1022) or to the saintly and severe Godehard (1022–

38). It seems reasonable to assume that it refers obliquely to the same phenomenon the author of the *Fundatio* observed. It incorporates both the known events of Azelinus's term of office — the importation of courtly ways and the burning down of the church. Apparently Otloh projects the events into the past in order to mute the criticism, to which the present bishop, Hezilo, may still be sensitive.

An anecdote attached to a manuscript of the *Translatio S. Epiphanii* also refers to the Hildesheim crisis. The person who penned it claims to have read it in the *Vita Bernwardi.* It tells how the ghost of Empress Theophanu, dressed in wretched rags, appears to a nun in her sleep, and begs her prayers. The nun asks why she suffers, and the former empress tells her that she is doing penance for having imported "many superfluous and luxurious ornaments for women, common in Greece, but until then unknown in German or French lands." The result of her innovations was that many women began to desire these vanities. Then follows the story of the burning of the Hildesheim church as punishment for vain and ostentatious clothing and the loosening of discipline, more or less as in Otloh (MGH SS 4, 888).

Clearly the critics of worldly ways had their eyes on the Hildesheim reforms, but the criticism is oddly indirect and muted. We are far from the atmosphere of Liège, where no nonsense was tolerated, and blatant resistance against the emperor and his minions was an admired stance.

The real nature of the Hildesheim reforms becomes apparent when we compare Azelinus's social innovations with his educational measures, which the *Vita* of Benno of Osnabrück reveals. Benno was an up-and-coming young talent in the emperor's service when he came to the attention of Bishop Azelinus. The bishop of Hildesheim was the winner in what Norbert describes as a competition of prominent men for the services of Benno.[63] Azelinus lured him away "with grand promises," and made him *scholarum magister.*

At Hildesheim he found the local clergy "educated in a rustic way, almost totally illiterate and unlearned,"[64] and he set to work with great energy to change that. He soon had inspired them with the love of learning and transformed Hildesheim to the point where no place in the kingdom could equal it. The level of the clergy was raised so high, Norbert continues, that they distinguished themselves both in the "honesty of claustral discipline" and in the "ardor for learning the science of letters."[65] Benno became known as "the enlightener (*illustrator*) of that place and, as it were, the new founder of an ecclesiastical order there" — rightly so, Norbert assures us.

This text, compared with the *Fundatio,* gives a clear picture of the circumstances which the team of Azelinus and Benno changed: both agree from their very different perspectives that the diocese had been rustic, and ignorant.[66] For the chronicler this is praise; for the biographer blame. Both agree that the advent of Azelinus and Benno brought important changes in the discipline of the church: the *Fundatio* says it was relaxed and secularized; Norbert that it was restored to "claustral discipline" *claustralis honestas disciplinae*. It is indisputable that Hildesheim swerved toward courtly luxury in mid-century: the historical traditions of Hildesheim agree unanimously on that. Why does Norbert of Iburg make such a claim in his Vita of Benno? Because no doubt the reforms of Azelinus aimed not only at letters but also at manners. What the anonymous historian saw as corruption of discipline, Norbert saw as a program of civilizing, and "claustral discipline" meant something different to him than to, say, Anselm of Liège. The Vita of Benno was written, also in Saxony, at a time (1090–1100) when the eleventh-century traditions of Hildesheim were still well known. I would suggest that the importation of the ways of the court into a rigorously monastic diocese might well have been seen in the imperial heartland as a major improvement. That is the justification for referring to Azelinus's influence as "reform." What the *Fundatio* sees as neglect, Norbert sees as a program.

This leaves us with a picture of Benno implanting in the rustics of Hildesheim a "zeal for the study of letters," while Azelinus introduced courtly refinements of manners: Benno, *litterae,* Azelinus *mores et curialitas* or *curialis facetia.* The diocese was reformed according to a program of "letters and manners." The imperial court was the source of this program, both in its social and its intellectual thrust.

Clearly the *Fundatio* has given a biased picture of the influence of Bishop Azelinus on the church. None of his fellow Saxons who commented on this bishop shares the view of him as a corrupter. He was a serious reformer, whose reforms aimed at instituting a program of court education. If he had been the epicurean corrupter the *Fundatio* makes of him, he surely would not have gone to the trouble of courting a sought-after and expensive young man like Benno of Osnabrück. And conversely, a man like Benno with a brilliant career in front of him would probably not have left the royal court at Goslar to follow a corrupt bishop into the backwoods.

In the clash of novel customs with conservative resistance at Hildesheim, the court and the imperial traditions won the day, the opposite result from Liège. The reforms of Azelinus and Benno were sustained through the bishopric of Azelinus's successor, Hezilo, and some of the fruits were a variety of historical works and the Hildesheim letter collection.[67]

The crisis at Hildesheim gives us contemporary perceptions of the two ways of life struggling to dominate northern European dioceses. We see the fronts between monastic rigor and imperial ways sharpened. The kind of reconciliation that Brun of Cologne had found was no longer attainable to Azelinus. On the contrary, what makes this situation into a crisis is precisely the extreme form of behavior and dress that came with his reforms. Luxurious clothing had been rejected by Brun, but Azelinus and Hezilo tolerated them. The extreme of luxury called forth an extreme, if limited, reaction. But the handwriting is on the wall: there is a serious division between the levels of clergy in northern Europe.

8. Old Learning Against New

Teacher Insulting

Gradually in the second half of the eleventh century and precipitously in the first half of the twelfth, the old learning became threatened by a new kind of teacher offering a new kind of studies: the disputatious philosopher-scholar-teacher in the stamp of Peter Abelard. Both Italy and the north apparently bred this type, because in reports from the monastic as well as the cathedral communities we see the schools teeming with cavillers whose breasts swell with pride in their knowledge, who dispute, cast doubt, redefine old usage, violate the laws of *reverentia* and *pietas* right and left, and have the nerve to contradict and show up their own teachers.[1]

Some early examples of teachers insulted and authority defied help locate a fundamental characteristic of the old learning and a fundamental weakness.

When Wolfgang of Regensburg was a student at Würzburg in the mid-tenth century, his fellow students asked him for a commentary on Martianus Capella, because they were not content with the reading of their teacher, Stefan of Novara, the Italian master called to the north by Otto the Great. Wolfgang complied, and he commented so astutely on Martianus that his erudition became an affront to his teacher. Stung to anger and threatened with the loss of his students, Stefan undertook to stifle Wolfgang's further progress. But the inner flame of divine erudition only burned the more brightly for the attempt to snuff it out, "as a fire flares when fanned by blasts of wind."[2] Wolfgang eventually moved to Trier as school master; he progressed to the bishopric of Regensburg (972–994), and ultimately to sainthood. But the future saint might have saved himself a good deal of trouble by not giving offense at all, especially to this sensitive foreigner.[3] An important point of conduct was violated when Wolfgang produced a commentary superior to that of the master. The circumstances in this case are quite different from the offense given by the poet of Worms to the Würzburg school master, Pernolf (see Chapter 3 above). Here the master's own student has the effrontery to understand more than his teacher and to let the whole school know it. These circumstances are close to those in which the young Peter Abelard outdid Anselm of Laon in biblical exegesis.

Abelard's intellectual arrogance is foreshadowed also in the insult dealt to the clergy of Limoges by a Lombard grammarian, Benedict of Chiusa, who visited Limoges in 1028 and disputed the claim that the local patron, St. Martial, was an apostle. Our source, Ademar of Chabannes, tells the story by way of holding this pompous windbag up to ridicule. He quotes a long speech, which he attributes to Benedict. In it the latter boasts of his knowledge of grammar and claims that all of Aquitaine and most of France are ignorant of this art, that after nine years of study his own wisdom is so perfect no one under the sun can match him.[4] It is a discrediting speech, fabricated to display intellectual arrogance. The monks of St. Denis a century later would undoubtedly have liked to place such words in the mouth of Peter Abelard, whom, out of the arrogance of his learning, they took to be diminishing the authority of their patron.[5]

It may be that Benedict and Abelard were entirely right in disputing the beliefs of the local monks. The validity of the claims against those beliefs, the historical truths at stake, did not matter. Reasoning and proof, when pitted against venerable authority, textual or personal, were pernicious instruments of pride that invited discrediting and were seen as deserving it.

But gradually knowledge, reasoning, success in disputation and in proof become ends in themselves. Grave and dignified orations, elegant gait and gestures, lose their importance in the schools; thought frees itself from its subordination to discipline. By the early twelfth century, the "discipline of manners" has been largely displaced at the schools and replaced by definitions and systematizing, frameworks of argumentation and harmonizing of inconsistencies.

The contest between old and new learning is as much a part of twelfth-century intellectual life as is the clash between the new learning and monastic orthodoxy, though the latter has commanded much more interest from historians. In many ways the old learning and monasticism were allied in opposition to the new. They had, it is true, a traditional antagonistic relationship in the eleventh century (polemics of monks against worldly professors), but at the same time an easy reciprocal relationship (many professors converted to monastic life). The rise of the new learning brought their common interests and characteristics into clear focus. Representatives of both joined forces against Berengar of Tours and Peter Abelard. The intellectual world of the monasteries had much in common with that of the schools. Philosophical Realism was fundamental to both, as was mistrust of doubt, of skepticism, and of curiosity. Also common to both was authority as the basis of thought, argumentation, and instruction. The basic intellectual reorientation of the period has long been regarded, rightly I believe, as the clash between reason and authority.[6] But some understanding of the old learning helps us to see the nature of authority in a clearer light. It does not only reside in texts and traditions: it is also a human quality.

Magisterial Authority and Its Mood Music

A letter from Adelman of Liège to Berengar of Tours cited in an earlier chapter shows us this form of authority at work in the eucharist controversy. The letter is a trenchant rejection of Berengar's position on the divine presence in the sacrament, but it is written in a tone of loving correction from one former student of Fulbert of Chartres to another. The body of the letter is a dossier of arguments and texts against reasoning, novelties, and heresy. Of interest to us is its introduction. Adelman evokes at length the figure of Fulbert, and in doing so recreates vividly and emotionally the atmosphere of the old learning:

> I have called you my fellow suckling and foster brother in memory of that sweetest and most pleasant of times we spent together, you a mere youth, I somewhat older, at the Academy of Chartres under our venerable Socrates. We have more cause to glory in the common life of studies [*convictus*] shared with him than had Plato, who gave thanks to nature for bringing him forth as a man rather than as an animal in the days when Socrates was teaching.[7]

Berengar and Adelman have experienced (*experti sumus*) the more saintly life and sound doctrine of Fulbert, and now can hope to benefit from his prayers in heaven, since the regard and Christlike charity in which he held them, as in a maternal womb, still live on; indeed, his death has only intensified them. Adelman conjures Fulbert looking down from heaven upon his two students and calling on them with his vows and prayers,

> entreating us through all those intimate evening colloquies he used to hold with us in the little garden next to the chapel in the city . . . and beseeching us, by the tears which broke forth and interrupted his lecture whenever the force of divine ardor overflowed within him, to hasten thither with all diligence,

treading in a straight path the royal road, adhering with utmost observance to the footsteps of the holy fathers, lest we should be detoured, turning aside into some new and false path and succumbing to the snares of scandal. (pp. 476–47, ll. 14–21)

In other words, Adelman conjures him by the person of their former teacher; if Berengar holds the memory of Fulbert dear, he will not deviate from the path of the fathers. These are arguments from authority: the personal authority of the great man. He dissuades Berengar from "false" opinions by the force and authority of Fulbert's personality, by pulling him back into the orbit of the master's charisma. The nostalgia of the scene he paints — Fulbert weeping during evening colloquies, overcome by the force of divinity breaking forth in his lectures — illustrates well the ideal atmosphere of the old learning. We see how true the statement by Wibald of Stablo rings, that students defend what their teachers say because they love the men, not the truth in their pronouncements.[8] "I conjure you by the tears of our teacher": this is the poetry and the mood music of the cathedral schools, unthinkable in a scholastic disputation, powerful in an atmosphere where love of teacher substitutes for thought, where the teacher's person constitutes a kind of orthodoxy. For Adelman there was more truth in Fulbert's tears than in Berengar's logic.

This gives us the common strand in the examples of authority defied: the old learning responded to conflict and intellectual challenge by asserting and defending the authority of the masters. An ideal of demonstrable truth approachable through arguments represented a powerful threat to men whose instruction was based on eloquence and personality. This points up the fundamentally irrational nature of an education based on the formation of character. It relies on the personal moral authority of the teacher, and reasoning — certainly critical, independent thought — can become an offense against him and diminish his authority. The old learning made the masters into an image of God, and the student's goal was to fashion himself in that image.[9] Disputation and reasoning are fundamentally at odds with this goal. Awe and reverence are appropriate to it.

Critical thought combined with the willingness to contradict was fateful for the masters of the old learning. The combination of reason and impudence answered their riddle and dissolved the magic spell of their authority. They were as vulnerable as their aura of venerability: tarnish it and they fell, contradict them convincingly and they faced early retirement. They had only faith, charisma, and tradition to fall back on, not a systematically worked out philosophical position. Stefan of Novara might have been pleased at having a talented student in Wolfgang of Regensburg. But he was not. He sensed that a systematic commentary by his own student on Martianus Capella, one that satisfied the intellectual curiosity of his students, was a serious threat to his authority as a teacher. The fate of William of Champeaux in the early twelfth century shows such fears to be well founded: his teaching career was seriously deflected because he lost to his student Abelard in their exchanges on the nature of universals. The very foundation of the old learning — personal authority — was its Achilles heel.

Early Retirement and the Collapse of Discipline: The Letter of Goswin of Mainz

Both Goswin of Mainz and Guibert of Nogent experienced and wrote down their observations on the passing of the old learning and the advent of the new, but they judged the development very differently. For Goswin the change spells the end of religion and the disciplined life, for Guibert the beginning of serious instruction.

Goswin decided to retire around 1065 after a full life of teaching and public administration.[10] He had become master of the school at Liège in 1044 and chancellor in 1050. Fairly soon thereafter he followed the invitation of Archbishop Liutpold of Mainz (1051–59) to teach at the school of Mainz. But in leaving Liège he had unwisely written an invective against the city, calling it a "vile heap of slag" compared with Mainz.[11] This indiscreet statement put him in a difficult position when some fifteen years later he decided to retire to Liège and wrote to his former student Walcherus to test the waters he had muddied.[12] We know how sensitive students were to criticism of their towns and their schools (the case of Würzburg). Goswin had created animosities that had to be drowned in torrents of rhetoric.

That is fortunate for us. His letter is full of lively and vivid observations on the schools around mid-century and their decline. It is a showcase of cathedral school learning that may have dazzled its recipients but has to aggravate and tantalize the modern reader by its endless sentences, heavy overlay of allusions, and obscure diction. I include a translation of the letter in Appendix B. Here I will deal only with those passages which relate to the decline of the old learning.

THE NEW TEACHERS

"Liberal studies are now given over to mimes and actors, who seem to go begging through taverns, where they hold forth in philosophical discourses on money."[13] These men set their students' ears itching with "vain and pestiferous novelties of phrasings and questions."[14] They are blown about like light chaff in every wind of doctrine (628), and having seized a single scrap of arcane knowledge they set out to wander like vagabonds through the fields of learning discoursing to no one's satisfaction," but filled with the conviction of their own expertise (XXVII.32.635ff.). He stresses their uprootedness: "Some men, made pseudo-masters by instruction of a sort, wander about here and there through villages, town and cities, since they know nothing of a fixed lodging" (XXVIII.32.640ff.).

When he brings it down to cases, it is Berengar of Tours who is the source of this new teaching:

> Observe, if you will, how sane are the doctrines and how salubrious the disciplines of the theologians who emerge from the academy of Tours. Its headmaster is that apostle of Satan, Berengar. Observe, I say, how pestilential, or rather how venomous are the scorpions and basilisks who break forth from the caverns of our contemporary Babylon, what heresiarchs, drunk on their must and smeared with their poison, introduce sacrilegious novelties concerning sacred things, useful for nothing except the subversion of the auditors, whose speech creeps like a cancer, because knowledge which puffs up does not edify, it subverts. (XXIX.32.652ff.)

These teachers have no reverence (XXIX.32.663, 699). They refuse to recognize anything beyond the grasp of reason. This is impudence and overweening. They dissolve mysteries and reduce God to the boundaries of nature (cf. chapter XXXI). They eat the paschal lamb raw or boiled (XXX.33.674ff.).

Complaints against this type of teaching are common from mid-century on.[15] We hear similar complaints enriched by social barbs in the Regensburg Rhetorical Letters (*Regensburg. Rhet. Briefe*, ed. Fickermann, epist. 6, p. 292), and Meinhard of Bamberg places the decline of studies in the same context as Goswin: the collapse of moral discipline (*Weitere Briefe Meinhards*, epist. 24, p. 221).

Discipline Fades

The new teaching is clearly in competition precisely with moral training. Discipline in the broader and the narrower sense is the very thing caviling logicians threaten. Liège in the golden age of Notker had had her students under her maternal wing and made them models of civil conduct, says Goswin:

> [Mother Liège] gathers her sons beneath her wings like a mother hen her chicks, favors and nourishes them, and educates, informs and instructs them in all that pertains to the conduct of life both personal or civil.[16]

But that age has passed. Now men cannot govern themselves, let alone the state, with the rudder of reason, since the hurricane blast of worldliness throws them off course.[17] When Henry III and Liutpold of Mainz were laid into the earth, all religion, equity, justice, moral discipline and liberal studies were buried with them, and the whole flourishing of the "manifold beauty of virtues and prolific burgeoning of liberal letters" that they had experienced, passed from the face of the earth (XXXIV.36–37.773–85). Now the pursuit of fame and vainglory have superseded the "dignity and modesty of the religious life" (XXXV.37.795–96).

Avarice is at fault. From it is sprung "that fatal rejection of manners and of discipline."[18] Whipping students to maintain discipline has fallen completely out of usage, and the result is that vices spring up like weeds in this newly created laxity. Instead of submitting to "the scholars' rod" students give themselves to stupidity, laziness and to their god, the stomach:

> Fleeing instruction in the gravity of moral discipline, they are blown about like light chaff in every wind of doctrine . . . those meant to be formed by artist's hand from wet and malleable clay into vessels of glory on the wheel of discipline leap off and take flight in trivialities, and are thus deformed into vessels of contumely. (XXVII.31–2.627ff.)

The image of discipline the sculptor or potter turning young men into exquisite works of art recurs in other documents of the old learning.[19] But this aging master imagines the moral sculptor working with the whip and deprived of his tools by pernicious novelty, and this is a throwback to a cruder side of discipline.[20]

Goswin comes close to suggesting that the pseudo-masters' pied-piper effect on students rests on the promise of laxer discipline:

> The youths . . . they lure into their company and out of the refuge of discipline, and guide them down the cliffs of voluptuousness. They put to flight the reverence for discipline, the subjection to obedience, the observance of religion, and in the end destroy all the fortifications of the regulated life through a most pernicious corruption of manners. (XXVIII.32.644ff.)

The same had been suggested by Anselm of Liège in his criticism of the new license that students could find at "the courts of kings and bishops." This breed also "disdained the yoke of discipline" in giving themselves over to levity (see Anselm, *Gesta*, Chapter 6, p. 203 above). Goswin calls this trend a disease which is poisoning the entire church (XXXII.34.708ff.).[21]

Others agreed that the trend was spreading. Meinhard of Bamberg also polemicizes against the "inept insolence and insolent ineptness" of certain teachers who, having hardly progressed beyond the rudiments of grammar, fancy themselves sages. These men swarm everywhere like a plague of frogs and bring down ruin on "manners and discipline" (*moribus et disciplinae*), infecting them with the turpitude of their licentious lives. The occasion of the letter is to announce to the recipient (not identified) that Meinhard is sending his nephew to his school. He does this not for any lack of lettered men in Bamberg, but "desirous of discipline, which I doubt not continues strong in your school, though everywhere else it is virtually extinct."[22]

The dying out of moral discipline in the stricter sense of a school subject is a concern of a group of teachers we have studied: Anselm of Liège, Meinhard of Bamberg, and Goswin of Mainz. Goswin seems to claim the near-extinction of "discipline" elsewhere in the empire:

> There is virtually no one who will either work for the true institutes of a good life [*vera bonae vitae instituta*] or reward the one who does as befits, and for this reason that handful of workers remaining is overcome by exasperation and resigns from the labor. (XXXII.34.711ff.)

Two letters from Bishop Hezilo of Hildesheim throw some light on the crisis of "discipline" both at Bamberg and Hildesheim. Some twenty years into his long period of office (1054–79) Hezilo was forced much against his will to remove a young man named Kuno from the provostship of St. Moritz of Hildesheim. Kuno had looked like a perfect choice for the office. He was a relative of Hezilo, and the bishop had sent him to the school of Bamberg (where he studied with Meinhard), much the way Meinhard sent his own nephew to another school. A well-educated relative must have been an ideal candidate for office. But Hezilo had a particular purpose. Hildesheim needed a warden of discipline, as he explained later to the Bamberg community:

> The moral discipline of my house had either been altogether ignored, or consigned to a status of neglect. Therefore I was desirous to reform and revive it with your institutes, and so I appointed this same lord . . . provost . . . believing him of that odor with which he had been imbued since boyhood at Bamberg and therefore useful for the good of the brothers and the education of the cloister.[23]

Hezilo could not have been more deceived. Kuno lorded it over the brothers with an intolerable pride and made a comfortable life for himself, enriching himself with the goods of the church. As soon as he ran into resistance, he bolted, stealing "piles of riches" from the church and heading for the royal court, where he did his best to damage his relative and former benefactor, Bishop Hezilo (cf. epist. 22, ed. Erdmann, p. 53). The incident resonates with Goswin's complaints: discipline does indeed seem to be dwindling. The bishop who has been in a position to observe for some twenty years cannot claim that he inherited a mess from his predecessor (Azelinus, who imported courtliness; see Chapter 7 above). Very late in the game, he sets about to appoint a teacher who will restore the teaching of discipline. But, as Goswin said, avarice and self-interest are in the saddle. These and not moral discipline were the forces that moved Provost Kuno.[24]

Old Masters Retire

Why did Goswin of Mainz want to retire? He was old and tired enough:

> . . . my career has drained my spent energy with the incessant demands of its labors to the point where hardly any is left, and it has sprinkled my head with early snow. I fear an untimely death will be the result, unless I retire betimes into quiet and leisure. (XXXIII.35.730ff.)

But he also feels all but isolated in his efforts and watches as the "handful of laborers remaining . . . retire" (713–14). He sees the best of his generation going into early retirement:

> With wise contempt many men of distinction and high authority have observed all these circumstances: Hermann of Rheims, Drogo of Paris, Huzmann of Speyer, Meinhard of Bamberg and many others. Having abandoned their ambitions and resigned their labors, they have bid farewell to studies.[25]

We may well imagine that the disappointment of these teachers was real, but their moral disgust at the decline of the good life probably is Goswin's extension of the real cause: "the collapse of moral discipline" means the fading of a certain kind of teaching at the schools. It is a school subject, not just a personal attainment. That subject is passing away as the dominant force in school curriculum. If humanists in the late twentieth century complained that "humanity is extinguished," and meant by the phrase that their classes were dwindling, we would have a comparable situation. Meinhard of Bamberg apparently had withdrawn from the school by around 1065, the date of Goswin's letter. But he did not drift off to inactivity. In 1085 he was appointed bishop of Würzburg. There can be many reasons for his leaving his teaching duties twenty years earlier, but his own and others' complaints about students running off to new teachers who do not whip them into vessels of perfection is the best attested of those reasons. "Manners" are fading as a major course of studies at cathedral schools.

Guibert of Nogent

Guibert of Nogent gives a vivid and lively record of the old learning as observed by a man who has moved on to the intellectual positions of the new.[26]

Guibert's teacher, it is true, is as far from Brun of Cologne, Gerbert of Rheims, or Meinhard of Bamberg as Ichabod Crane is from Leibniz and Gibbon, though these three may also have made very different use of a common education. Guibert's teacher had only one subject that he knew and taught with any competence: manners. That subject at least he had in common with Brun, Gerbert, and Meinhard.

Here is what Guibert tells us about his learning of manners:

1. His teacher was deficient in letters, having started his study of the subject at a late age, but what he lacked in letters he made up for in "modesty" and "propriety" or "moral excellence" (*honestum*).[27]

2. His tutor kept a close watch over the "vices which commonly spring up in youth"[28]; he spent all his time in the teacher's company, who kept an unrelenting vigilance on his carriage: "in everything I had to show self-control, in speech, in the governance of my eyes, in my actions."[29] Guibert takes this rigor to be more monkish than clerical.[30]

3. His teaching in letters was a waste of time, but the profit in manners was great:

> [in six years of rigorous training] . . . I got no reward worth the time it took. Yet otherwise, in respect to all that is associated with a foundation in good conduct,[31] he devoted himself completely to my improvement. Most faithfully and lovingly he instilled in me all that was temperate and modest and outwardly elegant.[32]

Guibert, it is clear, was under the tutelage of a teacher of *honestas*. Assuming this master to be between 50 and 65 (he was already *grandaevus* when he began the study of letters) at the time he taught Guibert (ca. 1070–1076), he would have received his own education in France ca. 1015–1030. We know that just at this time a student named Hubert received an education in *honestas* first at Chartres, then at Rheims.[33] We know also that at the same time Wazo taught both letters and manners at Liège, but favored manners over letters.[34] In other words, Guibert's teacher provided his pupil with an education that was prominent in the first half of the eleventh century and may still have been in place at some cathedrals in the twelfth,[35] and what looks to Guibert like a serious pedagogic failure — neglect of letters — might at least have been tolerated by some teachers. Wazo of Liège would have approved of the priorities of Guibert's teacher (though no one would have approved of his total ignorance of letters).

Finally, we know that, for the more intellectually inclined, "elegant but ignorant" was a reproach that could be hurled at the representatives of the old learning. Guitmund of Aversa criticized Berengar of Tours as "almost wholly ignorant," while affecting "grandeur and distinction" and "simulating the dignity of a teacher in his manner rather than by the substance of his teaching."[36] Guibert complains of the obscurity and nebulousness of his teacher's thought (chapter 5, p. 36), as Abelard complained about the obscure thought and incompetent philosophizing of the eloquent and elegant Anselm of Laon. Guibert's teacher was on an uncomfortable footing with the intellect and its tasks, and in this he embodied what was widely perceived as a weakness of the old learning.

The pedagogue tolerated no contradiction and taught garbled nonsense as unquestionable truth ("sua omnia sensa autentica aestimans"; "pro certo docere" — chapter 5, p. 36). He knew next to nothing, but he gave his uninformed utterances the weight of truths. That is, his teaching rested on personal authority, and no doubt part of the lesson was to accept that authority unquestioningly. The kinds of objections Guibert raised in his autobiography would undoubtedly have been seen and treated by his teacher as pernicious violations of the laws of love, reverence, and piety.

The whipping of Guibert is also approved pedagogy in the old learning. Goswin of Mainz would not have had a bad word to say about the method in principle, though one hopes he would not countenance turning students into scapegoats for incompetent masters. Probably the rule applied: the greater the teacher's ignorance, the greater the need for the whip (see n. 20 above).

"Love and fear" was another underpinning of the old learning, and whipping operated at its negative pole. But its positive pole, love, is the dominant in the relation between Guibert and his teacher. Their relationship starts with a dream of the master. His dream represents a virtual contract drawn up on the basis of love: a white-haired old man appears to him leading Guibert by the hand. "Go to him," the apparition says to Guibert, "for he will love you very much." Guibert kissed him repeatedly, and the master "conceived such affection" for the pupil, that he brushed aside all other considerations and accepted him as his student (chapter 4, p. 28). This affection sets the tone for their relationship: "Although he crushed me by his severity . . . he loved me as well as he did himself"; "I conceived much love for him"; "through a sort of love deeply implanted in my heart, I obeyed him in utter forgetfulness of his severity."[37] The beatings clearly are presented throughout as a factor that, dreadful as they were, could not damage so strong an affection. The teacher's brutality has predominated in the modern view of this pedagogue,[38] but it is balanced and to some degree compensated for in Guibert's mind by his love.

We know something about the status and previous employment of Guibert's teacher. He belonged to the class of clerics attached to a noble house, responsible for the religious life of a court and for the education of the lord's children. Guibert's mother makes contact with him through some men called "chaplains," and it is not unreasonable to assume that he was called by the same title. He was attached to the house of some of Guibert's relatives (referred to as *nobilis*—p. 28, in fact a distinguished family, a branch of the lords of Clermont), and "had been educated at their court" (*quorum innutritus curiae*).[39]

This all adds up to a case distinctly classifiable in the categories and terms of eleventh-century society and school life: a minor cleric who learned manners without letters in his school days — spent at least in part at a court of high French nobility — teaches Guibert what he himself has learned: how to behave circumspectly, "honestly," with prudence, modesty, and "external elegance." Guibert says his tutelage was more appropriate to a monk, and in severity and constancy of surveillance[40] this may be true. But the values of *temperantia*, *modestia*, *honestas*, self-control in speech, countenance, and actions, are more at home in cathedral schools, while *exterior elegantia* belongs exclusively to a worldly education. The tutor's instruction relies on love and fear, enforced by authority.

So what was Guibert's problem? He received a good education from a tough but loving master of *honestas*. Why didn't he count his lucky stars and accept happily training with which Thomas Becket and the favored students of Wazo of Liège were content? Probably the answer is that Guibert wanted to learn: "I would rather die than give up the study of letters" ("Si . . . proinde mori contingeret, non desistam, quin literas discam et clericus fiam!"—chapter 6, p. 40). His famous statement that in his youth there were hardly any "grammarians," and those there were had but meager learning (*scientia*), has to be read in this sense. *Scientia* is the cutting edge that separated old from new: Guibert sought knowledge, and the teachers he might have found at Rheims, Chartres or Liège diluted it with ethics, since for them knowledge was still a colony of *honestas*.

Guibert also says that the erudition of the teachers in his youth was not comparable to that of the "wandering scholars of the present day."[41] This phrase shows that Guibert is measuring the old learning against the standard of the new. We have learned to evaluate "wandering clerics" from the point of view of the old (Goswin and Anselm of Liège). For Guibert they have become the measure of learning.

That does not mean that Guibert was a representative of the new. He is notoriously difficult to categorize (see Benton's introduction to *Self and Society*). In his commentary on Hosea he wrote against new grammarians, who revise the opinions of God and the fathers (see Benton, *Self and Society*, p. 20). Still, in his autobiography, the new learning was the perspective from which he viewed his own early training.

The conventional reading of Guibert's education has created a misleading picture of an educational scene in eleventh-century France that was a wasteland in his youth and a blossoming garden in his maturity. That is true only from the point of view of the new masters. What was available in Guibert's youth was instruction in *mores* and *honestas*. It was not abundantly available. Guibert's mother had to lure a dubious candidate away from her own relatives, and she would presumably have taken an easier route, were such men readily available. But we should be careful in generalizing from Guibert's autobiography on this point. Guibert's mother wanted a private tutor, and the one she hired devoted six years of his life to a single student night and day, weekends and holidays. Such men are never available in abundance.

Peter Abelard

The opposition to the old learning had its sharpest edge in the teaching and writing of Peter Abelard. My purpose here is not to describe the thought and method of Abelard.[42] I want to regard Abelard strictly in his relation to the old learning. The point is to gain a clearer view of that education through the eyes of a major player in its demise.

SUBSTANCE VERSUS STYLE

Some of Abelard's most penetrating comments on teaching and learning are in the poem he wrote for his son Astralabe. It is an ambling collection of proverbial and personal wisdom.[43] The first subject it treats is study:

> Care not who speaks but what the value of his words are. Things well said give an author his reputation. Neither put your faith in the words of a master out of love for him, nor let a learned man hold you in his influence by his love alone. We are nourished not by the leaves of trees, but by their fruits. The meaning is to be preferred to the mere words. The rhetoric of ornate words may capture minds effectively, but true learning prefers plain speech. A wealth of words conceals a poverty of understanding. If you see that a man's teaching is inconsistent in itself you may take it that there is nothing reliable for you in it.[44]

With a few strokes of his pen, Abelard here cuts away some of the underlying principles of the old learning. He rules out eloquence that substitutes for understanding and rational consistency; he questions first love then authority as the basis of the student-teacher relationship; and he calls for something approaching systematic thinking in a teacher (doctrine that is not contradictory).

Some of the basic ideas of this passage recur in Abelard's criticism of the teaching of Anselm of Laon in the *Historia calamitatum*:

> Anyone who knocked at his door to seek an answer to some question went away more uncertain than he came. Anselm could win the admiration of an audience, but he was useless when put to the question. He had a remarkable command of words but their meaning was worthless and devoid of all sense. The fire he kindled filled his house with smoke but not with light; he was a tree in full leaf which could be seen from afar, but on closer and more careful inspection proved to be barren. I had come to this tree to gather fruit, but I found it was the fig tree which the Lord cursed.[45]

New confronts old here in as sharp an opposition as we could hope for. Anselm is teaching by eloquence, charisma (he can command admiration) and inertia. Abelard himself makes sense through plain speech and reasoning that addresses the understanding more than the emotions. Abelard has genius, Anselm has slowly acquired polish.[46]

AUTHORITY

Abelard's clash with authority had two phases: his opposition to his early masters and their advocates, ending at the council of Soissons (1121), and his clash with the Cistercians, ending at the council of Sens (1140). His account of his conflicts with William of Champeaux and with his accusers at the council of Soissons also make it clear that his opponents were dabbling in argumentation, but hoping reverence would carry the day against the terrors of irreverent students and no-holds-barred public disputation. But

Abelard did not spare his opponents; he exercised the lethal weapons of contradiction, intellectual consistency and plain speech; no mood music rescued weak positions from attack, and no Orphic strains slowed the charge of the rhinoceros.

An incident at the council of Soissons can help turn up a basic fallacy of authority that weakened the old learning and its representatives.

Abelard had written a tract on the Trinity. His students were asking for "human and logical reasons on this subject." They demanded "something intelligible rather than mere words," because "nothing could be believed unless it was first understood" (*Historia*, trans. Radice, p. 78). Difficult as the questions involved were, the subtlety of Abelard's answers and proofs is up to the task (Abelard tells us), and the book became popular. Called to account for his teaching at a church council arranged by two former students of Anselm of Laon, now masters of the school of Rheims, he put forward his book and explained his religion in public. Nothing heretical could be found, and his explanations proved popular. His enemies were suddenly in trouble; the tide of events threatened to turn against them. Alberic of Rheims faced him in public and asked him to account for his claim that God did not beget himself. Abelard was about to explain, when Alberic interrupted: "'We take no account of human reasoning,' he answered, 'nor of your interpretation in such matters; we recognize only the words of authority.'"[47] Abelard immediately located — in his tract — a quotation from Augustine on the Trinity that fully supported his position. Alberic was taken aback and stammered something that made no sense but saved face. Abelard offered to prove to Alberic that Alberic had himself fallen into a dangerous heresy by claiming that God begets himself.

What was Alberic relying on in facing off with Abelard on a point that had been addressed and answered satisfactorily in Abelard's own book — the one at issue? Hadn't he read the book? He asked for authorities that were there all the time. Abelard outplayed him on his own grounds. Naturally, Abelard wrote the scenario for the confrontation, and he cast himself in the role of winner. But even if his version is badly skewed, it shows us the issues as Abelard conceived them. Alberic's entire support in that confrontation was the false and wholly irrational assurance that he would not be contradicted.

In facing a master of rational disputation armed only with that conviction, Alberic committed a fundamental and representative error for any learning based on authority: he confused his *personal authority* with the authority of texts and ideas. The enthusiastic cry of Sigebert of Gembloux's

St. Maurice, "Who needs examples? You yourselves are the examples" (see above, p. 189) is good rhetoric but bad logic. The reverence for authority placed personal and ancient authority on the same plane, and the slippage on this spectrum always or ordinarily favored the living example.[48] When masters of the old learning spoke about authority, it was easy for them to fall into the illusion that it meant whatever they said. Guibert of Nogent's teacher, to take one example, was the lesson: he had nothing else to teach but himself. Authority is a comforting voice whispering to the old masters that they do not really have to make sense and their positions will still prevail. That means, of course, a sloppy and uncritical habit of mind secured against criticism by loving tyranny. In the scene cited above, Abelard uses authority as an instrument of rational, critical proof, and all Alberic has is the assertion: I don't care what you say. You're wrong anyway.

Abelard, on the other hand, appears to have regularly underestimated the power of irrational authority. It is a martyr-making fallacy whose results probably took him by surprise. Abelard's fallacy is that nothing can resist the strength of a powerful idea. The fallacy rests in failing to see that authority, which in its mythical or hagiographical mode embodies supernatural force, is in its everyday mode a mask for power. The comparatively harmless whip of the classroom is a poor relative of torture instruments, the pyre, the stake and the cross. The next move in the council of Soissons is the assertion of power behind authority. The council deteriorates into intrigues and ends with Abelard forced to recite the Athanasian creed and throw his book into the fire.

The development of the Paris schools, the university, and scholastic philosophy proved Abelard the winner in the long run. Reason and ideas take their time; they work slowly on the reshaping of consciousness and institutions. Authority is for the moment. Like so much of the old learning, it was oriented to the body and to personal presence. It is dramatically successful in controlling the immediate present, but it extends only as far as it can reach. If truth is the daughter of time, authority is the daughter of the present moment. Its gains are dramatic but short-lived, especially when they involve the removal of uncomfortable human beings like Abelard.

An incident that Bernard of Clairvaux tells in his Life of St. Malachy confirms this analysis of the role of irrational, personal authority and has a strong resonance with the events at Soissons. A certain learned cleric doubted the real presence of God in the sacrament, the story runs. Malachy called a public synod to debate the question. The cleric defended his viewpoint with great skill and ingenuity and powerful arguments. But in the end Malachy won the debate, and his opponent called foul: "He claimed that he had not been conquered by reason but pressured by episcopal authority."[49] The cleric continues, "You've confuted me without good reason, speaking against truths and your conscience. You all curry favor with one man instead of considering the truth. I shall not accept this person and so desert the truth."[50] Bernard is remarkably accurate in formulating the position of the rationalist. He opposes authority and the person. He claims truth for his own reasoning and sees it obscured by personal authority: "veritas potius quam homo," to turn around Bernard's phrase.

This is a generic confrontation. It applies well to the trials of Berengar of Tours, Abelard at Soissons and Abelard at Sens. It applies generally to the forces of authority opposing the forces of intellect in the century between Berengar's emergence and Bernard's death. It shows authority opposing reason and overwhelming it by no other instrument than authority itself. The story mystifies authority, making a simple exertion of it appear like the working of a miracle.

The wish dream of an embattled mentality is that its forces will expand magically to overwhelm the enemy pressing in on it. But the opposite was happening at the schools. Authority was giving way to reasoned debate. One of the major effects of Abelard's thought and method was to create a philosophy that removed the element of personality and personal authority from teaching and thinking.

THE INNER AND THE OUTER MAN

Abelard's ethical thinking likewise tends to undermine the idea that external appearance is the guarantor of inner virtue, and that is one of the main pillars of *cultus virtutum*.[51] He says in the poem to Astralabe, "There is no idea that learned men accept as a more certain truth than this: external things do not commend us to God. Your habit may make you proud, but not saintly" (*Ad Astralab.*, ll. 301–3, p. 123). Virtually every cathedral school master and student from the late tenth century on would have disagreed. All were at work making their students and themselves works of art that beam piety, reverence, modesty, and so on. The suggestion that God is indifferent to posture, gait, gestures, speech, table manners, and clothing is — given the presuppositions of *cultus virtutum* — outrageous. A number of learned men in Paris contemporary with Abelard would have disagreed also, and that certainly includes anyone at the school of St. Victor. Hugh of St. Victor wrote his *De institutione novitiorum* to show the way to god "through the discipline of virtue" (PL 176, 926B–C), which he later defines as

> good and proper behavior, to attain which it is not enough just to avoid evil. It
> strives also to *appear* above reproach in all things that it does well.[52]

It probably is no coincidence that the discipline described by Hugh of St.
Victor is to a great extent designed by Abelard's former teacher, William of
Champeaux, in fact no doubt just in the early days of St. Victor when
Abelard was still his student. It is not possible that Abelard was ignorant of
the fact that a long tradition of moral discipline depended precisely on
making virtue visible in external things.[53] If that discipline was not pleasing
to God, then a great many people were wasting their time.

The thrust of Abelard's ethical thought was to abolish the outer man as
the textbook and artwork of moral training. Defining sin as consent to evil
rather than commission of it makes the obligation to *appear* irreproachable
superfluous, in fact hypocritical.

The issues are strongly presented in Heloise's second letter to Abelard.[54] She paints the picture of herself as an unrepentant sinner, still sighing
for the lost state of sin more than for forgiveness and redemption. But
outwardly she seems penitent and chaste:

> Men call me chaste; they do not know the hypocrite I am. They consider purity
> of the flesh a virtue, though virtue belongs not to the body but to the soul. I
> can win praise in the eyes of men but deserve none before God.[55]

The times are bad, she continues. There is hardly any religion that is not
hypocrisy. "Whoever does not offend the opinions of men receives the
highest praise" (trans. Radice, p. 133; ed. Muckle, p. 81). She could well
cite Hugh of St. Victor's definition of discipline that insists on "appearing"
good, though the importance of doing good in that definition does not
serve Heloise's purpose, and she says as much:

> ... perhaps there is some merit ... if a person ... gives no offence to the church
> in his outward behaviour, . . . does not disgrace the order of his profession
> amongst the worldly. And this too is a gift of God's grace and comes through
> his bounty. (p. 134)

But outward show that receives praise is her object of attack.[56] She musters
biblical support and formulates some attacks of her own: "No one with
medical knowledge diagnoses an internal ailment by examining only outward appearance" (p. 135).

Heloise is the opposite of the virgin Sophia, whom angels envy as a
receptacle of visible virtue. No angels envy the unrepentant sinner Heloise,
since her visible virtue masks her desire for her lover.

ABELARD'S MORALS

This ethic of extreme inwardness that declares outer acts morally indifferent may be consistent with an ascetic strain in Christian moral thought,[57] but it is also an ethic of a man (and woman) who have caused scandal, and suffered disgrace and persecution as a result. It was comforting for Abelard to assure himself that the outer world was morally indifferent. He transformed himself in the years between the councils of Soissons and Sens into a kind of martyr figure, suffering calmly and passively the blows of fortune that were his lot. His wordy defense at Soissons compared with his Christlike silence nineteen years later at Sens signals this change.[58]

But another interesting response to his ethical stumbling is in his own reasoning about ethics. He shared much in common with St. Augustine. They both developed the fine and subtle sense of morality and humanity peculiar to the reformed sinner. There are probably few experiences that sharpen the sense of right and wrong, justice and injustice, more than guilt and contrition. In this also he is representative of a strong strain in the culture of the twelfth century. He shares the sinner's heightened moral-ethical sense also with Hartmann von Aue's Gregorius and Wolfram von Eschenbach's Parzival.

Abelard came to the ethics of the old learning by betraying them. The language of the old learning occurs in the poem to Astralabe, and in all cases it occurs in the form of self-castigation. He argues against himself and warns against his own example:

> This above all: do no damage to your reputation. Then you can do good to many others and to yourself. Old sins make new ones plausible, and your life until now bears witness to your life from now on.[59]

> No man becomes wise by mere sharpness of mind. Character [or good behavior: *mores*] and a good life make a man wise. Wisdom professes itself in actions, not in words, and this gift is conferred only on good men.[60]

> Be careful first to live the Good and only afterwards to teach it. Otherwise you will be at odds with yourself.[61] It is proper for a just man to . . . restrain the illicit impulses of a modest mind, especially in the midst of wealth.[62]

> Examine prudently what the nature of vice and of virtue is, and if you lose that knowledge, you cease to be what you are.[63]

> Strive with all your might to avoid scandals in the eyes of men, then you will incur no scandals in the eyes of God.[64]

At St. Victor and other surviving bastions of the old learning, they would have found little to quarrel with in the rudimentary common sense of these precepts. In fact one might almost imagine Abelard formulating lessons that Hugh of St. Victor had directed against him in the 1120s: "Unpraiseworthy is learning stained by a shameless life. Therefore let him who would seek learning above all take care not to neglect discipline."[65] But Abelard was an ethical thinker, not a pious moralizer. He made allowances for the man of talent that Hugh of St. Victor did not:

> Do not fault a man's skills because of his failings: Many a bad man is a good artist.[66]

Abelard forced a wedge between letters and philosophy on the one side and manners on the other. In his thought philosophy emancipated itself from its attachment to good behavior. The brilliance of his teaching and writing and the strength of his personal and intellectual charisma stood in sharp contrast to the scandals he caused and suffered.

*   *   *

There is a profound connection between Abelard's life and the general tendencies in the schools of the time. An entire system of education was caught in a conflict between a traditional kind of teaching that tended toward the acquisition of human qualities and a new kind that tended toward knowledge and rational inquiry. The representatives of the old warned that morals were going to the devil[67] and being replaced by irreverent caviling; representatives of the new scorned the elegant mediocrity of the old masters, and wrangled for the understanding that reverence had denied them. The clash between Abelard and Anselm of Laon exemplifies these tendencies strikingly. It is as if whatever forces of history shaped the general conflict designed Abelard and Anselm to embody it: they brewed the intellect and character of Anselm with an overbalance in favor of *mores* and eloquence (the products of the old learning), and then, like chemists performing an experiment, exactly reversed the proportions in brewing Abelard. Anselm and the type he represented may have lacked penetration and analytical sharpness, but they were masters of the discipline of living well. Abelard may have known a great deal and possessed a keenly analytical mind, but he was a failure at the discipline of life.[68]

Part Three

The Twelfth Century: Seeking New Homes

Introduction to Part 3

Peter Abelard drew crowds. His friends and enemies alike agree on that:

> What king or philosopher could match your fame? What district, town or village did not long to see you? When you appeared in public, who did not hurry to catch a glimpse of you, or crane his neck and strain his eyes to follow your departure?[1]

Otto of Freising says that Abelard drew a "great crowd of followers" wherever he went.[2] This charismatic quality was one of the things that made him appear dangerous to William of St. Thierry and Bernard of Clairvaux. Bernard wrote to Cardinal Guido di Castello: "He comes forward not by himself, like Moses, to the cloud hiding God, but with a great throng and with his disciples."[3] Where he could not go, his writings did: "His books fly everywhere. . . . In castles and towns they replace light with darkness. . . . They pass from one race to another, and from one kingdom to another"[4]; "His books cross the oceans, they leap over the Alps . . . they spread through the provinces and the kingdoms, they are preached as famous works."[5] One of his epitaphs calls him "the light of the student throng."[6] It was no doubt partly due to his influence that the student population of Paris swelled from whatever the cathedral of Notre Dame could accommodate by itself in 1100 (certainly not more than about 100 students) to 2000–3000 by 1140.[7]

While these crowds ran after Abelard, the old fashioned humanistic masters languished. A strain of stoic resolve on the part of the student-less teacher runs through the work *Philosophia mundi* of William of Conches. He says that he cares not for the multitude, but only for the probity and love of truth of the few.[8] He says that the true teacher teaches from love of learning, not from an urge for popularity, and that he continues his work "even when the crowd of followers fails him."[9] No-one was saying about William of Conches what the author of the "Metamorphosis Goliae" said about the major philosophers of mid-century: "et professi plurimi sunt Abaielardum" ("many of them are professed followers of Abelard")[10]

Manegold of Lautenbach in the previous century could have been writing for William of Conches when he said in his Glosses on Cicero's *De inventione*: "The dignity of a few good men excels by far the boundless multitude of the bad."[11] "A few good men" were always enough for the old learning. It was elitist and exclusive, and elitism maintains itself in part by gestures of exclusion. But the rush of the throng to other classrooms wounds even the firmest pride of the elitist teacher. William of Conches's expansive attitude was surely a face-saving accommodation to a crisis, not a confident posture of exclusion broadly available to well-situated humanist masters. John of Salisbury tells us that William "retired" along with his (John's) other teacher, Robert the Bishop, "when the onslaught of the ignorant crowd conquered" them.[12] The wording is unclear, but it certainly does not mean that they were "overwhelmed" by crowds of the ignorant seeking their instruction. More likely the crowds were running past and away from their schools and to teachers who promised greater success with shorter terms of study.[13]

Not all teachers of humanistic subjects lost their students. Bernard of Chartres maintained a high standing, and Thierry of Chartres was a famous teacher, called by one of his students, "the anchor immovably fixed during these changing times of fluctuating studies."[14] But the handwriting is on the wall and its message is clear.

What happened to *mores* as a school discipline in the flux of studies in the early twelfth century? That is the subject of the next chapters. But we need to observe at the outset that in the burgeoning French cathedral schools and the independent schools of Paris *mores* is nowhere in evidence as a discipline in the sense in which it appeared in the late tenth and eleventh centuries. We cannot do for twelfth-century France what we did for eleventh-century Germany and France: give an inventory of references to the teaching and learning of moral discipline at the cathedral schools. No masters lament the time they spend teaching *mores*, as Meinhard had done; no students — or few — are mentioned as seeking out the cathedral schools of France *causa discendae honestatis*, as the pupil of Fulbert of Chartres had done[15]; no masters are praised for favoring the teaching of *mores* over that of letters, as was Wazo of Liège. The schools of Germany, however, appear to have hung on to this discipline as handed down from the imperial cathedral schools of the pre-investiture controversy period. Wibald of Stablo at least still speaks the language of the old learning in urging Balderich, a schoolmaster of Trier, around mid-century,

> Let your mere presence be a course of studies for your students. . . . Your position requires more than mere teaching. You must exercise strict severity, for you are, as you know, also one who supervises the correction of manners. This teaching and this exercise is more subtle and in its fruits more important than any other.[16]

For the dialecticians of Paris, the entire plan of studies Wibald commends, but especially the suggestion that the correction of conduct is the "subtlest" of the arts, could have stirred only a snicker at such an impossibly backwoods attitude, one that would have been laughed out of the Paris schools.[17]

The Paris schools had released themselves from their tie to the bishop's court. It was possible to set up independent schools in which a single master could accommodate large numbers of students.[18] These circumstances made discipline as the elementary introduction to studies impossible in the old form.

Crowds of dialecticians: the nightmare of Goswin of Mainz. It meant that ideals like suave and gentle manners, loving correction, an aura of benign kindness spreading over the whole school and fusing its members into a brotherhood of love, were a thing of the past. In the catalogue of masters of the "Metamorphosis Goliae" (ca. 1142), a very different view of teachers emerges:

> There can be seen that doctor of Chartres whose sharp tongue cuts like a sword. Here also stands that prelate of prelates of Poitiers, the true knight and soldier of the wedding couple.

> Among these and others . . . the resident of the Petit Pont . . . disputed with i-shaped fingers.

> Reginald the monk contended clamorously and with insinuating words rebuked many a contender. No man of self-examination, he refutes this one and that one, suspending our Porphyry himself in his snare.[19]

The days of loving and emotional colloquies in cloister gardens between a revered master and a handful of socially and intellectually elite disciples were past, and in their place was an atmosphere of strident contention idealized and described in the language of military combat.[20]

There is another body of texts from and around the school milieu: criticism directed by virtually every group of learned society against the new schools. Stephen Ferruolo has studied these critics, and argues that they pointed to problems and conditions to which the new institution of the university was the answer.[21] A leitmotif of many of the texts Ferruolo treats is the collapse of moral discipline at the schools. The previous chapters suggest that such criticism had a distinct historical context. It may well have been more than topos-like calls for the restoration of a golden age. Their authors probably recalled a day when moral discipline had dominated the schools.

Something called *disciplina* had to exist at a bishop's household and had to be taught to new members of the community. Bernard of Clairvaux set out this obligation in the language of ethical training in his *De consideratione*. He paints the picture of a pope's or bishop's household dominated by the virtue of *honestas*: the bishop himself must provide for *disciplina*. Moderation should guide him between the extremes of austerity and frivolity, cruelty and laxness: "Sanctity befits the house of a bishop [Ps. 92: 5], as do moderation and ethical conduct [*honestas*]; discipline is their guardian." He must be strict in disciplining the servants of the household:

> Allow nothing disgraceful, nothing improper to remain in the appearance of those who are around you, or in their deportment of their carriage ["In vultu, in habitu, in incessu . . . nihil impudicum . . . indecens patiaris"]. Let your fellow bishops learn from you not to have boys with luxuriously curled hair and foppish young men in their retinue.[22]

He should preside with gravity but not austerity, moderation being the guide. His servants should love him, and while he keeps a close guard on his own speech, he should not exclude "gracious affability" (*affabilitatis gratia*). He should be "serene in appearance and guarded in speech." In general, the bishop's own example must provide the model for the entire household.[23]

Little has changed, it would seem, in the ideals of administration of a bishop's household. We hear themes and motifs that were commonplace in the cathedrals of the eleventh century.[24] But the discipline at the *schools* of cathedrals has no profile any longer in the twelfth century. Probably as a practiced discipline in cathedral communities, it has been lowered from the status of the chief goal of the school to a household discipline.

An odd situation: The language of *ethica*, its image of the ideal human being, is present at the cathedrals of the twelfth century. But it has shifted its context subtly. The medium is different. Lived ideals have been transformed into discourse; the language of school discipline becomes the language of humanistic poetry and philosophy. Gradually in the course of the century noble society generally begins to speak this language: it emerges in monastic communities, in communities of canons regular, and especially at worldly courts both in Latin and the vernacular. It is taken up into writings instructing in court behavior, the training of noble children, the "honest" pursuit of courtly love. It influences the iconography of the vices and virtues in Gothic sculpture.

The pressure exerted by the new trends on *mores* and *ethica* at the cathedral schools pressed and compressed this malleable subject so that it disappeared from the surface of instruction. But it leaked, seeped out at every edge, and spilled out into other areas. It was fragile as pedagogy but durable as an ideal of human perfection. The old learning had formulated a marvelous image of the human being as a work of art, an exquisite sculpture and a "vessel of perfection" turned on the artist's wheel: gentle, modest, affable, controlled, charming, and graceful. And while the teaching that had developed at cathedrals in the tenth and eleventh centuries no longer is visible in the new schools of the twelfth, its contents gain a life of their own and are transformed into widely shared social ideals and literary models.

This section observes that process of transformation, and we begin with a community that offers the best documentation in medieval Europe on the *disciplina morum* and its training. The school of St. Victor at Paris not only retained the pedagogic practice of the eleventh-century schools in the training of novices, it also recorded it in detail.

9. Humanism and Ethics at the School of St. Victor

William of Champeaux taught dialectic at the school of Notre Dame in Paris. Abelard calls him the "supreme master" of this art, which "had long been particularly flourishing."[1] Abelard may exaggerate both of these statements to give highlight to his victory in the conflict that developed between the two. He joined William's class and successfully challenged some of his arguments, an event that evidently shook the master's authority as a teacher of dialectic. A typical constellation ended in this case untypically: the master left the school of which he had been head, and the irreverent student stayed and eventually took over his position.

Whatever his motives,[2] William of Champeaux "retired" in 1108 to an abandoned hermitage on the south side of the Seine just outside of the city walls of Paris and founded there a community of canons regular dedicated to St. Victor. He continued to teach in the new community, which grew into one of the most illustrious schools of the twelfth century, and this, according to Abelard, irritated many people and cast doubt on the sincerity of his conversion.[3]

Schola virtutum: *Venustas morum* as Curriculum

What did he teach there? We know from Abelard that he taught rhetoric, since he himself studied the subject with William at the new school. It was here that Abelard dealt him his final defeat on the question of universals.[4] Another witness to William's teaching is a student from Bamberg who studied with him in the early years of St. Victor. The student wrote a letter to his prior in Germany basically asking for money, but also praising master William who "gave up all his possessions to live in some miserable little church to serve only God. There he showed himself kind and devoted to all who came to him, and he received them gratis." The master's words, he says, were so sweet that he seemed more like an angel than a man. The student seeks *bonum sapientiae* and *scientia cum caritate* from William. His *doctrina et studium* erase vice, inculcate virtue, and arm the mind against the attacks of this life.[5] The pious stance is somewhat suspect, since the writer has a financial incentive for putting the best face on his studies. But the array of offerings — eloquence and virtue — is a framework with which we are familiar.

More illuminating is a letter William received from Hildebert of Lavardin shortly after his retirement to St. Victor. This letter helps us deal with the question of what William taught at St. Victor. The occasion of writing is to oppose the voices criticizing William for his continued teaching activity and to encourage him to persist. It begins:

> My soul rejoices and exults in your conduct and conversion [*de conversatione et conversione*], giving thanks for these acts of grace to Him from whose gift you have at long last decided to begin philosophy. For what you have done until now did not savor of philosophy. You merely gathered knowledge from philosophers; you did not bring forth in yourself beauty of conduct [*morum venustatem*]. But now you begin to draw out from it [*ex ea*, i.e., beauty of manners] the pattern of good behavior [*bene agendi formula*] like honey from the comb.[6]

The philosophy abandoned is an ungenuine one, mere acquired knowledge; the philosophy embraced is pressed out of the very self, like honey from the comb, and is called "beauty of manners." This change occurs, Hildebert says, because William has subjected himself to a new rule of the religious life, which makes him into a true philosopher. Against the advice of those who urge William to give up teaching, Hildebert says, "Virtue is to administer the material of virtue, even to one who will not put it to good use" (142B).

The point is clear: he now has a new curriculum to administer, *virtus* and *morum venustas*. Its content (*bene agendi formula*[7]) is the honey that flows from the comb of beauty of manners. The letter is not an admonition to continue the teachings of the schools, but to administer the rule of a new life, and the "new" philosophy he urges him to teach is conduct. Hence his rejoicing both at his conduct and conversion (*conversatio et conversio*).

It is fairly clear that William of Champeaux has retreated from new learning back into the old. "Philosophy" regains its ancient and early medieval meaning of *bene vivendi disciplina*, and some of the goals of *ethica* are represented in his new curriculum: *morum venustas* and *bene agendi formula*.

This testimony to the "philosophy" of behavior at St. Victor is not isolated. One of the few witnesses to the teaching of Hugh of St. Victor is his student, Lawrence of Westminster, who confirms the prominence of ethical discipline. The student tells what drew him to the master:

> With all possible despatch I chose that excellent and unique doctor, and I embraced his teaching with supreme diligence, since the moral excellence of his life [*vitae honestas*] decorates his learning, and the saintliness of this teacher illuminates his polished doctrine with beauty of manners [*morum venustate*].[8]

Godfrey of St. Victor entered the community around 1155 or 1160, after completing ten years of study in liberal arts and sacred letters, and he explained its attractions in his quasi-biographical poem, *Fons philosophiae*. The life of canons regular drew him because it is a "faultless" norm learned from the "great examples" of the fathers. They are men "instructed in the salutary ways of the sacred rule, equal in manner of living, dressing, eating and gesturing" (*Vita, votis, habitu, victu, gestu pares*). The "master's elegance, the assessor's probity, the minister's skill" drew him. The "mere appearance of things" (*ipsa rerum facie[s]*) compels him to sit at the master's feet. After his entrance, he studied *ethica* and theology. Ethics removed all childish emotions and impulses (*pueriles motus*) from his mind and at the same time bathed him in "miraculous newness."[9] He learned to govern his tongue. Finally his mind was strengthened and his vagrant body restrained to a fixed measure (*figitur ut meta*).[10]

These witnesses confirm that something called *venustas morum* was prominent among the subjects that drew students to St. Victor, and Hildebert's letter strongly suggests that this was the curriculum instituted originally by William of Champeaux. It had powerful attractions, even for men like Godfrey and Lawrence of Westminster, who had received an education in the arts elsewhere prior to entering St. Victor.

We should stress that William of Champeaux's foundation was different from the provincial communities of canons regular. It was an urban community, or at least sub-urban. It attracted many noble clerics of high learning.[11] It enjoyed royal patronage.[12] A visit from the king was as much to be reckoned with as a visit from the local bishop, and the *Liber ordinis Sancti Victoris* makes provisions for receiving him.[13] It had excellent connections at the highest levels of church and state administration.[14] Its school was open to outsiders until approximately the death of Hugh of St. Victor in 1141,[15] and its traditions of ethical training persisted at least until the death of Richard of St. Victor in 1173. According to Jean Châtillon's formula that the more communities of canons tend to the monastic life, the more their schools disappear,[16] the life of St. Victor prior to Hugh's death was non-monastic, open to the exciting atmosphere of ideas in the other schools of Paris, though in regard to method, intellectual orientation and ethical training, conservative. Dialectic and disputation never found a home there.

The *Liber ordinis Sancti Victoris* and Other Rules

Important as ethical training was at cathedral schools of the eleventh century, there are no primary texts describing it. We have no customary or tract setting forth goals and methods. We have relied on peripheral evidence, and the result is that some of the basic questions remain unanswered: how long did this training take? At what age did it begin? How was it carried out in practice?

The houses of canons regular that burgeoned after the end of the eleventh century did produce texts on the training of novices.[17] These communities based the instruction of novices on spiritual formation according to several documents that went under the name "Rule of St. Augustine,"[18] according to Carolingian customs formulated in the *Regula canonicorum* of Aix from 816, and according to customs formulated individually by communities for their own use, often leaning on the previously mentioned documents and the Rule of St. Benedict. The command of St. Augustine that each canon should make himself an example for all others to imitate translated into formal arrangements and an ethos of life in which virtually the entire house could regard itself as a school.[19] The duty of teaching through example was for canons regular what pastoral duties were for secular clergy. It also distinguished them from monastic communities, where teaching and learning had a very different status and could not be regarded as an entirely legitimate activity of monks.[20]

These communities produced two kinds of documents that are evidence for training in *mores*: the *consuetudines* of the house,[21] which ordinarily include detailed prescriptions for receiving, initiating and instructing novices; and tracts that reflect on the nature and goals of the training of novices.[22] The earliest of these is Hugh of St. Victor's *De institutione novitiorum* written probably in the earlier twenties of the twelfth century.[23]

St. Victor has left the best documentation on ethical training from the period. The combination of its richly detailed customary, the *Liber ordinis*

Sancti Victoris[24] and Hugh's *De institutione novitiorum* gives us a uniquely clear picture of this instruction from the early twelfth century. Reading these works along with other tracts and letters from St. Victor shows us the life and teaching in that community united by a common core of ethical thought and a common ethical motive.[25] It also helps fill out an important aspect of the humanism of Hugh of St. Victor, easily overlooked, since it stands in the shadow of his major work on liberal studies, the *Didascalicon*.[26]

The *Liber* was written around 1116 by Gilduin, William's disciple and first abbot of St. Victor, probably with help from other members of the community.[27] It is longer and more detailed than any other customary known to me. Virtually every moment in the daily round is densely circumscribed by rules: rising, eating, communicating through signs, going to the choir, performing the liturgy, reading, going to bed. The rules are reinforced by a set of officers assigned for that purpose.

This closely examined life has a distinct style and flavor.

GOD'S MERCY AND YOUR SOCIETY: RECEIVING NOVICES

The reception and instruction of novices requires "the maximum of care and affection."[28] The house did not accept oblates. The minimum age was 15, and the rules for accepting novices generally are aimed at mature men (cf. 22, 7–94; 97–100; Godfrey of St. Victor had studied the arts for ten years before entering). All who are to be accepted should demonstrate "good manners" (*boni mores*), especially "gentleness, willingness to learn and patience with correction" (22, 16–19, 97). Once a brother is accepted, his perseverance and the sincerity of his profession tested, he is led by the *hospitarius* to the abbot in the chapter, at whose feet he prostrates himself and seeks indulgence. "What is your request, brother," asks the abbot. "I seek God's mercy and your society." The abbot responds, "May the lord grant you the society of his elect" (22, 95–107; 101).

When the first rituals of acceptance are performed, the novice is given into the charge of the *magister novitiorum*, who provides new clothing and a place for him in the dormitory. Once shaved and dressed, he is led by the master to the *scola*, where the novices are taught. During his novitiate, he leaves the school only to eat and sleep. His first instruction is in the immediate necessities of the community life. This primary instruction is described into the minutest details: where he is to stand, where to sit, where to keep silent; the master leads him to the washroom having "diligently instructed him in the things to be done there" (22, 162–63; 103). A novice goes nowhere without his master: ". . . the master is always present with them to keep watch over their discipline, to lead them to and from wherever necessity takes them" (22, 275–76; 108). The relationship of master to student is extraordinarily close: "His master must tend to him with the utmost diligence, giving him consolation in sickness and teaching and instruction in health" (22, 280–82; 108). In the school, the master

> instructs him diligently in the bows, in walking and standing, in his every gesture, how he should array his clothing in accordance with the particular act he is performing, how to compose his members in an ordinate way, keep his eyes lowered, speak gently and not too fast, swear no oaths . . . how to speak to the abbot or to his other masters, to the brother, to inferiors.[29]

He is to learn his actions and his speech by hearing and observing the master, who both speaks and acts in the appropriate way and then has the novice repeat and re-perform. Behavior is rehearsed, in other words, like movement, gestures, and speeches in a drama. The goal is to learn, by hearing and by practice, the "good measure and appropriate moderation in all words and acts" (*bonum modum et competentem mensuram in omnibus verbis et actionibus* — 22, 245; 107). This sense of rehearsing life before living it clearly looms large in this community:

> all things which he is to do in public he should first try out in advance in private and thus familiarize himself with them. (22, 247–48)

This kind of intensive teaching and custody continues for a month. At the abbot's discretion the novice is then admitted to the chapter. After full admission to the chapter, the novice remains in the custody of the master, but it is relaxed. The master speaks with him regularly, attends to his needs, corrects and encourages him; he "observes his daily behavior and his study," correcting and instructing him privately (23, 2–7; 111). Whenever speech is permitted, the novice must be in the master's presence, who maintains the same close scrutiny of his ward's speech as in his first month.

This second stage continues also about a month, though the prohibition of speaking except in the presence of the master continues up to a year.

The *Liber* does not specify the time the novice spends between admission to the house and his profession, which makes him a full member of the chapter. In other houses, the novitiate lasts approximately one year, and there is no reason to assume it was less at St. Victor.[30]

This rule gives us, for the first time in this study, a clear look at *disciplina* as it was taught. The context is a community of canons regular, and this distinguishes it from cathedral communities. Reading, writing, and learning in the sense in which Hugh of St. Victor describes it in the *Didascalicon* is never mentioned. The *Liber* is about behavior appropriate to communal activities, including the liturgy. I stress that the *Liber* is written out of this narrower perspective of the needs of the community. The broader implications of this training for general education of the Victorines will be clearer when we read Hugh's *De institutione novitiorum*. of the next section.

THE SCHOOL

The apparatus of instruction as laid out in the *Liber* clearly is considerable. The task of the *magister novitiorum* is arduous and demanding. The concern with custody and surveillance is all the more striking since the novices were in no small part mature men. The previous life is being sluffed off, and the creation of a new man requires constant vigilance from the master. But at the same time it is important to note that this watchful guard set on behavior never ends. Surveillance and correction are specified as duties of several of the officers.[31]

Besides the *magister novitiorum*, the *Liber* also mentions a *magister puerorum*.[32] But while rigorous discipline was obligatory for novices, ordinary school learning was not. Literacy played no part in the early training.[33] Otherwise information about masters and pupils is scarce in the *Liber*.[34] Clearly learning from books and teachers went on, abundantly. But when the *Liber ordinis* mentions the school, it is the *schola novitiorum*, and the only instruction is in *ethica*.

The customary does convey the impression that reading is a frequent activity. It devotes a long chapter to describing the duties of the librarian (*armarius*),[35] and refers to reading and books throughout. The librarian must receive a pledge for every book lent, especially if the borrower is a stranger (19, 14; 79). This shows that the school was not restricted to the Victorine community (see above, p. 246 and note 15). The librarian provides writing material to anyone who needs to write (19; 79–80). The only function of the library deducible from the *Liber* is religious and liturgical. The only kinds of books mentioned are "maiores expositores et passionarii et vitae patrum et omeliarii" (19, 86–87; 82), but the same passage refers to "others."

Silent hours are to be spent in reading or singing, the two activities separated so as not to disturb the readers. The chapter dealing with silence (31) is in large part devoted to instructions for getting and taking care of books.

CARITAS ET HUMANITAS: VICTORINE COURTESY

The *Liber ordinis Sancti Victoris* has a distinctive character compared with other works of the genre. Its recent editor, Ludo Milis, characterizes the Victorines, as they represent themselves in the *Liber*, as "plus originaux dans la formation de leur genre de vie, plus courtois (même au sens littéral du mot) et plus urbains" (*Liber*, avant propos, p. vi). To my mind this observation touches one of the essential distinguishing features of this customary and the life it describes. What follows in this section are a few footnotes on it. The qualities Milis describes are evident in every chapter of the *Liber*. I believe William of Champeaux, Hildebert of Lavardin, Hugh of St. Victor, and many others would have called them *venustas morum*.

Virtually every act respecting another brother is to be performed "gently, affably, considerately" (*benigne, affabiliter*).[36] These qualities are most evident in the reception and treatment of guests.

The court yard gatekeeper (*Portarius curiae*) is the first to welcome arrivals. He must be

> a man of proven character, affable and kind-hearted, instructed in the discipline of manners and speech, who can serve as an example to all and embody the reputation of the entire house.[37]

Someone who troubles arriving guests with questions and delays is not suited, particularly if his rejoinders are abrasive or wounding. If he turns people away for any reason, he must beg their pardon humbly and explain himself, "lest they be hurt by his repulse" (*ne aliquatenus de repulsa sua perturbentur*). Guests arriving for the first time must be met *cum magna benignitate et humanitate*. If they arrive on horseback the porter should approach the one he takes to be the superior and with a smiling face (*hilari vultu*) receive his reins and stirrup and say, "May our lords be welcome" (cf. 15; 55–57). The authors of courtly romances were to depict welcoming scenes with manners, gestures, and emotions close to those represented in the *Liber*. Here is the reception of the knight Calogrenanz at an unknown castle in Chrétien de Troyes' *Yvain*:

> I saw the master of the castle with a moulted falcon upon his wrist. No sooner had I saluted him than he came forward to hold my stirrup and invited me to dismount. . . . Then he told me more than a hundred times at once that blessed was the road by which I had come thither.[38]

There is a strong strain of courtesy and humanity in the Benedictine Rule and the traditions it founded. A look at the welcoming ceremony in other rules and customaries gives the Victorine ritual sharper profile. The Benedictine Rule also calls for a humane and compassionate reception of guests.[39] The virtue of *caritas* is also invoked, but the mood and gestures are different. The ritual in the Rule has a liturgical cast. It prescribes that every guest be received as if he were Christ. The priors or the brothers welcome him *cum omni officio caritatis*. The welcomers and the newcomers then pray together. They show their humility either by bowing their heads or by lying prone before the guest. (*Ben. Reg.*, 53).[40]

Interesting is the proximity of the Victorine customs to the influential constitutions of Marbach,[41] which stipulate,

> The brother who serves guests should be sweet, kind, humane and discreet. . . .
> Above all however, his inward feelings should be outwardly visible, a good and
> generous will, a happy and handsome face, a lovely and honest affability. He
> should take in wanderers and strangers even more humanely and joyfully than
> his parents and acquaintances, since in them more than others he receives
> Christ.[42]

These comparisons give us a clear focus on the peculiar character of the Victorine ritual. The injunctions not to offend the feelings of guests, to receive them *hilari vultu*, with great kindness, charity and humanity, and to represent in their bearing inner virtues are best described with the terms Milis uses, "courtly and urbane." The Victorine prescripts provide a little mirror of courtly ritual.[43]

The moment of reception, the mood of good humor and humane kindness, the *Liber* explains, is especially important for reasons other than external etiquette:

> We enjoin that all these things [the welcoming ritual] should be scrupulously
> carried out, because those who come from outside are especially to be received
> with great kindness and humanity from the first moment of reception . . . so
> that from their first impressions of the outside they form an estimate of the
> things concealed within.[44]

This comment strikes a rich chord. It recalls Godfrey of St. Victor's first impression of the community: "The very appearance of things compelled me to sit at the master's feet" ("Ipsa rerum facie cogor assidere" — *Fons phil.*, l. 761). We will encounter the idea in Hugh's *De institutione* in the context of ethical training.

This ideal of putting that face on things which best registers the inner life of the house is embodied also in the *hospitarius*. He is to be a man "educated in manners and discipline" who knows how to treat arrivals "as religion and good behavior require" (*religio et honestas* — 17, 1–5; 59–60). Guests arriving at mealtime are to be treated *largiori humanitate* (17, 118; 64). The hospitaler should be present when anyone is sick and attend to their needs *cum omni humanitate et caritate* (17, 177–78; 66–67). Finally, the obligations of the hospitaler extend to all servants of the community, where guests are concerned: they should show them a cheerful and kind face (*hilarem ac benignam faciem ostendant*), do nothing to them or their servants that in any way violates discipline, and if injured by them, bear it humbly and patiently (17, 197–205; 67–68).

The courtesy of St. Victor must have been some of the honey pressed from *venustas morum*. It was clearly part of the discipline of novices, and of the communal life which that discipline prepared for. But it served the interests of the house as well. It made it attractive to converts. Just as the monastic communities put the cult of friendship to practical use in recruitment,[45] St. Victor beckoned to those outside with the attractions of its courteous and affable society. Odo of St. Victor wrote a letter to a brother living outside the community, recalling him to the cordiality of their society, their *dulce consortium* and *dulce colloquium*, and commending his brothers as

> amiable as company and useful as models to imitate. They are amiable company not only for the sanctity of their lives, but also for the suaveness of their manners.[46]

The teaching of *mores* at St. Victor had another use. It was seen as a means of promotion in the church. *Elegantia morum*, *venustas morum*, the result of a discipline in *ethica*, were not only private virtues; they were also qualifications for church office; they were among the constituents of *idoneitas*.[47] The letter of Richard of St. Victor to Robert of Melun congratulating him on his promotion to Bishop of Hereford gives an interesting insight into Victorine attitudes on the subject. Robert had taught briefly at St. Victor before his election. Richard writes,

> . . . all your students were filled with joyful hope [at the news of your promotion] and the entire school was heartened and roused to the love of letters and the cultivation of virtue [*ad cultum virtutis*] through the example of your efforts and your success.[48]

Joined to the study of letters, *disciplina* and *cultus virtutis* were not entirely disinterested personal ethical formation, not a kind of aesthetic-spiritual self-perfecting, but rather also a study that shaped men for the service of church and state.[49]

Hugh of St. Victor

Hugh of St. Victor is a truly universal scholar and teacher. His admonition to young scholars to learn everything and disdain no knowledge (*Didascalicon*, 3.13) is a reflection of his own universalism, and this in turn has a basis in his ethical thinking and that of his school. This is clear in a remarkable passage at the beginning of the *Didascalicon*:

> Wisdom illuminates man so that he may recognize himself. . . . It is written on the tripod of Apollo: *gnothi seauton*, that is "Know thyself." . . . An opinion approved among philosophers maintains that the soul is put together out of all the parts of nature . . . thus it is that one and the same mind, having the capacity for all things, is fitted together out of every substance and nature by the fact that it represents within itself their imaged likeness . . . the rational soul could by no means comprehend all things unless it were also composed of all of them. . . . This then is that dignity of our nature which all naturally possess in equal measure.[50]

It looks forward to similar pronouncements on human dignity and universality in the Italian Renaissance, notably by Pico della Mirandola in his "Oration on the Dignity of Man." For both the medieval and the Renaissance humanist there is a cognitive and an ethical aspect to universal man. For Hugh this comprehensive nature of the human mind is the image of God in man. But man has lost or darkened it through sensuality and sense impressions, and there are two ways to restore it:

> Now there are two things which restore the divine likeness in man, namely the contemplation of truth and the practice of virtue.[51]

In his major treatise on the sacraments, Hugh distinguished the two phases of God's image within (*imago* and *similitudo*) by assigning one to knowledge and one to ethics.[52] Here we have learning and manners (Hugh's conception is too broad to be encompassed by the old formula, "letters and manners") integrated into theology, the three of them forming a grand program of attaining man's dignity in earthly life.

DE INSTITUTIONE NOVITIORUM
Hugh's major work on the cultivation of virtue is his *De institutione novitiorum*. This is one of his most popular works[53] and one of his oddest. It is a

tract of spiritual instruction, but it lacks the gravity, coherence, and systematic conception of other representatives of the genre (like Hrabanus Maurus's *De institutione clericorum* or Philip of Harvengt's work of the same title). Regarded alongside comparable works, it appears positively eccentric. It reads like a first draft. The organizing principle is a quotation from Psalm 118: 66 (AV 119: 66): "Teach me goodness and discipline and knowledge" ("Bonitatem et disciplinam et scientiam doce me"). But the work is exclusively about *disciplina*. He treats *scientia* briefly, essentially as a category of ethical learning,[54] and polishes off *bonitas* with almost jocular brevity in the final line of the work: "We have said these few things to you, brothers, concerning learning and discipline. As for goodness, pray that God give it to you" (952B). From beginning to end the work is about how to behave and how to learn good behavior.[55] Typical of the work's priorities is that the chapter on gesturing takes up six full columns in the Patrologia edition (938A–943D), while the chapter on sacred scripture takes up nineteen lines, barely half a column (933D–34A).

The work's religious intent deserves a more critical analysis than it has received. The editors of the Patrologia edition placed it among Hugh's mystical works. While this is not the place to treat the question in detail, an example or two can characterize the problem. The purpose of the work as stated in the prologue is to show the way to God through the "discipline of virtue" to men "to whom all earthly glory and beauty is as a heap of dung" (926B–C). But this purpose is almost wholly absorbed in matters of external conduct. The fervent conjuring of *contemptus mundi* and the apostolic life in the prologue gives way to lessons on walking, talking, gesturing, and table manners.

In its second half the work takes on a tone that Hugh himself describes as "satirical." In a number of passages he shows a quality I have not found in any other work of his, a sense of humor. Here he describes ill-disciplined gesturing:

> Some men are incapable of listening without jaws agape, and as if meaning entered the mind via the mouth, they open it wide to take in the words of the speaker. And others (far worse!), when they do something or listen to someone, stick out their tongue like a thirsty dog and revolve it around their mouth like a millstone, twisting their lips from the effort. Others stick out their finger while speaking, raise their eyebrows and roll their eyes; or they stand rooted to the spot in profound meditation and an outward pretense of some inner magnificence. (941C–D)

It goes on in this vein until Hugh interrupts to remind himself that he is teaching, not writing satire and that modesty and restraint are called for.[56]

But the satire persists and the *modestia* he conjures is put aside to make way for it.[57]

The work's stated intention is at odds with its tone and contents. In its preoccupation with external decorum, it omits the major themes of the Benedictine and Augustinian traditions. The work does not treat fasting, penance, self-denial, and mortification of the flesh. *Obedientia*, the dominant virtue in the Benedictine Rule, occurs only twice, in a single sentence (932A), subordinated to the topic of following examples. Chastity, which looms large in both the rules of Benedict and Augustine, is not mentioned. Nor is *caritas*. This omission gains profile against a passage from another work of Hugh's accusing the gentile ethical philosophers of "severing the members from the body of goodness, which has no life apart from charity."[58] This criticism of pagan ethics can be turned against the *De institutione*: it deals with a few members from the body of virtue and pays no attention to their source, *caritas*.

DISCIPLINA

"Discipline" is the central ethical/pedagogical idea of the work. It occurs in a variety of formulations: *disciplina virtutis, morum disciplina*; the abbey is the *schola disciplinae*; *custodia disciplinae* is the maintenance of acquired virtue through vigilant self-examination; the human face is the *speculum disciplinae*; the end point of ethical learning is the *forma disciplinae*; *disciplina vivendi* is another term for ethics. It designates both the content and the process of ethical training.[59]

Throughout Hugh's works "discipline" is the process of learning virtue. The word has no other general area of application[60] except in the *Didascalicon*, where it occurs in the conventional sense of *disciplina* = *ars*, and *disciplinae* = "the disciplines."[61] The singularity of Hugh's usage is apparent in the definition he gives in the *De institutione* (and in the fact that he gives a definition at all, which shows that the term requires explanation and is not part of a shared conceptual vocabulary):

> Discipline is good and proper behavior, to attain which it is not enough just to avoid evil. It strives also to *appear* above reproach in all things that it does well. Discipline is also the governed movement of all members of the body and a seemly disposition in every state and action.[62]

This definition expressly limits its meaning to an etiquette of conduct, bearing, control and governance of the body. It also insists that good is not constituted only in the performance of good and omission of evil acts, but also in the *appearance* of goodness, its outward semblance. Goodness should be visible in the governed movement of the body.

We need to supply a context for this definition. We should note at once that Hugh's definition of *disciplina* has no roots in either monastic usage or the traditions of canons regular. In monastic and canonical rules *disciplina* commonly refers to the teaching and learning of the rule itself. Common formulations are *regularis disciplina, canonica disciplina, monachica disciplina, disciplina ecclesiastica, disciplina claustralis, disciplina ordinis.*[63] Its meaning in the *Liber ordinis Sancti Victoris* is quite restricted. It ordinarily refers to a restriction placed on behavior (e.g., 22, 318; 110). We can contrast Hugh's definition with an instructive passage from the Constitutions of Springiersbach on the reception and "discipline" of novices. It distinguishes between two kinds of lay converts: the one fit by youth and mental aptitude to study letters and become clerics; the other somewhat older and duller of mind. The latter should imitate the canonical life and be governed under a rule by means of a discipline appropriate to them.[64] In a "tracking" system of teaching novices, the older and duller of mind are assigned merely to discipline under "some rule." The suggestion that "discipline" is the slow track was not thinkable at St. Victor, where, on the contrary, ethics was a major attraction to recruits, in some cases representing the fulfillment of an extensive program of liberal studies taken elsewhere (the case of Godfrey of St. Victor).

Disciplina morum, disciplina vivendi, and other terms for ethical training from the *De institutione*[65] form part of the tradition of training inherited from classical antiquity and taught in worldly courts at least since Carolingian times and at courts and cathedral schools since Ottonian. Hugh of St. Victor and presumably the community of St. Victor, were the beneficiaries of the *disciplina morum* of the eleventh century cathedral schools. Elements of this tradition are taken over by other canonical and monastic communities in the course of the twelfth century and beyond.[66] A good indication of its affinities with court/courtly education is that the *De institutione* is appropriated in the thirteenth century by courtesy books[67] and "mirrors of princes."[68]

Disciplina vivendi and *bene vivendi disciplina* are originally Ciceronian formulations.[69] They have loomed large in earlier chapters and it can suffice here to point back to the introduction and the beginning of Chapter five. But it may be worthwhile to repeat the comment of Hincmar of Rheims in his letter of instruction to Louis the German that the king's court is

> a place of discipline, that is correction, since it corrects men's behavior, their bearing, their speech and actions [*habitu, incessu, verbo et actu*], and in general holds them to the norms of a good life.[70]

This passage brings us close to the context in which Hugh places discipline. Both texts identify it with the teaching and correction of *habitus, incessus, verbum et actus*. This gives us the two contexts of *disciplina* as Hugh defines it: ancient philosophy and worldly ethics. One other passage will help locate the worldly ethic which is the twelfth-century context for that definition. Otto of Bamberg was praised by one of his biographers for his

> . . . special gift of . . . elegant and urbane *discipline*. Never under any circumstances, in eating, drinking, in word, gesture or dress, would he tolerate anything indecorous . . . but rather in every act of the outer man he manifested the harmony within him, conspicuous as he was for his goodness, *discipline*, and farsighted wisdom.[71]

Here again the contents of discipline are table manners, speech, gesture and dress, and Hugh's *De institutione* places discipline in just that context.

IMITATION

The basic mode of learning for the cultivation of virtue and the discipline of *mores* is imitation. *De institutione* is the most serious and extensive reflection on teacher imitation known to me from the Middle Ages. The presupposition for imitating good and holy men (as for the study of reading[72]) is humility, says Hugh. It softens the obdurate mind and makes it receptive to the lessons of others, as warmth softens wax prior to receiving the impress of the seal:

> In them [i.e., good men] the form of the likeness of God is engraved, and when through the process of imitation we are pressed against that likeness, we too are moulded according to the image of that likeness. But you must know that unless the wax is first softened, it cannot receive the form, and thus also a man can not be kneaded to the form of virtue through the hand of another's actions, unless he is softened and all pride and stiff-necked contrariness removed. (*De inst. nov.* chapter 7, 932D–933A)

Hugh clearly thought of spiritual formation in terms of the model of human handcraft. The model to imitate is the artist's conception, the finished man, reformed to the image of a new life, is the work of art. The rest of the chapter develops this comparison:

... we who seek to be reformed through the example of good men, as through some marvelously sculpted seal, perceive in them the traces of actions, some of which are sublime and eminent, but others abject and debased. . . . When [saintly men] act in such a way as to arouse the admiration of human minds, then they appear as exquisite sculptures. What stands out [is outstanding — *eminet*] in them should be recreated inwardly in us.[73]

The other source of models to imitate is scripture. Hugh deals with this subject in a few lines, perhaps feeling that he had already made his major statement on divine reading in his *Didascalicon* written at approximately the same time as the *De institutione*. He explains the process in some detail in his *De arca Noe*. The good in scriptures is useless, he says, unless the reader takes it as an example of living. The inward contemplation of God's word is only effective,

> if I work to know *and* to perform good and useful acts and make the virtues of others, which I love and admire, into my own through the exercise of discipline and the form of right living.[74]

But the basic locus of imitation is the lives of good men. The title of his chapter, "De exemplis sanctorum" is misleading if read to mean the saints of the church. It means the good men living in the community of St. Victor. This principle of imitability was so prominent in the community of St. Victor that in his chapter on treating each person in the appropriate way, he ranks the brothers in order of imitatability (chapter 5, 929C–930A). In his *De sacramentis* he uses a rich image depicting this imitability of others' virtues as a book written in and on men: The two books written in man are an outward and an inward one. The outer book is to be read through imitation, the inner through contemplation.[75]

Hugh of St. Victor integrated moral discipline and the study of letters into man's pursuit of God (cf. *De inst. nov.* prol., 925B–C). By claiming that the image of God constitutes that principle of imitatability, he created a great scale of discipline beginning in the training of the body and ending in similitude to God. It is above all the imitation of good men through which we restore the likeness of God:

> Why do you think, my brothers, we are enjoined to imitate the life and conduct of good men, unless it be that by imitating them we are reformed to the likeness of a new life? For in them the form of the likeness of God is expressed, and when we impress ourselves on them through imitation, then we too are reshaped according to the image of that same likeness.[76]

This became the theological grounding of moral training at St. Victor. Richard of St. Victor articulates it often.[77]

THE BODY AND THE INNER LIFE

The ethical vocabulary of *De institutione* deserves a detailed study. Its leading terms and concepts are discretion or judgment (*discretio*)[78]; moderation and the golden mean (*mensuram et modum tenere, rationis moderamen*); the examined life (*custodia, assidua inspectio operum et morum, facta sua circumspicere*); imitation of the examples of good men; renewal and reformation of the self (*ad novae vitae similitudinem reformari, se reformare in melius*); gentleness and modesty of mind which display themselves in speech, disposition, gestures and carriage of the body. Here I will limit myself to what is far and away the dominant concept of Hugh's tract—and of the ethical thinking of the school of St. Victor generally: the importance of outward display as the guarantor of inner harmony and well-governed virtues. Gesture, carriage and speech are the media in which inner virtue comes outwardly to expression. The composition of the inner world is the job of *ethica*, and for Hugh of St. Victor the job begins with the body:

> Just as inconstancy of mind brings forth irregular motions of the body, so also the mind is strengthened and made constant when the body is restrained through the process of discipline. And little by little, the mind is composed inwardly to calm, when through the custody of discipline its bad motions [emotions] are not allowed free play outwardly. The perfection of virtue is attained when the members of the body are governed and ordered through the inner custody of the mind. (chapter 10, 935B)

This means that virtue is acquired through physical training and restraint. For a teacher with this presupposition, *exterior disciplina* (935D) and *usus corporis*[79] become identical with *cultus virtutis*, and indeed, Hugh states this outright:

> The members of the body are to be restrained, therefore, through discipline, so that the condition of the mind may be firmed up within and strengthened to the point where exterior vigilance is set against that interior flightiness which has to be controlled, so that in the end the mind may be consolidated in peace. . . . Little by little, as it becomes habitual, that same image of virtue is impressed on the mind which is maintained through outward discipline in the disposition of the body.[80]

If the body becomes the locus of virtue, then it is possible to read it like a book for the signs of virtue, an image Hugh himself used (see above, p.

259). He infers for instance from various styles of gesture and carriage the virtue or vice which governs each:

> There are six kinds of reprehensible gesture and movement, namely, an effeminate glide, a swagger, a listless shuffle, a hasty stride, a wanton strut, and a turbulent dash. The effeminate step indicates lasciviousness; the swagger, slovenliness; the shuffle, laziness; the stride, inconstancy; the strut, pride; the dash, wrathfulness.[81]

Hugh clearly has a sophisticated and articulated concept of the body as the concern of ethical discipline. He applies the principle of political governance to the command of the body: the body is "a kind of republic" (943A), each member of which has its own duty. Vice is when one usurps the duty of another. The ordinate functioning of all together produces *concordia universitatis*. Moderation is the virtue that holds contrary vices, to which the body is prone, in check and produces a particular grace:

> . . . a man's gestures ought to be graceful without effeminacy, nonchalant without swagger, grave without listlessness. . . . The turbulent dash tempers the effeminate gesture, and the effeminate tempers the turbulent . . . because the median line between opposing vices is virtue.[82]

When the entire body is governed through discipline and custody according to the virtues of *moderamen*, *modus*, and *mensura*, then "harmony of the whole" is attained (*concordia universitatis* — 943A). This reiterates that striking comment quoted earlier that "the perfection of virtue [*integritas virtutis*] is attained when the members of the body are governed and ordered through the inner custody of the mind" (935B).

This process of training, restraining, governing and inspecting takes place in four contexts particularly: in dress, in gestures (including walking), in speech, and in table manners. There is no point going through them in detail. We are now in a position to judge the underlying conception of moral discipline that commended these questions of etiquette as an introduction to the search for God. The first step on the path to God is governance of the body: the mastery of external things leads to mastery of the inner world, and the composed and mastered body gives testimony to the virtuous soul.

Now we should recall the description of the porter's duty in which the authors of the *Liber* say that a good humored, humane and kind conduct is especially important, since "from their first impressions of the outside [the visitors] form an estimate of the things concealed within" (above, p. 252).

It recalls Hugh's "reading" of the body for signs of the state of mind in the *De institutione*. This suggests a conceptual unity underlying the life of St. Victor, Hugh's ethical thought, and no doubt also that of William of Champeaux. Just as the exterior behavior of the disciplined man gives testimony to the virtues composing his mind, so also the behavior of the "outer man" — the man on the outside — the porter, symbolizes the interior ideals, *benignitas, humanitas, caritas*. I would suggest that this conceptual unity also takes in aspects of Hugh's theology. One could compare the duty of the porter with Hugh's definition of a sacrament:

> Pupil: Why is a sacrament called a sign of something sacred?
> Master: Because through that which one sees outwardly, something inward and invisible is signified.[83]

The congruence of inner and outer, and the hermeneutic it creates, was a widely shared idea in the school of St. Victor. It forms something like a unifying moral/ethical concept.[84]

Now we need to place this conception within the traditions of training in *mores* we have observed until now.

De institutione novitiorum and Cathedral School Traditions

The fundamental ideas of the *De institutione* are indebted more to the secular traditions of antiquity and the cathedral schools of the eleventh century than to monastic and canonical traditions. The roots of that work are easy to locate. It is full of echoes of ideas we have come across in the eleventh century. Clearly its central idea is the one we put in the center of an earlier chapter, "virtue made visible." At St. Victor it appears as the foundation of an actual discipline of conduct, a role we can assume with some certainty it played also at the cathedral schools of the previous century.

The idea of a harmony uniting the entire presence (*concordia universitatis, integritas virtutis*) was present in Godfrey of Rheims' portrait of Odo of Orleans ("Trois oeuvres de Godefroid," pp. 345–46; Chapter 4, p. 114 and n. 145), in whom "attitude, voice, speech, figure, gait and appearance gave off signs of an integrating harmony." Also shared by both is the logic of opposed vices brought to equilibrium by the moderating force of *mensura*: Godfrey of Rheims:

vice is ill-shunned when the shunning yokes you to its opposite vice . . . Odo
holds the middle road between both extremes. (ll. 40–45)

Hugh of St. Victor:

> The turbulent dash tempers the effeminate gesture, and the effeminate tempers
> the turbulent . . . because the median line between opposing vices is virtue."
> (*De inst. nov.* chapter 12, PL 176, 943C–D)

The process of "reading" the body for signs of virtue and vice is
another shared idea of the Rheims school and Hugh of St. Victor. Recall
Walter's dedication of a book on physiognomy to Marbod of Rennes
(*Carmina*, ed. Bulst, p. 18; see above, Chapter 4, pp. 116 and n. 147):

> . . . it opens the secrets of nature to view.
> It notes certain things marked with the signatures of secret
>   meanings,
> Like stature, countenance, posture, voice, gestures, grooming.
> It reveals the character of men of whom you know nothing [and
>   reveals]
> Whether this one is just, beautiful with the flower of virtues,
> Or evil, false, and overly bold at any crime.

Clearly Hugh's *De institutione* and the life of St. Victor represent the
diffusion of the program of education in *mores* that we have followed in
earlier chapters. The comparison with the *Moralium dogma philosophorum*
ascribed to William of Conches is instructive. This is a kind of summa of
Ciceronian ethics,[85] and at the same time a prescriptive formulation of an
ethic that had been at work in cathedral schools for at least a century
previous. The work dates from the first half of the twelfth century. The only
guide to a more specific dating is the uncertain identification of the "Henricus" of the prologue with the young Henry of Anjou, future Henry II of
England. Lacking positive evidence of date and authorship, the work cannot be fit into the dossier of connections between William of Conches and
Hugh of St. Victor.[86] But the ethical language and concepts shared by
Hugh and this Ciceronian-Senecan compendium make the comparison
valuable. Here are a few passages that demonstrate proximity of thought
and language:

Moral. dog. phil., p. 42:

Modesty is the restraining of grooming and movement and our every occupation so that there is neither too little nor too much. On this the poet says: "Things have their own measure, there are definite boundaries."

De inst. nov., 943b:

. . . the custody of discipline in gestures [sees to it that] each and every member performs its functions in just that measure and degree of moderation which is appropriate, that is neither too much nor too little.

Moral. dog. phil., p. 42:

An ill-ornamented exterior is the messenger of an ill-composed mind.

De inst. nov., 935B:

. . . from inconstancy of mind is born inordinate movement of the body . . .

Moral. dog. phil., p. 42:

In the motions of the body one must take care lest through excessive sluggishness we use effeminate gestures . . . or lest in hastening, our speed becomes excessive. When this happens, we gasp for breath, the face is distorted, the mouth twisted; these signs give a strong indication of the lack of constancy. . . . Therefore care should be taken that reason presides and restrains impulsiveness. For if the impulses do not obey reason . . . not only the soul, but the body too is disturbed. [Cf. Cicero, *De officiis*, 1.131]

De inst. nov., 938A–C:

Gestures . . . are found reprehensible . . . when they are either effeminate or swaggering or sluggish or hasty. . . . When the mind is released inwardly from custody, then the members are moved outwardly in an inordinate way at every action . . . in all that it does it ceases to be governed by any moderating force of reason.

These passages do not argue direct influence, but certainly indicate shared ethical concepts. The debt to Cicero is obvious in the case of the *Moralium dogma philosophorum* and not obvious but palpable in Hugh's work. Hugh is using different words for the same ideas.[87] The comparison makes evident the veiled Ciceronianism fundamental to Hugh's work.

Discipline as Crisis Control

We still face the puzzle why Hugh, in outlining a program of spiritual renewal, placed so little stress on the apostolic life and so much on an ethic inherited ultimately from antiquity and immediately from cathedral schools.

This is a problem for a study in greater depth carried out by an expert in the history of religious movements. I will only point to some of the factors.

The crisis of the old learning had two causes: the new learning was one, the "corruption" of lay and religious discipline was the other. The community of St. Victor faced both. The origin of the house was connected with the victory of a brash young dialectician over its founder, William of Champeaux. The residue of antagonism registers in the veiled references to Peter Abelard in Hugh's *Didascalicon*.[88] In order to observe its opposition to the "decline" of *mores*, we need to take a look at the community's prescriptions on clothing and eating.

Hugh's *De institutione* is directed to nobles. It enjoins on them an aristocratic ethic — its canonical elements notwithstanding. The *Liber ordinis* is at pains to stress the equality of all brothers and to remove ranking by birth as an element in the life of the house. But it is also clear that the members received novitial training aimed at equalizing them at the level of aristocracy, on the basis of values at home at royal and episcopal courts.

The *De institutione* also warns against vices typical of the aristocracy, at least vices imputed by other writers to the nobles. A passage warning against excessively dainty dishes illustrates both the social level addressed and its vices, and it gives another rare example of Hugh's sense of humor:

> Caution is required in the choice of food, lest one request things excessively lavish and delicate, or rare and unusual. Nor should one desire things prepared in an excessively sumptuous or refined way. . . . But there are some men whose gorges are afflicted with a quite laughable infirmity, in that they cannot swallow anything that is not rich and delicate. And if on occasion sparse and ordinary food is offered them, they pass it by, offering frivolous excuses, as for instance, that it will cause them indigestion or asthma or headaches. Others disdain culinary delicacies and luxuries with great constancy, but at the same time despise altogether the common cuisine in a way equally intolerable. They demand new and unusual kinds of food, so that often for the sake of one man's stomach, a throng of servants must run through all the nearby villages to return at length with some rare roots plucked from distant desert mountains, or with a few little fishies [*pauculos pisciculos*] fished through enormous effort from the deep, or with strawberries plucked out of season from the thirsting bramble bushes, all this to quell the petulance of one man's appetite.[89]

This warning presupposes men with delicate palates, sensitive nervous systems, and finicky stomachs. It also presupposes numbers of servants at their disposal whom they can send for the rare fish and berries that alone will satisfy their tastes.[90] Of course, there may not have been a single novice or member of the community who really indulged in this vice after his entry into the religious life. The satire does not require the actual abuse to have its impact. But it does require the unfulfilled inclination. The barb would be blunted and the humor diluted if none of them kept servants or if they were men to whom rude and impoverished lives, or even ascetic lives of renunciation, were an accepted norm.

The prescriptions on dress, gesture, and eating habits reject fashions of the secular world which other clerics in many places in Europe were attacking throughout the late eleventh and twelfth centuries. Hugh says that clothes should not be *nimis subtilia vel mollia*, nor in any way "distorted according to worldly vanity" (936A).[91] He numbers among the vanities clothes that flow too fully and those pulled so tight as to reveal every curve of the body. This he calls shameless turpitude and vain ostentation; such fashions make women, or rather prostitutes, of men, who seem to change their sex along with their clothes (936C–D). Men should show modesty and humility in their clothing. But there are certain hard and rebellious souls, he continues, who can only be reined in with a jagged bit.

The language that Hugh speaks here is widely shared and easy to locate. These vanities and worldly ways are part of a broad wave of fashion that swept the European aristocracy from the middle of the eleventh century on.[92] Worldly fashions may have been as extravagant before that time, but the church reform produced a reaction against them that brought them into sharp profile. From the mid-eleventh century, wherever men touched by the spirit of the reform come into contact with worldly men, complaints like Hugh's surface. The *De institutione* responds in no small part to the crisis discussed in an earlier chapter, an infestation of bad manners among the European nobles, lay and clerical.

Hugh and the community of St. Victor looked at the continuing alteration and distortion of manners that Anselm and the community of Liège had observed. Liège withdrew into its shell, retreated into the comfort of monastic severity, and the result was the swift decline of its school. Not everyone took this snail-like posture. St. Victor took a position that represents a tendency to social reform, a direct answer to the abusers of the law of moderation. The threat to religion and conduct was answered not only by polemics, but by a moral discipline that made moderated elegance into the sign of inner virtue. It is no coincidence that both moral discipline and polemics against over-refinement make up the substance of *De institutione*. It shows St. Victor engaged, through both criticism and communal self-fashioning, in the project of rebuking and reforming a society veering dangerously away from moderation in dress, gesture, table manners, and the virtues that govern them. St. Victor did not reject refined and urbane manners, as Liège did. It caught up the thrust toward extreme behavior inherent in the dynamic of court manners, and blunted and refashioned it according to the law of *moderamen*. This is a productive response to the "crisis of manners" developing in Europe. At the same time as the school of Liège was declining to insignificance, the school at St. Victor developed into one of the most illustrious of the Middle Ages.

It should not be surprising if this project commended itself to a master responsible for formulating the education of novices at an abbey near Paris attractive to noblemen, a community whose rigorously structured life was conceived as a curriculum and whose "teaching" was exercised in the very act of living that life.

*   *   *

The humanism of St. Victor is fed by the diffusion of an ethic that spread from the cathedral schools in the course of the eleventh century. It picks up ideals of "beautiful manners" and the congruence of inner world and outer appearance. The lives and customs of canons regular with their stress on humanity, charity, and irreproachable appearance in external things provided an ideal context for this ethic. The Ciceronian-Ambrosian ideals of beautiful conduct "sat" perfectly in this context. A worldly ethic stressing fine manners and courtesy tended to over-refinement and ostentation in secular and episcopal courts. But a canonical community could be held to stricter standards of moderation. In the quasi-cloistral atmosphere, it was possible to create an exemplary community as a model and a reproach for worldly men. The founders and early teachers at the school of St. Victor superimposed an ethic of gentle, refined, "courtly and urbane" bearing onto the ideals of the apostolic life: equality of manners and renunciation of possessions. This created a quasi-monastic courtesy, an ascetic Ciceronianism, with a degree of legitimacy that the old imperial program of cathedral school education with its more worldly Ciceronianism could never again attain in the wake of the investiture controversy and religious reform. It occupies a middle position between the worldly ethic of the secular courts and the asceticism of the new monastic movements.

But apart from its social and historical context, Victorine humanism had its own content. Acquisition of virtue through training of the body, self-presentation made into a work of art, carriage and bearing as a symbolic code that conveys through outward elegance inner beauty and harmony: these are what the training of novices at St. Victor promised, and they must have represented powerful incentives to conversion. They spoke to worldly men of high nobility and to others who without license of birth might want to acquire noble manners. If men wanted asceticism, escape from the self, sainthood, they went to monastic communities. St. Victor offered "letters," beautiful manners, theological illumination, the "good" — that is the or-dained and regulated — life, a life that left open the possibility of advance-ment in the church.

The first two constituted its particular form of humanism. The two major works that convey that humanism are Hugh's *Didascalicon* (letters) and *De institutione novitiorum* (manners). Impressive as the former is in its breadth and coherence, the eccentric and unevenly composed *De institu-tione* formulated the *studium vivendi*, at least as attractive and important in the schooling at St. Victor as the *studium legendi*.

10. Bernard of Clairvaux

The writings of Bernard of Chairvaux share many features of the language of ethics spoken at St. Victor. But there are two big differences. If Hugh of St. Victor believed that walking, gesturing, eating, and speaking well made men virtuous, Bernard believed that indwelling virtue made men (and, at long last we can add, women) walk, gesture, eat, and speak well. For Hugh of St. Victor discipline began with the control of the body and moved inward. For Bernard the cultivation of virtue begins in the conscience and moves outward. What for Hugh is the result of long and careful training is for Bernard an act of grace or genius.

That is the first difference. The second is that *ethica* has separated itself in Bernard's language from the actual disciplining of behavior in a community and has become a general discourse of human talents. For Hugh of St. Victor, discipline was tied to instruction for the Victorine life.

In many ways Bernard despises the very discipline that has been the subject of this study. But he also produced some of the most lyrical descriptions of the disciplined human being.

Beauty of Soul

The letter to the virgin Sophia is our beginning point.[1] He writes to commend her on her chastity and to strengthen her resolve to remain a virgin. The glory and praise due her are all the greater because she is a noble and a woman. Those are two inducements to vainglory and wantonness, says Bernard. Her strength in overcoming the inborn vices of birth and gender is the greater, since virtue freely chosen is worth more than virtue born of necessity. Humility and restraint are no victory in an ugly and lowborn man; in a high-born beautiful woman they are glorious. She has long-necked friends who walk and dress elegantly. If they chide her, she should think of the bridegroom to whom she is betrothed, his gifts, the bride's dowry, and the "blessings of sweetness." Let this bridegroom,

Christ, come into their midst dazzling in his beauty and dressed to make the angels envious, and then ask the "daughters of Babylon" if their adornments can compare. They dress in purple and fine linen, but their conscience is torn and ragged; their necklaces dazzle and their morals disgust ("fulgent monilibus, moribus sordent"). Sophia, however, is beautiful inwardly and would remain so even dressed in rags: "What delights is within" ("Intus est quod delectat"). Her silks, her purple, her cosmetics are not material ones; they consist in something greater and more spiritual: the pure conscience, purified through confession. Beauty that can be removed along with clothing belongs to the cloth, not the clothed. "Inborn and internal beauty" suffices for Sophia. Innate modesty suffuses her virginal cheeks with chaste ruddiness better than the earrings of queens. Now follows that rhapsodical praise quoted earlier:

> O, how composed does discipline render every posture of your girlish body, and even more so, of your mind! It sets the angle of the neck, arranges the eyebrows, composes the expression of the face, directs the position of the eyes, restrains laughter, moderates speech, suppresses appetite, controls anger, arranges the gait. . . . What glory can compare to virginity thus adorned? The glory of angels? An angel has virginity, but no body; he is happier for it certainly, but not stronger. The best and the most desirable is that ornament which even angels might envy.[2]

Discipline does for Sophia what it did for Godfrey of St. Victor (and many others): composes her body and gives her restraint and control. But there is in this case no formal discipline, no masters, no whips, no period of the novitiate. All this "beauty" and "ornament" come from virginity, that is, an internal quality and inner state. To keep it requires strength and virtue, and the maintenance of that strength confers beauty, grace, and all the qualities the foolish friends of Sophia try to produce by material adornments.

This kind of virtue is not attainable in school rooms. Essentially, if you do not have it, you will never acquire it. It is "innate" and "inborn," a condition that asserts itself outwardly by a kind of miracle of charisma. The master imposing discipline has moved into the soul of the individual, and continues his activity there. That makes a living teacher of the art of self-control superfluous.

Bernard had used the same logic to define "beauty of soul."[3] His sermon 85 on the Song of Songs turns on the themes of wisdom, virtue and outward beauty. The former two are "gifts from the Word," and "spiritual goods" (85.4.10; *Opera*, 2: 314. 3). But Christ the bridegroom is said to love the bride specifically for her beauty, not her spiritual gifts. Bernard asks,

> What then is beauty of the soul? Is it perhaps that quality we call ethical propriety [*honestum*]? . . . But propriety concerns outward behavior. It does not issue from it, but it is perceived through it. Its roots and dwellings are in the conscience; and the evidence of a good conscience is its beauty.[4]

Purity of conscience is a "light that shines in the mind." Its connection with external conduct is a fact of nature, not a product of cultivation, since outward grace and beauty are the overflowing of that inner light:

> . . . when the luminosity of this beauty fills the inner depths of the heart, it overflows and surges outward. . . . It makes the body into the very image of the mind; [the body] catches up this light glowing and bursting forth like the rays of the sun. All its senses and all its members are suffused with it, until its glow is seen in every act, in speech, in appearance, in the way of walking and laughing. . . . When the motions, the gestures and the habits of the body and the senses show forth their gravity, purity, modesty . . . then beauty of the soul becomes outwardly visible.[5]

It is essentially the same process of transformation experienced by Sophia: the inner state orders the body. The results are precisely the same as the end point of cultivation of virtue at St. Victor or the earlier cathedral schools: control of facial expression, serenity and good humor, gravity and modesty, beauty in walking, gesturing and "posing" (*habitus*). But the "discipline" from which this control of the body derives is purely inward: resistance of sin, persistence in virtue, strength of mind. It is also attainable through contemplation.[6]

"Discipline" in the sense we have encountered it in earlier chapters does not loom large in Bernard's thinking. He mentions it; he is aware of it as a kind of grooming necessary for novices, but it has a subordinate importance, comparable to the subordinate role of learning letters.[7] Teaching is a nuisance to a man with these convictions. It is cultivation of externals, a necessary undertaking but essentially a concession to the impurity of man:

> How I wish that all had the gift of teaching: I should be rid of the need to preach these sermons! It is a burden I should like to transfer to another, or rather I should prefer that none of you would need to exercise it, that all would be taught by God.[8]

To some extent his thinking is directed against a Victorine conception of discipline, against primping at the outer man with the hope of purifying the inner. He gives us a disapproving glimpse of discipline as practiced in more worldly schools in a letter to Thomas of St. Omer, who has ignored his vow to enter the Cistercian community to continue his studies. By this failure, he shows greater fear of the tongues of men than of the "devouring sword":

> Is this then that most beautiful composition of manners [*illa morum pulcher-rima compositio*] for which you contract yourself to the pursuit of that knowledge, for the study and love of which you burn so ardently that you do not fear compromising a sacred vow?[9]

For Bernard, the only true master of *mores* is Christ.[10]

Bernard of Clairvaux masters the discourse of *cultus virtutum*. His treatment of it represents the monastic appropriation of that language and its values: the results of inner purity are identical with the results of *cultus virtutum*. But it occupies a low level on the ladder of perfection. No human pedagogy can have anything more than a mediating role.[11]

Bernard is clearly adapting language inherited from the cathedral school traditions. Many echoes are audible in the passage from Meinhard's letter to G. discussed in an earlier chapter:

> [G.'s father was] a man instructed in every kind of virtue, a man who enjoyed to an astonishing degree all the charm and grace of humanity, qualities visible far and wide not only in his dazzling blaze of manners, but also in the bright good humor which shone most graciously from his eyes.[12]

This passage has in common with Bernardine beauty of soul a basically Ciceronian ethical vocabulary. Both writers believe that the body is or can be made into "the image of the mind." Both employ the metaphor of the powerful light breaking forth from within to express the relation of inner virtue to outward grace. But for Meinhard this is the result of "instruction in every kind of virtue." For Bernard it comes from within.

Authority and Human Greatness

In another sense Bernard of Clairvaux, as a personality and public figure, represented the fulfillment of one aspect of the old learning.[13] Like few others in the Middle Ages, he was the embodiment of authority that transmitted itself through the aura of physical presence. He represents charismatic pedagogy released from a particular curriculum. Hildebert of Lavardin addressed him in this sense: ". . . we have learned that you are the one in the church who is able to teach virtue by example and word."[14] Wibald of Stablo was nearly ecstatic in praising this quality: "The mere sight of him instructs you; the mere sound of his voice teaches you; following him perfects you."[15]

Bernard's biographers confirm his charismatic presence. They describe him in a language pre-formed in his own works. Geoffrey of Clairvaux observed his "beauty":

> In his flesh there was visible a certain gift [*gratia*], which was spiritual rather than physical. His face radiated celestial brightness [beauty, *claritas*], his eyes shone with angelic purity. So great was the beauty of the inner man, that it must needs break forth outwardly in visible signs.[16]

His biographer introduced the portrait of Bernard with the comment that his power of miracle working was remarkable, but it was minor compared to the great miracle that he himself was: "Primum maximumque miraculum, quod exhibuit, ipse fuit" (PL 185, 303B). The thought that miracles are subordinate to the inner gifts and virtues that produce them is a convention of hagiography.[17] Remarkable here is the stress this comment places on the personal presence of the saint, rather than on an invisibly working inner power experienced in supernatural deeds. It was possible to *see* in the man's outward presence the "grace" or "gift" (*gratia*) from which his miracles derived.

In the passages cited above, observers of Bernard speak a language they learned from Bernard himself. He had described St. Malachy with this phrase: [He performed many miracles] "but in my judgment, the first and greatest miracle was the man himself."[18] The Life of Malachy is instructive for Bernard's own values. He has projected himself into Malachy. He continues the above passage by saying that he will pass over the inner man, his beauty, strength and purity, and simply describe his *mores* and his way of living, since these gave abundant testimony to his inner richness:

> What was there in his way of walking, in his appearance, in his posture, in his facial expression, that was not edifying? Finally the serene good cheer of his face was not obscured by sadness, nor pushed to levity by laughter. Everything in him was disciplined, everything was a sign of virtue, an exemplar of perfection, grave but not austere in all things, occasionally relaxed, but never lax.[19]

Bernard makes Malachy into the representative of personal authority as the force that produces justice. For such a man, external gifts, a "certain grace that shows in the flesh," are instruments of authority. Bernard said this outright in interpreting the line of the canticle, "Your name is as oil poured forth." It applies to "any man who perceives that he is endowed with an exterior grace enabling him to influence [i.e. in turn pour it forth to] other men."[20] Malachy had this force of presence, according to Bernard. He "judged on ecclesiastical authorities like one of the apostles, with complete authority. And no one said to him, 'By what authority do you do these things?'" (14.32; *Opera*, 3: 340.2ff.). His authority beamed from him. It was that short range authority which loses its force when its personal embodiment is absent. Malachy at one point sends another bishop to make peace among warring factions. The man he sends declines the embassy, claiming that the parties will not listen to him; it requires Malachy's own presence. Malachy sends him anyway. The peace is made and, as the man predicted, broken. Malachy restores it through a miracle.[21]

Indwelling virtue also enables Malachy to conquer the learned cleric skeptical of Christ's presence in the eucharist by mere force of episcopal authority, which overwhelms the reasoning intellect (see above, Chapter 8).

Bernard's stress on charisma and personal authority lends a special weight to the obligation of *praeesse*, wielding authority over others. It is a paradox of the person of Bernard, the humble, meek ascetic. It reminds us generally of Nietzsche's dictum that the will to power has its roots in asceticism. And specifically it points us to the imperial tradition of training men "with the strength of kings and the sanctity of priests" to govern and to do good in the same degree. Undoubtedly Bernard's position in respect to governance of the church is closer to imperial positions than to the church reform.[22] Obedience to precepts and commands, in Bernard's view, properly results from respect for the person who gives them: "The gravity of the precept depends primarily on the authority of him who issues it."[23] The alien character of authority rooted in person rather than in an abstraction is especially distinct in this definition. There is no appeal to law or the will of God as the unchanging and impersonal basis of authority. The subjective and personal in the law, far from diminishing its authority, constitutes it.

It is possible to see this concept at work in Bernard's own wielding of authority. Hayden White has cited examples of Bernard championing virtue and inner grace as a factor in episcopal elections (both of the electors and the elected) against the reform party's more rational program of canonical procedure (note 22 above). If the electing bishops are good men, then matters of procedure have only a minor importance. When God is working through you, you do not have to consult law books on due procedure, cite precedent and appeal to charters.

Virtue even overrides breaches of accepted procedures. In bringing Peter Abelard to trial at Sens in 1140, he did not scruple to call a meeting of the presiding bishops and the papal legate, on the evening prior to the hearing, at which the list of charges was finalized and a verdict of guilty agreed upon in advance. The verdict, in other words, preceded the trial. This action was so far from offending anyone's sense of due process that the bishops refer to it without apology in their report to the pope.[24] Clearly this is a case of Bernard replaying (or pre-playing) the confrontation of Malachy and the sceptical cleric. He crushed Abelard by the mere force of personal authority, against which the shrewdly reasoning intellect was powerless.

Bernard of Clairvaux as public man was in many ways what the old learning aimed at: mellifluous and persuasive eloquence (letters), backed by the force of charismatic presence (manners); *praeesse* at least as important as *prodesse*.[25] Whatever his attitude to the old learning, Bernard became in some sense its last great representative. He did not represent its institutions or certainly its narrower contents; the "miracle" that he was had little or no admixture of affability, charm, bright good humor. In a peculiarly ascetic monastic configuration, he represented eloquence and *mores* working with great effectiveness in the political and religious life. He embodied ideals like *praeesse* along with *prodesse* and "virtue made visible" at the point when these had ended their attachment to a particular institution and become a general ideal of human greatness.

Charismatic Bodies and Charismatic Texts

I said in an earlier chapter that, from the end of the eleventh to the thirteenth century, *ethica* and *moralitas* pass, "as in a massive transfusion," from persons to texts, and I tried to sketch the dynamic of interrelationships between charismatic human presence and charismatic representation. Bernard of Clairvaux is situated at an interesting stage in that transition: perfect balance. He distinguishes himself from every other charismatic figure we have dealt with because he combines charisma with writings. Texts were a major instrument of his effectiveness: sermons, tracts, biography, letters. His writings are powerfully evocative; he uses a lyrical language, charged with the imagery of the Song of Songs and so subtly overladen with the words of Christ, St. Paul and the prophets as to suggest that they are speaking through him. The power of his eloquence[26] is equal to that of his personal presence.

His biographer, Geoffrey of Clairvaux, noticed this coinciding of charismatic person and charismatic text. Chapter 8 of his biography has the title: "On St. Bernard's writings and the effigy of his soul expressed in them." It is a deepened and sharpened aesthetic sense that sees the silent and invisible presence of the author in the fabric of the text, in its style, diction, impact. But there is also a deepened sense of authorial identity and creativity that can activate this self-injection: something quite different from the biographer's urge to inject the personality and presence of the subject into the work.[27] This is personal charisma transfused into textual form *by the skill of its possessor*. Geoffrey of Clairvaux recognizes the paltriness of his attempt to recapture the living man's presence compared to the force of that presence in his writings:

> We have said these few things concerning the saintly manners and character [*moribus*] of our father. . . . But this is far more distinctly expressed in his books, and it emerges so clearly in his own writings, that it seems he had created an effigy and a mirror of himself in them.[28]

It is a peculiar feature of the exemplary life that it takes on literary forms, and tends to create new ones adequate to the individual in its wake.[29] "Life experienced as literature" is an interesting phenomenon. Geoffrey of Clairvaux seems to indicate that Bernard had this sense about his own life. He shows him at one point musing why God has chosen him for sanctity and miracle-making:

> Sometimes signs are made by holy and perfect men [*perfectos*], sometimes also by fictional men [*per fictos*]. I for my part am not aware either of being perfect or fictitious.[30]

The word play *perfectos—per fictos* neatly reproduces the glide from charismatic presence to charismatic text that is typical of Bernard as a figure active on the border between these two conditions. "As far as I know, I am not literature": it is the logic of the humility formula, affirming through negation his sense of being lived fiction, the ultimate state of charismatic pedagogy and the exemplary life.

Bernard shows the trend towards fictionalizing of moral philosophy in his letter to the virgin Sophia with which this chapter began. This is evident if we ask, who *was* the virgin Sophia? No historical person has turned up as the recipient of his Epist. 113. It seems all but certain that Bernard invented her. The name itself suggests fictionalizing: she is wisdom personified, and the juxtaposition of the wise virgin to the foolish friends (non-virgins, we can assume) suggests intentional schematizing. Jean Leclercq pointed out that the letter was painstakingly revised in several drafts, worked over like a piece of fiction.[31] Sophia is most likely a "literary" creation. The "real presence" has passed out of this particular textual representation of moral philosophy.

11. Twelfth-Century Humanism

From the end of the eleventh century on, a peculiarly medieval humanism asserted itself in lyric poetry, in some grand allegorical-philosophical epics, in Latin prose style, in architecture and sculpture, and in some of the vernacular courtly romances. It is easy to imagine that this movement sprang out of nothing with the spontaneity and historical illogic for which the term "renaissance" is the facilitating code word. The school life of the eleventh century with its curriculum of *mores* and poetry has played no part in forming our picture of twelfth-century humanism and its sources.[1] But all that has been said until now makes it clear that they need to be included in the discussion. Writing the history and describing the profile of medieval humanism without the eleventh-century cathedral schools misses at least one essential point in its historical development: the humanism of the twelfth century reflects on that of the eleventh.

Compendia of the Arts

It is worth noting that some of its most important documents are compendia of liberal learning. Hugh of St. Victor's *Didascalicon* and Thierry of Chartres's *Heptateuchon* are summations of an education in the arts. But these are not fresh and innovative works pointing in new directions; they are conservative attempts to prop up an embattled form of education that is passing from the scene. The fate of the arts curriculum in Paris and in the other schools of France makes that evident.

The most important witness to the crisis of the arts education is John of Salisbury's *Metalogicon*. John sees studies and all civilized life threatened by the tendency of contemporary scholars and teachers to cultivate specialized subjects, to privilege dialectic, to separate learning from ethics, and thus to end the fruitful relationship between philosophy and state or church administration. Especially dangerous, he believes, is the indifference to eloquence in the schools. It is eloquence, he says, varying Ciceronian themes, that has created cities, allied kingdoms to each other in friendship, and knit people together in "bonds of love":

> One who would eliminate the teaching of eloquence from philosophical studies, begrudges Mercury his possession of Philology. . . . Although he may seem to attack eloquence alone, he undermines and uproots all liberal studies, assails the whole structure of philosophy, tears to shreds humanity's social contract, and destroys the means of brotherly charity.[2]

The stakes in this conflict are immense, in John's opinion, and the hyperbole of his rhetoric may well be an indication of the hopelessness of his position. In a passage that is a touchstone for his concerns, he complains about the tendency to regard dialectic as separable from other disciplines and from the active life. To exercise dialectic without broad learning and a practical context for it is senseless and harmful, like a pigmy trying to swing the sword of Hercules. Learning must find its fulfillment in domestic life or at court or in the church, not remain merely a "school" discipline. Dialectic is an exercise, not the object of learning, and it is to be abandoned, along with other school exercises, when it has fulfilled its purpose. Learning that remains merely verbal is "scholastic," and necessarily sterile.[3]

The *Metalogicon* attempts what the other arts compendia do not: it aims at reconciling the old with the new learning. This humanistic rearguard action was ill-conceived and destined to fail. The arts course was no longer the means of entry into the active life, poetry and rhetoric no longer the vital instruments of influencing kings and bishops. But the polemical edge of John's plea for the arts brings out an aspect of the earlier arts compendia not evident in the works themselves: their conservatism. An old program of learning is wrapping itself in the funeral shroud of charismatic teaching, the treatise. The compendium of the arts saves them from extinction, as a time capsule saves its contents. But they would not have sought textual preservation if they had not been threatened with extinction.

The Cult of Friendship

In one point I agree strongly with R. W. Southern's definition of humanism (see n. 1 above): "Without the cultivation of friendship there can be no true humanism" ("Medieval Humanism," p. 34). But Southern thought the cult of friendship was monastic in origin and took Anselm of Canterbury's letters as an early representative of it. We know now that the cult of friendship was not monastic, but worldly, in its origins and early practice.[4] It appears in full blossom in Gerbert's letter collection from the late tenth century, in the Worms letter collection (1030s), in the Hildesheim collection (1060–70). The indications of these letters were reaffirmed in the panegyric to Gerbert's friend Constantine, in the Würzburg poem, in Goswin's letter to Walcher. In short, Southern was appropriating for late eleventh- and twelfth-century monasticism a phenomenon that Anselm and Aelred of Rievaulx had received from the earlier cathedral schools or secular courts or both.

The writings on friendship from the twelfth century do not have the character of summarizing previous ideals, as do the arts compendia. They codify living and practiced social ideals. But they do represent the continued diaspora of the subjects and practices of the tenth- and eleventh-century schools following on their exodus in the late eleventh and early twelfth century. The diffusion of the cult of friendship was broad, and its history is still to be written. It had an important impact on "courtly love,"[5] and on monastic friendship. These are some of the "new homes" sought and found by cathedral school ideals during their transformation into general social ideals.

The Ideal Man

R. W. Southern claims that the greatest accomplishment of twelfth century humanism was "to make God seem human" ("Medieval Humanism," p. 37). I would argue the reverse: it made man seem godlike. Discipline and learning deified the student. Sigebert of Gembloux felt a "god-like" power conferred on him through nature and study, and he and his generation formulated one of their highest intellectual goals as "outbidding the gods" and "overcoming nature." Benzo of Alba defined the first goal of *cultus virtutum* — virtue — as "dignity of mind, nobility of soul, which makes man not just an object of wonder, but divine." Baudri of Bourgueil claims that the milk of mother Philosophy turns her sucklings into "gods, not men." The Orphic God of Amadeus of Lausanne "introduced men into the society of the gods" by "composing them morally" and overcoming the impulsiveness of their "uncultivated barbarism." Alan of Lille's "new man" is to be a *divinus homo* (1.236), who will transmit his own virtues to others' characters by the strength of his human divinity.[6]

The two works generally regarded as the high point of medieval humanism, Bernard Silvester's *Cosmographia* and Alan of Lille's *Anticlaudianus*, reap the harvest of this idealizing tendency. Both are based on the assumption of man's essential dignity and perfectibility. Both are allegories of the creation of the perfect man. The grand undertaking of creating man ends in his preparation to enter life and engage in battle with vice (in the *Anticlaudianus*; the *Cosmographia* is unfinished). That means they are also allegories of preparation for the active life through education.

BERNARD SILVESTER'S *COSMOGRAPHIA*

The structure of Bernard's work is given by the *Timaeus*: the creation of man is preceded by the creation of the cosmos and relates to it as microcosm to macrocosm.[7] The fashioning of the universe, however, is not creation in the ordinary Christian sense, *ex nihilo*, from the mind and word of God. It is a process of refining, reforming, and shaping a chaotic mass. In describing this move from chaos to order, Bernard uses a richly articulated vocabulary of formation. The cosmos is not magically evoked; pre-existing chaotic matter is tamed and disciplined.

Macrocosm

The primal state is strife, contention, warfare.[8] In the very depths of the primal mass is an intractable evil.[9] But Noys, the mind of God, combats this strain — though it cannot remove it altogether — by "polishing," "disciplining," "refining" it:

> . . . she resolved to separate mixed natures, to give order to their confusion and to refine their unformed condition [*informibus expolitione consuluit*]. She imposed law and restrained their freedom of motion. Rude though they were , she effected a balance of properties among her undisciplined and recalcitrant [*rudes . . . indisciplinatas reluctantesque*] materials.[10]

The guiding metaphor is a move from hostility to friendship and love: "I will instil amity [*amiciciam*] in the universe" (2.2, p. 99). The bonds of "reconciling friendship" (*federantis amicicie ligaminibus*) force the "rough and undisciplined" matter to convert from obstinacy to cooperation (2.7, p. 101). The "discordant band" lays aside its weapons and is joined in a condition of "peaceful unity" (*ad pacificam ingressus est unitatem* — 2.10, p. 101). The reconciling force of number and music contribute to create a universal harmony. When Bernard reflects on the accomplishment of Noys at the beginning of *Microcosmus*, he summarizes it in terms familiar from education in *mores*:

> Now . . . Silva had been reborn to her true beauty [*decor*], and was a universe worthy of the name. If her ancient origin intruded any trace of roughness, the artificer's hand sought it out everywhere and banished it, until, no longer resisting, Silva presented herself as well-mannered [*morigeratam*]. (*Microcosm*, 2, adapting Wetherbee's trans., p. 93)

Whether or not these passages are in any direct way a reflection on the civilizing process of the eleventh and early twelfth centuries, they unquestionably speak the language of that movement. There is a great deal of the spirit of "Orphic poetry" in the fashioning of this allegorical universe. The universe moves from "evil," a litigious and contentious state, to amicability and love. The mind of God, Noys, is a kind of *magistra*, who polishes, disciplines, and refines "rude" and unformed matter, rendering it "well-mannered." The combating of strife and imposition of harmony was the first step in creation. Matter is made malleable, docile and ready for the second step, which is the creation of the world soul, its wedding-like union with disciplined matter, and the creation of the forms of life from that union. Matter and soul of course are resistant to union, and so there must be a preliminary process of "tuning," which is accomplished by the harmonizing force of number and music. Once their "manners are changed to amicability" (*moribus ad gratiam inmutatis*), the figure called Endelechia is wed to her husband, reformed matter, creating a bond of friendship and love which fuses the spiritual and material substance of the universe (2.15, p. 103). From this union the species of created life emerge. The process involves the imprinting of forms on substance; matter is conformed to the life- and form-giving idea appropriate to it; Endelechia is full of a vast number of archetypes, which stamp themselves onto docile but yet-unformed matter.

This process in its entirety, whatever the precedents in classical science of its individual elements,[11] is abstracted from the disciplining of *mores*. Unformed matter plays the role of the student; Noys and Endelechia are the masters/mistresses of discipline. This model is evident by comparison with some texts discussed in earlier chapters. The metaphors of sculpting a block of marble, turning a pot on a potter's wheel, sharpening steel by steel are closely related to the initial harmonizing of discordant matter. The proximity of language and the shared educational conception is evident in a passage quoted earlier from Sigebert's *Passio Thebeorum*:

> Just as the frequent exercise of study has extracted many sharpenable mountain stones from the veins of nature, so also it has hammered out and fashioned

many arts as from the mountain's marble. It polished one stone with another and refined one art with another, and these buffed our rough minds of their dense rust, sharpened and refined them.[12]

In the context of a process of personal formation, the early chapters of Hugh's *De institutione novitiorum* offer similarly striking parallels. The overarching metaphor of Hugh's work is a seal imprinting its image on wax. But before the wax can receive the impress, it must be softened. That is, the student must learn humility, obedience, modesty and measure. Chapter 6 gives the preliminaries for profiting from education ("Quales se debeant exhibere qui per doctrinam proficere volunt"). They are that the student must give up contentiousness in word and deed; he must avoid anger, shun contumely and malice, and keep to "moderation and the golden mean" in speech, gesture, action, and dress (*mensuram et modum*). Then follows the process of imitating good men (chapter 7), which Hugh describes in the image of the seal and wax. The student is to be "re-formed for the better" (*in melius reformari*). *Disciplina morum*, then, involves an initial phase of attunement to harmony, amicability, the removal of "malice" and contentiousness, followed by the true act of creation where a higher model is impressed on the now malleable raw substance of the character. This is essentially the process by which primal matter is transformed into phenomena and the forms of life, and it is fairly clear that Bernard Silvester has abstracted from character formation the process of cosmic formation.

Microcosm

It should not be surprising if a model of human education suggested itself to Bernardus as a model for the fashioning of the universe. For one thing, education is one of the main subjects in his other works.[13] And for another, the greater world is a model for the smaller, and that means that the spiritual formation of the human being must be answered by a corresponding process in nature. Indeed, the newly formed man is to learn the composition of his exterior, as well as his manners, from the heavens: "From the firmament let her learn a comely appearance, spiritual grace, and the laws of her behavior [*morum causas*]" (*Micro.*, 4, trans. Wetherbee, p. 98).

Noys maps out the plan of man's creation (*Micro.* 3). He is to be the "worthy consummation" of the universe, and therefore will receive the "distinctive attribute of dignity" (trans. Wetherbee, p. 94). Nature seeks out the help of Urania and Physis, and from the former receives a closer definition of her task:

> Let the work be perfect, let his beauty consist in the joining of his parts; it is
> God's will that nothing be lacking in his composition. It is God's will that the
> mixture be balanced, that balance effect a bond, that this divine bond bestow
> harmonious relation. (4, trans. Wetherbee, p. 97)

Noys gives the final instruction to the team (10, ed. Dronke, p. 140–41;
trans. Wetherbee, p. 113). Man must be divine in mind, and his body must
be appropriate to his mind, so that a harmonious bond can be effected:

> . . . man alone, his stature bearing witness to the majesty of his mind, will lift up
> his noble head toward the stars, that he may employ the laws of the spheres and
> their unalterable courses as a pattern for his own course of life.

This is the last passage that speaks the language of the old learning. It is
possible to tease out other reminiscences, but the fact is that Bernard
Silvester has no interest in the details of ethical discipline: gait, gesture,
speech. His work builds on the fundamentals of *cultus virtutum*, but also
takes leave from them. He has created a universe with a moral base (macrocosm-microcosm), and a human being capable of receiving the lessons of
ethica, who is destined to replay in his personal development the shift of
primal chaos from evil and strife to "well-mannered" and virtuous disposition, and thence to a productive and creative engagement in the world. But
Bernard's work is moving away from the particular concerns of the old
learning and toward natural science. He has no interest in the virtues, but
describes the physical constitution of the human body at length. It may be
that he planned a description of the education and moral formation of the
ideal man and never got to it. But not necessarily. His concerns are probably
closer to those of William of Conches, who likewise in his *Philosophia mundi*
progresses from the nature of the universe to the nature of man, but
restricts his interests to the physical constitution of both.

It suffices for our purpose to show how the general shaping of world
and man is set into the structure of an education of personal formation.[14]

ALAN OF LILLE'S *ANTICLAUDIANUS*

In a grand allegory of man's creation or recreation written some forty years
after the *Cosmographia*, Alan of Lille moves in the opposite direction. He
returns to the immediate concerns of the old learning. This work might well
be included among the compendia of studies mentioned earlier. More
directly than Bernard's *Cosmographia*, the *Anticlaudian* is an allegory of
education. As such it is comprehensive. It covers the entire range of learn-

ing starting with the rudiments of grammar, progressing through all the liberal arts and ending in theology. But in its allegorical frame it comprehends central ideas of the old learning, of which it is the fullest summation the Middle Ages produced. The education mapped out in previous chapters is set in the embracing framework of formation by the virtues, and this is of interest to the present study.

The work's central event is the creation of the perfect human being. In contrast to the *Cosmographia*, human perfection is to be restored, not set new into the world. Human nature is in a state of decline at the beginning of the work, and the summit meeting of the virtues that begins the work is an emergency session convoked by Nature to repair the ruin of her noblest creation.

The meeting takes place in the dwelling of Nature. On one of the palace walls is a mural depicting "the characters of men" (*hominum mores*).[15] The author introduces this mural with a comparison of the two arts, painting and logic. Both "arts" have the power to make illusion appear truth, but the former does so more successfully and impressively than the latter. The victory given to art as depicter of *mores* against logic the simulator of truth is significant within the contest of old and new. The medium appropriate to the old—representation of *mores*—is given priority. The opposition of art and logic stands for the two lines of development leading away from charismatic culture: the one, memorialization through art; the other rational, intellectual inquiry that looks away from charisma and individual authority to some kind of objective, discursive formulation of Truth (see above, Introduction, pp. 6–7). That Alan of Lille gives priority to artistic representation states his position clearly. Along with other old-guard humanists, he opposes excessive reliance on logic. Unlike John of Salisbury, however, he prefers artistic representation of human character to logical proofs.

Of course, it is Nature's house, and she prefers art because art imitates and reproduces nature. Logic is indifferent to nature.

The pictures in the mural are in part of great representers of human *mores* (Plato, Aristotle—expressly given second place to Plato—Cicero, Seneca, Virgil), and following the authors, their characters (figures from the story of the Trojan war and from ancient mythology). The only contemporary poets present are poetasters, included so that bad art will also be represented. It is striking how "literary" the representation of *mores* has become. Alan does not show Socrates and Aeneas as real and living presences, but rather as the products of the authors who have represented them.

It is textualized virtue, and the textualizers have the place of honor. If Sigebert's St. Maurice set living examples above those in books ("What need of examples; you yourselves are the examples!"), Alan might sympathize with the reverse: "What need of you yourselves? We have examples from books!" The cult of representation replaces the cult of the real presence, and the old learning rigidifies to artifacts. This mediated relation to virtue suggests that "envy" is at work in the conception of Alan's poem. Alongside the main task of restoring the ideal human being, the *Anticlaudianus* represents a subordinate task: evoking the artistic means of recapturing and holding firm images of lost or fading human greatness.

The congress of the virtues, presided over by Nature, decides to form a new man. Here is the fundamental conception of the work: the perfect human being owes its origin to Nature and to Prudence, Reason, and other virtues. The liberal arts and theology are means to that end; God ultimately presides over the process, but the idea, the will, and the effort are products of virtue consulting with nature and reason. That places us squarely in the conceptual world of *cultus virtutum*. The virtues are described as embodying the qualities they represent, and these descriptions — along with much in the poem — confirm the connection of the *Anticlaudianus* with the discipline of *mores*. Prudentia is the main figure in the allegory. Her appearance is described:

> Girded about by moderation in her placid countenance and her modest gestures, Prudence arises.[16]

Moderation is the dominant theme in the description of her body. A few details. Her golden hair is held in check by a pin, which "imposes its rule upon them" (1.271–72, trans. Sheridan, p. 56). Her brows are "well-ordered" and arranged "in proper balance" (loc. cit.). Her neck is the perfect length, not too long or too short (1.287ff.). Her hips "unite the upper and lower parts of her body" in "fitting restraint" (*modulo decenti* — 1.292ff.). Her height changes, but at present she "chastens herself with our rein" (1.302).

This is a portrait of a character made into what she appears by acts of restraint. Nothing is natural; all is controlled and held in place by discipline and conscious effort to achieve a mean. "Rule" is imposed on her every posture, gesture, and expression. The external details are the signs of the inner nature of the virtue they express: Prudence, discretion, good judgment. Prudence's appearance makes virtue visible.

At the end of the work, the virtues return to give their qualities to the

New Man. Phronesis has completed her journey to God transported by the cart of the liberal arts, drawn by the horses of the five senses, guided first by Reason, then Theology. She returns with the archetype of the perfect man's soul. Soul is joined to body, and the completed man is celebrated in a parade of the virtues. Each virtue showers her gifts on the new man to prepare him for his battle with the vices. This passage also must be read against the background of *cultus virtutum*, strikingly present in the four virtues, Modesty, Constancy, Reason, and *honestas*. Modesty gives her gifts abundantly, without forgetting due moderation:

> She composes the whole man, moderates his actions, measures his speech, determines his silences, weighs his attitudes, considers his postures and curbs his impulses. . . . She outlines the correct posture for his head and tastefully raises his face to an equally correct level, lest with face aloft, turning toward the beings above, he seem to spurn our mortal race and disdain to look upon our type of life, or with face turned overmuch to earth, show the signs of an inactive and vacant mind. It is raised, then, to a somewhat moderately controlled position and neither rises nor falls beyond due measure.[17]

The concerns are well known to us. The act of moral composition is so much the clearer for occurring in a strictly fictional portrait. The poet is unhindered by any sense of obligation to realistic portraiture. The "composition" is constructed to be "read." The physiognomy speaks and bespeaks the author of its appearance, Modesty.

The role of Constancy hardly differs from that of her sister virtue:

> Constancy . . . forbids buffoonish gestures, rejects an excessively grave gait. . . . She warns the man not to stoop to thrusting forth base arms like a buffoon nor to work his forearms in unseemly gestures nor, in a display of pride, so to position his elbows that something bow-like is produced. She secures his gait with regular tread to prevent him from mincing his steps and touching the earth with his toes but barely making contact with earth-bound things. Lest hair, over-ornamented with excessive treatment, reach the level of feminine excess and rob his sex of its honoured position, or lest it hang dishevelled . . . she insists on a style between both extremes and arranges the hair in a style of her own selection. She does not make the style of his dress shine with excessive splendour or degrade it with drabness: she observes the mean in all things . . . she disciplines the eyes and ears and curbs the nose. She moderates the sense of taste. She arranges the sense of touch.[18]

While the concern with external culture is evident, this passage strikes a different note from the previous one. It touches on the topics of criticism of courtly and aristocratic fashions. I will return to this point later.

Next comes Reason, who gives him good sense for making judgments in practical affairs, prevents him from taking any course of action hastily, and teaches him to prepare all undertakings carefully, to make few promises and give many gifts wisely, and to distinguish flattery from due praise.

Honestas then gives him the affection of his fellow men (makes him "all things to all men") while preserving the integrity of his inner life.

A series of recent studies has shown that the court and the civil duties of the court administrator are the context in which these passages are to be located.[19] Michael Wilks calls the *Anticlaudianus* "a species of court poetry," and compares it with the genre of tracts on the education of the prince. This characterization seems to me to bring us much closer to the social context of Alan's work than previous scholarship, which hardly recognized that the work had a social context. But I doubt that Alan intended a specific reference to Philip Augustus and a prediction of his victory over the Plantagenets, as Wilks and Linda Marshall argue.[20] The court and administrative activity are undoubtedly what this ideal formation aims at. But instruction for the ruler narrows its object too much. The virtues and intellectual powers of Alan's new man are a summing up of the old learning. As a preparation for court life, it applied to courtiers no less than to kings. It is an education through civil virtues for battle against civil vices. The gifts of Reason associate the passage especially clearly with the product of *ethica*, the ideal statesman/administrator. Alan's *ratio* is that force by which both the composed human being, the state and the cosmos ("O, qui perpetua mundum *ratione* gubernas") were governed. Her gifts are those appropriate to the statesman, and have next to nothing to do with the schoolman, with analysis, argumentation, or speculation.

Alan is evidently out of step with the life of the schools in Paris in the second half of the twelfth century. The concept of *ratio* had undergone a fundamental revaluation at the hands of the early scholastics, its meaning transferred from the civic to the intellectual realm.[21] Alan's *ratio* comes into effect in administrative activity, and this shows him clinging to an older, Platonic — Boethian — Ciceronian conception far from the cutting edge. Alan's new man receives no gifts or instruction from Law. Legal training plays no role in the fashioning of the perfect man, and rational argumentation, dialectic, is given a subordinate role defined with hardly concealed scorn. Clearly the author is looking back in time for his ideas, not forward.

None of the virtues that give the final polish to the newly created man are abstract inner qualities, cloistered, scholastic, or intellectual virtues. Their gifts aim at good grooming. What Constancy gives is not loyalty, not faith to oaths and vows, not steadfastness, but an elegant gait, measured gestures, correct clothes, and a fitting hairdo. The virtues do not bestow the inner qualities they govern: rather they *are themselves* those qualities, and what they bestow are the external signs of their presence. The logic at work is that of virtues made visible, beauty or harmony of soul shining forth from every action, down to dress, gesture, personal grooming and manner of walking.

Alan's allegory resonates clearly with the letter of Meinhard of Bamberg to G., former student and probably candidate for the archbishopric of Cologne (see above, Chapter 4, p. 96). The purpose of the letter is to prepare G. for his entrance into Cologne and for the victory of virtue in the battle between the court of vice and the court of virtue. The court of virtue places its governance into his hands because of the "perfection" or "exemplarity of his manners" (*specimen morum*) and the sharpness of his mind. Meinhard reminds G. of the values he has always taught him: following the examples of illustrious ancestors, the importance of fame, reputation, *honestas*, and the obligation to maintain glory in the active life. He sums it up by reference to the virtues of G's father,

> a man instructed in every kind of virtue, a man who enjoys to an astonishing degree all the charm and grace of humanity, qualities visible far and wide not only in his dazzling blaze of manners, but also in the bright good humor which shone most graciously from his eyes.[22]

Both this letter and the *Anticlaudianus* prepare gifted men for the battle with the vices. In the case of Meinhard, the context is clear: the administration of the church. In Alan's work the context is masked by abstraction. In both cases the main preparation is the acquisition of virtue or the gifts of virtue. Alan of Lille encloses within the outer borders of the new man's education in virtue an extensive course of studies, including the liberal arts and theology, ending in the vision of God. Meinhard hardly mentions letters and other studies, indicating them only in praising G's mental acumen and commending the *Tusculan Disputations*. Alan's work is incomparably richer. But that is a difference of degree, not of kind. In both documents, the perfect, elegant, humane gentleman / courtier receives his armor from civil virtues, does battle with civil vices, and shows outwardly the beauty within.

What these common features suggest is that the fates of the old learning and twelfth-century humanism were linked; the one was the bearer and transmitter of the other, and the institutional basis of this humanism was the cathedral school in its relation to court service. The common features of the *Anticlaudianus* and the many texts from the previous century cited earlier also teach us to regard the humanism of the eleventh and twelfth centuries as a more or less homogeneous phenomenon, held together above all by the element of *cultus virtutum*, though sharing a fondness for classical literature as illustrator — painter, to use Alan's metaphor, of *mores*. Meinhard and Alan produce similar portraits of idealized future statesmen because they taught (or at least knew and preached) programs of *ethica* that were not essentially different in either content or purpose.

A difference closer to the concerns of this study is that whereas the letter of Meinhard of Bamberg is addressed to and talks about human beings, Alan and Bernard wrote allegories; their perfect men were abstractions. Meinhard wrote out of real need; Alan wrote out of "envy." He was recapturing and restoring something he admired which was lost or fading. In this the historical situation of his work mirrors the condition of man which is its point of departure. The ruined state of man requires repair, and there may be a nostalgic undertone in this motif implying that the ruined state of education in the virtues likewise requires restoration. Meinhard's medium was the letter, something written for an immediate occasion, not first and foremost a monument. Alan's was a literary composition with all sorts of predecessors, influences, topoi: literature turned into an overswollen, baroque display piece, its real concerns and human content so submerged in its tides of rhetoric as virtually to drown in them. It is monumentalizing on the grandest scale. Moving from the one to the other we move from experience to abstraction, from charismatic presence to charismatic text.

The shift from realism to symbolism is one of the features that distinguishes the eleventh from the twelfth century. Alan of Lille appears as a high point of a literary-philosophical symbolism. It is easy for us to read the bodies of his abstract embodiments without a sense that both the "text" and its hermeneutic were forged earlier in reference to the living body. The reading of the composed body had developed to a high sophistication over the course of the previous age. As early as the late tenth century, an anonymous poet was "reading" the appearance of his friend Constantine for the visible symbols of virtue,[23] and Walter, the friend of Marbod of Rennes, toward the end of the eleventh, was summing up a rich hermeneutic of the body when he characterized the treatise on physiognomy he sent to his friend:

> It notes certain things marked with the signatures of secret
>   meanings,
> Like stature, countenance, posture, voice, gestures, grooming.[24]

Alan of Lille's imagination populates a symbolic world whose characters are "marked with the signatures of secret meanings" and whose "stature, countenance, posture, voice, gestures, grooming" are the bearers of veiled messages. A sophisticated sense of hidden meanings systematically readable existed in the eleventh century, but it referred to the physical presence. From the point of view of *cultus virtutum*, that is the essential shift from earlier to later: from body to text.

*   *   *

The old learning flowed into and extensively informed some of the major works of twelfth-century humanism. The common features urge us to regard that humanism and the works that represent it as the last flowering of a movement, based on the alliance of school and court, learning and government, that preceded them by some two hundred years.

12. Court Society

The major works of twelfth-century humanism did not provide a "new home" for *cultus virtutum*. They provided some big, baroque funeral monuments. In its search for new accommodations, the still living discipline of *mores* found it in the institution that had originally accounted for its rise, or resuscitation, in the tenth century, the prince's court.

The move of the old learning into monastic and canonical communities is minor and piecemeal compared to its move to worldly courts. Its appropriation in what can be called after about 1150 "courtly society" is a vast topic.[1] Each of the areas I treat in this chapter could be the subject of a book in itself. A particularly abundant and rich area is the literature of courtly education: handbooks of courtesy and "mirrors of princes." Rather than brushing quickly over that topic, I am openly capitulating before its scope. I will draw on the didactic literature of courtesy peripherally, and hope that others will study it from the point of view of its ties to the old learning.

Court and School

Courts secular and ecclesiastical had been the hidden context of the old learning for the centuries of its prominence. The court of Charlemagne gave us our first look at it in the Middle Ages. Alcuin taught *civiles mores* and *mores venustos* to the emperor using Cicero's rhetorical and philosophical writings as the textbook. Its nearest relative in Carolingian times was found only at the imperial court. It did not extend into the teachings of cathedral and monastic schools (see above, ch. 1). The distinction between "civil" and "ecclesiastical" mores was a sharp one. It is possible that something like *cultus virtutum* had never died out but had been maintained at worldly courts since antiquity, though it only registered dully or not at all in documents.[2]

The remarkable change in Ottonian times was that cathedral schools entered the scene to share with the courts the task of civil education. The early cathedral schools took up the overflow from the court chapel and along with that the task of imparting *civiles mores* and preparing men for service in the chapel and ultimately in administrative positions in the imperial church.

This education flourished at its new setting for a little more than a century. Then orthodoxy began to reclaim its institutions. The old learning was forced out of the cathedrals as church separated from state, as education changed from personal discipline to reasoning, organizing, systematizing study. There was always an inner contradiction in the old learning: it effaced the sharp Carolingian distinction between civil and church disciplines and set "eclesiastical disciplines" alongside the discipline of virtues. In practice the cultivation of virtue tended to become a goal in itself and a requirement for advancement. That translated in practice into external culture, elegance and grooming. What was essentially and in origin the education of a Roman orator smuggled itself into the domain of Christian education. This was the genial idea of Otto I and Brun of Cologne, consistent with the integration of the church into the apparatus of state government, consistent with a vision of renewing the Roman empire. When the church was reclaimed for strictly ecclesiastical ends, the old cathedral schools gradually declined and the moral discipline of the old learning returned — much enriched — to the worldly courts, its original home.

The career of William of Conches is exemplary for this development.[3] He began teaching in Paris, Chartres, or both around 1120 or 1125. His student John of Salisbury tells us that he taught in the manner of Bernard of Chartres and that he had to withdraw from the schools because his students left him for other disciplines and for teachers who promised greater success with shorter studies. That comment guarantees the representative nature of his career, since it resonates so clearly with the careers of Goswin of Mainz, Meinhard of Bamberg, Drogo of Paris, Hermann of Rheims, and William of Champeaux.

William of Conches left the schools and consoled himself with a position as tutor to the young Plantagenet prince and future king Henry II of England. He had written his work *Philosophia mundi* under the influence of the *Timaeus* for use in the schools. Now he rewrote it for the instruction of the prince and gave it the title *Dragmaticon*. It was probably William who composed the work *Moralium dogma philosophorum*, which has stood in the center of the discussion of a "ritterliches Tugendsystem." The intended audience of the work is uncertain. It is dedicated to a "vir optimus atque liberalis Henricus," who may be Henry II.[4] The work is located, like William himself, between schools and secular courts. Whoever the "excellent and liberal Henry" of the *Moralium dogma* was, the work was appropriated by secular courts.

This is a case parallel to the departure of William of Champeaux from the schools of Paris. He returned to a curriculum of *venustas morum* and instituted it in the newly founded community of St. Victor. In comparable circumstances, William of Conches took ethical training based on classical models with him in his "retirement" to a secular court.

Brun of Cologne was representative of the shift of court education from the chapel to the cathedral schools in the tenth century, William of Conches for its return to the courts in the twelfth.

Court Education

There is an old controversy on the question whether actual schools existed at worldly courts.[5] The question is misleading, because as soon as we learn that in the post-Carolingian period schools at court no longer existed *as institutions*, we are also tempted to conclude that teachers and instruction had little role at court. The Carolingians needed schools at court. The schools in the kingdom were barely able to deal with the rudiments of a Christian education, let alone to serve as adjunct institutions to propagate the comparatively sophisticated subject of *civiles mores*. The idea of transferring the "civil" instruction to cathedral schools would not have made any sense at a time when those institutions were attempting to establish themselves at a more basic level of instruction. But we would over-shoot the mark if we turned this around and said, the Ottonian and Salian kings did not require palace schools, because the cathedral schools had taken over their function. They did so, but without depriving the court of that task. More accurate would be: from Carolingian times on there is no useful distinction to be made between the court school and the life of the court itself, and the schooling in *civiles mores* found an alternate venue in cathedral schools. After Otto I, the life of the court, the court school, and cathedral schools were so closely allied that Anselm of Liège in the mid-eleventh century could look back nostalgically to the Ottonian days, when "in the chapels of the emperor no less than in those of bishops nothing more was pursued than the discipline of manners along with the study of letters!"[6] Cathedral schools were annexed to the court school to instruct in *civiles mores*, and this move made that kind of instruction available more broadly than was possible as long as the court was its sole venue.

Hincmar formulated the ideal of the court as a school for Louis the German. The passage has been quoted often in this study:

> The king's court is indeed called a school, that is, a course of studies, not because it consists solely of schoolmen, men bred on learning and well trained in the conventional way, but rather a school in its own right, which we can take to mean a place of discipline, that is correction, since it corrects men's behavior, their bearing, their speech and actions, and in general holds them to the norms of a good life.[7]

Hincmar considered the court a school of *mores* to which might have been added formal instruction in letters. This does not change in Ottonian times. The statements of Ruotger that Brun of Cologne as chancellor at Otto the Great's court rescued the seven liberal arts from their decline, attracted philosophers and intellectual "refugees," held philosophical disputations, improved the Latin of the court members, and served personally as a exemplar of wisdom, piety and justice (*Vita Brun.*, chapter 5) cannot be emptied of their content just because no traces of an institutionalized court school can be found. Ruotger's words make perfect sense when we understand the nature and goal of the old learning and distance ourselves from a conception of education limited to notions of classroom and textbook, learned lecturing and writing. Ruotger speaks the language of the old learning clearly: letters combine with manners; the person of the teacher is a large part of the curriculum; philosophy, learning, and public life are inseparable. The masters of the old learning were courtiers in their capacity as teacher, and teachers in their capacity as courtier. What need was there for institutionalized schools at court? The court itself was a school, where the pedagogy of personal charisma was at work more immediately than at formally constituted schools. Every educated man at court was, ideally, philosophy embodied and translating itself into acts of public administration. What changed around 950 was that this education became more closely oriented to classical models of the statesman and orator,[8] and expanded into the adjunct institution of cathedral schools, where hitherto secular and sacred letters and ecclesiastical disciplines had formed the curriculum.

It may be that *civiles mores* were cultivated at royal courts and courts of lesser nobility in various places in Europe in our period. The few references I have found to court education in the period from 950 to 1100 indicate that this is the case. We recall that Guibert of Nogent's teacher had previously resided at the court of the lords of Clermont, teaching *honestas* and *exterior elegantia*, and that he had learned this curriculum at this or another secular court. Bishop Azelinus of Hildesheim had been a courtier at the court of Henry III, and the new customs he brought with him to the diocese of Hildesheim were so closely associated with the imperial court as to be called *curialitas*. The biographer of Wernher of Merseburg, writing shortly before 1150, gives us a picture of education at the court of Henry IV in his portrait of Wernher's brother, the knight Moricho:

> . . . nurtured in the flower of youth at the court of emperor Henry IV, he rose to a position of high trust and intimate favor with the emperor as a man of nobility and a splendid administrator [*liber et splendidae administrationis homo*]. . . . For he was impeccable in his conduct [*optimus moribus*], firm in respect to justice, foresighted in counsel, faithful in rendering aid, most liberal and of immaculate repute, courtly/civil in manners [*civilis in moribus*]. While still in the flower of manhood, he was steward of the royal table and most suited to all administrative tasks.[9]

The nature of court education in the period is an unanswered question. It becomes easier to deal with in the middle decades of the twelfth century. The fading of the old learning at cathedral schools coincides with the rise of an education that we must now call "courtly," no longer merely "for the court."[10] The example of William of Conches suggests that this was no coincidence. The institutional basis of *cultus virtutum* had been eroded, but not its content. The court valued the *mores* it cultivated; it appropriated them and transformed them into courtliness, amalgamating them with the social ideals of lay nobles. The sudden blossoming of courtly culture may well be directly connected with the eroding of that discipline at cathedral schools. At least we know that it left some teachers of the subject available for employment elsewhere. If William of Conches, John of Salisbury, Andreas Capellanus, Wace, Benoît de St.-Maure, Chrétien de Troyes, Gottfried von Strassburg, and all the other clerics engaged in the formulation of court ethics and literature had found employment in the schools of France, Germany, and England — and not at the secular courts — courtly society and literature would be very different from what they are, or from the way we see them at present.

The following sections analyze two areas of twelfth-century court culture that illustrate the flow of the old learning into court society.

Moral Philosophy in the Lives of Thomas Becket

The biographies of Thomas Becket are some of the richest sources on court life from the twelfth century. The earlier ones were written by the scholars and courtiers who had been on Becket's administrative staff.[11] The Lives of Becket are set apart from other bishops' Lives by their unshrinking representation of Becket's splendor and courtliness. I quote from these works at length, partly to recreate the atmosphere of court life they convey, which has not played the part it deserves in forming our picture of contemporary aristocratic life, but especially because of their peculiar relevance to our narrower topic. The major biographers all draw to varying degrees on the concepts and ideals of *moralis philosophia* and *disciplina morum*. Herbert of Bosham does this programmatically, and being the most prolix of the biographers, he provides a rich picture of moral philosophy functioning in the life of a high court official and archbishop. He presents his subject from the outset as exemplary in terms with which we are familiar:

> To you especially this exemplary man gave an example, such that whatever he did ought to serve you as a guide to action. Whence throughout this history I have described this exemplary man, not the man who should cause astonishment by his miracles, but who should inspire imitation in deeds.[12]

Herbert excuses his verbosity by explaining that he is not just rehearsing the saint's deeds but "explaining their causes, not just describing acts but the mind of the actor."[13] In this and other Lives of Becket the narration is informed and in some cases structured by the ideas of the old learning.

THE YOUNG COURTIER
This influence is evident from the outset in the portraits of Becket that occur in the early sections of the major biographies.[14] According to John of Salisbury, he was

> tall of stature, handsome of form, keen of mind, sweet and jocund in his speech, and amiable for the beauty of his manners [*venustate morum*] given his age.[15]

William Fitzstephen observes some of the same qualities:

> He was of a placid and beautiful countenance, noble in stature, his nose long and straight, his body vigorous and adept; he was skilled in eloquence, subtle

in mind, great in soul, and because he tread the path of virtue in a higher sense, he showed himself amiable to all men . . . generous and witty [or sophisticated or courtly —*facetus*].[16]

Herbert of Bosham has a long treatise on the virtues and vices of the young Becket, too long to quote in full here. He describes the battle of virtue against vice that the young must fight, and suggests that Becket, for all his juvenile faults, fought this battle successfully because of his prominent virtue of physical chastity (2.6.170). It was like an "integrating vessel," preserving all the "spiritual aromata" and gifts of grace and nature from their natural admixture of vices. Herbert reflects on the "two-fold gift" of some men, whereby they please both God and the world. The young Becket pleased the world more than God, having an overbalance of that virtue which is "civil, urbane, kind and gentle, sweet, social, an invitation to affection, but more pleasing to the world and less to God."[17]

Becket's impressive appearance and his mastery of virtue are leitmotifs of the *Vitae*.[18] Herbert describes an especially telling incident that occurs later in Becket's life when he was traveling through England incognito, heading into exile. The archbishop had entered an inn dressed as a monk, with the assumed name Christianus. At table he took the last and least place among the traveling companions. But the innkeeper noted the "style of eating and distributing food" which distinguished "brother Christian," and this called for a closer look:

> . . . then he observed the composition of the whole man and his way of gesturing, the noble stature of his body, his broad forehead and grave aspect, his long and handsome face, the shape of his large hands, the harmonious and in a way exquisite fit and reach of his fingers.[19]

The innkeeper recognized the difference between him and the others, realized that this must be "some great man" (*magnum aliquem virum*), and took him to be the Archbishop of Canterbury. Herbert is at pains to make this recognition seem explicable: he tells that a rumor was about that the Archbishop of Canterbury was fleeing through the countryside. But he has obviously adapted the motif of the miraculous recognition of a saint or king from hagiography. In this case the charisma that beams from Thomas is located physically in the shape and form of his body and his hands, and it registers in his table manners and his gestures. Elegance and grace, the products of moral training, betray to the viewer a "great man" and thwart concealment.

As a young man Becket joined the court of a nobleman, Richer de l'Aigle, where he devoted himself to worldly pursuits and learned hunting with dogs and birds. Here also he "began to show excellent manners."[20] John of Salisbury observed the same turn in his life. After his studies, he gave himself to "the pastimes of the courts," but even in juvenile pursuits a certain zeal for the faith and "magnificence of soul" were apparent in him. At the same time he was immoderately fond of popularity. He was proud and vain, and "on occasion, he foolishly took on the appearance and spoke the words of lovers," though for chastity of body he was admirable.[21]

The biographers are perfectly willing to criticize the future saint as a young courtier. His vices are exemplary, and are not glossed over. Herbert of Bosham says forthrightly,

> he was intent on the kinds of things that are sweet and familiar to that age . . . courtiers' trifles, empty and vain pursuits. And so that he would stand out among the others, he cultivated clothes and an appearance more refined than that of others. . . . Nor would it be correct to imagine that this whole mode of fashioning derived more from virtue than from prurience. (2.1. 165–66)[22]

THE KING'S CHANCELLOR

"Magnificence" recurs like a leitmotif in Herbert's work to characterize Becket as king's chancellor.[23] He had already shown royal manners while on Archbishop Theobald's staff: he had thrown aside all priestly moderation and competed for *magnificentia* with the king's servants (2.7.172). And the same is true to an even greater degree in the chancellor's office, where

> he tended to grandeur and magnificence beyond what his office—a heavy enough burden, as many know—called for. He was extraordinarily lavish, generous to all, excelling all in sumptuousness and grandeur, as great in heart as he was grand in appearance. Nothing could be around him but what was splendid and magnificent. (Herbert, *Vita Thomae*, 2.11.176)

Becket became an immensely successful courtier. He helped the king in diplomatic and military undertakings, occasionally himself leading troops and fighting. To court the daughter of the French king for young prince Henry, he organized and conducted a splendid procession, which passed through England and France and aroused admiration for the English king and his emissary by its splendor.[24] He maintained a household that rivaled that of the king for pomp and magnificence. He loved and regularly took part in court games and pastimes like chess and hunting with dogs and birds. He gave splendid banquets. He became popular and beloved of the courtiers, clergy, and populace because of his many virtues, his "greatness of soul and the many merits inherent in his mind" (Fitzstephen, p. 24, ch. 14). His friendship with the king was so close that they "play together like boys once their business is over" (loc. cit.). Fitzstephen relates a charming incident to illustrate this friendship. It is worthwhile quoting in full to illustrate the chancellor's "magnificence" and the atmosphere of personal and social relations — at their best — at the king's court:

> One day they rode together in a street of London. A biting winter wind blew. The king spied an old pauper coming up the street in the distance, dressed in a thin, tattered garment, and said to the chancellor, "Do you see this man?"
> "I see him," replied the chancellor.
> "How poor, how wretched, how naked," said the king. "Would it not be a great act of charity to give him a thick and warm cape?"
> "Great indeed," replied the chancellor, "and it behooves you as king to think and act so."
> In the meantime they had reached the pauper. The king dismounted, and the chancellor with him. The king took the old man aside gently and asked if he would like a good cape. The pauper, not recognizing them, thought some joke was being played on him.
> "This great act of charity shall be yours," said the king to his chancellor, and laying his hands on Becket's cape, which happened to be new and splendid, of scarlet trimmed in grey fur, he strained to pull it off the chancellor, who struggled to retain it. Soon there was a great pulling and shoving. The potentates and knights in their train hurried up, wondering at the cause of this sudden struggle between the two, and neither [the king nor Becket] could tell them, since each thought only of his grip on the cape. At last the chancellor reluctantly gave in and bending forward let the king remove his cape, which he gave to the poor man. Then the king turned to his courtiers and explained what had happened. Amidst uproarious laughter, various of them offered their coats to the chancellor. The pauper went off wearing the chancellor's cape, enriched beyond his wildest hopes and giving thanks to God. (RS 67: 3, pp. 24–25, chapter 14)

The king plays a charming joke on his worldly chancellor. He forces Becket into the dilemma of showing deference and generosity and parting with his splendid coat, or keeping his coat and appearing niggardly and *inhumanus*. A man of Becket's "magnificence" is reluctant to part with so fine a coat for a mere beggar. Both the king and the chancellor, pretending deference to each other, do their best to remain outside the strictures of obligatory generosity and to force the other into them. Becket is pushed or pulled into the role of St. Martin by main force. This courtier who could make the king a gift of three ships fully equipped and manned[25] now struggles with the king to deprive a freezing beggar of his mantle. Or makes the gestures of struggling. It is all play, put on in the kind of jest that the court would have called *urbanitas* and *facetia*.[26]

BECKET THE EDUCATOR

Rich, popular, famous, and burdened with the tasks of chancellor, Becket takes over the job of court tutor. The king places his own son and heir, Prince Henry, in his care. This is the beginning of a close personal friendship between the prince and Becket. Herbert says that the king made his chancellor the young prince's "tutor and father through grace, as he [Henry] was his father through nature" (2.11.176–77). Also many princes of the land send their sons to serve at his court and receive education at his hands.[27]

What did he teach them? The passages from Herbert and Fitzstephen give us only an oblique hint. Fitzstephen tells that Becket himself prepares the prince and other young nobles for knighting, instructing them *honesta nutritura et doctrina*, finally sending some of them as trained knights back to their fathers *cum honore*, and keeping others in his own retinue. We learn from Fitzstephen also that instruction at court and service there were identical ("they sent their children to serve [*servituros*], and he himself instructed them" — Fitzstephen, chapter 12, p. 22). The prince at least, if not all the sons of nobles, may have received instruction in letters and the liberal arts,[28] but the busy chancellor surely did not dispense this technical instruction himself[29]; nor presumably did he teach them the art of combat, but left this also to subordinates. We are left with the question, what did Becket *ipse* teach them? The answer is no doubt, *mores*. Becket's biographies are about a man who had pursued *mores* and *moralitas* more than letters in his own education, both at court and school, and who had excelled in this "subject" (above, n. 18). What he taught at court was the sum total of what he was, and the education received by the prince and his cohorts was no doubt gotten by charismatic pedagogy enforced by "correction."

The best sources on the subject are the descriptions of Becket's banqueting customs.

LIVING WELL

The chancellor's and archbishop's table receives much comment from the biographers.[30] Table manners had been one of the contexts of *disciplina morum* at St. Victor. Herbert of Bosham makes Becket's dining arrangements at the archbishop's court into a schoolroom of "honest" behavior. It is a long and important passage, which I will partly paraphrase, partly translate.

The seating arrangements have Becket's scholars and learned clerics seated at his right hand; at his left, monks and other religious. Knights, however, no matter how famous or powerful, are seated at a separate table so as not to be disturbed by the readings and learned discussions going on at the archbishop's table — or embarrassed and irritated by not understanding them. But to compensate for their exclusion, their table was especially sumptuous. After the benediction the meal is served:

> One of the older men, a knight, stood before the archbishop, received the dishes brought by the others and set them before him. But many others of high nobility, handsome youths well instructed in such things [*in talibus eruditi*], stood by ready to serve. On one side stood adolescents, pink [of skin] and purple [of dress] like spring-time flowers; on the other, however, young boys, like the fresh and tender sprouts of noble gardens, as it were ornamenting and beautifying the entire table, who served the pontiff and those disposed at his right and left, all of them thoroughly prepared to serve and often performing their duties on their own with no commands.
>
> He had so many sons of the nobles at his disposal because by an ancient law of his predecessors all the second-born sons of the nobility of the land were sent, still in puberty and before receiving the belt of knighthood, to the archbishop. . . . Whence it happened that many flooded to his service, drawn by the man's magnificence, which was taught to them in so civil and urbane a manner [*propter viri magnificentiam tam civiliter eruditam et tam urbane edoctam*]. . . . Among and above all of whom the excellent boy mentioned earlier took the first place, the son of the king and heir of the realm, Henry, ward of the bishop himself, who would procede surrounded by his fellows and attendants like a crown set with purple and violets. . . . How shall I go on? This banquet was altogether splendid: the banqueters splendid, the attendants splendid, the servants splendid, the food most splendid of all. Everything, I repeat, was splendid, everything was delicious and opulent. For to tell the truth . . . nothing in the bishop's house could bring sadness like a meager table; nothing could bring joy like an opulent one. For this reason he himself used to keep a close watch over the proceedings . . . not in a conspicuous manner, but subtly and with courtly breeding [*modesto quodam modo et civiliter erudito*] . . . so that he could observe the order of the guests and accord honor where honor was due. And if perchance among so many someone should be seated in a low place who deserved to preside, he compensated him with frequent gifts of his own cup and of dishes, thus raising the honor of his place. (3.15.226–28)

The passage continues from this point for more than a page in the Rolls Series edition, describing Becket's supervision of the table. What interests Herbert is the distribution of honors for guests and servants and the correction of incautiousness on the part of the servers. The secular meal is watched over with a scrupulousness that would be appropriate for the liturgy and the sacred meal, and that is in fact the frame in which Herbert himself places his description: first the "spiritual table" (Becket performing the liturgy, ch. 13), then the "corporal." This exacting custody of the latter is described as "civil and courtly" [*civilem et domesticam custodiam*]. The narrator has his eye on the awarding of honor and precedence, on behavior that is *urbanum* and *civile*, and particularly on the archbishop, who is *urbane edoctus* (p. 229). The passage ends with more enthusiastic praise and jubilant apologetics for the entire banqueting rite:

> But what is the purpose of all this? Why all these magnificent trappings and so lavish a description of a table fit for an emperor? This seems more like Caesar's table than a bishop's. . . . But you who think thus, whoever you may be, stand here; go not away, judge not, but look upon this and wonder and imitate, if you can, this beast of many eyes and man of many faces. Behold the disciple made all things to all men on the model of his master, rejoicing with those who rejoice, weeping with those who weep, rendering unto the world what is worldly and to God what is God's. . . . "There is a time for all things," and the bishop's special gift is to obey the times, to indulge them and conform himself to them. (p. 230)

The following chapter is an essay on the virtues the bishop displays at table. It is one of the longest chapters in Herbert's long *vita* (pp. 231–38). Chief among his virtues are temperance and sobriety. His sobriety was of a "civil," courtly kind (*civiliter sobrius*, p. 232), and he joined abstinence to his sobriety, though he tended to "conceal his abstinence for the sake of his table companions with a courtly dissimulation, so that he might seem to rejoice with those rejoicing and feast with those feasting" (p. 232). In other words, he pretended courteously to indulge, so that his fellows would not take his abstention as a reproach. He frequently interrupted the eating to discuss some passage in scripture, but he did this in moderation. No music was allowed at the bishop's table. He presided over everything "with a placid countenance and amiable good humor." Then follows (p. 233) a brief discourse on "the three demands of abstinence": namely, what, when, and how much we should take.[31] Lessons and examples of moderation in eating illustrate the three points (pp. 233–34). "Nothing in excess" is the upshot, and "discretion is the charioteer of all the virtues" (p. 235).[32] Thomas is the *magister* of the table, showing moderation to his *condiscipuli*, a model for all priests and pontiffs to imitate (pp. 235–36). He rehearses the qualities the "prince of the table" embodies: he is *magnificus, erudite circumspectus, curialiter eruditus, civiliter sobrius.* He ends the entire chapter by commending Becket's habits to all bishops: "And you, the bishops who sit at his table by invitation, be apprised that it behoves you to do the same" ("Vos autem, invitati pontifices qui sedistis ad mensam, scitote et vos similia debere parare" — 238).

That is Herbert of Bosham's remarkable description of the archbishop's table. The other biographers tend to underplay Becket's magnificence and stress the piety and asceticism it conceals, but Herbert of Bosham hardly conceals his own admiration and astonishment at the well-bred opulence of the scene.[33]

Herbert's purpose in this long description is to recreate the educating force of the archbishop's presence. In these passages we have the clearest and most vivid representation of a "cathedral school" we have yet come across in this study of cathedral schools. It is the court of the primate of England, not of some emperor or worldly courtier, as Herbert stresses. And while it may be "magnificent," "splendid," and worldly, it is in the moral control and custody of the man at its center, who is a veritable force-field of discipline, holding servants and guests alike to the unwritten rules of the house by the radiation of his virtues. Education in *mores* is the framework in which Herbert himself places the scene: Becket is the *magister*, the guests are *discipuli* and *condiscipuli*.[34]

The boys on the staff[35] are "pupils" in a direct and literal sense: their service is a form of learning the "urbanity," "courtliness," and *honestas* of their master. Herbert points out that they are all "well educated" in their tasks (*in talibus eruditi*), and so well "prepared" that they carry out their duties with no commands.[36] They are getting what they came there for. They were drawn by the man's magnificence, and it is taught to them in an "urbane and civil" or "courtly manner."[37] "Educated" is one of the predominant terms of personal description in the passage.[38] We are no doubt justified in seeing in the banqueting scene a partial but distinct answer to the question, what Prince Henry and other noble sons studied under Becket as tutor. They are learning *civiles mores* and *honestas*.

They are not the only students in this school. Herbert twice holds up the scene as a model for other bishops: Becket's moderate and sober use of wine was "commendable and admirable, a model to imitate for any priest, but especially for bishops" (p. 236); and he ends by admonishing all pontiffs to take Becket's table arrangements as a model.

The "subjects" taught in this school pertain to the fourth cardinal virtue, temperance. Becket is himself the model of restraint and moderation. The rule of "nothing in excess" is enjoined by precept and embodied in the practice of the "master" and "prince of the table."

The arrangements show a remarkably delicate and humane sensibility toward guests and staff, and these certainly are part of the lessons in *temperantia*. The knights (including all secular nobles) are seated at a separate table. This could be seen as a hierarchic arrangement, or even as a rebuke to the unlettered and perhaps less polished laity. But it is made to seem an act of humane consideration: they should not be bored by the readings and discussions in Latin. Nor should they be made to feel their own ignorance. And they are compensated for any implied slight in the seating arrangement by having a table more sumptuous than that of the clerics. This is the sensitive considerateness of a man who is *curialiter eruditus*.

The same applies to Becket's own pretense of indulgence. He "concealed his abstinence for the sake of his table companions with a courtly dissimulation [*civili dissimulatione*]" (p. 232). The point of this seemingly arch gesture is that his companions must not feel rebuked by their bishop's abstinence, and so he forgoes the prestige of ascetic restraint and pretends to eat as much as they do. Anyone who wishes to can see this as a case of license smuggled in under the cloak of virtue, but whatever Becket's motives in indulging, the sensibility that understood and approved feigned indulgence as an act of courteous consideration was obviously alive and strong in his disciple, Herbert.[39] Respect, consideration, courtesy, and deference are the ancillary virtues of temperance, and for that reason they are appropriate at a banquet conceived as a school of manners.

This then is a "cathedral school." Like many of its eleventh-century predecessors, it integrates lessons in virtue and its cultivation into the practical activities of a bishop's court; it exemplifies discipline; the bishop is the "master," teaching by the force of his person; he is surrounded by students, official, and unofficial. Of course the more technical kinds of instruction do not register in this scene, but we cannot doubt that they were offered, since waiting on tables is not a full preparation for knighthood or court service. The curriculum in this particular classroom we are allowed to look into is *honestas*.

What then distinguishes Thomas Becket's household from that of, say, Fulbert of Chartres or Wazo of Liège? Probably not the religious elements, which are strongly present at Becket's court, though not stressed in my description: the meal begins and ends with readings and discussions of scripture. Nor is worldliness by itself the distinguishing feature, since a bishop's court had to accommodate soldiers and nobles and customarily educated their sons, in the eleventh no less than the twelfth century. Probably the distinguishing feature is indicated in the words "courtly and urbane." If either Fulbert or Wazo had been called *urbanus* or *curialiter eruditus*, he probably would have taken it as an insult.[40] Azelinus of Hildesheim tried to import a code named for its association with the emperor's court into his household in the early 1050s, and was criticized for it. Now a code called by the same name is fully integrated into *cultus virtutum*, and that is a distinct difference between eleventh and twelfth century bishops' courts. The archbishop of Canterbury is a man, like Azelinus, who is famed for winning the favor of worldly lords, and who, also like Azelinus, brought some of the customs of the king's court with him to a see previously known for its ascetic rigor. Becket may well have been criticized for his "splendor" and "magnificence" as chancellor and as archbishop, but the dominant voice is praise. "Courtliness" has gained legitimacy. The biographer himself admits that the scene he describes would do honor to an emperor's court.

While the dominant in Herbert of Bosham's chapters on the archbishop's table is imperial magnificence, he injects enough religious elements to raise the question whether the *conception* of the banquet as a school of *mores* came from the traditions of Canterbury or those of the royal court. There is an important text that helps us answer it. It is John of Salisbury's *Policraticus*, dedicated to Becket and finished in 1159, when Becket's term as chancellor was at its highpoint.

In five chapters (Book 8, chapters 6–10) John discusses and analyses ancient and Christian banqueting customs, and develops some guidelines for the king's chancellor. He distinguishes three kinds of banquets: the philosophical, the civil and the popular (*philosophica, civilia*, and *plebeia* — 8.6, ed. Webb 2: 253; cited henceforth as 8.6, p. 253). The kind he develops for Becket's edification combines philosophical and civil. A whole raft of vices beckons to "those who feast splendidly every day," and it is important to impose on these dangers the virtues and discipline of *modestia* and *temperantia*:

> The words of Portunianus were both elegant and true when he said that no one banquets in a civil way who does not impose on himself the rule of frugality and modesty in food and drink. Lack of moderation in food or drink drives away that ordering minister of all duties, Temperance. (8.6, p. 257)

He praises the learned poet who reckoned it appropriate to the "dignity of the ancients" that they "admitted nothing in the civil gathering which did not accord with nature or the instruction of manners."[41] The philosophical should not be separated from the civil banquet, because "philosophy brings moderation to all things [*philosophia rerum omnium moderatrix*]." Nothing is either civil or in accord with duty unless Philosophy has paved the way for it, and it is important that her ideas become realized in practice, because

> What good does it do to huff and puff about duties in the schools of virtue, if they are then not carried out in actions and in behavior. (8.6, p. 272)

That makes of the civil banquet the ideal stage for lived philosophy. Some may think the convivia of Socrates and his disciples uncivil because of their austerity and philosophical intensity, John says:

> But civil banquets are . . . freer and less restrained, though not dissolute, more opulent, and they tend — while not neglecting modesty — more to a general cheerfulness and good humor than to philosophical rigor. (8.6, p. 273)

Civil banqueting involves an amiable face and generous hand lightening the general atmosphere while diligently carrying out duties, serving individuals in accord with a careful account of the person, the place, and the time; the philosophical is altogether chaste, restrained, and subject to its rules, but:

> These duties, sober and purified from any trace of turpitude, do not prevent Socrates from expounding positive justice . . . do not forbid Timaeus to explain the causes of all things, nor do they restrain anyone from the display of any virtue. . . . Delights and pleasures are present without turpitude; dignity is present without excluding good humor. (8.6, p. 273)

Later he sums up the purpose and essence of the philosophical banquet:

> Finally, there is one goal at which the entire striving of the philosophical gathering aims, namely an honorable conclusion [*finis honestus*] and a happy and cheerful outcome, and philosophy will not accomplish this end unless she imposes Considerateness [*verecundiam*] as the overseer in every workshop and on all those who execute duties, for she is the parent . . . of all honorable counsel, the ward of solemn duties, the mistress [teacher] of innocence . . . who shows a favorable and approving countenance at all times and in all places. (8.9, p. 283)

In chapter 9 John includes, almost apologetically, the testimony of holy scripture. It may seem to pertain more to religion than to civility, he says, but for his part he refuses to make a sharp distinction between the two, "since nothing is more civil than the cultivation of virtue [*cultui virtutis*]"

(8.9, p. 280). But after side tracks into Christian customs he apologizes to those who may consider them "more superstitious than civil" (8.10, p. 284) and returns to where his heart is, the classical tradition.

He develops at great length Macrobius's prescriptions for banqueting from the *Saturnalia*. There is much material relevant to Becket's household in these passages also,[42] but the passages just discussed establish my point: John's discourse on banqueting for the chancellor virtually repeats the conceptual framework within which Herbert of Bosham describes the archbishop's table. In fact it raises the question whether Herbert consulted the *Policraticus* in describing Becket's table. The banqueting chapters of the *Policraticus* give us a clear answer to our question: the archbishop's table, as described by Herbert of Bosham, continues customs of the royal, not the episcopal court as prescribed by John of Salisbury. Their provenance is distinctly classical, not Christian; their social context worldly, not religious.

This book started by showing the limited role of *civiles mores* in Carolingian education in contrast to "ecclesiastical disciplines." A little more than three centuries later, the relationship has changed considerably: *civiles mores* are an object of instruction at the episcopal court that can command most of the attention of a bishop's/saint's biographer.

But there are severe limits on this comment. Few bishops' courts in the years 1155–60 will have reached the degree of sophistication and reflection of Canterbury under Archbishop Thomas Becket, as Herbert of Bosham depicts it. It may be that not even Canterbury attained it. We are dealing with a stylist whose avowed purpose is to create in Becket an exemplum of *honestas vitae*. But whatever really happened at Canterbury there can be no doubt that the chancellor's "school of manners" was informed by ideals that fully integrated *cultus virtutum* into a chivalric-courtly program of education.

DYING WELL

The moment of death, particularly a martyr's death, makes all superfluous things, thoughts, values, fall away as time gives way to eternity and the present to the beyond. Herbert of Bosham represents Becket's death as such a reversion to the essential. Becket showed fortitude and constancy, piety, devotion to church and so on. Along with these the martyr retains his external composure as an essential of this critical moment. Like most of Herbert's version, the chapter praising Becket's patience in meeting death (6.9, pp. 507–13) is long-winded. Here is the critical passage:

> As up to this point [we have observed] not only the signs of inner virtue, but also of outer polish [*ornatus*] and, as it were, of the beauty [*decus*] of martyr-

dom granted to him as his special privilege, so also [in the moment of death] our lord and patron embellished his martyrdom outwardly with a fitting and decent composition of the outer man, as though he regarded it as inappropriate to die for Christ if he did not die becomingly [*decenter*] for Christ.[43]

Among the elements appropriate for a martyr's death, Herbert of Bosham includes decorum, good manners, a certain well-proportioned and seemly posture, indicated in *decenter*. Even in the moment of death — perhaps especially then — his hero cannot do without that outward composition which bespeaks inner virtue: "This very composition of his body was a prayer to the lord" ("ipsa corporis compositio oraret Dominum" — 6.9, p. 508).

This insistent praise of virtue joined to decorum recalls a precept of *disciplina morum* from Hugh of St. Victor: for discipline it is not sufficient merely to do good things, but one must also *appear* impeccable while doing them; discipline also requires "the governed movement of all members of the body and a seemly disposition [*dispositio decens*] in every posture and act."[44] And more distantly, but distinctly, Herbert's vocabulary recalls the Ciceronian vocabulary of *decorum*: *ornatus, decus, decenti exterius membrorum compositione decoravit, decenter.*

The passage goes on at length, essentially repeating what was quoted above. What C. S. Lewis said of Alan of Lille applies well to Herbert of Bosham: he seems to feel that if a thing is worth saying once it is worth saying three times. He ends with the observation that Becket's combination of virtue and decorum will be a thing of admiration for ages to come, though few will be able to imitate it, because this weak, tepid age produces only self-seeking, vain human beings (p. 509).

For all its literary faults, Herbert of Bosham's Life of Becket is the first narrative we have come across in this study in which the *ethica* of the cathedral schools has consistently supplied the informing ethos of the work. Up to now we have relied on particular passages in letters and biographies, personal descriptions embedded in other contexts. In Herbert's *Vita Thomae*, *ethica* consistently guides the representation of events and provides the terms and concepts that describe education and human excellence.

*   *   *

From the later twelfth century on, lessons in manners become the primary subject of works instructing in chivalric education. A new kind of literature arises with a strong didactic cast to it: the courtly romance. At the same time as the king's chancellor was training future knights in courtesy, the king himself and his wife were avidly cultivating and patronizing a form of literature that made the courtly knight a mythical, exemplary figure.

To what extent did courtly romance arise as a vehicle for a chivalric transformation of the old learning? We know that since the end of the eleventh century clerics had felt it their obligation to teach knights and the lay nobility civilized manners. The author of "De nuptiis" (ca. 1080) listed something like this among the functions of Rhetoric:

> This art . . . holds kings to the rule of moderation,
> It reforms the knighthood, who bear the weapons of Mars,
> Teaching them the doctrine of vigilance and lordly ways.
> It regulates the manners of youths. . . .
> Holding them to civil laws in constant moderation.[45]

We know also that literature — poetry at least — played a role in softening and civilizing the manners of kings and princes. The Latin epic *Ruodlieb* represented the ideals of forgiveness, deference, wisdom, courtesy, and courtship that were in the air in the late eleventh century by projecting them onto a wandering knight educated at a king's court.

The clerical concern to civilize the lay nobility found its most popular instrument in the courtly romance. Whether King Arthur and his knights were fetched from the prop-box of Celtic mythology in order to illustrate courtly social ideals, or whether those ideals imposed themselves on what was already a popular form among the knighthood, the symbiosis of the knightly life and the values of *cultus virtutum* is a reality of European culture from ca. 1150 on. This point has been made recently in Aldo Scaglione's important study, *Knights at Court: Courtliness, Chivalry and Courtesy from Ottonian Germany to the Italian Renaissance*. Scaglione connects chivalric-courtly ideals with the moral discipline of the cathedral schools, and shows a consistent development of these ideals from the knighthood of the high Middle Ages to the Renaissance. He also demonstrates that courtly litera-ture — lyric, narrative and didactic — provided important links in this chain. Instead of repeating Scaglione's argument, I will refer the interested reader to his book, and move to the final subject of this chapter.

Courtly Love

The music Isolde plays (see Chapter 5 above) did not bring tears to the eyes of furies and soothe the raging spirit of kings. It inspired love. But there is a logical progression from Orphic music in the eleventh century to Isoldean in the twelfth and thirteenth. A certain kind of love takes over the function of civilizing brutes and "reforming the manners of knights."

The study of courtly love[46] is in the same methodological bind as the study of medieval education. The twelfth century brought startling innovations. These were in effect the foundation of modern sensibilities and intellectual orientations. It is a powerful constellation: both love and rational, critical thought appear on the scene seemingly without precedent; ergo, study the twelfth century and we study the beginnings of the way we love and think. It encourages us to declare in many areas "the birth (or rebirth) of"; "the origins of"; "the discovery of"; and many are the studies of twelfth-century culture and intellectual life with those words or some variant in the title. But it also obscures the rich and complex modes of thinking and feeling that preceded, flowed into, amalgamated with, and ultimately were abandoned by the new, the original, and the reborn. Since eleventh-century worldly culture appears to us as a blank spot, it is easy to accept uncritically, or half-critically, the notion that the twelfth century was created *ex nihilo* from the minds and hearts of a generation or two of original geniuses. As with medieval humanism and courtly ethics, so also with romantic love, there was something there before which flowed into, amalgamated with, and ultimately was abandoned by it.

WHAT WAS THERE BEFORE

The eleventh-century foundations of courtly love were, first, a conception of love that defined friendship as love of virtue in another human being[47]; second, an ethic and its discipline that aimed at the cultivation of virtue.

The phenomenon is more complex, but reducing it to these two factors highlights two essential driving forces of love as a public discourse of aristocratic society prior to the twelfth century, and while reduction means loss, it also means focus. In this case it gives us a sharp focus on what was and remained one of love's major features when *cultus virtutum* moved out of the schools and back to the courts in the twelfth century: its ennobling force.

"Love" is the ideal mood at secular courts as at cathedral schools.[48] The relatedness of the two institutions is obvious: cathedral schools prepared young clerics for court service. The atmosphere of peace and love at school prepared for the ideal atmosphere of the court. The learned courtier transplanted and maintained it in the worldly setting, partly in order to win the favor of the king and his court, partly in order to civilize the unruly lay nobles, and the two goals were closely connected. A standard Latin word for favor is *amor*. The many descriptions of clerics "loved" by the king testify to the successful pursuit of that goal. Otto III so loved his cleric Tammo that the two shared the same clothes and at table ate from the same bowl, joining their hands together when they met in the dish.[49] Bishop Adalbert of Prague shared the same room with Otto III night and day, because "he loved him."[50] Such comments in bishops' and saints' lives are far from indicating any kind of sexual preference. Interpreting them as signs of homosexuality tolerated has some oblique validity,[51] but it should not obscure the primary purpose of this discourse of love: it is part of the economy of honor, prestige and standing at court or in any community. If the king loves a courtier, it is because he has shown particular virtue, or is able to mediate virtue to the king. This Ciceronian conception of friendship was of course available to the Middle Ages through Cicero's most popular work, *De amicitia*. But we should not imagine a sensibility created by the reading of a classical work. It was certainly informed, shaped, and structured by that work, but the sensibility had probably inhered in aristocratic society since Greek antiquity. Love and refinement of feelings were one of the many means at the disposal of the aristocracy of showing forth and rewarding virtue. Passionate friendship distinguished nobles from non-nobles, just as other codes of behavior did: warrior honor and a refined, cultivated way of speaking, gesturing, dressing, and living. Passionate friendship is in many ways the counterpart in peace of warrior honor in combat.

If the love of medieval kings prior to the late eleventh century signaled sexual preference, then surely there would be some mention of kings who loved women, and shared their food and bed with them. But there are none (as Dinzelbacher has shown, "Entdeckung der Liebe"). For the earlier period a comment that a king so loved such and such a woman that he shared his food, clothes, and bed with her, would be as inappropriate as an announcement that the king had sexual relations with men. It would represent a ludicrous intrusion of the private sphere into a discourse and social custom that was essentially public and ceremonial.[52] Women belonged to the private sphere, and they could not participate in a discourse of love until they emerged into the public sphere. Things written guaranteed the public and representative nature of the subject and gave any statements the protection of discursive innocence.[53]

A suggestion of lust in love relations would deprive the discourse of that which fueled it: the display of impulse mastered and disciplined. The king's love mixed with his lust would confer no honor at all, just the opposite, and that means that the libidinous had no part in ceremonial love relationships, which represent a claim of the mastery of libido. Needless to say, behind the mask of ceremony the whole range of private love relationships played themselves out. Raising the mask was a concern of later ages. How firmly this discourse was still in place in the twelfth century is shown in the comment of Roger of Howden, historian of the reign of Henry II, that King Philip Augustus of France "so honored" Richard Lionheart of England that he "loved him like his own soul," shared his clothes and his bed with him.[54]

The letters and poems of friendship from the eleventh-century schools express the idea of an exalting love, which makes common cause with discipline and *cultus virtutum*.

A poem from the first half of the eleventh century (probably from the vicinity of St. Emmeram), the "Satyra de amicicia," celebrates friendship based on virtue.[55] It begins by lamenting the strife in the world. The poet conjures Amphion singing to restore harmony and to soften pain and sorrow while his boorish foe Zethus sows discord, unmoved by the music. Friendship is like music, the poem continues. It composes men to like-mindedness (a Ciceronian strain) while the harsh law causes discord. Virtue creates loyal friendships that bind men together, since it constantly seeks the good (*honesta*) and repels evil. The poet's wish is that virtue will hold him and his addressee together and join their hearts in firm bonds, so that they may rejoice to be called brothers and comrades. Since the occasion is the poet's joy at his lord's generous act of releasing him from his unfree status, we can infer that friendship creates equality. Orphic music appears as a relative of Ciceronian friendship in this early poem. It is a significant parallel, since it shows friendship based on virtue as part of that civilizing program borne by the medium of music, hence central to contemporary culture. Both Orphic music and friendship appear here as the adversaries of rustic boorishness and the "harsh law."

We see the cult of friendship keeping close company with moral discipline in a number of the Hildesheim letters. One of the letters directed to a student from a friend, begins:

> When I heard about your safety and well-being, which I fervently desired . . . , and when I received your greeting, my soul was so filled with joy that the simple and undivided Easter celebration which others were intent upon became for me a double festival: the one was the gross, palpable and corporal festivity all were celebrating; the other, inspired by your letter, is mine alone, private and unique: the festive and spiritual celebration of your love. Departing from you was like a descent into grave and gloomy Egyptian darkness

where my mind was held captive. . . . But upon receiving your divine letters, by which you deified me, I was as one led . . . into his own promised land . . . .

But if the shadowed thought of you and your sun-like words gave me so great a cause and occasion for joy, how much greater, how much fuller when you enrich me with your bodily presence and I rejoice to embrace you and speak with you, exult in this joy, and my whole body dances inwardly! How long shall I be deprived of your presence with no consolation? How long shall I be separated from you, my lord and most beloved? . . . But think not that these tearful interrogations are the result of despair . . . because the more I seek you with my constant desire, the greater will be my satisfaction at the dear and sweet delight of some day being with you. I consider our separation nothing other than the discipline of conserving what is one day to be shared together [*conservande olim conservantie disciplinatio*].[56]

All this was a prelude to the business of the letter. The recipient has asked the letter writer for advice in finding a teacher appropriate for his studies. The writer says that he has been hard at work, and has recommended him as "good and glorious" to French, Normans and Germans. Indeed he has been so industrious that his friend's fame now precedes him, and the faithful services of many are promised to him. He assures him that, humble and lowly as he is, a mere nobody in both letters and in the requisite virtue for the task, he nonetheless has striven to raise his friend to the pinnacle of honors. He urges him for his part to further his efforts by his own virtues:

You however, who have received as a gift of nature the highest nobility, an impressive beauty of bodily shape, see to it, keep on your guard, and be ever vigilant that your noble humility should make you beloved of all, approved of all, the intimate friend of all, and that your probity of holy manners [*sanctissimorum morum probitas*] should win you favor. (p. 77)

He warns his friend against a teacher at Beauvais, and asks for criticism of his own unpolished letters:

They come to you unkempt like barefoot country girls to their boy friends, having hastened in the middle of the night on their way to you their lover, frivolously uncomposed, forgetting their cosmetics.

The words of love the letter is couched in all but swallow up its meager business, to find a school for the wandering scholar.

Inseparable from their love is the writer's concern for his friend's reputation and standing. With his own feeble efforts he works to raise them, but he also exhorts him to guard his humility (to which his high nobility is presumably a danger). This urging is part and parcel of their friendship.

The teacher is protecting his friend, guiding him through dangers, by watching out for his honor and his virtue. Successful study depends on virtue, and the love of a friend is both a stimulus to heighten it and a medium for its cultivation. The conserving of their mutual desire is a positive form of discipline.

Baudri of Bourgueil wrote a poem to a young boy with similar strains. It plays on themes of homosexual love poetry,[57] but it is a poem of moral correction teaching essentially the same lesson as the Hildesheim letter. Baudri speaks to the boy as teacher to disciple. The boy has every gift of nature outwardly: he is beautiful, his hair is blonde, his skin is ivory, his voice is lovely and indistinguishable from a girl's, his cheeks just receiving their first down, his body "divinely" shaped. These features of the boy please Baudri, and he is also pleased that, given these charms, he refuses "to be Ganymede to Jove." Baudri praises this in him, and urges him not to be corrupted by false love. While everything else in the boy pleases Baudri, the boy's manners do not. His problem is arrogance, which Baudri castigates as *improbitas morum*: he hardly deigns to look at others; when they greet him, he passes by silently. He acts as though he thought he alone ruled on earth. God has created many more beautiful, more decorous than he, and this outer form will fade soon, like the beauty of flowers. He should soften his hard heart, give up his arrogance:

> I love a humble appearance and despise a stiff neck.
> Therefore, if you wish, boy, to please me,
> Put aside these lofty airs,
> Smile at him who smiles at you, make fitting responses.
> Soften that stiff head and rigid eyes. (ll. 56–59)

There can be no question of Baudri courting a desirable boy. He is plainly correcting his manners, making him fit for a worthy love. The master is tuning the boy's *mores* to his body, his inner to his outer world, and imposing due temperance and moderation all the more urgently the greater the physical beauty. The "lesson" repeats the "moral" correction of the Hildesheim letter just discussed: do not let the gifts of nature make you arrogant; study to win men's affection. The boy is courting the teacher, not vice versa; he wants to please Baudri, and is not doing so. There is a tinge of the erotic in the poem, of course, but that was probably inherently present in student—teacher relations in the old learning. It can be a useful pedagogic instrument. Love and affection were precisely the medium in which moral correction could take place without resentment. It must have been particularly important when a teacher dealt with high nobility. It was the medium in which Guibert of Nogent received instruction in *mores*. He received brutal correction with gratitude because he loved his teacher so. It even neutralized contempt for the teacher's ignorance.

Love in pedagogy means control of the student's will: he surrenders his will to his teacher, who puts his absolute control over the student to whatever purpose he sees fit. Some no doubt took advantage of that dominance to ravish their students.[58] Baudri is clearly putting his power over the boy to use to correct, not to ravish him. His poem is about cultivation of virtue, and that reading must be regarded as primary to any suggestion of homosexual courtship.[59]

The problem of whether homosexuality is concealing itself behind moral instruction, or vice versa, is not easily answered, and the "joke" (in Bond's sense — see n. 47 above) may be on both homo- and anti-sexual readers. The ambiguity of the discourse is part of its nature. For my point at present it is enough to show that passionate love and correction of *mores* made common cause. The correction of a youth's arrogance in the framework and through the language of erotic love, is an arrangement of moral discipline. Whatever play with erotic motives is present, the accepted, normative, legitimate discourse at work here is that of *cultus virtutum*.

WHAT WAS NEW IN THE TWELFTH CENTURY

What does this have to do with courtly love? I would suggest that it opens to view the foundations of its ethical aspects. These few texts show us clearly that the schools practised a ceremonial love which demonstrated the presence of virtue in the lovers and served as a medium to heighten the virtue and increase the honor of both partners, but especially of the student partner. *Cultus virtutum* took place in this medium — or was supposed to. It spoke the language of passionate love and played on its erotic elements while accounting it the part of virtue to control eros. The same language had played an important part also at worldly courts at least since Carolingian times in describing favor relationships between king and courtiers. Alcuin and Charlemagne, Adalbert and Otto III, show that the love relation of king to tutor is present at early medieval courts. Given the close connection between court and school from the mid-tenth century on, we can assume a connection between court love or the king's love and *cultus virtutum*.

Two essential innovations occur in this discourse at the end of the eleventh century: women are admitted to it and gradually assume the role of educator (at least are represented in this role); and with them, private elements enter what was previously a public, ceremonial discourse and begin to imbue that discourse with an overtly masking character that previously it had only had covertly. One of the symptoms of the shift is that Ovid supersedes Cicero as the ancient authority on love relationships.[60]

Hennig Brinkmann (n. 47 above) argues that courtly love in its origins was a creation of learned clerical poets, like Marbod, Baudri and Hildebert, who brought their classical learning to bear in letters and poems written to high courtly ladies. Of the various theories on the origins of courtly love, this one has the advantage of providing a social context for the phenomenon. The Loire circle had close contacts to Duke William IX of Aquitaine, the first troubador.

What this study can add to Brinkmann's model is the insight that a pedagogy of moral discipline had a major role to play in the formation of the ethical aspects of courtly love.

Since the late eleventh century we can observe the tendency to transfer the language of *cultus virtutum* onto a sphere of life that previously had been mute: love relations between men and women.[61] The poet of *Ruodlieb* (ca. 1070) has his proto-chivalric hero seek a bride who "would not be unbefitting our noble blood, but who would also ornament our nobility with her manners and with the inborn nobility of her conduct." The hero's advisor then recommends a young lady who is "your equal in probity of manners [*moris honestate*], virtue and nobility." Such a woman could give Ruodlieb a son who would be "the heir of your manners, your virtues, your goods."[62] Virtue and good manners register here as important qualities in a woman regarded as potential lover and spouse. This shows women admitted to the gentleman's club of a discourse on virtuous love. It is generally agreed that the *Ruodlieb* anticipates and creates social values rather than recording current practice among the aristocracy. If that is the case with virtue and manners as a criterion of a good wife, then we have a fairly clear case of a learned cleric imposing the neo-classical language of *cultus virtutum* onto the representation of courtship customs.

Baudri of Bourgueil writes poems of courtship to women (in the mode of the *iocus amoris*) which amalgamate the language of flirtatious wooing with the practice of *disciplina morum*. To Lady Constance, he proposes a chaste love (*castus amor*) which lacks all the dangers of erotic love.[63] In his "song of love" (*carmen amoris*) he pleads, "Let our hearts be joined, but our bodies remain sundered; for all the play [*iocus*] in our writing, let there be purity in our deeds."[64] Though Baudri claims not to be torn by his passion, or titillated in his flesh and innards, yet he loves her:

> I love you vehemently; all of me loves all of you.
> You alone do I enfold in my bosom.
> This kind of love, it is clear,
> Is not common, but special,
> A special love, not subject to the flesh,
> Nor marked by illicit desire. (ll. 72–80)

Indifferent to her flesh, except its purity, he depicts her outward form with only one end in mind, "that your outer shape should show forth the form of your character." The "flowered" virgin puts forth "florid manners" so that she may flourish inwardly more than outwardly (ll. 86–88). Many a young man has tried to play Jupiter and Mars to her Juno, Danae, Io and Venus, but she remains a chaste Diana. The two of them should take a new path, free of panderers: "Let us take the path of virtues and climb to the stars" (113).

Here a desirable woman, courted by many youths, receives an invitation to play a "game" of love whose purpose is the cultivation of virtue and the attunement of outer beauty to inner. It depends on a love seen as "special" and distinguished for being chaste.[65]

Another poem by Baudri shows us courtship, with many affinities to courtly love, practiced within the context of court society. Brinkmann points out Baudri's long poem to Countess Adela of Blois as a bridge between learned Latin poetry (there is an elaborate allegory of learning in the description of the countess's bedchamber) and courtly love.[66] The chaste, honest countess has many handsome suitors distinguished for their *probitas*. But those who have tried to tempt the countess have found their efforts fruitless, since her marriage bed is protected by an inviolable pact. Baudri understands the efforts of her suitors:

> Her unusual beauty and incomparable loveliness
> Commend her, as does her pleasant conversation.
> But who could soften her flinty resolve?
> Their gazing on her is pointless, though delightful.
> Nourished by empty hopes, they dream of grand rewards,
> And strain their eyes with gawking. (ll. 67–72)

So here we have the distant *domna* drawing the men of court to her by her virtue and beauty but thwarting their vain hopes by her chastity and loyalty. He does not say that she sends them out to polish their manners and accomplish bold feats before granting them any hope. It is the framework of courtly love without, for the moment, its educating aspect. The educating force of love is present in other poems of this circle to women, however.[67]

The cult of love that finds expression in Provencal and Old French love lyric from the early twelfth century on draws on the concepts and terminology of *cultus virtutum*. There is massive testimony to this influence,[68] but we can observe it best by staying with expressions of courtly love in Latin. The classic work on the subject was written by a learned cleric, chaplain of the king of France, to a young man named Walter who wishes to learn the ways of worldly love. Andreas Capellanus's *De amore* (ca. 1174), however one judges the nature of its discourse and the attitude of its author toward its subject,[69] is informed by the language of moral discipline. The two aspects of love that predominate in the work emerge in his chapter on "The Effects of Love."[70] Love turns the avaricious man generous; it makes the rough, uncultivated man blossom with beauty; it enriches even the low-born with "nobility of manners" (*nobilitate morum*); it turns arrogant men humble, and it "decorates" a man with the virtue of chastity (because he seeks only a single lover). Andreas's summarizing praise: "What a wonderful thing is love, since it makes a man shine with such virtues, and teaches him to abound in good manners [*docet . . . bonis moribus abundare*]" (1.4.1–3, p. 38).

In opening the long chapter on "How love is won" (1.6), Andreas cites five "modes": beauty of appearance, honesty of character, fluent and eloquent speech, great wealth, and easy granting of favors. He at once excludes the last two from serious consideration. That leaves the "modes": *formae venustas, morum probitas*, and *copiosa sermonis facundia*. The latter two are of course goals so central to cathedral school teaching as to be a variant of the formula, "letters and manners." The first tends to keep close company with the other two in descriptions of well educated men.[71] And of course the logic of virtue made visible commended both eloquent speech and physical beauty as outward indicators of inner beauty — in students no less than in lovers.

A distinctive feature of Andreas' conception is the image of love as an instructor (*docet*), whose curriculum is virtue and good manners. *Probitas morum* is the common formulation in Andreas, though he also speaks of *honestas morum*, *nobilitas morum*, *cultura morum*, *boni mores*, and simply *mores*. Virtue appears now as a prerequisite and now as a result of love, and those two contradictory roles can become the object of debate in the dialogues between women and their suitors. It is worth wondering whether love's ability to make a plain man handsome is a reminiscence of the old learning's ambition to "overcome nature."

Andreas consistently depicts women as teachers and men as students. In a passage of the dialogue between a man of the lower class (*plebeius*) and a woman of the higher nobility (*nobilior*) the man admires the woman's "comprehensive knowledge of the art of love" (*omnino in amoris arte instructam* — 1.6.146, p. 80) and requests that she become his teacher (*vestram in amore deposco doctrinam*). He is all the more urgent in pressing this request since he knows that all urbanity (*urbanitas*), all good deeds, and all kindness (*bonitas*) are due to love's teaching (147). The woman reproaches him for having requested first her love, then her teaching, thus showing his first request unworthy (*velut indoctus in amoris petis disciplina doceri* — 148). But she accedes to his request, lest she set a miserly example if "experts" (*periti*) should refuse their instruction (*sua documenta*) to the "less learned seeking instruction" (*minus eruditis quum postulant edoceri*).

Her instruction follows. A lover must show generosity through acts of charity, particularly to impoverished nobles. He must be "humble to all and ready to serve all." He must never speak ill of anyone, but where he sees evil men, he should discreetly reprove their bad behavior. He should never mock someone in distress. He should not be prone to quarrels and arguments (*litigiosus vel ad rixas faciendas promptus esse non debet*), but rather should strive to reconcile disputes and arguments. He should moderate his laughter, especially in the presence of women. The "governance of love" requires great wisdom: *In amoris . . . gubernatione prudentia grandis exigitur*. He should "enthusiastically study and aspire to the great achievements of the ancients." He must bear himself with courage and wisdom in battle. He must not adorn his body excessively. He must show himself as "prudent, sociable and pleasant to all" (*sapientem atque tractabilem et suavem . . . omnibus*). He should avoid lying, excessive talking and excessive silence. If anyone deceives him or treats him in an uncourtly manner, he must "reciprocate with kindness and render him service in every way, thus prudently forcing him to acknowledge his fault." He must be hospitable, must honor clerics and the church (cf. 1.146–60, pp. 80–84).

Some of the main themes of cathedral school teaching are touched on here: a learned teacher of virtue passes on to her student admonitions to humility, generosity, gentleness, deference, kindness etc. Virtually none of the lessons would have been out of place in the moral discipline of the schools (bold combat is the one exception), and some of them are central virtues of that discipline.

Two of the most common features of *cultus virtutum* are missing from this list of virtues: the notion of virtue made visible, and well-disciplined gesturing and walking. Both occur in the *De amore*, though they are not prominent features.[72]

In their role as teachers women also take on charismatic functions, in Andreas as elsewhere in the literature of courtly love. The *vir nobilior* opens his address by saying that nothing a man does is of any value unless he acts to do the will of a lady, since "all good things manifestly derive from women." This imposes on women the obligation to heighten man's virtue by the power that flows from their eyes: "To men who perform good deeds they must show themselves in such a light that the worth of such men seems to grow in every way from virtue to virtue under their gaze."[73] This is like that charismatic radiation which flowed "in a living stream" from the breast of Pernolf of Würzburg, also like the transforming power of Bernard of Clairvaux: "You need merely see him and you are edified, you need only hear his voice and you are learned." The force of Isolde's presence is similarly charged: "Whoever gazes at Isolde, his heart and soul are refined like gold in the white-hot flame; his life becomes a joy to live. . . . Her beauty makes others beautiful."[74]

One final point on *De amore*: Andreas (or the cleric of his dialogue) opposes "pure love" to "mixed love" (*amor purus, amor mixtus* — 1.6.470– 75, p. 180). "Pure love" is preferable; it is the source of all goodness (*totius probitatis origo*) and it is constantly growing. The woman doubts that such a love can exist, but concedes that a man able to love thus would be "most worthy of all honor." Marbod and Baudri had also propounded a *castus amor* of both women and men, and opposed it to the carnal love which they rejected.

It would be possible to analyse the ethical language of the *De amore* in much greater detail,[75] but it would only underscore the point already made: the work draws heavily on the vocabulary and concepts of *cultus virtutum*. Where else should a learned worldly cleric have found the matter for a treatise on the art of loving *honeste* than from the ethic of *honestas* of the cathedral schools? In place of a loved, charismatic teacher, we now have a loved woman; in place of "perfection," *sublimitas*, the granting of the lord's "love" and favor as consummating points of this curriculum, we now have the granting of a woman's love. These affinities are present in Andreas's work whatever ambiguities inform his presentation and his attitude toward courtly love.

This is far from an argument that courtly love originates in the old learning. It focuses on one aspect of a phenomenon that is richer and more complex. That aspect is one of the many paradoxes of courtly love, perhaps its central one: it subjects eros to rigorous ethical discipline. The discipline of the schools had always sought to restrain the *motus animi* and the *motus corporis*, to sublimate and channel them into "virtue." It had always striven to "overcome nature." But the move of "honest love" from men/men to men/women relations made the mastery of eros a virtuoso act, and no longer just a difficult one. It also made women for the first time presentable as players and speakers in a public discourse on love that granted virtue, prestige and honor.

*　*　*

A clear pattern emerges in the movement of *disciplina morum* into worldly courts. Bad manners of the lay aristocracy provoke a response from learned clerics (who regard it as one of their main duties to instruct and correct the laity); abuses draw clerical values into the worldly sphere as civilizing, moderating forces; the conflict of challenge (lay boorishness and brutality) and clerical response eventually resolves itself in a new social ideal. Some instances:

1. The peace movement has been outside the scope of this study, but it appeared on the periphery (Orphic poetry, Chapter 5). The violence, lawlessness, and depradations of the French nobles are met by a program of social and spiritual sanctions, and the conflict of lay violence with clerical pacification ends in the ideal of the Christian militia.[76]

2. The development of courtly manners: lay (and sometimes clerical) aristocracy — abstracting their social values from those appropriate to warfare — idealize a harsh, militant, abrasive social persona, and this is answered by clerical opposition (e.g., the conflict of Walo of St. Arnulf with Manasses of Rheims), ending in a code of restrained, refined manners called "courtliness" (*curialitas, facetia*).

3. The cult of woman in courtly literature: lay nobles treat women with brutality and contempt, and an ideal of refined, gentle, submissive behavior in love, appropriated at least in part from a clerical ideal of love and friendship, infuses the representation of male — female love relationships.[77]

4. Conduct and etiquette: lay nobles dress extravagantly, eat crudely, speak foully, walk in affected and exotic ways. Clerics protest, and lay nobles are soon hedged in by ideals of "beautiful manners" and "discipline."[78]

The phenomenon I referred to earlier as "crisis control" shows up any time the mores of lay aristocracy assert themselves against the values of learned worldly clerics. The laity's bad manners are met by clerical resistance motivated by a civilizing impulse.

Learned men were at virtually every court. There had to be tutors of princes. As polished manners became part of a code of the aristocracy, courtly education became imperative. Learned men were present at court to spiritualize and civilize courtly social norms, transforming them through their knowledge and experience of ethical discipline. The biographers of Thomas Becket represented him as injecting the learning of *mores* into a court which rather rose to his standards than raising him to theirs. Just as Becket transformed the worldly banquet into a school of urbanity and *honestas*, joining philosophy and civility, others will have tried to reshape and transform carnal love and the pursuit of women in the same direction. (We recall that Thomas Becket himself was not a stranger to court love practices. John of Salisbury admitted it reluctantly.) Andreas Capellanus, writing a Latin tract on refined courtship and seduction practices, subjects the pursuit of the erotic to a pedagogy of fine manners, and this is — apart from Andreas's self-undermining discourse — a good parallel to the biographers of Becket.

At the end of this chapter it is important to raise the question whether courtliness and courtly love were anything other than discourse. Have we just been observing the enculturation of living social ideals, or the textualization and imaginative transformation of dead or dying ones? It is at present impossible to say. Some of the best scholarship on the question argues the unreality of courtly ideals: Bumke, *Höfische Kultur* and Schnell, "Höfische Liebe als höfischer Diskurs über die Liebe," to mention only two. I am skeptical about the wholesale denial of the reality and institutionalizing of these codes and have suggested some ways of falsifying or confirming the two opposed positions.[79] What is beyond doubt is that courtliness and courtly love experienced a discursive explosion in the years after about 1150.

That places us in an odd situation: documentation seems to stand in an inverse proportion to the reality of the phenomena documented. The attestation of *cultus virtutum* for the late tenth and eleventh centuries was sparse but decisive: that curriculum existed and was a practiced code at cathedral schools. The statements of masters and students and the institutional accommodation assure us of its "reality." It was instrumental in creating a human type demonstrably at work shaping men according to the requirements of high administrative positions of church and state. From the second half of the twelfth century on, we have massive testimony to similar ideals in court society, but serious scholars can deny their reality as social practices.

The texts cited from Becket's biographies pose the problem clearly: modes of behavior are brought to bear in describing the archbishop's habits that demonstrably derive from *cultus virtutum*. The archbishop's table becomes a school of moderation and temperance. But we cannot say for certain that those descriptions represent actual practice at Becket's court. They may be responses to John of Salisbury's banqueting sections of the *Policraticus*, cribbed from Macrobius's *Saturnalia*, prescriptive and not descriptive. No other school in Europe contemporary with Becket to my knowledge was a school of virtue comparable to the Canterbury of the Becket biographies. But in the eleventh and early twelfth century, such "schools" of virtue had existed in fact.

Given the current uncertainty about the reality of courtly ideals after courtly literature, it seems prudent to put forward a model of development in the form of probable surmise. We can identify two stages: from 950 to ca. 1100 a school curriculum and a practice of schools and courts generated a discourse; whereas from ca. 1150 to the end of the Middle Ages and beyond, a discourse generated social ideals.

Conclusion

This study ends with some general reflections on its subject rather than a summary. The movement it has observed is the second of three major events in the development of European education in the Middle Ages. Each produced changes in western thought, culture, and institutions.

The first were the Carolingian educational reforms. They shaped or reshaped the seven liberal arts as a school curriculum and as the basic framework of education. They made rudimentary grammatical, rhetorical and scriptural learning available on a broader scale and created a literate culture in Europe where there had been virtually none before.[1] The institutional shift that made the spread of learning possible on a large scale was the revitalizing of monastic and cathedral schools.

The second began in the Ottonian educational innovations and flowed into the intellectual trend I have referred to as medieval humanism. Its institutional basis was the cathedral school as conveyor of "civil manners" (*civiles mores*) and educator of future administrators in worldly and ecclesiastical courts. It considerably broadened the basis on which court and civil education were available. Its contribution to rational thought was minimal, in fact retarding, since it was based on personal authority and discouraged skeptical, critical thinking. Its cultural contribution, however, was the social values of the European aristocracy, at least that side of their social values that set gentleness and modesty against harshness and arrogance, the codes of behavior we know as civility and courtesy.

The third change occurred in the course of the twelfth century. It represented a shift to rational inquiry and systematic critical thought. Its institutional foundation were the independent schools in Paris which emerged in the course of the twelfth century as a result of the end of the bishop's monopoly on instruction. Its intellectual contribution was scholasticism. Its cultural contribution was minimal[2]; the individual schools evolved into the institution of the university, and its bequest is that institution with its traditions of systematic, critical thought.

Monasticism gave Europe new ways of studying; humanism gave it new ways of behaving; scholasticism gave it new ways of thinking. Political policy and patronage stood behind each of these shifts. The first was Carolingian, the second Ottonian, the third Capetian.

The first and third of these movements have commanded the attention of intellectual historians. The history of the second has still to be written. I have tried to formulate a typology of its curriculum, an outline of its development and a conceptual framework within which its history can be described. Its main points are —

in its origins:

1) The institutional move from royal/imperial court to cathedral schools.
2) A curriculum involving the broadening of the orator's education of antiquity to a general medieval education in conduct, from *civiles mores* to *civilitas*.

in its development and decline:

3) A culture of personal charisma and authority ceding to an intellectual culture based on systematized rational thinking that required the written text as its ultimate medium.[3]
4) The transformation of a charismatic school culture into a textualized court culture, which in turn generated or helped generate social ideals and narrative forms based on personal charisma (courtliness, courtly literature, courtly love).

The research for this study has made me skeptical of terms like "Christian ethics," "medieval ethics," "the ethics of the Christian Middle Ages" as they are currently used. Handbook accounts of these concepts ordinarily move from Augustine to Abelard to Thomas Aquinas, and locate the subject within the field of thought and influences set in place by those three figures; that is, they follow the logical but misleading criterion of textual wealth. No history of ethics or philosophy I know of takes into account the pre-Abelardian school discipline known as *ethica, moralis philosophia, moralitas*. These terms have a clear and distinct content. The curriculum and the concepts they express dominated the cathedral schools from the late tenth to the early twelfth centuries. They deserve a place in the history of thought and education.

They are also useful in social, literary, and political analysis of the Middle Ages. The conceptual and pedagogic apparatus of *cultus virtutum* provides categories for understanding and judging behavior and conduct. They get us into the fabric of human interrelationships; they equip us with the contemporary language of friendship, love, and conflict, and with a vocabulary for describing a whole spectrum of "attitudes" (*habitus, status*) that created and defined issues. They are important in analyzing social and political conflict, for instance that of the schools of Würzburg and Worms; of Wazo of Liège with the imperial court; of Bishop Azelinus with the conservative clergy of Hildesheim; of Walo of St. Arnulf and others with Archbishop Manasses of Rheims. They show the real social issues at stake, for instance in a "school poem" as opaque and obscure as the eleventh-century "De nuptiis Mercurii et Philologiae." That poem's Orpheus sang in the underworld with essentially the same motive as Walo of St. Arnulf "mitigating the fury" of Archbishop Manasses and the starving students of Hildesheim pleading for mercy with Bishop Hezilo.

These are things that are as elusive as motives and sensibilities. They are difficult to get at for the Middle Ages, since its historical sources tend to place little stress on behavior and its analysis, and the literary-didactic sources that do are stymied by hermeneutic indeterminism. In the current critical climate, very few readers of courtly literature and courtesy books would venture an estimate of the social reality to which the literature of courtesy refers. That climate for medieval literary studies is dominated by the opposition of the real to the ideal.[4] This conceptual opposition banishes the conveyors of courtly ideals to a detached aesthetic realm with no ties to social reality. The study of medieval literature has been strongly under the influence of E. R. Curtius,[5] and that means it is haunted by the wan ghosts called "topoi." Curtius helped us look on medieval literature as a composite of received forms, as texts generated by other texts. But many of the "mere" topoi from antiquity on which Curtius based his great study turn out to be the clothing for vital ideas, alive, powerful, and at work transforming the society that produced them via the medium of literature.

A discipline of conduct was a reality at cathedral schools. We know some of its central values and virtues: love, friendship and peace that make possible the cultivation of gentleness and humane kindness; elegance and beauty of manners, composed bearing, restrained and moderated conduct in gesturing, walking, eating, laughing; joviality, charm, grace, and good humor. We know that these concepts made their way outward from the schools to influence conduct and its pedagogy in other areas of society:

communities of canons regular, monks (though I have found no evidence that monastic communities adopted them), and, above all, worldly courts. The literature of the courts after ca. 1155 appears like a literature of pure fantasy and high-flung fairy-tale ideals when read in isolation. But when read against the background of *cultus virtutum*, it appears as the bearer of a long-established code of refined manners.

The discourse of the old learning is the shadow and cipher of life. The virtue it taught made no sense apart from embodied, lived and experienced virtue. *Compositio morum* is an abstraction from the body, hence it has to have one. The body of virtue can be either living or fictional. But the history of cultivating virtue from the tenth to the twelfth century makes it clear that it began with embodied virtue and moved to textualized. The letter of Meinhard to G. of Cologne once again is paradigmatic for those priorities: the teacher says to his student, in effect, think constantly of your father, what he was and what you owe him, and, by the way, do not forget the *Tusculan Disputations*; the greatest work of ancient philosophy can be helpful also. The textbook is fine, but it cannot compare in immediacy of impact with the real or recollected presence of a human being. Those priorities assure us that *cultus virtutum* had to be, in its origins, lived and embodied ideals. They became abstract and cut themselves off from real embodiment when they lost their institutional base. At that point ideals were, so to speak, placed on their own. Their embodiment came to depend on the charisma of their representation, though Thomas Becket is a possible exception, if his charismatic presence inspired the texts which convey it to us — and that is an entirely reasonable assumption.

The history of *cultus virtutum* also tells us something about the way European social values were made in the Middle Ages. They began as a school discipline, one conceived and implemented at and around the royal/imperial court, initially to serve it. This discipline drew on ancient social and political ideals. "Renewal of the Roman empire" was a political program, and this influenced the educational program that served imperial ends. Also, Roman writers had given the most sophisticated formulations to some of the goals of cathedral school education: the preparation for state service through training in eloquence and *civiles mores*. Once this elite discipline moved from the court into the cathedral schools, it trained far more people than the imperial and royal courts could accommodate. But that was all right, because everybody wanted to behave the way the king or emperor and his retinue behaved, and that behavior came to be a desirable quality for administrative service at cathedrals as well. And so an applied education became a general education. The training of a "splendid man of administration" simply became the training of a "splendid man," and ultimately also of a splendid woman. What began as applied educational goals developed into social values.

Finally, this study provides a closer look at the worldly culture of the eleventh century, especially in the schools but also to some degree in the courts. That secret garden all but shut its doors to later generations, and its secretive gardeners were oblivious to the problems that their silence and obscurity were going to cause historians centuries later. They did not leave us texts, and modern scholarship, its apparatus created to deal with texts and to process words, has understandably asked what they read and what they wrote. When Pernolf of Würzburg taught he had his voice, body, facial expressions, a few books, and a memory filled to overflowing. That equipment was adequate. It allowed the "beauty of many poets" to beam from him and the "living stream of learning" to flow from his breast.

Insofar as historians have wondered about the eleventh-century school culture at all, their evaluation was guided necessarily by the presuppositions of a book culture. Those presuppositions make it hard to distinguish a great philosopher-teacher who wrote nothing from a mediocrity who wrote nothing. The example of Pernolf of Würzburg and others like him focuses our attention on the tyranny of documentation to which the historian is subject. Tucked away in the modern historical consciousness are a few embedded commands that say to the silent "philosophers" and school masters of the eleventh century: Why can't you be more like Peter Abelard, or Peter Lombard, or Alan of Lille?

Treating the early cathedral schools as institutions of a charismatic culture helps judge the age by the criteria that apply to it. It urges us to regard the humanist monuments of the twelfth-century renaissance as in part responses to the fading vitality of the previous age, and it encourages us to ask to what extent the eleventh century was the *auctor absconditus* or *architectus absconditus* of the twelfth.

Appendix A. Moral Discipline and Gothic Sculpture: The Wise and Foolish Virgins of the Strassburg Cathedral

The move from hieratic stiffness to realism and plasticity that occurs in sculpture in the course of the twelfth and thirteenth centuries poses a problem for the historian of art and of ideas. Whose hieratic rigidity of thought and feeling produced the stiffness of early Gothic? And whose humanism created the supple nuanced humanity of high Gothic? When a certain conception of the human figure is expressed in stone, where does it come from? It is a short-circuiting of historical thought to say, "The late thirteenth century represented the human figure so beautifully, so supplely, so individualistically — what a high concept of humanity and individualism that age must have had!" Comparing moral discipline at the schools with its representation in sculpture offers a model case of the infusion of *cultus virtutum* into art — and shows sculpture as a latecomer to ideals of grace, beauty and restraint in the human figure.

The wise and foolish virgins on the south portal of the west façade of Strassburg cathedral are our test case. These figures have stood in the shadow of the great statues of Ecclesia and Synagoge, created in Strassburg some forty years earlier. But along with their older sisters they are no doubt among the most beautiful representations of women that remain to us from the Middle Ages. The statues date from ca. 1290. They are products of high Gothic sculpture in its full blossom, the height of its plasticity, dynamism, and realism (illustrations 1–8).[1] The extraordinary nuancing in posture and facial expression created a series of portraits in which the sculptor's individualizing and idealizing impulses are in perfect concord.

Perhaps their most striking feature is what we might call their moral transparency. They are representations of vices and virtues, but this meaning has to be read from their bodies, their posture, their facial expressions, the tilt of their heads. It is a decisive break with tradition. The tradition of representing the vices and virtues required some sort of emblem or external

Figure 1. Christ and wise virgins. Source: Reinhardt, *La cathédrale de Strasbourg,* Pl. 112.

Figure 2. The tempter and foolish virgins. Source: Reinhardt, *La cathé-drale de Strasbourg*, Pl. 111.

Figure 3. The tempter with foolish virgin. Source: Schmitt, *Gotische Skulpturen des Strassburger Münsters,* vol. 2, Ill. 134.

Figure 4. Foolish virgins. Source: Schmitt, *Gotische Skulpturen,* vol. 2, Ill. 135.

Figure 5. Wise virgin. Source: Reinhardt,
La cathédrale de Strasbourg, Pl. 109.

Figure 6. Wise virgin. Source: Schmitt, *Gotische Skulpturen*, vol. 2, Ill. 144.

Figure 7. Wise virgin. Source: Schmitt, *Gotische Skulpturen,* vol. 2, Ill. 141.

narrative device to make the quality represented visible.[2] Facial expression, stature and posture played no part in identifying the symbolic meaning of the figure. In fact often enough the "good" forces are identical with the "evil" — "isocephalic," as the art historians say — and the difference is signaled only by some patched-on device. The virtues and vices at Notre Dame of Paris (1210) are virtually indistinguishable. Each figure holds a circle that contains an emblem. These and not their physical appearance constitute their identity.[3]

The Strassburg virgins, by contrast, carry their emblems in the contours of their bodies. They dramatize and enact virtue or vice rather than wearing its symbol as a badge. The medium of representation has moved from the external narrative device to the flesh; the mode of representation has shifted from abstract signalizing to incarnation.

As long as virtue could be externalized in an emblem, individuality and plasticity of representation had no role to play. Once it was conceived as inherent in posture and facial expression, the sculptor faced a new challenge and required new techniques of realism to make the ideals of virtue visible in the flesh.

Each of the virgins is recognizable and distinct from each of the others. But it is not apparent that they represent individual virtues. It is possible to recognize them as individuals, but not as symbols. We cannot say that one shows chastity, another humility, and another modesty. It seems rather that a whole complex of virtues coalesces in each of the figures.

The beauty of the wise virgins is startling. Each has full swelling lips and a well-shaped nose. The dimples in chin and cheeks lend realism to the portraits and suggest that the sculpting is the observable molding that occurs in the human body, not an artificial device of the sculptor in stone (cf. illustrations 6–7 and frontispiece).

But the expressiveness of the group is constituted especially by posture and facial expression. The tilt of the head is made to suggest extraordinary nuances of character and mood. The round-faced wise virgin looking to her left (illustration 6) seems to be drawing back as though in questioning retreat, but also is perfectly poised to respond to whatever she is facing. This tension is created by angling the chin back very slightly from the forehead. The posture conveys restrained strength and testing scrutiny, a quality conveyed in the human form in reality when the head is tilted forward while the eyes fasten on something straight ahead. The impression is strengthened in this figure by the narrowing of her eyes. The Strassburg virgin exudes both wisdom and fortitude, and she seems tensed to exercise those virtues in the imaginary moment in which the sculptor caught her. But for the figure as a whole, any suggestion of tenseness and challenge is dissolved in the relaxed poise of the body (illustration 5). The left hand drops limply from the mantle-string, and the body is shifted slightly, its weight placed on the right foot. She is at her ease and not on her guard. This backward tilt of the body answers the forward tilt of the head. The over-all impression is of strength coupled with restraint and of a mean struck between opposing tensions.

The figure third from Christ's left (frontispiece) has a nobly elongated nose. Her full, sensual lips are set off by a distinct tuck from her dimpled chin. Her face is narrower and longer than the others. What seems to me to give this figure her extraordinary aura is the tension between sensuality and morality. The forward tilt of the head expresses a range of qualities from humility to contemplativeness. There is a suggestion of submissiveness, perhaps even shame, but it competes so directly with serenity, that this figure too confronts us with complexity of expression, and any analysis ends in ambiguity and questioning rather than in a univocal interpretation. She conveys the sexual promise and erotic potential of virginity, an impression that is strengthened rather than diminished by the reverence expressed in the angle of the head. That conflict constitutes her peculiar character: being the most beautiful and most sensual of the group, she is also the most virginal. In the soft line of her lips there is the bemused early awareness of sexuality. But the overall impression is of control and restraint. A woman so in control of her feelings as to maintain this serene half-smile is also the mistress of her own awakening sexuality. This figure shows the heroism that Bernard of Clairvaux ascribed to the virgin Sophia, whose victory over temptation was the greater since she was the more beautiful and noble. The beauty of this wise virgin expresses both temptation and its mastery. Her face shows forth the glorious victory that restraint and humility represent in a beautiful and high-born woman.[4]

The slight downward tilt of the head in illustration 6 and the front-ispiece is not programmatic for this group. This is not a monastic posture, nor are any of these women nuns. The figure next to Christ (illustrations 1 and 7) does not look down at all, but slightly to the right; the vertical of the head shows no angle. She is the strongest of the group. She lacks the femininity and quizzical character of figure 6 and the sensuality of the frontispiece figure. She is somewhat plain and severe by comparison with any of the others; her dominant qualities are strength and resolve.

The wise virgins are realizations of virtue made visible. Abstract and generalized as they are in their individuality, the entire group embodies serenity and moderation. They bear the expression of the soul in their face, to use Otto Schmitt's phrase (p. 18). Schmitt sees the statues of the Ecclesia master characterized by "nobility of body and mind" (Schmitt, p. 16), and this applies as well to the wise virgins. Their faces and figures show us not the battle ground of virtues and vices, but the results of the peace arrangements; they are the offspring of wedded antinomies. In their expressions various psychomachias settle into composure.

The language to describe this group of statues is best supplied by the moral discipline of the cathedral schools. Godfrey of Rheims's lines on Odo of Orléans are a good formulation of the ideals they embody:

Doubt not that his attitude, voice, speech, figure,
His gait and appearance all gave off signs of an integrating harmony.
He was not austere with morose gravity — which I hate —
But rather serene with bright spirited countenance — which I love.
His face was not twisted nor intimidating with grim glances,
Nor were his brows rigid and severe,
But rather mild, gentle and placid as a dove, [warming] as the
    summer sun.
Nor was he so gay and facile to look on
That he would have neglected a modest appearance.
Nor would he tempt shame by frivolous speech
Or turn his appearance into that of a petulant boy . . .
Odo holds the middle road between both extremes,
And considers moderation safe from faults.
He adorns himself so with temperance that his mark is
Light good humor mixed with gravity . . .
This posture, this attitude are decorous . . .
A sublime head set on a noble body
Magnified his appearance of height.[5]

Or in Bernard of Clairvaux's definition of beauty of soul,

When the motions, the gestures and the habits of the body and the senses show forth their gravity, purity and modesty . . . then beauty of the soul becomes outwardly visible.[6]

Whatever the degree of interdependence, it is evident that the formulators of moral discipline and the high Gothic sculptor share a single idiom expressed in different media. The art of the sculptor has accomplished in stone what discipline, according to Bernard, has accomplished in the virgin Sophia: it renders every posture of their girlish bodies composed, it sets the angle of the neck, arranges the eyebrows, composes the expression of the face, directs the eyes, restrains laughter, controls anger, arranges the gait. Discipline produces moderation and an "integrating harmony" holding dissonant forces in balance. The living and the sculpted virgins also share what I called moral transparency: the outer appearance leads the mind to a perception of the inner state. About one hundred and fifty years after Bernard of Clairvaux had praised the virgin named for wisdom — Sophia — for those qualities, these stone artifacts at Strassburg are made to embody something like the glory that even angels might envy.

The best argument that moral discipline provided the conceptual idiom of the Strassburg virgins is in their smiles. Are the wise virgins smiling at all? It is hard to say. They show hardly more than the faintest smile, just enough to suggest serene good humor. It seems less a smile than a hovering state, a psychomachia resolved between gravity and gaiety. Like Odo of Orléans, their faces hold the mean between austerity and levity, which come to equilibrium in a person "serene with bright spirited countenance . . . , mild, gentle, placid as a dove, warming as the summer sun." Like Odo, their mark is "light good humor mixed with gravity."

This is different from smiling and laughter. Hilarity has an important role in the group, but it is decidedly in the realm of the foolish virgins and their leader, the tempter (see illustrations 2 and 3). Both the tempter and the foolish virgin on his left smile broadly. The man's smile almost turns down and this gives him a sinister aura. His smile is without humor; it seems forced and hypocritical. The virgin, however, smiles broadly, and there is little to read in her face besides abundant good cheer. In fact her expression places her close to the famous smiling angels of the annunciation and visitation scenes on Rheims cathedral.[7] Both have a puckish, full grin, and the comparison legitimizes the smile of the Strassburg virgin, foolish though she is. The sculptor did not want to convey a vice, but a virtue unrestrained and undisciplined.

What does a foolish virgin have to smile at? The overturned lamp at her feet, the worms and snakes writhing in the back of the tempter, and the judgment scene on the tympanum of the same porch are gloomy enough portents of the fate that awaits her. This broad smile on the face of a foolish virgin is unique in the tradition. No representation of this theme other than the Strassburg figures and the statues dependent on it (Freiburg), show a foolish virgin smiling and laughing.[8] The great predecessor of the Strassburg group, the Magdeburg wise and foolish virgins from ca. 1250–60 is instructive.[9] They show the same plasticity as the Strassburg group, though in this case there is an agitated restlessness of the garments and an extreme of passion in the faces. The Magdeburg foolish virgins present a scene of unmitigated woe. They are exemplary illustrations of mourning gestures: one wipes away her tears; another holds her head in her hands, the ancient gesture of melancholy; another covers her face; another beats her breast. The faces are twisted in grotesque exaggerations of suffering. This argues the uniqueness of the smiling foolish virgin at Strassburg. The smile did not come automatically with the techniques that made greater expressiveness possible. It is there because of an idea of foolishness that the sculptor / designer wanted to convey.

Conversely tradition has the wise virgins smiling. They smile, of course, because they are received by the bridegroom, that is, redeemed at the final judgment. The logic of the tradition depends on the symbols acting within the meaning *to which they are meant to refer*. Their gestures are tropological, not natural. Wise virgins smile because they are headed for heaven; foolish frown for the opposite reason. In the Strassburg statues, the foolish virgin laughs because excessive laughter is foolish *in social practice*. We see her in the grips of seduction, and there are few better visual realizations of foolishness than the smile of the seduced. The explanation of her expression is psychological, social, natural, not supernatural. The presupposition of this group is human social life, that of the tradition, apocalyptic symbolism. Frivolity is lived and embodied in the one; its moral and historical endpoint is made visible in the other. In the Strassburg group, the foolish virgin smiles and laughs — contrary to the tradition — because she is undisciplined.

Again the vocabulary of this stance is available in the documents on moral discipline. Odo of Orléans avoided precisely excessive gaiety in holding the mean between extremes:

Nor was he so gay and facile to look on
That he would have neglected a modest appearance.

Hugh of St. Victor commended discipline as a means of restraining levity.[10] Bernard of Clairvaux noted that discipline restrained excessive laughter in the virgin Sophia, and in his tract *On the Steps of Humility and Pride* he makes "foolish happiness" (*inepta laetitia*) into the third step of pride.[11] The happy fool behaves accordingly:

> . . . over-cheerful in appearance, swaggering in his bearing, always ready for a joke, any little thing quickly gets a laugh. . . . He is like a well-filled bladder that has been pricked and squeezed. The air, not finding a free vent, whistles out through the little hole with squeak after squeak.[12]

The foolish virgins are recognizable at first glance and distinguishable from the wise by the posture of head and body. Their bearing is the emblem of their foolishness. The tempter's partner (illustration 3) holds her head at a coquettish angle, and her body arcs in an almost dance-like pose. The unnatural angle of the fingers on her right hand shows affectation, and this is underscored by the precious gesture of hooking the folds of her garment around her little finger.

The two figures standing on her left show anger and spoiled petulance (illustration 4). They seem to embody those qualities Odo of Orléans rejected:

> His face was not twisted nor intimidating with grim glances,
> Nor were his brows rigid and severe.

Even if we did not see the extreme facial expressions, their bodies speak eloquently. The tilt of the head is at odds with the angle of the body, and they seem oddly cocked and awkwardly tensed. Some spring or inner tension has to be released, it seems, before they can settle into a relaxed stance. They lack the elegance and understated grace of the wise virgins altogether. Clearly their bodies are speaking the language of mores, *lingua morum*, and we are meant to read the state of their mind from the awkward angles of their posture. They would have provided a good cautionary lesson for the novices of St. Victor, where, 150 years before, students learned to read the irregular motions of the body and its uncontrolled postures as signs of inconstancy of mind.

*   *   *

Historians of Gothic sculpture tend to study its development in terms of the history of styles and techniques. It is generally agreed that a decisive shift in style occurs around 1180. Sauerländer connects this change with Nicholas of Verdun, in whose work we find "a hitherto unsuspected capacity to animate the human figure, a new exuberance of movement, gesture, and facial expression. It is as though medieval art had made its first encounter with the antique, in all its radiant sensuality. The stylistic origins remain a mystery."[13] I know of no other explanation of this change in recent work than the one Sauerländer points to. Erwin Panofsky also sees the new style in these terms: "[the schools of Laon, Senlis, Chartres, and Paris] reimparted to their figures a serene animation as close to Graeco-Roman *humanitas* as mediaeval art could ever come."[14]

For Panofsky and Sauerländer, Gothic sculpture becomes "humane" once it comes under classical influence. The change is referred to the solution of a problem of technique, a solution supplied by a model from an earlier period. Unquestionably the rediscovery of antiquity had a role to play in the emergence of the new style, but that rediscovery does not "explain" the shift to high Gothic, as Sauerländer himself stresses: "The stylistic origins remain a mystery." The problem of analysis is comparable to the role of ancient drama in French classicism or of medieval chivalric culture and *Don Quixote* in romanticism. The earlier model supplies the form, mood, and tone that the present age needs. But no one would be content with an "explanation" of French classicism in its appropriation of classical models or of Romanticism in its appropriation of medieval ones. The nourishing forces of those movements are far more complex, and the forces that nourished high Gothic sculpture were no doubt more complex. The new style is more than the discovery of technique.

The "capacity to animate the human figure" and to imbue it with "exuberance of movement, gesture and facial expression" may well have been first discovered by Nicholas of Verdun as an artist's skill, but that capacity, far from being "hitherto unsuspected," had existed in the schoolroom since the tenth century. That expressiveness that emerges in Gothic sculpture responded to an earlier awareness of the suppleness of human expression. Hugh of St. Victor shows a subtle comprehension of the expressiveness of the human face:

> There are thousands of masks, thousands of ways of flaring and contracting the nostrils, thousands of twists and turns of the lips which deform the beauty of the face and the harmony of discipline. For the face is a mirror of discipline and it is to be shaped with so much greater vigilance, since the sins which appear there cannot be concealed. . . . Let it always have a severe sweetness and sweet severity.[15]

A discipline of forming the human body, its postures, facial expressions, modes of standing, walking, dressing, gesturing and speaking, had been an everyday experience of life in the cathedral schools. This discipline sculpted the living human form to elegance, grace, modesty, restraint, and moderation. It made "beauty of soul" and "beauty of manners" appear in the contours of the face and body.

It seems very unlikely that the sculptor's art, which sought to mold stone to these ideals, developed independently and in ignorance of this discipline — especially since the sculptor's graceful and elegant human figures decorated the very buildings that had housed the old discipline of conduct.

It is not popular in medieval studies to appeal to experience or social practice as a ground of explanation for anything in art and literature. Historians of literature are uneasy at the thought of reality as a factor in imaginative fiction, and art historians show a shyness toward "explanation" in general.[16] But it does seem to me that the interrelatedness of moral discipline and Gothic representation of the human figure calls for an integrating "explanation" and represents a case where practical experience forms the imaginative capacities. The testimony in histories of Gothic sculpture to ancient influences (Panofsky) pales in confrontation with the spread throughout Germany and France of a discipline of conduct to which at least some major works of Gothic statuary refer. When Gothic sculptors discovered classical form and technique, it appealed to them not only as technique and as an answer to problems they sought to solve, but also because of that which its technique conveyed. Panofsky calls it something close to "Graeco-Roman *humanitas*." But it should be evident that this ancient ideal was borne first and foremost by its medieval counterpart, the *humanitas* and *venustas morum* cultivated at cathedral schools and embodied by learned clerics throughout the eleventh and twelfth centuries. The rediscovery of the sculpture of antiquity was decisively prepared by the moral discipline of the cathedral schools.

The Strassburg wise and foolish virgins make clear that the plasticity of conception of the human figure in moral discipline cannot be regarded as wholly separate from the plasticity of representation in Gothic sculpture. In terms of the legitimacy of a claim to influence, that discipline, for the group considered at least, must have priority over classical models, which may have contributed much, even decisively, to technique, but cannot claim exclusive title to the conception.[17]

The formulators of the practice of moral discipline saw an analogy between their pedagogy and the artist's work and called on images from the plastic arts to explain what they were doing: Goswin of Mainz imagined discipline as analogous to the potter making pots, and Hugh of St. Victor used sculpture as the metaphor for the shaping of moral-physical perfection:

> We long to be perfectly carved and sculpted in the image of good men, and when excellent and sublime qualities stand out in them, which arouse astonishment and admiration in men's minds, then they shine forth in them like the beauty in exquisite statues, and we strive to recreate these qualities in ourselves.

*   *   *

If the ideals of the cathedral schools deserve consideration in the history of Gothic style, then the hard historical problem posed by its inclusion is this: *the rise of the new style coincides with, or rather postdates, the death of instruction in moral discipline in cathedral schools.*

So where did the "idea" of the Strassburg group come from? From an anachronistically functioning school of *moralis disciplina* in the see of the bishop of Strassburg?[18] Or was the discipline by this time so thoroughly integrated into the life of the nobility, that we no longer need cathedral schools to explain its spread? Whose thoughts did the sculptor think and whose feelings did he feel? It would be possible to find a comparable conception of human elegance, poise, "moral" balance in Vincent of Beauvais on the education of noble children, more or less contemporary with the Strassburg group. But the passages we could cite would by and large be borrowed from Hugh of St. Victor. We could point to the late courtly romance in both France and Germany, which, however, by 1290 had fallen into a mood of epigonal gloom at the passing of the classical period of courtly narrative.

So if moral discipline deserves a place in the discussion of Gothic style, we are faced with the odd disjuncture that the "spirit of Gothic art," its humanism and plasticity, is a borrowing or adaptation from the preceding century.[19] And to bridge this disjuncture, I would suggest that we need the concept of "envy" as defined earlier. The Strassburg group is a nostalgic reconstruction of an ideal still mouthed and formulated by the sculptor's contemporaries but seldom attained in reality. While still enjoying the magic license of the hypothesis, we can construct a little drama of noble men and women looking at the Strassburg group (or virtually any other statue in the cathedral from the period), seized with an envious longing to be like those wise virgins. This drama is not entirely fanciful, because Hildebert of Lavardin staged and predicted it or something very like it in his poem "Par tibi Roma nihil." He imagined the ancient gods alive and looking at the statues of themselves carved by the Roman sculptors. He described the gods' unsettled reaction:

> Divinities themselves look awe-struck on divinities sculpted
> And wish themselves the equals of those sembled forms.
> Nature could not make gods as fair of face
> As man created images of gods.
> Carved likenesses improve these deities;
> The sculptor's art deserves worship more than
> their own divinity.[20]

We know that several generations of living human beings had valued grace, charm, serenity, beauty, striven for it in their own presence, had it beaten into them by whip-wielding masters, and imagined such qualities as constituting a godlikeness of the human form. The experience of finding those qualities better represented in stone than in their own flesh was available to the European aristocracy, educated and uneducated, as early as 1180–90. By that time, the human grace and beauty that astonished gods and made angels envious has passed out of the province of teachers and into that of sculptors.

Appendix B. The Letter of Goswin of Mainz to His Student Walcher (ca. 1065)

Edition: *Apologiae Duae: Gozechini epistola ad Walcherum; Burchardi . . . apologia de barbis*, ed. R. B. C. Huygens, intro. Giles Constable. CCCM 62 Turnholt: Brepols, 1985. pp. 11–43.

Older edition: PL 143, 885–908.

Numbers in parentheses refer to line numbers in Huygens's edition. I have identified only direct quotations. To identify allusions and indirect borrowings, I refer the reader to the documentation in that edition.

The Letter of Gozechinus the school master to his former pupil, Valcherus, likewise school master

To his brother and son, united with him in soul, brother Goswin sends his wish that the better part of existence may be a happy coexistence. Since you have renewed the many tokens of good will you used to show me so often, in turn I both cherish and pay out a wealth of favor to you, dearest friend; not only for the sweet, pleasant, and delectable memory of times past, but also for the joyous receipt of this new gift. For you have sent me the book I sought, transcribed in your own hand, in which you plainly show that you hold me in high regard and consider my wishes not among the least important things. That book has recalled so vividly to mind all those gifts of charity for which I am in your debt that the present moment seems to restore to me in one gift the sum total of all previous ones. (11)

Hence when I first saw your gift, when I first took it into my hands and recognized your writing, or rather you yourself in it, at the same moment my deep affection for you was rekindled as if for the first time. Truly my soul rejoiced that I had once guided you with my own hand in forming those crude characters and made you atone with strokes on your back for those ill-turned lines and other sins of tender youth, since now I can rejoice in the rich harvest of fruit from our little tree, having [once] thought its luxuriant growth of sheaves and leaves excessive. For who would plant a vine and not accept its fruit? I at least have reaped again and again the sweet fruit of my labor, for God has granted increase to those slips which I have planted and irrigated. But however great the harvest from others, it was you who pleased me with the greatest abundance of fruits. (24)

II. Would that I had nourished all the members of both my schoolrooms in the same way! Would that I could find among them even one such as you as a crutch for my old age! As the divine oracle laments through his prophet: nourish and exalt your sons today, only to have them — very few excepted — spurn their exalter. But let such men take care lest for contempt of the father who admonishes them wisely, they should be deprived of the bequest of their eternal inheritance by the father of fathers. (32)

III. But you, my dearest son, continue on the way you have begun; increase those goods you have received from me, make them greater and better, nor ever stint in your abundant goodness to me, for which he who sent you to me will reward you with eternal inheritance. Nor, if you show yourself kind to me, will you be acting in a new or unaccustomed way; but even though you have long wept beneath the teacher's rod, still you served me with the same kindness. And that goodness which fear alone sufficed to extort from others, you showed of your own free will, as is natural for a man like you. You hung on the very motion of my lips, lest any of my words should fall to the earth. I began to love you as a boy for this and for certain other eminent signs of virtue; and now as you mature, I place yet higher hopes in you with each passing day, seeing the strength of your industry in clarifying obscure readings, your wisdom and vigilance, and the sharpness of your acute mind in pursuing subtle points. While other auditors of our lessons were not equal to the words of the teacher, be they spoken or written, you seemed able to transform yourself altogether into the master. Whence I gloried, along with your brother and other friends, to see so rich a spice spring up in that little garden I planted — I mean you, a wise youth among mature men. (52)

IV. How deeply I rejoiced in your company seeing your maturity of character, your virtuous conduct. What was there in life more gratifying to me, more cherished than you! How could anyone or anything intervene to reduce you in my favor? It is said that the constant presence of many things and of men is wont to produce satiety. But our intimacy, be it at home or in public, only served to enshrine you more deeply in my regard, and each passing day rendered you dearer and fresher. Rightly so. For in all things you showed yourself of one mind with me. You not only rejoiced at my successes, but you bore the burden of aggravation and indignation for my setbacks. Even then there was occasion to test the value of your counsel: in good times you zealously applauded, in adversity you bravely carried on, and often you guided our affairs for the better. But if ever external business consumed my time, you carried out the tasks of the absent master among the students in my care so well that if any complex problems arose, be it in reading or disputing, in theological or sophistical matters, you wisely unravelled them with your subtle mind, and in bandying them about dealt with them to complete satisfaction. (71)

V. Since all this and much more is true of you, how, I pray, could I fail to mention your probity, your diligence, your kindness and many other obligatory features of circumspect conduct in you, and moreover, how could my love for you fail, even if I wished it so? Rather I now embrace with all my heart that same mature youth and young man wise beyond his years in whom as a boy I once recognized such brilliant promise. Nor does anything oppress me more than that I am deprived of your sweet presence and seem to be living out my days as it were in some desert solitude. Not that I lack for frequent companions and dearest colleagues; but there is none among them, or hardly any, in whose lap I may lay my head, or rather my soul, sweetly to rest. So it is that I would assail the ears of divine piety — were it permissible and sensible — with unending prayers, and beg admission to that holy sanctuary where prayers are heard: that God may settle me at length in some place where I may enjoy the kindness of you and others with whom I have grown so close in mind or whom I once taught, and that I may once again as in earlier days glory in a life shared with you and in that same kindness that once brought such joy to me. (87)

VI. For while it is true that this noble city Mainz, this golden crown of the kingdom, has rained on me liberal showers from those sweet flowing rivers of its bounty which flow on all sides and has reserved for me a place of no humble rank in the most splendid diadem of its sacred senate, still, I say it without prejudice to Mainz: that corner of our land beckons to me above all

others which Mother Liège in the strength and vigor of her virtues shows to
be as delightful as it is pleasant to its natives. Erected on the gentle inclines
of her western hills, nestled in the double bays of its Mons Publicus which
nourishes the four flocks of the regulated life [i.e., four monastic commu-
nities] on the gently sloping pastures of its landward side, and in her
double-bayed hill, as I said, gathers her sons beneath her wings like a
mother hen her chicks, she, as you know, pampers and nourishes them,
educates, informs and instructs them in all that pertains to the conduct of
life both personal and civil. And she always provides the means either to
govern abundance or to temper want. And the two forked Meuse, so
superior to our Belgian rivers, laps pleasingly and gently against the city
adding at once to its fortification and to its bounty. It brings a rich abundance of fish not only to citizens but also to the peasants on nearby lands, it
conveniently provides various routes for merchants' goods, highly conducive to all kinds of commerce, except (if with your leave I may speak
satirically, albeit not in verse) on those occasions when Meuse has sat at the
table of the gods, where Aeolus, raising his cup with wonted frequency,
reigns as king in the palace of Juno with his brothers the cloud-born rain
showers, only to return exhausted from its long labors [of eating and
drinking], and inebriated from snows and rains. And once swelled with the
torrents of the rivers feeding it, it rages like an assembled army in a mad
course through the surrounding countryside, trampling and ravaging whatever stands in its way. It punishes the nocturnal poaching of fishermen, and
so enforces the prohibition, often ignored with impunity, of this much
lamented practice. It tears up and washes away the crops which avid farmers
sprinkled, having violated with wanton furrows the grassy banks where the
river likes to nap at midday. And in its indignation at our choosing to dwell
in the seaside chambers of its watery court and at the frequent annoyances it
suffers from our serfs, it enters our houses without waiting for our permission. And having expelled us all, it pays us violent visits, ignoring all
formalities. And because we are prone to supplicate frequently and inti-
mately a god inimical to it, it drives away the household gods of those
whom it torments; and all the relics of that envied divinity, cinders and
ashes, it extinguishes and washes away. And when at length our patience
can take no more, and we give up our futile resistance, it returns to its
channel only half-placated, and, leaving great scars behind, it betakes itself
once more to its palace. (126)

All over our suburbs are sweetly fragrant olive groves and gardens
filled with rubicund fruits, and where they stretch their viny arms toward

higher realms, the outer leaves of the grapes and their trunks receive the final touches from rain showers.

While our Liège is bountifully enriched with many such blessings, still there are far greater and more worthy ones. For that flower of tripartite Gaul and that second Athens luxuriates nobly in the study of the liberal arts, and, more excellent yet, the observance of divine worship flourishes. And, if I may say so with the indulgence of the churches, where the study of letters is concerned, Plato's Academy did not offer better; and in respect to the practice of religion, Leo's Rome was not superior. (138)

VII. Hence spreading forth in every direction the good fragrance of Christ, it attracts and receives a great multitude that flocks to it. No one who has applied himself here has failed to advance and improve himself, except the lazy and neglectful. Since our Liège is what it is, let anyone who maligns it, anyone who does not love it having once known it, have the hate of God, to put it in the rustic way. So it is, my dear friend, that I constantly strike out with oaths, for though I may dwell elsewhere, yet in my soul I reside there with you. (146)

VIII. But perhaps you will accuse me of levity, as if I would now seek a place where life is easy, leisure abundant and where I can rest on my laurels; for that is the way of a vain mind, and your sharp reply is thus: that now from homesickness and nostalgia I praise so fervently the location, the pleasant-ness, the affluence, and the wisdom of our Liège, whom I earlier aban-doned, preferring the glory of Mainz. You will say that I vacillate with such inconstancy of mind that once located in Liège I long for Mainz; and when planted in Mainz I race back in my mind to Liège. And to strengthen your case you cite that testimony of Horace, so that the tumor you think you are cutting away can be rubbed all the sorer with the salt of satire:

> Those who hurry to cross oceans change their location, not their mind. [Horace, Epist. 1.2.27]

And again:

> The mind that never escapes itself merits blame. [Epist. 1.14.13]

I don't mean to suggest that you would say dark things against me, nor by the same token have I set myself up against you to stir up conflict. (160) It is just that I know well those dogs who are always ready to snap at others from behind and gnaw at them with slanders, while they themselves attend the banquet of vice in disguise and wallow in iniquity. I conjure these detractors to oppose them face to face and put them behind me, and you are the occasion. I prepare an answer to them in your name, though I suspect nothing sinister of you. I do this so that by subtly introducing these cavillers now, I can deflect all the arrows that these men have ever shot at me from the bow of envy and render harmless the bitter slanders of their odious, serpent-like hissing. Please remember one thing in the meanderings of this long discourse: that whatever I have said in these polemics that is excellent, elegant, amiable, applies to you; and whatever is harsh, abrasive, biting, to my detractors. (173)

IX. [continues attack on detractors]

X. Perhaps I did once, in abandoning Liège, write a scurrilous attack on it, perhaps I did prefer the glory of Mainz and seemed to regard Liège as a vile heap of slag. (210) But now in pressing me with the enemy's weapon and asking, what is Liège to me? you have wandered far from the path of truth, or rather you have abandoned the truth altogether. Tell me now, I ask you, you who beneath your sheep's clothing snarl like a wolf, tell me which of two men is preferable: he who makes or he who receives a petition? Why do you hesitate to answer? Do you imagine that a trap is being laid for you? Hence your silence? Of course you must concede that he who is petitioned by others is held to be superior. Tell me, then, whether I did not harvest a title of glory for Liège, when it received a petition on my behalf from a city yet greater than itself. No, rather Liège was exalted when at the invitation or command of the greatest men of that golden age I was called to Mainz. Did I thus rebuff Mother Liège? Or did I show insolence and contempt for her whom I never forsook but rather embraced with the loving tenderness due a mother? I tell you it was not to divorce her that I left, as you would have it in your carping, but to glorify her; not to place an epitaph on her tombstone, but a crown of honor on her head. I spoke eloquently, but only what rose to my lips from her [i.e. Liège's] heart; I contributed to the treasury of her [i.e. Mainz's] affluence, but only what I had gathered from the treasures of her [Liège's] wisdom. Nor will you ever elude me now by any means, even if you are a second Proteus, until you admit honestly that a sensible change of location does no injury, as long as it is not accompanied by a change of good intentions. Admit too that it behooves the wise man to measure all of life's motives according to time and place, and not to imagine, as did vain Diogenes, that all things hang upon a single center-point. (230)

XI. That saying of Horace you would brand on me as a mark of vice, whether you take it as poetry or philosophy, serves its author's argument and makes its point well, but not necessarily when taken literally, because those who hasten to cross oceans can change their minds along with the sky above them, as for instance if some uneducated, insipid fellow — if you will pardon the phrase — should wander or sail to Athens, and there, infused with the salt of learning, should transform his ignorance into wisdom. But that following passage, where he remains silent about changing places and the sky above and reproaches the changing of mind, he means in terms of reason: that a change of location in itself is neither harmful nor beneficial in terms of leading the good life, unless it occurs with a fixed and reasoned resolve. (240) However, that mind which does not shun such a place as produces corruption and vice is much to be reproached, The same applies to one who does not head toward self-knowledge on the narrow path of moral discipline, as can be attained in the school of virtues.

But truly the pursuit of such subtle arguments is not my task either at leisure or at work. Let us leave them for now, with your permission, to that tribe who are consumed in body and mind, in leisure and in work, by verbose disputations, by sophistic cavillings in their teaching or learning. (247)

XII. But we have testimony more ancient than these, which argues the idea that the homeland or any place whatsoever neither confer nor detract anything from the wise man's quest to live well. But rather virtue by itself suffices altogether for a good and blessed life. When Teucer, for instance, was prevented from returning home without his brother and had shunned the isle of Salamis and his own father, he was asked by his homesick comrades where he would choose to stay now, and he replied: "Home is wherever life is good" [Cicero, *Tusc. disp.*, 5. 37. 107]. I cannot see what could be said more to the point on this question of where to live, if we take "where life is good" as it is meant. Socrates also, when asked what citizenship he claimed, replied, "of the world," that is, a citizen and resident not of any one place, but rather of the entire world, indicating by this reply that wherever he may be, he would be the same, since his commitment to virtue does not change, and that he shares citizenship in common with all reasoning men in the whole world. Moreover the most noble philosophers, as we read in the records of the ancients, chose for themselves no fixed place of habitation for leading the good life — Xenocrates, Crantor and Crisippus, Aristotle, Carneades, Panaetius, and others beyond number — but rather having once set out on the quest for that wisdom which eludes the whole world, they never again returned home. Such is the life of the perfect and consummate wise man, that neither torture nor the bull of Phalaris nor any change of place budge him from the gravity of his resolve and the rigor of his purpose, since to him the entire world is a single place for the good and blessed life. But why go on like this? Only to demonstrate clearly that location and residence and change of them are no obstacle to the wise man's resolve to remain constant in virtue wherever he may be. (274)

XIII. But what do we care for these pagan examples? The holy apostles elected by the creator of the world, first educated by the sound of the living voice under the tutelage of the heavenly master in the school of Truth, then sent forth like the rays of the true sun to spread light and dispersed like the salt of the earth as purge and condiment: they possessed neither fatherland nor home, neither field nor house, nor any sort of worldly possession, but rather for the saving of souls they first devoted themselves to the extremely hard task of preaching in spite of freezing and starvation, in spite of a host of dangers, finally they laid down their lives for their brothers, following the example of their master, than which there can be no greater love. But all that blessed posterity descended from this spiritual procreation, that chosen people, which by God's choice succeeded as the race of the elect and the royal priesthood having been adopted into Israelitic dignity by martyrdom for Christ, all those, I say, entered onto the path of life, albeit with varying distinction of rank and office. Since they toiled in an alien land not for themselves but for others, since they sought the city of the future, lacking a present one, they entered into the promised land of the sons of Israel through Him who in his resurrection led captivity captive, and there they were made citizens of the saints and servants of the lord. (293)

XIV. Nor should you think my vision blurred either by the blindness of ignorance or by the fogs of forgetfulness, in that I ignore the ordained phalanges of the Christian militia or imply some judgment against them with the petulant arrogance of a man freed from duty and released to a vagrant state. This militia is commanded to stand guard with the armor of God in the towers of New Jerusalem to protect not only themselves but also the more frail members of the church with the armor of God and are forbidden to alter the rule of a regular life or to change the guard post of their military vigil by abandoning it. For we have seen in the divine edicts of the fathers that caution is necessary lest anyone wander to alien places except for an excellent reason, and lest anyone lure away a cleric from afar. (303)

Nonetheless we also are aware that it is freely permitted, if a church be lacking in any of the various functions of its ranks and ministries, that its petition to another church that is amply staffed may not be denied: in respect to ranks when for instance it seeks the ordination of a bishop or a priest from another church; in respect to ministries when it seeks the installment of a regular prelate or a master of letters. We know too that among those flocks of the spiritual life there are those to whom the sweet and happy leisure of the contemplative life appeals, and others engaged in winning souls through the evangelical business of the active dispensation. Some men are like circles of gold, others like staves, others yet bearers of the new ark of the testament, who set it in eternal life to the praise and glory of allmighty God. This is that distinction of ranks and ministries and radiance of good works performed through them which the prophet saw in the splendid accoutrements of the queen, who standing in her golden vestments at the right hand of her spouse the king shines forth in the splendor of her various garments. The same prophet viewed this same distinction in an enigma when, wondering at the marvelous name of the lord through all the earth, seeing His magnificence exalted above the heavens, wondering, I say, at the son of man made a little lower than the angels and crowned with glory and honor [Ps. 8:6] through the passion of death in the courtroom of the Father, he said, "You have subjected all things beneath His feet, the sheep, the cattle, the flocks of the field, the birds of the sky, the fish of the sea" [Ps. 8:8–9]. Blessed is he who has seen such things, blessed also the church of the saints, which and for which and in which he has predicted such things! For there beneath the feet of Christ he saw the pious birds of heaven distinct from those which, with the hooked beak of avarice, with the curved talon of rapacity, devour the more gentle birds in the air, distinct also from those which plunge into the waters, submerging in the profound depths of lust, to feed their insatiable maw with the rapacious capture of wretched fish; distinct also are those gentle birds of the heavens, who, covered with the bright plumes of good works and having too the feathers of the virtues and the two wings of charity, fly like doves to their windows.

There too are the stars of the heavens which Abraham referred to in his promise, "I will multiply your seed like the stars of the sky and like the sands of the seashore" [Gen. 22:17]. These stars, crystalline in the purity of their conduct, shine out in the firmament of the church, radiant in words, brilliant in examples. (338)

XV. But what are the birds of the sky to us, what to us are the stars of the heavens? For we are the wretched fish of the sea, we are the sands of the seashore, we are pounded by the waves of earthly life like the sands, we are swept away in the tides of worldly incertitude. And so what comparison is there between us and the pious birds of the sky? What correlation with the bright stars? Only if we can compare nothing to something, and only then if it seems reasonable to call it a comparison. (345)

O that we might rest together in some spiritual hollow far from tempests, that we might hide away in some secret place beneath the cliff of life, where the winds of fortune cannot blast us and make us their plaything! My choice and my desire, then, as this grotto of rest and this refuge from the cliffs of life is our Liège, though you may well rub away my levity in the salt of your abrasive Horace. I say, then, I would choose Liège, the mother of studies, the font also of subtle genius and the place fertile in divine wisdom, as the city which the finger of God has favored many times over, and which by the grace of God will continue forever to bring forth men of its own kind. (354)

But what have I said? As if, being insufficient in herself, she were in need of my praise! She does not require anyone's painted praise and she needs not the fictional effigy of a blessed city colored by the words of any man, because this city is alive in reality and blessed in fact, living in the institutes and laws of divine religion. (359)

Since therefore the august head of our nurse and mother radiates from its venerable hair a whiteness of ancient wisdom whiter than snow, since she wears in her turreted crown the diadem of divine religion, and since she shines in her priestess robes woven with the gold of glorious deeds and is desirable in every way, adorned everywhere with abundant virtues, are you, then, in your right mind if you urge that I do not seek the shelter of her wings—which is tantamount to urging me to hate her? Not, surely, so that you might drink of her public and general benefits and joys, keeping them for your private enjoyment? Far be it from your modesty and probity, far be it from my soul that I should ever believe this of you, whom I have known for so long. But so unlikely is it that I should ever hold her in contempt, that I would love her most vehemently even if I were forbidden to do so. (369)

XVI. By saying this I do not claim that the bountiful city where I now live does not show me the face of a father and the breasts of a mother. But rather I am either bantering with you, or uttering the wish-dreams of one granted the grace of God without the prejudice of honor. Nor ought you to set down as a failing of mine what outstanding men did not hesitate to do if the situation called for it. Antiquity and modern times alike provide plenty of examples of many highly illustrious men who with good reason moved from one place to another, fleeing not the places but that in them which was alien to their character and way of life, or migrating to others where many could derive benefits from their presence. Abraham the patriarch, for one, and his sons would certainly not have changed places so often, would not have dug so many wells in search of living water, if they had found in any one place all things which constituted a good life for them. (381) Jacob too, no less prophet than patriarch, would never have descended into Egypt with seventy people (a mystical number), finding first bounty then servitude, unless he were fleeing the famine in Canaan. Joseph also, sold by his envious brothers, did well to change his home, since in the time of want he saved the lives of many. This man, first taught by the rod of temptation and purified in the furnace of tribulations, rose up thence to become lord of Egypt, bending his shoulder to the burdens of patience and setting his hands in servitude to the pots of obedience. (369)

XVII. I could adduce innumerable examples of this kind, if I were not persuaded that these suffice to chasten you. These few then will serve as a response to your Horace with his comments about the sky and the mind, a response more chastening than its quantity might suggest, and let him henceforth not rashly carp at any other man's plans. Then cast aside this Horace with his sky and take up the psalter with me. If this is not to your liking, love him and have him all to yourself with no rival. But it has been shown above with the light of unexceptionable arguments, though your Horace falls silent, that the place of the good life is wherever you happen to be, and, if your equanimity fail you not, it too is your Ulubris. (400)

XVIII–XIX, 400–419: [caution in the choice of traveling companions commended]

At any rate, brother, so it is. It belongs to the human condition generally, at least to the condition of men, always to be in a state of combat testing them beyond their strength, never to give the mind over to the sweetness of divine contemplation, constantly to be buffetted by head-long assaults, never to enjoy the peace of inner repose. (423) Now however, you will find a weapon in the saying of that ancient sage, Musonius, piercing as an enemy's spear, "The soul's leisure is the soul's loss," and your shield is the word of the Christian sage, "Never is the good man spared combats and conflicts" [C. Musonius Rufus, quoted from Aulus Gellius, *Attic Nights*, 18.2.1] To these words I shall respond, that indeed the soul's leisure is its loss, when it is given over to delights and pleasures and released to indulge worldly desires and when it throws over those things that work for its salvation and protection. But when the soul raises itself aloft and transcends the hurly-burly of worldly affairs — as much as man can be freed from them — when the storm clouds of cares are dissipated, the gusts and hales of slandering tongues and the tempests and whirlwinds of false brothers abate, when it is relieved of the rigorous discipline of the armed camp to give itself over entirely to the most placid and lucid peace of divine contemplation, then truly it is not lost but rather saved, or rather, far more important, it seems at long last to come to life. (436)

But as to the saying of our theologian, that the Christian's duty is always to struggle, I would not dare or seek to change a word of it. And yet the perfect constancy of virtue may be allowed to call it quits and end its labors, if the wars and seditions against false brethren cease outwardly, while inwardly the force of our striving against the temptations of the ancient enemy press on until, having conquered them with the battle gear of God, we accept the repose of eternal peace as Christ's reward for our struggles. (443)

XX. Arguing up to this point in your vivacious way, you claim that both kinds of struggle have taken place in the camps of the Christian militia and that Augustine, Ambrose, Athanasius and innumerable fathers whose names are well known have fought hard both outwardly against apostles and disciples of Satan and inwardly against spiritual wickedness, persisting until crowned with victory. And in fact, brother, I assent to these things which you argue, sometimes in truth and other times in fancy, but you seem to me not quite to include every church of the elect that deserves it in this stage of the struggle. For if you collect annals of Christian soldiers from calendars and chronicles, or rather from the genuine monuments of the scriptures, you will surely see that they have pleased God with theoretical as well as practical virtues, that is with the virtues of leisure as well as with those of public life. (455) And, if I may touch on a few of these and bring them into the argument on faith, consider those living in the shadow of the law, Joshua, Gideon, David, and the crown of the Maccabees, then Moses and Aaron, Elias and Elijah and the choir of prophets, and finally, recall what Paul says of these same ancient fathers: "who through faith subdued kingdoms" down to where he says, "they wandered in deserts and in mountains," until he at length concludes having enumerated them all, "and these all were tested and proven through faith" [Hebrews 11:33–39]. (462) If you direct your loving consideration to these and others like them, you will surely see patriarchs involved most intensively in quite practical affairs, while the prophets with serene mind bask in the quiet of contemplation. For how else could the one group defend the well-being of their people with might and main, or the other receive blessed visions with the calm eye of the mind? Nor do I deny that in either order there were some committed to the other, but as a general rule this distinction separates the two orders. (470)

When however the night of the old testament had passed, in the firmament of which the above-mentioned fathers shone like the brightest stars, and when the day dawned which the Lord ordained and the sun of justice, Jesus Christ, rose, behold how Peter Bar-Jonah and that vessel of election Paul, persisted in the battle until crowned with martyrdom, while John, the theologian of angelical virginity and Luke the fire of the gospel, the first of whom warred powerfully against the beast Domitian, the others against the antichrists, but then, once the furies of these beasts were allayed, turned to theology in the ensuing quiet, and dipping their reeds in the mysteries of the gospel, grew old together in peace. (479)

But Luke, along with the peripatetic Paul and other messengers of the gospel, labored early on in many places, later retired to the calm of theology and, weaving the sacred history of the incarnate Word, at length died a peaceful and blessed death. Here you see, then, how those Augustines and Ambroses you allude to persisted successfully in both modes of battle, as you justly assert, but note at the same time also how these Pauls and Antonys and innumerable other martyrs of Christ lived virtually free of the turbulence of the active life and in addition, with God's help, turned away from inner battles and struggles to live as it were already among the citizens of heaven together with him, who said, "our life is in heaven" [Phil. 3:20]. (490)

XXI. Not only the theologians, radiant with the brilliance of evangelical light, but also innumerable earlier philosophers and heroes, obscured though they were in the clouds of paganism — the sun of justice had yet to rise — passed their days in highly astute cultivation of the Moral and the Beneficial [*honestum et utile*]. In this they exercised the virtues of both private and public life, which they attained partly as a gift of nature and partly as a result of liberal studies. On the one side there were those devoted to the art of warfare and those engaged in public administration. They gained a fame they supposed immortal by their wise actions at home and in the public forum, or by their brave combat in the field or at sea. On the other were those given to a noble leisure, having withdrawn, some as a well earned retirement from their toils, others out of contempt for secular affairs. They furnished guidance both for themselves and for the state either by their writings or their discoursing. (502)

XXII. If now you who bubble over with arguments engage in staunch battle against the line of thought just presented, Truth herself will join the fray, girded about with the reserve troops of her wise sayings, and will support those in her camp unstintingly. And to confirm the truth of our assertions with more reliable testimony, She drafts into the guard troops of faith some figures from both testaments: from the one, Rachel and Leah, from the other Martha and Mary. But to what purpose? To this: that you should learn for certain that, just as has been argued, the elect of God please Him as much through public as through private virtues. He never favors the one over the other, for just as God embraces the labors of the active life, he also does not banish from his favor the fruits of the contemplative. (513)

XXIII. Marvelous to behold, oh brother, what a subtle web of arguments you weave! Like a capped mushroom you cover yourself at every point. Just as I began to think you were settling back and giving way either under pressure from the speaker's authority or — more importantly — from the gravity of the things said, behold! again the trumpet sounds, again the call to arms rings out. Once more your pleas impugn the mind that embraces leisure and quiet and issue a warning: that you will force inactivity and apathy cloaking themselves in the mantle of "reflection" to show their true colors and will drag them into the light of day from the shelter which hides them. You go back to the aforementioned prophet and make him into an example of unstinting labor at chastising perverters and removing the poison of scorpions. The sharpness of his attack answers the fury goading them on to repulse and destroy him. You also recall those words scourging the indigent by which Horace, masking himself in the satiric comment of his Damasippus, accuses himself of laziness: "You seek to placate envy by abandoning virtue?! O contemptible wretch!" [Serm. 2.3.13–14]. (527)

XXIV. Or you might do better yet by citing that greatest comfort to perseverance uttered by Paul, that vessel of election and most solid anvil of ancient persecution against the elect: "All who would live godly in Christ will suffer persecution" [2 Tim. 3:12], and "only he who struggles lawfully will wear a crown" [cf. 2 Tim. 2:5]. Moreover you may well call for that shield of divine protection by which the lord sent comfort to his prophet in contention with his enemies: "Be not afraid of their faces, for I am with you to deliver you, says the lord" [Jer. 1:8]. (535)

XXV. I certainly admit, dearest friend, even those things that you assert concerning the rustic Minerva of the satirist Damasippus, where the poetic figment has a philosophical argument, or those arguments you produce concerning the divine oracle, where the truth of logical proof shines clear without any fog of fable: I tell you they are true and altogether fitting, though not altogether efficacious in persuading when the mind chooses with stubborn persistence some proposition at odds with these.

For you have learned from the teachings of Cicero the function and end of the orator: his function is to speak in a way suited to persuade; his end, to persuade by speech. The first of these you fulfill admirably with your persuasive speech. At the second however, you fail. Your speech does not persuade, and therefore you miss your goal. You are well aware that a duty which remains without effect is like seed unsown. Accordingly you fulfill your duty correctly when speaking of labor, but when you turn to him who chooses quiet and leisure, you fail to persuade and, as said above, miss your goal. (550)

For who in these days would not prefer leisure to the life of affairs. If you labor, your work falls into a pit; if you cease, the result is the same. For who would not grow cool to toils seeing the man of leisure more rewarded than the toiler, who receives not even the coin he had come for. Well then let him put his leisure to good use! But what man in his right mind would persist in seeding thorn fields at such a time when the bad earth, shuddering at the thistles of genuine perversity, spurns the ordering hand of the gardner and the good seed of the word? But happy is the land where the word of God is sown through the word of man. This land renders fruit hundredfold to the grainaries of the lord its God, when the clouds of teachers rain upon and irrigate it. (560)

That land of lead, on the other hand, deserves its sky of bronze, which, accepting the unfructified seed, gathers thorns and tares into its bundles at harvest time, and is sent to the eternal fire. Finally, the pater familias grows angry at such a land and such a vineyard which ignores the gardners, and threatens them in the words of his prophet: "There shall be neither thinking nor digging, and I shall command the clouds to withold their rain from it" [Is. 5:6]. He means those predestined by the design of providence to hell, and separates them with this word from those predestined to conform to the image of His son. Thence also, I believe, the bringer of the law and lord of prophets in his gospel, on which the law and the prophets depend, says, "give not what is holy to dogs nor cast pearls before swine" [Mt. 7:6], separating by this word again the damned from the blessed, lest by preaching to the deaf the pious fervor of the laborer should go to waste. (574)

XXVI. Now at long last, my dearest one, you will confess, I believe, that my choice of retirement at this point in time was neither fruitless nor lazy — not for me, for you, or for all good men — especially since the life of affairs satisfies neither the Good nor the Beneficial, nor indeed their more ancient relative, salvation. And so you concede, conquered, I believe, by true arguments and guided into our camp by the allurement of peace and quiet, and, if you are wise, you will no longer take the part of the opponent of leisure against its defender. (581)

But so that you may know for certain the main purpose of this lengthy missive, I for one require this desirable leisure as an old soldier who has done his tour of duty three and four times beyond the length of ordinary service. But not only for myself, for you too, green and fresh though you may still be, and for all good men. Because I fear, or rather see for a fact, that in your labors you revolve the wheel of nativity in vain. It would be superfluous in disciplined discourse to repeat my earlier argumentation in explaining why it is in vain. Besides, you know that the levites are constrained by legal mandate to take up the ministry at the age of 25 and beyond, and that at age 50 — the jubilaum year and a number famed for its mystical meanings — they become custodians of the vessels. (591)

And in more recent times young recruits for the military are enlisted by army law for the same term of service. So also the professor's chair, like military discipline, has its own term of basic training and preliminary instruction. But the master's tenure of office lasts much longer and retirement comes much later. The proper term of this office has been set by wise men at seven years, since there is no task more difficult under the sun and none that more thoroughly saps the strength of its practitioner — the exception being one who presides by his authority rather than by his labor. (599)

You, my dearest son, have reached some of these deadlines; I have reached them all, and more — and still we groan beneath our burden, still we sweat at our toils, while no distinctions and no honors of the emeritus smile upon us, which would justly compensate us for so great a labor. If there are any at all who would now take up that task, they are very few. For liberal studies are now given over to mimes and actors, who seem to go begging through taverns, where they hold forth in philosophical discourses on money. Mammon now rules in all ways over kings and monarchs. In the end beastly avarice holds sway over all the rewards of virtue and ambition takes inventory of its merchandise in the kingdom of money. And what shall we believe is to be our part of such wretched leavings, when the stones of the sanctuary are dispersed through all the streets? But what ministry of dignities or custody of spiritual vessels could be hoped for or desired, where not the vessels of compassion shaped for glory, but the vessels of wrath leading to death, are seen everywhere, from vessels of the minor arts to every vessel of the higher arts? (615)

XXVII. From this same poisoned root of avarice and from these barren tare-seeds is sprung and is still sprouting abundantly today that fatal rejection of manners and of discipline. Nowhere where the regulated life is taught is it permitted to employ the solemn censure of the seniors or the rod. But where one is willing to spare the twistings and turnings of vice and withdraw the hand from the rod and the stimulus of discipline, there the seniors will find a multitude of fellow vices springing forth as their champions, or money stepping forward as their defender. For the minors, however, either ill-mannered license or flight, the liberator, will intercede with her winged feet. But better to be silent about the seniors, for telling the truth stirs hatred. (625)

But those who should still receive their training beneath the scholar's rod give themselves over to stupidity, laziness, and their god the stomach. Fleeing instruction in the gravity of moral discipline, they are blown about like light chaff in every wind of doctrine. And according to that same apostle, they do not endure sound doctrine, but for their own desires accumulate masters who set their ears itching. They do homage to vain and pestiferous novelties of phrasings and questions, and those meant to be formed by artist's hand from wet and malleable clay into vessels of glory on the wheel of discipline leap off and take flight in trivialities, and are thus deformed into vessels of contumely. Also if they gather some scrap of arcane or verbose knowledge, they wander like vagabonds through the fields of learning discoursing to no one's satisfaction. Because questions of morals are either last on their list or not present at all, they revert to their own kind; they shake off the yoke of fear from their unbending necks, they tear the reins of discipline, they charge the precipice, dragging themselves down by a perverse life and others by the corrupting ferment of their malice. (640)

XXVIII. Some men, made pseudo-masters by instruction of a sort, wander about here and there through villages, towns and cities, since they know nothing of a fixed lodging and have no house of their own to retreat to, pass along novel readings of the psalter, of Paul, of the Apocalypse. The youths — servitors of levity — fleeing from discipline, ever eager for novelty, they lure into their company and guide them down the cliffs of voluptuousness. They undermine the reverence for discipline, the subjection to obedience, the observance of religion, and in the end destroy all the fortifications of the regulated life through a most pernicious corruption of manners. (649)

XXIX. And lest you think I cast the weapons of detraction against this brood and weave invidious affronts against things which are new, perhaps even better, you need not believe my words alone. Believe rather your own eyes and ears. Observe, if you will, how sane are the doctrines and how salubrious the disciplines of the theologians who emerge from the academy of Tours. Its headmaster is that apostle of Satan, Berengar. Observe, I say, how pestilential, or rather how venomous are the scorpions and serpents who break forth from the caverns of our contemporary Babylon, what heresiarchs, drunk on their must and smeared with their poison, introduce sacrilegious novelties concerning sacred things, useful for nothing except the subversion of the auditors. Their speech creeps like a cancer, because knowledge which puffs up does not edify, it subverts. (660)

XXX. These men hammer out new and vagrant interpretations concerning things sacrosanct, namely concerning the heavenly sacraments, which the holy fathers, when they dared stretch their hands towards them, seeing that they surpassed not only human language, but also human reason, approached reverently and, where necessary, they had the key of David with the subtle judgment to open and close, and they explained them in a catholic way and with the sobriety sufficient to the wise. The heavenly sacraments themselves, which are consecrated at the altar, they claim to be shadow and not truth—at which the tongue balks and the hearing shudders. They maintain that they are subject to the stomach and the privy in accord with nature's necessity. These mysteries the lord of nature has, of course, created from his omnipotence as a sacrament and a bond of human reconciliation and has given them to the Christian soul as a spiritual nourishment, from which it may live in eternal life. (674)

These men take that same paschal lamb, which prepared and consecrated those same sacraments for us and transformed them in itself in a way that defies explanation, and eat it raw or boiled in water, not roasted in fire. And they do not burn in the fire that which remains (and always will, because no mortal, however holy, has ever in this life been able or will ever be able to penetrate to the mystery of the incarnate Word with full understanding). These men lay in wait for incautious and simple-minded brothers and especially for those who frivolously run after intellectual curiosities, and lure them with the bait of a new teaching. For a start they explain the literal level of scripture as if to show them a broad path to the home of seven-columned wisdom, and as if to guide them down the right path to the haven of salvation. But then once snared in the toils of sophistic disputation and blunted by the sharpness of carnal understanding, they are lead through the captious labyrinth of necessary argumentation, until with a superfluous novelty of questions alien to salvation they are elegantly instructed to their own ruin, and they sink into the pit of destruction. (689)

XXXI. Since men like this do not acknowledge that the things of God defy the speech of man and the world, and that honey should be eaten to satisfy and not to cloy, they prop themselves up on their wisdom and investigate the profound secrets of a majesty far beyond them. Hurled from those heights of glory, they plunge into its abysses, and, striving with the impudence of carnal wisdom to fix the fever-reddened eyes of the animal man, who sees not what is God's, on the true sun, they are hurled back into the outer darknesses of their errors by the rays of that unapproachable light. In the form of impious cavillings these same men audaciously worship the divine mysteries of the sacraments, which merit constant reverence and never are approachable through human senses or reason. But they produce nothing worthy of a sane mind. They seek to encompass God within the boundaries of nature, and to confine within human reason that which surpasses the reason of any rational creature. In doing so they truly dash against the stone of offence and the rock of scandal, and they contend to press from the pious breasts of sane doctrine not milk, but butter or blood. May Jesus Christ eradicate this plague of lethal doctrine from his church before this crumb of ferment infects the whole body. (708)

XXXII.In this way the entire church is being poisoned on all sides not just by this toxin but also by the multiform corrupting force of malice and evil, while at the same time the pure unleavened bread of sincerity and truth receives next to no homage. There is virtually no one who will either work for the true institutes of a good life or reward the one who does as befits, and for this reason that handful of workers remaining is overcome by exasperation and resigns from the labor. Who under these circumstances would not prefer the life of leisure to that of public affairs? who would not prefer quiet and silence to futile toil and unheeded shouting? "I have placed a guard upon my words," he says, "since they constantly sin against me; I fall mute, and I am humbled and remain silent from good things" [Ps. 38:2–3]. And we learn from Jeremiah what behooves men thus humbled and silent from the good, when he says: "He will sit in isolation and will remain silent, because he elevated himself above himself" [Lam. 3:28]. (720)

XXXIII.With wise contempt many men of distinction and high authority have observed all these circumstances: Hermann of Rheims, Drogo of Paris, Huzmann of Speyer, Meinhard of Bamberg and many others. Having abandoned their ambitions and resigned their labors, they have bid farewell to studies, and, following wise counsel, have retired into the leisure of theological pursuits. But as for me, what should I do? Why should I not for my part choose the same course? Gladly! Even if the general lament of all the pious or the present circumstances did not urge me to it, the course of my life and the outcome of all my strivings would abundantly commend that decision to me. For my career has drained my spent energy with the incessant demands of its labors to the point where hardly any is left, and it has sprinkled my head with early snow. I fear an untimely death will be the result, unless I retire betimes into quiet and leisure. (733)

In my present circumstances I am blessed abundantly with the good things of life, but impoverished of what is best, namely all that I mentioned earlier from the golden age of our forefathers, those happier days of our memories which I saw with my own eyes. Those things are genuine faith and impartial truth, keeping the word of the lord one and all, preferring nothing to justice and equity, insisting on discipline and religion with all due gravity, tolerating nothing which is not to the public honor and benefit, along with all that goes with these concerns, which can edify the golden minds placed in these mud baskets [i.e., the body] and restore the longed-for treasures in those earthen vessels. These are the things that in those better days of our memories I have rejoiced to witness and to play a serious part in. But now, seeing them pass almost altogether out of existence, I weep not so much for my own as for the general misery. (747)

XXXIV. But enough of those earlier — and therefore better — times. Now let us talk of those things which in part we ourselves have seen and in part have learned recently from faithful report. I mean from the days of Lord Notker [of Liège], bishop of our city, and of those bishops, his contemporaries, who at that time flourished as the most distinguished men in the church, including those two luminaries, which by now have miserably faded away, compassion and truth. [In those days] they were united, if I may put it that way, and justice and peace kissed. But now truth has been removed from the earth and justice has returned to heaven, and by a swift blow of fortune and a monstrous overturning of things, all is turned inside-out and upside-down and, in short, just the contrary of what I described earlier. Now if anyone should attempt to govern himself and the things entrusted to him, steering through the tempests of worldly life with the same rudder of reason and along the same path of commandments, following as it were the guidance of celestial stars, such a man would be forced to abandon his intention, once blasted by the violence of that whirlwind. (760) It is diffi-cult for anyone to explain how dreadful and monstrous this is. For we read that that noble age of gold of an earlier time degenerated gradually and over long periods into silver or other metals of inferior value, and that it did not lose at one stroke the beauty of its color. But now, as I said earlier, by a monstrous and unprecedented disturbance of order, all things are subverted as it were in a single moment. Nor is there anyone left who tends to the legitimate pursuits of his ordained status and duty. Now that desirable gold of our time has deteriorated, not as in earlier times little by little, but at a single swift stroke, not into silver or any other metal of whatever value, but into stubble and chaff, if not dust and ashes. (772)

And now, let me recall in a compendious epilogue all that I earlier complained of so bitterly in responding to your objections. When those two greatest lights of the church, which God lit too late and extinguished too soon, sheltering them in the darkness of his presence from the plottings of men — I mean emperor Henry III and archbishop Liutpold of Mainz, in whom the boundaries of the age of gold reached their outermost limits with the greatest perfection of beauty — when these two brightest lights, I say, were lifted up (we hope and pray) from these depths to the true light, from which even now they shine down onto the orb of the earth, then all divine religion, all equity and justice, all liberal studies and all moral discipline that had flourished anywhere, as at that time the church flourished both with a variegated beauty of virtues and with a manifold burgeoning of liberal letters — all this was buried with them, or rather received into heaven, so that hardly any vestiges of them are left on earth apart from a few wretched traces, and even those the mere empty shadow. (787)

XXXV. In the first place, virtually all those magistrates and leaders who hold the place of rule among the people of God serve only their own interests, not the common good or that of others. They do not respect the God who sees all, nor do they fear correction from men. Since they know no fear of God, there is pain and unhappiness in all their ways. And how should those who "devour my people like nourishing bread" [Ps. 13:4] know the path of peace? But since there is no one who will call them to account and reprove them, the interests of factions have invalidated the study of divine scriptures; the pursuit of fame and vainglory have superseded the dignity and modesty of the religious life, and while they thrill to compete the one against the other for wealth and distinctions, these vain minds also do not shrink from indulging in intrigues and contentions. Nor do they care in the least that their rule is an exercise in tyranny, and not just rule at all, an end to which such things are bound to tend, bringing destruction in their wake. (800)

If some day this sort of majesty and this form of power should sit in the place of the tribunal to examine the deeds of its subjects, ignoring the beam in its own eye while removing the mote from that of others, then it would have Lady Avarice as its assistant standing at its right hand to declaim law suits, toil at trials and cases, deplore the fact that right and wrong, sacred and profane, are lumped together, call with tears in her eyes upon the compassion of the judges, the authority of the laws, on divine and human justice, and if perchance accusations against a rich man should not lead to a fat fine, she complains that it means the collapse of order in all courts. Then when all are struck with terror by this thunderous speech, she inclines her head to defendant and plaintiff alike, who whisper to her from each side, and scowling grimly invites bribes from each of them. She stretches out her rapacious hand to both of the promise-makers. Hardly has she finished accusing him who has what she covets, at once she pardons him for giving what she demands. Then when the case has been fully argued and she has assumed the seat between Violence and Rapacity and other fellow lawyers, she reads from her law book what is just, and, with the assent of the others, who confirm the legality by oath, she issues judgment on the accused based on the money-lender-law, and a man who has been in chains for however long is held guilty until the God Mammon absolves him, and someone she has just crucified by Cecilian law as a Labeo, she awards the seat of office to as a Cato in accord with the money-law. But in every assembly of this court, the authority of the laws proposes this one rule, and the court worthies agree in this one point: that he who cannot release himself by an immense fortune, should do it with the moderate means he has scraped together, and if he lacks means altogether, he should be mercilessly crucified. (823)

XXXVI. Hence it is that we see the holy gospel displayed in the market places and in the church [we see] doves for sale, vendors' booths, and not far from these the tables of money-lenders. For these days nothing is received gratis and nothing is given gratis. When we see these things, I say, we spend more time in the market than the choir, more intent on usury than Scripture, more concerned with merchandising than with religion, more given to filling large purses than pursuing liberal studies. Putting aside all ecclesiastical disciplines which gospel truth, apostolic teaching and the authority of the holy fathers have sanctioned, we pant for the things of this world; we spend all our time accumulating wealth, as if we might earn the purchase of eternal life at this price. Why? Because "you are what you own" [Horace, Serm. 1.1.62]. As that poet says whom you know well: every thing,

> virtue, fame, glory, things human and divine,
> all bow to lovely riches. Famous is he
> who attains them, courageous, just and wise —
> kings and everything else included. [Horace, Serm. 2.3.95–98]

Since, then, from this root of all evils, avarice, such a horrible thicket of brambles grows, it is easy — nay rather terrible — to see what fruit these thorns bear. (843)

Hence while we languish in pursuit of acquisitions, vying for honors without excelling in honor, having altered the ancient face of divine religion and having nearly reduced the traditional institutes of moral discipline to the level of fable, we are filled with envy one brother against another; we attack one another with slander, we provoke civil wars with our accusations and stab our brothers through the very heart with the sharp thorns of our words. With deception in our heart and a false smile on our face, we proffer falsehood in our words, and in utter iniquity we regard all the command-ments of God as insignificant in comparison with money. And in the end we are blown about like reeds in the wind by levity and inconstancy of charac-ter, so that one can hardly even remember today what one strove for vehemently yesterday. And what can we hope for in the future? Only this: that the lord will drive all of this sort from the temple with a scourge. (857)

Greatly to be feared is that three-fold scourge of divine reproach, which the lord indicated to his sinning people when, through the mouth of his prophet, he said: "Behold, I shall send forth a sword against them, hunger and pestilence, and I shall disperse them to all the winds." [Cf. Ez. 6:3, and Jer. 24:10] But even now we see as it were the first sprouts of this scourge rising slowly from the earth as warnings, when bit by bit the lord grinds away the staff of the bread and [banishes] the mirth from wine. And at the same time we hear of wars waged and seditions launched among Christians, and of frequent incursions of pagans against Christians. Whence it is easy to prophesy that what remains will not long be postponed, unless God can be propitiated by our correction. (866)

XXXVII. Go now, brother, act against leisure and rest, and him who desires them at this time call lazy and apathetic. (And o! would that, having de-spaired of any rewards for our labors, we could obtain them in that longed-for and health-giving quiet which admits no labor but enters the senate of the celestial court with glory.) If, brother, you know a better state, then, honest friend that you are, tell me openly. If not, then enjoy this one with me. If the noble strength of your great soul has until now not given in to them [leisure and rest] and does not flinch before any arduous task, seek then another fellow-in-arms than me, because you shall not have me as your comrade in war at this time. Or seek another Marius and entrust this task to him. But see that you can attribute to him a better outcome of good beginnings than was the lot of that Roman. I for my part, chained and sentenced to long internment as I am in that deadly prison, I shall find solace for my spent forces to the extent possible in peace, and I hope that at length my prayers will be heard and my deep sighs for the desired mission will win for me retirement, if not with high distinction, then at least with honor, and I shall transfer my sad realm to another. But placing no faith in my own will or intention, I shall return to my potter all the clay from which he made me: let Him fix me in the wheel of the world order as it suits his whim, and just as he turns me on the lathe by his power, I shall add nothing except that solemn word of obedience: "Thy will be done" [Matt. 6:10]. (885)

XXXVIII.But now, brother, why have we wandered off? Why have we deflected our course from the straight line of the correct path? To what end have you thus led unsuspecting me so far astray? To what diversions of speech have you drawn me, intoxicated with the sweetness of your love? Behold and beware, my brother, lest while we follow the fixed stars of scripture with insufficient caution we suffer Charibdean shipwreck, having been lured to the cliffs and sandy shores, beware, I say, even though unwillingly, lest more should be said than appropriate, since the blow of the scourge makes only bruises, but the scourge of the tongue crushes the body. (893)

Let our discourse therefore return now to its point of departure and come back to you, that point whence its flow took its first source. It began in love, and now let it end in love. Let charity never fade, but let it give a foretaste, once seeded and rooted here, of its true plenitude in eternal life. What I said earlier in this letter must suffice to praise your excellent character, your dignity, modesty and constancy and other virtues of the good life, but your affection, kindness, and other virtues of humanity can never be sufficiently praised, neither here not elsewhere. (901)

This alone I beg of you: strive always for better and greater things, and finally, strive for that plenitude of growth in which you need never fear diminution. Indeed, because you serve this desirable treasure in its earthen vessel, I think it not superfluous to remind you to guard it lovingly with constant vigilance. This you would do if you would hold all the gates of your citadel and all the windows of this earthen dwelling under the lock and bolt of humility, if also you would equip all the entrances and exits of this clay vessel with the bars of virtues, lest any opening appear either to those guarded within or those laying in ambush without. For if frivolous pride should permit those things to flow out which the busy hand of diligent labor has gathered up within, the wind of overweening will blow and disperse them into vanities' perdition, never to be recovered again. But if the door is open from without so that the malignant armies break through, they will violently pillage and plunder those things which you have gathered up within you with such great labor and leave nothing to the conquered but hell's flames. (916)

Accordingly let all the good talents God implanted in you, all the divine gifts enshrined in the treasury of your conscience, be imputed neither to me who planted and watered them, nor to you who bore fruit in this fertile earth, but let them all be referred to the father of lights, from whom is every good present and every perfect gift. (921)

XXXIX. I could certainly praise your perfect gifts more fully and completely, were it not that dignity and modesty shun the mark of flattery. But I find in all my worldly goods nothing adequate to return your great kindness and repay you appropriately for the book which you wrote for me and which was the occasion for this letter. Your book has stolen into my very soul and endeared all of you to me, from the very joints of your fingers to your eyes and soul, the angle of your neck and the labor of your mind. I can only ask Him from whom you have received all these gifts to recompense you for such kindness by writing your name in golden letters in the book of life. My willing devotion to you will know no rest if the occasion to repay you should come about — given the modest means at my disposal — to the extent that it redounds to our mutual honor. (935)

XL. I have at long last said all that I have to say, to the extent that other obligations permitted. Now let my reed-pen circumcise itself anew with the new scalpel of the scribe, not as Jews, but as scholars do it, and let it [my letter] prepare itself to receive you, to salute you, to celebrate you, not so much through its size as through its elegance. I would not like to send you away, whom I hold inwardly embraced in the bosom of Christ, unless you had enjoyed an elegant reception. And you should know that you owe a debt of gratitude for a feast whose festive table-mate and companion you have shown yourself to be. (943)

Of the many surrounding me, few join me in saluting you, either because the residents of the city I serve who know with how great a gift of virtues you ornament your untiring mind, are few, or because there are few good critical minds able to judge things clearly. For those who have a trained and practiced judgment would surely love you if they knew you and judged you according to your merits. I salute you along with all our fellow workers who studied the good life and ascended from our academy to claim the master's chair in the highest places. I salute you along with our pupils who labor at present in the halls of school, the most noble flower of talent, who ponder their subjects as my words dictate even beneath the rod. If you were to read their names in writing you would not recognize them, having never seen them. (I say this though I refute myself with my very words, because if you measured recognition by the face, you would not know yourself, since you yourself never see your own face.) Above all I salute you with that same charity by which I suckled you in the cradle of discipline with the milk of elementary learning, leading you to the solid food of higher subjects, so that you my comrade in arms and my fellow toiler in the fields would be my heavenly countryman and co-heir of the bequest of eternity. Thus greeted, greet also in my humble name my brothers, not those related in flesh and blood, but reborn in water and spirit and joined by adoption, that as co-heirs of Christ we should receive the lot of eternal beatitude in the kingdom of God the father by the testament of blood. Greet also fathers and lords, brothers and friends, fathers in administering, lords in governing, brothers in God the father, friends in charity. Greet each one of them, I say, as befits his place with me or with you. My greeting be to you all, so that with the aid of Him in whom we believe, we will all equally share eternal life.

Notes

Introduction

1. Haskins, *The Renaissance of the Twelfth Century*, p. 16.
2. Representative is the survey of cathedral schools, 800–1150, in Joseph H. Lynch, *The Medieval Church: A Brief History*, pp. 243–46. See also Specht; Clerval; Lèsne; Paré, Tremblay, and Brunet; Delhaye, "L'organisation scolaire"; Wallach, "Education and Culture"; Liebeschütz, "The Debate on Philosophical Learning"; Gibson, "The Continuity of Learning"; Riché; Lutz; Zielinski and Köhn (see bibliography). A number of essays bearing on the topic appear in the two volumes of *La scuola nell' occidente latino dell' alto medioevo*. Contreni, "The Tenth Century: The Perspective from the Schools," pp. 379–87.
3. It is important to recognize the very minor role of scriptural studies at the worldly schools before the investiture controversy. Beryl Smalley calls the tenth and eleventh centuries "a dramatic pause in the history of Bible studies" (*The Study of the Bible*, p. 44). She includes monasteries and cathedral schools in this judgment. At cathedral schools, she says, "the masters were more interested in the arts and sciences than theology" (p. 45). Lèsne agrees (*Les écoles*, p. 642). The present study bears out this judgment.
4. See Glauche, *Schullektüre* and Köhn, "Schulbildung und Trivium," in *Schulen und Studium*, ed. Fried.
5. Goswin (Gozechinus), *Epist. ad Walcherum*, chapter XXVII, pp. 32, ll. 627–635.
6. I will use the English of these terms interchangeably to refer to cathedral school discipline, and in doing so am following eleventh- and twelfth-century usage.
7. Haskins, *Renaissance of the Twelfth Century*, p. 16: "As we come into the eleventh century, German culture shows little vitality from within." The same must be said of French, of course, where the same conditions predominate.
8. The two major voices that have addressed the transition from the eleventh to the twelfth century recently are those of Charles Radding, *A World Made by Men*, and Brian Stock, *The Implications of Literacy*. Radding adapts a model of historical development from Jean Piaget's studies of cognitive development. He associates the evolution of mentalities with rising stages of cognition. Stock's model operates on the opposition of orality to literacy. Both are progressive, evolutionary models, suggesting a rise from more to less primitive in social and cognitive change. Both are formulated to analyze the new. Neither model comes to terms with the sense of superiority of the old and contempt for that which supersedes it, and neither can deal with "reversion" from a "higher" to a "lower" stage.

9. *Tusc. Disp.* 4.2.3: "... praecepta quaedam occultius tradere et mentes suas a cogitationum intentione cantu fidibusque ad tranquillitatem traducere ..."

10. 4.3.5: "... hanc amplissimam omnium artium, bene vivendi disciplinam, vita magis quam litteris persecuti sunt." Here and throughout, I will translate *vita* in this context as "conduct," "way of living."

11. Eric Havelock, *Preface to Plato*. Werner Jaeger, *Paideia*, 2: 17ff.

12. This comment leaves out the mainstream of Platonic influence, Neoplatonism. While Neoplatonism is important to acknowledge, the two branches of influence of interest to me are the memorializing of Socrates and the opposition to his doctrine.

13. Southern, *The Making of the Middle Ages*; Grabmann, *Geschichte der scholastischen Methode*; Radding, *A World made by Men*; Stock, *Implications of Literacy*.

14. On itinerant kingship, see the survey by Joachim Bumke in *Höfische Kultur*, pp. 71–76; on administrative kingship, C. Warren Hollister and John Baldwin, "The Rise of Administrative Kingship: Henry I and Philip Augustus."

15. Tellenbach, *Church, State and Society*, and White, "The Gregorian Ideal and Saint Bernard of Clairvaux." Also below, Chapter 10, pp. 274–75 and n. 22.

16. On "performance" in the context of a shift from oral to written literature, see Paul Zumthor, *Oral Poetry: An Introduction*.

17. Hugh, *De Sacramentis* 1.6.5., PL 176, 267A: [referring to the incarnation] "... et positus est liber scriptus intus et foris; in humanitate foris, intus in divinitate, ut foris legeretur per imitationem, intus per contemplationem ..."

18. Herbert of Bosham, *Vita Thomae* 3.13, RS 67: 3, p. 208: "Sed novum nostrum exemplar replicemus, et in ipso relegamus adhuc. Fructuosius quippe virtutum opera leguntur in viris quam in libris, quanto efficacior est vox operum quam sermonum."

19. Some thoughts on these problems in a number of essays in *Materialität der Kommunikation*, ed. Gumbrecht & Pfeiffer.

20. See Zumthor, *Oral Poetry*, on voice and text.

21. *Institutio oratoria* 2.13.9: "... recti quidem corporis vel minima gratia est; nempe enim adversa sit facies et demissa brachia et iuncti pedes at a summis ad ima rigens opus. Flexus ille et, ut sic dixerim, motus dat actum quendam et adfectum. Ideo nec ad unum modum formatae manus et in vultu mille species.... Quam quidem gratiam et delectationem adferunt figurae ..."

22. *Bede's Ecclesiastical History of the English People* 3.5, p. 226.

23. *Das Leben der Liutbirg* (880), chapter 8, ed. Ottokar Menzel, MGH Deutsches Mittelalter, Kritische Studientexte 3 (Leipzig, 1937; rpt. Stuttgart, 1978), p. 15, lines 18–20. The passage is especially rich in translation problems which derive from the identification of behavior and morality common to a charismatic culture.

24. Ruotger, *Vita Brun.* chapter 21, LB, p. 210.

25. Sigebert of Gembloux, *Gesta Abb. Gembl.* chapter 4, MGH SS 8, p. 525. line 9.

26. Otto III writing to Gerbert of Aurillac, requesting instruction from his book of mathematics, "... ut pleniter eius [= the book's] instructi documentis aliquid priorum intelligamus subtilitatis." *Briefsammlung Gerberts* epist. 186, p. 222.

27. English preserves the meaning "embodied lesson" well into the modern period. Laertes calls Ophelia "a document in madness" (*Hamlet* 4.1.178.)

28. *De institutione novitiorum* chapter 10, PL 176, 935D. See below, Chapter 9.

29. Emil Lèsne's expansive work (*Les écoles*) on the schools from the eighth to the twelfth century is an exception.

30. Paravicini can point to a passage in the "Ecbasis captivi," currently dated 1043–1046, which quotes the "Quid suum virtutis."

31. Hauréau, *Les mélanges poétiques d'Hildebert de Lavardin* (Paris, 1882), p. 41; Curtius, "Die Musen im Mittelalter," *ZRPH* 59 (1939), pp. 183–84.

32. Charles Radding and Ronald Witt are preparing studies of Italian schools in the eleventh century.

Chapter 1: Two Models of Carolingian Education

1. On education in the Carolingian period see Lèsne, *Les écoles*; Josef Flecken-stein, *Die Bildungsreform Karls des Grossen als Verwirklichung der norma rectitudinis*; M.L.W. Laistner, *Thought and Letters in Western Europe A.D. 500 to 900*; Wolfgang Edelstein, *Eruditio et sapientia: Weltbild und Erziehung in der Karolingerzeit*; Pierre Riché, *Les écoles et l'enseignement*.

2. See Beryl Smalley, *The Study of the Bible in the Middle Ages*, pp. 37ff.; Laistner, *Thought and Letters*, pp. 189ff.

3. *Die Vita Sturmi des Eigil von Fulda* chapter 2, pp. 132–33: ". . . presbyter sanctus puerum Sturmen ad Dei omnipotentis servitium instruere studuit. Psalmis tenaci memoriae traditis, lectionibusque quam plurimis perenni commemoratione firmatis, sacram coepit Christi puer scripturam spiritali intelligere sensu, quatuor evangeliorum Christi mysteria studiosissime curavit addiscere, novum quoque ac vetus testamentum, in quantum sufficiebat, lectionis assiduitate in cordis sui thesauro recondere curavit. Erat quippe, ut scriptum est, 'meditatio eius in lege Domini die ac nocte.'"

4. "Sacred letters" are one of the most common topics in descriptions of education, frequently the only element mentioned. Cf. Altfrid, *Vita Liudgeri*, MGH SS 2, 410 (chapter 19): "sacris litteris imbutum"; Pope Benedict III, *Vita*, PL 115, 683A: "sacrorum voluminum didicit lectiones"; Pope Leo IV, PL 128, 1303: "quousque sacras litteras plenitus disceret . . ."; *Vita vel passio S. Eulogii* PL 115, 707C: ". . . litteris ecclesiasticis haerens . . ."; Ansgar, *Vita Willehadi* MGH SS 2, 380, l. 4ff.: ". . . ab infantia sacris eruditus litteris, ac spiritalibus instructus disciplinis . . ."; Alcuin, *Vita Willibrordi*, PL 101, 696A: "[W. sent to monastery] . . . religiosis studiis et sacris litteris erudiendum."

5. Eigil's own biographer (Candidus or Brun of Fulda) paints the same picture: Eigil studied at Fulda (under Sturmi), where divine law was taught "in inexhaustible exertions" (*jugi exercitatione*), and studied "with the utmost industry" (*cum summa industria*, PL 105, 385B). The warning of Hrabanus Maurus to students that it is better to memorize less and understand more underscores the point (PL 107, 407A).

6. On this aspect of Carolingian education, see Heinrich Fichtenau, *The*

Carolingian Empire, trans. Peter Munz, esp. pp. 90–103, and Smalley, *The Study of the Bible*, pp. 37ff.

7. This is not to ignore the philosophical accomplishments of the period, those of John the Scot for instance. Our concern is with the education instituted in monasteries and cathedrals, which came as an innovation of the period, and a view of this scene underscores the exceptional nature of the brilliant accomplishment of a few Carolingian scholar-philosophers.

8. "ad discendos libros divinos." *Vita Gregorii*, chapter 2, MGH SS 15: p. 68. ll. 1ff.

9. Cf. Laistner, *Thought and Letters*, p. 194: "Charles repeatedly stresses the need of good preachers, who, instead of always addressing their flock in the language of the church, were permitted and even directed to use the vernacular, if their hearers were unable to follow in Latin."

10. Hrabanus Maurus, *De clericorum institutione* 3.27, PL 107, 406B: ". . . quem antiqua diffinitio affirmat, virum bonum et dicendi peritum esse debere. Si ergo haec definitio in oratoribus gentilium observabatur, multo magis in oratoribus Christi observari convenit, quorum non solum sermo, imo etiam tota vita doctrina virtutum debet esse." On the definition of the virtues in the period, see Edelstein, *Eruditio et Sapientia* and Sibylle Mähl, *Quadriga virtutum: Die Kardinaltugenden in der Geistesgeschichte der Karolingerzeit*.

11. *De inst. cler.* 3. 28, PL 107, 407A: "Sapienter autem dicit homo tanto magis vel minus, quanto in scripturis sanctis majus minusve proficit." Scripture is the basis of all wisdom, according to Hrabanus, 3.2, PL 107, 379B: "Fundamentum . . . et perfectio prudentiae scientia est sanctarum Scripturarum . . ."

12. Laistner, *Thought and Letters*, pp. 207ff.

13. PL 105, 800C: "Tandem a parentibus traditus in liberalibus artibus erudiendus . . . coepit . . . juxta scientiae doctrinalis augmentum incrementum religionis suscipere: ut non solum in liberalibus, verum etiam in spiritualibus disciplinis efficaciter instrueretur."

14. On *convictus* in monastic communities in the early Middle Ages, see Detlef Illmer, *Formen der Erziehung und Wissensvermittlung im frühen Mittelalter*, pp. 58ff.; Jean Leclerq, "Pédagogie et formation spirituelle du VIe au IXe siècle," pp. 285–86. Among the clergy in general, Richard Stachnik, *Die Bildung des Weltklerus im Frankenreiche von Karl Martell bis auf Ludwig den Frommen*, pp. 3–4.

15. PL 115, 629Af.: "Ubi non solum litteras didicit, verum etiam in studio sanctae conversationis, non quasi puer . . . sed velut perfec tus monachus mansit."

16. MGH SS 2, 41–42: "litterarum scientia sublimatus, virtutum sectator morumque laudabilium possessor sacerdotii gradum conscendit."

17. Ep. 271, Epist. 4, Karol. aevi 2, p. 430: ". . . erudite pueros et adolescentulos vestros cum omni diligentia, in castitate et sanctitate, et disciplina ecclesiastica, ut digni habeantur vestrum post vos tenere locum . . ."

18. *Vita Lamberti*, chapter 1, sec. 5–6, PL 132, 645–46: ". . . peritissimis viris traditur educandus. Ecclesiastica religione admodum insignitur, et coelestium mysteriorum igneo amore penetraliter inflammatur, tantoque celerius liberalium fluenta artium epotavit, quanto ardentius in amore Dei totum se olim transfudit . . . Instructus tandem divinis dogmatibus, et ubertim vigoratus monasticis sanctioni-

bus . . ." (645C); ". . . nitens totis viribus vir fieri perfectus . . ." (646B); "Huic [=
Bp. Theodard] . . . Lantbertus, nobilitate cluentissimus, forma corporis elegan-
tissimus commendatur, in aula regia educandus . . ." (646C). Cf. *Vita . . . S. Eulogii*
PL 115, 707Cf.: "Ab ipsis . . . incunabulis litteris ecclesiasticis haerens, et quotidie
per studia bonorum operum crescens, perfectionem adeptus est . . . magistrorum
doctor est factus." *De Vita S. Odulphi*, PL 133, 857: ". . . litterarum studiis traditus, et
sanctis ac deo devotis hominibus, ut ab illis canonica religione imbueretur, com-
mendatus est. . . . aetatem suam, licet annis necdum maturam, divinis disciplinis, et
dogmatibus egregie ornaret"; ". . . in virum perfectum . . ." (859A).

19. *Epistola de litteris colendis*, MGH Leges 2, Capit. regum Franc. 1, p. 79, ll. 9–
15: ". . . consideravimus utile esse, ut episcopia et monasteria nobis Christo propitio
ad gubernandum commissa praeter regularis vitae ordinem atque sanctae religionis
conversationem etiam in litterarum meditationibus eis qui donante Domino discere
possunt secundum uniuscuiusque capacitatem docendi studium debeant impendere, qualiter, sicut regularis norma honestatem morum, ita quoque docendi et
discendi instantia ordinet et ornet seriem verborum, ut, qui Deo placere appetunt
recte vivendo, ei etiam placere non negligant recte loquendo."

20. *Epist. de litt.col.*, p. 79, ll. 38–39: ". . . et interius devotos et exterius doctos
castosque bene vivendo et scholasticos bene loquendo . . ."

21. Cf. the resolution of the Council of Lestinnes (Liptinensis, near Lobbes)
from 743 enjoining reform. MGH Leges 2, Capit. 1, p. 28, ll. 1–2: "[representatives
of the entire clergy] . . . promiserunt se velle ecclesiastica iura moribus et doctrinis et
ministerio recuperare." Stachnik, *Die Bildung des Weltklerus*, p. 24.

22. On the moral thrust of pre-Carolingian education in monastic communities, see Illmer, *Wissensvermittlung*, pp. 51ff., and in early Christian education in
general, Joseph McCarthy, "Clement of Alexandria and the Foundations of Christian Educational Theory," *History of Education Society Bulletin* 7 (1971), 11–18.

23. Two decades after the emergence of educational reform, Charlemagne
found it necessary to issue an edict (in 811) cautioning against favoring study of
letters and the chant to the neglect of *bona conversatio*. Bishops apparently courted
large numbers of clerics, attending more to their literacy than to discipline and
institutional identity: ". . . plus studet [pastor vel magister] ut suus clericus vel
monachus bene cantet et legat quam iuste et beate vivat . . ." Both are to be
cultivated, but ". . . tolerabilius . . . ferendum nobis videtur inperfectione [sic]
cantandi quam vivendi" (MGH Leges 2, Capit. regum Franc. 1, p. 164, nr. 72). The
indication is clearly that the strong initial emphasis on letters and church duties
brought a neglect of the other side of the curriculum, personal discipline. See the
comments of Stachnik, *Die Bildung des Weltklerus*, pp. 60–61.

24. See the article, "Perfection chrétienne", in *Dictionnaire de théologie catholique* 12: 1219–51.

25. PL 126, 993B: ". . . in paucis annis omni maturitate et scientiae et virtutum
perfectus enituit." *Vir perfectus* is biblical (Luke 6:40): "Every disciple who becomes
like his master is perfect." But it is an ideal shared with Roman antiquity (Quintilian,
Inst. orat. 12.2.25 & 27), and not restricted to any period of western Christianity,
though the phrase runs like a leitmotif through Carolingian biographies. One
example that epitomizes the Carolingian educational tradition, *Vita Leonis* 4, PL

115, 629B: "... non solum litteras didicit, verum etiam in studio sanctae conversationis, non quasi puer ... sed velut perfectus monachus ..." Alcuin gives a definition with a classical flavor in his dialogue *Grammatica*, PL 101, 851A: [the master quotes the dictum, "nothing in excess," and the pupils ask how to judge proper moderation] "Discip: 'Perfectorum esse arbitramus hujusmodi rationis frenis animarum cursus coercere.' — Mag.: 'Ad hanc scilicet perfectionem ... vos cohortor.'"

26. *Vita Sturmi*, chapter 2, p. 133: "... profundus in sensu, sagax in cogitatione, prudens in sermone, pulcro adspectu, gressu composito, honestis moribus, vita immaculata, caritate, humilitate, mansuetudine, alacritate, omnium in se traxit amorem."

27. MGH SS 2, p. 407, chapter 9: "... vir mirae mansuetudinis, vultu hilari, non tamen facilis in risu, et in omnibus actibus prudentiam cum temperantia amplectens. Erat enim assiduus meditator divinae scripturae, et eius precipue, quae ad laudem Dei et ad doctrinam pertinebat catholicam ..."

28. MGH SS 2, p. 407, chapter 11: "Erat consueto more omnibus carus, eo quod esset ornatus moribus bonis et studiis sanctis." As a result of his studies with Alcuin he became "in monasticis eruditionibus illustr[ior]" (p. 408, chapter 12).

29. *Epistola ad clericos et monachos Ludgunenses de modo regiminis ecclesiastici*, PL 104, 195C: "Omnis ergo qui praeponitur caeteris, sive clericus sive monachus, si ita videtur benevolus et mansuetus atque affabilis, ut subditorum corda in sui amorem et propriam laudem convertat, adulter est, et regimen animarum suscipere nunquam debet."

30. *De Carolo Magno*, I, 3, ed Jaffé, Bibl. rer. germ. 4, p. 633: "'Nunc ergo ad perfectum attingere studete; et dabo vobis episcopia et monasteria permagnifica, et semper honorabiles eritis in oculis meis.'"

31. There is general agreement on this point. Cf. Fleckenstein, *Bildungsreform*, p. 23 and passim; Franz Brunhölzl, "Der Bildungsauftrag der Hofschule," p. 32; Rosamond McKitterick, *The Frankish Kingdoms Under the Carolingians, 751–987*, pp. 147–48. Beryl Smalley treats Biblical studies at "Monastic and Cathedral Schools" (the title of her second chapter) as if there were no distinctions to make between the two.

32. *Vita Bardonis*, ed. Jaffé, Bibl. rer. germ., 3, p. 525. On Wazo's contested election, MGH SS 7, p. 219, ll. 39–44 and below, Chapter 7.

33. *Epist. de litt. colendis*, MGH Leges 2, Capit. 1, Nr. 29, p. 79. 9: "... episcopia et monasteria ... docendi studium debeant impendere"; line 43: "Huius epistolae ... exemplaria ad omnes suffragantes tuosque coepiscopos et per universa monasteria dirigi ..." The *Admonitio generalis* commands, "Psalmos, notas, cantus, compotum, grammaticam per singula monasteria vel episcopia et libros catholicos bene emendate." Recall also Charlemagne's words to the diligent sons of poor men: "... dabo vobis episcopia et monasteria permagnifica ..." (above, n. 30). This suggests that the two institutions were indistinguishable in terms of the education offered and that educated men were prepared for pastoral care, administrative service and the religious life alike at either.

34. Alcuin writes to the emperor describing his teaching activity at St. Martin's (sacred scripture, "ancient studies," grammar and astronomy). Its purpose: "ad profectum sanctae Dei ecclesiae et ad decorem imperialis regni vestri" (MGH Epist.

4, Ep. Karolini Aevi 2, pp. 176–77, nr. 121), and he urges Charlemagne to exhort the "youths in the palace" to achieve the same kind of wisdom (p. 177, ll. 29–30). Fleckenstein argues that the court was the breeding and testing ground of the educational program, and that from the court it spread to cathedral and monastery (*Bildungsreform*, esp. p. 28). On the Carolingian court or palace school in general see Lèsne, *Les écoles*, pp. 39ff.; Brunhölzl, "Der Bildungsauftrag," who argues, against Albert Hauck, that there is no meaningful distinction between court and ecclesiastical schools (pp. 29–30); Fichtenau, *Carolingian Empire*, pp. 79 ff.; Fleckenstein, *Bildungsreform*; see also his "Karl der Grosse und sein Hof," and "Die Struktur des Hofes Karls des Grossen im Spiegel von Hinkmars *De ordine palatii*"; Rosamond McKitterick, "The Palace School of Charles the Bald."

35. Pierre Riché, *Education and Culture in the Barbarian West from the Sixth Through the Eighth Century*, p. 239. Riché refers to Waldregisil, trained at court *militaribus gestis et aulicis disciplinis*.

36. Epist. Syn. Karisiac. XII, MGH Leges 2, Capit. 2, p. 436, ll. 2–6: "Et ideo domus regis scola dicitur, id est disciplina; quia non tantum scolastici, id est disciplinati et bene correcti, sunt, sicut alii, sed potius, ipsa scola, quae interpretatur disciplina, id est correctio, dicitur quae alios habitu, incessu, verbo et actu atque totius bonitatis continentia corrigat." Heiric of Auxerre praised the court of Charles the Bald also as a school. MGH Poetae 3: 429, l. 37: ". . . merito vocitetur scola palatium, cuius apex non minus scolaribus quam militaribus consuescit cotidie disciplinis."

37. Stachnik had shown the pedagogic thrust of the religious life as early as the sixth century and into the eighth ("Fritzlar ist also in erster Linie mehr Schule als Kloster; Schule in klösterlichem Gewande, nicht Kloster mit Schule" — p. 19). Fleckenstein and his student Illmer take up the idea and point to the essentially personal, charismatic nature of instruction in Carolingian times and before and to the problems of applying the word "school" uncritically to this learning. Jean Leclerq came to similar insights in his "Pédagogie et formation spirituelle," esp. p. 268: "Il n'y a pas d'écoles monastiques' à proprement parler, il n'y a même pas d'écoles dans les monastères . . . l'école, c'est tout le monastère."

38. Riché, *Education and Culture*, p. 238. "Schola palatina" designated the elite troops attached to the royal court. Cf. O. Seeck, "Scholae Palatinae," Pauly-Wissowa, 2nd ser. 2, 261.

39. Cf. Alcuin to Bp. Eanbald of York, urging him to maintain the school there as "totius bonitatis et eruditionis fons," as a drinking fountain for those who thirst for *ecclesiastica disciplina* (Epist. 114, MGH Epist. 4, Ep. Karol. Aevi 2, p. 169, 15ff.

40. Cf. n. 26 above: praise of Sturmi, *gressu composito*. See also J.-C. Schmitt, *La raison des gestes*, pp. 93–133. His only Carolingian examples are secular, and he concentrates on interpreting the representation of gestures in illuminated manuscripts.

41. *Einharti vita Caroli magni*, chapter 19, ed. Jaffé, Bibl. rer. Germ. 4, 526: ". . . primo liberalibus studiis, quibus et ipse operam dabat, erudirentur. Tum filios, cum primum aetas patiebatur, more Francorum equitare, armis ac venatibus exerceri fecit; filias vero lanificio adsuescere, coloque ac fuso, ne per otium torperent, operam inpendere atque ad omnem honestatem erudiri iussit."

42. Ermenrici epist. ad Grimaldum, MGH Epist. 5, Ep. Aev. Karol. Aevi 3, p. 536, ll. 10ff.: ". . . veste septemplici, quam Sophia sibi suis manibus texuerat, indutus mirifice procedis, preter haec etiam gemmis omnium virtutum adornatus. . . . Et non inmerito his virtutum alis ceteros precellis, qui a primo aetatis flosculo inter aulicos beatorum augustorum mores decentissimos enutritus es. Tam dogma totius discipline quam normam recte vivendi ab eis didicisti . . ."

43. Paschasius Radbertus, *Vita Adalhardi*, chapter 7, MGH SS 2, p. 525.

44. *Grammatica* PL 101, 849–902; *De dialectica* PL 101, 949–76; *De rhetorica et virtutibus*, *The Rhetoric of Alcuin and Charlemagne*, ed. Howell (see bibliography). See Liutpold Wallach, *Alcuin and Charlemagne: Studies in Carolingian History and Literature*.

45. "inter curas aulae." *The Rhetoric of Alcuin and Charlemagne*, p. 66, l. 34.

46. *The Rhetoric of Alcuin*, p. 66, lines 12 ff.: ". . . te olim memini dixisse, totam eius artis vim in civilibus versari quaestionibus. Sed ut optime nosti propter occupationes regni et curas palatii in huiuscemodi quaestionibus assidue nos versari solere, et ridiculum videtur eius artis nescisse praecepta, cuius cotidie occupatione involvi necesse est."

47. For instance, chapter 3, p. 70, ll. 67 ff.: "rhetoricae disciplinae regulas pande nobis: iam cotidiana occupationum necessitas cogit nos exerceri in illis."

48. PL 101, 919:

Qui, rogo, civiles cupiat cognoscere mores
Haec praecepta legat quae liber iste tenet.

49. p. 142, ll. 1149 ff.: ". . . illis sermocinandi ratio, qui causis civilibus et *negotiis saecularibus* interesse aestimandi sunt, mox a pueritia multo studio habenda est . . ." (emphasis added)

50. PL 101, 613–38. See Liutpold Wallach, "Alcuin on Virtues and Vices: A Manual for a Carolingian Soldier."

51. See Samuel Jaffé, "Antiquity and Innovation in Notker's *Nova rhetorica*: The Doctrine of Invention" and bibliography in that article on early medieval rhetoric.

52. See Howell's introduction, *Alcuin's Rhetoric*, pp. 22–33 and his notes.

53. Cf. Cicero, *De inventione* 1.1.1ff. See Jerrold Seigel, *Rhetoric and Philosophy in Renaissance Humanism*, on the tradition in the Middle Ages, pp. 173–99, though with a tendency to underestimate its importance. Also see below, Chapter 5.

54. Seigel denies the connection, but points to Alcuin's treatment of style. The joining of wisdom and eloquence is addressed mainly in the section on delivery.

55. *The Rhetoric of Alcuin*, p. 142, ll. 1156–57: "Nam ut in castris miles, sic in domo orator debet erudiri, ut quod solus exercuerat, inter multos facere non formidet." *In domo* in this context must be translated "at court" rather than "at home", as Howell renders it (p. 143).

56. *The Rhetoric of Alcuin*, p. 142, ll. 1167ff.: ". . . verba sint lecta, honesta, lucida, simplicia, plano ore, vultu quieto, facie conposita, sine immoderato cacchino, clamore nullo prolata. Nam bonus modus est in loquendo, tamquam in ambulando, clementer ire, sine saltu, sine mora, quatenus omnia medii moder-

aminis temperantia fulgeant, quae est una de quatuor virtutibus, de quibus caeterae quasi radicibus procedant virtutes, in quibus animae est nobilitas, vitae dignitas, morum honestas, laus disciplinae." See Schmitt's commentary, *La raison des gestes*, pp. 93–95.

57. See *The Rhetoric of Alcuin*, p. 144, ll. 1204ff.

58. These verses are not printed either by Howell or by Karl Halm in his edition of Alcuin, *Rhetores latini minores*, 523–50. The editor of the Migne edition comments that they occur in all the manuscripts he consulted (PL 101, 949A). Neither Howell nor Halm comments on the lines or their omission. Wallach takes them as genuine lines of Alcuin not originally attached to the *De rhetorica* (*Alcuin and Charlemagne*, pp. 86–88).

59. Cf. Alcuin's Ep. 229, MGH Epist. 4, Ep. Karol. Aevi 2, 373. 2ff., urging Charlemagne to become a philosopher-prince by practicing *sapientia* in which is found *decus, pulchritudo vitae praesentis* and glory of perpetual beatitude. Imbedded in Ciceronian/Alcuinian ideals is the use of "beauty" as a modifier of conduct of the present life as opposed to eternal life.

60. But this definition is common: cf. in Halm, Cassiodorus, Isidor and Alcuin.

61. Hrabanus, *De cler. inst.* 3.19, PL 107, 396C–D: "Sed haec diffinitio licet ad mundanam sapientiam videatur pertinere, tamen non est extranea ab ecclesiastica disciplina. Quidquid enim orator et praedicator divinae legis diserte et decenter profert in docendo, vel quidquid apte et eleganter depromit in dictando, ad hujus artis congruit peritiam; nec utique peccare debet arbitrari, qui hanc artem in congrua aetate legit . . ."

62. *De cler. inst.* 3.27, PL 107, 406B.

63. On Carolingian Fürstenspiegel, Jonas of Orleans, *De institutione regia*, ed. J. Reviron, in *Les idées politico-religieuses d'un évêque du IXe siècle: Jonas d'Orléans et son De inst. reg.* (Paris, 1930). Hans Hubert Anton, *Fürstenspiegel und Herrscherethos in der Karolingerzeit.*

64. Einhard, *Vita Caroli magni*, chapter 25, pp. 531–32: "Erat eloquentia copiosus et exuberans; poteratque, quicquid vellet, apertissime exprimere . . . apud quem [=Alcuin] et rethoricae et dialecticae . . . ediscendae plurimum et temporis et laboris inpertivit." On the position of rhetoric and an orator's education in the ninth century see Laistner, *Thought and Learning*, pp. 217–18.

65. Thompson, *The Literacy of the Laity in the Middle Ages*, pp. 27–52.

66. See Howell, *The Rhetoric of Alcuin*, pp. 8ff.

Chapter 2: Court and School in Ottonian Times

1. *Ruotgers Lebensbeschreibung des Erzbischofs Bruno von Köln*, chapters 5–8, LB, pp. 186–190. On Brun's influence as teacher, see Gunther Wolf, "Erzbischof Brun I. von Köln und die Förderung der gelehrten Studien in Köln" with earlier literature.

2. Sigebert of Gembloux, *Vita Deoderici ep. Mettensis*, MGH SS 4, p. 464, ll. 43ff.: ". . . in sanctae Halberstadensis ecclesiae gremio a primis annis maternae

pietatis ubere ablactatus, et sublimiter ut competebat educatus, naturae et morum dulces et uberes repromittebat fructus." On Dietrich see DGQ 1. 182–85.

3. *Vita Deoderici*, pp. 464.48–465.16:

> Et quia erat quondam in castris coelestis militiae civiliter militaturus, sub eo in sanctae Coloniensis ecclesiae gimnasio per diutina diludia liberali tyrocinio est exercitatus, et per diuturna proludia laudabiliter probatus. Discebat ibi humiliter subesse, qui debebat multis aliquando utiliter praeesse, et subiectis humili et discreta praelatione utillime prodesse. Erat in utroque, quod uterque in alterutro amplecteretur; et sicut ferrum ferro acuitur, sic alter alterius bona aemulatione aedificabatur. . . .
>
> Nec in vanum cedere poterat, quod vir, qui in Christo et in aecclesia talis tantusque futurus erat, quem mater aecclesia ad ornamentum et firmamentum sui nutrierat, quem natura, immo ipsius auctor naturae, nativo ingenii bono ditabat, talis tantique magistri studio et doctrina institui et expoliri meruerat. Ut enim ait quidam:
> Doctrina vim promovet insitam
> Rectique cultus pectora roborant,
> Utcumque defecere mores,
> Dedecorant bene nata culpae.

4. On the muting of sainthood in Brun's Vita, see Patrick Corbet, *Les saints ottoniens: Sainteté dynastique, sainteté royale et sainteté féminine autour de l'an Mil*, esp. pp. 51–58, 74–80.

5. *Benedicti regula* 64.8, ed. Hanslik, p. 149: "sciatque sibi oportere prodesse magis quam praeesse."

6. Cf. Augustine, Sermo 340.1, PL 38, 1484; *De civitate Dei* 19.19, PL 41, 647; *Contra Faustum* 22.56, PL 42, 436. Gregory the Great, *Regula pastoralis* 2.6, PL 77, 34C; *Moralia* 21.15 (22–24), CC 143A, 1082–83 (benefit others without being set above them [*praeesse*]). Hincmar, *De divortio*, PL 125, 772 (everyone should by "ruled and benefited" by episcopal authority and the royal office). I am grateful to George Brown and Greg Rose for the first of these references. The latter two are from John van Engen, "Sacred Sanctions" (forthcoming). Also Sigebert, *Passio Thebeorum* 1.379–81, ed. Dümmler, p. 58: "His isti presunt primatus ordine, prosunt / Exemplis vite fideique pari pietate. / Qui presunt subsunt, qui subsunt hi quoque presunt." See also the discussion of the importance of unquestioned authority in the running of the bishop's household in Bernard of Clairvaux, *De consideratione* 4.6.18, which gives particular stress to *praeesse*. See below, Chapter 7 on Wazo of Liège.

7. Cf. Ruotger, *Vita Brun.*, chapter 21, LB, p. 210: "exemplum et documentum factus est omnibus. . . ." Also chapter 29, p. 220; chapter 30, p. 224; chapter 33, p. 227. Pointed out and discussed by Hartmut Hoffmann, "Politik und Kultur im ottonischen Reichskirchensystem: Zur Interpretation der Vita Brunonis des Ruotger," p. 49.

8. Ruotger, *Vita Brun.*, chapter 1, LB, p. 180: "Ineffabili igitur providentia bonitatis Dei collatum est electis eius, ut et gratis copiosis gratie muneribus ditentur

et tamen hoc ipsum, quo munerantur, quodammodo per gratiam mereantur, alius sic, alius vero sic, unusquisque secundum quod in eo operatur unus atque idem spiritus dividens singulis prout vult."

9. *Vita Deoderici*, chapter 3, p. 465, ll. 27ff.:

Nam caeteris quibus pollebat artibus etiam hoc addiderat, quod principibus cuiusque ordinis, in quibus columbae innocentiam, serpentis astuciam, et praecipue tutae fidei simplicitatem vigere videbat, his adprime amicitiam suam accommodabat, his gratiam regis cumulatius conciliabat. Si quos talium privata adhuc vita oscurabat, hos oportune in loco defunctorum illustrium virorum sua opera suffectos, ad bene agendum accendebat. Omnia quippe omnibus factus erat. . . .

Ruotger says as much of Brun, chapter 37, LB, p. 234:

Quesivit interea summa diligentia pius pastor Bruno . . . navos et industrios viros, qui rem publicam suo quisque loco fide et viribus tuerentur . . . hos ipse inter summos et familiares habebat, eisdem imperatorem, germanum suum, adprime conciliabat. . . .

10. On the incident see Karl Uhlirz, *Jahrbücher des deutschen Reiches unter Otto II. und Otto III.*, 1: 178–79.

11. Alpert, *De episcopis Mettensibus libellus*, MGH SS 4, p. 699, ll. 41ff.:

Verum dum omnium virorum nostrorum causas sublimium considero, nihil in eis repperio, quod non eius vitae eligantia superet; et hoc quisque etiam crimen arrogantiae subit, si existimet, se vitae Deoderici cuiusque iudicio posse comparari. Multi namque non a se ipsis, set ex aliorum beneficiis vel etiam rapinis, locupletes et clari effecti; Deodericus vero longe aliter generositate parentum et excellentia maiorum, ex innata quoque copia magna praediorum clarissimus habetur.

12. See my *Origins of Courtliness*, pp. 35–36.

13. MGH SS 8, pp. 536–37 (chapters 26–29). On the text see Max Manitius, *Geschichte der lateinischen Literatur des Mittelalters*, 3: 340ff.

14. Cf. pp. 537.1ff.:

. . . ut prudenter indisciplinatos mores eorum corrigeret, pravas vias eorum, quibus illicite vagando aberrare solebant, spinis regularis disciplinae sepiebat; . . . exemplo evangelici Samaritani ulceribus eorum vinum severitatis et oleum pietatis infundebat . . . Sciens quippe quia otiositas inimica est animae, suos iam satis imbutos sancta religione, studiis etiam litterarum docuit studiose insistere; ut dum per semitas scripturarum oculis atque animis relegerent patrum vestigia, scirent indubitanter errorum cavere a via. . . .

Here discipline of conduct is a scourge to sinfulness and letters is a kind of penal servitude in advance, a check on laziness.

15. The term has survived a recent brush with opposition. See Timothy Reuter, "The 'Imperial Church System' of the Ottonian and Salian Rulers: A Reconsideration." Reuter was answered by Josef Fleckenstein, "Problematik und Gestalt der ottonisch-salischen Reichskirche." For a survey of earlier research, see Oskar Köhler, "Die Ottonische Reichskirche: Ein Forschungsbericht." In the discussion here I am following Fleckenstein, especially "Problematik und Gestalt."

16. Hans-Walter Klewitz, "Königtum, Hofkapelle und Domkapitel im 10. und 11. Jahrhundert"; cited here from the 1960 reprint, p. 14.

17. See Oskar Köhler, *Das Bild des geistlichen Fürsten in den Viten des 10., 11. und 12. Jahrhunderts*; and Jaeger, "The Courtier Bishop in Vitae from the Tenth to the Twelfth Century," and *Origins of Courtliness*, pp. 21ff.

18. See Hoffmann, "Politik und Kultur," and Josef Fleckenstein, "Königshof und Bischofsschule unter Otto dem Grossen."

19. Ruotger, *Vita Brun.*, chapter 20, LB, p. 206:

> . . . hoc est, quod in acerbis meis rebus me maxime consolatur, cum video per Dei omnipotentis gratiam nostro imperio regale sacerdotium accessisse. In te namque et sacerdotalis religio et regia pollet fortitudo. . . . Nec abesse tibi iam dudum perpendi ipsam ingenuarum arcium matrem et vere virtutem philosophie, que te ad hanc modestiam magnitudinemque animi erudivit.

20. Cicero, *Tusculan Disputations*, 1.26.64: "philosophia vero, omnium mater artium . . . nos primum ad illorum [deorum] cultum . . . tum ad modestiam magnitudinemque animi erudivit. . . ." Striking in Ruotger's borrowing is the omission: Cicero named as Philosophy's first lesson the worship of the gods.

21. See *Origins of Courtliness*, pp. 35–36.

22. Sigebert names a number of eminent bishops from Brun's school, hand picked by Brun himself: "It is easy to know what sort of men they were, since they were colleagues of our Dietrich, rendered illustrious by the teaching of Brun, in whose judgment they merited advancement to the bishopric" (". . . qui quales fuerint, vel hinc potest sciri, quia collegae fuerunt huius nostri Deoderici, ex disciplina Brunonis incliti, cuius etiam iudicio ad gradum pontificatus meruerunt provehi" — *Vita Deod.*, chapter 7, p. 467, ll. 46–48). Sigebert's praise of Ottonian times and the "highly distinguished pastors" (*pastores clarissimi*) is worth citing. He breaks into praise of the "happy times of Otto" (*felicia tempora Ottonis* — l. 36); the "famous prelates and wise men" taught and picked by Brun "reformed the republic, restored the peace to the churches, recreated the *honestas religionis*." It was the fulfillment of the possibilities of philosophers and kings ruling the republic in common (ll. 37ff.).

23. See the study by James H. Forse, "Bruno of Cologne and the Networking of the Episcopate in Tenth-Century Germany," pp. 267–68: ". . . the pontificates of forty-seven bishops and archbishops fall within the period of Bruno's career. *Forty-five* of them can be linked directly or indirectly with Bruno's family, tutelage, patronage, or activities as chancellor, archbishop of Cologne, duke of Lorraine, or regent."

24. Cf. Fleckenstein, "Königshof und Bischofsschule."

25. Fleckenstein, *Die Hofkapelle der deutschen Könige*, 2: 50–51.

26. See Herbert Zielinski, *Der Reichsepiskopat in spätottonischer und salischer Zeit (1002–1125)*, p. 99. He shows that of 75 bishops between 1002 and 1125 whose place of study is known, 13 studied in monasteries and 58 in cathedral schools.

27. For references and bibliography on individual schools, see Jaeger, "Cathedral Schools and Humanist Learning," p. 572, n. 12, and ff.

28. The poem is by Abbot Gerhard of Seeon. MGH Poet. Lat., 5, p. 398 (ll. 33–34): "Non minus ista Sepher Cariath [cf. Joshua 15: 15: Sepher Cariath = civitas litterarum] cluit arte scienter, / Inferior Stoicis nequaquam, maior Athenis."

29. See Lèsne, *Les écoles de la fin du VIIIe siècle* and Specht, *Geschichte des Unterrichtswesens in Deutschland*, on individual schools. The French schools following Gerbert and Fulbert: Arles, Tours, Angers, Orléans, Toulouse, Tournai, Troyes. Bayeux developed a school from the mid-eleventh century under the influence of Liège (Lèsne, p. 109). The illustrious Carolingian schools follow a consistent pattern: they maintain their traditions until the mid- or late tenth century, then disappear from view until the late eleventh or twelfth: Lyon (Lèsne, pp. 80–81); Autun (pp. 94–95); Auxerre (pp. 96–97); Soissons, (pp. 310–311). For Tours two masters are mentioned between 909 and the advent of Berengar ca. 1040; but Berengar, a student of Fulbert, had his early education at Tours, so the school was alive, if ill-documented and no longer illustrious, in the early eleventh century (Lèsne, pp. 137ff.). Clearly the Carolingian impulses subsided by the late tenth century, and the new education exerted its influence through Liège, Rheims, and Chartres in the course of the eleventh.

30. Otloh, *Vita Wolfkangi*, chapter 7, MGH SS 4, p. 529, ll. 3–4: "Juvenes . . . non solum liberalibus exercebat doctrinis, verum etiam moralibus informabat disciplinis."

31. Anselm of Liège, *Gesta ep. Leod.*, chapter 40, MGH SS 7, p. 210, ll. 30ff.: "In quarum [scolarum] studio tam morum quam litterarum vigilantissime exercuit disciplinam, eos qui pro his moribus essent, licet minus litteratos, longe his anteponens, quibus, ut in plerisque solet, scientia litterarum vanae gloriae peperisset stulticiam."

32. Bernward at school, *Vita Bernwardi*, chapter 1, LB, p. 274: ". . . literis imbuendus, moribus etiam instituendus deputatur." And as tutor to Otto III, chapter 2, p. 278, he gained the empress's favor so greatly, ". . . ut domnum regem fidei illius literis imbuendum moribusque instituendum consensu cunctorum procerum commendaret."

33. *Die ältere Wormser Briefsammlung*, ed. Bulst, MGH Briefe der deutschen Kaiserzeit 3, p. 127, ll. 264–65: "Istinc si discis, statim sensu resipiscis, / Recte vivendi potans et dogma loquendi." See the discussion, below Chapter 3.

34. *Briefsammlungen der Zeit Heinrichs IV.*, pp. 238–39:

Cum me negociosissimi magistratus cura implicueris, urgues tamen et instas . . . ut novam operam, non tam arduam et difficilem quam plane impossibilem suscipiam. . . . Equidem si excubie nostre solis adolescentum ingeniis liberali erudicione excolendis assiderent, quod unicum curriculum pleraque veterum studia sibi vindicarunt, laboris mala fame nominisque momenta mihi pensarent. Verum nunc qui prefecti scolarum habentur, gemina pro ecclesiastico usu functione multantur: primas enim partes formandis moribus impendunt, secundas vero litterarum doctrine insumunt.

Erdmann takes the letter to be the dedication to Meinhard's work *De fide*. See Erdmann's *Studien zur Briefliteratur Deutschlands im elften Jahrhundert*, p. 23.

35. *Gozechini epistola ad Walcherum*, ed. Huygens, p. 35, ll. 721–26: ". . . precisis spebus et abdicatis laboribus, studiis valefecerunt et sapienti consilio usi in theologiae otium concesserunt."

36. *Briefsammlungen, Weitere Briefe Meinhards*, epist. 19, ed. Erdmann, p. 213:

Verum inter alia gravia et luctuosa hunc dolorem quasi capitalem deplorastis studium lumenque litterarum penitus apud vos occidisse nec minus disciplinam moralem egregie apud vos antiquitus institutam situ quodam et negligentia nunc dissolutam iam iamque obisse, immo sepultam esse. Quas ob res adolescentem vestrum officine nostre erudiendum informandumque tradidistis, ut duo pignora vestra, mores dico litterasque [sic], per eum vobis . . . resuscitentur."

37. *Udalrici codex*, nr. 172, Bibl. rer. germ., ed. Jaffé, vol. V. Monumenta Bambergensia, p. 305: "in litterarum sciencia, in rerum agendarum pericia, in honestate morum, in gratia discretionum."

Chapter 3: The New Education Institutionalized

1. Zielinski, *Reichsepiskopat*, p. 84.
2. *Vita Wolfhelmi*, chapter 4, MGH SS 12, p. 183, ll. 17–28:

. . . quicquid poeta cecinit, orator facundus disseruit, philosophus excogitavit, quadam penna altioris sensus penetravit. . . . Tanta autem gravitas, tanta morum illi inerat maturitas, ut palam cunctis daretur intelligi, vas illum electionis exsistere. . . . Ineptas etiam fabulas iuvenumque lasciviam declinabat, venenatas adulantium linguas abhorrebat; vaniloquium, levitatem oculorum, totiusque motus corporis anchora cohibebat gravitatis. Considerans itaque et perpendens magister scholarum hunc illius in omnium virtutum disciplinis profectum, gaudebat doctrinae illi impendisse studium, quem perfectionis cernebat attigisse fastigium.

3. On Eraclius and the rise of Liège's schools, see Cora Lutz, *Schoolmasters of the Tenth Century*, p. 21; Jean-Louis Kupper, *Liège et l'église impériale*, pp. 375ff.; *DGQ*, 1.132–33; John van Engen, *Rupert of Deutz*, pp. 16ff, 42ff.

4. Anselm, *Gesta ep. Leod.*, chapter 24, MGH SS 7, p. 201, ll. 26–27: "Everacrus . . . 45. nobis constitutus est episcopus, *annuente Brunone archiepiscopo*, eodemque ut aiunt duce." Cf. Folcuin, *Gesta abb. Lob.*, chapter 27, MGH SS 4, p. 69, ll. 7–8: ". . . Evracrus ex Bonna decanus, *Brunone concedente*, efficitur episcopus, vir inge-

nuarum artium litteratus" (emphasis added). Kupper cautions against accepting the twelfth-century biographer's claim of his Saxon origins uncritically (*Liège et l'église impériale*, p. 115 & n. 26).

5. Anselm, *Gesta ep. Leod.*, chapter 24, MGH SS 7, p. 201, ll. 30ff.:

> Hic cum eleganti morum probitate, liberali adprime honestatis scientia, cum iam pridem aput illius temporis nostrates funditus liberale studium cum memoria absolvisset, ille scolas per claustra stabilire curavit.

Does the comment "iam pridem aput . . . nostrates . . . liberale studium . . . absolvisset" show that "letters" and the arts were taught in Liège prior to Eraclius, hence implying that his innovation is the introduction of *elegans morum probitas* and *honestatis scientia*? The author of the *Chronicon sancti Laurentii Leodiensis* claims that until Eraclius, Liège had no tradition of learning:

> Totam Leodiensem ecclesiam, immo totam provinciam, nullis hactenus studiis illustratam, ad studium coaptavit, scholas constituit, per itos quaquaversum clericos collegit, eosque magistros instituens sua ope liberaliter pavit. (chapter 1, MGH SS 8, p. 262, ll. 41–43)

But see *DGQ* 2.658–59 & n. 76 on this source. It is hard to share Kupper's conviction that "l'enseignement dans cette terre d'Empire qu'est le pays mosan, a ses sources vives en France et notamment dans les écoles de Reims et de Chartres" (*Liège et l'église impériale*, p. 377). Both bishops credited with founding the schools (Everacrus and Notker) were Germans, both were closely associated with Brun of Cologne and the imperial court, and their influence in Cologne precedes the blossoming of the Rheims school under Gerbert. The school of Chartres is unknown prior to Fulbert. The sources suggest (though not reliably) some "liberal learning" in Liège prior to Everacrus, but make it clear that he and Notker imported *honestas*, *probitas*, and *elegantia* as the foundation of the schools. There is no historical justification for Kupper's claim of a French tradition.

6. The passage contains a few puzzles. What does the phrase "liberal learning of virtue" (*liberali honestatis scientia*) mean? It suggests the assimilation of *honestas* to the arts. The formulation *liberale studium cum memoria* is unique.

7. Cf. Sylvain Balau, *Les sources de l'histoire de Liège au moyen âge*, p. 118: "Notger est le véritable créateur de la ville et de la principauté de Liège." The standard work on Notker is Godefroid Kurth, *Notger de Liège et la civilisation au Xe siècle*.

8. *Vita Notgeri*, ed. Kurth in *Notger de Liège et la civilisation au Xe siècle*, 2: 10:

> A litterali ergo scientia morum quoque ornamenta accepit et in utraque disciplina laudabiliter promotus, de scolis ad palatium transferri meruit. Ibi inter prudentes et bonos viros, qui eo tempore soli regalibus obsequiis aderant, consilii et operationis virtute claruit, adeo ut honestatis sue prerogativa de palatio ad regimen Leodiensis ecclesie votis et petitione cleri et populi et favore principis transierit. Tunc demum tamquam competentem materiam in qua virtus clarissimi viri operaretur adeptus spem de se habitam ad rem perduxit.

9. Anselm, *Gesta ep. Leod.*, chapter 25, MGH SS 7, p. 203, ll. 1–2: ". . . Notkerus, genere quidem Alamannus, sed admodum omni morum elegantia insignitus . . ." The suggestion in "quidem . . . sed" that Anselm would not expect this quality of a German, at least of an *Alamannus*, indicates a source of tensions in Liège that surface in the context of Wazo's conflict with Henry III's court. More on this issue in Chapter 7.

10. The isolated statement of the Hildesheim annalist for the year 1008 that Notker was provost at St. Gall cannot be confirmed and has been rejected. *Annal. Hildesh. cont.*, MGH SS 3, p. 92, l. 25. Balau argues that the biographer's comment that Notker progressed "from the schools to the palace" contradicts the Hildesheim chronicle, and should be given priority. Balau, *Les sources*, p. 118. See also Zielinski, *Reichsepiskopat*, p. 78, n. 25.

11. Anselm, *Gesta ep. Leod.*, chapter 30, MGH SS 7, p. 206, l. 27:

> Cuius exemplis inbutus et doctrinis instructus, adiectis insuper propriis ex divino munere virtutibus, nostris quoque magistrum repraesentare studuit temporibus.

12. *Gesta ep. Leod.*, chapter 68, MGH SS 7, p. 230, ll. 50–51:

> Miserum me, vix fateri audeo, cum me indignissimum et confusione plenum dulcissimo illo suo excellentis scientiae et elegantis ingenii sale condito dignaretur alloquio.

13. *Gesta ep. Leod.*, chapter 40, MGH SS 7, p. 210–11, ll. 29 ff.:

> In quarum studio tam morum quam litterarum vigilantissime exercuit disciplinam, eos qui pro his moribus essent, licet minus litteratos, longe his anteponens, quibus, ut in plerisque solet, scientia litterarum vanae gloriae peperisset stulticiam . . . Discedebant alii litteris, moribus et religione instructi . . .

On Wazo see Albert Bittner, *Wazo und die Schulen von Lüttich*.

14. *Gesta ep. Leod.*, chapter 28, MGH SS 7, p. 205, ll. 16–17:

> . . . o si nostris temporibus tam aurea possent revocari secula, ut in capellis tam imperatoris quam episcoporum nil magis appeteretur quam cum litterarum studio morum disciplina!

15. On the little that can be gleaned of Goswin as a personality see R. B. C. Huygens in the introduction to his edition of the letter *Gozechini epistola*, pp. 3–6.

16. Goswin, *Gozechini epistola*, chapter VI, ed. Huygens, p. 14, ll. 98–100: ". . . filios suos . . . ad omne quod civile sit et moribus conducat informat et instruit." See below, Appendix B, p. 352.

17. On Gerbert as school master, see Oscar Darlington, "Gerbert the Teacher"; John R. Williams, "The Cathedral School of Rheims in the Eleventh Century"; Uta Lindgren, *Gerbert von Aurillac und das Quadrivium: Untersuchungen*

zur Bildung im Zeitalter der Ottonen; Hélène Gasc, "Gerbert et la pédagogie des arts libéraux à la fin du dixième siècle."

18. The much-discussed passage in Richer's *Histoire de France* needs to be read critically in the light of its conservatism. It is a throwback to Carolingian educational values. It stresses the liberal arts and the zeal, energy and sweat expended in the pursuit of them. Cf. Richer, *Histoire de France*, chapters 46–54, ed. & trans. Robert Latouche, 2: 54 ff.: Aristotle on interpretation and Boethius on rhetoric are studied by labor (chapter 47, p. 56). "Quantus sudor expensus sit" is Richer's perspective on mathematics (chapter 49, p. 56); on geometry Gerbert expended no less labor than on astronomy (chapter 54, p. 62). This picture of an athlete in the liberal arts is the Carolingian muscular approach to studies, though with no mention of religion. Richer's account now must be read against the background of Charles Radding's study, "The Geography of Learning in Early Eleventh-Century Europe: Lanfranc of Bec and Berengar of Tours Revisited."

19. *Die Briefsammlung Gerberts*, ed. Weigle, epist., 186, p. 222.

20. Epist. 187, ed. Weigle, p. 224: ". . . nisi moralis philosophie gravitatem amplecteremini, non ita verbis vestris *custos omnium virtutum* impressa esset humilitas."

21. Epist. 158, ed. Weigle, p. 187: ". . . in otio et negotio praeceptorum M. Tullii diligens fui executor."

22. Epist. 44, ed. Weigle, p. 73: "Cumque ratio morum dicendique ratio a philosophia non separentur, cum studio bene vivendi semper coniuncxi studium bene dicendi."

23. This context also evident in the fact that Robert the Pious was Gerbert's pupil. Robert's biographer, Helgaud, says that Robert was sent to Gerbert (after 983) by his mother, Adelaide, to introduce him to the knowledge of the liberal arts, and to make him agreeable to the lord through the practice of the holy virtues (*Vita Roberti*, ed. Bautier, p. 65). Cited in Riché, "Les conditions de la production littéraire: maîtres et écoles," p. 419 and n. 37.

24. Edition by Ernst Dümmler, "Gedichte aus Frankreich." On the poem and its subject see Manitius, *Geschichte der lateinischen Literatur*, 2: 506–9; F. M. Warren, "Constantine of Fleury, 985–1014"; Fritz Weigle, "Studien zur Überlieferung der Briefsammlung Gerberts von Reims"; K. F. Werner, "Zur Überlieferung der Briefe Gerberts von Aurillac," pp. 99–100, 113–18.

25. I try to approximate the unintelligibility of the original here, *psalmatio regum* (*hapax legomenon*, as far as I could determine). Either he sings the praises of kings or they sing his.

26. ll. 48–51:

Denique si verum constat, quod corporis actus
Signum sit mentis, animus quoque panditur actu,
Corporis es nostro tali tunc dignus honore
Iudicio, qualem suffit tibi fama per orbem.

27. Gerbert praises him as "nobilis scolasticus, adprime eruditus michique in amicicia coniunctissimus" (epist. 92, ed. Weigle, p. 122). Gerbert dedicated no

fewer than five of his writings to Constantine; cf. Werner, "Zur Überlieferung der Briefe Gerberts," p. 113.

28. The second poem of the three edited by Dümmler, clearly written in the same community, if not by the same monk, places a similar stress on the composition of poetry with classical inspiration: the author is grateful to his adressee, a scholar named Bovo, who has sung odes of praise to him ("Gedichte aus Frankreich," ed. Dümmler, p. 228, l. 19); *physis, prudentia, poesis,* and *sophia* are his school masters (22, 23, 28); Bovo is "a constant friend of the Pieride muses, since the Pierides have made you into a learned poet" (*doctum poetam* — 36ff.). The poet himself complains that he has never bathed his lips in the well of Pegasus (*fons caballinus*) nor has he received the dreams of Parnassus, snoring in his sleep (cf. 44ff.).

29. See below, Chapter 4. Now the indispensable guide to the subject is McGuire, *Friendship and Community.*

30. McGuire, *Friendship,* pp. 146–56.

31. See Williams, "Cathedral School of Rheims," p. 662; Georges Duby, *The Three Orders,* pp. 21–43.

32. *Gesta ep. Camerac.,* 3.1, MGH SS 7, p. 465, ll. 32–33: "Sub cuius liberali eruditione et normam aecclesiasticae religionis et mundanae disciplinam satis viderat honestatis."

33. Hugh of Flavigny, *Chronicon,* MGH SS 8, p. 368, ll. 40–44:

Quae aecclesia tanto tunc vernabat religionis decore, tot personarum nobilium et religiosarum, quas ipsa in se educaverat, sibi adplaudebat honesta numerositate et decenti honestate, ut religione ipsa praemineret omnibus aecclesiis Belgicae, formaque esset omnibus honeste vivendi recteque conversandi in castitate, in scientia, in disciplina, in correptione morum, in exibitione bonorum operum.

34. *Vita Richardi,* Chapter 2, MGH SS 11, p. 281, ll. 41ff.:

. . . in puerilibus annis ecclesiae beatae virginis Mariae Remis sacris litteris erudiendus et canonica regula instituendus traditus fuit; ubi Deo se gubernante secundum incrementa corporis morum et doctrinae proficiens incrementis, in brevi ad summum apicem caelicae doctrinae pertingere studuit. Deinde per singulos sacrae pro motionis gradus conscendens . . . in ordinibus sacris, sic moribus dignis sese conspicabilem reddidit. Unde factum est, ut tam scientiae gratia quam vitae et morum elegantia, praecentoris et decani in ipsa ecclesia sortiretur officia.

35. *The Letters and Poems of Fulbert of Chartres,* ed. and trans. Frederick Behrends, p. 136 (epist. 76): "[Hubertus] qui de patria sua causa discendae honestatis egressus . . . Nunc vero eadem causa permotus, monasterium beati Remigii . . . visitare disposuit." Behrends translates the phrase "for the sake of acquiring a sound education," but this obscures the intent. Clerval's rendering also does not render the term: ". . . qui a quitté son pays pour venir étudier les lettres chez nous" (Clerval, *Les écoles de Chartres,* p. 99).

36. If there is anything to credit in the view of the author of the *Gesta episcoporum cameracensium*, then the school of Rheims under Ebalus was a bad choice on any score. He calls Ebalus "a man of no discipline whatsoever, who knew nothing of letters apart from a few syllogistic arguments, by which he was wont to dupe ignorant and simple-minded men" (*Gesta*, 3: 25, MGH SS 7, p. 473, ll. 46–47). But there was probably not much worth crediting. As a check to this criticism see Williams, "Cathedral School of Rheims," p. 663, n. 13.

37. *Briefsammlungen der Zeit Heinrichs IV., Hannoversche Briefsammlung*, epist. 65, ed. Erdmann, pp. 112–13:

Neque enim convictu vestro, quo apud vos humanissime acceptus sum, quicquam potest esse liberalius neque studio illo, tametsi mea ingenii malignitas me uberiorem eius fructum defraudavit, studio inquam illo nihil esse potest vel ad utilitatem efficacius vel ad elegantiam accuratius vel ad sublimitatem exquisitius.

On the identification of the recipient with Hermann of Rheims, see Erdmann, *Studien zur Briefliteratur*, pp. 38–39.

38. See Williams, "Cathedral School of Rheims," pp. 665–66.

39. PL 152, 602, Epitaph no. 173.

40. Williams, "Manasses I" and "Godfrey of Rheims."

41. *Baldricus Burgulianus Carmina*, ed. Hilbert, nr. 99, pp. 112–18 (ed. Abrahams, *Les oeuvres poétiques de Baudri*, nr. 161, p. 151–57).

42. *Vita Angelranni*, chapter 3, PL 141, 1406A.

43. The critical edition of Adelman's poem by J. Havet is printed by Clerval, *Les écoles de Chartres*, pp. 59–61. Here, p. 59:

Eheu! quanta dignitate moralis industriae,
Quanta rerum gravitate, verborum dulcedine,
Explicabat altioris archana scientiae!

44. Ibid., p. 60: "Is magistrum referebat vultu, voce, moribus."

45. Fulbert, epist. 95, ed. Behrends, pp. 172–75.

46. Cf. the letters from Chartres edited by Lucien Merlet, "Lettres d'Ive de Chartres et d'autres personnages de son temps."

47. Edition and analysis in Peter Vossen, *Der Libellus Scolasticus des Walther von Speyer: Ein Schulbericht aus dem Jahre 984*; another edition by Karl Strecker in MGH Poet. Lat. 5, 1:1–26.

48. Specht, *Geschichte des Unterrichtswesens in Deutschland*, pp. 322, 334; DGQ 1. 213.

49. Wilhelm Wattenbach provides an introduction and edition of *Colores rhetorici* in his "Magister Onulf von Speier." The entire work skillfully combines moral and rhetorical lessons. The prologue fragment begins, ". . . arti rhetoricae: morum elegantiam, compositionem habitus, vitae dignitatem amplectere" (p. 369). It probably completes the thought, "The art of rhetoric is not confined to the framing of

speeches, but includes the cultivation of elegant manners, composed bearing and dignity of conduct." See below, Chapter 5, pp. ***

50. *Vita Bennonis II.*, Chapter 4, LB, p. 378:

. . . plurima eodem tempore de toto regno illuc undique clericorum turba concurreret, eo quod circumquaque flagrans imperiale studium studium etiam litterarum inibi ardentissimum florere fecisset . . .

51. See Zielinski, *Reichsepiskopat*, p. 87, arguing against F. Weber, *Die Domschule von Speyer im Mittelalter*, p. 65, who calls it a "Diplomatenschule."

52. See Zielinski, *Reichsepiskopat*, pp. 84–86. See Carl Erdmann, "Die Bamberger Domschule im Investiturstreit"; and Claudia Märtl, "Die Bamberger Schulen: Ein Bildungszentrum des Salierreiches."

53. *Briefsammlungen der Zeit Heinrichs IV., Weitere Briefe Meinhards*, epist. 36, ed. Erdmann, pp. 234–35: ". . . ut in officina scolari tam moribus quam disciplina excoctus . . . intra nostre ecclesie ornamenta resplendeat."

54. See *Origins of Courtliness*, pp. 49–53.

55. *Udalrici codex*, epist. 114, Bibl. rer. Germ., ed. Jaffé, 5: p. 226:

Quia morum tuorum qualitatem, vitae conversationem, liberalium studiorum maturitatem, cum adhuc nobiscum conversareris, exper imento didicimus, in te unanimiter intendimus, utque unus ex nobis fias invitamus.

56. Ibid., epist. 172, p. 305: "Comperi enim, eum esse filium Babenbergensis ecclesiae in litterarum scientia, in rerum agendarum pericia, in honestate morum, in gratia discretionum."

57. See *DGQ*, 1.7–8. Also on Stefan, see L. F. Benedetto, "Stephanus grammaticus da Novara"; Fleckenstein, "Königshof und Bischofsschule," pp. 53–54.

58. Otloh of St. Emmeram, *Vita Wolfkangi*, chapters 4, 5, MGH SS 4, p. 528.

59. On Otloh in Würzburg, see Manitius, *Geschichte*, 2:83–84, 86.

60. MGH Poetae, 5. 555: "Ast Popo antistes hanc me perduxit in urbem, / Qua sophie studiis dogmata crebra dedi."

61. On the Würzburg school, see Rudolf Blank, *Weltdarstellung und Weltbild in Würzburg und Bamberg*, pp. 47–75; J. Kempf, *Zur Kulturgeschichte Frankens während der sächsischen und salischen Kaiser. Mit einem Excurs: Über einen Schulstreit zwischen Würzburg und Worms im 11. Jahrhundert*; Zielinski, *Reichsepiskopat*, pp. 86–87.

62. Zielinski takes "Gaul" to mean Lorraine. *Reichsepiskopat*, p. 81, n. 43.

63. Anonymus Haserensis, *De episcopis Eichstetensibus*, chapter 28, MGH SS 7, p. 261.

64. A "Bernolf" appears as signatory on a document from the Würzburg cathedral from 1057. See Georg Schepss, "Zu Froumunds Briefcodex und zu Ruodlieb," p. 427 & n. 2.

65. The most recent edition is in *Die ältere Wormser Briefsammlung*, ed. Walther Bulst, pp. 119–127 (references here are to this edition); also *Die Tegernseer Briefsammlung*, ed. Karl Strecker, pp. 125–134. The earlier ascription to Froumund

of Tegernsee is not tenable. For commentary see Georg Schepss, "Zu Froumunds Briefcodex und zu Ruodlieb"; Elisabeth Häfner, *Die Wormser Briefsammlung des 11. Jahrhunderts*; and Kempf, *Zur Kulturgeschichte Frankens* (n. 61 above).

66. *Wormser Briefsammlung*, epist. 15, p. 32: ". . . litem, quam cum Herbipolensibus exercitii causa habuimus."

67. Würzburg poem ll. 1–82, *Wormser Briefsammlung*, pp. 119–21.

68. l. 25: *scripture studium*. On the translation see below, n. 69.

69. Cf. l. 160, where *scriptura* refers clearly to the Worms poem to which the Würzburgers are responding: ". . . Quod cor non celat, quoniam scriptura revelat / Versibus oblatis mendacibus inmodulatis." Cf. also the usage in *Wormser Briefsammlung*, epist. 19, p. 36, l. 10: "De scriptura [= the outer shell, the written form] non erit curandum, cum magis ad sententie nucleum . . . sit respiciendum." And a poem in the *Tegernseer Briefsammlung*, ed. Strecker, nr. XLI, p. 122: "Me bene scribentem faciat, precor omnipotentiam. / . . . / Artem scripture sectandi sit tibi cure."

70. At Worms they pursue *spiritualia monstra* (206); they revive the gods of the underworld to their peril, since they lack the lyre of Orpheus to soften their anger (212ff.); they revive the cult of iniquitous gods (219) and of black demons (225).

71. The last line is confusing. See Strecker's (p. 130) and Bulst's (p. 123) puzzlement. But the sense is fairly clear: Many who can't end their disputes will marvel at the model of conciliatory restraint and loving friendship these two friends provide.

72. Anyone who wrestles his way through the Würzburg poem with its confused grammar and forced rhymes will recognize this as a case of the pot calling the kettle black.

73. See the study of this virtue in *Origins of Courtliness*, pp. 36–42, 149–50.

74. Cf. l. 102: "Quatinus in pena sis propter tale poema."

75. The story of Wolfgang of Regensburg correcting the teaching of Stefan of Novara has to appear somewhat suspect against this background. Such contradiction could not have gone without retribution. Otloh tells of Stefan's failed attempts at revenge, which also do not harmonize with the picture of utopian peace and sanctions on the breach of it painted in the Würzburg poem. Wolfgang left Würzburg for Trier. But Otloh is a monk suspicious of worldly learning. He is telling a story of an embarrassment dealt to a foreign school master at a time when the north was experiencing an infestation of dialectics, in part imported from Italy. Furthermore Würzburg was not Otloh's favorite place. This casts doubt on his story. It was more possible to spite a school master in 1070 than 100 years earlier.

76. *Wormser Briefsammlung*, epist. 25, pp. 46–47.

77. They were not all invulnerable. See Ludwig Gompf, " 'Querela magistri Treverensis': Das sogenannte 'Carmen Winrici.'" (An Italian teacher at the Trier cathedral school complains of being given humiliating duties in the kitchen in a satirical poem written ca. 1042.) Wazo of Liège resigned his teaching position and was forced out of Liège altogether because of conflict with the provost. The particular constellation at Würzburg must have made the situation sensitive: the distinguished head of the school is attacked by students of a competing school.

78. Some of the best known descriptions of monastic education in the period

refer only to *litterae*. Abbo of Fleury was sent to school *litteris imbuendus* (PL 139, 389A). At Ramsey Abbo is said to have taught *litterarum scientia*, and in a long description of his teaching, no mention is made in any form of *mores* (ibid., 392B). Otloh of St. Emmeram was sent to school *pro litteris discendis* (PL 146, 38B); Cf. ibid., 56D: " . . . scholari disciplinae traditus . . . litterasque celeritus didicissem"; ibid., 357C: " . . . ad monast. Herveldense scribendi causa transmissus fuissem." A good example of a monastic career is that of Abbot Gervinus of St. Riquier. Hariulf tells that as a young man he went to Rheims to study letters (*litterarum studiis imbuendus*), where he managed with God's help to resist the seductive influence of the poets during his grammar studies. Although he was a canon at the cathedral of Rheims, his study of *mores* is not mentioned. However, when he seeks admission to the community of St. Vannes under Abbot Richard, he is introduced to the Rule of St. Benedict. The subjection to the rule is separable in the monastery from the discipline of "beautiful" or "elegant" manners, but not in cathedral communities. Some sifting on the biographer's part will have occurred here, since he was interested in Gervinus' mastering of the rule at St. Vannes and indifferent to any study of *mores* at Rheims. Hariulf, *Chronique de l'Abbaye de Saint-Riquier*, 4.13–14, pp. 207–10.

Chapter 4: Cultus Virtutum

1. The discipline of ethics in the earlier Middle Ages is normally approached through the texts read: Cicero's *De officiis* and the adaptation of this work by Ambrose; the Distichs of Cato, Seneca's letters, and medieval works like the *Moralium dogma philosophorum*. The studies of Philippe Delhaye are the most illuminating works in this direction, esp. "L'enseignement de la philosophie morale au XIIe siècle"; "Grammatica et ethica au XIIe siècle"; "La place de l'éthique parmi les classifications scientifiques au XIIe siècle."

2. On rehearsal of gestures and words at St. Victor of Paris, see below, Chapter 9, pp. 258ff.

3. Some comments on charismatic pedagogy in the early Middle Ages in Illmer, *Formen der Erziehung und Wissensvermittlung*, p. 56ff. See also his index under "Charisma."

4. Henry IV Part 2, II, iii, 18–33.

5. See Werner Jaeger, *Paideia: The Ideals of Greek Culture*, passim, on the transition from charismatic to textual pedagogy, 2: 13ff.; Eric Havelock, *Preface to Plato*.

6. Seneca, *Epist. ad Lucilium*, 6, 5: "Plus . . . tibi et viva vox et convictus quam oratio proderit. . . . longum iter est per praecepta, breve et efficax per exempla."

7. *Epist. ad Luc.*, 52, 8–9: "Illum elige adiutorem quem magis admireris, cum videris, quam cum audieris."

8. Cited in Georges Pire, *Stoicisme et pédagogie de Zénon à Marc-Aurèle, de Sénèque à Montaigne et à J.-J. Rousseau*, p. 24, with ref. to von Arnim, *Stoicorum veterum fragmenta* (Leipzig, 1921), 1: Z233.

9. *Epist. ad Luc.*, 11, 8: [quoting Epicurus] "'Aliquis vir bonus nobis dili-

gendus est et semper ante oculos habendus, ut sic tamquam illo spectante vivamus et omnia tamquam illo vidente faciamus." Cf. Ep. 25, 5.

10. Cicero, *De oratore*, II, 90.

11. See Illmer, *Erziehung*; Jean Leclerq, "Pédagogie et formation spirituelle du VIe au IXe siècle"; Peter Brown, "The Saint as Exemplar in Late Antiquity"; Joseph McCarthy, "Clement of Alexandria and the Foundations of Christian Educational Theory."

12. *De off. min.*, 2.20, PL 16, 137B. The passage is quoted by Manegold of Lautenbach in his Epistola ad Gebehardum chapter 9, MGH Libelli de lite 1: 327–28.

13. Luke 6: 40, "Every [disciple] that is perfect shall be as his master"; Ambrose, *De off. min.*, 2.20; Posidius, *Vita Augustini*, ch. 31, PL 32, 64: "ego arbitror plus ex eo proficere potuisse, qui eum et loquentem in ecclesia praesentem audire et videre potuerunt, et eius praesertim inter homines conversationem non ignoraverunt" (cited in Illmer, *Erziehung*, p. 59). See the discussion of teacher imitation among the desert fathers in Ph. Rousseau, *Ascetics, Authority and the Church in the Age of Jerome and Cassian* (Oxford: Oxford University Press, 1978), pp. 20ff. Especially worth quoting, the praise of one holy man: "Just by remaining near him, you will gain instruction" (pp. 20–21).

14. Gregory the Great, *Moralia*, 24, 8, 16, PL 76, 295B: "Viva lectio est vita bonorum." Cf. Illmer, *Erziehung*, pp. 101ff., 136ff.; Leclerq, "Pédagogie et formation spirituelle," p. 281.

15. Alcuin, epist. 280, MGH Epistolae 4, p. 437: "Non solum verbis ammoneant iuniores suos, verum etiam bonis exemplis erudiant illos. Ergo magistri . . . sapientia doctoris fulgeat in honestate morum." Cf. Alcuin, *Vita Sancti Vedasti*, PL 101, 666Aff. Hrabanus Maurus, *De clericorum instructione*, 3. 27, PL 107, 406B: ". . . in oratoribus Christi . . . non solum sermo, imo etiam tota vita doctrina virtutum debet esse." Wolfgang Edelstein, *Eruditio und sapientia: Weltbild und Erziehung in der Karolingerzeit*, p. 69; Fleckenstein, *Bildungsreform*, pp. 27ff.; and his "Struktur des Hofes Karls des Grossen," p. 43.

16. *Libellus de Willigisi consuetudinibus*, chapter 4, MGH SS 15: 2, p. 745, ll. 31–32: "Amatores virtutis, qualiter honesta moralitate deberent vivere, docuit in re, non ore, lingua magis morum quam lingua verborum." Cf. Marbod of Rennes, *Vita Magnobodi*, PL 171, 1549D–50A: ". . . morum doctrinam etiam lingua tacens poterat, vita loquens, minoribus exhibere."

17. On Willigis's person as an ethical curriculum: he was "vitae honestissimae speculum" (p. 743, l. 35); "[from his life] possunt exempla vivendi honestissima sumere qui student honestissime vivere" (p. 744, ll. 4–5); "per assiduae lectionis honestaeque moralitatis [note the pair, letters and manners] exemplum honestissimum vitam non cessavit honestare multorum" (p. 744, ll. 42–43).

18. *Gesta ep. Virdun.*, Contin., chapter 8, MGH SS 4, p. 48, l. 5: "Vita huius spectabilis vitam multorum reddidit spectabilem."

19. Cited from Hauréau's edition in Clerval, *Les écoles de Chartres*, p. 60: "Is magistrum referebat vultu, voce, moribus."

20. *Epist. ad Walcherum*, chapter III, p. 12, ll. 47–49: ". . . cum ceteri nostrae cataceseos auditores verba magistri dictis vel scriptis nequiverint aequiperare, tu etiam

totum magistrum in te videreris transfundere." The image is of the master's words bouncing off all the others, whereas the entire master, words, gestures, body, soul and all, get transferred into Walcher. The translation, "You transformed yourself into the master," is not literal, but it gives the sense of "digesting the master whole."

21. See the fundamental study by Carolyn Walker Bynum, *Docere verbo et exemplo: An Aspect of Twelfth Century Spirituality*. See also below, Chapter 9, on the school of St. Victor at Paris.

22. *Das Moralium Dogma Philosophorum des Guillaume de Conches*, p. 26, ll. 16ff.:

> Reverentia est virtus personis gravibus vel aliqua prelatione sublimatis debite honorificationis cultum exhibens. Huius officium est imitari maiores. Optimum est enim maiorum vestigia sequi, si recta precedunt. Eligendus est autem nobis vir bonus et semper ante occulos habendus, ut sic tamquam illo spectante vivamus et omnia tamquam illo vidente faciamus.

23. *Der wälsche Gast des Thomasin von Zirclaria*, ll. 617–20: "er sol ouch haben den muot, / merke waz der beste tuot, / wan die vrumen liute sint / und suln sîn spiegel dem kint"; 627–29: "In sînem muot man stille sol / einn vrumen man erweln wol / und sol sich rihten gar nâch im"; 641–43: "Ein kint sol haben den muot / daz in dunke, swaz er tuot, / daz in sehe ein biderbe man"; 647–49: "man sol gern volgen dem man / der bezzer ist ze sehen an / denn ze hoeren."

24. *Wibaldi epistolae*, epist. 91, p. 165:

> Presentia tua tuis auditoribus disciplina sit. . . . Plus habet locus tuus quam docendi officium; nam et censoriam exhibere debes severitatem, quoniam et corrigendis moribus prefectum te esse noveris. Quae disciplina et exercitatio omnibus est subtilior et in fructu cunctis propensior.

25. Epist. 167, p. 286: "Quem si aspicias, doceris; si audias, instrueris; si sequare, perficeris." The addressee of the letter cited in the previous note, Balderich of Trier, used the turn of thought to describe Hyacinth (presumably Hyacinth Bobo, Cardinal, then Pope Celestine III, a supporter of Abelard in his confrontation with Bernard of Clairvaux at Sens in 1140): ". . . qui omnem iacinctum splendore suae virtutis vincebat . . . quem audire atque videre, honestatem discere erat" (*Vita Alberonis*, chapter 23, LB p. 596).

26. Cf. Bynum, *Docere verbo et exemplo*, p. 41: "life almost becomes a form (a more effective form) of speech."

27. The main "teacher" of a school may well not have been the *magister scholarum*. Brun of Cologne, Willigis of Mainz, and Fulbert of Chartres, for instance, were influential as teachers in their capacity as bishop. This was possible as long as personal authority carried a pedagogic charge. Goswin of Mainz articulates the distinction between those who preside through *auctoritas* and those who teach by *labor*. The latter should not stay in this occupation, "than which there is none more arduous under the sun," longer than seven years. The former are not so limited. *Epist. ad Walcherum*, chapter XXVI, p. 30, ll. 596–99: "Cuius laboris

tempus, quia nichil difficilius sub sole geritur vel quod magis operarii sui vires exhauriat, a sapientibus prefinitum est septuenne, nisi de cetero is qui preest auctoritate presideat, non labore."

28. Cf. Lèsne, *Les écoles*, pp. 511–12.

29. Helmold, *Chron. Slav.*, LXV, MGH SS 21, p. 47, ll. 8ff.: [Vicelin went to Laon to study with Ralph, Anselm's brother, where] "ad ea solum enisus est, que sobrio intellectui et moribus instruendis sufficerent."

30. Abelard, *Historia calamitatum: Texte critique avec une introduction*, p. 68. English in text from *The Letters of Abelard and Heloise*, trans. B. Radice, p. 62.

31. PL 149, 1428B: "cujusdam excellentiae gloriam venari, qualitercunque poterat, affectabat: factumque est ut pompatico incessu, sublimi prae caeteris suggestu, dignitatem magistri potius simulans quam rebus ostendens, profunda quodque inclusione inter cucullum, ac simulatione longae meditationis, et vix tandem satis desideratae diu vocis lentissimo quodam quasi plangore incautos decipiens, doctorem sese artium pene inscius profiteretur."

32. On Berengar's career as teacher, see Lèsne, *Les écoles*, 1: 121–23, 139–41; also R. W. Southern, "Lanfranc of Bec and Berengar of Tours."

33. *Wibaldi epistolae*, epist. 167, p. 277: "Discipuli magistrorum sentencias tuentur, non quia verae sunt, set quod auctores amant; scola adversus scolam debachatur, odio vel amore magistrorum." Cf. William of Conches's observation that students should love their teachers more than their parents: *Philosophia mundi*, 4.30, pp. 114–15 (in the Migne ed., 4.38, PL 172, 100A–B). And Abelard's, that students should not be duped by love of their teachers into believing that they make sense: Peter Abelard, *Carmen ad Astralabium*, p. 107, vv. 9–12: "nec tibi dilecti iures in verba magistri / nec te detineat doctor amore suo. / Fructu, non foliis pomorum quisque cibatur, / et sensus verbis anteferendus erit."

34. *Wormser Briefsammlung*, epist. 52, p. 89: "Hinc divina providentia, cum te nostre rei publice regende necessarium previdisset, ad pastoralis cure apicem perduxit, ut quod inter secreta otia didiceras, in actum publice administrationis transferres. Magistra itaque Virtutum in te elegit sedem, ut in cunctis actibus tuis illius vestigia sequi videaris." Cf. Boethius, *De cons. phil.*, I. 4.7: "Quod a te inter secreta otia didiceram, transferre in actu publicae administrationis optavi."

35. On the combining of the intellectual and civil life in the empire, see Hoffmann, "Politik und Kultur im Ottonischen Reichskirchensystem"; Zielinski, *Der Reichsepiskopat*, passim. For England, R. W. Southern, "The Place of England in the Twelfth Century Renaissance," pp. 158–80, esp. pp. 174ff. Also Beryl Smalley, *The Becket Conflict and the Schools: A Study of Intellectuals in Politics*.

36. *Briefsammlungen der Zeit Heinrichs IV., Weitere Briefe Meinhards*, epist. 1, ed. Erdmann, p. 193: "Unde hortor, ut Tusculanis tuis plurimus insideas, quibus Latina philosophia Cicerone parente nichil illustrius edidit."

37. *Tusc. Disp.*, 4.3.5–6. The turn of thought is quoted or referred to in *Regensburger rhet. Briefe*, epist. 1, p. 275; epist. 11. p. 329; epist. 12, p. 331–32; epist. 13, p. 333; epist. 16, p. 336; epist. 22, p. 348.

38. On the assimilation of *philosophia* to formation of *mores*, see the following chapter.

39. Richard of St. Victor, epist. 1, PL 196, 1225A: "Magnam de promotione vestra concepit Ecclesia nostra laetitiam, et spe non modica hilarati sunt auditores vestri, tum universi scholares animati ad amorem litterarum, et cultum virtutum, vestri laboris et successus exemplo." On the connection between studies and promotion to the bishopric, see Zielinski, *Reichsepiskopat*, pp. 110ff.

40. Jaeger, *Origins of Courtliness*, pp. 19–48; "The Courtier Bishop in Vitae from the Tenth to the Twelfth Century."

41. Lampert, *Annales* (1065), p. 99: ". . . vir preter morum gloriam et animae divicias corporis quoque bonis adprime ornatus . . . tum statura et formae elegantia ac tocius corporis integritate . . . caeteris eminens mortalibus . . ."

42. William of Malmesbury, *De gestis pontificum Anglorum* 1.6, p. 14.

43. Cicero, *De officiis* 1. 26. 90: ". . . quanto superiores simus, tanto nos geramus summissius." Cf. Ecclus. 3: 20, "quanto magnus es humilia te in omnibus." See the discussion in *Origins of Courtliness*, pp. 35–36.

44. The older *Vita Licinii* is cited from AS Boland., Feb. XIII, 678D–679A; Marbod from *Vita Licinii*, PL 171, 1495A–1496D.

45. See the discussion of *mansuetudo*, *patientia*, and *modestia* in *Origins of Courtliness*, pp. 36–42.

46. Alpert of St. Symphorian, *De ep. Mett. libellus*, MGH SS 4, p. 699, ll. 45–46: "Deodericus vero longe aliter generositate parentum et excellentia maiorum, ex innata quoque copia magna praediorum clarissimus habetur."

47. See G. M. Vogt, "Gleanings for the History of a Sentiment: Generositas virtus, non sanguis"; Karl Vossler, "Adel der Geburt und der Gesinnung bei den Romanen"; M. L. Colker, "De nobilitate animi"; Karl Heinz Borck, "Tugend, Adel und Geblüt: Thesen und Beobachtungen zur Vorstellung des Tugendadels in der deutschen Literatur des 12. und 13. Jahrhunderts"; William C. McDonald, "The 'Nobility of Soul': Uncharted Echoes of the Peraldean Tradition in Late Medieval German Literature."

48. *Vita Brun.*, chapter 3, LB p. 184: ". . . rex, pater huius magni viri"; chapter 2, p. 182: ". . . lineamentorum gratia, artium gloria et omnigena animi . . . industria."

49. Folcuin, *Gesta abb. Lobb.*, chapter 28, MGH SS 4, p. 70, l. 16: ". . . spiritus Dei donum singulare . . . veritatis et fidei."

50. "It seemed to us that his bountiful eloquence gave him a style of speech appropriate to the majesty of his person." *Vita Notgeri*, chapter 9, in Kurth, 2.14: ". . . visum est nobis, copia dicendi stilum ipsum magestati [sic] persone convenire."

51. *Briefsammlungen der Zeit Heinrichs IV.*, *Hannov. Samml.*, epist. 106, ed. Erdmann, p. 178: ". . . facile tolerabimus detrimentum nominis, modo accedat incrementum honoris et splendor persone."

52. *Vita prior.*, chapter 1, MGH SS 11, p. 170, ll. 48–50: ". . . plerosque vanae nobilitatis arroganti superbia elatiores, multimodae ingeniositatis elegantia privatim ac publice praecesserit. Nemo enim nobilis nisi quem virtus nobilitat."

53. Richer, *Historiae*, 3.67, ed. Latouche, 2: 82: "Otto . . . rem publicam strenue atque utiliter amministravit, vir magni ingenii totiusque virtutis, liberalium litterarum scientia clarus adeo . . ."

54. Benzo of Alba, *Ad Heinricum*, 4.7.3, MGH SS 11, p. 673, ll. 20–21: "Virtus est mentis dignitas, et animi nobilitas, / Quae homines mirificat, insuper et deificat."

55. Benzo, 4.12, p. 645, esp. ll. 33–36.

56. Benzo, 1.26, p. 609, ll. 34ff.

57. It is consistent with the idea of "charismatic leadership" opposing the legalistic, office-sanctioned idea of authority pressed by the church reformers. See Hayden White, "The Gregorian Ideal and Saint Bernard of Clairvaux"; also John Sommerfeldt, "Charismatic and Gregorian Leadership in the Thought of Bernard of Clairvaux"; also below, Chapter 10.

58. See also the discussion of *elegantia, suavitas, venustas, pulchritudo morum* in *Origins of Courtliness*, pp. 32–34, 128–43.

59. Alcuin had commended *mores venustos* to those who wished to learn *civiles mores* (see above, p. 33 and n. 59). The term occurs in the context of the religious life. Cf. Hugeburc, *Vita Willibaldi* (ca. 778), ch. 5, MGH SS 15, p. 102, ll. 21–25: "non solum verbis, sed morum venustatis [sic] visitando docebat et recte constitutionis formam et cenobialis vitae normam in semet ipso ostendendo prebebat."

60. Cf. *Origins of Courtliness*, pp. 32–33.

61. *Vita posterior* (ca. 1115–20), MGH SS 12, p. 254, l. 26: "delectabilium morum suavitas"; and l. 29: "recte vivendi forma."

62. *Das Leben des Bischofs Meinwerk von Paderborn*, chapter 5, p. 7: "Meinwercus autem, regia stirpe genitus, regio obsequiuo morum elegantia idoneus adiudicatur evocatusque ad palatium regius capellanus efficitur."

63. John of Salisbury, *Policraticus*, 5.1, ed. Webb, 1: 281: "Modestiam tuam noveram non appetere principatum, quem tamen semper morum elegantia mereri studuisti."

64. On the debate over this intricate question, see recently Max Kerner, "Randbemerkungen zur Institutio Traiani," in *The World of John of Salisbury*, ed. Michael Wilks (Oxford: Blackwell, 1984), 203–6. Kerner reviews the scholarship on the question.

65. Gerald of Wales, *De principis instructione* 1.1, RS 21: 8, p. 9: "Cum autem morum venustas cuilibet ad se regendum apprime in vita sit utilis et accommoda, nulli tamen adeo ut illi qui multitudinem regit est necessaria."

66. *Weitere Briefe Meinhards*, epist. 1, ed. Erdmann, pp. 192–94. See Erdmann, *Studien zur Briefliteratur*, p. 282. Erdmann's interpretation depends on the final words of the letter: ". . . sic te age, ut qui hoc convictu Coloniam Christo mediante tibi despondeas." "Make yourself the bridegroom of Cologne," "Become engaged to Cologne." For our purpose it is worth noting that the *behavior* enjoined on G. by Meinhard is the qualification for becoming the fiancé of Cologne: "sic te age, ut . . . hoc *convictu.*"

67. As E. R. Curtius suggested, privately to Erdmann. *Studien zur Brief-literatur*, p. 282.

68. On the competition for "sought after men" (*viri expetibiles*) see *Origins of Courtliness*, p. 52.

69. *Weitere Briefe Meinhards*, epist. 1, p. 193:

Sepenumero advertisti me de nobilitate in utramvis partem vel glorie vel ignominie disputantem, quam grave scilicet onus insignis maiorum industria humeris posterorum imponat, quibus vite honestas morumque observantia non tam gloriosa quam necessaria, qui etsi vigilantissime egerint, non tam laudem merentur quam vitant reprehensionem, utpote quibus in maxima fortuna minima sit licentia. Nam si a via, quam eis gloria parentum editissimo virtutis loco stravit, inde inquam si tantillum quid exorbitaverint, o mi G., in quantum precipicium fame, nominis, honorum ruituri sunt! Hec inquam vel et multa id genus et his similia . . . me audistis predicantem.

70. P. 193:

Est enim vir ille omni genere virtutis instructus, omni lepore humanitatis mirifice conditus, que in eo non solum flagrantia morum latissime redolet, sed ex ipsa oculorum hilaritate gratiosissime renidet. Atque sic in te animi ornamenta redundent, ut illa ocularis gratia relucet.

71. Peter von Moos, *Hildebert von Lavardin, 1056–1133: Humanitas an der Schwelle des höfischen Zeitalters*, is still the major study on *humanitas* in the high Middle Ages. See esp. pp. 147ff. Von Moos locates Hildebert's *humanitas* as a social and ethical virtue close to *mansuetudo*. My comments expand von Moos's and show the foundation and context of Hildebert's idea in earlier texts. See also Wolfram von den Steinen, "Humanismus um 1100," p. 208, and Eckhard Kessler, *Das Problem des frühen Humanismus: Seine philosophische Bedeutung bei Coluccio Salutati*.

72. *Tusc. disp.* 5. 55: ". . . C. Caesaris, in quo mihi videtur specimen fuisse humanitatis, salis, suavitas, leporis."

73. *De oratore* 2. 270: ". . . Socratem opinor in hac ironia dissimulantiaque longe lepore et humanitate omnibus praestitisse." Meinhard did not know *De oratore*. At least he never quotes from it.

74. See esp. Friedrich Klingner, "Humanität und Humanitas"; Wolfgang Schadewalt, "Humanitas Romana"; Karl Büchner, "Humanitas in der römischen Welt"; Heinz Haffter, "Die römische Humanitas"; Eckhard Kessler, *Das Problem des frühen Humanismus*, pp. 56–62.

75. *Weitere Briefe Meinhards*, epist. 65, pp. 112–13. Quoted above, p. 60, n. 37.

76. *Weitere Briefe Meinhards*, epist. 14, p. 206: "Quam suavi et imperioso regno caritas tua per dulcissima humanitatis tue condimenta cordi nostro dominetur, vix ullis eloquentie viribus explicetur."

77. Some comments on this sense of the word in Rolf Sprandel, *Ivo von Chartres und seine Stellung in der Kirchengeschichte*, pp. 24–28.

78. *Benedicti regula*, 53.9, ed. Hanslik, p. 124: "Legatur coram hospite lex divina, ut aedificetur. Et post haec omnis ei exhibeatur humanitas."

79. Gerbert, *De informatione episcoporum*, PL 139, 172D–173A: "Et post haec addit: Hospitalem; ut humanitatis intuitu hospitio recipiat non habentem hospitium, et egenum sine tecto in domum inducat suam . . ."

80. *Vita Radbodi* chapter 5, PL 132, 542C: "Ejusmodi studiis et officiis humanitatis et misericordiae die noctuque . . . vacabat." Cf. Otloh, *Vita Wolfkangi*, chapter 4, PL 146, 397C: ". . . omnem humanitatem, quae discendi ac peregrinandi necessitas exigit, promitteret." Anselm of Liège, *Gesta ep. Leod.*, MGH SS 7, p. 217, l. 52: "Sentiebant humanitatem eius egritudines decumbentium, labores exulum."

81. The arch-humanist John of Salisbury uses it in this sense (*Policraticus*, 8.13, ed. Webb, 2: 325): "Qui vero humanitatem exhibet hospiti et caritatem implet, nichil eorum subtrahit quae ratio permittit exponi . . . Est itaque in hospitem peregrinum omnis humanitas et sobria liberalitas exercenda."

82. *Vita Udalrici posterior* (ca. 1115–20), MGH SS 12, p. 259, ll. 40ff.: ". . . hilari vultu eum [aemulum suum] suscepit . . . Cui . . . ut filius pacis pacem obtulit in amplexu et osculo caritatis, dulci illum demulcens alloquio, omnique humanitatis refovens obsequio."

83. *Vita Prima*, 3.7, PL 185, 320A: "Et corporeas . . . necessitates piissimo miserabatur affectu; cujus tanta erat humanitas, ut non modo hominibus, sed irrationabilibus etiam animantibus . . . compateretur." Cf. ibid., 315C: "Dulcissimis enim affectibus plenum pectus ipse gerebat . . . humanissimus in affectione." In this sense, generalizing from hospitality and mercy, also *Udalrici Codex*, epist. 202, ed. Jaffé, 5:368: [A canon who left the Utrecht community returns and begs to be accepted again] ". . . cepit . . . misericordiam et humanitatem postulare." Hugh of St. Victor, *De institutione novitiorum*, PL 176, 945D: "Exhortemur . . . ad humanitatem parcos."

84. Goscelin of Canterbury, *Vita Swithuni*, PL 155, 58C: "humanitate et mansuetudine studere"; Thomas Becket, epist. 246, RS 67: 6, p. 49: [The king of France showed me] "benignissime et liberalissime . . . plurimam humanitatem." Herbert of Bosham, *Vita Thomae*, 4. 21, RS 67: 3, p. 408: "Dulcis [Francia] . . . propter eximiam gentis humanitatem et inolitam principum benignitatem; dulcissima vero propter caelitus datam regibus terrae mansuetudinem."

85. Otto of Freising, *Gesta Friderici*, 3.41, MGH SS 20, p. 439, ll. 50–51: "Princeps pro regali mansuetudine, pro humanitate naturali cives civitati . . . servare cupiens." Also Gerald of Wales, *De princ. instr.* 1. 2, p. 11: "Principalibus viris induatur humanitas in conclavi."

86. See Lothar Bornscheuer, *Miserae Regum: Untersuchungen zum Krisen- und Todesgedanken in den herrschaftstheologischen Vorstellungen der ottonisch-salischen Zeit*, pp. 131–36.

87. *De princ. instr.*, 1.5, p. 16: "Patientia Trajani . . . potissime in exemplum humanitatis et benignitatis est trahenda."

88. Gerald of Wales, *De princ. instr.*, 1.5, p. 16.

89. The classic definition of this conception is in Aulus Gellius, *Attic Nights*, 13.17. See Eugenio Garin, "Retorica e 'Studia humanitatis' nella cultura del Quattrocento." Gerald Bond finds in Baudri of Bourgueil the idea that classical literature creates or decorates *mores* ("'Iocus amoris,'" p. 190). Cf. Baudri, Carmen 130, ed. Hilbert, p. 147, vv. 1–3 (ed. Abrahams, Carmen 192, p. 194): ". . . format tibi littera mores, / Moribus es, qualis clericus esse solet; / Scilicet urbanus, alacer, iocundus, amicus." Bond's translation: "Classical letters shape your character." Also Carmen 162, ed. Hilbert, p. 242, vv. 5–6 (ed. Abrahams, Carmen 65, p. 69): "Ad decus hunc morum ditarat littera multa, / Copia quam torrens extulit ingenii." And similarly Carmen 194, ed. Hilbert, p. 259, vv. 15–17 (ed. Abrahams, Carmen 232, p. 330).

90. *Vita Bern. Tiron.* chapter 1, PL 172, 1373A: ". . . honestis et religiosis parentibus fuit oriundus, hospitalitatis ac humanitatis studia sectantibus." Parallel to

the praise of Radbod of Utrecht's kindness to paupers as among the *studia et officia humanitatis et misericordiae* (n. 80 above).

91. Thierry of Chartres, "Prologue to Heptateuchon," p. 174.

92. The word is fairly common in Thierry's works, but his usage has no ethical aspect: *humanitas* = humankind in general. See *Commentaries on Boethius by Thierry of Chartres and his School*, index.

93. William of Conches, *Glosae super Platonem: Texte critique avec introduction, notes et tables*, ed. Jeauneau, p. 65:

> commendat Osium sic: florente animo studiis humanitatis. Studium est vehe-mens et assidua animi applicatio ad aliquid agendum cum magna voluntate. Sed studia, alia sunt humanitatis ut practice, alia divinitatis ut theorice. Sed, cum iste in omnibus floreret, maxime in studiis humanitatis, quia humanus homo erat, floruit. Vel studia humanitatis dicantur omnia que ab homine sciri possunt, in quibus omnibus iste florebat.

Cf. ibid., p. 83: "Critiam scimus adprime . . . vigere . . . in omnibus studiis humanitatis id est ethica, economica, politica, vel in omnibus studiis que hominibus possunt inesse." Jeauneau elsewhere ("Deux rédactions des gloses de Guillaume de Conches sur Priscien," pp. 237–38, n. 89) discusses these glosses in their possible conceptual relatedness to the *studia humanitatis* as defined by Leonardo Bruni in his letter to Niccolo Strozzi, a *locus classicus* for the definition of humanism.

94. Wibald, epist. 331, ed. Jaffé, p. 462: "Neque enim mores nostros ita instituit et formavit illa vestra doctrix et domina, rerum divinarum et humanarum magistra et educatrix, philosophia . . . vestra industria cum omni humanitate et placiditate animi efficere curabit, ne spes pacis abrumpatur."

95. It is interesting to compare Meinhard's portrait of G's father with Cas-tiglione's of Duchess Eleanora Gonzaga, *The Book of the Courtier* 4. 3, trans. Charles Singleton, (New York: Doubleday, 1959), p. 287: ". . . if ever there were joined in a single person wisdom, grace, beauty, intelligence, discreet manners, humanity, and every other gentle quality — they are so joined in her that they form a chain that comprises and adorns her every movement, uniting all these qualities at once." Cf. Coluccio Salutati's portrait of Carlo Malatesta, *Epistolario de Coluccio Salutati*, epist. 18, ed. Francesco Novati (Rome, 1896), 3: 534–36. A strong argument for the validity of such comparisons is Aldo Scaglione's *Knights at Court: Courtliness, Chiv-alry and Courtesy from Ottonian Germany to the Italian Renaissance*.

96. For references see *Origins of Courtliness*, p. 143.

97. *Vita Brun.* chapter 8, LB, p. 190: "Nullo autem hoc egit supercilio, sed cum domestico lepore tum urbana gravitate." On the translation "courtly" for *domesticus*, see Niermeyer, *Med. Lat. Lex.*, pp. 347–48.

98. Ambrose, *De off. min.* 2.7.29, PL 16, 118B–C:

> Ac primum noverimus nihil tam utile, quam diligi: nihil tam inutile, quam non amari . . . Popularis enim et grata est omnibus bonitas, nihilque quod tam facile illabatur humanis sensibus. Et si mansuetudine morum ac facilitate, tum moderatione praecepti, et affabilitate sermonis, verborum honore, patienti

quoque sermonum vice, modestiaeque adjuvetur gratia, incredibile quantum procedit ad cumulum dilectionis.

99. Cf. Edgar N. Johnson, *The Secular Activities of the German Episcopate, 919–1024*, p. 248: "Perhaps the adjectives most commonly applied to these bishops are *affabilis* and *hilaris*."

100. *Vita Norberti*, chapter 1, LB, p. 452: ". . . forma et habilitate corporis beneficio naturae gaudens et cum scientia litterarum eloquio praeminens, morum ornatu cunctis qui eum noverant gratum se exhibebat."

101. Cf. Cicero, *De amicitia*, 9.30–31; 14.50; 14.51 and 21. On Ciceronian friendship in the "Loire circle" of poets, see Bond, "Iocus amoris," pp. 162ff.

102. See Jaeger, "L'amour des rois: Structure sociale d'une forme de sensibilité aristocratique."

103. A few examples in *Origins of Courtliness*, p. 45. See also "L'amour des rois."

104. See Brian P. McGuire, *Friendship and Community: The Monastic Experience, 350–1250*.

105. The wealth of documentation in McGuire's work makes it clear that the beginnings of a cult of monastic friendship in the late tenth and early eleventh centuries lay in the cathedral communities and worldly courts, not the monasteries. Cf. McGuire, p. 164: "The new learning of the eleventh-century cathedral school and not tenth-century reformed monasticism first articulated friendship as a conscious and important matter for men in the church." He shows the vocabulary of friendship penetrating Cluny via two channels, Fulbert and the community of Chartres, and the imperial court.

106. Cf. *Vita Brun.* chapter 2, LB p. 182–84.

107. See Edelstein, *Eruditio et sapientia*, p. 73 (Alcuin's letters); William of Conches, *Philosophia mundi* 4.30, ed. Maurach, pp. 114–15 (students should love their teachers more than their parents); also his *Glosses on Priscian* ("Deux rédactions"), ed. Jeauneau, p. 224 (the first masters, loving their pupils like fathers, composed works for them); p. 233 (the master in some sense has begotten his pupil in wisdom and in this sense confers being on him more truly than his father). John of Salisbury says (with ref. to Quintilian, *Inst. orat.*, 2.9) that the seventh key of learning is love of teacher—*Policraticus*, 7.14, ed. Webb, 2: 152: "In libro Quintiliani . . . septima discentium clavis ponitur amor docentium, quo praeceptores ut parentes amandi sunt et colendi." As the parents create the body, the teachers create the soul; pupils are glad to listen to those they love; they believe them and desire to be like them; under the impulse of loyalty and affection they are eager and glad to be among the throngs of students; eloquence cannot mature unless a spirit of harmony reigns between teachers and students. Against this kind of attitude, Wibald of Stablo's complaint about students who love their teachers and not the truth in their statements is understandable (epist. 167, ed. Jaffé, p. 277).

108. Numerous examples in the Worms letter collection (esp. epistolae 60 & 61) and the Hildesheim collection, of which McGuire makes abundant use (*Friendship and Community*, pp. 188–92). Guibert of Nogent's love for his teacher developed in spite of the man's ignorance and brutality. Cf. *De vita sua* 1.4–6, ed. Labande, pp. 26–42. Also, below, Chapter 8, pp. 226ff.

109. Adelman in "Textes latins du XIe au XIIIe siècle," ed. Huygens, p. 476, ll. 3–8: "Conlactaneum te meum vocavi propter dulcissimum illud contubernium, quod tecum adolescentulo, ipse ego maiusculus, in achademia Carnotensi sub nostro illo venerabili Socrate iocundissime duxi, cuius de convictu gloriari nobis dignius licet quam gloriabatur Plato, gratias agens naturae eo, quod in diebus Socratis sui hominem se et non pecudem peperisset."

110. *Gozechini epistola*, ed. Huygens, pp. 11–13.

111. The imagery of light and fire is not classical. If it does occur in post-classical Latin, I suspect the eleventh-century had it most directly as an appropriation from imperial forms of representation. Ralph Glaber uses the language of virtue made visible in describing the royal insignia, *Historiae* 1. 23, ed. Bulst, pp. 38–40. See Herwig Wolfram, *Splendor Imperii: Die Epiphanie von Tugend und Heil in Herrschaft und Reich*.

112. See Werner Jaeger, *Paideia*, 1.3–4 and 1.416, n. 4. Also Hermann Wankel, *Kalos kai agathos*; Walter Donlan, *The Aristocratic Ideal in Ancient Greece: Attitudes of Superiority from Homer to the End of the Fifth Century B. C.*, esp. pp. 129ff., summarizing his article, "The Origin of Kaloskagathos"; Robert Philippson, "Das Sittlich-schöne bei Panaitios."

113. *De off. min.*, 1.19, PL 16, 52–53.

114. E.g., Poeta Saxo, 5, MGH Poet. Lat. 4, 1, p. 60, vv. 211–220. See Alexandru Cizek, "Der 'Charakterismos' in der Vita Adalhardi des Radbert von Corbie," p. 188 and n. 13.

115. "Drei Gedichte," ed. Dümmler, p. 225–26, vv. 48–51: "Denique si verum constat, quod corporis actus / Signum sit mentis, animus quoque panditur actu, / Corporis es nostro tali tunc dignus honore / Iudicio, qualem suffit tibi fama per orbem."

116. Alpert, *De diversitate temporum* 1.11, MGH SS 4, p. 705, ll. 41ff.: "Sermo eius ita mediocritate et discretione temperatus, ut non comici nostri dictum: 'Ne quid nimis,' supergrederetur. Sed et hoc adnectendum, quia ex moderatione suorum verborum facile compositio et honestas eius occulti cordis ab audientibus intellegi potuit."

117. *Vita Udalrici*, chapter 2, PL 142, 1186B: "Incipiebat enim tunc inter coaevulos modeste conversari . . . ac . . . in corporis motu, gestu, incessu, foris ostendere, qualis habitus formaretur intus in mente."

118. Leo IX, Epist. et decret. pontif. 22, PL 143, 623C–D: ". . . cum episcopali officio, etiam archiepiscopalia insignia eidem Hugoni archiepiscopo per hanc paginam concedimus et confirmamus, crucem videlicet et pallium et quidquid antecessores ejus ab antecessoribus nostris constat promeruisse, ut qui pollet meritorum laudabili dignitate, tam in virtutum [emending from *virtute*] scientia quam in morum honestate, polleat etiam ornamentorum pulchritudine in omni archiepiscopalis culminis plenitudine, semper meminerit in exteriore decore interiorem decorem procurare . . . virtutem pontificatus simul cum nomine habens."

119. Lampert, *Annales* (a. 1065), ed. Holder-Egger, p. 99: ". . . vir preter morum gloriam et animae divicias corporis quoque bonis adprime ornatus . . . lingua promptus et consilio, litteris eruditus tam divinis quam humanis, tum statura et formae elegantia ac tocius corporis integritate ita caeteris eminens mortalibus."

The sentence is completed with a story of a crowd gathering around a church in Jerusalem where Gunther stopped on his crusade, which prevented his leaving until they had gotten a glimpse of his fabled beauty.

120. *Vita Wulfstani*, PL 179, 1740D: "Cumulabat pectoris gratiam speciosi tam corporis; quam licet inter virtutes non numerem, non tamen omnino excludo, quia sicut ars opificis in commodiore materia elucet, ita virtus in pulchritudine formae splendidius eminet." Second part of the sentence adapted from Ambrose, *De off. min.*, 1. 19. 83, PL 16, 52B–C.

121. Hugh of St. Victor, *De inst. nov.*, PL 176, 935C: "Integritas ergo virtutis est, quando per internam mentis custodiam ordinate reguntur membra corporis."

122. *The Letters of John of Salisbury*, epist. 34, ed. Millor, Butler, rev. Brooke, 1: 61: "Recte quidem, eo quod . . . illud [sal] Deo offertis examinato eloquii casti argento, et aureae virtutum imagines in speculo verbi et operis renident intuentibus eosque provocant, ut imitatione virtutum possint esse speculum aliorum."

123. Vincent of Beauvais, *De eruditione filiorum nobilium*, chapter 31, ed. Steiner, pp. 117–23.

124. *Vita Odilonis*, chapter 2, PL 142, 899C: "Qui considerans in eo praestantem elegantiam corporis et nobilitatem generis, magnum quiddam et divinum oculis interioribus in eo praevidens, totus in ejus amorem illabitur."

125. Chapter 4, PL 142, 900D. Cf. Ambrose, *De off. min.*, 1.18.71, PL 16, 48D–49A: "Est etiam in ipso motu, gestu, incessu tenenda verecundia. Habitus enim mentis in corporis statu cernitur. . . . Itaque vox quaedam est animi corporis motus."

126. Chapter 5, PL 142, 900D–901A:

Erat mediocris in eo statura. Vultus ipse plenus auctoritatis et gratiae; mansuetis hilaris et blandus, superbis vero et offensis, ut vix sufferri posset, terribilis. Macie validus, pallore ornatus, canitie decoratus. Oculi illius veluti quodam splendore fulgentes, intuentibus et terrori erant et admirationi. . . . Renitebat etiam in ipsius motu, gestu, incessu, species auctoritatis, pondus gravitatis tranquillitatisque vestigium.

127. Hildebert of Lavardin's description of Hugh of Cluny presiding over the baptism of the infant Henry IV in the presence of the imperial court may be relevant here (see PL 159, 864B–C), though it is not clear whose ethical language is being spoken in the passage, that of Hildebert, of Hugh, or of the German court.

128. Odo of Cluny, *Vita Geraldi*, 1. 16, PL 133, 653D. His portrait of Gerald is set in opposition to this abuse; cf. 1.12, PL 133, 650.

129. Conrad of Hirsau, *Dialogus de mundi contemptu vel amore*, ed. R. Bultot, Analecta Mediaevalia Namurcensia 19 (Louvain, 1966), pp. 62–63: ". . . nihil vero prodesse cultum exteriorem virtutum gressus mentientem. . . . Iunge utrumque, et habitum et animum, et summa voti perfectionis calculo constabit."

130. Nicholas of Clairvaux, Ep. 8, PL 196, 1603: ". . . apud vos, ubi plus est auri, plus creditur et esse meriti; ubi plus palliorum, plus morum; ubi plus epularum et vestium, ibi verior observatio mandato rum." See John van Engen, "The 'Crisis of Cenobitism' Reconsidered: Benedictine Monasticism in the Years 1050–1150," pp. 285ff. (attacks on idea of link between material and spiritual among Benedictines).

131. Walter Müller's study, *Das Problem der Seelenschönheit im Mittelalter: Eine begriffsgeschichtliche Untersuchung*, draws largely on Bernard for his treatment of the twelfth-century. This is useful as a collection of material, but not for its analysis.

132. *Super Cant. Sermo*, 85.10–11, *Sancti Bernardi Opera*, 2: 314:

In quo ergo animae decor? An forte in eo quod honestum dicitur? Hoc interim sentiamus, si melius non occurrit. De honesto autem exterior interrogetur conversatio: non quod ex ea honestum prodeat, sed per eam. . . . Siquidem claritas eius testimonium conscientiae. . . . Cum autem decoris huius claritas abundantius intima cordis repleverit, prodeat foras necesse est. . . . Porro effulgentem et veluti quibusdam suis radiis erumpentem mentis simulacrum corpus excipit, et diffundit per membra et sensus, quatenus omnis inde reluceat actio, sermo, aspectus, incessus, risus. . . . Horum et aliorum profecto artuum sensuumque motus, gestus et usus, cum apparuerit serius, purus, modestus . . . pulchritudo animae palam erit.

133. *De officiis*, 1.126: ". . . decorum illud in omnibus factis, dictis, in corporis denique motu et statu cernitur idque positum est in tribus rebus, formositate, ordine, ornatu ad actionem apto."

134. *De officiis*, 1.128–29: "status incessus, sessio accubitio, vultus oculi manuum motus teneat illud decorum. Quibus in rebus duo maxime sunt fugienda, ne quid effeminatum aut molle et ne quid durum aut rusticum sit." Of basic importance for what follow is Jean-Claude Schmitt, *La raison des gestes*.

135. *De officiis*, 1.131: "Cavendum autem est, ne aut tarditatibus utamur in ingressu mollioribus . . . aut in festinationibus suscipiamus nimias celeritates, quae cum fiunt, anhelitus moventur, vultus mutantur, ora torquentur; ex quibus magna significatio fit non adesse constantiam."

136. *De oratore*, 3.222: "Est actio quasi sermo corporis." *Orator*, 55: "Est enim actio quasi corporis quaedam eloquentia."

137. *De off. min.*, 1.18.71, PL 16, 48D–49A, quoted above, n. 125.

138. Ibid., 49C: "Est etiam gressus probabilis in quo sit species auctoritatis, gravitatisque pondus, tranquillitatis vestigium."

139. Eigil, *Vita Sturmi*, Chapter 2, p. 133; "gressu composito."

140. See Chapter 1 above and Schmitt, pp. 93ff. The only sources Schmitt cites with echoes of the classical sources are Alcuin's *De rhetorica et virtutibus* and the "mirrors of princes."

141. *Epist. syn. Karisiac.*, 12, MGH Leges 2, Capit. 2, p. 436, ll. 2–6: "Et ideo domus regis scola dicitur, id est disciplina; quia non tan tum scolastici, id est disciplinati et bene correcti sunt, sicut alii, sed potius, ipsa scola, quae interpretatur disciplina, id est correctio, dicitur quae alios habitu, incessu, verbo et actu atque totius bonitatis continentia corrigat."

142. Cf. *Rule of St. Augustine, Praeceptum*, 4.2. (*Règle de St. Augustin*, ed. Verheijen, 1: 423): "Quando proceditis, simul ambulate; cum veneritis quo itis, simul state. In incessu, in statu, in omnibus motibus vestris nihil fiat quod cuiusquam offendat aspectum." *Regula canonicorum* of Aix (816), in *Concilia Aevi Karolini*, ed. Werminghoff, chapter 123, p. 403, ll. 20–21: ". . . intus, forisque non

solum habitu et actu, sed etiam ipso incessu inreprehensibiles existant." Ibid.,
chapter 131, p. 408, ll. 4–5: [clerics should enter the church] ". . . non pompatice aut
inhoneste vel inconposite, sed cum reverentia."

143. "Drei Gedichte, ed. Dümmler, pp. 225–26, vv. 48–51: "Denique si verum
constat, quod corporis actus / Signum sit mentis, animus quoque panditur actu, /
Corporis es nostro tali tunc dignus honore / Iudicio, qualem suffit tibi fama per
orbem." See discussion above, Chapter 3, pp. 57ff.

144. Bern of Reichenau, *Vita Udalrici*, chapter 2, PL 142, 1186B: ". . . in
corporis motu, gestu, incessu, foris ostendere [incipiebat], qualis habitus formaretur intus in mente."

145. "Trois oeuvres inédites de Godefroid de Reims," ed. Boutemy. On Godfrey and these three poems see John R. Williams, "Godfrey of Rheims, A Humanist
of the Eleventh Century." Williams characterizes the poetry as marked by a "truly
pagan spirit" (p. 44). The verses translated are 27–74 (ed. Boutemy, pp. 345–46):

> Non poteram falli cognitione viri,
> Quoque minus dubites, habitus, vox, sermo, figura,
> Gressus et aspectus consona signa dabant.
> Non erat austerus mesta gravitate, quod odi,
> Sed, quod amo, leta fronte serenus erat.
> Non obliqua sibi facies, nec lumine toruo
> Horrida, nec rigidis seva superciliis,
> Sed facies mitis, clemens placideque columbe
> Instar et estiuis solibus equa fuit.
> At non sic hilaris fuerat facilisque videndus
> Ut neglecta sibi forma modesta foret.
> Nec sic iocundo dampnarat in ore pudorem
> Ut fieret pueri frons petulantis ei,
> Nam male quisque fugit uicium cum sic fugit illud
> Rursus ut opposito det sua colla iugo.
> Non bene luxurie maculam lavat helluo cum se
> Mergit in obscene crimen auaritie.
> Odo tenens medium que sit uidet inter utrumque
> Semita, nec culpas in mediata putat.
> Temperie se sic decorarat ut esset eidem
> Morosa mixtus cum grauitate iocus.
> . . . .
> Temperie rapidi solis aguntur equi,
> Temperie messes formant calor atque pruina,
> Temperie uitis uuaque vina parit.
> Hic status, hec habitudo decent; inglorius erret
> Qui de mendaci relligione tumet.
> Exulet in siluis taciturnus amarus et asper
> Et comes Hircanis tygribus esse velit.
> Par hiemi censendus erit Boreeque niuoso,
> Gaudia qui dampnat tristiciamque probat.

. . . .
Talis tamque decens et in hoc moderamine vultus
Adstiterat nostro uatis imago thoro.
Adstandis non forma fuit brevis atque pusilla.
Sed fuit ingentis ardua forma viri.
Nam sublime caput procero corpore tollens,
Altior ac soleat suspiciendus erat.

146. See Gerald Bond, "Natural Poetics: Marbod at Angers and the Lessons of Eloquence"; *Carmina Leodiensia*, ed. Bulst; also Maurice Delbouille, "Un mystérieux ami de Marbode: Le 'redoutable poète' Gautier." The physiognomic treatise is published by Richard Foerster, *Scriptores Physiognomonici* (Leipzig, 1893), 2. 3–145. I could not find a study of physiognomy in the earlier Middle Ages. On the subject in the later Middle Ages, see John Block Friedman, "Another Look at Chaucer and the Physiognomists," *Studies in Philology* 78 (1981), 138–52.

147. *Carmina*, ed. Bulst, p. 18:

Ergo librum talem, modicum licet ac manualem,
Distinctum flore per singula multicolore,
Mellifluis sulcis, miratur Francia dulcis.
Ut fatear verum: scrutentur ut abdita rerum,
Hic notat obscuris quedam signata figuris,
Ut status, ut uultus habitus uox motio cultus
Absque nota morum commendet quemque uirorum,
Utrum sit iustus, uirtutum flore uenustus,
An nequam, fallax et ad omne scelus nimis audax.

148. See *Origins of Courtliness*, chapter 7, pp. 113–26.

Chapter 5: Ethics Colonizing the Liberal Arts

1. On this topic see the study by Marie-Thérèse D'Alverny, "La sagesse et ses sept filles: recherches sur les allégories de la philosophie et des arts libéraux du IXe au XIIe siècle." Other schemes set ethics parallel to the arts, for example, Logic, Physics, Ethics (Conrad of Hirsau, *Dialogus*, ed. Bultot, p. 131). Also the late eleventh-century poem "De nuptiis Mercurii et Philogiae," ed. A. Boutemy, esp. p. 49, ll. 77–85, where Wisdom presents the seven liberal arts in their two parts, the trivium and quadrivium; ethics is the "special companion" of each.

2. *De officiis*, 2.5–6, trans. Miller, pp. 172–73. Cf. also *In L. Pisonem*, 71: "Philosophia, ut fertur, virtutis continet et officii et bene vivendi disciplinam." On Cicero's idea of philosophy, see Josef Mancal, *Zum Begriff der Philosophie bei M. Tullius Cicero*, Humanistische Bibliothek 1.39 (Munich, 1982).

3. Also worth noting in this context is Seneca's virtual identification of philosophy and ethics, to the exclusion of "science":

Philosophy . . . gives form and fabric to the soul, it orders life, governs actions, points to what should and should not be done. (*Epist. ad Lucil.*, 16.3)

Neither can there be philosophy without virtue, nor virtue without philosophy. Philosophy is the study of virtue. (89.8)

The commandment of philosophy is this: to remain cheerful, brave and serene in the face of death and for that matter in any condition of the body, nor to lose heart, even when all is lost. (30.3)

4. On the idea of philosophy in the earlier Middle Ages, see Leclercq, *Études sur le vocabulaire monastique*, 39–79; idem, "Pour l'histoire de l'expression 'philosophie chrétienne' "; idem, *The Love of Learning and the Desire for God*, pp. 107–8; E. R. Curtius, "Zur Geschichte des Wortes Philosophia im Mittelalter," pp. 304ff.; Peter von Moos, *Hildebert von Lavardin*, pp. 103–5.

5. Isidore, *Etymologiae*, 2.24.1, ed. W. M. Lindsay (Oxford: Oxford University Press, 1911) (unpaged).

6. Alcuin, *De dialectica*, chapter 1, PL 101, 952A. Cf. also *De grammatica,* PL 101, 849C, 852D.

7. *De universo*, 15.1, PL 111, 413.

8. Gerbert, epist. 44, ed. Weigle, p. 73:

Cumque ratio morum dicendique ratio a philosophia non separentur, cum studio bene vivendi semper coniuncxi studium bene dicendi, quamvis solum bene vivere praestantius sit eo, quod est bene dicere, curisque regiminis absoluto, alterum satis sit sine altero. An nobis in re publica occupatis utraque necessaria.

9. This definition is evident in monastic usage. See the studies by Leclercq in note 4 above. The regulated life of the monastery could be called *phylosophya Benedicti.* Cf. Brun. *Vita Adalberti*, chapter 27, MGH SS 4, p. 609, l. 25.

10. *Wormser Briefsammlung*, epist. 52, ed. Bulst, p. 89 (see above, p. 83).

11. Boethius, *De cons. phil.*, 1. Prose 4.15ff.

12. Sigebert of Gembloux alludes to Plato's idea of the philosopher king in referring to the wise men serving Otto I: Brun, Dietrich of Metz, and others of Brun's students: *Vita Deoderici*, chapter 7, MGH SS 4, p. 467, ll. 38ff.

13. *Vita Brun.*, chapter 20, LB, p. 206: "Nec abesse tibi iam dudum perpendi ipsam ingenuarum arcium matrem et vere virtutem philosophie, que te ad hanc modestiam magnitudinemque animi erudivit."

14. *Briefsammlungen der Zeit Heinrichs IV., Regensburger Rhet. Briefe*, pp. 274–76.

15. *Regensburger Rhet. Briefe*, ed. Fickermann, epist. 1, p. 275: ". . . virtutem querere, virtuti studium adhibere, virtutis insudare exerciciis non solum honestati, verum utilitati consulere est."

16. Meinhard of Bamberg had recommended the same work to G. as "the best that Latin philosophy has produced" (*Briefsammlungen der Zeit Heinrichs IV., Weitere Briefe Meinhards*, ed. Erdmann, epist. 1, p. 193).

17. No doubt a symptom of an educational scene barren of logic. See Charles M. Radding, "The Geography of Learning in Early Eleventh-Century Europe: Lanfranc of Bec and Berengar of Tours Revisited."

18. *Vita Burchardi*, chapters 18 and 19, MGH SS 4, pp. 840–43.

19. Clerval, *Les écoles de Chartres*, p. 59; quoted above, Chapter 3, n. 43.

20. See the passage from an anonymous twelfth-century commentary from Ms. Pistoie, Archivio capitolare, C. 80, f. 72 cited in Leclercq, *Études sur le vocabulaire monastique du moyen âge*, p. 60, n. 16.

21. John of Salisbury, *Metalogicon*, prol. ed. Hall, CCCM 98, p. 11, ll. 76–78; trans. adapted from McGarry, p. 6.

22. A detailed exposition in *Policraticus* 7.8, ed. Webb, 2.118–22; trans. Pike, pp. 240–43. Cf. *Entheticus maior*, part 2, ll. 1247ff. (Parag. 80), *John of Salisbury's Entheticus Maior and Minor*, ed. and trans. van Laarhoven, 1.186–87: "Nam quamvis linguam formet, componat et actus, / vivere praecipue Philosophia docet. / Vivere sincere pars optima philosophandi est." Here as in the *Policraticus* the intellectual side of learning has no role assigned to it in philosophy, and where it does appear, its role tends to be negative. Cf. Epist. 185, *Letters of John of Salisbury*, ed. Millor and Brooke, 2.224–45. The synthesis of the three arts of the trivium proposed in the *Metalogicon* has a more conciliatory attitude to the intellectual.

23. *The Latin Rhetorical Commentaries by Thierry of Chartres*, ed. Fredborg, p. 59.

24. Cf. David Knowles, "The Humanism of the Twelfth Century," p. 19. Also Köhn, "Schulbildung und Trivium," p. 248.

25. Wibald, epist. 331, ed. Jaffé, p. 462: "Neque enim mores nostros ita instituit et formavit illa vestra doctrix et domina, rerum divinarum et humanarum magistra et educatrix, philosophia."

26. *Reineri Vita Eraclii* chapter 1, MGH, SS 20, p. 562, ll. 9ff.: "Ipse apud Coloniam Agripinensem ad litterarum dispositus rudimenta, tantam postmodum in divinis aeque et humanis assecutus est scientiam, ut summis par esse philosophis iure censeretur, presertim cum venustatem corporis mores etiam inaurarent splendidi, et iuxta Salomonem in facie prudentis luceret sapientia."

27. Radding's study "The Geography of Learning," has shown the rudimentary nature of logic in the eleventh century. The same cannot be said of rhetoric and poetry.

28. See von Moos, *Geschichte als Topik*.

29. See the discussion of the school of St. Victor below, Chapter 9.

30. Delhaye's idea that the connection played the role of rescuing and legitimizing the reading of the classics ("Grammatica et ethica," pp. 91ff.) is certainly true at some level. It was a secondary result of the programmatic thrust of learning to maintain the strict coordination of letters and manners.

31. See the analysis above, Chapter 3. *Wormser Briefsammlung*, ed. Bulst, p. 120, ll. 24–44:

Ipse poetarum fulget decus omnigenarum.
Imperio Christi moderando sceptra magistri
Preter scripture studium nihil est sibi cure,

Cultor virtutis manet eterneque salutis,
Vim talem mentis dono tenet omnipotentis.
Doctrine rivus fluit eius pectore vivus,
Eternum numen sermonum dat sibi flumen,
Est ornamentum nobis huius documentum,
Ut verni flores cui crescunt semper honores.
Indoctis lumen cum fert seu mentis acumen,
Grammaticas partes ac cunctas instruit artes,
Tempore nocturno neque vult cessare diurno
Dicta peritorum depromens orthographorum.
Tanto pastori numquam sunt scripta labori,
Ceu solis lumen sibi sed patet omne volumen.
Ingenio mundum faciens vernare rotundum,
Strennuus et iustus, gemmis virtutis onustus,
Dat pernox Argus documenti fercula largus . . .
Propter sollertes non umquam spernit inertes . . .

32. *Metalogicon*, ed. Hall, pp. 52–54; trans. McGarry, pp. 67–70.

33. It is the core of Ciceronian teaching. Cf. especially *De inventione, De officiis*, and *De oratore*. Also the pseudo-Ciceronian *Rhetorica ad Herennium*; Quintilian, *Inst. Orat.*, 2.1–5. On the connection in Hellenic education, Werner Jaeger, *Paideia*, 1.293 94. In Roman education, H. I. Marrou, *A History of Education in Antiquity*, pp. 196, 198; Stanley F. Bonner, *Education in Ancient Rome from the Elder Cato to the Younger Pliny*, pp. 172–73.

34. On the study of Cicero's *De inventione* in the Middle Ages see Karin Fredborg, "Twelfth-Century Ciceronian Rhetoric: Its Doctrinal Development and Influences"; also the introduction to Fredborg's edition of *The Latin Rhetorical Commentaries by Thierry of Chartres*.

35. "Une version médiévale de la légende d'Orphée," ed. Boutemy. The title, "De nuptiis Mercurii et Philologie," is confusing, but is the one given the poem in the two manuscripts preserving it. I put it in quotation marks to distinguish it from the work by Martianus Capella, given in italics.

36. "De nuptiis," ed. Boutemy, p. 50, ll. 136–45:

Ars docet hoc, leges tenet in moderamine reges,
Milicie gentem Mavorcia tela gerentem
Doctrina vigili studioque reformat herili,
Hoc iuvenum mores struit, instituit seniores,
Perpete mensura cohibens civilia iura.
Quatuor ornatur virtutibus et decoratur.
Omnia discrete moderatur, cuncta quiete
Temperat, est iuste fortis prudensque venuste.
His veluti summis firme subnixa columpnis
Stat quasi quadrate satis eque collaterata.

37. *Regensburger Rhet. Briefe*, epist. 20, pp. 344–45.

38. Ch. 3, PL 172, 1244A: "Tullius itinerantes ornate loqui instruit, quatuor

virtutibus . . . mores componit. Huic urbi subjacent historiae, fabulae, libri oratorie et ethice conscripti, per quos gressus mentis ad patriam sunt dirigendi."

39. See Ward, *Artificiosa eloquentia in the Middle Ages*, pp. 65ff.; Mary Dickey, "Some Commentaries on the *De inventione* and *Ad Herennium* of the Eleventh and Early Twelfth Centuries," pp. 12ff. Dickey identifies "Menegaldus" with Manegold of Lautenbach. On the difficulty of this identification, see Wilfried Hartmann, "Manegold von Lautenbach und die Anfänge der Frühscholastik," pp. 49ff.

40. Cited in Ward, *Artificiosa eloquentia*, p. 70. Cf. *De inventione*, 1.2.

41. Anselm of Liège relates that Wazo prevented Henry I from invading Aix by writing a persuasive letter, and Anselm comments that the wisdom and eloquence of a single man can thus prevent undertakings that would consume great armies. The incident has a Ciceronian model, *De officiis*, 1.79. Cf. Godfrey of Rheims's poem to Enguerrand de Coucy, ll. 91–94 (referring to Cicero thwarting Catiline): "Armed only with the toga, he subdued his weapons. A powerful thing is genius, and stronger than the sharp sword. The [orator's] skilled tongue cuts through the duke's armor." "Trois oeuvres inédites de Godefroid de Reims," ed. Boutemy, p. 342.

42. Onulf, ed. Wattenbach, "Magister Onulf von Speyer," pp. 361–86.

43. Manitius understandably found the work "odd" (*Geschichte*, 2.715). On Onulf see also L. Wallach, "Onulf of Speyer: A Humanist of the Eleventh Century," pp. 35–56; and Carl Erdmann, "Onulf von Speyer und Amarcius."

44. Onulf, ed. Wattenbach, p. 370: "Quid enim tuae saluti conducet haec exornatio, cum sola morum et habitus exornatio, sicut sola est, sic et appelari sola debeat exornatio?"

45. Pp. 382–83, Verse parag. 11:

Ut placeas pueris, senibus juvenumque catervae,
Te mores, habitus, sapientia mentis adornent.
Mandat, amat, probat hoc Deus, angelus, ac homo doctus.
Te colat, optet, amet vir, femina, dives, egenus.
Aetas, condicio, sexus veneretur, honoret.
Vox, habitus, facies pia, dulcis, amabilis extet.

46. Cf. Curtius's observations on the "rejection of the muses" in his study, "Die Musen im Mittelalter." The studies appear condensed in idem, *European Literature*, pp. 228–46.

47. PL 171, 1690A (parag. 13):

Similiter desinens est, cum, tametsi casus non insunt, verbi tamen similes sunt exitus; hoc pacto:
Censu ditari, virtute petis vacuari.
Sed nec dives eris, donec virtute carebis.
Molliter affaris, fallaciter insidiaris.
Inquiris blande, prodis commissa nefande.

48. Curtius, *European Literature*, p. 468 (Excursus 7: "The Mode of Existence of the Medieval Poet").

49. *De sancta simplicitate* chapter 7, S. Pier Damiani, *De divina omnipotentia e altri opuscoli*, ed. Brezzi and Nardi, p. 188; in the Migne edition, PL 145, Opusc. 45, 700C–D.

50. Rudolf Schieffer's case for identifying the Archpoet with a school master of Cologne gains persuasiveness from this point of view, even though the stature of poetry had been changing radically since the beginning of the twelfth century: "Bleibt der Archipoeta anonym?" The evidence is not yet fully persuasive for this identification. Johannes Fried takes up Schieffer's line of thought and comes to a different identification, still in the milieu of the high clergy of Cologne: "Der Archipoeta: Ein Kölner Scholaster?"

51. "*Carmina Cantabrigensia*," nr. 37, ed. Bulst, p. 65:

Ad mensam philosophie   sitientes currite
et saporis tripertiti   septem rivos bibite,
uno fonte procedentes   non eodem tramite,
      Hinc fluit gramma prima,
      hinc poetica ydra,
      lanx hinc satiricorum,
      plausus hinc comicorum,
      letificat convivia
      Mantuana fistula.

52. The sense of outbidding antiquity is evident in much of the school poetry. It imposed an obligation on the poet which had disastrous effects on his Latin style. Cf. Anselm of Besate, dedicatory letter to *Rhetorimachia*, ed. Manitius, pp. 97 and 100. He associates the deeds of Henry with Augustus Caesar and himself with Virgil, whose task was to praise the deeds of Augustus. Since Henry's are more famous than Caesar's, it follows—though it is not stated outright—that poetic talents beyond Virgil's are called for, and Anselm is his man—that is stated outright. Anselm was offered a position in Henry III's chapel, presumably as a response to his *Rhetorimachia*. See Carl Erdmann, "Anselm der Peripatetiker, Kaplan Heinrichs III." Two recent studies of Anselm's style, Beth S. Bennett, "The Significance of the *Rhetorimachia* of Anselm de Besate to the History of Rhetoric," *Rhetorica* 5 (1987), 231–50; idem, "The Rhetoric of Martianus Capella and Anselm de Besate in the Tradition of Menippean Satire," *Philosophy and Rhetoric* 24 (1991), 128–42. See Curtius's excursus on "Poetic Pride" in *European Literature*, pp. 485–86.

53. Guibert of Nogent claimed that in his youth he had "immersed my soul beyond all measure in poetry so I considered scripture ridiculous vanity." He read Ovid and the bucolics, and composed love poetry himself. See Peter Stotz, "Dichten als Schulfach: Aspekte mittelalterlicher Schuldichtung," esp. pp. 9ff.

54. The poem is from someone either in or acquainted with the Rheims circle of poets. He knew the work of Godfrey of Rheims and Marbod of Rennes. Boutemy's edition presents it as "Une version inconnue de la légende d'Orphée," and both that title and Boutemy's commentary tend to stress the Orpheus section (second half only) and to conceal the programmatic thrust of the poem read as a whole.

55. I know of no other version from any period in which Eurydice herself

performs as a singer. The extravagant reward seems to aim at legitimizing praise of women. Cf. ll. 398–400: "Leta cohors superum *laudes probans mulierum* / Euridicis totis referunt preconia votis, / Utque decet lauro, gemmis redimitur et auro." Can anyone explain this untypical bit of feminist advocacy? Possibly because some sources make her into a daughter of Apollo? Cf. Mythographus Vaticanus I, 75, 1–2: "Orpheus Oeagri et Caliope muse filius, ut quidam putant, Appolinis filiam habuit uxorem Euridicen." *Mythographi Vaticani I and II*, ed. Peter Kulcsar, CCSL 91C (Turnholt: Brepols, 1987), p. 33. This still doesn't explain *laudes probans mulierum*. The article on Eurydice in Pauly-Wissowa (6.1.1322–27) does not mention a singing Eurydice or a daughter of Apollo. It may have to do with the cultivation of poems of women in the Loire circle. See Peter Dronke, *Women Writers of the Middle Ages*, pp. 84–97.

56. The distinction between music and poetry is not always clear in the period. I will deal with music in a later section, but here it is worth noting another allegorical representation of the high status of song: Baudri of Bourgueil assigned the same preeminent role to music. The headboard of the allegorical bed in Countess Adela of Blois's bedchamber is inscribed with a representation of Philosophy and the liberal arts. Music is located at the right hand (l. 975), or at the feet (l. 1002) of Philosophy herself, because she is the force that keeps the other sisters in harmony with each other. Baudri, ed. Hilbert, Carmen 134, ll. 999–1004, p. 175.

57. A few details confirm that the poet was working within a structure where poetry fulfills the arts. The "ethereal chorus of philosophy" sings, in praise of *sapientia*, "At hominum sensus, duce te, sapiendo remensus / Appetit internas herebi penetrare cavernas, / Discutiens utique secreta polique solisque" (227–29). This marks the catabasis as symbolic of the continuing quest for understanding; to "penetrate the caverns of the underworld" means to investigate the secrets of the heavens. Boutemy points to the lines as foreshadowing the descent of Orpheus (p. 52 and note), but he regards the Orpheus story as tacked on, not the fulfillment of learning. Likewise the striking parallel between the role of rhetoric as presented by Calliope (136–59) and the judicial pleading for Eurydice in the underworld (593–616), discussed below.

58. "Eine Bamberger Ars Dictaminis," ed. Bittner, p. 156, ll. 31–39:

> Fateor me iudice nemo,
> Si concedis idem, carissime, doctus ad unguem
> Nec perfectus erit, qui nil componere novit
> Auditu dignum; quod maius dic rogo signum
> Aut argumentum, quod certius est documentum
> Divitis ingenii, frater dulcissime, quam si
> Dictator mentes et grate mulceat aures?
> Hic est aut nusquam quod quaerimus, hic erit inquam
> Fructus longorum, ni fallor ego, studiorum.

componere here refers to poetry as well as prose. Cf. ll. 58–59: "Nam versus dulces scribendo pectora mulces, / Mulces egregie scribens metri sine lege." On Ulrich's so-called *ars dictandi* and its two introductory poems, see I. S. Robinson, "The 'colores rhetorici' in the Investiture Contest."

59. For more details, see my study "Orpheus in the Eleventh Century"; also McDonough, "Orpheus, Ulysses, and Penelope." On Orpheus, see Heitmann, "Orpheus im Mittelalter"; J. B. Friedman, *Orpheus in the Middle Ages*; Wetherbee, *Platonism and Poetry in the Twelfth Century*; Brinkmann, *Mittelalterliche Hermeneutik*.

60. The judicial nature of the proceedings is quite apparent. The chorus gives the "king" advice on the treatment of the accused and convicted in general: "Parcere prostratis decus est et honor pietatis" (594). They invoke points of law: "ne modo maiora pereant concede minora, / Ne vicio regis titubet sententia legis" (598–99). They appeal to "the law" itself (*sententia legis* — 599; *lex tua* — 604). The issue glides from death versus life over into innocence versus guilt: "Innocuos dure non sit tibi perdere cure / Sitque satis diram pretendere sontibus iram" (607–8). Eurydice's plight is a *casus* (610) and a *causa* (611). They demand that condemnation be based on proof: "Non bene dampnatur qui non meruisse probatur" (609). A near-contemporary text describing (satirically) legal procedures and drawing on the same vocabulary: Goswin of Mainz, *Gozechini epistola*, ed. Huygens, chapter XXXV, pp. 37–38, ll. 800–823.

61. See Heitmann, "Orpheus im Mittelalter," pp. 267–69; for the Renaissance, John Warden, "Orpheus and Ficino," pp. 89–91, with some parallels to the eleventh-century figure. Cf. p. 90: Orphic song in its civilizing capacity is "a social and political program."

62. Ovid has no interest in this aspect of the myth (see *Metam.* 10.1–63, 11.1–66); nor does Virgil, *Georgics* 4. 453ff.; Quintilian makes of Orpheus a musician, philosopher and poet in one, who by the power of his song "rudes quoque atque agrestes animos admiratione mulceret"; Horace presents him as the primal civilizer: "Silvestres homines sacer interpresque deorum / caedibus et victu foedo deterruit Orpheus, / dictus ob hoc lenire tigris rabidosque leones" (*Ars Poetica*, 391–93); Boethius mentions the softening effect of song with the casualness of a received motif (*De cons. phil.*, III m. 12), though he was to treat the civilizing aspect of music at length in his *De inst. musica*. For classical authors, Orphic song is a producer of *mirabilia*, not a force aimed at a widely accepted social mission. The more detailed description of his civilizing power in Eusebius (see Friedman, pp. 56–57) suggests that it is a product of Christian modeling of the ancient myth. On Orpheus in Merovingian and Carolingian sources, see Peter Godman, *Poets and Emperors: Frankish Politics and Carolingian Poetry*, pp. 1–37, also Jaeger, "Orpheus."

63. "*Quid suum virtutis*": *Eine Lehrdichtung des 11. Jahrhunderts*, ed. A. Paravicini. The poem has been attributed to Thierry of St. Trond and Hildebert of Lavardin (see above, Introduction, p. 16). The most recent editor suggests an anonymous poet writing under the pseudonym of Mamucius (possibly also Kalphurnius) and a date prior to 1043–46 (based convincingly on an allusion to the poem in *Ecbasis captivi* — Paravicini, pp. 8–9). Its origin remains uncertain. The distribution of manuscripts suggests that it was popular in southern Germany, but also in Belgium and northern France (p. 14). Paravicini conjectures that it may have

been written for the instruction of a prince, possibly for Henry III by a member of his chapel (p. 10). (See above, Introduction, pp. ***.)

64. Ll. 499–504:

> Arti materne iunctum sudando laborem
> > Manibus extorsit Orpheus Euridicen.
> Non hic frenaret fluvios, non saxa moveret,
> > Vellet si blande se dare desidie,
> Sed studio dictante sagax dum temperat odas
> > Muse demulcens omnia blandiciis.

65. "Quem non invitat, que non precordia mulcet / Musica? . . ." (675–76); ". . . dulcedine tali / . . . permulcebat . . ." (749–50); ". . . ira resedit, / . . . pax et adest animi" (781–82); "Exhilarant umbre frontem presente Megera, / Dum lira permulcet, pena dolore caret. / Ad nectar cantus hilarescit ovans Rhadamantus, / Ridet permulsus carmine trux Eacus" (953–56).

66. ". . . pisces muti vocis dulcedine capti" (677); "Dulcis eum Muse sola fames tenuit" (692); "Sic Musa dulci dulcis fuit Orpheus orbi" (721); "Huius Musa viri mundum dulcedine tali / Dum permulcebat . . ." (749–50); ". . . Musa tui, sacer Orpheu, / Tanti dulcoris extiterat superis" (809–10).

67. "Tot res et tante letantur eo modulante, / Has et que vegetat musica letificat" (723–24); "Leta . . . / Stix, qua nil umquam tristius esse potest" (829–30); "Numquam leta prius, Charon, tua . . . senectus / . . . gaudet . . ." (943–44); ". . . Parce / . . . hilares" (991–92).

68. "Mox, ut spondei succinuit gravitas, / . . . ira resedit, / . . . pax et adest animi" (780–82).

69. Ll. 749–64:

> Huius Musa viri mundum dulcedine tali
> > Dum permulcebat, esse palam dederat,
> Vis armonie quia rerum temperet esse
> > Unanimi nodo dissona concilians, . . .
> Et que maioris eadem moderando minoris
> > Naturam mundi lex copulat numeri . . .
> Hec anime corpus, hec federat ima supernis,
> > Hec mores ornat, membra dolore levat.

70. Ll. 799–802:

> Et cum nunc mulcet, nunc asperat et modo pacat
> > Affectum mentis musica temperies,
> Certo certius est hominis subsistere totum
> > Apte coniungi temperie numeri.

71. Ll. 809–12:

Nec mirum dictu, quod musa tui, sacer Orpheu,
  Tanti dulcoris extiterat superis:
Tartara flexisti, legem Stigis annichilasti,
  Te modulante madent Eumenides lacrimis.

72. Ll. 921–22:

Quelibet in portu Stigio stabulantia monstra
  Alternis gradibus membra movent fidibus.

73. Or "leaps out of sight" (*Excedens visum niger estuat ignis in altum* — l. 963). The urge to overwhelm is so prominent in the rest of the passage, the more powerful reading seems preferable.

74. Ll. 989–90:

Miratur flecti frendens furor ipsius Orci
  Mansuescendo stupens se periisse sibi.

75. *Ovans Rhadamantus* (955). *Ovans* is the festive mood for the triumphal entry: "ovans urbem ingrederetur" (Liv., 5.31); "ovans triumphavit" (P. Velleius Paterculus, 2.96.3). Glosses from Lewis and Short, *Latin Dictionary*, p. 1285.

76. The motif is from Boethius, *De cons. phil.*, III m. 12, 47–48.

77. "Muse confisus rursum fidicen generosus / Squalores imi mox repetens baratri / Conciliante lira molliret saxea corda, / Placaret Parcas, flecteret Eumenides, / Deflens pulsaret, pulsando preces iteraret, / Sollers effectum nec negat ingenium" (1013–18). Orpheus's urge to return and engage hell again is present in Ovid (*Metamorphoses*, 10.72), but is thwarted by the ferryman. The eleventh-century poet makes the power of poetry into the motivating force, frustrated by the poet's revulsion at the thought of hell's evil. The lines leave some room for seeing here a second descent and successful rescue of Eurydice. Cf. Peter Dronke, "Return of Eurydice," p. 199. A successful return is an outcome more consistent with the poet's faith in powerful song and genius. It would also eliminate the awkward artifice of an Orpheus ready and willing to return but repelled by the thought of dealing with such monsters, "even bearing gifts." But the subjunctives (*molliret, placaret* etc.) followed by "Sed fugit exosus Stigios . . . / Indignans supplex nequitie fieri" seem clear, and the upbeat conclusion ("Fortiter extorsit a Stige, quod voluit. / Sic ars naturam vicit . . .") probably looks backward past the poet's failure through love to the initial success through song. Read this way, the conclusion states: "what powerful song accomplished, ungovernable love undid."

78. "Numine sic artis fidens industria mentis / Fortiter extorsit a Stige, quod voluit. / Sic ars naturam vicit studio mediante / Virtuti domine cedere cuncta probans" (1021–24).

79. *Carmina Leodiensia*, ed. Bulst, 11–12.

80. See Maurice Delbouille, "Un mystérieux ami de Marbode."

81. Ed. Bulst, ll. 1–3: "Carmine leniti tenet Orpheus antra Cocyti / . . . /

Carmine placavit quod quisque mali toleravit." The seven-fold repetition of *carmine* and *carmina* in the first eight lines suggests that the poet knew Godfrey of Rheims's poem to Enguerrand of Soissons, in which an anaphora with *carmine* is sustained over five lines; likewise the power of poetry is the theme. See Godfrey, in "Trois oeuvres," ed. Boutemy, p. 342, ll. 99–103.

82. Cf. "Satyra de amicicia . . . (Clm 29111): Das Freundschaftsideal eines Freigelassenen," ed. Raedle, p. 180, ll. 2ff). Also Froumund of Tegernsee, in *Tegernseer Briefsammlung*, nr. 32, p. 81: "Nunc facito versus, omnis, qui scribere nosti, / Ut modo pellatur mentibus ira suis." Hildebert still cultivated a poetry aimed at calming, soothing and consoling. Cf. Peter von Moos, *Hildebert*, pp. 26–27: "[H.] . . . sieht den höchsten Sinn der Dichtung in der Vermittlung menschlicher Gunst, im Freundesdienst. . . . Dichtung soll 'erleichtern,' die Sorgen vergessen lassen, das Dasein angenehmer machen. . . . [Der Dichter] hilft den anderen, beschwichtigt, bringt Ruhe und Ordnung in bedrängte und erregte Herzen."

83. The *vir perfectus* is the fulfillment of moral training. Cf. Martin of Braga, *Formula vitae honestae*, VI 1ff., p. 247; and the work of Hildebert dependent on it, *Libellus de quatuor virtutibus vitae honestae*, PL 171, 1055–56C: "Quarum [namely the four virtues] se formis si mens humana coaptet, / Perfectum faciet integra vita virum"; ibid., 1063B: "His . . . formis virtutes commemoratas / Perfectum constat reddere posse virum." Also PL 132, 645; PL 157, 671C; PL 207, 377B; Alan of Lille, *Anticlaudianus* passim.

84. Ll. 56–62:

> quis te subtilem nesciat esse?
> Ingenii venam tibi quis neget esse benignam?
> Nam versus dulces scribendo pectora mulces,
> Mulces egregie scribens metri sine lege.
> Moribus haec ornas, cum sit tibi prona voluntas
> Semper ad omne bonum.

85. Ll. 213–16:

> Inferni divos cur optabis redivivos?
> Quos lex Plutonis damnavit fauce draconis,
> Non resonante lira cuius mulcebitur ira,
> Quicquid hic acceptat, nullius iam prece reddat.

86. The early date of the poem (1031) can put to rest any reservations about the advent of the Orpheus figure in the capacity as restorer of peace and love. The indirectness of the treatment suggests this interpretation of the myth is well known.

87. Ll. 130–35:

> Inter nos ire fugiat discordia dire,
> Expertes belli nos simus amore gemelli,
> Fedus Davidis mecum Ionatheque subibis,
> Nil nosmet sevum conturbet nunc et in evum.

Multum mirantur nam, talia cum speculantur,
Sunt qui cum rixis nobis in pignore fixis.

The last line is confusing. See Strecker's (*Tegernseer Briefsammlung*, p. 130) and Bulst's (*Wormser Briefsammlung*, p. 123) puzzlement. But the sense is fairly clear: many who cannot end their disputes will marvel at the model of conciliatory restraint and loving friendship these two provide, having been transformed from bitter enemies to a David and Jonathan.

88. See *Origins of Courtliness*, pp. 36–42, 149–50, 198–99.

89. "Istic prescriptum metrico modulamine dictum, / Cum precor eius opem necnon venerabile nomen, / De cuius donis modulo fungor rationis, / . . . / Nobis ductores verbi dum posco satores / Agrum divinum plantantes semine primum" (273–79).

90. The later letters addressing the conflict at Würzburg (*Wormser Briefsamm-lung*, epist. 15, 25, 26) suggest some legal action was taken, at least threatened, against the perpetrators, as we have seen. Another case is that of Wazo of Liège. See below, Chapter 7.

91. *Briefsammlungen der Zeit Heinrichs IV.*, epist. 27, p. 61: "Domno patri et episcoporum dignissimo H. famelici et vix herentes ossibus Hiltinisheimensium scholarum hospites uberem celestis gratie societatem, plenam panis vivi, qui est Christi, refectionem." The editors identify *vix herentes ossibus* as an echo of Virgil, *Eclogae*, 3.102.

92. P. 63: "Si Erudicen ab inferis ignoscere nescientibus Orphei liberaverat lira, quelibet optanda benedictissime tue anime apud Dominum impetrabit nostre devotionis cythara."

93. *Briefsammlungen der Zeit Heinrichs IV.*, *Hannoversche Briefsammlung*, epist. 109, p. 184. On Walo's conflict with Manasses, see Manitius, *Geschichte der lat. Lit.*, 2: 724–25; Williams, "Manasses I of Rheims and Gregory VII," pp. 809–10.

94. See Curtius, "Die Musen im Mittelalter," pp. 129–88.

95. On the frequent comparison of David and Orpheus see J. B. Friedman, *Orpheus in the Middle Ages*, pp. 148–55; Peter Dronke, "The Return of Eurydice," esp. pp. 206ff.; E. Irwin, "The Songs of Orpheus and the New Songs of Christ," in *Orpheus: The Metamorphosis of a Myth*, ed. Warden, pp. 51–62 (a dense and informative study). Walo is the only monk quoted so far. It may be that in monastic communities the Old Testament figure was the preferred calmer of rage. Also noteworthy for its omission in favor of Orpheus in hell: Christ harrowing hell. Cf. Dronke, "The Return of Eurydice," p. 208.

96. *Sigeberts von Gembloux Passio Sanctae Luciae Virginis und Passio Sanctorum Thebeorum*, ed. Dümmler.

97. *Passio*, 1.12.613–27, pp. 65–66: "nec civilis multum, nec amicus amicis, . . . Est trux ira animos . . . / Nunquam corde reses, ceu mansuescens leo deses . . . ; *ferox et naturaliter atrox*, . . . *barbaricus sensus*." Cf. 3.2.204ff., pp. 101–3.

98. 2.2.36–37, p. 72: "nec vos miseratio flectat. / Non sit qui parcat, nullus sit qui miserescat."

99. 2.2.67–70, pp. 72–73:

Pluto duritia vincens adamantina saxa,
Non potuit flecti lacrimosis cantibus Orphei,
Quis tygres, rupes, silvas flectebat et amnes,
Ut daret Euridicis vitam pretium modulanti."

100. This episode shows how casually variable and governed by authorial intention the fate of Eurydice is. The purpose of the individual author can override tradition and "Stoffzwang."

101. Cf. Walafrid Strabo, *In Natalem S. Mammetis Hymnus*, MGH Poetae 2: 296, 5–6: "Mitis domans immitia, / illisque promens mystica, / Vivebat inter bestias, / quo cive gaudent angeli. / Adiutus armis spiritus / *vicit furores principum*, / saevi draconis conterens / sacris caput conatibus" (emphasis added).

102. *Briefsammlung Gerberts*, ed. Weigle, epist. 44, p. 73: ". . . nobis in re publica occupatis utraque necessaria. Nam et apposite dicere ad persuadendum et *animos furentium suavi oratione ab impetu retinere* summa utilitas" (emphasis mine).

103. This phrase becomes the formula for describing victories over foreign invaders or rebellious states. Cf. the dedicatory poem believed written by Brun for Otto the Great: "Caeca secula barbaries / Seva premebat et error iners. / At tua dextra ubi sceptra tenet, / Publica res sibi tuta placet" (MGH Poetae, 5:2.378, ll. 23–27). Anselm of Besate, *Rhetorimachia*, ed. Manitius, epist. to Henry III: "[it is matter of praise for him that] gentes feras et atrocissimas domuisti animos crudos nefarios ab humanitate derelictos."

104. *Vita Brun.*, chapter 2, LB, pp. 182–84: ". . . nominis quoque eius fama, quousque pervenit, bella sedaret, pacem formaret, studium in omnibus bonis artibus firmaret." Cf. also chapter 25, p. 216, Brun's *pietas* renders battle-hardened men warshy and timid: ". . . quos nulla umquam acies, nulla inflexit asperitas, hos huius viri pietas inbelles et timidos faciebat." Chapters 18 and 19 show Brun attempting to pacify and reconcile Otto the Great's rebellious brother Liudolf. It is oratory (*vir bonus, dicendi peritus*—p. 204) at its Ottonian best, working to mitigate the fury (Liudolf is possessed by an "Erinye") of princes with the suasions of eloquence—the ideal function of the statesman as Gerbert would formulate it (above, pp. 153–54).

105. Sigebert, *Gesta Abb. Gembl.*, chapter 3, MGH SS 8, p. 524, ll. 32–41:

Quam patiens et quam dulcis quantumque benignus
Iugiter extiterit, quis memorare queat?
Nam placidus degens lenibat corda furentum
In mores pacis de feritate vocans.
Alloquia blandus, mira gravitate modestus,
Non asper, non trux, non violentus erat . . .
Quem mestum vidit, quem tristem quemque dolentem,
Affectu patris subveniebat ei;
Affatu dulci merentia pectora mulcens.

On the text see *DGQ*, 1.149 and n. 220. Cf. the commemorative lines by Eugenius Vulgarius (southern Italy, ca. 911): "Iohannes / Inferior nulli veterum probitate priorum, / Cuius in octonis mundus suffragia clamat / Quatinus *indomitas evi demulceat iras* / Ingentesque animi curarum mitiget estus." Paul Mayvaert, "A

Metrical Calendar by Eugenius Vulgarius," *Analecta Bollandia* 84 (1966), 364, ll. 104–8.

106. Odo of Cluny praises Gerald of Aurillac for exercising this influence in Aurillac in his *Vita Geraldi*, 4.8, PL 133, 700D: "Incolae autem regionis illius mores valde ferinos habere solebant, sed aliquantulum exemplo vel reverentia sancti hominis esse mitiores videntur." Passage cited in Thomas Bisson, "The Organized Peace in Southern France and Catalonia," p. 292.

107. Fulbert, epist. 95, *Letters*, ed. Behrends, p. 172: ". . . te propter mores tuos matura sanctitate suavissime redolentes erga tibi subditos eo animo esse intelligo, ut bonos sinceri amoris gratia conplectaris."

108. Epist. 94, ed. Behrends, pp. 170–71. Cf. also his poem to peace, ed. Behrends, pp. 262–63. Peter Damian is going about the same duty in his tract "De frenanda ira et simultatibus exstirpandis," (Opusc. 40, PL 145, 649–60). Cf. also the example of Thierry of St. Hubert and Manasses of Rheims (note 111 below).

109. Ed. Behrends, pp. 262–63: "Ad normam redigit qui subdita secla pravitati, / Potens novandi sicut et creandi, / . . . / Iam proceres legum racionibus ante desueti / Quae recta discunt strenue capessunt."

110. This observation is based on a reading of the sources in Ludwig Huberti, *Studien zur Rechtsgeschichte der Gottesfrieden und Landfrieden* (Ansbach, 1892), and on the documents in MGH, Leges 4, Constit. 1, pp. 596–617. That the contemporary commentary on peace, its legislation and its ends could draw on Orphic discourse is evident in a speech of Archbishop Guido of Vienne in the Council of Langres (1116) Concilium Lingonense, RHF 14. 223, and Mansi, Collect. Suppl. vol. 2. 159. Guido's speech to open the council lamented the depradations on the church. The effect of his speech, delivered in *mellita oratione*: "His et huiuscemodi declamatis a viro facundissimo coepere audientium mitescere pectora et in pacis modestiaeque velle concurrere sacramenta." Cited in Huberti, *Studien*, p. 430. Also the speech of this same Guido (now Pope Calixtus II) at the council of Rheims (1119), after hearing much bickering and contention from a host of complainants: *The Ecclesiastical History of Orderic Vitalis*, ed. Chibnall, p. 262 (12. 21). Cited in Huberti, pp. 431–32.

111. *Vita Theod. Abb. Andaginensis*, chapter 20, MGH SS 12, p. 49, ll. 9ff.:

. . . natura et moribus plus quam oporteret ferus, propter laudabilem conversationem eius sibi amicum eum fecerat. . . . Multum ergo feritatis ab eo admonitus deposuit . . . et cum pluribus esset frequenter immitis et truculentus, huic uni . . . semper fuit mitis et placidus.

Writing ca. 1090, the biographer of Abbot Thierry of St. Hubert (Ardennes) wrongly takes Manasses's predecessor to be the object of this pacifying activity. On the error, see Williams, "Manasses I," p. 806, n. 7. Walo, in accepting the abbacy of St. Remi, let his good judgment be overruled by the prospect of "tempering the truculence" of Manasses (PL 150, 879–80) and sought to transform his "canine manners," "savageness of mind," and "bestiality of manners" into "most gentle charity and charitable gentleness" (*Briefsammlungen der Zeit Heinrichs IV.*, Hannover Collect. epist. 108, p. 183).

112. *Die Briefe des Abtes Bern von Reichenau*, ed. Schmale, pp. 55–64. For a commentary see Karl Schnith, "Recht und Friede."

113. Schmale cites Isidore as Bern's source for this etymology, but it is evident from the passage in *Etymologiae* (9.3.19–20) that the idea of a transition from barbarity to reason inspired by "sacred religion" is Bern's addition.

114. See *Origins of Courtliness*, pp. 211–35. I now believe that the peace movement was a vital precursor of medieval courtliness. Se Georges Duby, "The Laity and the Peace of God."

115. See Karl Hauck, "Heinrich III und der Ruodlieb."

116. *Ruodlieb*, ed. Vollmann, 5.405–7:

> . . . "absit, ut is de me tribuletur <ut hostis,>
> A quo sum numquam minimam commotus in <iram,>
> Quin irascentem me mitem reddit ut ag<num> . . . "

Ruodlieb's personal qualities are tailored to this effect. He is *mitis* and *benignus* (5.400), "ready to serve and in all things well mannered," envious of none, and dear to all, the king's "most beloved" and "dearest of all the retinue": ". . . promptus eras et in omni morigerebas; / Hinc habeo grates tibi, dilectissime, grandes. / Invidus es nulli sed plebi karus es omni / . . . karissime cunctigenorum" (5.419–22). (*invidus* seems to be preferable to Vollmann's conjecture *gravis* in l. 421.) The atmosphere of the king's court is determined by *amor*, *mansuetudo*, and *clementia*. See Helena Gamer, "Studien zum Ruodlieb." Even the tamed wild animals that the court teems with become representatives of the civilizing power of these virtues. Likewise the king's generous and merciful treatment of his conquered adversary illustrates the nobility of not seeking revenge but reconciling enemies through friendship and love, and invites comparison with Henry III (see Chapter 8). These values were represented as institutionalized at the school of Würzburg in the poem from 1031 discussed in Chapter 3.

117. See my "Orpheus in the Eleventh Century," pp. 161–67.

118. See my essay "L'amour des rois."

119. *Die Werke Wipos*, ed. Bresslau, ll. 225–27:

> Et post iudicium veniae mulcedo sequatur . . .
> Lex odium regi generat feriendo nocentes;
> Ut sit carus item rex idem, Gratia suadet.

120. Evidently Wipo's invention. Cf. Breslau's note, p. 83, n. 6. The admonition to compassion does not occur in any preserved royal ordination.

121. Ll. 249–53:

> Dum rex iratus fueris, miserando quiesce.
> Dura foventur agens, durescunt lenia flammis,
> Alternatque vices moderatae ius rationis.
> Hinc adamas durus solvetur sanguine molli . . .
> Et natura iubet mutari tristia blandis.

122. For instance, Peter Damian's tract on suppressing anger, *De frenanda ira et simultatibus extirpandis* (Opusc. 40), PL 145, 649–60; Hildebert's letter to Countess Adela of Blois (epist. 1.3, PL 171, 144–45), a little treatise on clemency, drawing on Seneca and using the language of Orphic discourse; Bernard of Clairvaux, *Sermo super cant.*, 12, *Sancti Bernardi Opera*, 1.60–67; Peter of Blois's fictional dialogue against royal anger between Henry II and the abbot of Bonneval (PL 207, 975–88).

123. Adam of Bremen says that Bishop Adalbert (d. 1072), though not partial to *fidices*, called on them to "relieve his anxieties": "Raro fidices admittebat quos tamen propter alleviandas anxietatum curas aliquando censuit esse necessarios." *Hamburgische Kirchengeschichte*, ed. Schmeidler, 3.39, p. 183, l. 2. But this is probably standard medical practice with little evocation of the Orpheus figure.

124. Cf. Fulcoius's epitaph: "Legem, consilium, rationem, carmina, linguam / Sparsa quis hospitio colligit huic simili? / Quis queat actorem titulare? Quis anser olorem / Hunc pro tot titulis carminibusque suis?" Cited in "Fulcoii Belvacensis Epistulae," ed. Colker, p. 192. On Fulcoius, see also Williams, "Manasses I," pp. 808, 813–14. André Boutemy and Fernand Vercauteren, "Fulcoie de Beauvais et l'intérêt pour l'archéologie antique au XIe et au XIIe siècle." Manitius, *Geschichte*, 3:836–40 (p. 836 on the uncertainty of his dates), and Bernt, "Fulcoius von Beauvais," in *Lexikon des Mittelalters*.

125. Bernard Silvester's treatment in his commentary on Virgil's *Aeneid* is instructive. He develops the myth in the interpretation that became shared by the "School of Chartres": Orpheus is Reason, which combines wisdom and eloquence, Eurydice is natural desire and so on. The only trace that remains of the eleventh-century Orpheus is the comment on his lyre: "Lenimen huius ad aliquod honestum opus pigros excitat, instabiles ad constantiam vocat, *truculentos mitigat.*" *Commentary on the First Six Books of the Aeneid of Vergil commonly attributed to Bernardus Silvestris*, 6.119, ed. Jones and Jones, p. 54 (emphasis added). There is a clear reminiscence of the eleventh-century Orpheus in John of Salisbury's *Policraticus*, 5.10, ed. Webb, 1.326, ll. 20–27.

126. Amadeus of Lausanne, *Huit homélies mariales*, ed. G. Bavaud, Sources Chrétiennes 72 (Paris: Éditions du Cerf, 1960), 4.17–22, pp. 110–12:

> . . . suavitate mirificae cantilenae suscitavit [deus] de lapidibus filios Abrahae, et ligna silvarum, id est corda gentilium ad fidem commovit. Feras quoque, id est feros motus et incultam barbariem moraliter composuit, et homines ab hominibus eductos in numerum deorum instituit.

127. See Heitmann, "Orpheus im Mittelalter"; Wetherbee, *Platonism and Poetry*; Brinkmann, *Mittelalterliche Hermeneutik*.

128. *Passio Thebeorum* 3.8, ed. Dümmler, p. 112, ll. 595–601:

> Omne, quod in mundo geritur variamine tanto,
> Repperit aut studium, levis aut rotat orbita rerum . . .
> Nature columen per nostrum excrevit acumen,
> Venis nature studii dum plurimus usus
> Montis acutibiles tanquam de marmore cotes
> Elicuit plures excudit et extudit artes.

129. Prol. Bk. 2, p. 69, ll. 1–24, esp. 21–2: "Nos quoque laudemus, qui plus laudare valemus, / Quos similes domino mens facit et ratio."

130. *Carmina Leodiensia*, nr. 3, ed. Bulst, p. 11, ll. 3–4: "Omnia que crescunt pereunt et adulta senescunt, / Aes aurum squalent, carmina sola valent." On the introductory lines see Bulst's comments, pp. 21–22.

131. Godfrey, "Trois oeuvres," ed. Boutemy, p. 357, ll. 180–205.

132. "Trois oeuvres," ed. Boutemy, p. 348, l. 126: "Te . . . Amphyon, rigidi montes sequerentur / Parerentque tue saxa vocata lire."

133. "Trois oeuvres," p. 342, ll. 93–94: "Res valida ingenium strictoque potentior ense, / Percutit armatum lingua diserta ducem."

134. Ll. 99–104:

Carmine si libeat super ethera ferre potentes,
Carmine quemque super ethera ferre potes.
Carmine presignem fieri si intendis amicum,
Carmine presignis factus amicus erit.
Carmine si infensum lesisse paraveris hostem,
Infensus hostis carmine lesus erit.

135. Guibert, *Autobographie, De vita sua* 1.11, ed. Labande, p. 64: "Bonus . . . esset Remensis archiepiscopatus, si non missas inde cantari oporteret." On Manasses and Godfrey, see J. R. Williams, "The Cathedral School of Rheims in the Eleventh Century," esp. pp. 670–72; and idem, "Manasses I."

136. See Curtius's chapter on Mannerism in *European Literature*, pp. 273–301.

137. Hildebert, *Carmina minora*, ed. Scott, Carmen 36, p. 24, ll. 29–36:

cura hominum potuit tantam componere Romam,
quantam non potuit solvere cura deum.
hic superum formas superi mirantur et ipsi,
et cupiunt fictis vultibus esse pares.
non potuit Natura deos hoc ore creare,
quo miranda deum signa creavit homo.
vultus adest his numinibus, potiusque coluntur
artificum studio quam deitate sua.

For a commentary see Peter von Moos, *Hildebert*, pp. 240ff. and his exchange with Otto Zwierlein in *Mittellateinisches Jahrbuch* 11 (1976), 92–94 and 14 (1979), 119–26. The reading of l. 35, *adest* = "improves," "is advantageous to", is von Moos's suggestion.

138. The proximity of these two comments on art surpassing nature shows why the earlier poem might have been taken for the work of Hildebert. The difference is worth stressing. Lacking in "Quid suum virtutis" from the mid-century is the nostalgia for the Roman past from which Hildebert's poem lives. The earlier poet considered the overcoming of nature through art a goal fully attainable by his contemporaries, at least those who pursue studies and virtue. But in Hildebert's poem the Roman past is unrecoverable, and neither nature nor presumably the present age is equal to it: "par tibi *nihil.*"

Nostalgia for the Roman past was a shared feature of the Rheims—Loire poets. Godfrey of Rheims looked back on ancient poetry as an unrecoverable goal. Cf. "Trois oeuvres," Poem 1, ed. Boutemy, p. 342, ll. 105–8: "Of course, the writings of the ancients rise from a more dignified source, / nor does the divine inspiration of Virgil have its equal; / but while you cannot rival them in terms of genius, / it is good to stay close to them as men":

Scripta quidem veterum surgunt graviore camena,
Nec divina parem musa Maronis habet;
Sed licet ingeniis nequeas equare poetas,
Proderit a tantis haud procul esse viris.

Odo of Orléans writes poetry, so Godfrey claims, "stamped so with the mark of the ancients, / it seemed true poetry reborn, / as if the ancient poets had not yet passed away / and the golden age returned" (Poem 2, p. 347, ll. 107–10):

. . . veteri sic sunt impressa moneta
Ut sit visa mihi vera poesis agi,
Ut rear antiquos nondum occubuisse poetas
Et superesse modo secula prisca putem.

139. Here I am following the study by Gerald Bond, "Natural Poetics: Marbod at Angers and the Lessons of Eloquence." Bond is one of the few readers to comment persuasively on the poetry of the Loire circle from the point of view of medieval poetics and the humanism of the twelfth century. See also Wolfram von den Steinen, "Humanismus um 1100."

140. This and several other mildly erotic poems are not included in the Migne edition of Marbod's poetry. See the texts in Walther Bulst's edition, "Liebesbriefgedichte Marbods," in *Liber Floridus: Mittellateinische Studien Paul Lehmann . . . gewidmet*, ed. Bernhard Bischoff, "De molesta recreatione," p. 296. Latin text with translation in Bond, "Natural Poetics." English translation quoted here is Bond's.

141. Hennig Brinkmann points to verbal reminiscences of Ovid's story of Pyramus and Thisbe, whom he takes to be the lovers. *Mittelalterliche Hermeneutik*, p. 206 and note 939. But if Marbod had wanted an explicit identification, he could have made it. *Quidam miles* suggests he wanted "any" knight.

142. It is worth noting that the two motifs prominent in the eleventh-century Orpheus poems—partial or full revival of the dead and the softening, sweetening effect—are both negated here: the fictional knight remains dead and the real listener is "troubled," not soothed.

143. "To speak with the voice of the gods," if not better, is a turn of thought I know only from this period. It defies the logic of inspiration through a muse, since it gives credit to the human artist and sets him equal to or above the gods. Cf. Hildebert (besides the Rome poem), verses in praise of the nun Muriel's poetry (*Carmina minora*, ed. Scott, nr. 26, p. 17): "It is not human to be up to such sacred accomplishments, and I can only believe that not you are speaking, but divinities through you. The weight of your words, the dignity of meaning, the beauty of

structure have the semblance of the divine." Sigebert's St. Exuperius rouses the doomed Theban legion with "music" whose effect we can well assess: "Your rhythm modulates their hearts like the music of an organ . . . you who with the skillful sound of a single plectrum and the varied chords of the cithara tune the dissonant hearts of the multitude and make dissimilar strokes produce unified sound. Exuperius, filled with divine strength . . . rendered godly voices in human speech . . ." *Passio Thebeorum* 11.2.643–50, ed. Dümmler, p. 89.

144. Ulrich of Bamberg, excerpting Cicero's *De oratore*, urges using words that "are proper and correct, as though the very names of things were almost born as one creature along with the things themselves" (*Ars dictaminis*, p. 157; cf. *De oratore* 3.37.149).

145. For a survey of research on the subject, see R. P. Winnington-Ingram, "Ancient Greek Music 1932–1957," 5–57, esp. pp. 48–55 ("Music and Education: Ethos").

146. Plutarch, On Music, *Moralia* 1140B, with reference to Plato, *Republic* 3.401ff.

147. *Tusc. disp.*, 1.19: "Aristoxenus, musicus idemque philosophus, ipsius corporis intentionem quandam, velut in cantu et fidibus quae harmonia dicitur, sic ex corporis totius natura et figura varios motus cieri tamquam in cantu sonos."

148. The Latin text, *Anicii Manlii Torquati Severini Boetii De institutione Arithmetica libri duo, De institutione Musica libri quinque*, ed. Godfredus Friedlein (Leipzig, 1867). A recent English translation with commentary, *Fundamentals of Music: Anicius Manlius Severinus Boethius*, trans. Bower; a general treatment with bibliography and review of research, John Caldwell, "The *De institutione arithmetica* and the *De institutione musica*." Also D. S. Chamberlain, "Philosophy of Music in the Consolatio of Boethius."

149. ". . . tota nostrae animae corporisque compago musica coaptatione conjuncta" (p. 186, ll. 3–4); ". . . non potest dubitari quin nostrae animae et corporis status, eisdem quoddammodo proportionibus . . . compositus, quibus harmonicas modulationes posterior disputatio conjungi copularique monstrabit" (p. 186, ll. 9–13).

150. See Rudolf Allers, "Microcosmus from Anaximandros to Paracelsus," on numbers and music esp. pp. 371–77.

151. Some studies in history of music that treat the survival of ancient conceptions in the Middle Ages: Hermann Abert, *Die Musikanschauung des Mittelalters*; G. Pietzsch, *Die Musik im Erziehungs- und Bildungsideal des ausgehenden Altertums und frühen Mittelalters*; Heinrich Hueschen, "Antike Einflüsse in der mittelalterlichen Musikanschauung"; Leo Spitzer, *Classical and Christian Ideas of World Harmony*; Hans Martin Klinkenberg, "Der Verfall des Quadriviums im frühen Mittelalter"; Karl Gustav Fellerer, "Die Musica in den Artes Liberales." Jean-Claude Schmitt cites a passage from Clement of Alexandria that formulates the notion we want to pursue, *La raison des gestes*, pp. 67–68: "il donne au corps en mouvement une harmonie pensée sur le mode musical. Le corps est comme un instrument de musique dont les cordes se tendent et se relâchent: 'Il faut nous gouverner nous-même avec mesure, accordant une détente harmonieuse au sérieux et à la tension de notre bonne volonté sans les relâcher jusqu'à la dissonance . . .'" Passage cited from *Le pédagogue*, ed. Cl.

Moutdesert and Marrou, p. 70. Cf. also Augustine, *De musica*, PL 32, 1083 (1.2), 1085 (1.3, 1.4ff.) and book 6, passim. On Augustine and the ethics of music, see Klinkenberg, "Verfall des Quadriviums," p. 7. Cassiodorus took up and elaborated a number of themes of Boethius's tract on music in his letter to the author. He argued that music harmonizes thought and creates beauty in speech, and measure in gestures: "Per hanc competenter cogitamus, pulchre loquimur, convenienter movemus." For Cassiodorus music is the symbol of the Christian life, since in the formal beauty of music we admire the sonorous projection of a perfect, virtuous life (Letter to Boethius, MGH Auct. Antiq. 12, Var 2, epist. 40. Cited in Edgar De Bruyne, *Études d'esthétique médiévale*, 1:64.

152. See Alison White, "Boethius in the Medieval Quadrivium". On *musica humana* see esp. De Bruyne, *Études d'esthétique médiévale* (see index, "musique humaine"). On the assimilation of *musica humana* and *instrumentalis* see for instance Adalbold of Utrecht, *Epist. cum tractatu de musica instrumentali, humanaque ac mundana*, ed. Smits de Waesbrugge, p. 28; also John Cotto, Gerbert 2, p. 134 A–B; De Bruyne, *Études*, 2:114. See Calvin M. Brown, "Natural and Artificial Music," p. 21.

153. *Die Briefe des Abtes Bern von Reichenau*, epist. 17, ed. Schmale, pp. 50–51. Passage cited at note, p. 51: ". . . tota animae nostrae corporisque compago musica coaptatione coniungitur, animus quoque tuus sonora artis huius dulcedine suavius delectetur." On the letter, its origin and connection to Bern's *Tonarius* see Manitius, *Geschichte*, 2:64, 69–70.

154. "Quid suum virtutis," ll. 799–802: "Et cum nunc mulcet, nunc asperat et modo pacat / Affectum mentis musica temperies, / Certo certius est hominis subsistere totum / Apte coniungi temperie numeri."

155. *Carmina*, ed. Hilbert, Carmen 134, pp. 174ff. (ed. Abrahams, Carmen 196, pp. 220–21.)

156. See d'Alverney, "La sagesse et ses sept filles," p. 260.

157. *Carmina*, ed. Hilbert, p. 175, ll. 1001–3: "Fecerat hanc ideo sibi Philosophia secundam, / Iusserat et pedibus semper adesse suis. / Quippe per hanc alie sibi consensere sorores."

158. *Carmina*, ed. Hilbert, ll. 979–85, p. 175 (ed. Abrahams, ll. 978–84, pp. 221–22): "Hec demulcebat homines dulcedine tanta, / Ut recreare hominis ipsam animam valeat. / Nam status humane, vigor et modulatio vite / Quodam concentu, nescio quo, regitur, / Ut de quadrata videatur surgere forma, / Que formis reliquis amplius est solida / . . . / Hic harmonie typicalis compotus atque / Celestis rithmus corpora nostra regit." The meaning of the phrase *harmonie typicalis compotus* escapes me. A translation that retains the obscurity of the original would be "This construct [computation?] of type-bound harmony" (though it may also be "construct" that is "type-bound"). Also conceivable is "This type-bound [typical?] numbering of harmony." But none of this makes sense, and I suspect that the original phrase also did not make sense. The form *typicalis* occurs in no gloss or lexicon, medieval or modern, I was able to consult.

159. *Carmina*, ed. Hilbert, nr. 218, pp. 287–88 (ed. Abrahams, nr. 251): "Organa, que pariter concordi voce resultant, / Sunt quedam nostre concors modulatio vite" (Thus we live in one mood [mode?] and go together): ". . . Sic Deus et

mores et corpora nostra coaptet, / Ut placeat nostre symphonia mistica vite." On the generalizing of *organum* to "musical instrument," see Spitzer, *Classical and Christian Ideas*, p. 48. Music became a circumlocution for harmonious cooperation. Wibald writes, epist. 168, ed. Jaffé, p. 288: "Cum haec persona illustrat aecclesiam et aecclesia ornat personam, dulcis armonia est et salutaris utique rei simphonia."

160. The glosses were recognized as Bernard's and recently published by Paul E. Dutton, *Bernard of Chartres, Glosae super Platonem*, pp. 216–17 (7.437–43): ". . . valet [auditus] ad correctionem morum. Auditis enim consonantiis musicis, debemus in moribus nostris virtutum consonantia reformari. Licet enim anima secundum consonantias sit compacta, tamen ipsae consonantiae ex corporum coniunctione dissonae fiunt et reformandae sunt per exteriorem musicam. Et hoc est: tota musica data est hominibus non ad delectationem, sed ad morum compositionem."

161. 7.449–52, p. 217: ". . . non solum musicae consonantiae valent ad morum compositionem, sed etiam rithmus. Rithmus est aequalis numerus sillabarum et, secundum eius aequalitatem, statuenda est aequalitas in moribus nostris."

162. 3.64–68, p. 147: ". . . ita nutriendi sunt tutores patriae, ut prompti ad laborem et affabiles sint obedientibus. Quod prompti sint per exercitium, scilicet cursum, venatum, et ludos gymnasii; quod mites et affabiles, per delinimenta praeparatur musicae, quae per sonorum convenientiam morum docet concordiam."

163. Honorius, *De animi exsilio et patria*, chapter 6, PL 172, 1244D: "In hac urbe docentur viantes per modulamen morum transire ad concentum caelorum."

164. *Didascalicon*, 2.12, ed. Buttimer, pp. 32–33: "musica inter corpus et animam est illa natauralis amicitia qua anima corpori non corporeis vinculis, sed affectibus quibusdam colligatur, ad movendum et sensificandum ipsum corpus." William of Conches repeats this scheme: "humane [musice] tres [sunt species], humoralis in humoribus, virtualis in anime virtutibus, coniunctiva in coniunctione corporis et anime" ("Un brano inedito," p. 27).

165. Amadeus of Lausanne, *Hom.*, 4.19–20, ed. Bavaud: "Feras . . . id est feros motus et incultam barbariem moraliter composuit."

166. *Des Adelard von Bath Traktat de eodem et diverso*, ed. Willner, p. 26, ll. 11 ff.:

> Adeo haec vis animae imperativa est. Nam ut fabulosa praetermittam, quae musicis instrumentis muros crevisse, silvas artificem secutas esse asserunt: id saltem dubium non est, si quis delectationis suae reminisci volet, quin et animum ex turbiditate in quietem, ex quiete vero in pietatem haec ipsa constituat. In senectute vero tantam hoc decus efficaciam obtinet, ut non solum vocum concordiam haec aetas exposcat, verum et mores et facta universa in ethicam consonantiam redigere et gaudeat et nitatur.

167. Gottfried, *Tristan*, ed. Ranke, ll. 7969–8149.

168. Ll. 8112–31: si sanc in maneges herzen muot / offenlîchen unde tougen / durch ôren und durch ougen. / ir sanc, dens offenliche tete / beide anderswâ und an der stete, / daz was ir süeze singen, / ir senftez seiten clingen, / daz lûte und offenlîche / durch der ôren kuenicrîche / hin nider in diu herzen clanc. / so was der tougenliche sanc / ir wunderlichiu schoene, / diu mit ir muotgedoene / verholne unde tougen / durch diu venster der ougen / in vil manic edele herze sleich / und

daz zouber dar in streich, / daz die gedanke zehant / vienc und vahende bant / mit sene und mit seneder nôt.

[She sang to the very heart and soul of many a listener, both openly and secretly, both through their ears and their eyes. The song which she sang openly was her sweet singing, her gentle stroking of the strings, which made its way audibly and publicly through the kingdom of the ears down into the heart. The secret song was her miraculous beauty, which crept with its spiritual strains into many a noble heart and smoothed on the magic salve that in an instant seized and bound thoughts in the toils of love-longing and its pain.]

169. Max Wehrli suggests the connection between this passage and *musica humana* in his essay "Der Tristan Gottfrieds," p. 117.

170. The standard translation for Gottfried's phrase *brieve und schanzune* (8139), "words and songs" or some variation, is not tenable. Gottfried's meaning is clear: she composed letters and songs; she was skilled at both administrative tasks and courtly pastimes; she applied her talents in both *otium* and *negotium*.

171. See Hermann Abert, "Die Musikästhetik der *Echecs amoureux*." The passages on music from this fourteenth century chess allegory show the persistence of *musica humana*. The poet tells of the musical construction of the universe and the inaudible music the heavenly bodies sing (p. 896). The construction of the human body also rests on musical proportions. Its "delightful harmonies" are visible signs of the soul's high dignity and excellence. Music inclines individuals "to virtue, to good manners and to good acts." It restrains the passions, foolish inclinations and evil leanings, and turns cowardly hearts courageous (cf. p. 912, lines 1057ff.).

172. See Maximilian Forschner, *Die stoische Ethik: Über den Zusammenhang von Natur-, Sprach-, und Moralphilosophie im altstoischen System*.

173. *De legibus* 1.21.56: ". . . certe ita res se habet ut <aut> ex natura vivere summum bonum sit . . . aut naturam sequi et eius quasi lege vivere." For Quintilian the study of nature and physics has become a principle of the orator's education. Cf. *Inst. orat.* 12.2.4, and 12.2.20ff.

·   174. *Policraticus*, 4.1 (ed. Webb, 1:235), 6. 21 (ed. Webb, 2: 60). See the study by Tilman Struve, "Vita civilis naturam imitetur: Der Gedanke der Nachahmung der Natur als Grundlage der organologischen Staatskonzeption Johannes von Salisbury." On the same subject generally in the twelfth century, Gaines Post, *Studies in Medieval Legal Thought*, pp. 517ff. Alan of Lille has the virtue of *honestas* teach the new man to "love nature" and to embrace whatever nature has created (*Anticlaudianus*, 7.208ff., ed. Bossuat, p. 163). This is an allegorical assertion of the connection between nature and morality.

175. *De cons. phil.*, 1, Prose 4, trans. Stewart, p. 142: ". . . mores nostros totiusque vitae rationem ad caelestis ordinis exempla formares."

176. Juvenal, Satire 11.27. Quoted in Macrobius, *Commentary on the Dream of Scipio* 1.9.2. On the origin of virtue and the nature of souls see ibid., 1.9.1ff. Cf. also ibid., 1.1.3 (reasons for Cicero's describing celestial circles, orbits and spheres, and planetary motions to illuminate regulations of governing commonwealths.

177. See Brian Stock, *Myth and Science in the Twelfth Century: A Study of Bernard Silvester*, pp. 163–87. He calls the section describing the heavenly journey "a type of Bildungsroman" (p. 164).

178. See Margaret Gibson, "The Study of the 'Timaeus' in the Eleventh and Twelfth Centuries"; also Tullio Gregory, "The Platonic Inheritance."

179. See the study of manuscripts in Waszing's edition of Chalcidius, *Timaeus a Calcidio translatus commentarioque instructus*, Corpus Platonicum Medii Aevi, Plato Latinus 4 (London, 1975), pp. CVI–CXXXI. The analysis of its distribution given here is taken from R. W. Southern, *Platonism, Scholastic Method, and the School of Chartres*, p. 14.

180. Quoted in Gibson, "The Study of the Timaeus," p. 192.

181. *Regensburger Rhet. Briefe*, epist. 9, ed. Fickermann, p. 316.

182. PL 171, 1717A: "Moribus esse feris prohibet me gratia veris, / Et formam mentis mihi mutuor ex elementis." Quoted and discussed in Bond, "Natural Poetics."

183. On Macrobius see Wilfried Hartmann, "Manegold von Lautenbach und die Anfänge der Frühscholastik" (with bibliography). On Plato, Tullio Gregory, *Platonismo medievale: studi e ricerchi*, p. 20; idem, "The Platonic Inheritance"; P. E. Dutton, "'Illustre civitatis et populi exemplum': Plato's Timaeus and the Transmission from Calcidius to the End of the Twelfth Century of a Tri-Partite Scheme of Society"; and Dutton's introduction to Bernard's *Glosae super Platonem*.

184. *Liber contra Wolfhelmum*, ed. Wilfried Hartmann, MGH Quellen zur Geistesgeschichte des Mittelalters 8 (Weimar: Böhlau, 1972). See the studies of this work in Hartmann's and Gregory's articles cited in the previous note.

185. This is one of the important findings in Hartmann's study of Manegold, pp. 77ff.

186. N. M. Häring, "The Creation and the Creator of the World according to Thierry of Chartres and Clarenbaldus of Arras," *AHDLMA* 22 (1955), 137–216. The text of Thierry's tract is also printed in Häring's edition *Commentaries on Boethius by Thierry of Chartres and his School*. See the comments of Southern, *Platonism*, pp. 25ff.

187. Manegold, *Liber contra Wolf.*, XXII, pp. 93–94: "ecclesiastici rectores et gubernatores divine rei publice." Manegold himself was the author of a commentary on the *Timaeus*, or at least a commentary was ascribed to him. See Gibson, "The Study of the 'Timaeus,'" p. 185. In any case he knew the tradition closely, and Hartmann's suggestion that he taught worldly philosophy before his conversion is convincing ("Manegold," pp. 49ff.).

188. William of Conches, *Glosae super Platonem: Texte critique*, ed. Jeauneau, Prol. p. 57.

189. *Commentaries on Boethius by Thierry*, ed. Häring, p. 555, parag. 1, ll. 2ff.: "... primam Geneseos partem secundum phisicam et ad litteram ego expositurus ... ut et allegoricam et moralem lectionem que a sanctis doctoribus aperte execute sunt ex toto pretermittam."

190. *Didascalicon*, 6.5, trans. Taylor, p. 145; ed. Buttimer, p. 123: "in illa [= significatione rerum] enim naturalis iustitia est, ex qua disciplina morum nostrorum, id est, positiva iustitia nascitur. contemplando quid fecerit Deus, quid nobis faciendum sit agnoscimus. omnis natura Deum loquitur, omnis natura hominem docet."

191. *Glosae super Platonem*, ed. Jeauneau, p. 59 (parag. 3): "Unde possumus

dicere quod materia huius libri est naturalis iusticia vel creatio mundi: de ea enim propter naturalem iusticiam agit."

192. Cf. Delhaye, "L'enseignement de la philosophie morale," p. 83, n. 13.

193. *Glosae super Platonem*, 151, ed. Jeauneau, p. 254. This is only a slight variation from the position of William's master, Bernard of Chartres, who says also that vision is necessary for moral discipline "because through vision we note the rational movement of *aplanos*, which both moves itself without error and tempers the erratic motions of the planets. Noting this we should educate the *aplanos* of our own mind in such a way that it moves itself without error and restrains the erroneous motions of the vices" (*Glosae super Platonem* 7.388–93, ed. Dutton, p. 215). See also Dutton's comments on the moral thrust of Bernard's *Timaeus* commentary, *Glosae*, intro. pp. 57–62.

194. An interesting study by Bernhard Dietrich Haage looks at trends in learning in cosmology and medicine in the twelfth century and draws compelling parallels to vernacular courtly literature: "Wissenschafts- und bildungstheoretische Reminiszenzen nordfranzösischer Schulen."

195. The author of the entry on "astronomy" in the *Dictionary of the Middle Ages* comments (1: 611) that the eleventh century had not been intellectually prepared to meet the challenge of sophisticated measuring and calculating instruments. This is on the whole right. To raise Hermann of Reichenau's treatise on the astrolabe (PL 143, 390ff.) against it would be quibbling. But the author's argument does not credit the ethical purpose of cosmology at the cathedral schools.

Chapter 6: Conclusion to Part I

1. The eleventh century merits only a few words in Dronke's *History of Twelfth Century Philosophy*. The break between eleventh and twelfth century philosophy is so great that the twelfth seems to have appeared out of thin air, neither growing out of nor superseding the eleventh.

2. For recent literature, see Sigebert von Gembloux, *Liber decennalis*, ed. Wiesenbach; *Catalogus Sigeberti Gemblacensis Monachi de viris illustribus*, ed. Witte. In Manitius's judgment (*Geschichte*, 3.332–50), "Einer der vielseitigsten und bedeutendsten Schriftsteller des 11. und beginnenden 12. Jahrhunderts" (p. 332). Nonetheless Sigebert is hardly mentioned in scholarship except as an apologist for the imperial party in the investiture controversy.

3. Prol. ll. 5–6, ed. Dümmler, p. 44: "Est pars magna spei patronis officiari, / Nec nihil est, regis si famuler famulis."

4. See Robert G. Babcock, "Sigebert of Gembloux and the 'Waltharius.'"

5. 2.574–45, ed. Dümmler, p. 111: "Que deceant fortem vel que deceant sapientem, / Pectore mellito declamat et ore perito."

6. The following is a partial translation of *Pass. Theb.*, 3.8, ed. Dümmler, pp. 111–13. There are complications of phrasing in the passage that mock normal Latin reading skills. I am thankful to Peter von Moos, Peter Godman, Sieglinde Pontow and Anders Winroth for help with the translation.

7. Some elements of the preceding lines were adapted from Cicero, *Tusc.*

Disp., 3.28.69: Theophrastus on his death bed complains to Nature for having given the stags and crows a long life but letting man die comparatively early. Men would use a long life to perfect all the arts and enrich human life, whereas the gift is wasted on the animals. The differences are striking: Sigebert shows the long-lived animals marveling at Victor's even longer and more vital life; what was a lament on man's shortcomings turns into a praise of his accomplishments.

8. I am emending the manuscript's *vel* to make the line logical. Chance clearly disturbs the process of discovery, it does not aid it, as the formulation in Dümmler's edition indicates.

9. The abbreviated thought is that the arts are hewed out of the raw matter of learning as a statue is hewn from mountain marble.

10. *Pass. Theb.*, 1.221–24, ed. Dümmler, p. 54: "Quicquid natura vel te, doctrina, magistra / Omnis ab antiquo belli dictaverat ordo, / Edidicit docili studio Thebea iuventus"

11. 1.260–61, p. 55: "Quando potens virtus naturam vincere gestit, / Hic opus est ultra nature tendere iura."

12. "Quid suum virtutis," ll. 1022–23: "Sic ars naturam vicit studio mediante / Virtuti domine cedere cuncta probans."

13. Marbod, *Vita Sancti Licinii*, PL 171, 1495B. See above, pp. 92ff.

14. *Commentaries on de inventione*, in Thierry, *Latin Rhetorical Commentaries*, ed. Fredborg, p. 62, l. 100.

15. In *Carmina minora*, ed. Scott, p. 24, ll. 33–34: "non potuit Natura deos hoc ore creare, / quo miranda deum signa creavit homo."

16. *Pass. Theb.*, Prohem. 2.21–22, p. 69: "Nos quoque laudemus, qui plus laudare valemus, / Quos similes domino mens facit et ratio." The singer like a god: also in the *Pass. Theb.*, St. Exuperius oration to the legion: the speech of this *rethor et orator, dialecticus atque soritor* (2.605, p. 87) has the effect of Orphic music on the listeners: the spirit of the lord spoke through him, sending a single rhythm pulsing through many hearts and "filling two flutes with one voice. Hearts that went various paths are now tuned to a single chord," and he commences his speach "rendering divine voices in the human voice" (2.643–50, pp. 88–89). Cf. Baudri's praise of Godfrey of Rheims's art: "You could lure Jove himself out of the heavens and make the mind of Jove be that of Caesar" (Baudri, *Carmen* 99, ed. Hilbert, ll. 69–70).

17. Amadeus of Lausanne, *Homily* 4.19, ed. Bavaud, p. 110. See above, p. 158 and n. 126.

18. Bernard, epist. 133, *Sancti Bernardi Opera*, 7: 290.

19. The variations on the theme in the twelfth century would make an interesting subject. John of Salisbury's objection to the "Cornificians" in the *Metalogicon* is in part that they find nature and natural talent sufficient, hence feel no need to "conquer nature." The Archpoet may well have had the motif obliquely in mind when he "confessed," "A difficult thing it is to conquer nature" ("Res est arduissima vincere naturam". *Die Gedichte des Archipoeta*, ed. Watenphul, Krefeld, p. 74 ("Estuans interius," St. 7.1).

20. PL 171, 1365–80. See the study by Peter Godman, "Ambiguity in the 'Mathematicus' of Bernardus Silvestris," also on transmission, editions, translations, and previous scholarship.

21. *Cantus* 12, PL 171, 1377A–B: "Nostra quid aethereis mens est cognatior astris, / Si durae Lachesis triste necesse ferat. / Frustra patricidam divinae mentis habemus, / Si nequeat ratio nostra cavere sibi. / Sic elementa Deus, sic ignea sidera fecit, / Ut neque sideribus subditus esset homo. / Sic puri datur ingenii solertia major, / Possit ut objectis obvius ire minor."

22. Sigebert used a similar image to describe the effect of Brun's teaching on Dietrich of Metz. See above, Chapter 2, pp. 37ff.

23. This is against the Pauline text "Fides per auditum" (Romans 10: 17).

24. *Pass. Theb.*, 2.505–13, p. 85: "Legimus hactenus hec, audivimus hactenus istec, / Sanctorum tanti recitantur in orbe triumphi, / Hic video coram fieri que facta legebam. / Dicite prudentes . . . / Auriculis oculisne fides est certior istis. / . . . / Me moveant oculis subiecta fideliter istis; / Auditis alii credant, oculis ego credam. / En mihi quos imiter, sunt presto quos bene mirer"

25. Sigebert, *Vita Wicberti*, chapter 17, MGH SS 8, 515, ll. 6ff.: ". . . vir Dei consummatus in virtutum gratia, quod maius est quam si claruisset miraculorum gloria — miraculis quippe nonnumquam virtutes offuscantur, miracula vero solis virtutibus commendantur." The cult of virtues could combine with that of miracles. Gerhoh of Reichersberg says that a person can be healed by looking on a citizen of Jerusalem, from whose example he is refreshed as from a fountain (*Liber de aedificatione Dei*, PL 194, 1305C). On admiring miracles but imitating virtues, see Benedicta Ward, *Miracles and the Medieval Mind*, p. 25, also the general discussion in William D. McCready, *Signs of Sanctity: Miracles in Gregory the Great*.

26. *Vita prima*, 3.1, PL 185, 303B: "primum maximumque miraculum, quod exhibuit, ipse fuit." Bernard had used the phrase to describe St. Malachy, *Vita Malachiae*, chapter 19.43, *Opera*, 3: 348. 13ff.

27. See above, Introduction, pp. 10ff.

28. Beaujouan, "The Transformation of the Quadrivium," p. 464; also his study "L'enseignement du quadrivium."

29. This process has been sharply analysed by Eric Havelock in his *Preface to Plato*. See also Werner Jaeger, *Paideia*, 2: 18 where he argues that the dialogues and memoirs by the members of Socrates's circle are "new literary forms invented by the Socratic circle . . . to recreate the incomparable personality of the master." Cited in Goody and Watt, "The Consequences of Literacy," p. 63, n. 1.

30. Ruotger, *Vita Brun.*, chapter 2, LB p. 182: "We believe that many can be instructed by the example of his conduct, if we retell the essence from his childhood on."

31. *Gesta Chuonradi*, Prol., *Die Werke Wipos*, ed. Bresslau, pp. 4–5.

32. See the comments in the Introduction (above, pp. 11–12) on rhetorical terminology abstracted from the human body. An interesting case of this equation of human postures with literary style is the appropriation in Elizabethan books of poetics of schemes and terms from books of courtesy. See Daniel Javitch, *Poetry and Courtliness in Renaissance England* (Princeton, NJ: Princeton University Press, 1978).

33. See the study by Stephan Maksymiuk, *Knowledge, Politics and Magic: The Figure of the Court Magician in Medieval German Literature*, Dissertation, University of Washington, 1992.

Chapter 7: Two Crises

1. See Henri Platelle, "Le problème du scandale: Les nouvelles modes man-sulines aux XIe et XIIe siècles"; Jaeger, *Origins of Courtliness,* pp. 176–94.

2. Brun of Cologne is praised for avoiding "soft and fine clothing" at royal courts, where he was surrounded with "purple garbed courtiers and knights radiant in gold" (Ruotger, *Vita Brun.,* chapter 30, LB, p. 222). When he moved to the cathedral of Cologne, he banished "excesses of dress, inordinate mores, and all that was effeminate and indecent" ("vestium superfluitas, morum inequalitas et quic-quid hoc modo effeminatum et indecens in eius ecclesia videretur"—chapter 21, p. 210). Courtly excess prior to the polemics of church reformers goes under the fairly neutral name of *inaequalitas morum.* Gebhard of Regensburg, chaplain under Otto III, astonished Thietmar of Merseburg because of his exotic "conduct and rare pomp and magnificence" (*moribus et raris apparatibus*) and his cultivation of exotic foreign customs (*Chronicon,* 6.41, ed. Holtzmann, pp. 324–26). It may well have been the Byzantine connection at the Ottonian courts that generated this thrust toward exotic refinement. Cf. the anecdote of Theophanu in hell (below, p. 214).

3. See Platelle, "Le problème du scandale," pp. 1073ff. and *Origins of Courtliness,* pp. 178ff. My earlier cautioning that such cries of alarm are topoi on the occasion of the marriage of a king with a foreign queen is correct, but should not be read to suggest that the customs observed and castigated by William of St. Benigne of Dijon, Ralph Glaber, Siegfried of Gorze, and others were not a real social phenomenon.

4. See Heinz Thomas, "Zur Kritik an der Ehe Heinrichs III. mit Agnes von Poitou." Thomas is mainly concerned with the reproach of incest made by the Abbot of Gorze.

5. Letter of Siegfried of Gorze to Poppo of Stablo, edited by Wilhelm von Giesebrecht, *Geschichte der deutschen Kaiserzeit* 5th ed., 2: 718.

6. See Fleckenstein, *Hofkapelle* 2:268ff. and Jaeger, *Origins of Courtliness,* pp. 122–26 and n. 34.

7. *Chronic. Novalic. app.,* chapter 17: "Heinricus imperator bene pericia lit-terarum imbutus"; Benzo of Alba, *Ad Heinricum IV.* MGH SS 11, p. 667: "septem artibus ornatus ad instar Pompilii"; Goswin of Mainz, *Epist. ad Walcherum* chapter 34, p. 37, ll. 783–85: "tunc temporis aecclesia et vario virtutum decore et multiplici liberalium litterarum propagine florebat." On Henry's learning and support of studies see James W. Thompson, *The Literacy of the Laity in the Middle Ages,* pp. 88–89; Giesebrecht, *Geschichte der deutschen Kaiserzeit,* 2: 632–33.

8. Eckehard of Aura. *Chronicon* (1106), MGH SS 6, p. 239: "More patris sui clericos et maxime literatos adherere sibi voluit . . . liberalium artium inquisitione secum familiarius occupavit."

9. *Annales Augustani* (Annals of Augsburg) for year 1041, MGH SS 3, p. 125, ll. 52–53: "Huius astipulatione et industria plurimi eo tempore in artibus, in aedificiis, in auctoribus, in omni genere doctrinae pollebant. Studiumque ubique famosissimum." Cited in Reto Bezzola, *Les origines et la formation de la littérature courtoise en occident (500–1200)* (Paris: Champion, 1958), 1: 279.

10. The suggestion of Werner Braun, *Studien zum Ruodlieb,* of a dating ca.

1100 has not found acceptance. Still persuasive is Hauck, "Heinrich III und der Ruodlieb."

11. See Friedrich Prinz, "Kaiser Heinrich III: Seine widerspruechliche Beurteilung und deren Gründe"; Fleckenstein, *Hofkapelle*, 2: 234ff.

12. This is not to suggest that his peacemaking efforts were ultimately successful. See Monika Minninger, "Heinrichs III interne Friedensmassnahmen und ihre etwaigen Gegner in Lothringen"; Karl Schnith, "Recht und Friede: Zum Königsgedanken im Umkreis Heinrichs III"; J. Gernhuber, *Die Landfriedensbewegung in Deutschland;* Gerhard Ladner, *Theologie und Politik vor dem Investiturstreit,* esp. pp. 70–78.

13. *Briefe des Abtes Bern,* ed. Schmale, epist. 26, p. 55:

. . . hi, qui nunc reges dicuntur, olim ob crudelem morum ferocitatem tyranni vocabantur, sed crescente sacrae religionis studio reges appellati sunt a recte regendo, dum bestiales motus comprimunt et per discretionis vim se rationales ostendunt.

14. In a later letter he praises the king for uniting in his own heart mercy and truth, justice and peace (an echo of Psalm 84: 11). These unions have "composed such bonds of concord in the kingdom as are unheard of in all previous ages. No traces of any discord, no frauds and intrigues remain; theft has fled, sacrilege passed out of being. All things are pacified" (*Briefe des Abtes Bern,* epist. 27, p. 57). Henry is that "soft, humble, gentle" David who conquered the giant Goliath. He loves his enemies and joins all in his kingdom "beneath one bond of love and peace." Far from seeking revenge against those who have wronged him, he favors them with a miraculous feeling of charity (p. 59). He has recalled all to the "unanimity of peace and concord" (p. 60). Henry's civilizing mission is evident also in Anselm of Besate's praise for him in the dedicatory letter of his *Rhetorimachia* to Henry: [his conquest of foreign peoples is the matter of great praise] "vicisti enim gentes feras et atrocissimas, domuisti animos crudos, nefarios, ab humanitate derelictos" (Anselm of Besate, *Rhetorimachia,* ed. Manitius, p. 98). Conquest over foreigners stylized as a victory of civilization over barbarism had been conventional since Ottonian times. In one of the *Visiones* of Otloh of St. Emmeram, a cleric visits hell and sees the opponents of Henry's peace efforts roasting in a metal bowl (Visio 11, MGH SS 11, p. 382, ll. 41ff.)

15. Siegfried of Gorze's letter, n. 5 above. Likewise Anselm of Liège pointed to the flatterers as a bad influence on the king, *Gesta ep. Leod.,* chapter 50, MGH SS 7, p. 219, ll. 39–40; also Gerhard of Cambrai urging Henry to heed advice from those nearest him, not from outsiders and peace-breakers (*Gesta ep. Cam.,* ed. Bethmann, chapter 60, MGH SS 7, p. 488). Cf. Egon Boshof, "Lothringen, Frankreich und das Reich in der Regierungszeit Heinrichs III," pp. 123–24.

16. See Thomas, "Zur Kritik an der Ehe Heinrichs III."

17. Hermann of Reichenau, *Chronicon* (1053), MGH SS 5, p. 132. ll. 32ff. Quoted and analyzed in Prinz, "Kaiser Heinrich III," pp. 539ff.

18. Koepke's text has *e scolaribus alis* (p. 205, l. 8), which can be emended to *e scolaribus aulis.*

19. Did Anselm get confused in the course of this lengthy comparison? Or are

there problems with the text? I have translated the text as is, but the antithesis of the first "if . . . then" clause to the second is lost.

20. *Gesta,* chapter 28, MGH SS 7, p. 205, ll. 1ff.:

Maxima illi circa educandos pueros erat sollicitudo, eosdemque cum aecclesiasticis disciplinis instruendos, adeo ut quocumque vel ad proxima vel ad longinqua loca pergeret, scolares adolescentes, qui uni ex capellanis sub artissima non aliter quam in scolis parerent disciplina, secum duceret, cumque his librorum copiam ceteraque arma scolaria circumferri faceret. Sicque fiebat ut quos plerumque rudes et illiteratos a claustro abduxisset, et ipsos quos prius magistros habuerant, in litterarum perfectione redeuntes superarent. Sed vereor, ne huiuscemodi se tueantur exemplo, qui e scolaribus a[u]lis in curias regum et episcoporum querunt erumpere, et disciplinae iugum detrectantes, levitati animum dare contendunt, quos ego felices iudicaverim, si in nullo ab istius exempli disciplina exorbitaverint. Nam si nunc temporis inter strepitus curiarum studia bonarum arcium haut secus quam in claustri quiete constiterit valere, de remissiori ad arciorem discendi viam non negamus convolari debere. Sin autem longe est res e contrario, immo quia est, cesset ultra lasciva aetas falsas instabilitati suae causas praetendere, quia quod in tranquillitate claustri neglexit, verum est quod nequaquam in tumultuantis seculi turbine possit assequi, quamque o si nostris temporibus tam aurea possent revocari secula, ut in capellis tam imperatoris quam episcoporum nil magis appeteretur quam cum litterarum studio morum disciplina!

21. Goswin of Mainz, former school master under Wazo at Liège, agrees. Cf. *Epist. ad Walch.,* chapter XXVII, ed. Huygens, p. 31, ll. 625ff.: "instrui refugiunt ad gravitatem moralis disciplinae." The golden age of Notker is past, he complains, and now "holy religion, equity and justice, the liberal arts, and moral discipline" are abandoned (p. 37, ll. 781ff.). In this case, the death of Henry III is a symptom of the golden age's passing. Instead of "gravity and modesty," men pursue "glory and the glorification of vain pride" (ll. 795–96).

22. Anselm regularly holds up the bishops of Liège as examples of rigorous discipline. Bishop Balderich founded a monastery, "where the more rigorous life beneath the rule of blessed Benedict was led, so that the minds of the inhabitants would be the more intent on prayer for being freed from the hurly-burly of secular cares" (chapter 31, p. 207, ll. 6–7: ". . . ubi arcior vita sub beati Benedicti regula duceretur, ut eorum mens qui ibidem inessent, eo magis studio orationis esset intenta, quanto a saecularium curarum turbine esset libera"). Anselm describes the monastic life with the same language as he does the school discipline of Liège: *artissima disciplina* (Notker's school); *arcior vita* (Balderich's foundation). In both cases he also opposes the quiet of the claustral life to the "whirlwind of the turbulent world" (*tumultuantis seculi turbine*) and the "whirlwind of worldly cares" (*saecularium curarum turbine*).

Anselm praises Balderich's successor, Wolbodo, for studying the "ecclesiastical disciplines of the claustral life" under "very religious fathers" in Utrecht. His own students he "constrained in their years of laxness [lasciviousness] under more rigorous discipline [*arciori disciplina*]" and permitted them no opportunity for wandering and straying from the path of holy religion (chapter 32, p. 207, ll. 23–24: "nullus . . . alicui locus evagandi, aut quoquam a sanctae religionis tramite exorbitandi sub eo locus erat"). Cf. the ironical description of the chaplain's criterion for a good bishop: "it was wrong [they claim] to make a man bishop who had not been accustomed to wander with the royal court" ("nisi quem constiterit in curte regia evagari"—chapter 50, p. 219, l. 43). His personal presence had an effect that cured precisely the ailment afflicting the students of Anselm's day: "He converted many from the levity they were previously given to, to dignity of conduct" (chapter 34, p. 208, ll. 35–37: ". . . erga subditos tam monitis quam exemplis aecclesiasticis rigorem auxit disciplinis. Multique a levitate, quam retro fuerant sectati, ad gravitatem morum conversi . . .").

23. Chapter 28, p. 205, ll. 1–2; chapter 32, p. 207, l. 16; chapter 34, p. 208, l. 35.

24. The bishops who emerged from Notker's school are listed and praised for "correcting as many churches as possible" ("quam plurimae correctae sunt aecclesiae"—chapter 29, p. 205, ll. 26ff.). A certain Otbert is praised for "striving to return the life of the clerics of Aix, who had been depraved once again by the contagion of pernicious disorder [licentia], back to the norm of holy religion" ("Otbertus . . . vitam Aquensium clericorum, perneciosae contagio licentiae retro depravatam, ad sanctae religionis . . . normam reducere studuit" (ll. 32–33).

25. Chapter 34, p. 208, ll. 27ff.: "Sicque magis celebre . . . effectum, quam aliorum quorumque praesulum, qui creditas sibi spoliantes aecclesias, mimos caeterosque palatinos canes ditare contendunt, ipsique scurrilibus stultiloquio et turpissimis circa reges adulationibus inservire non erubescunt."

26. Chapter 57, p. 223, ll. 47ff.: ". . . difficile est, ut mentis oculus, hinc gloria et divitiis, hinc variis dispensandae rei publicae curis, hinc mille adulantium linguis in diversa raptatus, aliquando a veritatis luce non cecutiat . . ." Anselm gives a vivid illustration of Bishop Wazo himself deprived of judgment by the "whirlwind" of the court. Accused of conspiring with the Frisians while the emperor is waging war against them, the aged and ailing bishop is summoned to court and made to stand during a long consultation. Ready to defend himself, he is unable to do so, assailed from one side "by the shouts and clamor of the party of royal flatterers," from the other by the admonishing cheers of his fellow bishops: ". . . finding himself caught alone in such a whirlwind [in tanto turbine]," and with "the insane din of the shouters" buffeting his ears ("insano fragore obstrepentium"—p. 229, l. 46), he resists the emperor's powerful will as long as possible, then makes a false admission of guilt, just in order to end the situation—and regrets the admission for the rest of his life (cf. chapter 66, p. 229, ll. 32–41).

27. On the background to this conflict, see Bittner, *Wazo und die Schulen*, pp. 13ff. Charles Dereine pointed to the value of Wazo's letter to provost John as a "commentaire des chapitres de la règle relatifs aux fonctions de doyen et de prévôt." ("L'école canonique liègoise et la réforme Grégorienne," pp. 86–87 and n. 1).

28. His generosity in his days as school master to paupers and guests arouses the envy of men who are "more noble and more wealthy," indignant at seeing themselves bested by the "virtue and glory of this less powerful man" (Anselm, chapter 40, p. 211, ll. 16ff.).

29. Chapter 42, p. 215, ll. 25–27: ". . . quae sua sunt non querens sed quae Iesu Christi. Quod haut secus esse, patuit paulo post in propositurae et postmodum in episcopatus amministratione."

30. The letter comprises chapter 41 of the *Gesta*. Cf. p. 211, l. 39: "plurimum seculari potentiae confideres"; p. 211, l. 41: "Dicis te praepositum potenter esse constitutum"; p. 212, l. 22: "pluris existimas opes religione"; p. 212, l. 23: "gloriaris te praepositum esse"; p. 212, l. 42: ". . . ne solus praepositus . . . possit superbire"; p. 213, l. 9: ". . . si gloriosissimus esses, per humilitatem hanc dominationis ambicionem cavere deberes"; p. 213, l. 23: "contendis vocari praepositus potens"; p. 214, l. 7: "quanto maiores sumus in seculi dignitatibus, tanto nos humiliemus in omnibus" (quoting Eccles. 3:20 with Wazo's addition, *in seculi dignitatibus*).

31. P. 212, l. 2: ". . . si tibi ambitionem michique lenieris invidiam"; p. 213, l. 10: "hanc dominationis ambicionem cavere deberes"; p. 214, l. 22: "non ambitiosa karitas quae Dei sunt, sed quae sua rimatur" [emending Koepke's "non quae sua rimatur"].

32. P. 212, l. 45: ". . . tu solus singulariter tibi . . . vendicas dominium"; p. 213, l. 10: "dominationis ambicionem"; p. 213, l. 22: "cur tanto fastu queris dominari?"; p. 213, l. 25: "deposito dominationis fastigio fias parvulus"; p. 213, l. 38: "administrationem secundum regulam, non dominationem collige"; p. 214, l. 8: "Avariciae dominationisque altitudinem fugiamus."

33. P. 212, ll. 20ff.: "Spiritualia enim secularibus digne praeponuntur, quantum stolido corpori racionalis anima principatur; hanc institutionem immobiliter servant occidentalia claustra et monachorum quotquot sunt ubiubi coenobia."

34. Cf. Wazo's position in the dispute over the bishop of Ravenna some years later (cf. chapter 58, p. 224). Also Wazo's comparison of his own consecration and anointing with the emperor's: "There can be no doubt: as life surpasses death in excellence, so far does my annointing surpass yours" ("unde quantum vita morte praestantior, tantum nostra vestra unctione sine dubio est excellentior" — Cf. chapters 65–66, 228–30. Passage cited, chapter 66, p. 230, ll. 6–7). See the analyses of the events by Benson, *The Bishop Elect*, pp. 207–9; Gerd Tellenbach, *Church, State and Christian Society at the Time of the Investiture Contest*, pp. 103–5; Ute-Renate Blumenthal, *The Investiture Controversy: Church and Monarchy from the Ninth to the Twelfth Century*, pp. 87–89. Anselm casts the emperor in the same role in which Wazo had earlier depicted John: "The emperor however was the sort of man who sought to usurp power over bishops prompted by the guidance of fleshly values, or rather by ambition" ("Imperator vero, utpote qui eiusmodi homo esset, qui sibi super episcopos nimis carnaliter, ne dicam ambiciose, quereret usurpare" — chapter 66, p. 229, ll. 49–50). In both cases Wazo boldly and bravely opposed worldly men, men given to arrogant overstepping of the boundaries of their power, driven by fleshly considerations and by ambition.

35. P. 212, ll. 25–26: "Hinc religionis divinae, pro dolor! ruina suboritur, litteralis disciplinae studium penitus destituitur." The complaint finds an echo in Adelman's poem on Fulbert's school (written between 1028 and 1033): "Legia, magnarum quondam artium nutricula, / Non sic, o! nunc dominante virtuti pecunia" (Adelman, *De viris illust.*, in Clerval, *Les écoles de Chartres*, p. 61).

36. P. 215, ll. 11ff.: "Scolaris oboedientiae ministerium, cum nullum studium

discendi, nulla facultas cohercendi . . . rationaliter subterfugi." His resignation is also due to John's high-handed act of restoring to honor a student who had confessed to twenty thefts and conspired against Wazo's life (p. 215, ll. 13–14).

37. Anselm refers to the Benedictine Rule throughout as simply "the rule" (*regula*). Cf. p. 212, l. 15.

38. P. 214, ll. 39ff.: [Wazo asks] ". . . quare . . . me soles iracundum vocare? . . . imputas mihi propter iracundiae magnitudinem nostrique obstinationem penitus hoc agere."

39. Bittner argues that the change in bishop from the comparatively strict Durandus to the allegedly simoniac Reginhard in 1025 accounts for Wazo's fall and John's success in turning the heads of the chapter against him (*Wazo und die Schulen*, p. 25). This argument is not persuasive. We know that Wazo's letter was written around 1021, still during Durand's administration. John would not have waited some four years for a change in bishop to present his inflamed reaction to Wazo's letter. If Wazo's departure had been the result of the bad judgment of a corrupt bishop, Anselm surely would have mentioned it. Koepke, editor of the *Gesta*, agrees (p. 215, n. 74). Anselm has high praise for Reginhard and no blame. He polished off Durandus in a few lines.

40. Ch. 42, p. 215, ll. 28ff.: "Iohannes . . . persuasibilibus terrenae sapientiae verbis episcopi caeterorumque priorum animos nichilominus in eius odium accendit, quaeque fideliter ab eo gesta potius deputans studio litigii, quam fidelitatis devotioni." Later the king's advisors raise the same objection to Wazo, claiming he allied himself with Godfrey of Lorraine in his rebellion against Henry "out of his customary contentiousness and arrogance" ("Wazo, non . . . imperatoriae fidelitatis gratiae, sed ex contentionis usu, propriae inservierit arrogantiae" — chapter 57, p. 223, ll. 51ff.).

41. Cf. chapter 50, p. 219, ll. 27ff. He conjures an angry God sending Wazo before him as his soldier to the "stern field of contention." Also chapter 55, p. 221, ll. 47ff.: ". . . ecce bellator Christi inexpugnabilis et inperterritus lorica iusticiae induitur, gladio spirituali accingitur, praevia cruce Christi . . . pro lancea utitur." Chapter 56, p. 223, l. 31: "propugnator"; chapter 59, p. 224, ll. 47ff.: the lord sent "his pugilist" to exhibit "the virile strength of this fighter through the hard labors of many a struggle" ("per duros certaminum labores virile pugnatoris robur . . . exponere voluit").

42. In the one case where Wazo capitulates to the King, he regrets his act of submission the rest of his life, and, given the chance would rather have died than repeat it. (Cf. chapter 66, p. 229, ll. 36ff.).

43. Cf. chapter 56, p. 223, ll. 38ff.

44. Ch. 56, p. 223, ll. 25ff. Steindorff has read this passage as a report of an actual event (*Jahrbücher des deutschen Reiches unter Heinrich III* 2: 23). But Wazo says only that he was prepared to do this, not that he did it.

45. The controversy is recorded in three letters of the Hildesheim collection, *Briefsammlungen der Zeit Heinrichs IV.*, ed. Erdmann and Fickermann, pp. 52–61 (epist. 22, 24, 26).

46. Provost John was getting just the kind of support Bernard of Clairvaux prescribes a century later to bishops in dealing with the provosts of their house-

holds. He says that to rule successfully the provost must have unquestioned authority: "Everyone must be subject to this man; let no one oppose him." Bernard seems to be addressing just the issues operating in the opposition of Wazo and John, and siding strongly with the provost: "Let there be no one who says, 'Why did you do this?' Let him have the power to exclude and to admit whom he wants." And Bernard also speaks the language of the imperial statesman/administrator: "Let him be in charge of all [*praesse*] so he may benefit all [*prodesse*] in every way." Bernard of Clairvaux, *Five Books on Consideration*, 4.6.18, p. 132.

47. *Ben. reg.*, 64.8, ed. Hanslik, p. 149. See above, Chapter 2, pp. 38–39. The Regensburg Rhetorical Letters develop the theme of a necessary balance between the two administrative duties, using Ciceronian terms (*Regensburger Rhet. Briefe,* epist. 20, ed. Fickermann, p. 344).

48. Ch. 43, p. 216, ll. 8ff. On the death of Provost John, he was reluctant to return to Liège, lest anyone think he coveted the provostship rather than claustral peace (p. 216, ll. 38–39). He declined the bishopric of Liège in favor of his student Neithard, "using the authority of his power to maintain his commitment to humility, not to seize a position of importance" (chapter 49, p. 219, ll. 1ff.). He tended to secular business not out of any wish to do so, but out of necessity, so as not to displease God (chapter 56, p. 223, l. 20).

49. Ch. 50, p. 219, ll. 42f.: ". . . nisi quem constiterit in curte regia evagari." The sense of aimless vagabondage is intentional. Cf. Anselm's earlier formulation: the rigorous discipline of Bishop Wolbodo left his students no room for "wandering or straying from the path of sacred religion" ("nullus alicui locus evagandi, aut quoquam a sanctae religionis tramite exorbitandi" — chapter 32, p. 207, l. 23).

50. Ch. 50, p. 219, ll. 39–44: "Nec defuere adulantium linguae, qui electionem sine regio favore factam asseverarent causam fore. Ex capellanis pocius episcopum constituendum, Wazonem numquam in curte regia desudasse, ut talem promereretur honorem; quod vero nefas sit alium episcopari, nisi quem constiterit in curte regia evagari, ac non potius talem eligi oportere, qui informatus subiectione claustralis oboedientiae, non tam praesse quam prodesse didicerit."

51. See Zielinski, *Reichsepiskopat,* pp. 175–76; Bittner, *Wazo und die Schulen,* p. 18; Köhler, *Das Bild,* p. 72 with some discussion of Anselm's confused wording. Steindorff, *Jahrbücher des deutschen Reiches unter Heinrich III.,* 2:23, interprets the passage to mean that Wazo has insufficient monastic discipline; Köhler correctly reads past the confused syntax. The meaning is perfectly clear when read against the background of the education of Dietrich of Metz. "Governing" (*praeesse*) became a virtual requirement of an imperial bishop, as did service in the chapel. This is clearly Brun's tradition, which the chaplains support and Wazo violates.

52. Otto I writing to Brun, in Ruotger, *Vita Brun.,* chapter 20, LB, p. 206. See Chapter 2, p. 44 and n. 19.

53. From Evraclius to Wazo (959–1048), six of eight bishops of Liège had served in the royal chapel. From Wazo to Albero (d. 1128), one of five moves from the chapel to the bishopric. See *Series Episcoporum,* ed. Weinfurter and Engels, 1: 66–76. Also Zielinski, *Reichsepiskopat* and Fleckenstein, *Hofkapelle.* Bishop Durandus (1021–25) is an uncertain case, but Fleckenstein considers it possible that he was a chaplain (*Hofkapelle* 2: 202–3).

54. Charlotte Renardy, "Les écoles liégeoises du IXe au XII siècle: grandes lignes de leur évolution," pp. 320–26.

55. This section reinterprets and adds to materials I discussed in another context in *Origins of Courtliness*, pp. 153–54. A fuller interpretation is useful not only for the present topic, but also to keep the name of Azelinus of Hildesheim visible. The abundant literature on courtliness and courtly culture in the past ten years has taken no notice of him. His name is not mentioned in the collection of studies whose title first occurs in connection with Azelinus: *Curialitas: Studien zu Grundfragen der höfisch-ritterlichen Kultur*, ed. Fleckenstein. As far as the historical sources are concerned, Azelinus is the first representative of medieval courtesy. A second commendation of this set of texts and historical circumstances to colleagues in history clearly cannot hurt.

56. For the general line of Azelinus's career, see Hans Götting, *Das Bistum Hildesheim 3*, pp. 263–71. Götting shows no interest in the nature of Azelinus's reforms (cf. p. 266).

57. *Fundatio ecclesiae Hildesheimensis*, chapter 4, MGH SS 30: 2, pp. 944–45 (on the text see *DGQ* 2: 576):

> His igitur presidentibus . . . clerus tam districta religione et religiosa districtione Dei obsequio se mancipaverat, ut in professione canonica districtione gauderet monachica. Nam — ut taceatur, quam severe animadvertebatur si quis choro, mensae, dormitorio, non dico deesset, sed vel tardius advenisset, nisi aut gravi necessitate irretitus aut licentia munitus hoc facere praesumpsisset — scholaris disciplinae iugo absoluti strictiori habena in claustro servabantur . . . Delicatioris enim vestitus tam nulla illis erat cura, ut gulas quibus nunc clerus ardet, nescirent, linguas pelliciales ac manicas non pallio, sed nigrato panno ornarent. . . . Sic ergo rusticalem stultitiam curiali facetiae pretulerant . . . nec altiora, quam de claustro administrabantur affectando, ut tam interius quam exterius claustrali restrictione clausi renunciato nondum seculo seculum nescirent. Hunc ergo statum claustri Heinrico imperatori . . . referunt in tantum placuisse, ut ab exterioris eorum hominis compositissimo habitu interioris religionem sibi experto credendam protestatus suae Bavenbergensi ecclesiae cum studio Leodicensi optaret etiam rigorem Hildensemensis claustri.
>
> Haec censura claustri permansit usque ad tempora Azelini episcopi XVI. Eo enim presidente irrepsit ambitiosa curialitas, quae dum in vestitu mollior, in victu lautior, in omni cultu accuratior amari quam timeri maluit, disciplinae mollito rigore claustri claustra relaxavit.

58. Ibid., chapter 6, p. 945, ll. 25–26: ". . . magis . . . prodesse quam preesse volens Hezilo, non tam presul quam pater . . . Hildensemensem suscepit ecclesiam."

59. *Ben. Reg.*, 64.15, ed. Hanslik, p. 165: "studeat plus amari quam timeri."

60. "Trois oeuvres," ed. Boutemy, pp. 345–46, ll. 30–56. See Chapter 4, pp. 114–15 and n. 145.

61. Wolfhere, author of two Vitae of Godehard of Hildesheim, has high praise for Azelinus as ". . . regius capellanus, in divinis scilicet et humanis feliciter strenuus" (*Vita posterior*, ed. Pertz, chapter 33, MGH SS 11, p. 215, ll. 44ff.). He even lauds his

close relationship to the emperor: "Qui . . . apud imperatorem et primates ad summum mundanae felicitatis apicem honorifice profecit" (ll. 51–52). This testimony is the more valuable, since Godehard was undoubtedly the originator of the monastic rigor that long dominated Hildesheim, and the author Wolfhere was a canon at Hildesheim under both Godehard and Azelinus. He wrote the *Vita posterior* shortly after 1068, and so is closer to Azelinus than either of the chroniclers from around 1080. But he reproaches Azelinus for "removing" much of the church's possessions and claims he "was at fault in many ways" ("multipliciter deliquit"—chapter 33, p. 216, ll. 3ff.). Norbert of Iburg calls Azelinus "venerabilis eiusdem loci Ezelinus episcopus" (*Vita Bennonis,* chapter 5, LB, p. 380).

But the picture is not entirely rosy. The *Chronicon Hildesheimense,* written ca. 1079, criticizes him for tearing down the destroyed church without consulting the brothers, but otherwise has only good words for him ("Azelinus, regius capellanus . . . successit; qui pluralem utilitatem suae ecclesiae diversa acquisitione contulit, veruntamen, ut veremur, ante Deum reus extitit, quot monasterium nostrum igne consumptum inconsulte deiecit"—chapter 16, MGH SS 7, p. 853). This writer makes his successor, Hezilo, either still alive or newly dead at the time of the writing, responsible for tolerating if not introducing relaxed rigor and "superfluous clothing" ("institutionem nostri ordinis in abbreviatione divini officii, in superfluitate vestium, in relaxando regularis vitae districtionem, non dico mutavit, sed mutantibus non contradixit"—chapter 17, p. 854). This passage and the description of Azelinus from the *Fundatio* are repeated by the Saxon Annalist, MGH SS 6, p. 690, ll. 3ff. (a. 1054).

62. *Visio quinta,* PL 146, 357–59.

63. *Vita Bennonis,* chapter 5, LB, p. 380.

64. *Vita Bennonis,* chapter 5, LB, p. 380: ". . . eatenus ecclesiae illius clerici rusticano quodam more educati, pene sine litteris ac idiotae fuissent."

65. *Vita Bennonis,* chapter 5, LB, p. 380: "Egregius enim exinde ibi clerus adolescere coepit cum claustralis honestate disciplinae, tum litterarum scientiam ardore discendi."

66. *Fundatio:* "rusticalis stultitia"; *Vita Bennonis:* "rusticano more educati, pene sine litteris ac idiotae."

67. *Briefsammlungen der Zeit Heinrichs IV.,* ed. Erdmann and Fickermann, pp. 15–106.

Chapter 8: Old Learning Against New

1. Contradicting the teacher is no minor breach of etiquette. Cf. William of Conches's "Glosses on Priscian," 18.5, "Deux rédactions des gloses de Guillaume de Conches sur Priscien," ed. Jeauneau, p. 234: "magistri nostri quibus non fas est contra dicere." The Pseudo-Boethian work *De disciplina scholari,* written in the twelfth century and still formulating a conservative humanistic program against the new, writes: "qui se non novit subjici, non noscat se magistrari" (PL 64, 1226D); 1227C: "Non est ergo dignus scientia qui scientiae insurgit praeceptori."

2. Otloh of St. Emmeram, *Vita Wolfkangi,* chapters 4–5, MGH SS 4, p. 528.

3. One wonders whether Italian masters were fair game in the north. They certainly were sensitive to contradiction. Stefan's countryman Gunzo of Novara had his grammar corrected by the monks of St. Gall, and responded in dudgeon with a long tract justifying himself.

4. Ademar, *Epistola de S. Martiali*, PL 141, 107–9. See H. E. J. Cowdrey, "Anselm of Besate and some North-Italian Masters of the Eleventh Century," p. 119.

5. Abelard, *Historia calamitatum: Texte critique avec une introduction*, ed. Monfrin, p. 90, ll. 963ff.

6. Grabmann, *Geschichte der scholastischen Methode*, 1: 215–34, and on Anselm of Canterbury, 1: 265–339. Radding, *A World Made by Men*, pp. 153–99.

7. Adelman, Letter to Berengar, in "Textes latins du XIe au XIIIe siècle," ed. Huygens, p. 476, ll. 3–8. (For Latin quote, see above, Chapter 4, p. 105 and n. 109). On the letter, see Radding, *A World Made by Men*, pp. 165–66, and Southern, *Making of the Middle Ages*, pp. 197–98.

8. Wibald, epist. 167, ed. Jaffé, p. 277: "Discipuli magistrorum sentencias tuentur, non quia verae sunt, set quod auctores amant; scola adversus scolam debachatur, odio vel amore magistrorum."

9. Cf. Hugh of St. Victor, *De institutione novitiorum*, chapter 6, PL 176, 932D.

10. On Goswin see the introduction to his letter by R. B. C. Huygens in his edition, *Apologiae duae: Gozechini epistola ad Walcherum*, pp. 3–9; also the article by F. J. Worstbrock, "Gozwin von Mainz," in *Verfasserlexikon*, 2nd ed.; Riché, *Écoles et enseignement*, p. 337; Manitius, *Geschichte der lateinischen Literatur*, 2: 470–78; S. Balau, *Étude critique des sources de l'histoire du pays de Liège*, pp. 172–74; O. Holder-Egger, "Goswin und Gozechin: Domscholaster zu Mainz."

11. *Gozechini epistola ad Walcherum*, chapter X, ed. Huygens, p. 18, ll. 207ff.: "Perhaps I did once, in abandoning Liège, write a scurrilous attack on it, perhaps I did prefer the glory of Mainz and seemed to regard Liège as a vile heap of slag."

12. This conjecture seems the most probable explanation of the length and detail of the letter. It does not require some thirty to forty pages of dense prose to inquire whether he would be welcome. He must overcome strong barriers, no doubt put in place by his ungracious exit. The long arguments against detractors (among whom the recipient Walcher almost certainly numbers), who attack men for changing their place of residence, does not make alot of sense without a reason for pressing such arguments against Goswin himself. For whatever reasons, he did not make it back, but lived out his life in Mainz and died in 1075.

13. *Epist. ad Walcherum*, chapter XXVI, pp. 30–31, ll. 604ff. From now on I will cite the letter in the form: XXVI.30–31. 604ff. (= chapter.page.lines).

14. XXVII.32.636: ". . . vanis et pestiferis inserviunt vocum vel quaestionum novitatibus." The "novelty" of these teachings is repeatedly stressed: "novas psalterii, Pauli, Apocalipsis lectiones tradunt" (XXVIII.32.643–44). The teachers draw into their following "iuventutem novorum cupidam" (644–45); "de sacris sacrilegas introducunt novitates questionum" (657–58); "de his . . . rebus et sacramentis et novas et peregrinas ducunt a fide intelligentias" (XXX. 33. 665–66); "novo quodam docendi lenocinio" (682); "extranea et a salute peregrina questionum novitate pulchre ad perniciem instructos" (687–89).

15. On opposition to worldly learning in general, see Grabmann, *Geschichte der*

scholastischen Methode, 1: 215ff.; Riché, *Écoles et enseignement*, pp. 335–44. On Otloh's opposition to worldly learning, Helga Schauwecker, *Otloh von St. Emmeram: Ein Beitrag zur Bildungs- und Frömmigkeitsgeschichte des 11. Jahrhunderts*, pp. 165ff. On Peter Damian, J. A. Endres, *Petrus Damiani und die weltliche Wissenschaft*; A. Cantin, *Les sciences séculières et la foi: Les deux voies de la science au jugement de S. Pierre Damien.*

16. VI.14.98–100: "haec filios suos . . . fovet et nutrit et ad omne quod civile sit et moribus conducat informat et instruit."

17. XXXIV.36.760: "turbinis violentia," referring to worldly affairs, is an image of which Goswin's former colleague, Anselm of Liège, also was fond.

18. XXVII.31.618: "exitialis morum et disciplinae iactura."

19. Hugh of St. Victor, *De inst. nov.* chapter 7, PL 176, 932D–933D.

20. The whip was in common use (cf. Specht, *Geschichte des Unterrichtswesens*, p. 75, 203ff., 209, 346; Lèsne, *Les écoles*, 2: 540–41; Köhn, "Schulbildung und Trivium," p. 242), but there were voices in favor of moderation, and no voices advocating the use to which for instance Guibert of Nogent's master put it. The Würzburg master, Pernolf, is praised around 1031 for his moderate use of the whip (Würzburg poem, *Wormser Briefsammlung*, ed. Bulst, l. 25). Rather of Verona and Meinwerk of Paderborn argued for, Egbert of Liège against it. See Louis Halphen, "Un pédagogue," pp. 282–83. Whipping a student had legal sanction. A Lombard truce of God contract forbids hitting anyone in anger "except a master his student" ("nisi magister discipulum"—MGH Leges 4, Constit. 1, p. 598, Nr. 420, chapter 4).

21. A letter included among Meinhard of Bamberg's appeals to Rheims to return a cleric who ran away from Bamberg because he could not bear the school discipline. *Weitere Briefe Meinhards*, epist. 3, ed. Erdmann, p. 195.

22. *Weitere Briefe Meinhards*, epist. 24, ed. Erdmann, p. 221: "Non adeo fortassis domestica litterarum inopia merces peregrinas persequimur, sed discipline desiderium id nos sollicitat; que cum ubique fere sit extincta, non dubitem illam in vestra calere officina." The suggestion that moral discipline has died out at Bamberg would seem to date this letter considerably after Meinhard's epist. 39 (*Weitere Briefe Meinhards*, pp. 238–39) complaining to Bishop Gunther about the dual discipline of "letters and manners." See Chapter 4, p. ***). The tone and content of this letter suggest that it was written shortly before his "retirement" as school master.

23. *Hildesheimer Briefe*, ed. Erdmann, epist. 24, p. 57.

24. On Bishop Hezilo and Kuno, see Erdmann, *Studien zur Briefliteratur*, pp. 128–30. Kuno's career was advanced by fleeing his post at Hildesheim. He found support at the royal court and wound up as Bishop of Brescia. It is an odd phenomenon: men of talent in trouble in their churches turn to the royal courts and find safe haven and succor there. This is the case with Rather of Verona, Gerbert of Aurillac, Wazo of Liège, Manasses I of Rheims, and William of Conches. Ruotger called the court of Otto the Great under Brun's chancellorship a haven for intellectual refugees. *Vita Brunonis*, chapter 5, LB, p. 186: ". . . ab omnibus calumnia qualibet oppressis hoc asylum unicum petebatur."

25. XXXIII. 35. 721ff. On the teachers mentioned, see Erdmann, *Studien zur Briefliteratur*, p. 22, n. 2; Riché, *Écoles et enseignement*, p. 180, 184.

26. R. T. Moore, "Guibert of Nogent and his World"; Edmond-René Labande, "Guibert de Nogent, Disciple et Témoin de Saint Anselme au Bec"; Georg Misch, *Geschichte der Autogiobraphie* 3, 1: 108–62; Louis Halphen, "Un pédagogue";

Paré, Tremblay, Brunet, *La renaissance*, pp. 22–23; Bernard Monod, "La pédagogie et l'éducation au moyen âge d'après les souvenirs d'un moine du XIe siècle"; Chris D. Ferguson, "Autobiography as Therapy: Guibert de Nogent, Peter Abelard, and the Making of Medieval Autobiography"; Delhaye, "L'organisation scolaire," 243–46; Auguste Mollard, "L'imitation de Quintilien dans Guibert de Nogent"; idem, "Interpretation d'un passage du *De Vita sua.*"

27. Guibert de Nogent, *Autobiographie*, chapter 4, ed. Labande, p. 26: "Tantae vero modestiae fuerat, ut quod deficiebat in literis, suppleret honesto."

28. English translations of Guibert taken in part from the revision of C. C. Swinton Bland by John Benton, *Self and Society in Medieval France: The Memoirs of Abbot Guibert of Nogent (1064?–c. 1125)*, here p. 46.

29. Chapter 5, p. 30: "nihil non temperanter, non in verbo, non in respectu, non opere, agere."

30. Chapter 5, p. 30: "ut non clericatum, quin potius monachatum a me videretur exigere."

31. A vital point not conveyed by Bland's and Benton's rendering, "in all that is supposed to count for good training." Guibert wrote: "ad totius *honestatis* rudimentum" (chapter 5, ed. Labande, p. 32). Labande comes closer: "tout ce qui regarde les principes du parfait honnête homme."

32. Chapter 5, p. 32: ". . . nihil quantum ad tantum temporis attinet inde extuli operae pretium. Alias autem quantum ad totius honestatis rudimentum spectare dinoscitur, nihil fuit quod non meis utilitatibus impendisset; quidquid modestiae, quidquid pudicum ac exterioris elegantiae fuit, eo fidelissime et amanter me imbuit."

33. Fulbert of Chartres, epist. 76, *Letters and Poems*, ed. Behrends, p. 136. See above, Chapter 3, p. 60.

34. Anselm, *Gesta Ep. Leod.*, chapter 40, MGH SS 7, p. 210, ll. 30ff. See above, Chapter 3, p. 56 and n. 13.

35. Thomas Becket could still be mentioned as putting his efforts into *mores* and *moralitas*, rather than letters, but the passage also shows less patience with his unimpressive performance in letters. See below, p. 470, n. 18.

36. PL 149, 1428B. See above, Chapter 4, pp. 81–82 and note 31.

37. Chapter 6, p. 38; trans. Bland and Benton, p. 49.

38. See esp. Halphen, "Un pédagogue."

39. Cf. chapter 4, pp. 26–28.

40. Lèsne gives examples of constant surveillance in monastic communities (*Les écoles*, 2: 538–39). It was also the case at St. Victor of Paris.

41. Chapter 6, p. 40: "nec etiam moderni temporis clericulis vagantibus comparari poterat." On the state of liberal learning in France in the eleventh century, see Radding, "The Geography of Learning."

42. For a recent survey, see D. E. Luscombe, "Peter Abelard."

43. In the recent critical edition, Peter Abelard, *Carmen ad Astralabium*, J. Rubingh-Boscher suggests a date in the mid-1130s.

44. *Carmen ad Astralab.*, ed. Rubingh-Boscher, p. 107, ll. 7–18:

non a quo sed quid dicatur sit tibi cure:
    auctori nomen dant bene dicta suo;
nec tibi dilecti iures in verba magistri

nec te detineat doctor amore suo.
Fructu, non foliis pomorum quisque cibatur
    et sensus verbis anteferendus erit.
ornatis animos captet persuasio verbis;
    doctrine magis est debita planicies.
copia verborum est ubi non est copia sensus,
    constat et errantem multiplicare vias.
cuius doctrinam sibi dissentire videbis
    nil illam certi constet habere tibi.

45. *Letters of Abelard and Heloise*, trans. Radice, p. 62.; *Historia cal.*, ed. Monfrin, p. 68, ll. 165–76.

46. Anselm may not have been the mediocrity Abelard made him out to be (see Marcia Colish, "Another Look at the School of Laon"), but he was no match for Abelard, and the passage quoted makes it clear that he was aiming not just at an individual, but at an entire education that offered, in his formulation, leaves but no fruit.

47. Trans. p. 80, here with slight variations; ed. Monfrin, p. 84, ll. 757–59).

48. See the chapter of Hugh of St. Victor's *De inst. novit.* on imitating the examples of saints (chapter 7, "De exemplis sanctorum imitandis," PL 176, 932–33). The title seems to indicate biblical models and Christian saints, but actually refers to good and saintly men alive and active in St. Victor.

49. *Vita Malachiae*, *Sancti Bernardi Opera*, 3: 360.18–19: "Dicebat autem se non ratione victum, sed episcopi pressum auctoritate."

50. *Opera*, 3: 360.25–361.1: "'Omnes,' inquit, 'favetis homini potius quam veritati; ego personam non accipio, ut deseram veritatem.'"

51. See the introduction to *Peter Abelard's Ethics*, ed. and trans. Luscombe.

52. *De inst. nov.*, chapter 10, 935A–B: "Disciplina est conversatio bona et honesta, cui parum est mala non facere, sed studet etiam in iis qua bene agit per cuncta irreprehensibilis *apparere*" (emphasis added).

53. His treatment of the philosopher in the *Dialogue of a Philosopher with a Jew and a Christian* shows no interest in practical training in behavior. It is about speculative ethics, the writings of the ancient philosophers and the definition of the *summum bonum*.

54. Epist. 3 (4 in editions including *Hist. cal.* among the letters, PL 178), J. T. Muckle, "The Personal Letters Between Abelard and Heloise." On the vexed question of authorship, see the summary by Adalbert Podlech, *Abälard und Héloïse oder die Theologie der Liebe*, pp. 476–77. Barbara Newman's case for Heloise as the author of the letters ascribed to her is patent good sense—not that common in this authenticity dispute: "Authority, Authenticity, and the Repression of Heloise." I will talk about the letter as if Heloise were the unique and genuine author who has taken over ideas of her teacher-lover-husband and analyzed her own situation using them.

55. Trans. Radice, p. 133; ed. Muckle, p. 81: "Munditiam carnis conferunt in virtutem, cum non sit corporis, sed animi virtus."

56. The point is made strongly in Heloise's letter requesting a rule for nuns (epist. 5 in Muckle's numbering, in that of PL 178, epist. 6), here pointed distinctly

against *honestas* as an ideal of outward comportment. See J. T. Muckle, ed., "The Letter of Heloise on Religious Life and Abelard's First Reply," p. 250. Also the commentary by Linda Georgianna, "Any Corner of Heaven: Heloise's Critique of Monasticism," p. 242.

57. See Luscombe, intro. to *Abelard's Ethics* and Jaeger, "Peter Abelard's Silence at the Council of Sens," esp. pp. 44–45.

58. See "Abelard's Silence," previous note.

59. P. 107, ll. 33–36: "Detrimenta tue caveas super omnia fame / ut multis possis et tibi proficere. / que precesserunt, credi nova crimina cogunt / et prior in testem vita sequentis erit."

60. P. 109, ll. 55–58: "ingenii sapiens fit nullus acumine magni; / hunc pocius mores et bona vita creant. / factis, non verbis sapiencia se profitetur; / solis concessa est gracia tanta bonis."

61. P. 109, ll. 71–72: "Sit tibi cura prior faciendi, deinde docendi / que bona sunt, ne sis dissonus ipse tibi."

62. P. 111, ll. 85–88: "Est iusti proprium . . . / illicitos animi motus frenare modesti / tunc cum succedunt prospera precipue."

63. Ll. 93–94: "quid vicii, quid sit virtutis discute prudens; / quod si perdideris, desinis esse quod es."

64. P. 113, ll. 107–8: "Scandala quam possis hominum vitare labora, / ut tamen incurras scandala nulla dei."

65. *Didascalicon*, 3.12, trans. Taylor, p. 94. On Hugh of St. Victor's oblique and "quiet" criticism of Abelard's doctrine, see D. E. Luscombe, *The School of Peter Abelard: The Influence of Abelard's Thought in the Early Scholastic Period*, pp. 183–97.

66. Ll. 425–26: "Ex hominis vicio ne culpes illius artem: / est homo sepe malus qui bonus est opifex." The editor gives three further passages in Abelard's works where the idea occurs. On Abelard as a rigorous moral thinker, see Georgianna, "Heloise's Critique," pp. 248–49.

67. Massive documentation of the resistance to change and complaints about the collapse of *mores* in Stephen C. Ferruolo, *The Origins of the University: The Schools of Paris and Their Critics, 1100–1215*, pp. 47–277.

68. I do not mean this to blame and indict Abelard, but in the strict sense of violating the *disciplina* and *ars bene vivendi* idealized and cultivated at the major schools of his contemporaries. His later life was evidently irreproachable (though his fateful penchant to make enemies abated very late), his last days were, according to Peter the Venerable, a model for others, and in his own words, "A good death pays all debts" ("Cum bene quis moritur persolvit debita cuncta"—*Carmen ad Astralab.* p. 141, l. 615). The point is, whatever good can be said of the mature and old Abelard was lost in the perceptions that had been set in his earlier life and the enmities he had aroused.

Introduction to Part III

1. Heloise to Abelard, epist. 1, *Letters,* trans. Radice, p. 115; "Personal Letters," ed. Muckle, p. 71.

2. Otto, *Gesta Frid.*, 1.48, MGH SS 20, p. 337, ll. 21–22: "maximamque post se sociorum multitudinem traheret . . ."

3. Bernard, epist. 332, *Opera*, 8.271.12ff.: "Accedit non solus, sicut Moyses, ad caliginem in qua erat Deus, sed cum turba multa et discipulis suis."

4. Bernard, epist. 189, *Opera*, 8.13.18ff.

5. William of St. Thierry to Bernard and Geoffrey of Chartres (among Bernard's letters), epist. 326, PL 182, 531B. Ed. Jean Leclercq, *Revue Bénédictine* 79 (1969), 376–78.

6. PL 178, 105: "turbae lucerna scholaris."

7. See R. W. Southern, "The Schools of Paris and Chartres," in *Renaissance and Renewal*, p. 128.

8. William of Conches, *Philosophia mundi*, ed. Maurach, II. prol., p. 41: ". . . nihil de multitudine, sed de paucorum probitate gloriantes soli veritati insudamus." Similarly Thierry of Chartres in his commentary on Cicero's *De inventione:* "I have carried out my resolve to shut out, at my whim, the ignorant mob and the mish-mash of the schools." Quoted in Dronke, "Thierry of Chartres," in *History of Twelfth Century Philosophy*, p. 362 (Dronke's translation).

9. *Phil. mundi*, ed. Maurach, 4.30, p. 114: "nec, si deficiat multitudo sociorum, deficiet [alt. desinet]."

10. "Metamorphosis Goliae," ed. R. B. C. Huygens, "Mitteilungen aus Handschriften," *Studi Medievali* Ser. 3, 3 (1962), p. 771, stanza 50, 4.

11. Cited by John Ward, *Artificiosa Eloquentia*, 2: 61: "dignitas paucorum bonorum longe excellit infinitam multitudinem malorum."

12. John of Salisbury, *Metalogicon*, 1.24, ed. Hall, p. 54: ". . . impetu multitudinis imperitae victi cesserunt."

13. In this sense also William's attack on teachers who fawn on students and on students who pass judgment on their masters (*Phil. mundi*, 4.Prol., ed. Maurach, p. 88). The loss of students puts him on the defensive.

The statement of Everard of Ypres that he had heard Gilbert of Poitiers lecture in Chartres to an audience of four and in Paris to an audience of some three hundred must surely be a reflection of these priorities. Cited in N. M. Häring, "Chartres and Paris Revisited," in *Essays in Honour of Anton Charles Pegis*, p. 283 and note 41.

14. On the popularity of Chartrian masters, see Häring, "Chartres and Paris," passim, and Peter Dronke, "Thierry of Chartres," in *History of Twelfth Century Philosophy*, p. 363.

15. An exception: the education of Vicelin, described in Helmold's *Chron. Slav.*, chapter 65, MGH SS 21, 47, 1.8ff. He went to Laon to study with Ralph, the brother of Anselm, where ". . . ad ea solum enisus est, que sobrio intellectui et moribus instruendis sufficerent."

16. Wibald, epist. 91, ed. Jaffé, p. 165: "Presentia tua tuis auditoribus disciplina sit. . . . Plus habet locus tuus quam docendi officium; nam et censoriam exhibere debes severitatem, quoniam et corrigendis moribus prefectum te esse noveris. Quae disciplina et exercitatio omnibus est subtilior et in fructu cunctis propensior." Cf. also his epist. 167 to Manegold of Paderborn, ed. Jaffé, pp. 276–88. The letter is a sophisticated presentation of a liberal education, with stress on classical learning. *Mores* are mentioned as the ultimate goal (p. 281f., p. 283), but

receive no more than a mention. See also the study by Wilhelm Hemmen, "Der Brief des Magisters Manegold an Abt Wibald von Corvey (1149)."

17. On what was laughed out of the Paris schools, see John of Salisbury, *Metalogicon*, 1.3, trans. McGarry, p. 15: "Poets who related history were considered reprobate, and if anyone applied himself to studying the ancients, he became a marked man and the laughingstock of all."

18. On this development see Southern, "Schools of Paris and Chartres," p. 120. For Southern the breaking of the chancellor of Paris's monopoly on teaching is the decisive moment in the development of the independent schools.

19. Ed. Huygens (n. 10 above), p. 771 (stanzas 48–51): "Ibi doctor cernitur ille Carnotensis, / cuius lingua vehemens truncat velud ensis, / et hic presul presulum stat Pictaviensis, / proprius nubencium miles et castrensis. / Inter hos et alios in parte remota / Parvi Pontis incola, non loquor ignota, / disputabat digitis directis in iota / et quecumque dixerat erant per se nota. / . . . / Reginaldus monachus clamose contendit / et obliquis singulos verbis reprehendit, / hos et hos redarguit nec in se descendit, / qui nostrum Porphirium laqueo suspendit."

20. John of Salisbury describes this transition in *Metalogicon* 1.3.

21. Ferruolo, *The Origins of the University*.

22. Bernard of Clairvaux, *Five Books on Consideration: Advice to a Pope*, trans. Anderson and Kennan, Book 4, chapter 6, paragraph 21. *Opera*, 3: 464.23–26.

23. This was a summary of *De consideratione*, 4.6.21–22. *Opera*, 3: 464–65, and trans. Anderson and Kennan, pp. 130–37.

24. Cf. the comment on Vicelin's study at Laon (note 15 above) with the statutes of Laon (ca. 1190), one of the few "rules" of a twelfth century cathedral community. On the *doctrina et officia* to be taught to junior members of the church: PL 199, 1117A: [The servant of the church] "verecundiam in omnibus debet servare, in motu corporis, in actu operis, in gestu omnium membrorum, in incessu ut mature incedat . . . in loquendo. . . . Pulchrae igitur virtutes sunt verecundia, patientia, et remissio injuriarum, et suavis est gratia." 1117B: "Speculum mentis . . . refulget in verbis." 1117C: "Verecundia bene morigerati." 1118A: "in ipso motu, gestu, incessu, tenenda verecundia omnibus clericis . . . quia habitus mentis in corporis statu cernitur. . . . Vox quaedam est animi motus." 1118D: "Sunt . . . qui . . . ambulando imitantur histrionicos gressus, et quasi quaedam fercula pomparum et statuarum status imitantium . . . gressus suos probabiles ostendere."

Chapter 9: Humanism and Ethics at the School of St. Victor

1. *Historia calamitatum*, trans. Radice, p. 58; ed. Monfrin, p. 64, ll. 31–34.

2. The tendency of scholars to advocate William of Champeaux by denying Abelard's account of a resounding defeat has persisted since Fourier Bonnard, *Histoire de l'abbaye royale et de l'ordre des chanoines reguliers de St.-Victor de Paris*, 1: 4–5. Cf. also J. C. Dickinson, *The Origins of the Austin Canons*, p. 85 and Jean Châtillon, *Théologie, spiritualité et métaphysique dans l'oeuvre oratoire d'Achard de Saint-Victor*, p. 55. Since Abelard is the only one to report it, this scepticism might have some credibility, but seen against parallel examples of the demise of established masters at

the hands of young turks, Abelard's report does not seem just a product of his ego, however much he may have favored himself in the account. Discussion of the political background to these shifts; see Robert-Henri Bautier, "Paris au temps d'Abelard," in *Abélard en son temps*, ed. Jolivet; Podlech, *Abälard und Heloise*, pp. 83–87.

3. *Historia calamitatum*, trans. Radice, p. 61; ed. Monfrin, p. 65, ll. 78ff.

4. Debate on the philosophical subject was possible because William evidently tended to mix questions of dialectic into his teachings on rhetoric. See Karin Fredborg, "The Commentaries on Cicero's *De inventione* and *Rhetorica ad Herennium* by William of Champeaux," esp. p. 16.

5. *Codex Udalrici*, epist. 160, ed. Jaffé, p. 286. Southern interprets the writer's phrase *magnum studium* ("The Schools of Paris and Chartres,") as meaning large crowds. The meaning of the phrase is not clear, however.

6. Hildebert, *Epistolae*, PL 171, 141A. On the letter, see Châtillon, *Achard de St.-Victor*, pp. 56–57.

7. Hildebert's poem, *Formula vivendi*, gives an idea of his conception of the meaning of that term. See *Carmen* 16, *Carmina minora*, ed. Scott, p. 5: ". . . pauca loquaris, / plurima fac: sit utrisque comes modus, utile, pulchrum."

8. Bernard Bischoff, "Aus der Schule Hugos von St. Viktor," in *Aus der Geisteswelt des Mittelalters: Studien und Texte Martin Grabmann . . . gewidmet*, ed. Lang et al.; edition of letter and passage cited on p. 250.

9. See Giles Constable, "Renewal and Reform in Religious Life: Concepts and Realities," on "newness" and "renewal" as topoi of entry into a religious community.

10. Godfrey of St. Victor, *Fons philosophiae*, ed. Michaud-Quantin, ll. 741–84. Further comments on ethical training in ll. 401–4. The Victorine masters identify the "path of morality" with "beautiful manners" (*pulchri mores*). These distinguish the individual, help govern the family and the state. This is the threefold division of *practica* in Hugh's *Didascalicon* 3.1, ed. Buttimer, p. 48: "practica dividitur in solitariam, privatam, publicam." *Fons phil.*, ll. 413–16 place among the masters of *practica* (meaning ethics) some whom probity has made kings of the church, dukes (i.e. leaders) of souls, and even secular princes of lands, who govern many people. Clearly *practica* aims at administering and governing.

11. Robert of Torigny, *De immutatione ordinis monachorum*, chapter 5, PL 202, 1313B: "Sub cuius [i.e. Abbot Gilduin's] regimine multi clerici nobiles saecularibus et divinis litteris instructi, ad illum locum habitaturi convenerunt."

12. Bonnard, *Histoire* (n. 2 above), chapters 1, 2, and 3.

13. *Liber ordinis Sancti Victoris*, chapter 33, ed. Jocqué and Milis, p. 162, l. 168: "Si rex vel episcopus vel abbas in capitulum adducitur, fratres assurgentes omnes ei inclinent . . ."

14. Dickinson, *Austin Canons* (n. 2 above), p. 86: "Favoured by the highest officials of Church and State, esteemed all over the Western world, the haven of scholars and nursery of bishops, St. Victor's displayed perhaps more than any other house the potential of the regular canonical life."

15. Beryl Smalley, *The Study of the Bible in the Middle Ages*, p. 83–84; Ferruolo, *Origins of the University*, p. 32.

16. Jean Châtillon, "Les écoles de Chartres et de Saint-Victor," p. 812.

17. See the fundamental works by Charles Dereine, *Les chanoines réguliers au diocèse de Liège avant Saint Norbert*; art. "Chanoines," in *Dictionnaire d'histoire et géographie ecclésiastique* (1953), 12: 353–405; "Vie commune, règle de S. Augustin et chanoines réguliers au XIe siècle"; "Les origines de Prémontré." Also Dickinson, *Austin Canons*; Caroline Bynum, *Docere verbo et exemplo*; eadem, "The Spirituality of Regular Canons in the Twelfth Century: A New Approach"; Jean Châtillon, "La crise de l'église aux XIe et XIIe siècles et les origines des grandes fédérations canoniales"; M.-D. Chenu, "Monks, Canons, and Laymen in Search of the Apostolic Life"; Ludo Milis, "Ermites et chanoines réguliers au XIIe siècle"; Barbara Newman, "Flaws in the Golden Bowl: Gender and Spiritual Formation in the Twelfth Century."

18. On the so-called rule of St. Augustine, see *La règle de Saint Augustin*, ed. Luc Verheijen.

19. Bynum's *Docere verbo et exemplo* is the major study of this phenomenon and the works that express it.

20. See for instance, Bynum, *Docere verbo et exemplo*, pp. 4–5, 18–21; Ph. Delhaye, "L'organisation scolaire au XIIe siècle," pp. 225ff.

21. On customaries see Ch. Dereine, "Chanoines," pp. 386–91; idem, "Coutumiers et ordinaires de chanoines réguliers"; idem, "Les coutumiers de Saint-Quentin de Beauvais et de Springiersbach"; idem, "Saint-Ruf et ses coutumes aux XIe et XIIe siècles"; Josef Siegwart, *Die Consuetudines des Augustiner-Chorherrenstiftes Marbach im Elsass (12. Jahrhundert)*, pp. 4–14.

22. The subject of Bynum's study, *Docere verbo et exemplo*, the best guide to sources. Now also Newman, "Gender and Spiritual Formation" (n. 17 above), pp. 144–46, expanding Bynum's list to include nuns.

23. On the date of the work, see Damien Van den Eynde, *Essai sur la succession et la date des écrits de Hugues de Saint-Victor*, pp. 113ff. Van den Eynde places it just after the *Didascalicon*, that is, prior to 1125. But Roger Baron is sceptical about a specific dating: *Études sur Hugues de Saint-Victor*, pp. 69–89, esp. p. 71.

24. On this work see, besides the introduction to the edition of Jocqué and Milis, Bonnard, *Histoire*, 1: 47ff.; Châtillon, *Achard de Saint Victor*, pp. 63–67. Jocqué is preparing a monographic study of the *liber*.

25. On the school of Saint Victor see Bonnard, *Histoire*, 1: 85–140; Smalley, *The Study of the Bible*, pp. 83–195; Jean Châtillon, "De Guillaume de Champeaux à Thomas Gallus: Chronique d'histoire littéraire et doctrinale de l'école de Saint-Victor"; idem, "Les écoles de Chartres et de Saint-Victor"; idem, *Achard*, pp. 53–85; M.-D. Chenu, "Civilisation urbaine et théologie: L'école de Saint-Victor au XIIe siècle"; Jean-Pierre Willesme, "Saint-Victor au temps d'Abélard"; Ferruolo, *Origins of the University*, pp. 27–44. The earlier works by E. Michaud, *Guillaume de Champeaux et les écoles de Paris au XIIe siècle* and Martin Grabmann, *Geschichte der scholastischen Methode*, 2: 229–322, are still valuable.

26. R. Baron in his *Science et sagesse chez Hugues de Saint-Victor* defines Hugh's humanism in terms of thought, not behavior. Cf. p. 95: "L'humanisme de Hugues est essentiellement un humanisme de pensée. Il est à la recherche de la vérité."

27. See Milis's introduction to the *Liber*.

28. *Liber*, chapter 22, ll. 1–2, p. 96. Since Milis and Jocqué have numbered lines within chapters (i.e., not pages), I will cite brief references as 22, 1–2; 96 (= chapter, lines; page).

29. 22, 229–36; 106: "In scola diligenter instruendus est de inclinationibus, de incessu et statu, et omni gestu suo, et quomodo vestimenta sua in omni actione circa se coaptare debeat, et membra sua ordinate componere, oculos demissos habere, submisse et non festinanter loqui, iuramenta non facere . . . quomodo ad abbatem vel ceteros magistros suos loqui debeat, quomodo ad fratres vel alios compares, et quomodo ad inferiores."

30. The Benedictine Rule stipulates one year (*Ben. Reg.*, 58.9–13, ed. Hanslik, pp. 134–35).

31. Cf. chapter 8: the subprior sees to it that the brothers stand and sit *ordinate* when in the choir, and "quicquid corrigendum perspexerit corrigere [debet]" (8, 8–11; 29–30). The *circator*, a kind of ombudsman, circulates throughout the monastery observing the brothers, looking for neglects and breeches of the order. Where brothers talk, he checks lest they speak *inordinate* (chapter 41; pp. 194–95).

32. Chapter 25, 124; p. 130.

33. Cf. the comment that the novices write their own profession, "or, if they cannot write, they call on some one else" (24, 15–17; p. 113). But it need not mean much. It is borrowed from *Ben. Reg.*, 58.20, ed. Hanslik, p. 136.

34. Châtillon, *Achard*, pp. 72–73, notes that the *Liber* is interested only in the instruction of novices, not philosophy and the arts: "Cet enseignement . . . n'avait rien de scolaire."

35. Chapter 19; 78–86. The Marbach customs mention a librarian only once for his functions in the burial ritual. He writes the dead brother's name in the memorial book (*Consuetudines*, chapter 154, parag. 352, ed. Siegwart, p. 258). Arrouaise has books and an *armarium*, evidently just a place where books are kept, but no *armarius* (*Constit. Arroas.*, chapter 7, ed. Milis and Becquet, pp. 43–44). The customs of Springiersbach mention neither library nor librarian. By contrast the *Liber* with its details of a check-out system and descriptions of the librarian's duties, is exceptional.

36. The *vestiarius* should admonish anyone requesting superfluous clothing *amicabiliter et caritative* that such clothing is good for his body but bad for his soul (18, 114–19; 75). If any brother meets a guest of other members of the community, he should show them good cheer (*laetam faciem demonstret*) and speak to them courteously (*benigne eos alloquatur* — 17, 218–22; 68). If anyone sees that a brother needs something at table, he should indicate by a nod to the head of the refectory (35, 124–26; 171–2). Any and all conflict is proscribed (16, 27–29; 59).

37. 15, 1–5; 55: "Portarius unus de conversis fratribus eligi debet, probatus moribus, affabilis et benignus, qui, morum atque verborum disciplina instructus, cunctis quasi exemplum et titulus tocius domus proponatur."

38. *Yvain*, ll. 197ff. Cited from Chrétien de Troyes, *Arthurian Romances*, trans. W. W. Comfort (London and New York: Oxford University Press, 1975), p. 182.

39. Cf. *Ben. Reg.*, 53.

40. The Rule of St. Augustine gives no precepts for receiving guests. The rule of Chrodegang of Metz calls for a porter who is *probabilis vitae, sobrius, patiens et*

sapiens, a man who knows how to receive and render a response, who does his job *summa obedientia et humilitate*. He should not be drawn into any nonsense by outsiders, but should receive guests *cum charitate* and close the door well (Chrodegang, *Regula canonicorum*, chapter 12; Amort 1: 248). The *Decreta* of Lanfranc are dry and practical: the brother who receives guests should have various kinds of equipment ready: beds, towels, etc. (*The Monastic Constitutions of Lanfranc*, ed. Knowles, p. 87). The Premonstratensian custom is positively dour: when a guest knocks, the porter opens, asks humbly who it is and what he wants (*Instit. Praemonstrat.* 2. 15, in *De antiquis ecclesiae ritibus*, ed. Martène, 3: 913). The *Regula clericorum* ("Petrus de Honestis") is more concerned with the porter's character, but is not very interested in the reception of guests (PL 163, 747–48). The customs of Springiersbach (*Consuet. Springersb.*, ed Weinfurter) and Arrouaise (*Constitut. Arroas.*, ed. Milis and Becquet) give no rules for receiving guests.

41. The customs of Marbach are the earliest rule to show a strong influx of the vocabulary of courtesy. Cf. ed. Siegwart, chapter 149, p. 254 (on the prior): "Sit sermo edificans, vita imitabilis. Sit caritate eminens, mansuetus, humanus, hilaris, severus, largus, cunctis affabilis atque amabilis." On the Latin vocabulary of courtesy, see *Origins of Courtliness*, pp. 127–75. It is tempting to pursue this lead and a possible connection with the urbane humanity of St. Victor, since the author of the earliest sections of this rule is Manegold of Lautenbach, possibly the same as that Manegold, *modernorum magister magistrorum*, who was the teacher of William of Champeaux. The Bamberg student who studied with William in the early days of St. Victor (see n. 5 above, *Udalrici Codex*, p. 286) said that the founder of St. Victor "showed himself kind and devoted to all who came to him, and he received them gratis . . . *in the manner of Master Manegold of blessed memory*" (emphasis mine). This student was in a good position to observe William's cordiality and liberality and to judge them as the continuing influence of Manegold. Of course his comment does not tell us whether this was the same as that Manegold of Lautenbach, author of the core of the Marbach customs. Both this connection and the dating of the Marbach customs are too uncertain to allow any easy conclusion. Manegold's contributions to the rule date from around 1103; other sections were added between 1122 and 1136. See J. Siegwart in the introduction to the *Consuetudines Marbacenses*, p. 31. On Manegold and the problems of identifying him in his relations to William of Champeaux, see Wilfried Hartmann, "Manegold von Lautenbach und die Anfänge der Frühscholastik."

42. *Consuet. Marbach*, ed. Siegwart, chapter 127, p. 231. "Frater qui hospitibus servit dulcis debet esse, benignus, humanus et discretus. . . . Super omnia vero debet apparere affectus animi, voluntas bona et larga, vultus hilaris et clarus, affabilitas pulchra et honesta. . . . Peregrinos autem et extraneos majori humanitate et hilaritate quam etiam parentes et notos colligere oportet, quia in his maxime Christus suscipitur." This last sentence neatly combines values of courtesy with the prescription of the Benedictine Rule to receives guests as Christ. On the influence of the Marbach customs, see Dickinson, *Austin Canons*, p. 46.

43. The precepts for receiving guests bear comparison with Andreas Capellanus's advice to women for the courtly reception of their lovers. See *Andreas Capellanus on Love*, ed. and trans. Walsh, pl. 160, l. 410: ". . . hilari scilicet facie et

urbanitatis quemlibet receptu suscipiant"; p. 162, l. 414: "hilari vultu in suo quemlibet adventu suscipere et suavia sibi responsa praestare" [= *opus curialitatis*]; p. 162,
l. 414: "ad vos venientes hilari receptione suscipitis et curialitatis verba secum
adinvicem confertis."

44. 15, 18–22; 55–56: "Haec omnia ita diligenter exequenda praecipimus,
quia hii, qui deforis adveniunt, praecipue primo occursu cum magna benignitate et
humanitate recipiendi sunt . . . ut ex his, quae extrinsecus vident, eorum, quae
intrinsecus latent, existimationem colligant."

45. Jean Leclercq, *Monks and Love in Twelfth-Century France*, pp. 8–23.

46. Odo of St. Victor, epist. 2, PL 196, 1403C: "ad societatem amabiles, ad
imitandum utiles. Sunt inquam amabiles ad societatem, tum pro vitae sanctitate,
tum pro morum suavitate." For some commentary on his letters, see Bynum, *Docere
verbo et exemplo*, 44–45, 81–82.

47. See *Origins of Courtliness*, pp. 32–34.

48. PL 196, 1225A. Perhaps somewhat revealing on the connection between
the life of canons regular and promotion in the church is Abelard's accusation that
William of Champeaux converted "ut quo religiosior crederetur ad majoris prela-
tionis gradum promoveretur" (Abelard, *Hist. calam.*, ed. Monfrin, p. 65, ll. 74–75).
The suggestion that the canonical life had this effect must have weight whether or
not that was William's intention.

49. See the discussion in my "Cathedral Schools," pp. 594ff.

50. Hugh, *Didascalicon*, trans. Taylor, pp. 46–47.

51. *Didasc.*, 1.8, tr. Taylor, pp. 54–55, ed. Buttimer, p. 15: "Duo vero sunt quae
divinam in homine similitudinem reparant, id est speculatio veritatis et virtutis
exercitium." Cf. 1.1, trans. Taylor, p. 47: ". . . we are restored through instruction so
that we may recognize our nature." Also 2.1, p. 61: "This then is what the arts are
concerned with, this is what they intend, namely, to restore within us the divine
likeness . . ."

52. *De sacramentis*, 1.6.2, PL 176, 264C–D: "Factus est homo ad imaginem et
similitudinem Dei. . . . Imago secundum rationem, similitudo secundum dilectionem; imago secundum cognitionem veritatis, similitudo secundum amorem
virtutis."

53. 172 manuscripts have survived as compared to 125 for the *Didascalicon*. See
Rudolf Goy, *Die Überlieferung der Werke Hugos von St. Viktor*, pp. 340–66 (*De Inst.*),
pp. 14–34 (*Didasc.*).

54. Cf. chapter 1, PL 176, 927A: ". . . scientia[m] (quae ad institutionem recte
et honeste vivendi pertinet)."

55. I believe Jean-Claude Schmitt is the first to recognize the work as essentially concerned with comportment: *La raison des gestes dans l'occident médiéval*. He
also suggests the proximity of Hugh's comments on gestures to humanism (pp.
193–94) and to courtly manners (p. 197). He points out the importance of the
"aesthetic dimension" to Hugh's ideas (p. 178). Roger Baron, coming at the work
from the point of view of Hugh's intellectual achievement, has trouble locating it
among his other works: "On pourrait se demander si le contenu de cet ouvrage (qui
traite surtout du comportement extérieur) est en accord avec ce que nous savons de
Hugues" (*Science et sagesse*, p. xxix, n. 48). Baron excuses the work referring to

Hugh's comment that everything is worth learning. But the suggestion of an inferior work qualifying for Hugh's authorship by a generous extension of boundaries does it an injustice. It is in a sense the heart of Hugh's and of Victorine thinking.

56. Chapter 12, 942C: [after quoting Horace] "Sed ne forte satiram potius quam doctrinam edere videamur . . . modestiae hic quoque oblivisci non debemus."

57. An especially rich satirical passage is against delicate table manners: chapter 19, 950A–B. Quoted below, p. 265 and n. 89.

58. *De scripturis et scriptoribus sanctis*, PL 175, 9f.

59. 946A: "Sunt . . . loca . . . pro disciplina et instructione morum"; 946B: "in illis locis ubi de disciplina agendum est."

60. Even in *Didasc.* the major area of reference of *disciplina* is ethical. Cf. *Didasc.*, ed. Buttimer, Praef. pp. 2–3: ". . . legentibus vitae suae disciplinam praescribit"; 3.3, p. 61: ". . . cavendum ei qui quaerit scientiam, ut non negligit disciplinam"; 1.11, p. 22: "practica, quae morum disciplinam considerat"; 3.6, p. 57: [the three things necessary to study: *natura, exercitium, disciplina*] "disciplina, ut laudabiliter vivens mores cum scientia componat"; same passage in *De modo dicendi et meditandi*, PL 176, 877C. Cf. also *Epitome Dindimi in philosophiam*, 2.19, ed. Baron, p. 195: "Ethica . . . ordinem modumque virtutum ac morum disciplinam, que ad probitatem et religionem spectant, instituit"; *Epitome Dindimi*, 2.22, p. 196: "Ethica moralis interpretatur, ex re nomen sumens, quia morum disciplinam instituit"; *Expositio in Hierarchiam Coelestem Sancti Dionysii*, 1.1, PL 175, 927B: ". . ethica . . . quae modum vivendi rectum, et disciplinae formam secundum virtutum instituta disponit"; *De arca Noe morali*, 2.6, PL 176, 640A: [mere knowledge is not useful in itself, unless one strives to imitate the virtues he admires in others and to make them his own] "per exercitium disciplinae et formam recte vivendi." *Didasc.* trans. Taylor, p. 213, n. 49, refers to Cicero, Quintilian, Augustine, and Boethius as sources for the idea, but qualifies it, "Note, however, that in the words which follow Hugh gives his own definition to each term, altering particularly the sense of *disciplina* from "art" to moral excellence." See also Ferruolo, *Origins*, pp. 37–38, on the unconventional narrowing of *disciplina*: "Hugh defines discipline not as academic training but as moral excellence. This definition seems intended to suggest the clear advantage of studying at St. Victor, where the rules of learning were inseparable from the rules of the canonical life."

61. *Didasc.*, 1.11, ed. Buttimer, p. 20: "logicae peritia disciplinae"; 1.11, p. 22: [the invention of the arts =] "disciplinae exordium"; 2.1, p. 23: "artes et disciplinae"; 2.1, p. 24: "disciplina [est] quae in speculatione consistit et per solam explicatur ratiocinationem"; 2.6, p. 30: "astronomicae disciplinae peritia."

62. Chapter 10, 935A–B: "Disciplina est conversatio bona et honesta, cui parum est mala non facere, sed studet etiam in iis quae bene agit per cuncta irreprehensibilis *apparere*. Item disciplina est membrorum omnium motus ordinatus, et dispositio decens in omni habitu et actione" (emphasis added).

63. Fairly standard is Sigebert of Gembloux's description of the education of his teacher, Abbot Olbert: "in disciplina monachica regulariter nutritus" (*Gesta*, MGH SS 8, p. 536, l. 4). Ulrich of Cluny is talking about "the rule" plain and simple, when he says, "Since we are treating the training of novices . . . let us now

take in proper sequence the discipline to which those are strictly held who wish to share our life." This usage (*disciplina* = the rule or the learning of it) is consistent with patristic usage. Cf. Walter Dürig, "'Disciplina'"; M.-D. Chenu, "Disciplina."

64. *Consuetudines Springirsbacenses-Rodenses*, chapter 40, ed. Weinfurter, p. 124, parag. 233: ". . . alii provectiores et natura hebetiores in eo, quo sunt statu, imitantur vitam canonicam et sub quadam regula positi reguntur per congruam sibi disciplinam."

65. *disciplina virtutis* (925B); *scientia vere discretionis* (926A); *scientia . . . ad institutionem recte et honeste vivendi* (927A); *schola virtutum* (931B); *schola disciplinae* (933D); *peritia bene agendi* (932C). A useful comparison with the last formulation: a letter from the canons of Worms to their colleagues at Bamberg ca. 1115 asking for support of their newly elected bishop, who had studied in Bamberg and acquired "litterarum scientia, *rerum agendarum pericia*, honestas morum, gratia discretionum." *Udalrici codex*, epist 172, ed. Jaffé, p. 305.

66. Cf. Adam of Perseigne, *Lettres*, ed. Bouvet, epist. 5.59, p. 124: "'Bonitatem,' inquit, 'et disciplinam et scientiam doce me,' [Psalm 118:66] . . . Maturum quippe reddit hominem disciplina quae est membrorum omnium motus ordinatus et compositio decens in omni habitu et actione"; ibid., p. 122: "elegantia disciplinae." Cf. Pseudo-Hugh of St. Victor, *Expositio Regulae S. Augustini*, PL 176, 898C: "Tunc enim religiose vivimus, si membra et sensus nostros studeamus restringere, ut non possint lasciviae et levitati deservire, ut aspectus noster sit simplex et humilis . . . ut sit . . . in incessu gravitas, status cum reverentia, motus cum maturitate, habitus cum religione, quatenus ubique resplendeat sanctitas, supereminaet honestas"; ibid., 897C: "Nostrae divitiae, nostra pulchritudo boni mores sunt." Adam of Dryburgh (ca. 1170) has appropriated the discourse of *cultus virtutum* though he is more indebted to St. Ambrose, *De off. min.* than to Hugh of St. Victor. Cf. *De ordine praemonst.*, Sermo 2.11, PL 198, 459B. The Pseudo-Vincent of Beauvais compendium, *Speculum morale* (late thirteenth century), 1.3.42, *Speculum maius* (Douai, 1624; rpt. 1964), 3.307–8, quotes Hugh's definition of discipline in full. For further references, see Dilwyn Knox, "The Origins of European Civility," pp. 113–15.

67. Thomasin of Zirclaere unmistakably appropriates Hugh's definition in prescribing the education of courtly damsels, *Der Wälsche Gast*, ll. 199–208: "A woman may perform good acts, but if her gestures are not appropriate and her speech not elegant, her good deeds remain uncrowned. For elegant gestures and appropriate speech are crowns on a woman's actions. I tell you that her good deeds can never remain constant, if she is unable to comport herself well and speak as is appropriate" ("swâ ein vrouwe reht tuot, / ist ir gebaerde niht guot / und ist ouch niht ir rede schône, / ir guot getât ist âne krône, / wan schoene gebaerde und rede guot / die kroenent daz ein vrouwe tuot. / ich sagiu daz ir guot getât / mac ouch nimmer wesen stat, / kan si niht gebâren wol / und reden daz si reden sol.") My thanks to Elke Brüggen for this reference.

68. Vincent of Beauvais borrows wholesale from *De inst. nov.* in his *De eruditione filiorum nobilium*, ed. Steiner. His chapter 31 is a cento of quotations from Hugh's work, including his definition of *disciplina* word for word. The *De inst.* is quoted and adapted in many other passages. Aegidius Romanus adapts Hugh's

work in his influential *De regimine principum.* E.g., 2.2. 13: "Gestus autem dicuntur quilibet motus membrorum ex quibus iudicari possunt motus animae. . . . Disciplina autem, quae est danda in gestibus, est, ut quodlibet membrum ordinetur ad opus sibi debitum. Homo enim non audit per os, sed per aurem." *D. Aegidii Romani . . . De regimine principum libri III* (Rome, 1556), 192r–193v. My thanks to David Fowler for pointing out this passage to me.

69. See *Tusc. Disp.*, 4.3.5. and the discussion of this passage, above, Introduction.

70. Epist. Syn. Karisiac., XII, MGH Leges 2, Capit. 2, p. 436, 4–6. See above, Chapter 1, note 36.

71. *Herbordi dialogus*, 2.16, p. 90. The last line raises the question whether the influence of Hugh's *De institutione* shows in this biography written ca. 1155. The resonance between Herbord's *bonitas, disciplina et prudenci[a]* and Hugh's *bonitas, disciplina et scientia* is worth noting. The Psalm quotation is probably not the mediator, since the ethic of elegance and "virtue made visible" is the prominent factor pointing to Hugh. On the diffusion of the *De institutione* see R. Goy, *Die Überlieferung*, pp. 340–67, 496–500. Bavaria was an interested recipient of the work (Goy, p. 367). But of course the echoes do not require the explanation of direct influence, just a shared ethical language and curriculum in *mores*.

72. Cf. *Didasc.* 3.13. This also reiterates the stipulation of the *Liber ordinis Sancti Victoris* that the first requirement for the acceptance of novices, prior to their novitial training, is that they be "mansueti ac tractabiles . . . correctionisque suae non impacientes" (22, 16–19; 97).

73. 933B–C. The passage depends on elaborate word plays on the raised and depressed areas on the surface of a seal. The former are "eminent, sublime, outstanding," the latter "depressed and abject" — in Latin the meaning is both moral and spatial. The eminences of the model become the interior of the copy, its depressions become his eminences.

74. *De arca Noe morali*, 2.6, PL 176, 640A.

75. *De sacramentis*, 1.6.5, PL 176, 267A.

76. *De inst. nov.*, chapter 7, PL 176, 932D: "Quare putatis, fratres, vitam et conversationem bonorum imitari praecipimur, nisi ut per eorum imitationem ad novae vitae similitudinem reformemur? In ipsis siquidem similitudinis Dei forma expressa est, et idcirco cum eis per imitationem imprimimur, ad ejusdem similitudinis imaginem nos quoque figuramur." Richard of St. Victor took over the idea and developed it, clearly in the context of ethical training, into a means of mystical union with God; cf. *Explicat. Cant.*, PL 196, 412D–413B: ". . . a perfectis primo quaerit exempla. Considerat quam arcta se lege vivendi constrinxerunt. . . . Cum enim in istis imago Dei et magna ex parte similitudo resplendeat, et quantum hos imitari potuerit, eisque assimilari, tantum Deo meritur uniri tantumque Deum in se suscepit, quantum similitudinem ejus assumpserit." Cf. also ibid., 443D: "in eorum vita et conversatione formam ei, quam imitetur ostendit." A major statement of the connection of judgment, self-knowledge and the image of God in his *Benjamin minor*, chapters 71 and 72, PL 196, 51–52.

77. *Explicat. Cant.*, chapter 2, PL 196, 412A–413C (paraphrasing): Through its struggles to seek quiet and tranquility, the soul arrives at humility. Once this

happens, it can turn away from worldliness and "look about through the congregation of good men, so that in he may find examples of a better life and instructions in the virtues." Then he strives "to transfuse them through imitation into his own manners and to ornament the house of his mind with them." He bends all his efforts to cultivating their virtues (*excolendis virtutibus operam dat*). Through these men, he seeks God, "Since the image of God is in them, and to a great extent, that likeness shines forth . . . therefore you form the image of God in yourself by forming the virtues." He cautions this God-seeker not to despise the examples of those who have won fame in secular life (413C).

78. Also the subject of Richard of St. Victor's *Benjamin minor*.

79. Hugh gives three contexts for "propriety in every act" (927A): worship and the liturgy, human duties (*humana officia*), and the governance of the body (*quae ad usum corporis pertinent* — 927B). The focus of *De inst. nov.* is exclusively on the latter two.

80. Chapter 10, 935D: "Liganda ergo sunt foris per disciplinam membra corporis, ut intrinsecus solidetur status mentis, quatenus dum undique exterior custodia interiori mobilitati coercendae opponitur, tandem mens ad pacem in seipsa colligatur. . . . Paulatimque eadem virtutis forma per consuetudinem menti imprimitur, quae foris per disciplinam in habitu corporis conservatur."

81. Chapter 12, 938A–B: ". . . sex modis reprehensibilis invenitur, scilicet, si est aut mollis, aut dissolutus, aut tardus, aut citatus, aut procax, aut turbidus. Mollis significat lasciviam, dissolutus negligentiam, tardus pigritiam, citatus inconstantiam, procax superbiam, turbidus iracundiam." Jean-Claude Schmitt has interpreted this passage and the entire set of concerns in Hugh's treatment of gestures in his *La raison des gestes*, pp. 179ff., and in his essay, "The Ethics of Gesture."

82. Chapter 12, 943C–D: ". . . gestus hominis in omni actu esse debet gratiosus sine mollitie, quietus sine dissolutione, gravis sine tarditate. . . . Mollem gestum temperat turbidus, et turbidum mollis . . . quia inter vitia contraria medius limes virtus est." On the presence of this Aristotelian definition of virtue in the earlier Middle Ages, see C. J. Nederman, "Aristotelian Ethics before the *Nichomachean Ethics*: Alternate Sources of Aristotle's Concept of Virtue in the Twelfth Century."

83. *De sacramentis legis naturalis et scripturae*, PL 175, 34B. Cf. *De sacramentis*, 9.2, PL 176, 317C. Here the comparison between sacrament and significatum, the human body and soul, and scriptural letter and meaning, suggests a common symbolic structure uniting theology (sacraments), ethics (body-soul), and textual studies (Scripture).

84. Cf. Richard of St. Victor, *Explicat. in Cant.* PL 196, 461C–463D; 462A: ". . . custodia et disciplina loquendi mentem decorat . . . et foris pulchram animam demonstrat . . . composita verba . . . testimonium dant constantiae mentis." Also Hugh, *De sacramentis*, 1.6.21, PL 176, 276D; 1.8.5, 309D; 1.9.2, 317C.

85. *Das Moralium Dogma Philosophorum des Guillaume de Conches: Lateinisch, Altfranzösisch und Mittelnieder-fränkisch*, ed. Holmberg, p. 77: "intentio . . . est summatim docere ethicam Tullianam et Tullium et Senecam imitari."

86. Taylor's notes to the *Didascalicon*, which constitute an important study of Hugh's intellectual obligations, suggest strong connections between him and William of Conches. Cf. esp. intro. pp. 6–7 and notes 15, 16.

87. One example where the reader wonders if Hugh read the work: the *Moral. dog. phil.* (*Mdp*) treats *providentia* and *circumspectio* one after the other (pp. 9–10). Hugh's chapter 9 urges: ". . . homo sit circumspectus et providus" (934B); these virtues foresee *futurum eventum* and *rerum exitus* (*Mdp*); in *De inst.* it is the *finis actionis* and *finis operis* (934C, D). The *Mdp* commends caution: "Cautio est discernere a virtutibus vitia virtutum speciem preferentia"; it helps the cautious avoid deception through *occultiores insidie* (pp. 10, ll. 18ff.). Cf. *De inst. nov.*, 934C: [through circumspection] ". . . plane vitium esse dignoscitur, in quo prius sibi animus falso de virtute blandiebatur" and it helps him avoid future deception if once he has succumbed to *insidiis inimici* (934D).

88. Cf. 3.13, the chapter on humility, part of which is clearly directed against Abelard (see also Taylor's note, p. 215, n. 68).

89. Chapter 19, 950A–B. This passage has the flavor of Roman satire, but I have not been able to turn up a model for it, even with the help of the Argus computer concordance of Latin literature.

90. Bonnard, *Histoire*, 1: 68, says that the *Liber ordinis* forbids guests to send their servants out for special dishes. I could not find the passage and Bonnard gives no reference. It does forbid guests to bring their own cooks with them: "Just as all guests receive our care, so all must eat our fare" (*Liber*, 17, 243ff.; 69).

91. This is again consistent with the *Liber*, which enjoins the *vestiarius* to permit no clothes that are "too long, or hang down in differing lengths, or flowing out too far, or in any way distorted or inappropriately fashioned" (18, 14–15; 70: "nimis longa . . . vel inaequaliter dependentia, aut fluxa nimis, sive quolibet alio modo distorta, vel inepte composita"). It is the duty of the prior of the cloister to examine all clothes issued to those with duties outside of the house, and this is followed by an extensive list of current fashions that are not permitted (18, 18ff.; 70ff.). The linen vestments may not be "nimis subtilia aut pretiosa" (18, 37; 71).

92. See the studies by Platelle ("Le problème du scandale") and Jaeger cited above, Chapter 7 and the discussion of the Hildesheim "crisis," above, pp. 210–16.

Chapter 10: Bernard of Clairvaux

1. Bernard, epist. 113, *Opera*, 7: 287–91. The character Bernard addresses is a beautiful woman of high nobility living in the world, not a nun. See Jean Leclercq, *La femme et les femmes dans l'oeuvre de Saint Bernard*, pp. 57–62. Also M. D'Elia Angiolillo, "L'Epistolario femminile de S. Bernardo," *Analecta S. Ordinis Cisterciensis* 15 (1959): 46.

2. Epist. 113.5; *Opera*, 7: 290:

O quam compositum reddit omnem puellaris corporis statum, nedum et mentis habitum, disciplina? Cervicem submittit, ponit supercilia, componit vultum, ligat oculos, cachinnos cohibet, moderatur linguam, gulam frenat, iram sedat, format incessum. . . . Istiusmodi circumdata varietate virginitas, cui gloriae merito non praefertur? Angelicae? Angelus habet virginitatem, sed non carnem, sane felicior quam fortior in hac parte. Optimus et optabilis valde ornatus iste, qui et angelis possit esse invidiosus.

3. *Decor animae*. See Müller, *Das Problem der Seelenschönheit*.

4. *Serm. Cant.*, 85.10–11; *Opera*, 2: 314. See Chapter 4 above, p. *** and n. 132.

5. *Serm. Cant.*, 85.11; *Opera*, 2: 314:

> Cum autem decoris huius claritas abundantius intima cordis repleverit, prodeat foras necesse est. . . . Porro effulgentem et veluti quibusdam suis radiis erumpentem mentis simulacrum corpus excipit, et diffundit per membra et sensus, quatenus omnis inde reluceat actio, sermo, aspectus, incessus, risus. . . . Horum et aliorum profecto actuum sensuumque motus, gestus et usus, cum appareverit serius, purus, modestus . . . pulchritudo animae palam erit.

The translation in the text is freely adapted from *Bernard of Clairvaux on the Song of Songs IV*, trans. Irene Edmonds, pp. 206–7. Edmonds renders *honestum* as "honor," which invites confusion with the warrior ideal *honos*. I have translated it "propriety" or "ethical propriety."

6. *De consideratione*, 1.7.8, *Opera*, 3: 404.1ff.: Consideration purifies the mind, stirs affection, directs acts, corrects excess, composes manners, "vitam honestat et ordinat."

7. This kind of insight is facilitated by the concordance to Bernard's works: *Thesaurus Sancti Bernardi*. A basic statement on discipline is in *Serm. Cant.*, 86.1.1–2. But even here discipline aims at strengthening and maintaining "inborn purity." Also significant, *Serm. Cant.*, 23.3.5–6: the king's three chambers are "discipline," "nature," and "grace." One is guided to the first chamber by moral principles, and one discovers there one's inferiority to others. The purpose of discipline is "to tame wilfulness of character by submission." The disciplined man "becomes pleasant and temperate." But here too discipline as pedagogy is inferior to spontaneous acts of a pure will: ". . . to curb with firm discipline the flesh's immoderate appetites, is by no means as easy . . . as to live in the harmony of spontaneous affection with our companions; to live agreeably with them at the prompting of the will is different from a life where the rod is the check on manners" (trans. Killian Walsh, pp. 30–32). Cf. also *Serm. Cant.*, 63.6.

8. *Serm. Cant.*, 22.1.3, trans. Walsh, pp. 15–16. Cf. also *Serm. Cant.*, 63.6 (the disciplined appearance and proper deportment of novices are pleasant, but they are mere flowers, not fruits of the spiritual life).

9. Epist. 108, *Opera*, 7: 278.3ff.: "Haeccine est illa morum pulcherrima compositio, qua informari te scribis scientiae huius apprehensione, cuius studio et amore sic ferves, ut non verearis sancto proposito praeiudicium facere?"

10. Cf. *Serm. Cant.*, 21.2.3; *Opera*, 1: 124.4ff.: the bridegroom is the "leader and teacher." He is the "exemplar of her moral life, preparing the way of virtue" ("praeiret in via morum, et praepararet iter virtutum"). He teaches the bride to "become like himself." He gives her "the law of life and discipline," thus renders her beautiful, and is then attracted by her beauty.

11. On Bernard's ambiguous attitude to external beauty, see the sermons on the "blackness of the bride", esp. *Serm. Cant.*, 25.

12. *Weitere Briefe Meinhards*, epist. 1, *Briefsammlungen*, ed. Erdmann, p. 193. See Chapter 4, p. 97 and n. 70.

13. See Glenn W. Olsen, "Twelfth-Century Humanism Reconsidered: The Case of St. Bernard," who argues a development in Bernard away from an early asceticism toward positions close to humanist.

14. Hildebert, epist. 18, PL 171, 294C: ". . . didicimus, te in Ecclesia eum esse, qui ad eruditionem virtutis et exemplo sufficias et verbo."

15. Wibald, epist. 167, ed. Jaffé, p. 286: "Quem si aspicias, doceris; si audias, instrueris; si sequare, perficeris."

16. *Vita prima*, 3.1, PL 185, 303C: "Apparebat in carne ejus gratia quaedam, spiritualis potius quam carnalis. In vultu claritas praefulgebat . . . coelestis; in oculis angelica quaedam puritas. Tanta erat interioris ejus hominis pulchritudo, ut evidentibus quibusdam indiciis foras erumperet." Also quoted in *Vita secunda*, chapter 5, PL 185, 479D.

17. A good point of comparison is Sigebert of Gembloux's *Vita Wicberti*. The biographer praised Wicbert's "gift of virtues, which is something greater than if he had shone with the glory of miracles. Miracles can often . . . obscure virtues, but miracles derive their value only from virtues." Chapter 17, MGH SS 8, p. 515, ll. 6ff.: "Vir Dei consummatus est in virtutum gratia, quod maius est quam si claruisset miraculorum gloria — miraculis quippe nonnumquam virtutes offuscantur, miracula vero solis virtutibus commendantur." See Benedicta Ward, *Miracles and the Medieval Mind*, p. 25; William D. McCready, *Signs of Sanctity: Miracles in Gregory the Great*, esp. pp. 84–110.

18. *Vita Malachiae*, chapter 19.43, *Opera*, 3: 348.13ff.

19. *Vita Malachiae*, chapter 19.43, *Opera*, 3: 348.18ff.

20. *Serm. Cant.*, 18.1; *Opera*, 1: 104.5f.; trans. Walsh, p. 133. Walsh has translated *refundere* as "influence," which is a good interpretation. In the original, Bernard is speaking within the metaphor of "pouring forth" (*fundere*), which occurs in a chain, so that the one who receives the "oil" of grace "repours" it to others, that is, reshapes and "influences" them.

21. Chapter 27.58–59; *Opera*, 3: 361–63. This recalls the discussion of authority in the bishop's household in *De consideratione*. (See above, Introduction to Part 3, p. 242, n. 22.)

22. See especially Hayden F. White, "The Gregorian Ideal and Saint Bernard of Clairvaux"; also John Sommerfeldt, "Charismatic and Gregorian Leadership in the Thought of Bernard of Clairvaux"; Bernard Jacqueline, *Episcopat et papauté chez Saint Bernard de Clairvaux*.

23. *De praecepto et dispensatione*, 7.15, *Opera*, 3: 263–64; Bernard of Clairvaux, *Treatises I*, trans. Greenia, p. 116.

24. Among Bernard's letters in the Migne edition, Epist. 337, PL 182, 542B. See Jaeger, "Peter Abelard's Silence," p. 32 and n. 19.

25. I cannot agree with Bernard Jacqueline that the priority of the Benedictine Rule ("prodesse *magis quam* praeesse") looms large (*Episc. et papauté*, pp. 150ff.). Jacqueline's references are all to *dominium*, a bad word in the abbot's vocabulary. *Praeesse* is something else; it designates an important obligation, never to be separated from *prodesse*, but also not to be subordinated to it.

26. On Bernard's style, see Jean Leclercq, "S. Bernard écrivain," in his *Recueil d'études sur Saint Bernard et ses éccrits* (Rome, 1962), 1: 321–35; also Christine

Mohrmann, "Observations sur la langue et le style de Saint Bernard," Intro. to *Opera*, 2: ix–xxxiii.

27. Cf. the cases of Ruotger/Brun and Wipo/Conrad. Above, p. 191.

28. *Vita Prima* 3.8, PL 185, 320C: "Haec nos quidem de sacris moribus Patris nostri . . . perstrinximus. Caeterum longe eminentius in suis ille libris apparet, et ex litteris propriis innotescit, id quibus ita suam videtur expressisse imaginem, et exhibuisse speculum quoddam sui . . ."

29. Cf. Christ and Socrates. W. Jaeger, *Paideia*, 2: 17.

30. *Vita Prima* 3.7, PL 185, 314D–315A: "facta sunt aliquando signa per sanctos homines et perfectos: facta sunt et per fictos. Ego mihi nec perfectionis conscius sum, nec fictionis."

31. Leclercq, *La femme et les femmes*, p. 58. He infers its "caractère hautement littéraire."

Chapter 11: Twelfth-Century Humanism

1. Current and past views on the nature and history of medieval humanism are widely divergent. On the one hand David Knowles, Wolfram von den Steinen, and Peter von Moos see it as a revival of classicism and ideals of human dignity in Hildebert, Bernard Silvester, John of Salisbury, and Alan of Lille's *Anticlaudianus*, which died out soon after the mid-twelfth century. On the other hand, Étienne Gilson and R. W. Southern argue that the early twelfth century represents fledgling beginnings, which come to fruition in the great achievement of high scholasticism. Southern sees the beginnings of humanism in monastic communities and in the cult of friendship, and takes Anselm of Bec/Canterbury as its earliest representative. Gilson and Southern include Aristotle as a representative of classicism, and take theology as the high point of humanism. See Knowles, "The Humanism of the Twelfth Century"; Wolfram von den Steinen, "Humanismus um 1100"; von Moos, *Hildebert*, passim; Étienne Gilson, "L'humanisme médiévale"; R. W. Southern, "Medieval Humanism." See the recent trenchant criticism of Southern along with an original rereading of medieval humanism by Glenn W. Olsen, "Twelfth Century Humanism Reconsidered: The Case of St. Bernard," with extensive bibliography.

2. *Metalogicon*, 1.1, trans. McGarry, p. 11; ed. Hall, p. 13.

3. *Metalogicon*, 2.9, ed. Webb, p. 77; trans. McGarry, p. 94; ed. Hall, p. 69.

4. Southern had no thorough study of medieval friendship at his disposal. In the meantime, B. P. McGuire's work, *Friendship and Community*, has made it clear that the monastic cult of friendship is an appropriation from the schools.

5. Some thoughts on this in my study, "L'amour des rois."

6. Sigebert of Gembloux, *Pass. Theb.*, prohem, 2.21–22, ed. Dümmler, p. 69 (above, Chapter 6. p. ***); Benzo of Alba, *Ad Heinricum IV.*, 7.3, MGH SS 11, p. 673; Baudri, ed. Hilbert, nr. 153, p. 204. ll. 49–50 (ed. Abrahams, nr. 215, p. 272): "Sunt dii, non homines, quos lactat philosophia, / Nec deberent dii vivere sicut homo"; Amadeus of Lausanne, *Homélies* 4.22, ed. Bavaud, p. 112 (above, Chapter 5, p. ***, n. 126); Alan, *Anticlaudianus*, 6.366–67: "Sic ad nos divinus homo descendat, ut upsis / Virtutum titulis aliorum moribus instet." Cf. 1.240–41: "Sic

homo sicque Deus fiet, sic factus uterque / Quod neuter mediaque via tutissimus ibit."

7. The same structure occurs in a discursive mode in William of Conches's *Philosophia mundi*.

8. Bernard Silvester, *Cosmographia*, ed. Dronke. Cf. p. 100 ("Megacosmus," 2.6): the seeds of contrary qualities in Silva's womb are at war (*repugnantia sibi semina*); and they move about "with the clash of contradictory tendencies" (*contrariis motibus*). English translations from *The Cosmographia of Bernardus Silvestris*, trans. Wetherbee, p. 71.

9. Hyle's condition is "two-faced" or "ambiguous" (*anceps*), inclined to good and evil, but favoring evil (*preponderante malitia — Cosmographia*, 2.2, ed. Dronke, p. 99). Rooted in her seedbed is an inborn strain of malice (*quaedam malignitatis antiquior nota —* 2.6, p. 100).

10. Trans. Wetherbee, p. 71; ed. Dronke, 2.7, p. 100.

11. Closely analysed in Brian Stock, *Myth and Science in the Twelfth Century: A Study of Bernard Silvester*. Stock clearly has found the source for the "evil" (*malitia* and *carentia*) inherent in unformed matter and its need to receive "cultivation and beauty" (*cultum ornatumque*): it is Chalcidius's reception of Aristotle's Physics on matter (Stock, pp. 114–17). But that passage gives no antecedents for the transformation of matter from *rudis*, *indisciplinatus*, to *expolitus*, *morigeratus*, and *disciplinatus*; from contentious, litigious, and warring to *pax*, *amor*, and *amicitia*, a change described as *moribus ad gratiam inmutatis*. These conceptions and their vocabulary are abstracted from education.

12. Sigebert, *Pass. Theb.*, 3.8, ed. Dümmler, p. 112, ll. 599–604. See above, Chapter 6, p. 183.

13. For instance, the commentary on the first six books of the *Aeneid*, and, if the ascription is correct, the commentary on Martianus Capella.

14. Brian Stock calls the work "a type of the *Bildungsroman*" (*Myth and Science*, p. 164).

15. *Anticlaud.*, 1.119: "Hic hominum mores picture gracia scribit." Latin references to Alan of Lille, *Anticlaudianus: Texte critique avec une introduction et des tables*, ed. Bossuat, here p. 60. English from Alan of Lille *Anticlaudianus, or The Good and Perfect Man*, trans. Sheridan.

16. My translation. Sheridan's is accurate but oblique. 1.270–71, p. 65: "Surgit ad hoc placidi vultus gestusque modesti / Circumscripta modum Prudencia."

17. 7.121–38, trans. Sheridan, pp. 176–77, ed. Bossuat, pp. 160–61:

Totum componit hominem, contemperat actus
Verbaque metitur, libratque silencia, gestus
Ponderat, appendit habitus sensusque refrenat . . .
Describit gestum capitis faciemque venuste
Suscitat ad recti libram, ne fronte supina
Ad superos tendens, videatur spernere nostros
Mortales, nostram dedignans visere vitam,
Vel nimis in faciem terre demissus, inhertem
Desertumque notet animum; moderancius ergo

Erigitur, nec enim surgit vel decidit ultra
Mensuram. . . .

18. 7.138–63, trans. Sheridan pp. 177–8, ed. Bossuat, p. 161:

. . . Constancia vultus
Scurriles prohibet gestus nimiumque severos
Abdicat incessus . . .
Et ne degeneres scurrili more lacertos
Exerat et turpi vexet sua brachia gestu,
Aut fastum signans ulnas exemplet in arcum,
Admonet illa virum, vel ne delibet eundo
Articulisque pedum terram, vix terrea tangens,
Eius legitimo firmat vestigia gressu.
Ne cultu nimium crinis lascivus adequet
Femineos luxus sexusque recidat honorem,
Aut nimis incomptus iaceat . . .
. . . tenet inter utrumque
Illa modum proprioque locat de more capillos.
Non habitum cultus nimio splendore serenat,
Non scalore premit, mediocriter omnia pensat.
Ne vitanda foris oculus venetur et auris,
. . . visum castigat et aurem,
Frenat odoratum . . .
        sensus gustus contemperat, usum
Tactus componit.

19. Linda Marshall, "The Identity of the 'New Man' in the 'Anticlaudianus' of Alan of Lille"; Michael Wilks, "Alan of Lille and the New Man." Also of interest for our topic is P. G. Walsh, "Alan of Lille as a Renaissance Figure."

20. Cf. also John Baldwin's skepticism on this point, *The Government of Philip Augustus*, p. 571.

21. Cf. Grabmann, *Geschichte der scholastischen Methode*, 1: 272–336.

22. *Briefsammlungen der Zeit Heinrichs IV.*, ed. Erdmann, *Weitere Briefe Meinhards*, epist. 1, p. 193.

23. "Gedichte aus Frankreich," ed. Dümmler, ll. 48–51. See above, Chapter 3, p. 58.

24. Marbod, *Carmina*, ed. Bulst, p. 18. See above, Chapter 4, p. 116.

Chapter 12: Court Society

1. Bumke's *Höfische Kultur* is an important study. See also his recent, extensive survey of research, "Höfische Kultur: Versuch einer kritischen Bestandsaufnahme."

2. On the Merovingian palace school see Riché, *Education and Culture*, pp. 238–39. Riché's treatment of early medieval court education does not suggest that

the neo-classical curriculum observable at Carolingian, Ottonian and many later courts played any prominent role.

3. On William's career, see R. L. Poole, *Illustrations of the History of Medieval Thought and Learning*, 2nd ed., pp. 106–12; J. M. Parent, *La doctrine de la création dans l'école de Chartres* (Paris, 1938), esp. pp. 11–25; Manitius, *Geschichte*, 3: 215ff.; Jeauneau, *Glosae super Platonem*, pp. 9ff.; Bradford Wilson in his edition, Guillaume de Conches, *Glosae in Iuvenalem*, pp. 75ff. John Newell, "William of Conches," in *Dictionary of Literary Biography*. The article by Dorothy Elford on William in the *History of Twelfth Century Western Philosophy*, ed. Dronke, is a good summarizing of his thought and influence, but is not interested in his biography.

4. The editor of the *Moralium dogma*, John Holmberg, takes this to be Henry II (pp. 6–7) against the skepticism of Manitius, *Geschichte*, 3: 219.

5. See Lèsne, *Les écoles*, pp. 39ff.; Fleckenstein, "Königshof und Bischofsschule," pp. 40f.; idem, *Die Bildungsreform Karls des Grossen*, pp. 24ff.; Brunhölzl, "Der Bildungsauftrag der Hofschule," pp. 28f.; Rosamond McKitterick, "The Palace School of Charles the Bald."

6. Anselm of Liège, *Gesta ep. Leod.*, chapter 28, MGH SS 7, p. 205. See above, Chapter 7, p. 203 and n. 20.

7. *Epist. syn. Karisiac.* 12, MGH Leges 2, Capit. 2, p. 436, ll. 2–6. See above, Chapter 4, p. 113 and n. 141.

8. A recent article by Louis Holtz shows that one of the distinct changes in the teaching of grammar in the course of the tenth century is the swell of classical authors read in the second half: "Les nouvelles tendances de la pédagogie grammaticale au Xe siècle."

9. MGH SS 12, p. 245. ll. 9ff. See the discussion of this and other texts on court education in *Origins of Courtliness*, pp. 215–18.

10. The contemporary terms are *aulica* or *curialis nutritura*, or *aulicae/curiales disciplinae*. See *Origins of Courtliness*, pp. 215–16.

11. The Vitae I treat are by John of Salisbury, Edward Grim, William of Canterbury, and especially William Fitzstephen and Herbert of Bosham. They are published in Rolls Series 67: 1–3. For brief biographies of the biographers, see David Knowles, *Thomas Becket*, pp. 172ff.; also Frank Barlow, *Thomas Becket*. On Becket and the climate of ideas, see Beryl Smalley, *The Becket Conflict and the Schools*. Another recent biography is by Pierre Aube, *Thomas Becket*. See also H. Vollrath, " 'Gewissensmoral' und Konfliktverständnis: Thomas Becket in der Darstellung seiner Biographen"; A. Duggan, "John of Salisbury and Thomas Becket," in *The World of John of Salisbury*, ed. Wilks, pp. 427–38.

12. Herbert of Bosham, *Vita Thomae*, 1.Pref; RS 67: 3, p. 156 (Prefatory letter to Baldwin of Canterbury):

Vobis enim praesertim exemplum dedit exemplaris iste vir, ut, quemadmodum fecit ipse, et vos similiter faciatis. Unde et per totam historiam hanc virum descripsi exemplarem, non quidem mirandum in signis, sed imitandum in operibus.

(I will cite this *Vita* in the form, Herbert, 3.13.208 = Book 3, chapter 13, p. 208.) Several times Herbert draws on this significant conceit: Becket is or was in his own person a book which we can read. Cf. 1.Pref.156: "I have wished to restore to you . . . the uncorrupt exemplar [i.e., the man himself], by which you should live and govern, and in which you should read every day" ("exemplar restitui vobis desidero; exemplar quippe hoc incorruptum, secundum quod vivere, secundum quod regere, in quo et quotidie legere debeatis"). Also 3.13.208: "Let us now fold back anew the pages of our exemplar [= Thomas himself] and continue to read in it. For acts of virtue are certainly read more fruitfully in men themselves than books, just as deeds speak more effectively than words" (Latin text given above, Introduction, p. 11 and n. 18).

13. 3.18.248: ". . . non solum pontificis opera, sed et causas operum . . . non solum facta, sed et animum facientis . . ."

14. A brief portrait of the young man's *mores*, virtues and physical appearance was an obligatory topic of a bishop's biography. See *Origins of Courtliness*, pp. 32ff.

15. RS 67: 2, p. 302 (chapter 1): "statura procerus, decorus forma, ingenio perspicax, dulcis et jucundus eloquio, et venustate morum pro aetate amabilis . . ."

16. RS 67: 3.7.17 (the chapter heading is "De statura illius et moralitate"): "Erat siquidem placido vultu et venusto, statura procerus, naso eminentiore et parum inflexo, sensibus corporeis vegetus, eloquio comptus, ingenio subtilis, animo magnus, virtutum iter jam altius ingrediens, omnibus amabilem se exhibens . . . munificus et facetus . . . statim prudens hujus saeculi filius."

17. 2.1.163: "Duplex enim est in hominibus gratia; est quippe civilis quaedam gratia, urbana, benigna, dulcis, socialis et ad sui dilectionem invitans, qua homo plus placet saeculo, sed Deo minus."

18. Cf. William Fitzstephen, RS 67: 3, chapter 5, p. 16, comparing Becket to the other men of high learning at the court of Archbishop Theobald of Canterbury: "Thomas was less a man of letters; but far superior is the rule of manners to that of letters [*ratio morum quam litterarum*], and he strove to pursue moral training [*moralitas*] and prudence." Also ibid., chapter 28, pp. 39–40 ("Reason the queen reigned within him, commanding lusts and base impulses of the mind. Led by Reason he progressed in virtue, possessing the four cardinal virtues. This 'fourfold chord' [*diatessaron*] is the highest harmony attainable on earth"). In the next chapter he says that Becket "took pains to perform all his duties with constancy, splendor, dignity, honesty [*constanter, splendide, graviter, honeste*]; to consult wisdom in all things, to govern himself . . . to believe himself born not for himself, but for all in need of his help" (chapter 29, p. 40). Edward Grim says that the young Becket was worldly and ambitious of honors. He "poured his soul into external things." "There was in him a mature wisdom unique in one so young. His counsels were those of an experienced man. He had a charm and dignity of manners [*morum jocunditas, gravitas*] that won him the admiration and love of all men" (RS 67: 2, p. 361, chapter 11). Also William of Canterbury, RS 67: 1, p. 3, chapter 1.

19. Herbert 4.4.327: ". . . totius hominis compositionem intuebatur et gestum, corporis videlicet proceritatem egregiam, frontem amplam et aspectum severum, faciem oblongam et venustam, formam manuum oblongarum, et articulorum in manibus congruam et quasi exquisitam his protensionem."

20. Edward Grim, RS 67: 2, p. 359, chapter 8: "optimis coepit pollere moribus."

21. RS 67: 2, p. 303, chapter 3: ". . . etsi superbus esset et vanus, et interdum faciem praetenderet insipienter amantium et verba proferret, admirandus tamen et imitandus erat in corporis castitate."

22. This penchant continues, Herbert asserts, even when Becket entered the staff of Theobald of Canterbury and rose to the position of archdeacon (2.7.172).

23. Cf. 2.8.173: "in apparatu magnificum"; 2.11.175: [the king favors him] "tantam cernente magnificentiam"; 2.11.175: his favor rises in relation to his *magnificentia*; 2.11.176: "ad ipsius revertar magnificentiam"; 2.11.176: "supra omnes et prae omnibus apparebat magnificus, sicut magnus corde magnus et corpore, magnus et apparatu. Nihil circa eum nisi magnum, nihil nisi magnificentia." See Barlow, *Becket*, pp. 43ff. and n. 4.

24. William Fitzstephen, RS 67: 3, pp. 29ff., chapters 19–20. See Barlow, pp. 55–57; analyzed in Brown / Jaeger, "Pageantry and Court Aesthetics."

25. Fitzstephen, RS 67:3, p. 26, chapter 16. On his generosity see also ibid., pp. 22–23, chapter 12.

26. See *Origins of Courtliness*, pp. 143–47, 162–65.

27. Fitzstephen, chapter 12, p. 22. On the education of pages in general, see Lutz Fenske, "Der Knappe: Erziehung und Funktion." On Becket as teacher of pages, pp. 60–61.

28. See Fenske, "Der Knappe," pp. 64–65.

29. Fitzstephen tells us that Becket as chancellor had fifty-two learned clerics in his service, most of whom were attached to his household staff (chapter 18, p. 29). There was no lack of learned tutors at court.

30. William of Canterbury RS 67: 1, p. 5, chapter 4. John of Salisbury, 67: 2, pp. 307–8. John of Salisbury has left the most extensive commentary on Becket's banqueting in the *Policraticus*. Fitzstephen on the chancellor's table, chapter 11, pp. 20–21; he describes the archbishop's table in describing his ascetic practices, but he indicates that the asceticism was behind the scenes, and leaves us to reconstruct a sumptuous foreground (chapter 26, pp. 37–38).

31. It sounds very much like one of those classifications Hugh of St. Victor is fond of, though the wording does not suggest that Herbert used the *De institutione novitiorum* as a model. Cf. *De inst. nov.* chapter 19, PL 176, 950A: "Sequitur triplex observatio disciplinae in cibo, observatio in eo quid sumat, . . . in quanto sumat, . . . in eo quomodo sumat."

32. In a later chapter Herbert castigates Thomas for excessive abstinence in eating. Asceticism, he argues, is itself a temptation, which one must resist no less than indulgence. The wise man follows the path of reason, restraint and moderation, governs his will with discretion. As a result of this lesson, Becket moderates his asceticism (Herbert 4.14.376–77).

33. A scene in Fitzstephen's biography gives us some insight into Herbert's character. In 1169 Henry received two emissaries from Becket. One of them was John of Salisbury, the other Herbert of Bosham. As Herbert entered the king's presence, Fitzstephen reports, the king whispered to his retinue, "Look now, how arrogant this next fellow is," and Fitzstephen explains, Herbert was "of noble stature, a handsome shape, dressed perhaps in an overly splendid manner" (RS 67: 3, p. 99, chapter 97: "Rex ait de eo, 'En videbitis quendam superbum intrare.' Ipse

quidem, statura ut erat procerus et forma venustus, etiam satis splendide erat indutus").

34. Throughout the vita, Herbert refers to Becket as *magister* and to himself as *discipulus*.

35. On Herbert's enthusiastic praise of their beauty, recall that Bernard of Clairvaux had reproached bishops for attracting "boys with luxuriously curled hair and foppish young men" to their retinue (*De consideratione*, 4.6). Otherwise Becket's household in Canterbury fits the picture Bernard draws of a well disciplined bishop's court. See above, Introduction to Part 3, p. 242.

36. P. 227: "ad obsequendum paratissimi, et saepius obsequentes injussi."

37. P. 227: "propter viri magnificentiam tam civiliter eruditam et tam urbane edoctam." I read this as indicating that instruction in magnificence passes from Becket to the boys, not as a comment on Becket's own education. The feminine adjective endings confirm this reading: erudit*am*, edoct*am*. The "magnificence" and not Becket is referred to.

38. Becket is *erudite circumspectus, curialiter eruditus, civiliter sobrius*. He observes and corrects the household "subtly and with courtly breeding" [*modesto quodam modo et civiliter erudito*].

39. In several of the biographies Becket is made to appear as a master of "courtly dissimulation," and that includes the business of the church. This is the formula by which in part the biographers transform Becket's apparent worldliness into secret service of the church. See esp. Herbert of Bosham, 2.9.173–74. Also the discussion in my *Medieval Humanism in Gottfried von Strassburg's Tristan und Isolde*, pp. 91–94.

40. On the gradual move of *curialitas* from abuse to praise see *Origins of Courtliness*, pp. 155–57.

41. 8.6.259: ". . . eleganter innuit in cantico citharedi poeta doctissimus veterum gravitatem, qui in cetu civili nichil admittebant nisi quod naturae aut morum instructione polleret."

42. Janet Martin is preparing a study of John of Salisbury's use of Macrobius on banqueting.

43. Herbert 6.9, p. 508:

> Et ut adhuc, quod non solum ad virtutem sed et ad ornatum attinet, et velut ad privilegiatum quoddam martyrii decus, quadam decenti exterius membrorum compositione exterioris hominis patronus hic noster paratum sibi decoravit martyrium, quasi indecens pro Christo mori judicans, nisi etiam decenter moreretur pro Christo.

44. *De inst. nov.*, chapter 10, PL 176, 935A–B. See above, Chapter 9, p. 256 and n. 62.

45. "De nuptiis," ed. Boutemy, p. 50, ll. 136–45. See above, Chapter 5, pp. 132–33 and n. 36.

46. It would not be useful to summarize the debate on courtly love here or its literature. For a recent study with earlier literature see Bumke, *Höfische Kultur*, pp. 503–82 and Schnell, "Die 'höfische Liebe' als 'höfischer Diskurs' über die Liebe."

47. Hennig Brinkmann, *Entstehungsgeschichte des Minnesangs*, pp. 18–44, and

Gerald Bond, "'Iocus amoris': The Poetry of Baudri of Bourgueil and the Formation of the Ovidian Subculture," have opened access to the eleventh-century roots of courtly love by pointing to the Loire circle of poets, Marbod, Baudri, Hildebert. Brinkmann argues that the vernacular poetry of courtly love emerges from the interchange among these poets and noble ladies at courts and in monasteries. Bond suggests that the poems and letters to men formed part of a public discourse of love that moved over to women. These insights produce three shifts in perspective that position us to see "what was there before": (1) Latin and not vernacular is its language; (2) men and not women were its original object; (3) public and ceremonial, not private discourse characterizes its mode. Some observations in my "L'amour des rois."

48. See Jaeger, "L'amour des rois," pp. 549ff.

49. Peter Damian, *Vita Romualdi*, chapter 25, PL 145, 975C. Further examples in "L'amour des rois," pp. 547–49.

50. *Vita Adalberti*, chapter 23, MGH SS 4, p. 591, ll. 32ff. This early work (ca. 997) already shows distinctly that the love of two men is the medium for moral instruction, not for sex. Adalbert shared the emperor's room night and day so that "with his sweet sayings, he could inflame the emperor with love of the celestial fatherland . . . instructing him also not to imagine he is great because he is emperor." See McGuire, *Friendship and Community*, p. 154, and "L'Amour des rois," p. 549 and n. 13.

51. John Boswell, *Christianity, Social Tolerance, and Homosexuality*. On the ambiguity of the discourse see Bond, "Iocus amoris."

52. That is the main reason, I believe, why Peter Dinzelbacher can find no traces of love defined as romantic, private emotion between men and women, prior to the twelfth century. See his "Über die Entdeckung der Liebe im Hochmittelalter"; also idem, "Sozial- und Mentalitätsgeschichte der Liebe im Mittelalter."

53. Baudri of Bourgueil states this principle outright — no doubt an indication that the innocence of discourse is eroding — in a poem to Godfrey of Rheims (ed. Hilbert, nr. 99; ed. Abrahams, nr. 161): "Carminibus meis sexus uterque placet. / Nam si quid vellem, si quid vehementer amarem, / Esset amoris tunc nescia carta mei. / Non promulgetur confessio carmine nostra; / Solus cum solo crimina confitear. / Non est in triviis alicuius amor recitandus" (ll. 187–94: ". . . both sexes are pleasing to my verse. . . . If I wanted something, if I loved something ardently, my parchment would be ignorant of this love. Let no confession be publicized in my poem; let me confess my crimes alone to a confidant. No one's love is to be recounted in public"). See Bond, "Iocus amoris," pp. 183–84. Bond's translation is cited here.

54. *Gesta regis Henrici secundi*, in *Chronicles of the Reigns of Henry II and Richard I*, ed. W. Stubbs, RS 49: 2.7. "L'amour des rois" is an analysis of this passage.

55. "Satyra de amicicia . . . (Clm 29111): Das Freundschaftsideal eines Freigelassenen," ed. Raedle.

56. *Hildesheimer Briefe*, epist. 36, ed. Erdmann, *Briefsammlungen der Zeit Heinrichs IV.*, pp. 76–79. Neither writer nor addressee has been identified. The letter was written prior to 1085 and probably after 1073 — the span of the datable letters in the collection.

57. Ed. Hilbert, nr. 3, p. 15–17, "Ad iuvenem nimis elatum." See Boswell, *Christianity*, p. 245

58. As did Abelard. He says that precisely the license to whip and beat Heloise served as a convenient camouflage of their love making.

59. The parallel to a poem by Marbod of Rennes underscores this interpretation, but also the problems of this discourse. It purports to retell a poem of Horace, describing a beautiful but arrogant boy. He is cruel and inhuman (*impius*). He kills others with his coldness and laughs at their suffering. Marbod comments that this fault of his *mores* takes all value from the beauty of his body: "a beautiful face seeks a good and patient mind / Not puffed up with pride, but ready for this and that." Beauty of the flesh fades soon. Therefore while in the bloom of youth, "take on the manners of a mature man." (PL 171, 1717D–18B). See the conflicting interpretations of Boswell, *Christianity, Social Tolerance, and Homosexuality*, p. 248 and McGuire, *Friendship and Community*, p. 247. Bond's suggestion that the contradiction of physical and spiritual love is resolved in the joke persuades me; see "Iocus amoris." Marbod is playing, writing a *satyra* (which means here only a happy, playful poem, not a "satire"), when he says the boy's problem is that he will not consent to love. Speaking the language of illicit love, he corrects the boy's arrogance. John Boswell's point remains, and is perhaps strengthened by this interpretation: a discourse of male love was so accepted that it could serve as the vehicle of moral correction.

60. See Ralph Hexter, *Ovid and Medieval Schooling*; John W. Baldwin, "L'ars amatoria au XIIe siècle en France: Ovide, Abélard, André le Chapelain et Pierre le Chantre."

61. The point of departure for Dinzelbacher's study, "Die Entdeckung der Liebe" (n. 52 above), is the near total silence of earlier medieval sources on the love of men and women.

62. *Ruodlieb*, ed. Vollmann, 16.55ff.: [tell me where I can find a wife] "Quae non indecor et nostrum genus, id sed inauret / Moribus ingenita vel vitae nobilitate". The advisor replies, ". . . dominam . . . unam scio, quae tibi par fit / Moris honestate virtute ve nobilitate."

63. Baudri, "Ad Dominam Constantiam," ed. Hilbert, nr. 200, pp. 266–71. Constance is a woman of high nobility and broad education, a nun at the time of their exchange, probably in the monastery of Le Ronceray at Angers. See Bond, "Iocus," p. 168 and n. 74.

64. Ll. 45–46: "Pectora iungantur, sed corpora semoveantur; / Sit pudor in facto, sit iocus in calamo."

65. "Chaste love" which is *honestus* opposed to destructive carnal love is also the theme of the "Parce continuis," a poem of love consolation from the late eleventh century. See David A. Trall, " 'Parce continuis': A New Text and Interpretative Notes." The poet urges a friend, who is weeping in the bonds of carnal passion, to a love which seeks only *honestas* and whose sole passion is *utilitas* (i.e., Ciceronian *amicitia*). He cites examples of friends joined by "a venerable bond" opposing them to lovers destroyed by passion. The image of Pyramus and Thisbe separated by the wall offers a metaphor for carnal passion controlled and forced into the strictures of spiritual love. The wall permitted only the passage of their souls, and restricted their

intercourse to *colloquia intima* (St. 4a, ll. 47ff.). Passion and desire controlled are an ideal.

66. Ed. Hilbert, nr. 134; ed. Abrahams, nr. 196. Abrahams dates the poem between 1099 and 1102 (p. 232). See Brinkmann, *Entstehungsgeschichte*, pp. 21ff. and Bond, "Iocus amoris," pp. 180–81.

67. See, for instance, Brinkmann, *Entstehungsgeschichte*, p. 25.

68. See Scaglione, *Knights at Court*, esp. pp. 89–111.

69. Cf. Alfred Karnein, *De Amore in Volkssprachlicher Literatur: Untersuchungen zur Andreas Capellanus-Rezeption in Mittelalter und Renaissance*; Rüdiger Schnell, *Andreas Capellanus: Zur Rezeption des römischen und kanonischen Rechts in De Amore*.

70. References to *Andreas Capellanus on Love*, ed. and trans. P. G. Walsh.

71. E.g., Peter Damian on the perfect worldly cleric: "pulcher aspectu quodammodo, sicut Tullius loquitur" (PL 145, 700C.); Lampert of Hersfeld on Gunther of Bamberg: "vir preter morum gloriam et animae divicias corporis quoque bonis adprime ornatus . . . tum statura et formae elegantia ac tocius corporis integritate . . . caeteris eminens mortalibus"; Lampert, *Annales* (1065), p. 99; Godfrey of Rheims on Odo of Orleans: "habitus, vox, sermo, figura, / Gressus et aspectus consona signa dabant" ("Trois oeuvres," ed. Boutemy, p. 345, ll. 28–29); Norbert of Xanten: "forma et habilitate corporis beneficio naturae gaudens et cum scientia litterarum eloquio praeeminens, morum ornatu cunctis qui eum noverant gratum se exhibebat" (*Vita Norberti*, chapter 1, LB p. 452).

72. In the dialogue between a man and woman of the high nobility, the man praises the woman for the youthful glow in her face, and comments, "Exterior enim habitus manifeste demonstrat qualis sit intus dispositio mentis" (1.6.446, p. 172). In enumerating the means of increasing love in book 2, he says, "Multam praeterea intensionem praestat amori gestus et incessus placabilis coamanti atque facundia pulchra loquendi suavitasque sermonis" (2.2.6, p. 228).

73. ". . . incumbit ut tales se debeant bona facientibus exhibere, ut eorum probitas earum intuitu de virtute in virtutem modis omnibus crescere videatur" (1.6.403–4, p. 158).

74. Gottfried, *Tristan*, ll. 8290–97; trans. Hatto, p. 150 (here with minor variations).

75. For instance, in the dialogue of *plebeius* with *plebeia* (1.6.49 - 55, pp. 52–4): a young boy courts an experienced woman, who turns him down as lacking either the "signs of probity" or fame of good deeds. He requests schooling from her (*bonis moribus informari*), arguing that a teacher (*doctor*) receives greater honor from the improvement of an inexperienced pupil (*discipulum imperitum*) through his teaching (*doctrina*), hence he seeks her teaching: ". . . in amore rudis te mihi peto magistram et tua doctrina plenius erudiri." She turns him down and suggests that he should go to the schools of Paris if he wants schooling. It is sarcasm, not a sober comment that women don't teach. On the contrary, she says she can get a learned lover (*doctus amator*), being herself a trained woman (*instructa mulier*). Cf. the case in the courts of love where a woman teaches a man courtesy (*in probis moribus propria . . . doctrina*). Her teaching renders him "decorous in every virtue of courtliness" (*in . . . qualibet curialitatis decorato virtute* – 2.13.28–30, p. 260).

76. This is not to suggest that the peace movement (or the clerical response in

any of the following conflicts cited) "resolved" the problem once and for all, established peace and courtesy as the dominant reality of aristocratic life; just that they established peace and restraint as the dominant social ideals. See the analysis by Georges Duby, "The Laity and the Peace of God"; also Gerd Althoff, "Nunc fiant Christi milites, qui dudum extiterunt raptores: Zur Entstehung von Rittertum und Ritterethos"; and my study of this dynamic of social transformation, "Courtliness and Social Change."

77. See Bumke's treatment of courtly love and the position of women in court society in *Höfische Kultur*, pp. 451–582.

78. See the criticisms of the knighthood in Peter of Blois's epist. 94 (PL 207, 293–97), analysed in "Courtliness and Social Change."

79. In "Courtliness and Social Change."

Conclusion

1. This is not to ignore the important findings of Pierre Riché on pre-Carolingian education. It was more extensive than had been believed. But Riché's studies have not changed the accepted view that Carolingian reforms accomplished a spread of learning not imaginable previously.

2. There are some imaginative readings of the connections between scholasticism and the culture in which it flourished, for instance Erwin Panofsky, *Gothic Architecture and Scholasticism*; Charles M. Radding and William W. Clark, *Medieval Architecture, Medieval Learning: Building and Masters in the Age of Romanesque and Gothic*; also Ullrich Langer, *Divine and Poetic Freedom in the Renaissance: Nominalist Theology and Literature in France and Italy*. But these have in common that they look at underlying shared mentalities, not direct connections. There are, however, direct and demonstrable historical connections between Carolingian education reforms and European literacy; between Ottonian reforms and European civility.

3. The disputation, one of its basic pedagogic arrangements, required presence and authority of a very different kind from the old learning.

4. See my "Courtliness and Social Change."

5. See the introduction to the most recent American edition of *European Literature and the Latin Middle Ages* (Princeton, NJ: Princeton University Press, 1990), by Peter Godman: "The Ideas of Ernst Robert Curtius and the Genesis of ELLMA," pp. 599–653.

Appendix A: Discipline and Sculpture

1. On the Strassburg sculptures, Georg Dehio, *Das Strassburger Münster* (Munich, 1922), esp. 25ff. Dehio cannot identify the source of the statues on the three west portals with any French school but considers them undoubtedly of French provenance (p. 32). On the sculpture of the Strassburg cathedral in general, Otto Schmitt, *Gotische Skulpturen des Strassburger Münsters*, 2 vols. (Frankfurt/ Main, 1924) with an analysis of the Wise and Foolish virgins, pp. 22–26. Schmitt

points to Rheims and Paris for lines of influence, though he also sees those lines as vague. Schmitt also stresses the later influence of the west portal statues of Strassburg. Also Willibald Sauerländer, *Von Sens bis Strassburg: Ein Beitrag zur kunstgeschichtlichen Stellung der Strassburger Querhausskulpturen* (Berlin, 1966); Hans Reinhardt, *La cathédrale de Strasbourg* (Strassburg: Arthaud, 1972).

2. On the representation of vices and virtues see Emil Mâle, *The Gothic Image: Religious Art in France of the Thirteenth Century*, trans. Dora Nussey (New York, Evanston, London, 1958), pp. 98–130; Adolf Katzenellenbogen, *Allegories of the Virtues and Vices in Mediaeval Art* (New York, 1964); Jennifer O'Reilly, *Studies in the Iconography of the Virtues and Vices in the Middle Ages* (New York and London: Oxford University Press, 1988).

The Strassburg virgins carry the conventional emblem of the upright and overturned lamps, but this portrayal only shows their traditional function in the context of Christ's parable (Matt. 25:1–13). They are ordinarily represented in early Gothic art in that context, as the damned and the elect at the last judgment. Strassburg changes this context decisively. The reference to the last judgment remains in the tympanum of the same portal. But the second and unconventional context is moral philosophy and the Christian life (Christ leading into the church) as opposed to the life of pleasure (the tempter leading away from it).

3. See Katzenellenbogen, *Virtues and Vices*, pp. 57–81.

4. Dehio's description of the Ecclesia—Synagoge figures applies to her as well: "Überzarte Gebilde, doch nicht aus weichlichem Stoff; in ihrer binsenschlanken Biegsamkeit spannkräftig wie feiner Stahl; adlig geborene Mädchen vom Scheitel bis zur Sohle. Das Gewand liegt über ihnen wie ein zarter Hauch, aber ein Geist der Keuschheit und Strenge macht es fest wie einen Panzer" (*Das Strassburger Münster*, p. 30).

5. "Trois oeuvres," ed. Boutemy, pp. 345–46, ll. 28–74. For full text and Latin, see above Chapter 4, pp. 114–15 and n. 145.

6. Bernard, *Super Cant. Sermo*, 85.10–11, *Sancti Bernardi Opera*, 2: 314. See above, Chapter 4, p. 111 and n. 132.

7. Rheims exterior, west façade, central portal, right jamb, ca. 1245–55.

8. I owe a very large debt of gratitude to Adelaide Bennet of the Princeton Index of Art, Princeton University, and to Shirley Wargon who consulted the Princeton Index for me at UCLA. Between the two of them I was able to survey some three hundred representations of the theme of the wise and foolish virgins in various media from the twelfth to the fourteenth centuries.

9. Exterior, north transept portal, left jamb. See James Snyder, *Medieval Art: Painting, Sculpture, Architecture, 4th–14th Century* (New York, 1989), p. 416 and fig. 541.

10. *De inst. nov.*, chapter 10, PL 176, 935B: "levitatem ligat."

11. Bernard, *De gradibus humilitatis et superbiae*, XII.40., *Opera*, 3: 47.

12. Bernard of Clairvaux, *The Steps of Humility and Pride*, trans. M. Ambrose Conway, p. 68.

13. Willibald Sauerländer, *Gothic Sculpture in France 1140–1270*, trans. Janet Sondheimer (London, 1972), p. 50. Classical influence is for Sauerländer the regular grounding of explanation. He juxtaposes works from the older and the

newer style and concludes: "Such comparisons make clear what deep significance lay behind the new interest in models from antiquity" (p. 51).

14. Erwin Panofsky, *Renaissance and Renascences in Western Art* (New York and Evanston: Harper and Row, 1972), p. 62.

15. *De inst. nov.*, chapter 12, PL 176, 942A.

16. Ernst Gombrich, *Art and Illusion: A Study in the Psychology of Pictorial Representation*, 2nd ed., Bollingen Series 35. 5 (New York, 1961), pp. 118–19.

17. Sauerländer insists on the distinction between "borrowing from antiquity in the visual arts and antique *tradition* in other areas of intellectual life." W. Sauerländer, "Architecture and the Figurative Arts: The North," p. 671 (emphasis in original).

18. O'Reilly, *Iconography of the Virtues and Vices* (note 2 above), devotes a chapter to the "didactic context" of the representation of vices and virtues in the thirteenth and fourteenth centuries. She locates it in lay education following upon the Fourth Lateran Council of 1215. The sermon literature offers the closest parallels to the cycles of virtues and vices she studies. But by way of extending her perspective it should be noted that the aristocracy had its own values and art media quite different from those O'Reilly considers. The context of popular religious instruction can hardly have much to do with the moral complexity and social sophistication of the high aristocratic ladies to whom the virgins are closest. A world of sensibility separates them from the figures in the book illuminations O'Reilly cites, which served to instruct the general populace.

19. Gombrich dealt with a similar problem and came up with a similar solution in his essay "Reflections on the Greek Revolution," in *Art and Illusion*, pp. 116–45. In the case of Greek sculpture the emergence of realistic representation had been treated by scholars as a matter of technique and of the overcoming of Egyptian models. Gombrich points to conceptions in Homeric narrative as predecessors of the revolution in sculpture. That is, the ideas and feelings of classical humanism were available in a narrative medium several centuries prior to their emergence in sculpture.

20. Ed. Scott, ll. 29–36.

Bibliography

PRIMARY SOURCES

This list includes the major sources used in this study for the period from the tenth through the twelfth century. It also includes frequently cited works from classical antiquity and the Carolingian period.

BIOGRAPHICAL WORKS

The subject of the biography is listed first, the biographer (if known) second.

Adalbert of Prague. Johannes Canaparius. *Vita antiquior S. Adalberti episcopi*. Ed. G. H. Pertz. MGH SS 4, 581–95.

———. Brun of Querfurt. *Vita secunda S. Adalberti episcopi*. Ed. G. H. Pertz. MGH SS 4, 596–612.

Balderic of Liège. *Vita Balderici episcopi Leodensis*. MGH SS 4, 724–738.

Benno of Osnabrück. Norbert of Iburg. *Vita Bennonis II*. LB, 372–441.

Bernard of Clairvaux. William of St. Thierry. *Vita prima, liber primus*. PL 185, 225–68.

———. Geoffrey of Clairvaux. *Vita prima, liber tertius*. PL 185, 301–68.

Bernward of Hildesheim. Thangmar. *Vita Sancti Bernwardi*. LB, 272–361.

Brun of Cologne. Ruotger. *Vita Sancti Brunonis*. LB, 178–261.

Burchard of Worms. *Vita Burchardi episcopi Wormatiensis*. Ed. D. G. Waitz. MGH SS 4, 829–46.

Dietrich of Metz. Sigebert of Gembloux. *Vita Deoderici episcopi Mettensis*. MGH SS 4, 461–83.

Eraclius of Liège. Reiner of Liège. *Reineri Vita Eraclii*. Ed. W. Arndt. MGH SS 20, 561–65.

Gerald of Aurillac. Odo of Cluny. *Vita Geraldi*. PL 133, 639–704.

Godehard of Hildesheim. Wolfher of Hildesheim. *Vita Godehardi prior*. Ed. G. H. Pertz. MGH SS 11, 167–96.

———. *Vita Godehardi posterior*. Ed. G. H. Pertz. MGH SS 11, 196–218.

Guibert of Nogent. *Autobiographie: de vita sua*. Ed. Edmond-René Labande. CHFMA 34. Paris: Les Belles Lettres, 1981.

———. *Self and Society in Medieval France: The Memoirs of Abbot Guibert of Nogent (1064?–c.1125)*. Trans C. C. Swinton Bland, rev. with commentary by John F. Benton. New York and Evanston: Harper and Row, 1970.

Heribert of Cologne. Lambert of Deutz. *Vita Herberti archiepiscopi Coloniensis*. MGH SS 4, 740–53.

Licinius of Angers. *Vita Licinii*. Acta Sanctorum Boland. Feb. XIII.5.2, 678–82.

——. Marbod of Rennes. *Vita Sancti Licinii*. PL 171, 1493–1505.

Magnobod of Angers. Marbod of Rennes. *Vita Sancti Magnobodi*. PL 171, 1547–62.

Malachy of Armagh. Bernard of CLairvaux. *Vita Sancti Malachiae*. In *Sancti Bernardi Opera*, 3: 307–78.

Meinwerk of Paderborn. *Das Leben des Bischofs Meinwerk von Paderborn*. Ed. Franz Tenckhoff. MGH SS rer. germ. in us. schol. 59. Hannover: Hahn, 1921.

Norbert of Xanten. *Vita Sancti Norberti*. LB, 452–541.

Notker of Liège. *Vita Notgeri*. Ed. Godefroid Kurth. Also in Kurth, *Notger de Liège et la civilisation au Xe siècle*. Vol. 2. Paris: A. Picard, 1905.

Otto of Bamberg. Herbord of St. Michel. *Herbordi dialogus de vita S. Ottonis*. Ed. Jan Wikarjak and Kazimierz Liman. Monumenta Poloniae Historica n.s. 7, fasc. 3. Warsaw: Państwowe Wydawn, 1974.

Richard of St. Vannes. *Vita Richardi*. Ed. Wilhelm Wattenbach. MGH SS 11, 280–90.

Robert the Pious. Helgaud of Fleury. *Vie de Robert le Pieux: Epitoma vitae regis Rotberti Pii*. Ed. Robert-Henri Bautier and Gillette Labory. Sources d'Histoire Médiévale 1. Paris: Editions de CNRS, 1965.

Sturmi. Eigel von Fulda. *Die Vita Sturmi des Eigil von Fulda*. Ed. Pius Engelbert. Veröffentlichung der Historischen Kommission für Hessen 29. Marburg: Elwert, 1968.

Thierry of St. Hubert. *Vita Theoderici abbatis Andaginensis*. Ed. Wilhelm Wattenbach. MGH SS 12, 36–57.

Thomas Becket. Edward Grim. *Vita et passio Sancti Thomae*. Ed. James Craigie Robertson. RS 67: 2, 353–450. London: Longman, 1875–77.

——. Herbert of Bosham. RS 67: 3, 155–534.

——. John of Salisbury. RS 67: 2, 299–322.

——. William of Canterbury. RS 67: 1, 1–136.

——. William Fitzstephen. RS 67: 3, 1–154.

Ulrich of Augsburg. Bern of Reichenau. *Vita Udalrici*. PL 142, 1183–1203.

——. Gerhard of Augsburg. *Vita Sancti Oudalrici episcopi Augustani*. LB, 46–167.

Ulrich of Cluny (Zell). *Ex vita Sancti Udalrici priorensis Cellensis*. Ed. Roger Wilmans. MGH SS 12. *Vita prior*, 251–53; *Vita posterior*, 253–67.

Wernher of Merseburg. *Vita Wernheri*. Ed. Roger Wilmans. MGH SS 12, 244–48.

Wicbert of Gembloux. Sigebert of Gembloux. *Vita Wicberti*. MGH SS 8, 507–16.

Willigis of Mainz. *Libellus de Willigisi consuetudinibus*. Ed. D. G. Waitz. MGH SS 15: 2, 742–45.

Wolbodo of Liège. Reiner of Liège. *Vita Wolbodonis*. Ed. Wilhelm Arndt. MGH SS 20, 565–71.

Wolfgang of Regensburg. Otloh of St. Emmeram. *Vita Wolfkangi episcopi*. Ed. D. G. Waitz. MGH SS 4, 521–42.

Wolfhelm of Brauweiler. Conrad of Brauweiler. *Vita Wolfhelmi*. Ed. Roger Wilmans. MGH SS 12, 181–95.

OTHER WORKS

Abelard, Peter. *Carmen ad Astralabium: A Critical Edition*. Ed. José M. A. Rubingh-Boscher. Groningen: J.M.A. Rubingh-Boscher, 1987.

———. *Historia calamitatum: texte critique avec une introduction*. Ed. J. Monfrin. Paris: J. Vrin, 1959.

———. *Peter Abelard's Ethics*. Ed. and trans. David. E. Luscombe. Oxford: Clarendon, 1971.

Abelard, Peter and Heloise. *The Letters of Abelard and Heloise*. Trans. Betty Radice. Harmondsworth: Penguin, 1974.

———. "The Personal Letters Between Abelard and Heloise." Ed. J. T. Muckle. *Mediaeval Studies* 15 (1953), 47–94.

———. "The Letter of Heloise on Religious Life and Abelard's First Reply." *Mediaeval Studies* 17 (1955), 240–81.

Adalbold of Utrecht. *Epistola cum tractatu de musica instrumentali, humanaque ac mundana*. Ed. Joseph Smits van Waesbrugge. Divitiae Musicae Artis, ser. A, Liber 2. Buren: F. Knuf, 1981.

Adam of Bremen. *Hamburgische Kirschengeschichte*. Ed. Bernhard Schmeidler. 3d. ed. MGH rer. germ. in us. schol. Hannover and Leipzig: Hahn, 1917; rpt. 1977.

Adam of Perseigne. *Lettres: Texte latin, introduction, traduction et notes*. Ed. Jean Bouvet. Sources Chrétiennes 66; Textes Monastiques de l'Occident 4. Paris: Éditions du Cerf, 1960.

Adelard of Bath. *Des Adelard von Bath Traktat de eodem et diverso*. Ed. Hans Willner. BGPMA 4, 1. Munich: Aschendorff, 1903.

Adelman of Liège. Letter to Berengar of Tours. "Textes latins du XIe au XIIIe siècle." Ed. R. B. C. Huygens. *Studi Medievali* 3d ser. 8 (1967), 476–93.

———. *De viris illustribus sui temporis*. Ed. J. Havet. In Clerval, *Les écoles de Chartres*, 59–61.

Ademar of Chabannes. *Epistola de apostolatu S. Martialis*. PL 142, 87–112.

———. *Historiarum libri tres*. PL 141, 19–80.

Alan of Lille. *Anticlaudianus: Texte critique avec une introduction et des tables*. Ed. Robert Bossuat. Paris: Vrin, 1955.

———. *Anticlaudianus, or The Good and Perfect Man*. Trans. James J. Sheridan. Toronto: Pontifical Institute of Mediaeval Studies, 1973.

Alcuin. *The Rhetoric of Alcuin and Charlemagne: A Translation with an Introduction, the Latin Text, and Notes*. Ed. and trans W. S. Howell. New York: Russell, 1965.

———. Letters. MGH Epist. 4, Ep. Karol. aevi 2. Ed. E. Dümmler.

Alpert of St. Symphorian (Metz). *De diversitate temporum*. MGH SS4, 700–723.

———. *De episcopis Mettensibus libellus*. MGH SS 4, 697–700.

Die ältere Wormser Briefsammlung. Ed. Walther Bulst. MGH, Briefe der deutschen Kaiserzeit 3. Weimar: Böhlaus, 1949.

Ambrose. *Sancti Ambrosii Mediolanensis episcopi De officiis ministrorum libri tres*. PL 16, 23–194.

Andreas Capellanus. *Andreas Capellanus on Love*. Ed. and trans. P. G. Walsh. London: Duckworth, 1982

Annales Augustani. MGH SS 3, 123–36.

Annales Hildesheimenses continuatio. MGH SS 3, 90–103.

Anonymus Haserensis. *De episcopis Eichstetensibus*. Ed. L. C. Bethmann. MGH SS 7, 189–234.

Anselm of Besate. *Gunzo Epistola ad Augienses und Anselm von Besate Rhetorimachia*.

Ed. Karl Manitius. MGH Quellen zur Geistesgeschichte des Mittelalters 2. Weimar: Böhlau, 1958.

Anselm of Liège. *Gesta episcoporum Leodiensium*. Ed. R. Koepke. MGH SS 7, 189–234.

Antiqua statuta ecclesiae Lugdunensis. PL 199, 1091–1120.

Archpoet. *Die Gedichte des Archipoeta*. Ed. Heinrich Watenphul and Heinrich Krefeld. Heidelberg: Winter, 1958.

Baudri of Bourgueil. *Baldricus Burgulianus Carmina*. Ed. Karlheinz Hilbert. Editiones Heidelbergenses 19. Heidelberg: Winter, 1979.

——. *Les oeuvres poétiques de Baudri de Bourgueil (1046–1130)*. Ed. Phyllis Abrahams. Paris: Champion, 1926.

Bede. *Bede's Ecclesiastical History of the English People*. Ed. Bertram Colgrave and R. A. B. Mynors. Oxford: Clarendon Press,1969.

Benedicta regula. Ed. Rudolph Hanslik. CSEL 75. Vienna: Hölder, 1960.

Benzo of Alba. *Ad Heinricum IV. imperatorem libri VII*. Ed. K. Pertz. MGH SS 11, 591–681.

Bern of Reichenau. *Die Briefe des Abtes Bern von Reichenau*. Ed. Franz-Josef Schmale. Veröffentlichungen der Kommission für geschichtliche Landeskunde in Baden-Württemberg, Reihe A, Quellen 6. Stuttgart: Kohlhammer, 1961.

Bernard of Chartres. *Bernard of Chartres, Glosae super Platonem*. Ed. Paul E. Dutton. Pontifical Institute of Mediaeval Studies, Studies and Texts 107. Toronto: The Institute, 1991.

Bernard of Clairvaux. *De consideratione. Sancti Bernardi Opera* 3: 93–493.

——. *Bernard of Clairvaux on the Song of Songs*. I, II, trans. Killian Walsh; III, IV, trans. Irene Edmonds. Cistercian Fathers Series 4, 7, 31, 40. Kalamazoo, MI: Cistercian Publications, 1979, 1980.

——. *Epistolae. Sancti Bernardi Opera*, vols. 7, 8.

——. *Five Books on Consideration: Advice to a Pope*. Trans. John D. Anderson and Elizabeth T. Kennan. Kalamazoo, MI: Cistercian Publications, 1976.

——. *Sancti Bernardi Opera*. Ed. J. Leclercq, Charles H. Talbot, H. M. Rochais. Rome: Editiones Cistercienses, 1957.

——. *The Steps of Humility and Pride*. Trans. M. Ambrose Conway. Kalamazoo, MI: Cistercian Publications, 1989.

——. *Treatises I*. Trans. Conrad Greenia. Cistercian Fathers Series 1.1. Dublin etc.: Irish University Press, 1970.

Bernard Silvester. *The Commentary on the First Six Books of the Aeneid of Vergil commonly attributed to Bernardus Silvestris*. Ed. Julian Jones and Elizabeth Jones. Lincoln: University of Nebraska Press, 1977.

——. *The Commentary on Martianus Capella's De nuptiis Philologiae et Mercurii attributed to Bernardus Silvestris*. Ed. Haijo Jan Westra. Pontifical Institute of Mediaeval Studies, Studies and Texts 80. Toronto: The Institute, 1986.

——. *Cosmographia*. Ed. Peter Dronke. Leiden: Brill, 1978.

——. *The Cosmographia of Bernardus Silvestris*. Trans Winthrop Wetherbee. New York: Columbia University Press, 1973.

Boethius. *Anicii Manlii Torquati Severini Boetii, De institutione Arithmetica libri duo,*

De institutione Musica libri quinque. Ed. Godfredus Friedlein. Leipzig, 1867; rpt. Frankfurt am Main: Minerva, 1966.

———. *De consolatione philosophiae.* Trans, H. F. Stewart. Loeb Classical Library 74. Cambridge, MA: Harvard University Press, 1968.

———. *Fundamentals of Music: Anicius Manlius Severinus Boethius.* Trans. with introduction and commentary by Calvin M. Bower. New Haven, CT: Yale University Press, 1989.

Briefsammlungen der Zeit Heinrichs IV. Ed. Carl Erdmann and Norbert Fickermann. MGH, Briefe der deutschen Kaiserzeit 5. Weimar: Böhlau, 1950.

Carmen Winrici. " 'Querela magistri Treverensis': Das sogenannte 'Carmen Winrici.' " Ed. Ludwig Gompf. *Mittellateinisches Jahrbuch* 4 (1967): 91–121.

Carmina Cantabrigiensia. Ed. Walther Bulst. Heidelberg: Winter, 1950.

Carmina Leodiensia. Ed. Walther Bulst. Sitzungsberichte der Heidelberger Akademie der Wissenschaften, Phil-Hist. K. Abh. 1. Heidelberg: Winter, 1975, 5–47.

Chronicon episcoporum Hildesheimensium. MGH SS 7, 850–54.

Cicero. *De officiis.* Trans. Walter Miller. The Loeb Classical Library 30. Cambridge, MA: Harvard University Press, 1975.

———. *De amicitia.* Trans. William Armistead Falconer. The Loeb Classical Library 154. Cambridge, MA: Harvard University Press, 1979.

———. *De inventione.* Transl H. M. Hubbell. The Loeb Classical Library. Cambridge, MA: Harvard University Press, 1960.

———. *Tusculan Disputations.* Trans. J. E. King. The Loeb Classical Library 141. Cambridge, MA: Harvard University Press, 1971.

Conrad of Hirsau. *Dialogus de mundi contemptu vel amore.* Ed. R. Bultot. Analecta Mediaevalia Namurcensa 19. Louvain: Nauwelaerts, 1966.

Constitutiones canonicorum regularium Ordinis Arroasiensis. Ed. L. Milis and J. Becquet. CCCM 20. Turnhout: Brepols, 1970.

Consuetudines canonicorum regularium Springirsbacenses-Rodenses. Ed. Stefan Weinfurter. CCCM 48. Turnhout: Brepols, 1978

Consuetudines des Augustiner-Chorherrenstiftes Marbach im Elsass (12. Jahrhundert). Ed. Josef Siegwart. Spicilegium Friburgense 10. Freiburg: Universitätsverlag, 1965.

Le coutumier de Saint-Quentin de Beauvais. Ed. L. Milis. *Sacris Erudiri* 21 (1972/73), 435–81.

"De nuptiis Mercurii et Philologiae." "Une version médiévale inconnue de la légende d'Orphée." Ed. André Boutemy. In *Hommages à Joseph Bidez et à Franz Cumont.* Collection Latomus 2. Brussels: Latomus, 1941, 43–70.

"Drei Gedichte aus Frankreich." Ed. Ernst Dümmler. *Neues Archiv* 2 (1877). Poem to Constantine, 222–30.

Folcuin of Lobbes. *Gesta abbatum Lobiensium.* Ed. D. G. Waitz. MGH SS 4, 52–74.

Fulbert of Chartres. *The Letters and Poems of Fulbert of Chartres.* Ed. and trans. Frederick Behrends. Oxford Medieval Texts. Oxford: Clarendon Press, 1976.

Fulcoius of Beauvais. "Fulcoii Belvacensis Epistulae." Ed. Marvin L. Colker. *Traditio* 10 (1954), 191–273.

Fundatio ecclesiae Hildesheimensis. Ed. A. Hofmeister. MGH SS 30:2, 939–46.

Gerald of Wales. *De principis instructione liber*. Ed. George F. Warner. RS 21: 8. London, 1891

Gerbert of Aurillac. *Die Briefsammlung Gerberts von Reims*. Ed. Fritz Weigle. MGH Briefe der deutschen Kaiserzeit 2. Weimar: Böhlau, 1966.

———. *De informatione episcoporum*. PL 139, 1169–78.

Gesta episcoporum Cameracensium. Ed. L. C. Bethmann. MGH SS 7, 402–500.

Gesta episcoporum Virdunensium. Ed. D. G. Waitz. MGH SS 4, 36–51.

Godfrey of Rheims. "Trois oeuvres inédites de Godefroid de Reims." Ed. André Boutemy. *Revue du Moyen Âge Latin* 3 (1947): 335–66.

Godfrey of St. Victor. *Fons philosophiae*. Ed. Pierre Michaud-Quantin. Analecta Mediaevalia Namurcensia 8. Namur-Louvain-Lille: Nauwelaerts, 1956.

Gottfried von Strassburg. *Tristan*. Ed. Friedrich Ranke. 11th edition. Dublin and Zurich: Weidmann, 1967.

———. *Tristan with the 'Tristran' of Thomas*. Trans. A. T. Hatto. Harmondsworth: Penguin, 1985.

Gozechin (Goswin) of Mainz. *Apologiae duae: Gozechini epistola ad Walcherum; Burchardi, ut videtur, Abbatis Bellevallis apologia de barbis*. Ed. R. B. C. Huygens. CCCM 62. Turnhout: Brepols, 1985.

Hariulf. *Chronique de l'Abbaye de Saint-Riquier*. Ed. Ferdinand Lot. CTSEEH 17. Paris: A. Picard, 1894.

Hildebert of Lavardin. *Epistolae*. PL 171, 135–311.

———. *Hildeberti Cenomannensis Episcopi Carmina minora*. Ed. A. Brian Scott. Leipzig: Teubner, 1969.

———. *Libellus de quatuor virtutibus vitae honestae*. PL 171, 1055–67.

———. *Les mélanges poétiques d'Hildebert de Lavardin*. Ed. Hauréau. Paris, 1882.

Honorius Augustodunensis. *De animi exsilio et patria*. PL 172, 1241–46.

Hrabanus Maurus. *De clericorum institutione ad Haistulphum libri tres*. PL 107, 293–419.

Hugh of Flavigny. *Chronicon*. MGH SS 8, 280–503.

Hugh of St. Victor. *Hugonis de Sancto Victore Didascalicon De Studio legendi: A Critical Text*. Ed. Charles Henry Buttimer. Catholic University of America Studies in Medieval and Renaissance Latin 10. Washington, DC: Catholic University Press, 1939.

———. *The Didascalicon of Hugh of St. Victor: A Medieval Guide to the Arts*. Trans. Jerome Taylor. New York: Columbia University Press, 1961.

———. *De institutione novitiorum*. PL 176, 925–92.

———. *Epitome Dindimi in philosophiam. Hugonis de Sancto Victore opera propaedeutica*. Ed. Roger Baron. University of Notre Dame Publications in Mediaeval Studies 20. Notre Dame, IN: University of Notre Dame Press, 1966.

Insitutiones patrum Praemonstratensium. In *De antiquis ecclesiae ritibus*. 3 vols. Ed. Edmond Martène. Antwerp, 1737; rpt. Hildesheim: Olms, 1967.

Ivo of Chartres. "Lettres d'Ive de Chartres et d'autres personnages de son temps." Ed. Lucien Merlet." *Bibliothèque de l'École des Chartes* 16 (1854/55): 443–71.

John of Salisbury. *John of Salisbury's Entheticus Maior and Minor*. Ed. and trans. Jan van Laarhoven. 4 vols. Studien und Texte zur Geistesgeschichte des Mittelalters 17. Leiden: Brill, 1987.

——. *The Letters of John of Salisbury.* Ed. W. J. Millor and C. N. L. Brooke. 2 vols. Oxford: Clarendon Press, 1979; rev. 1986.

——. *Metalogicon.* Ed. J. B. Hall. CCCM 98. Turnhout: Brepols, 1991.

——. *Policraticus.* Ed. C. J. Webb. 2 vols. Oxford: Clarendon Press, 1909.

——. *The Metalogicon of John of Salisbury: A Twelfth-Century Defense of the Logical and Verbal Arts of the Trivium.* Trans. Daniel D. McGarry. Berkeley and Los Angeles: University of California Press, 1962.

Lampert of Hersfeld. *Annales* in *Lamberti monachi Hersfeldensis Opera.* Ed. O. Holder-Egger. MGH SS rer. germ. in us. schol. Leipzig: Hahn, 1894.

Lanfranc. *The Monastic Constitutions of Lanfranc.* Ed. David Knowles. New York: Nelson, 1951.

Lateinische Dichtungen des X. und XI. Jahrhunderts: Festgabe für Walther Bulst. Ed. W. Berschin and R. Düchting. Heidelberg: Winter, 1981.

Liber ordinis Sancti Victoris Parisiensis. Ed. Lucas Jocqué and Ludovicus Milis. CCCM 61. Turnhout: Brépols, 1984.

Manegold of Lautenbach. *Liber contra Wolfhelmum.* Ed. Wilfried Hartmann. MGH Quellen zur Geistesgeschichte des Mittelalters 8. Weimar: Böhlau, 1972.

Marbod of Rennes. "Liebesbriefgedichte Marbods." Ed. Walther Bulst. In *Liber Floridus: Mittellateinische Studien Paul Lehmann . . . gewidmet.* Ed. Bernhard Bischoff. St. Ottilien: Eos Verlag, 1950, 287–302.

——. *Carmina varia.* PL 171, 1692C–D 1717–36.

Martin of Braga. *Formula vitae honestae. Martini ep. Bracarensis opera omnia.* Ed. Claude Barlowe. New Haven, CT: Yale University Press, 1950.

Meinhard of Bamberg. Letters. In *Briefsammlungen der Zeit Heinrichs IV.* Ed. Carl Erdmann and Norbert Fickermann. MGH Briefe der deutschen Kaiserzeit 5. Weimar: Böhlau, 1950.

"Metamorphosis Goliae." Ed. R. B. C. Huygens. "Mitteilungen aus Handschriften." *Studi Medievali* 3d ser. 3 (1962), 764–72.

Onulf of Speyer. "Magister Onulf von Speier." Ed. Wilhelm Wattenbach. *Sitzungsberichte der Preussichen Akademie der Wissenschaften.* Berlin, 1894, 361–86.

Orderic Vitalis. *The Ecclesiastical History of Orderic Vitalis.* Ed. and trans. Marjorie Chibnall. 6 vols. Oxford: Oxford University Press, 1969–80.

Otloh of St. Emmeram. *Visiones.* Ed. Roger Wilmans. MGH SS 11, 378–87.

Otto of Freising. *Gesta Friderici.* Ed. Roger Wilmans. MGH SS 20, 338–496.

Papias. *Vocabulista.* Venice: Phillipus di Pinci, 1496; rpt. Torino: Bottego d'Erasmo, 1966.

"'Parce continuis': A New Text and Interpretative Notes." Ed. David A. Trall, *Mittellateinisches Jahrbuch* 21 (1986), 114–24.

Peter Damian. *De sancta simplicitate. De divina omnipotentia e altri opuscoli,* ed. P. Brezzi and B. Nardi. Florence: Vallecchi, 1943.

Peter of Blois. *Epistolae.* PL 207, 1–560.

Petrus de Honestis (so-called). *Regula clericorum.* PL 163, 691–748.

Pseudo-Boethius. *De disciplina scholari.* PL 64, 1223–38.

Pseudo-Hugh of St. Victor. *Expositio in regulam Beati Augustini.* PL 176, 882–924.

"Quid suum virtutis": *Eine Lehrdichtung des 11. Jahrhunderts.* Ed. B. A. Paravicini. Editiones Heidelbergenses 21. Heidelberg: Winter, 1980.

Die Regensburger Rhetorischen Briefe. In *Briefsammlungen der Zeit Heinrichs IV*. Ed. Norbert Fickermann. MGH Briefe der deutschen Kaiserzeit 5. Weimar: Böhlau, 1950.

La règle de Saint Augustin. Ed. Luc Verheijen. 2 vols. Paris: Études Augustiniennes, 1967.

Regula canonicorum of Aix (816). In *Concilia Aevi Karolini*, ed. Albertus Werminghoff. MGH Legum sec. 3, vol. 2, part 1. Hannover and Leipzig: Hahn, 1906; rpt. 1979.

Rhetores latini minores. Ed. Karl Halm. Leipzig: Hahn, 1863; rpt. Frankfurt: Minerva, 1964.

Richard of St. Victor. *Explicatio in cantica canticorum*. PL 196, 405–523.

Richer of St. Rémy. *Historiae* (*Histoire de France*). Ed. and trans. Robert Latouche. CHFMA 17. Paris: Didier, 1937.

Ruodlieb: Faksimile-Ausgabe des Codex Latinus Monacensis 19486 der Bayerischen Staatsbibliothek München und die Fragmente von St. Florian. Ed. Benedikt Vollman. Wiesbaden: L. Riechart, 1985.

Rupert of Deutz. *Ruperti Chronicon Sancti Laurentii Leodiensis*. Ed. Wilthelm Wattenbach. MGH SS 8, 261–79.

"Satyra de amicicia . . . (Clm 29111): Das Freundschaftsideal eines Freigelassenen." Ed. Fidel Raedle. In *Lateinische Dichtungen des X. und XI. Jahrhunderts: Festgabe für Walther Bulst*. Ed. Walther Berschin and Reinhard Düchting. Heidelberg: Winter, 1981.

Sigebert of Gembloux. *Catalogus Sigeberti Gemblacensis Monachi de viris illustribus*. Ed. Robert Witte. Lateinische Sprache und Literatur des Mittelalters 1. Bern and Frankfurt: Herbert and Peter Lang, 1974.

———. *Gesta abbatum Gemblacensium*. MGH SS 8, 523–42.

———. *Liber decennalis*. Ed. Joachim Wiesenbach. MGH Quellen zur Geistesgeschichte des Mittelalters 12. Weimar: Böhlau, 1986.

———. *Sigeberts von Gembloux Passio Sanctae Luciae Virginis und Passio Sanctorum Thebeorum*. Ed. Ernst Dümmler. Akademie der Wissenschaften, Berlin, Phil-Hist. Kl. Abh. 1. Berlin, 1893.

"Some Commentaries on the *De inventione* and *Ad Herennium* of the Eleventh and Early Twelfth Centuries." Ed. Mary Dicky. *Mediaeval and Renaissance Studies* 6 (1968), 1–41.

Die Tegernseer Briefsammlung. Ed. Karl Strecker. MGH Epistolae selectae 3. Berlin: Weidmannsche Buchhandlung, 1925.

Thierry of Chartres. *Commentaries on Boethius by Thierry of Chartres and His School*. Ed. Nikolaus M. Häring. Pontifical Institute of Mediaeval Studies, Studies and Texts 20. Toronto: The Institute, 1971.

———. *The Latin Rhetorical Commentaries by Thierry of Chartres*. Ed. Karin M. Fredborg. Pontifical Institute of Mediaeval Studies, Studies and Texts 84. Toronto: The Institute, 1988.

———. "Prologue to Heptateuchon." Ed. Edouard Jeauneau. *Mediaeval Studies* 16 (1954), 171–75; also in Jeauneau's "Note sur l'école de Chartres." *Studi Medievali* 3d ser. 5 (1964), 821–65.

Thietmar of Merseburg. *Die Chronik des Bischofs Thietmar von Merseburg*. Ed. Robert Holtzmann. 2nd ed. MGH SS rer. germ., N.S., vol 9. Berlin: Weidmann, 1955.

Thomasin of Zirclaere. *Der wälsche Gast des Thomasin von Zirclaria*. Ed. Heinrich Rückert. DNL vol. 30. Quedlinburg: Basse, 1852; rpt. Berlin: De Gruyter, 1975.

Ulrich of Bamberg. "Eine Bamberger Ars Dictaminis." Ed. Franz Bittner. *Historischer Verein für die Pflege der Geschichte des ehemaligen Fürstbistums Bamberg* 100 (1964), 145–71.

———. *Udalrici codex*. Ed. Philipp Jaffé. Bibliotheca rerum germanicarum 5: Monumenta Bambergensia.

Ulrich of Cluny. *Antiquiores consuetitudines Cluniacensis monasterii*. PL 149, 635–778.

Vincent of Beauvais. *De eruditione filiorum nobilium*. Ed. Arpad Steiner. Mediaeval Academy of America Publications 32. Cambridge, MA: Harvard University Press, 1938.

Walther of Speyer. *Der Libellus Scholasticus des Walther von Speyer: Ein Schulbericht aus dem Jahre 984*. Ed. Peter Vossen. Berlin: De Gruyter, 1962.

Werner of Basel. "Warnerii Basiliensis Paraclitus et Synodus." Ed. P.-W. Hoogterp. *ADHLMA* 8 (1933), 261–429.

Wibald of Stablo. *Wibaldi epistolae*. Ed. Philipp Jaffé. Bibliotheca rerum Germanicarum 1: Monumenta Corbeiensia. 1864; rpt. Aalen: Scientia, 1964.

William of Champeaux. "The Commentaries on Cicero's *De inventione* and *Rhetorica ad Herennium* by William of Champeaux." Ed. Karin Fredborg. *Cahiers de l'Institut du Moyen Âge Grec et Latin* 17 (1976), 1–39.

William of Conches. *Glosae in Iuvenalem*. Ed. Bradford Wilson. Textes Philosophiques du Moyen Âge 18. Paris: J. Vrin, 1980.

———. *Glosae super Platonem: Texte critique avec introduction, notes et tables*. Ed. Edouard Jeauneau. Textes philosophiques du moyen âge 13. Paris: J. Vrin, 1965.

———. *Das Moralium Dogma Philosophorum des Guillaume de Conches: Lateinisch, Altfranzözisch und Mittelniederfränkisch*. Ed. John Holmberg. Paris, 1929.

———. "Deux redactions des gloses de Guillaume de Conches sur Priscien." Ed. Edouard Jeauneau. *RTAM* 27 (1960), 212–47.

———. *Philosophia mundi*. Ed. G. Maurach. Pretoria: University of South Africa, 1980.

William of Malmesbury. *De gestis pontificum Anglorum*. Ed. N. E. Hamilton. RS 52. London, 1870.

Wipo. *Die Werke Wipos*. Ed. Harry Bresslau. 3d ed. MGH Script. rer. Germ. in us. schol. Hannover and Leipzig: Hahn, 1915; rpt. 1956.

Würzburg poet (anonymous). Poem against the school of Worms. In *Die ältere Wormser Briefsammlung*, ed. Bulst, 119–27; also in *Die Tegernseer Briefsammlung*, ed. Strecker, 125–34.

Secondary Sources

Abert, Hermann. "Die Müsikästhetik der Echecs amoureux." *Romanische Forschungen* 15 (1904), 884–925.

———. *Die Musikanschauung des Mittelalters und ihre Grundlagen*. Halle 1905; rpt. Tutzing: H. Schneider, 1964.

Allers, Rudolf. "Microcosmus from Anaximandros to Paracelsus." *Traditio* 1 (1943), 319–407.

Althoff, Gerd. "Nunc fiant Christi milites, qui dudum extiterunt raptores: Zur Entstehung von Rittertum und Ritterethos." *Saeculum* 32 (1981), 317–33.

Anton, Hans. *Fürstenspiegel und Herrscherethos in der Karolingerzeit*. Bonn: L. Röhrscheid, 1968.

Arts libéraux et philosophie au moyen âge. Actes du Quatrième Congrès International de Philosophie Médiévale, Université de Montréal, 27 août–2 septembre 1967. Montreal: Institut d'Études Médiévales, 1969.

Aube, Pierre. *Thomas Becket*. Paris: Fayard, 1988.

Auty, Robert, ed. *Lexikon des Mittelalters*. Munich and Zürich: Artemis Verlag, 1977.

Babcock, Robert G. "Sigebert of Gembloux and the 'Waltharius.'" *Mittellateinisches Jahrbuch* 21 (1986), 101–5.

Balau, Sylvain. *Les sources de l'histoire du pays de Liège au moyen âge*. Brussels: F. Hayez, 1903.

Baldwin, John. *The Government of Philip Augustus: Foundations of Royal Power in the Middle Ages*. Berkeley: University of California Press, 1986.

——. "Masters at Paris from 1179 to 1215: A Social Perspective." In Benson and Constable, eds., *Renaissance and Renewal*, 138–72.

——. "Five Discourses on Desire: Sexuality and Gender in Northern France Around 1200." *Speculum* 66 (1991), 797–819.

——. "L'ars amatoria au XIIe siècle en France: Ovide, Abélard, André le Chapelain et Pierre le Chantre." In *Histoire et société: Mélanges offerts à Georges Duby*, 1: 19–29. Aix-en-Provence: Université de Provence, 1992.

Barlow, Frank. *Thomas Becket and His Clerks*. Berkeley and London: University of California Press, 1986.

Baron, Roger. *Science et sagesse chez Hugues de Saint-Victor*. Paris: Lethielleux, 1957.

——. *Études sur Hugues de Saint-Victor*. Paris: Desclée, De Brouwer, 1963.

Bautier, Robert-Henri. "Paris au temps d'Abélard." In Jolivet, ed., *Abélard en son temps*, 21–77.

Beaujouan, Guy. "The Transformation of the Quadrivium." In Benson and Constable, eds., *Renaissance and Renewal*, 463–87.

——. "L'enseignement du quadrivium." In *La scuola*, 2: 639–723.

Benedetto, L. F. "Stephanus grammaticus da Novara." *Studi Medievali* 3 (1908–11), 499–508.

Benson, Robert L. *The Bishop Elect: A Study in Medieval Ecclesiastical Office*. Princeton, NJ: Princeton University Press, 1968.

Benson, Robert L. and Giles Constable, eds. *Renaissance and Renewal in the Twelfth Century*. Cambridge, MA: Harvard University Press, 1982.

Benton, John. *Self and Society in Medieval France: The Memoirs of Abbot Guibert of Nogent (1064?–c.1125)*. New York and Evanston: Harper and Row, 1970.

Bernt, G. "Fulcoius von Beauvais." In Auty, ed., *Lexikon des Mittelalters*, 4: 1019.

Berschin, Walter, ed. *Lateinische Kultur im X. Jahrhundert. Akten des I. Mittellateinerkongresses, Heidelberg 12.–15. IX. 1988. Mittellateinisches Jahrbuch* 24/25 (1989/90).

Bischoff, Bernhard. "Aus der Schule Hugos von St. Viktor." In *Aus der Geisteswelt des*

Mittelalters: Studien und Texte Martin Grabmann . . . gewidmet, ed. Albert Lang et al., eds. BGPTMA, Supplement vol. 3, 246–50. Munich, 1935; rpt. in his *Mittelalterliche Studien: Ausgewählte Aufsätze zur Schriftenkunde und Literaturgeschichte*, 2: 182–186. Stuttgart: Hiersemann, 1967.

Bisson, Thomas. "The Organized Peace in Southern France and Catalonia, ca. 1140–ca. 1233." *AHR* 82 (1977), 290–307.

Bittner, Albert. *Wazo und die Schulen von Lüttich*. Dissertation, Breslau, 1879.

Blank, Rudolf. *Weltdarstellung und Weltbild in Würzburg und Bamberg vom 8. bis zum Ende des 12. Jahrhunderts*. Bamberg: Selbstverlag des Historischen Vereins, 1968.

Blumenthal, Ute-Renate. *The Investiture Controversy: Church and Monarchy from the Ninth to the Twelfth Century*. Philadelphia: University of Pennsylvania Press, 1991.

Bond, Gerald. "Composing Yourself: Ovid's Heroides, Baudri of Bourgueil and the Problem of Persona." *Mediaevalia* 13 (1987), 83–117.

——. "'Iocus amoris': The Poetry of Baudri of Bourgueil and the Formation of the Ovidian Subculture." *Traditio* 42 (1986), 143–93.

——. "Natural Poetics: Marbod at Angers and the Lessons of Eloquence." Chapter 3 of *The Loving Subject: Desire, Eloquence and Power in Romanesque France*. Forthcoming.

Bonnard, Fourier. *Histoire de l'abbaye royale et de l'ordre des chanoines réguliers de St.-Victor de Paris*. 2 vols. Paris: A. Savaeta, 1904–1907.

Bonner, Stanley F. *Education in Ancient Rome from the Elder Cato to the Younger Pliny*. Berkeley: University of California Press, 1977.

Borck, Karl Heinz. "Tugend, Adel und Geblüt: Thesen und Beobachtungen zur Vorstellung des Tugendadels in der deutschen Literatur des 12. und 13. Jahrhunderts." *PBB* (West) 100 (1978), 423–57.

Bornscheuer, Lothar. *Miserae Regum: Untersuchungen zum Krisen- und Todesgedanken in den herrschaftstheologischen Vorstellungen der ottonisch-salischen Zeit*. Arbeiten zur Frühmittelalterforschung 4. Berlin: De Gruyter, 1968.

Boshof, Egon. "Lothringen, Frankreich und das Reich in der Regierungszeit Heinrichs III." *Rheinische Vierteljahrsblätter* 42 (1978), 63–127.

Boswell, John. *Christianity, Social Tolerance, and Homosexuality: Gay People in Western Europe from the Beginning of the Christian Era to the Fourteenth Century*. Chicago: University of Chicago Press, 1980.

Boutemy, André and Fernand Vercauteren. "Fulcoie de Beauvais et l'intérêt pour l'archéologie antique au XIe et au XIIe siècle." *Collections Latomus* 1, 173–86. Brussels: Latomus, 1937.

Braun, Werner. *Studien zum Ruodlieb*. Berlin: De Gruyter, 1962.

Brinkmann, Hennig. *Mittelalterliche Hermeneutik*. Tübingen: Niemeyer, 1980.

——. *Entstehungsgeschichte des Minnesangs*. Halle/Saale: Niemeyer, 1926; rpt. 1971.

Brown, Calvin M. "Natural and Artificial Music: The Origins and Development of an Aesthetic Concept." *Musica Disciplina* 25 (1971), 17–33.

Brown, Peter. "The Saint as Exemplar in Late Antiquity." In Richard Trexler, ed., *Persons in Groups: Social Behavior as Identity Formation in Medieval and Renais-*

sance Europe, 183–94. Binghamton, NY: Mediaeval and Renaissance Texts and Studies, 1985. Appeared in slightly different form in *Representations* 1 (1983).

Brown, Margaret and C. Stephen Jaeger. "Pageantry and Court Aesthetics in *Tristan*." In Roy Wisbey, ed., *Gottfried von Strassburg and the Medieval Tristan Legend*, 29–44. London: D. S. Brewer, 1990.

Brunhölzl, Franz. "Der Bildungsauftrag der Hofschule." In Bernhard Bischoff, ed., *Karl der Grosse: Lebenswerk und Nachleben*, Vol. II: Geistiges Leben. Düsseldorf: Schwann, 1965.

Bruyne, Edgar de. *Études d'esthétique médiévale*. 3 vols. Bruges, 1946; rpt. Geneva: Slatkine Reprints, 1975.

Büchner, Karl. "Humanitas in der römischen Welt." In his *Studien zur römischen Literatur*, 5: 47–65. Wiesbaden: Steiner, 1965.

Bumke, Joachim. *Höfische Kultur: Literatur und Gesellschaft im hohen Mittelalter*. Munich: Deutscher Taschenbuch Verlag, 1986.

——. "Höfische Kultur: Versuch einer kritischen Bestandsaufnahme." *PBB* (Tübingen) 114 (1992), 414–492.

Bynum, Caroline Walker. *Docere verbo et exemplo: An Aspect of Twelfth Century Spirituality*. Harvard Theological Studies 31. Missoula, MT: Scholars Press, 1979.

——. "The Spirituality of Canons Regular in the Twelfth Century: A New Approach." *Medievalia et Humanistica* n.s 4 (1973), 3–24.

Caldwell, John. "The De institutione arithmetica and the De institutione musica." In Gibson, ed., *Boethius: His Life, Thought, and Influence*, 135–54.

Cantin, A. *Les sciences séculières et la foi: Les deux voies de la science au jugement de S. Pierre Damien (1007–1072)*. Spoleto: Centro italiano di studi sull'alto Mediovo, 1975.

Chamberlain, D. S. "Philosophy of Music in the Consolatio of Boethius." *Speculum* 45 (1970), 80–97.

Châtillon, Jean. "La crise de l'église aux XIe et XIIe siècles et les origines des grandes fédérations canoniales." *Revue de l'Histoire de la Spiritualité* 53 (1977), 3–46.

——. "Les écoles de Chartres et de Saint-Victor." In *La scuola*, 2: 795–840.

——. "De Guillaume de Champeaux à Thomas Gallus: Chronique d'histoire littéraire et doctrinale de l'école de St. Victor." *Revue du Moyen Âge Latin* 8 (1952), 139–162 and 247–272.

——. *Théologie, spiritualité, et métaphysique dans l'oeuvre oratoire d'Achard de Saint-Victor*. Études de Philosophie Médiévale 58. Paris: J. Vrin, 1969.

Chenu, M.-D. "Civilisation urbaine et théologie: L'école de Saint-Victor au XIIe siècle." *Annales ESC* 29 (1974), 1253–64.

——. "Disciplina." *Revue des Sciences Philosophiques et Théologiques* 25 (1936), 686–92.

——. "Monks, Canons, and Laymen in Search of the Apostolic Life." In his *Man and Society in the Twelfth Century: Essays on New Theological Perspectives in the Latin West*, 202–38. Trans. Jerome Taylor and Lester Little. Chicago: University of Chicago Press, 1968.

Cizek, Alexandru. "Der 'Charakterismos' in der Vita Adalhardi des Radbert von Corbie." *Rhetorica* 7 (1989), 185–204.

Classen, Peter. "Die hohen Schulen und die Gesellschaft im 12. Jahrhundert." *AKG* 48 (1966), 155–80.

Clerval, A. *Les écoles de Chartres au moyen-âge du Ve au XVIe siècle.* Paris, 1895; rpt. Geneva: Slatkine Reprints, 1977.

Colish, Marcia. "Another Look at the School of Laon." *AHDLMA* 61 (1986), 7–22.

Colker, Marvin. L. "De nobilitate animi." *Mediaeval Studies* 23 (1961), 47–79.

Constable, Giles. "Renewal and Reform in Religious Life: Concepts and Realities." In Benson and Constable, eds., *Renaissance and Renewal*, 37–68.

Contreni, John J. "The Tenth Century: The Perspective from the Schools." In Claude Lepelley et al., eds., *Haut Moyen Âge: Culture, éducation et société: Études offertes à Pierre Riché*, 379–87. La Garennes-Colombes: Éditions Européennes, 1990.

Corbet, Patrick. *Les saints ottoniens: Sainteté dynastique, sainteté royale, et sainteté féminine autour de l'an Mil.* Beihefte der Francia 15. Sigmaringen: Thorbecke, 1986.

Cowdrey, H. E. J. "Anselm of Besate and Some North-Italian Masters of the Eleventh Century." *Journal of Ecclesiastical History* 23 (1972), 115–24.

Curtius, Ernst Robert. *European Literature and the Latin Middle Ages.* Trans. Willard Trask. New York and Evanston: Harper and Row, 1963.

———. "Zur Geschichte des Wortes Philosophia im Mittelalter." *Romanische Forschungen* 57 (1943), 291–309.

———. "Die Musen im Mittelalter." *ZRPH* 50 (1939), 129–88; also 63 (1943), 256–88.

D'Alverny, Marie-Thérèse. "La sagesse et ses sept filles: recherches sur les allégories de la philosophie et des arts libéraux du IXe au XIIe siècle." In *Melanges dédiés à la mémoire de Félix Grat*, 1: 245–78. Paris: Perqueur-Grat, 1946

Darlington, Oscar. "Gerbert the Teacher." *AHR* 52 (1946/47), 456–76.

Delbouille, Maurice. "Un mystérieux ami de Marbode: Le 'redoutable poète' Gautier." *Moyen Âge* 57 (1951), 205–40.

Delhaye, Philippe. "L'organisation scolaire au XIIe siècle." *Traditio* 5 (1947), 211–68.

———. "Une adaption du De officiis au XIIe siècle: Le *Moralium dogma philosophorum.*" *RTAM* 16 (1949), 227–58; and ibid. 17 (1950), 5–28.

———. "L'enseignement de la philosophie morale au XIIe siècle." *Mediaeval Studies* 11 (1950), 77–99.

———. "La place de l'éthique parmi les classifications scientifiques au XIIe siècle." In *Miscellanea moralia in honorem E.D.A. Janssen*, 79–94. Bibliotheca Ephemeridum theologicarum Lovaniensium, Ser. I, vols. 2–3. Louvain: Nauwelaerts, 1949.

———. "Grammatica et ethica au XIIe siècle." *RTAM* 25 (1958), 59–110.

Dereine, Charles. "Chanoines." In *Dictionnaire d'histoire et géographie ecclésiastique* (1953), 12: 353–405.

———. *Les chanoines réguliers au diocèse de Liège avant Saint Norbert.* Mémoires, Académie Royale de Belgique, 2nd ser., vol. 47. Brussels, 1952.

———. "Coutumiers et ordinaires de chanoines réguliers." *Scriptorium* 5 (1951), 107–13.

——. "Les coutumiers de Saint-Quentin de Beauvais et de Springiersbach." *RHE* 43 (1948), 411–42.

——. "L'école canonique liégoise et la réforme Grégorienne." *Annales du XXXIIIe Congrès de la Fédération Archéologique et Historique de Belgique* 2 (1951), 79–94.

——. "Les origines de Prémontré." *RHE* 42 (1947), 352–78.

——. "Saint-Ruf et ses coutumes aux XIe et XIIe siècles." *Revue Bénédictine* 59 (1949), 161–82.

——. "Vie commune, règle de S. Augustin et chanoines réguliers au XIe siècle." *RHE* 41 (1946), 365–406.

Dickey, Mary. "Some Commentaries on the *De inventione* and *Ad Herennium* of the Eleventh and Early Twelfth Centuries." *Mediaeval and Renaissance Studies* 6 (1968), 1–41.

Dickinson, J. C. *The Origins of the Austin Canons and Their Introduction into England*. London: S.P.C.K., 1950.

Dinzelbacher, Peter. "Über die Entdeckung der Liebe im Hochmittelalter." *Saeculum* 32 (1981), 185–208.

——. "Sozial- und Mentalitätsgeschichte der Liebe im Mittelalter." In Ulrich Müller, ed., *Minne ist ein swaerez spil: Neue Untersuchungen zum Minnesang und zur Geschichte der Liebe im Mittelalter*, 75–110. Göppingen: Kümmerle, 1986.

Donlan, Walter. *The Aristocratic Ideal in Ancient Greece: Attitudes of Superiority from Homer to the End of the Fifth Century B.C.* Lawrence, KN: Coronado Press, 1980.

——. "The Origin of Kaloskagathos." *American Journal of Philology* 94 (1973), 365–74.

Dronke, Peter, ed. *A History of Twelfth-Century Western Philosophy*. Cambridge: Cambridge University Press, 1988.

——. "The Return of Eurydice." *Classica et Mediaevalia* 23 (1962), 198–215.

——. *Women Writers of the Middle Ages: A Critical Study of Texts from Perpetua (d. 203) to Marguerite Porete (d.1310)*. Cambridge: Cambridge University Press, 1984.

Duby, Georges. "The Laity and the Peace of God." In his *The Chivalrous Society*, 123–33. Trans. Cynthia Postan. Berkeley and London: University of California Press, 1977.

——. *The Three Orders: Feudal Society Imagined*. Trans. Arthur Goldhammer. Chicago: University of Chicago Press, 1980.

Duggan, A. "John of Salisbury and Thomas Becket." In Wilks, ed., *The World of John of Salisbury*, 427–38.

Dürig, Walter. "'Disciplina': Eine Studie zum Bedeutungsumfang des Wortes in der Sprache der Liturgie und der Väter." *Sacris Erudiri* 4 (1952), 245–79

Dutton, P. E. "'Illustre civitatis et populi exemplum': Plato's Timaeus and the Transmission from Calcidius to the End of the Twelfth Century of a Tri-Partite Scheme of Society." *Mediaeval Studies* 45 (1983), 79–119.

Edelstein, Wolfgang. *Eruditio und sapientia: Weltbild und Erziehung in der Karolingerzeit: Untersuchungen zu Alcuins Briefen*. Freiburg: Rombach, 1965.

Elford, Dorothy. "William of Conches." In Dronke, ed., *History of Twelfth Century Philosophy*, 308–27.

Endres, J. A. *Petrus Damiani und die weltliche Wissenschaft.* BGPMA 8, 3. Munich: Aschendorffsche Buchhandlung, 1910.

Erdmann, Carl."Anselm der Peripatetiker, Kaplan Heinrichs III." In his *Forschungen zur politischen Ideenwelt des Frühmittelalters,* 119–24. Ed. Fr. Bäthgen. Berlin: Akademie-Verlag, 1951.

———. "Die Bamberger Domschule im Investiturstreit." *Zeitschrift für Bayerische Landesgeschichte* 9 (1936), 1–46

———. "Onulf von Speyer und Amarcius." In his *Forschungen zur politischen Ideenwelt,* 124–34.

———. *Studien zur Briefliteratur Deutschlands im elften Jahrhundert.* MGH, Schriften 1. Leipzig: Hiersemann, 1938.

Evans, Gillian. *Old Arts and New Theology: The Beginnings of Theology as an Academic Discipline.* Oxford: Clarendon Press, 1980.

Fellerer, Karl Gustav. "Die Musica in den Artes Liberales." In Koch, ed., *Artes Liberales,* 33–49.

Fenske, Lutz. "Der Knappe: Erziehung und Funktion." In Fleckenstein, ed., *Curialitas,* 55–127.

Ferruolo, Stephen C. *The Origins of the University: The Schools of Paris and Their Critics, 1100–1215.* Stanford, CA: Stanford University Press, 1985.

Fichtenau, Heinrich. *The Carolingian Empire.* Trans. Peter Munz. Oxford: Blackwell, 1957.

Fleckenstein, Josef. *Die Bildungsreform Karls des Grossen als Verwirklichung der norma rectitudinis.* Freiburg: Herder, 1953.

———, ed. *Curialitas: Studien zu Grundfragen der höfisch-ritterlichen Kultur.* Veröffentlichungen des Max-Planck-Instituts für Geschichte 100. Göttingen: Vandenhoeck and Ruprecht, 1990.

———. *Die Hofkapelle der deutschen Könige.* 2 vols. MGH Schriften 16, 1 & 2. Stuttgart: Hiersemann, 1959–66.

———. "Karl der Grosse und sein Hof." In Bernhard Bischoff, ed., *Karl der Grosse: Lebenswerk und Nachleben,* Vol. 2: *Geistiges Leben,* 24–50. Düsseldorf: Schwann, 1965.

———. "Königshof und Bischofsschule unter Otto dem Grossen." *AKG* 38 (1956), 38–62.

———. "Problematik und Gestalt der ottonisch-salischen Reichskirche." In Karl Schmid, ed., *Reich und Kirche vor dem Investiturstreit: Gerd Tellenbach zum 80. Geburtstag,* 83–98. Sigmaringen: Thorbecke, 1985.

———. "Die Struktur des Hofes Karls des Grossen im Spiegel von Hinkmars *De ordine palatii.*" *Zeitschrift des Aachener Geschichtsvereins* 83 (1976), 5–22; rpt. in his *Ordnungen und formende Kräfte des Mittelalters: Ausgewählte Beiträge,* 67–83. Göttingen: Vandenhoeck and Ruprecht, 1989.

Forschner, Maximilian. *Die stoische Ethik: Über den Zusammenhang von Natur-, Sprach-, und Moralphilosophie im altstoischen System.* Stuttgart: Klett-Cotta, 1981.

Forse, James H. "Bruno of Cologne and the Networking of the Episcopate in Tenth-Century Germany." *German History* 9 (1991), 263–77.

Fredborg, Karin. "Twelfth Century Ciceronian Rhetoric: Its Doctrinal Development and Influences." In Vickers, ed., *Rhetoric Revalued,* 87–97.

———. "The Commentaries on Cicero's *De inventione* and *Rhetorica ad Herennium* by William of Champeaux. *Cahiers de l'Institut du Moyen Âge Grec et Latin* 17 (1976), 1–39.

Fried, Johannes. "Der Archipoeta: Ein Kölner Scholaster?" In Klaus Herbers et al., eds., *Ex Ipsis Rerum Documentis: Beiträge zur Mediävistik: Festschrift für Harald Zimmermann*, 85–90. Sigmaringen: Thorbecke, 1991.

———. "Die Bamberger Domschule und die Rezeption von Frühscholastik und Rechtswissenschaft in ihrem Umkreis bis zum Ende der Stauferzeit." In Fried, ed., *Schulen und Studium*, 163–201.

———, ed. *Schulen und Studium im sozialen Wandel des hohen und späten Mittelalters.* Vorträge und Forschungen 30. Sigmaringen: Thorbecke, 1986.

Friedman, John Block. *Orpheus in the Middle Ages.* Cambridge, MA: Harvard University Press, 1970.

Gamer, Helena. "Studien zum Ruodlieb." *ZfdA* 88 (1957/58), 249–66.

Ganz, Peter, R. B. C. Huygens, and Friedrich Niewöhner, eds. *Auctoritas und ratio: Studien zu Berengar von Tours.* Wolfenbütteler Mittelalter-Studien 2. Wiesbaden: O. Harrassowitz, 1990.

Garin, Eugenio. "Retorica e 'Studia humanitatis' nella cultura del Quattrocento." In Vickers, ed., *Rhetoric Revalued*, 225–39.

Gasc, Hélène. "Gerbert et la pédagogie des arts libéraux à la fin du dixième siècle." *Journal of Medieval History* 12 (1986), 111–21.

Georgianna, Linda. "Any Corner of Heaven: Heloise's Critique of Monasticism." *Mediaeval Studies* 49 (1987), 221–53.

Gibson, Margaret, ed. *Boethius: His Life, Thought and Influence.* Oxford: Blackwell, 1981.

———. "The Continuity of Learning circa 850–circa 1050." *Viator* 6 (1975), 1–13.

———. "The Study of the 'Timaeus' in the Eleventh and Twelfth Centuries." *Pensamiento* 25 (1969), 183–94.

Giesebrecht, Wilhelm von. *Geschichte der deutschen Kaiserzeit.* 5th ed. Vols. 2, 3. Leipzig: Duncker and Humblot, 1885, 1890.

Gilson, Étienne. "L'humanisme médiévale." In his *Humanisme et renaissance.* Paris: J. Vrin, 1986; rpt. from *Les idées et les lettres*, 171–96. Paris: J. Vrin, 1955.

Glauche, Günter. "Die Rolle der Schulautoren im Unterricht von 800–1100." In *La scuola*, 2: 617–36.

———. *Schullektüre im Mittelalter: Entstehung und Wandlungen des Lektürekanons bis 1200 nach den Quellen dargestellt.* Münchener Beiträge zur Mediävistik und Renaissanceforschung 5. Munich: Arbeo, 1970.

Godman, Peter. "Ambiguity in the 'Mathematicus' of Bernardus Silvestris." *Studi Medievali* 3rd ser. 31 (1990), 583–648.

———. "The Ideas of Ernst Robert Curtius and the Genesis of ELLMA." Introduction to *European Literature and the Latin Middle Ages*, Princeton, NJ: Princeton University Press, 1990.

———. *Poets and Emperors: Frankish Politics and Carolingian Poetry.* Oxford: Clarendon Press, 1987.

Gompf, Ludwig. " 'Querela magistri Treverensis': Das sogenannte 'Carmen Winrici.' " *Mittellateinisches Jahrbuch* 4 (1967), 91–121.

Goody, Jack. *The Logic of Writing and the Organization of Society.* Cambridge: Cambridge University Press, 1989.

Goody, Jack and I. P. Watt. "The Consequences of Literacy." *Comparative Studies in Society and History* 5 (1963), 304–45.

Götting, Hans. *Das Bistum Hildesheim 3: Die Hildesheimer Bischöfe von 815 bis 1221 (1227).* Germania Sacra N.F. 20. Berlin and New York: De Gruyter, 1984.

Goy, Rudolf. *Die Überlieferung der Werke Hugos von St. Viktor: Ein Beitrag zur Kommunikationsgeschichte des Mittelalters.* Stuttgart: Hiersemann, 1976.

Grabmann, Martin. *Geschichte der scholastischen Methode: nach den gedruckten und ungedruckten Quellen.* Berlin: Akademie, 1957.

Gregory, Tullio. *Platonismo medievale: studi e ricerchi.* Rome: Istituto storico Italiano per il Medio Evo, 1958.

———. "The Platonic Inheritance." In Dronke, ed., *History of Twelfth Century Western Philosophy*, 54–80.

Gumbrecht, Hans U. and K. L. Pfeiffer, eds. *Materialität der Kommunikation.* Suhrkamp Taschenbuch Wissenschaft 750. Frankfurt am Main: Suhrkamp, 1988.

Haage, Bernhard Dietrich. "Wissenschafts- und bildungstheoretische Reminiszenzen nordfranzösischer Schulen bei Gottfried von Strassburg und Wolfram von Eschenbach." *Würzburger medizinhistorische Mitteilungen* 8 (1990), 91–35.

Haffter, Heinz. "Die römische Humanitas." In hans Oppermann, ed., *Römische Wertbegriffe*, 468–82. Wege der Forschung 14. Darmstadt: Wissenschaftliche Buchgesellschaft, 1974.

Häfner, Elisabeth. *Die Wormser Briefsammlung des 11. Jahrhunderts*, Erlanger Abhandlungen zur mittleren und neueren Geschichte 22. Erlangen: Palm and Enke, 1935.

Halphen, Louis. "Un pédagogue." In his *A travers l'histoire du moyen âge*,277–85. Paris: Presses Universitaires de France, 1950.

Häring, N. M. "The Creation and the Creator of the World According to Thierry of Chartres and Clarenbaldus of Arras." *AHDLMA* 22 (1955), 137–216.

———. "Chartres and Paris Revisited." In J. Reginald O'Donnell, ed., *Essays in Honour of Anton Charles Pegis*, 268–329. Toronto: Pontifical Institute of Mediaeval Studies, 1974.

Hartmann, Wilfried. "Manegold von Lautenbach und die Anfänge der Frühscholastik." *DA* 26 (1970), 47–149.

Haskins, Charles H. *The Renaissance of the Twelfth Century.* 1927; rpt. New York: New American Library, 1972.

Hauck, Albert. *Kirchengeschichte Deutschlands.* Leipzig: J. C. Heinrichs'sche Buchhandlung, 1920 (Vol. 3), 1913 (Vol. 4).

Hauck, Karl. "Heinrich III und der Ruodlieb." *PBB* 70 (1948), 372–419.

Havelock, Eric. *Preface to Plato.* Cambridge, MA: Harvard University Press, 1963.

Heitmann, Klaus. "Orpheus im Mittelalter." *AKG* 45 (1963), 253–94.

Hemmen, Wilhelm. "Der Brief des Magisters Manegold an Abt Wibald von Corvey (1149)." In Klemens Honselman, ed., *Von der Domschule zum Gymnasium in Paderborn*, 79–105. Paderborn: Bonifatius, 1962.

Hexter, Ralph. *Ovid and Medieval Schooling: Studies in Medieval School Commentaries* on *Ovid's Ars amatoria, Epistulae ex Ponto and Epistulae Heroidum*. Munich: Arbeo, 1986.

Hoffmann, Hartmut. "Politik und Kultur im ottonischen Reichskirchensystem: Zur Interpretation der Vita Brunonis des Ruotger." *Rheinische Vierteljahresblätter* 22 (1957), 31–55.

Holder-Egger, O. "Goswin und Gozechin: Domscholaster zu Mainz." *Neues Archiv* 13 (1887/88), 11–21.

Hollister, C. Warren and John Baldwin. "The Rise of Administrative Kingship: Henry I and Philip Augustus." *AHR* 83 (1978), 867–905.

Holtz, Louis. "Les nouvelles tendances de la pédagogie grammaticale au Xe siècle." *Mittellateinisches Jahrbuch* 24/25 (1989/90), 163–73.

Huberti, Ludwig. *Studien zur Rechtsgeschichte der Gottesfrieden und Landfrieden*. Ansbach: Brugel, 1892.

Hüschen, Heinrich. "Antike Einflüsse in der mittelalterlichen Musikanschauung." In Paul Wilpert, ed., *Antike und Orient im Mittelalter*, 80–95. Miscellanea Mediaevalia 1. Berlin: De Gruyter, 1962.

Illmer, Detlef. *Formen der Erziehung und Wissensvermittlung im frühen Mittelalter: Erziehung und Wissensvermittlung im frühen Mittelalter: Beiträge zur Entstehungsgeschichte der Schule*. Kastellaun/Hunsrück, 1979.

Jacqueline, Bernard. *Episcopat et papauté chez Saint Bernard de Clairvaux*. Thesis, University of Paris 1971; Lille: Université de Lille; Paris: Champion, 1975.

Jaeger, C. Stephen. "L'amour des rois: structure social d'une forme de sensibilité aristocratique." *Annales ESC* 46 (1991), 547–71.

———. "Peter Abelard's Silence at the Council of Sens." *Res Publica Litterarum* 3 (1980), 31–54.

———. "Cathedral Schools and Humanist Learning, 950–1150." *DVJS* 61 (1987), 569–616.

———. "The Courtier Bishop in Vitae from the Tenth to the Twelfth Century." *Speculum* 58 (1983), 291–325.

———. "Courtliness and Social Change." In *Cultures of Power: Lordship, Status and Process in Twelfth Century Europe*. Ed. T. Bisson. Philadelphia: University of Pennsylvania Press, 1995, forthcoming.

———. *Medieval Humanism in Gottfried von Strassburg's Tristan and Isolde*. Heidelberg: Carl Winter, 1977.

———. *Origins of Courtliness: Civilizing Trends and the Formation of Courtly Ideals, 939–1210*. Philadelphia: University of Pennsylvania Press, 1985.

———. "Orpheus in the Eleventh Century." *Mittellateinisches Jahrbuch* 27 (1992), 141–68.

Jaeger, Werner W. *Paideia: The Ideals of Greek Culture*. Trans. Gilbert Highet. 3 vols. New York: Oxford University Press, 1965.

Jaffe, Samuel. "Antiquity and Innovation in Notker's *Nova rhetorica*: The Doctrine of Invention." *Rhetorica* 3 (1985), 165–81.

Jolivet, Jean, ed. *Abélard en son temps: Actes du colloque international organisé à l'occasion du 9e centenaire de la naissance de Pierre Abélard*. Paris: Belles Lettres, 1981.

Johnson, Edgar N. *The Secular Activities of the German Episcopate, 919–1024*. University of Nebraska Studies 30. Lincoln: University of Nebraska Press, 1932.

Karnein, Alfred. *De Amore in Volkssprachlicher Literatur: Untersuchungen zur Andreas Capellanus-Rezeption in Mittelalter und Renaissance.* Heidelberg: Carl Winter, 1982.

Kempf, J. *Zur Kulturgeschichte Frankens während der sächsischen und salischen Kaiser. Mit einem Excurs: Über einen Schulstreit zwischen Würzburg und Worms im 11. Jahrhundert.* Programm d. k. Neuen Gymnasiums Würzburg 1914/15. Würzburg, 1915.

Kessler, Eckhard. *Das Problem des frühen Humanismus: Seine philosophische Bedeutung bei Coluccio Salutati.* Munich: W. Fink, 1968.

Klewitz, Hans-Walter. "Königtum, Hofkapelle und Domkapitel im 10. und 11. Jahrhundert." *Archiv für Urkundenforschung* 16 (1939), 102–56; rpt. Darmstadt: Wissenschaftliche Buchgesellschaft, 1960.

Klingner, Friedrich. "Humanität und Humanitas." In his Römische Geisteswelt: Essays zur lateinischen Literatur, ed. Karl Büchner, 704–46. Stuttgart: Reclam, 1979.

Klinkenberg, Hans Martin. "Der Verfall des Quadriviums im frühen Mittelalter." In Koch, ed., *Artes Liberales*, 1–32.

Knowles, David. "The Humanism of the Twelfth Century." In his *The Historian and Character and Other Essays.* Cambridge: Cambridge University Press, 1963.

———. *Thomas Becket.* Stanford, CA: Stanford University Press, 1971.

Knox, Dilwyn. "*Disciplina*: The Monastic and Clerical Origins of European Civility." In John Monfasani and Ronald G. Musto, eds., *Renaissance Society and Culture: Essays in Honor of Eugene F. Rice, Jr.*, 107–35. New York: Italica Press, 1991.

Koch, Josef, ed. *Artes Liberales von der antiken Bildung zur Wissenschaft des Mittelalters.* Studien und Texte zur Geistesgeschichte des Mittelalters 5. Leiden and Cologne: Brill, 1959.

Köhler, Oskar. *Das Bild des geistlichen Fürsten in den Viten des 10., 11. und 12. Jahrhunderts.* Abhandlungen zur mittleren und neueren Geschichte 77. Berlin: Verlag für Staatswissenschaften und Geschichte, 1935.

———. "Die Ottonische Reichskirche: Ein Forschungsbericht." In Josef Fleckenstein, ed., *Adel und Kirche: Gerd Tellenbach zum 65. Geburtstag*, 141–204. Freiburg: Herder, 1968.

Köhn, Rolf. "Schulbildung und Trivium im lateinischen Hochmittelalter und ihr möglicher praktischer Nutzen." In Fried, ed., *Schulen und Studium*, 203–84.

Kupper, Jean-Louis. *Liège et l'église impériale XIe–XIIe siècle.* Bibliothèque de la Faculté de Philosophie et Lettres de l'Université de Liège 228. Paris: Belles Lettres, 1981.

Kurth, Godefroid. *Notger de Liège et la civilisation au Xe siècle.* 2 vols. Paris-Brussels-Liège: A. Picard, 1905.

Ladner, Gerhard. *Theologie und Politik vor dem Investiturstreit.* Vienna: Rohrer, 1936.

Laistner, M. L. W. *Thought and Letters in Western Europe A.D. 500 to 900.* 2nd ed. Ithaca, NY: Cornell University Press, 1957.

Langer, Ullrich. *Divine and Poetic Freedom in the Renaissance: Nominalist Theology and Literature in France and Italy.* Princeton, NJ: Princeton University Press, 1990.

Leclercq, Jean. "Deux opuscules sur la formation des jeunes moines." *Revue d'Ascéti-que et de Mystique* 33 (1957), 387–99.

——. *Études sur le vocabulaire monastique du moyen âge*. Studia Anselmiana 48. Rome: Orbis Catholicus, Herder, 1961.

——. *La femme et les femmes dans l'oeuvre de Saint Bernard*. Paris: Tequi, 1983.

——. *The Love of Learning and the Desire for God: A Study of Monastic Culture*. Trans. Catherine Misrahi. New York: Fordham University Press, 1962.

——. *Monks and Love in Twelfth-Century France: Psycho-Historical Essays*. Oxford: Clarendon Press, 1979.

——. "Pédagogie et formation spirituelle du VIe au IXe siècle." In *La scuola*, 1: 255–90.

——. "Pour l'histoire de l'expression 'philosophie chrétienne.'" *Mélanges des Sciences Religieuses* 8 (1952), 221–26.

——. *Recueil d'études sur Saint Bernard et ses écrits*. 2 vols. Rome: Edizione di Storia e Letteratura, 1962.

Lèsne, Emil. *Les écoles de la fin du VIIIe siècle à la fin du XIIe siècle*. Vol. 5 of his *Histoire de la propriété ecclésiastique en France*. Lille: Faculté Catholique, 1940.

Liebeschütz, Hans. "The Debate on Philosophical Learning During the Transition Period (900–1080)." In Arthur H. Armstrong, ed., *The Cambridge History of Later Greek and Early Medieval Philosophy*, 587–610. Cambridge: Cambridge University Press, 1970.

——. "Kosmologische Motive in der Bildungswelt der Frühscholastik." *Vorträge der Bibliothek Warburg* 1923/24 (1926), 83–148.

Lindgren, Uta. *Gerbert von Aurillac und das Quadrivium: Untersuchungen zur Bildung im Zeitalter der Ottonen*. Sudhoffs Archiv, Beiheft 18. Wiesbaden: Steiner, 1976.

Luscombe, David E. "Peter Abelard." In Dronke, ed., *A History of Twelfth Century Philosophy*, 279–307.

——. *The School of Peter Abelard: The Influence of Abelard's Thought in the Early Scholastic Period*. Cambridge: Cambridge University Press, 1970.

Lutz, Cora. *Schoolmasters of the Tenth Century*. Hamden, CT: Archon Books, 1977.

Lynch, Joseph H. *The Medieval Church: A Brief History*. London and New York: Longman, 1992.

Mähl, Sibylle. *Quadriga virtutum: Die Kardinaltugenden in der Geistesgeschichte der Karolingerzeit*. Cologne and Vienna: Böhlau, 1969.

Maksymiuk, Stefan. *Knowledge, Politics and Magic: The Figure of the Court Magician in Medieval German Literature*. Dissertation University of Washington, 1992.

Mancal, Josef. *Zum Begriff der Philosophie bei M. Tullius Cicero*. Humanistische Bibliothek 1. 39. Munich: Fink, 1982.

Manitius, Max. *Geschichte der lateinischen Literatur des Mittelalters*, Handbuch der Altertumswissenschaft 9, 2. 3 vols. Munich: Beck, 1923; rpt. 1973.

Marrou, H. I. *A History of Education in Antiquity*. Trans. George Lamb. Madison: University of Wisconsin Press, 1956.

Marshall, Linda. "The Identity of the 'New Man' in the 'Anticlaudianus' of Alan of Lille." *Viator* 10 (1979), 77–94.

Märtl, Claudia. "Die Bamberger Schulen: Ein Bildungszentrum des Salierreiches." In Stefan Weinfurter, ed., *Die Salier und das Reich*. 3: 327–46.

McCarthy, Joseph. "Clement of Alexandria and the Foundations of Christian Educational Theory." *History of Education Society Bulletin* 7 (1971), 11–18.

———. *Humanistic Emphases in the Educational Thought of Vincent of Beauvais*. Studien und Texte zur Geistesgeschichte des Mittelalters 10. Leiden: Brill, 1976.

McCready, William D. *Signs of Sanctity: Miracles in Gregory the Great*. Toronto and Leiden: Pontifical Institute of Mediaeval Studies, 1989.

McDonald, William C. "The 'Nobility of Soul': Uncharted Echoes of the Peraldean Tradition in Late Medieval German Literature." *DVJS* 60 (1986), 543–571.

McDonough, Christopher. "Orpheus, Ulysses, and Penelope." *Studi Medievali* 3rd Ser. 31 (1990), 85–121.

McGuire, Brian P. *Friendship and Community: The Monastic Experience 350–1250*. Cistercian Studies Series 95. Kalamazoo, MI: Cistercian Publications, 1988.

McKitterick, Rosamond. *The Carolingians and the Written Word*. Cambridge: Cambridge University Press, 1989.

———. *The Frankish Kingdoms Under the Carolingians, 751–987*. London and New York: Longmans, 1983.

———. "The Palace School of Charles the Bald." In Margaret T. Gibson and Janet L. Nelson, eds., *Charles the Bald: Court and Kingdom*, 385–400. BAR International Series 101. Oxford: BAR, 1981.

———, ed. *The Uses of Literacy in Early Mediaeval Europe*. Cambridge: Cambridge University Press, 1990.

Michaud, E. *Guillaume de Champeaux et les écoles de Paris au XIIe siècle*. Paris: Didier, 1867.

Milis, Ludo. "Ermites et chanoines réguliers au XIIe siècle." *CCM* 22 (1979), 39–80.

Misch, Georg. *Geschichte der Autobiographie*. Vol. 3, parts 1 & 2. Frankfurt/Main: Schulte, Bulmke, 1959.

Monod, Bernard. "La pédagogie et l'éducation au moyen âge d'après les souvenirs d'un moine du XIe siècle." *Revue Universitaire* 13 (1904), 25–36.

Moore, R. T. "Guibert of Nogent and His World." In Henry Mayr-Harting and R. T. Moore, eds., *Studies in Medieval History Presented to R.H.C. Davis*, 107–17. London: Hambledon Press, 1985.

Müller, Walter. *Das Problem der Seelenschönheit im Mittelalter: Eine begriffsgeschichtliche Untersuchung*. Bern: Haupt, 1923.

Nederman, Cary J. "Aristotelian Ethics Before the *Nichomachean Ethics*: Alternate Sources of Aristotle's Concept of Virtue in the Twelfth Century." *Parergon* n.s. 7 (1989), 55–75.

———. "Nature, Sin and the Origins of Society: The Ciceronian Tradition in Medieval Political Thought." *Journal of the History of Ideas* 49 (1988), 3–26.

Newell, John H. Jr. "Grammaticus et Ethicus: William of Conches' Search for Order." In Simo Knuuttila, Monika Asztalos, John Murdoch, and Illka Nuniluoto, eds., *Knowledge and the Sciences in Medieval Philosophy: Proceedings of the Eighth International Congress of Medieval Philosophy, Helsinki 24–29 August, 1987*, 2: 275–84. Helsinki: Yliopistopaino, 1990.

——. "William of Conches." In *Dictionary of Literary Biography*, vol. 115, *Mediaeval Philosophers*. Detroit: Gale Research, 1992, 353–59.

Newman, Barbara. "Flaws in the Golden Bowl: Gender and Spiritual Formation in the Twelfth Century." *Traditio* 45 (1989/90), 111–46.

——. "Authority, Authenticity, and the Repression of Heloise." *Journal of Mediaeval and Renaissance Studies* 22 (1992), 121–57.

Olsen, Glen W. "Twelfth-Century Humanism Reconsidered: The Case of St. Bernard." *Studi Medievali* 3rd ser. 31 (1990), 27–53.

Ong, Walter J. *Orality and Literacy: The Technologizing of the Word*. London and New York: Methuen, 1982.

Panofsky, Erwin. *Gothic Architecture and Scholasticism*. New York: Meridian, 1957.

Paré, Gérard, P. Tremblay, and A. Brunet. *La renaissance du XIIe siècle: Les écoles et l'enseignement*. Publications de l'Institut des Études Médiévales d'Ottowa 3. Paris and Ottowa: J. Vrin, 1933.

Philippson, Robert. "Das Sittlichschöne bei Panaitios." *Philologus* 85 n.s. 39 (1930), 357–413.

Pietzsch, Gerhard. *Die Musik im Erziehungs- und Bildungsideal des ausgehenden Altertums und frühen Mittelalters*. Halle, 1932; rpt. Darmstadt: Wissenschaftliche Buchgesellschaft, 1969.

Pire, Georges. *Stoicisme et pédagogie de Zénon à Marc-Aurèle, de Sénèque à Montaigne et à J.-J. Rousseau*. Liège and Paris: Dessain, 1958.

Platelle, Henri. "Le problème du scandale: Les nouvelles modes masculines aux XIe et XIIe siècles." *Revue Belge de Philologie et d'Histoire* 53 (1975), 1071–96.

Podlech, Adalbert. *Abälard und Héloïse oder die Theologie der Liebe*. Munich and Zürich: Piper, 1990.

Poole, Reginald L. *Illustrations of the History of Medieval Thought and Learning*. 2nd ed. New York, 1920; rpt. New York: Dover, 1960.

——. "The Masters of the Schools at Paris and Chartres in John of Salisbury's Time." *English Historical Review* 139 (1920), 321–42.

Post, Gaines. *Studies in Medieval Legal Thought*. Princeton, NJ: Princeton University Press, 1964.

Prinz, Friedrich. "Kaiser Heinrich III: Seine widersprüchliche Beurteilung und deren Gründe." *HZ* 246 (1988), 529–48.

Radding, Charles M. "The Geography of Learning in Early Eleventh-Century Europe: Lanfranc of Bec and Berengar of Tours Revisited." *Bullettino dell'Istituto Storico Italiano per il Medio Evo e Archivio Muratoriano* (forthcoming).

——. *A World Made by Men: Cognition and Society, 400–1200*. Chapel Hill: University of North Carolina Press, 1985.

Radding, Charles M. and William W. Clark. *Medieval Architecture, Medieval Learning: Builders and Masters in the Age of Romanesque and Gothic*. New Haven, CT: Yale University Press, 1992.

Renardy, Charlotte. "Les écoles liégoises du IXe au XIIe siècle: grandes lignes de leur évolution." *Revue Belge de Philologie et d'Histoire* 57 (1979), 309–28.

Reuter, Timothy. "The 'Imperial Church System' of the Ottonian and Salian Rulers: A Reconsideration." *Journal of Ecclesiastical History* 33 (1982), 347–74.

Riché, Pierre. "Les conditions de la production littéraire: maîtres et écoles." *Mittellateinisches Jahrbuch* 24/25 (1989/90), 413–22.

——. *Les écoles et l'enseignement dans l'occident chrétien de la fin du Ve siècle au milieu du XIe siècle*. Paris, 1979.

——. *Education and Culture in the Barbarian West from the Sixth Through the Eighth Century*. Trans. J. Contreni. Columbia, SC: University of South Carolina Press, 1978.

——. "L'enseignement de Gerbert à Reims dans le contexte européen." In *Gerberto: Scienza, storia, et mito: atti del Gerberti Symposium, Bobbio 25–27 Iuglio, 1983*. Archivum Bobbiense, Studia 2. Bobbio and Piacenza: Editrice degli A.S.B., 1985.

Robinson, I. S. "The 'colores rhetorici' in the Investiture Contest." *Traditio* 32 (1976), 209–38.

Ruh, Kurt and Gundolf Keil, eds. *Die deutsche Literatur des Mittelalters: Verfasserlexikon*. 2nd ed. Berlin and New York: De Gruyter, 1977– .

Scaglione, Aldo D. *Knights at Court: Courtliness, Chivalry and Courtesy from Ottonian Germany to the Italian Renaissance*. Berkeley: University of California Press, 1991.

Schadewalt, Wolfgang. "Humanitas Romana." In Hildegard Temporini, ed., *Aufstieg und Niedergang der römischen Welt I: Von den Anfängen bis zum Ausgang der Republik*, 4: 43–62. Berlin: De Gruyter, 1973.

Schauwecker, Helga. *Otloh von St. Emmeram: Ein Beitrag zur Bildungs- und Frömmigkeitsgeschichte des 11. Jahrhunderts*. Dissertation, Würzburg, 1962.

Schepss, Georg. "Zu Froumunds Briefcodex und zu Ruodlieb." *ZfdPh* 15 (1883), 419–33.

Schieffer, Rudolf. "Bleibt der Archipoeta anonym?" *Mitteilungen des Instituts für Österreichische Geschichtsforschung* 98 (1990), 59–79.

Schmitt, Jean-Claude. "The Ethics of Gesture." In Michel Feher, ed., *Fragments for a History of the Human Body*, 128–47. New York: Zone, 1989.

——. *La raison des gestes dans l'occident médiéval*. Paris: Gallimard, 1990.

Schnell, Rüdiger. *Andreas Capellanus: Zur Rezeption des römischen und kanonischen Rechts in De Amore*. Munich: W. Fink, 1982.

——. *Causa amoris: Liebeskonzeption und Liebesdarstellung in der mittelalterlichen Literatur*. Bern: Francke, 1985.

——. "Die 'höfische Liebe' als 'höfischer Diskurs' über die Liebe." In Fleckenstein, ed., *Curialitas*, 231–301.

Schnith, Karl. "Recht und Friede: Zum Königsgedanken im Umkreis Heinrichs III." *HJb* 81 (1962), 22–57.

La scuola nell' occidente latino dell' alto medioevo. Settimane di studio del centro Italiano di studi sull' alto medioevo 19. 2 vols. Spoleto: Presso la sede del Centro, 1972.

Seigel, Jerrold. *Rhetoric and Philosophy in Renaissance Humanism: The Union of Eloquence and Wisdom, Petrarch to Valla*. Princeton, NJ: Princeton University Press, 1968.

Siegwart, Josef. *Die Consuetudines des Augustiner-Chorherrenstiftes Marbach im Elsass (12. Jahrhundert)*. Spicilegium Friburgense 10. Freiburg: Universitätsverlag, 1965.

Silvestre, Hubert. "Notice sur Adelman de Liége, évêque de Brescia (+1061)." *Revue d'Histoire Ecclésiastique* 56 (1961), 855–71.

Smalley, Beryl. *The Study of the Bible in the Middle Ages*. 2nd ed. Notre Dame, IN: Notre Dame University Press, 1970.

——. *The Becket Conflict and the Schools: A Study of Intellectuals in Politics*. Totowa, NJ: Rowman and Littlefield, 1973.

Sommerfeldt, John. "Charismatic and Gregorian Leadership in the Thought of Bernard of Clairvaux." In *Bernard of Clairvaux: Studies Presented to Dom Jean Leclercq*, 73–90. Washington, DC: Cistercian Publications, 1973.

Southern, R. W. "Lanfranc of Bec and Berengar of Tours." In R. W. Hunt, W. A. Pantin, and R. W. Southern, eds., *Studies in Medieval History presented to Frederick Maurice Powicke*, 27–48. Oxford: Clarendon Press, 1948.

——. *The Making of the Middle Ages*. New Haven, CT: Yale University Press, 1966.

——. "Medieval Humanism." In his *Medieval Humanism and Other Essays*, 29–60. New York: Harper and Row, 1970.

——. "The Place of England in the Twelfth Century Renaissance." *History* 45 (1960), 201–16; rpt. in his *Medieval Humanism and Other Essays*, 158–80.

——. *Platonism, Scholastic Method, and the School of Chartres*. The Stenton Lecture 1978. Reading: University of Reading, 1979.

——. "The Schools of Paris and Chartres." In Benson and Constable, eds., *Renaissance and Renewal*, 113–37.

Specht, Franz Anton. *Geschichte des Unterrichtswesens in Deutschland von den ältesten Zeiten bis zur Mitte des dreizehnten Jahrhunderts*. Stuttgart: Cotta, 1885.

Spitzer, Leo. *Classical and Christian Ideas of World Harmony: Prolegomena to an Interpretation of the Word "Stimmung"*. Ed. A. G. Hatcher. Baltimore: Johns Hopkins University Press, 1963.

Sprandel, Rolf. *Ivo von Chartres und seine Stellung in der Kirchengeschichte*. Stuttgart: Hiersemann,, 1962.

Stachnik, Richard. *Die Bildung des Weltklerus im Frankenreiche von Karl Martell bis auf Ludwig den Frommen: Eine Darstellung ihrer geschichtlichen Entwicklung*. Paderborn: F. Schöningh, 1926.

Steindorff, Ernst. *Jahrbücher des deutschen Reiches unter Heinrich III*. Leipzig, 1874–81; rpt. Darmstadt: Wissenschaftliche Buchgesellschaft, 1963.

Steinen, Wolfram von den. "Humanismus um 1100." In his *Menschen im Mittelalter: Gesammelte Forschungen, Betrachtungen, Bilder*, 196–214. Ed. Peter von Moos. Bern and Munich: Francke, 1967.

Stock, Brian. *The Implications of Literacy: Written Language and Models of Interpretation in the Eleventh and Twelfth Centuries*. Princeton, NJ: Princeton University Press, 1983.

——. *Myth and Science in the Twelfth Century: A Study of Bernard Silvester*. Princeton, NJ: Princeton University Press, 1972.

Stotz, Peter. "Dichten als Schulfach: Aspekte mittelalterlicher Schuldichtung." *Mittellateinisches Jahrbuch* 16 (1981), 1–16.

Strayer, Joseph, ed. *Dictionary of the Middle Ages*. New York: Scribners, 1982.

Struve, Tilman. "Vita civilis naturam imitetur: Der Gedanke der Nachahmung der Natur als Grundlage der organologischen Staatskonzeption Johannes von Salisbury." *Historisches Jahrbuch* 101 (1981), 341–61.

Tellenbach, Gerd. *Church, State and Christian Society at the Time of the Investiture Contest*. Trans. R. F. Bennett. Oxford: Blackwell, 1940.

Thomas, Heinz. "Zur Kritik an der Ehe Heinrichs III. mit Agnes von Poitou." In Kurt-Ulrich Jäschke and Reinhard Wenskus, eds., *Festschrift für Helmut Beumann zum 65. Geburtstag*, 224–35. Sigmaringen: Thorbecke, 1977.

Thompson, James W. *The Literacy of the Laity in the Middle Ages*. Berkeley: University of California Press, 1939; rpt. New York: B. Franklin, 1963.

Uhlirz, Karl. *Jahrbücher des deutschen Reiches unter Otto II. und Otto III.* 1902; rpt. Berlin: Duncker and Humblot, 1967.

Van den Eynde, Damien. *Essai sur la succession et la date des écrits de Hugues de Saint-Victor*. Spicilegium pontificii Athenaei Antoniani 13. Rome: Pontificum Athenaeum Antonianum, 1960.

Van Engen, John H. "The 'Crisis of Cenobitism' Reconsidered: Benedictine Monasticism in the Years 1050–1150." *Speculum* 61 (1986), 269–304.

——. *Rupert of Deutz*. Berkeley: University of California Press, 1983.

Vickers, Brian, ed. *Rhetoric Revalued: Papers from the International Society for the History of Rhetoric*. Binghamton, NY: Center for Medieval and Early Renaissance Studies, 1982.

Vogt, G. M. "Gleanings for the History of a Sentiment: Generositas virtus, non sanguis." *JEGP* 24 (1925), 102–24.

Vollrath, H. "'Gewissenmoral und Konfliktverständnis: Thomas Becket in der Darstellung seiner Biographen." *HJb* 109 (1989), 24–55.

von Moos, Peter. *Geschichte als Topik: Das rhetorische Exemplum von der Antike zur Neuzeit und die* historiae *im* Policraticus *Johanns von Salisbury*. Ordo 2. Hildesheim-Zürich-New York: G. Olms, 1988.

——. *Hildebert von Lavardin, 1056–1133: Humanitas an der Schwelle des höfischen Zeitalters*. Pariser Historische Studien 3. Stuttgart: Hiersemann, 1965.

——. "Par tibi, Roma, nihil: Eine Antwort." *Mittellateinisches Jahrbuch* 14 (1979), 119–26.

Vossen, Peter. *Der Libellus Scolasticus des Walther von Speyer: Ein Schulbericht aus dem Jahre 984*. Berlin: De Gruyter, 1962.

Vossler, Karl. "Adel der Geburt und der Gesinnung bei den Romanen." In his *Aus der romanischen Welt*, 44–52. 2nd ed. Karlsruhe: Stahlberg, 1948.

Wallach, Luitpold. *Alcuin and Charlemagne: Studies in Carolingian History and Literature*. Ithaca, NY: Cornell University Press, 1959.

——. "Alcuin on Virtues and Vices: A Manual for a Carolingian Soldier." *Harvard Theological Review* 48 (1955), 175–95.

——. "Education and Culture in the Tenth Century." *Mediaevalia et Humanistica* 9 (1955), 18–22.

——. "Onulf of Speyer: A Humanist of the Eleventh Century." *Medievalia et Humanistica* 6 (1950), 35–56.

Walsh, P. G. "Alan of Lille as a Renaissance Figure." *Studies in Church History* 14 (1977), 117–35.

Wankel, Hermann. *Kalos kai agathos*. Dissertation, Würzburg, 1961; rpt. New York: Arno, 1979.

Ward, Benedicta. *Miracles and the Medieval Mind: Theory, Record, and Event, 1000–1215*. Philadelphia: University of Pennsylvania Press, 1982.

Ward, John. *Artificiosa eloquentia in the Middle Ages*, Dissertation, Toronto, Pontifical Institute of Mediaeval Studies, 1972.

———. "The Date of the Commentary on Cicero's 'De inventione' by Thierry of Chartres (ca.1095–1160?) and the Cornifician Attack on the Liberal Arts." *Viator* 3 (1972), 219–73.

Warden, John. "Orpheus and Ficino." In John Warden, ed. *Orpheus: The Metamorphosis of a Myth*. Toronto: Toronto University Press, 1982.

Warren, F. M. "Constantine of Fleury, 985–1014." *Transactions of the Connecticut Academy of Arts and Sciences* 15 (1909), 285–92

Wattenbach, Wilhelm. "Magister Onulf von Speier." *Sitzungsberichte der Preussischen Akademie der Wissenschaften* (1894), 361–86.

Weber, F. *Die Domschule von Speyer im Mittelalter*. Dissertation, Freiburg, 1954.

Wehrli, Max. "Der Tristan Gottfrieds von Strassburg." In Alois Wolf, ed., *Gottfried von Strassburg*, 97–134. Wege der Forschung 320. Darmstadt: Wissenschaftliche Buchgesellschaft, 1973.

Weigle, Fritz. "Studien zur Überlieferung der Briefsammlung Gerberts von Reims." *DA* 14 (1958), 158–64

Weinfurter, Stefan, ed. *Die Salier und das Reich*. 3 vols. Sigmaringen: Thorbecke, 1991.

——— and Odilo Engels. *Series Episcoporum Ecclesiae Catholicae Occidentalis, Ser. 5: Germania, Bd. 1: Archiepiscopatus Coloniensis*. Stuttgart: Hiersemann, 1982.

Werner, K. F. "Zur Überlieferung der Briefe Gerberts von Aurillac." *DA* 17 (1961), 91–144.

Wetherbee, Winthrop. *Platonism and Poetry in the Twelfth Century*. Princeton, NJ: Princeton University Press, 1972

White, Alison. "Boethius in the Medieval Quadrivium." In Gibson, ed., *Boethius: His Life, Thought and Influence*, 162–205.

White, Hayden F. "The Gregorian Ideal and Saint Bernard of Clairvaux." *Journal of the History of Ideas* 21 (1960), 321–48.

Wilks, Michael. "Alan of Lille and the New Man." *Studies in Church History* 14 (1977), 117–35.

———, ed. *The World of John of Salisbury*. Studies in Church History, Subsidia 3. Oxford: Blackwell, 1984.

Willesme, Jean-Pierre. "Saint-Victor au temps d'Abélard." In Jolivet, ed., *Abélard en son temps*, 95–105.

Williams, John R. "The Cathedral School of Rheims in the Eleventh Century." *Speculum* 19 (1954), 661–77.

———. "Manasses I of Rheims and Gregory VII." *AHR* 54 (1949), 804–24.

———. "Godfrey of Rheims: A Humanist of the Eleventh Century." *Speculum* 22 (1947), 29–45.

Winnington-Ingram, R. P. "Ancient Greek Music 1932–1957." *Lustrum* 3 (1958), 5–57.

Wolf, Gunther. "Erzbischof Brun I. von Köln und die Förderung der gelehrten Studien in Köln." In Albert Zimmermann, ed., *Die Kölner Universität im Mittelalter: Geistige Wurzeln und soziale Wirklichkeit*, 299–311. Miscellanea Mediaevalia 20. Berlin and New York: De Gruyter, 1989.

Wolfram, Herwig. *Splendor Imperii: Die Epiphanie von Tugend und Heil in Herrschaft und Reich*. MIÖG Ergänzungsband 20, 3. Graz and Cologne: Böhlau, 1963.

Worstbrock, Franz Josef. "Gozwin von Mainz." In Ruh, ed., *Verfasserlexikon*, 2nd ed., 3: 205–7.

Zielinski, Herbert. *Der Reichsepiskopat in spätottonischer und salischer Zeit (1002–1125)*. Wiesbaden: Steiner, 1984.

Zumthor, Paul. *Oral Poetry: An Introduction*. Minneapolis: University of Minnesota Press, 1990.

———. "The Text and the Voice." *NLH* 16 (1984), 67–92.

Zwierlein, Otto. "Par tibi, Roma, nihil." *Mittellateinisches Jahrbuch* 11 (1976), 92–94.

Index

University of Pennsylvania Press
MIDDLE AGES SERIES
Edward Peters, General Editor

F. R. P. Akehurst, trans. *The* Coutumes de Beauvaisis *of Philippe de Beaumanoir.* 1992

Peter L. Allen. *The Art of Love: Amatory Fiction from Ovid to the* Romance of the Rose. 1992

David Anderson. *Before the Knight's Tale: Imitation of Classical Epic in Boccaccio's* Teseida. 1988

Benjamin Arnold. *Count and Bishop in Medieval Germany: A Study of Regional Power, 1100–1350.* 1991

Mark C. Bartusis. *The Late Byzantine Army: Arms and Society, 1204–1453.* 1992

J. M. W. Bean. *From Lord to Patron: Lordship in Late Medieval England.* 1990

Thomas N. Bisson, ed. *Cultures of Power: Lordship, Status, and Process in Twelfth-Century Europe.* 1995

Uta-Renate Blumenthal. *The Investiture Controversy: Church and Monarchy from the Ninth to the Twelfth Century.* 1988

Daniel Bornstein, trans. *Dino Compagni's* Chronicle *of Florence.* 1986

Maureen Boulton. *The Song in the Story: Lyric Insertions in French Narrative Fiction, 1200–1400.* 1993

Betsy Bowden. *Chaucer Aloud: The Varieties of Textual Interpretation.* 1987

Charles R. Bowlus. *Franks, Moravians, and Magyars: The Struggle for the Middle Danube, 788–907.* 1994

James William Brodman. *Ransoming Captives in Crusader Spain: The Order of Merced on the Christian-Islamic Frontier.* 1986

Kevin Brownlee and Sylvia Huot, eds. *Rethinking the* Romance of the Rose*: Text, Image, Reception.* 1992

Matilda Tomaryn Bruckner. *Shaping Romance: Interpretation, Truth, and Closure in Twelfth-Century French Fictions.* 1993

Otto Brunner (Howard Kaminsky and James Van Horn Melton, eds. and trans.). Land *and Lordship: Structures of Governance in Medieval Austria.* 1992

Robert I. Burns, S.J., ed. *Emperor of Culture: Alfonso X the Learned of Castile and His Thirteenth-Century Renaissance.* 1990

David Burr. *Olivi and Franciscan Poverty: The Origins of the* Usus Pauper *Controversy.* 1989

David Burr. *Olivi's Peaceable Kingdom: A Reading of the Apocalypse Commentary.* 1993

Thomas Cable. *The English Alliterative Tradition.* 1991

Anthony K. Cassell and Victoria Kirkham, eds. and trans. *Diana's Hunt/Caccia di Diana: Boccaccio's First Fiction.* 1991

John C. Cavadini. *The Last Christology of the West: Adoptionism in Spain and Gaul, 785–820.* 1993

Brigitte Cazelles. *The Lady as Saint: A Collection of French Hagiographic Romances of the Thirteenth Century.* 1991

Karen Cherewatuk and Ulrike Wiethaus, eds. *Dear Sister: Medieval Women and the Epistolary Genre.* 1993

Anne L. Clark. *Elisabeth of Schönau: A Twelfth-Century Visionary.* 1992

Willene B. Clark and Meradith T. McMunn, eds. *Beasts and Birds of the Middle Ages: The Bestiary and Its Legacy.* 1989

Richard C. Dales. *The Scientific Achievement of the Middle Ages.* 1973

Charles T. Davis. *Dante's Italy and Other Essays.* 1984

William J. Dohar. *The Black Death and Pastoral Leadership: The Diocese of Hereford in the Fourteenth Century.* 1994

Katherine Fischer Drew, trans. *The Burgundian Code.* 1972

Katherine Fischer Drew, trans. *The Laws of the Salian Franks.* 1991

Katherine Fischer Drew, trans. *The Lombard Laws.* 1973

Nancy Edwards. *The Archaeology of Early Medieval Ireland.* 1990

Margaret J. Ehrhart. *The Judgment of the Trojan Prince Paris in Medieval Literature.* 1987

Richard K. Emmerson and Ronald B. Herzman. *The Apocalyptic Imagination in Medieval Literature.* 1992

Theodore Evergates. *Feudal Society in Medieval France: Documents from the County of Champagne.* 1993

Felipe Fernández-Armesto. *Before Columbus: Exploration and Colonization from the Mediterranean to the Atlantic, 1229–1492.* 1987

Jerold C. Frakes. *Brides and Doom: Gender, Property, and Power in Medieval Women's Epic.* 1994

R. D. Fulk. *A History of Old English Meter.* 1992

Patrick J. Geary. *Aristocracy in Provence: The Rhône Basin at the Dawn of the Carolingian Age.* 1985

Peter Heath. *Allegory and Philosophy in Avicenna (Ibn Sînâ), with a Translation of the Book of the Prophet Muhammad's Ascent to Heaven.* 1992

J. N. Hillgarth, ed. *Christianity and Paganism, 350–750: The Conversion of Western Europe.* 1986

Richard C. Hoffmann. *Land, Liberties, and Lordship in a Late Medieval Countryside: Agrarian Structures and Change in the Duchy of Wrocław.* 1990

Robert Hollander. *Boccaccio's Last Fiction: Il Corbaccio.* 1988

Edward B. Irving, Jr. *Rereading* Beowulf. 1989

Richard A. Jackson, ed. *Texts and Ordines for the Coronation of Frankish Kings and Queens in the Middle Ages.* 1994

C. Stephen Jaeger. *The Envy of Angels: Cathedral Schools and Social Ideals in Medieval Europe, 950–1200.* 1994

C. Stephen Jaeger. *The Origins of Courtliness: Civilizing Trends and the Formation of Courtly Ideals, 939–1210.* 1985

William Chester Jordan. *The French Monarchy and the Jews: From Philip Augustus to the Last Capetians.* 1989

William Chester Jordan. *From Servitude to Freedom: Manumission in the Sénonais in the Thirteenth Century.* 1986

Donald J. Kagay, trans. *The Usatges of Barcelona: The Fundamental Law of Catalonia.* 1994

Richard Kay. *Dante's Christian Astrology.* 1994

Ellen E. Kittell. *From Ad Hoc to Routine: A Case Study in Medieval Bureaucracy.* 1991

Alan C. Kors and Edward Peters, eds. *Witchcraft in Europe, 1100–1700: A Documentary History.* 1972

Barbara M. Kreutz. *Before the Normans: Southern Italy in the Ninth and Tenth Centuries.* 1992

Michael P. Kucsynski. *Prophetic Song: The Psalms as Moral Discourse in Late Medieval England.* 1995

E. Ann Matter. *The Voice of My Beloved: The Song of Songs in Western Medieval Christianity.* 1990

A. J. Minnis. *Medieval Theory of Authorship.* 1988

Lawrence Nees. *A Tainted Mantle: Hercules and the Classical Tradition at the Carolingian Court.* 1991

Lynn H. Nelson, trans. *The Chronicle of San Juan de la Peña: A Fourteenth-Century Official History of the Crown of Aragon.* 1991

Barbara Newman. *From Virile Woman to WomanChrist: Studies in Medieval Religion and Literature.* 1995.

Joseph F. O'Callaghan. *The Cortes of Castile-León, 1188–1350.* 1989

Joseph F. O'Callaghan. *The Learned King: The Reign of Alfonso X of Castile.* 1993

Odo of Tournai (Irven M. Resnick, trans.). *Two Theological Treatises:* On Original Sin *and* A Disputation with the Jew, Leo, Concerning the Advent of Christ, the Son of God. 1994

David M. Olster. *Roman Defeat, Christian Response, and the Literary Construction of the Jew.* 1994

William D. Paden, ed. *The Voice of the Trobairitz: Perspectives on the Women Troubadours.* 1989

Edward Peters. *The Magician, the Witch, and the Law.* 1982

Edward Peters, ed. *Christian Society and the Crusades, 1198–1229: Sources in Translation, including* The Capture of Damietta *by Oliver of Paderborn.* 1971

Edward Peters, ed. *The First Crusade: The* Chronicle of Fulcher of Chartres *and Other Source Materials.* 1971

Edward Peters, ed. *Heresy and Authority in Medieval Europe.* 1980

James M. Powell. *Albertanus of Brescia: The Pursuit of Happiness in the Early Thirteenth Century.* 1992

James M. Powell. *Anatomy of a Crusade, 1213–1221.* 1986

Susan A. Rabe. *Faith, Art, and Politics at Saint-Riquier: The Symbolic Vision of Angilbert.* 1994

Jean Renart (Patricia Terry and Nancy Vine Durling, trans.). *The Romance of the Rose or Guillaume de Dole.* 1993

Michael Resler, trans. Erec *by Hartmann von Aue.* 1987

Pierre Riché (Michael Idomir Allen, trans.). *The Carolingians: A Family Who Forged Europe.* 1993

Pierre Riché (Jo Ann McNamara, trans.). *Daily Life in the World of Charlemagne.* 1978

Jonathan Riley-Smith. *The First Crusade and the Idea of Crusading.* 1986

Joel T. Rosenthal. *Patriarchy and Families of Privilege in Fifteenth-Century England.* 1991

Teofilo F. Ruiz. *Crisis and Continuity: Land and Town in Late Medieval Castile.* 1994

James A. Rushing, Jr. *Images of Adventure: Ywain in the Visual Arts.* 1995.

Steven D. Sargent, ed. and trans. *On the Threshold of Exact Science: Selected Writings of Anneliese Maier on Late Medieval Natural Philosophy.* 1982

Pamela Sheingorn, ed. and trans. *The Book of Saint Foy.* 1995.

Robin Chapman Stacey. *The Road to Judgment: From Custom to Court in Medieval Ireland and Wales.* 1994

Sarah Stanbury. *Seeing the* Gawain-*Poet: Description and the Act of Perception.* 1992

Robert D. Stevick. *The Earliest Irish and English Bookarts: Visual and Poetic Forms Before A.D. 1000.* 1994

Thomas C. Stillinger. *The Song of Troilus: Lyric Authority in the Medieval Book.* 1992

Susan Mosher Stuard. *A State of Deference: Ragusa/Dubrovnik in the Medieval Centuries.* 1992

Susan Mosher Stuard, ed. *Women in Medieval History and Historiography.* 1987

Susan Mosher Stuard, ed. *Women in Medieval Society.* 1976

Jonathan Sumption. *The Hundred Years War: Trial by Battle.* 1992

Ronald E. Surtz. *The Guitar of God: Gender, Power, and Authority in the Visionary World of Mother Juana de la Cruz (1481–1534).* 1990

William H. TeBrake. *A Plague of Insurrection: Popular Politics and Peasant Revolt in Flanders, 1323–1328.* 1993

Patricia Terry, trans. *Poems of the Elder Edda.* 1990

Hugh M. Thomas. *Vassals, Heiresses, Crusaders, and Thugs: The Gentry of Angevin Yorkshire, 1154–1215.* 1993

Ralph V. Turner. *Men Raised from the Dust: Administrative Service and Upward Mobility in Angevin England.* 1988

Mary F. Wack. *Lovesickness in the Middle Ages: The* Viaticum *and Its Commentaries.* 1990

Benedicta Ward. *Miracles and the Medieval Mind: Theory, Record, and Event, 1000–1215.* 1982

Suzanne Fonay Wemple. *Women in Frankish Society: Marriage and the Cloister, 500–900.* 1981

Kenneth Baxter Wolf. *Making History: The Normans and Their Historians in Eleventh-Century Italy.* 1995.

Jan M. Ziolkowski. *Talking Animals: Medieval Latin Beast Poetry, 750–1150.* 1993

This book has been set in Linotron Galliard. Galliard was designed for Mergenthaler in 1978 by Matthew Carter. Galliard retains many of the features of a sixteenth-century typeface cut by Robert Granjon but has some modifications that give it a more contemporary look.

Printed on acid-free paper.